AN
AMERICAN
PROPHET'S
RECORD

AN
AMERICAN PROPHET'S RECORD
THE
DIARIES
AND
JOURNALS
OF
JOSEPH SMITH

Edited By
Scott H. Faulring

Signature Books
in association with
Smith Research Associates
Salt Lake City
Utah
1989

This edition of *An American Prophet's Record: The Diaries and Journals of Joseph Smith* is published by arrangement with the Joseph Smith Family Association. The publisher, however, is solely responsible for its contents, editorial approach, design, and format. *An American Prophet's Record* is not an official publication of either the Reorganized Church of Jesus Christ of Latter Day Saints or The Church of Jesus Christ of Latter-day Saints.

© 1987 by Signature Books, Inc.
Signature Books is a registered trademark of Signature Books, Inc.
All rights reserved
Printed in the United States of America
First published in 1987 in a limited cloth edition of 500 copies
Second edition 1989

96 95 94 93 92 91 90 89   6 5 4 3 2

Library of Congress Cataloging-in-Publication Data

Smith, Joseph, 1805-1844.
    An American prophet's record.

    Bibliography: p.
    Includes index.
    1. Smith, Joseph, 1805-1844—Diaries.   2. Church of
Jesus Christ of Latter-day Saints—Biography.   3. Mormon
Church—Biography.   I. Faulring, Scott H.   II. Title.
BX8695.S6A3   1989   289.3'092   [B]   89-6219
ISBN 0-941214-78-8

Cover illustration: *Entering Nauvoo by Water,* by Gary E. Smith, 1975, oil on canvas

To the memory of
Joseph Smith

Table
of

CONTENTS

ACKNOWLEDGEMENTS

This book has its beginnings in the early 1980s when I was an undergraduate at Brigham Young University. As with any project of this size, I could not have compiled and edited the personal diaries and journals of Joseph Smith without the assistance of friends and associates. Still I accept complete responsibility for the presentation and editing of these manuscripts.

I wish to thank George D. Smith and Smith Research Associates for inviting me to edit these diaries and journals. Equally important was the encouragement of the heirs of Joseph Smith and the Joseph Smith Family Association, especially Paul M. Edwards and Daniel M. Larsen. This volume, the first in a series of the diaries, autobiographies, and personal reminiscences of significant Mormons, would not exist without their support.

I appreciate Gary James Bergera, Ronald L. Priddis, Connie Disney, and Mary Brockert of Signature Books for patiently assisting throughout the production of this volume.

I gratefully acknowledge Elizabeth Dehghan for her technical expertise and Mark McOmber, Kim Puzey, Susan Staker, and Gary Teaman for their constructive editorial criticisms. My gratitude to LaJean Purcell Carruth and Jani Fleet for their help in transcribing and deciphering the few, yet important, journal entries recorded in shorthand. I also appreciate the advice and counsel of Gary H. Moore, Beth H. Parker, and Andrew C. Hess.

I am indebted to Richard Bushman who, at a lecture given in the spring of 1978 at Cornell University, first prompted me to research and document the life of Joseph Smith. In addition, I have benefited greatly from the following scholars and researchers of Mormon history: Thomas G. Alexander, James B. Allen, Richard L. Anderson, Hyrum L. Andrus, Leonard J. Arrington, Milton V. Backman, Jr., Donald Q. Cannon, Lyndon W. Cook, James D'Arc, Chad Flake, Lawrence Foster, Harvard S. Heath, Marvin S. Hill, Dean C. Jessee, Truman G. Madsen, H. Michael Marquardt, Robert J. Matthews, H. Donl Peterson, Larry C. Porter, D. Michael Quinn, Dennis Rowley, and David J. Whittaker.

I appreciate the assistance and friendship of Ian G. Barber, E. Jay Bell, Sharol Ellermeier, Elaine Erickson, Gerald Evans, Leda Farley, Mark Grandstaff, Michael Gruse, Catherine Hall, Myron and Kalleen Hendrick, Ross Kincaid, Gary Robert Pettit, Douglas Shawn Herbert Charles MacDonald, Glenn McCoy, Hal Palmer, Alma-Jane Perkins, Tim Rathbone, Marqua Ratliff, Byron and Allison Sauer, Ernest Strack, Joseph and Barbara Sykes, Denise Rae Thayer, Ray and Stacy Welsh, and Kenneth D. Winward.

I am ever thankful for the loving support of my mother, Barbara R. Faulring, and father and step-mother, Richard and Doris Faulring. I love them for their encouragement and understanding.

Finally, I would like to express my heartfelt appreciation to my wife Barbara, who patiently assisted me in the transcription and editing of these writings. Our children—Jon, Spencer, Tiffany, and Joseph—also deserve my sincere thanks for their patience and understanding while I was working on this book.

INTRODUCTION

The Mormon prophet Joseph Smith (1805–44) is a well-known, controversial nineteenth-century religious figure. Partisans and detractors alike have devoted thousands of pages to explain his life. For some, he was a charlatan; for others, he was "Prophet, Seer, and Revelator" of Jesus Christ's true church restored to the earth in the latter-days. Today more than one hundred churches, with some seven million adherents worldwide, trace their origins to Joseph Smith and to his teachings. These churches include, most notably, The Church of Jesus Christ of Latter-day Saints, known as the Latter-day Saints (LDS) or Mormons, and the Reorganized Church of Jesus Christ of Latter Day Saints (RLDS), based in Independence, Missouri. Yet, while some of Joseph Smith's autobiographical writings have appeared in a variety of publications, there has surprisingly been no attempt to bring together in one volume the unfolding story of his life as recorded in his own diaries and journals. This volume seeks to remedy that situation by publishing for the first time all of the available diaries and journals of Joseph Smith.[1]

---

[1] From 1979 to 1982, H. Michael Marquardt published Joseph Smith's 1832 autobiographical sketch, his 1832–34 diary and journal, his 1835–36 diary and

For millions, Joseph Smith was, and remains, something of an enigma. Although he had little formal education, he claimed to translate, by the "gift and power of God," a complex religious record of an ancient American civilization, published in 1830 as The Book of Mormon. In addition, he dictated or recorded over 150 revelations and visions, gathered into a second volume of scripture known as the Doctrine and Covenants. A third volume, entitled The Pearl of Great Price, includes documents Joseph claimed were restorations of ancient Hebrew and Egyptian scriptures.[2] A contemporary LDS apostle has written of Joseph Smith's accomplishment, "From . . . one unlearned and untrained in theology, more printed pages of scripture have come down to us [from him] than from any mortal, including Moses, Paul, Luke, and Mormon."[3] Brigham H. Roberts, an early twentieth-century LDS historian, addressed his subject in these words: "Joseph Smith . . . is preeminently the American Prophet. He is not the 'boy prophet;' . . . He is not the 'Prophet of Palmyra' [New York]; he is the Prophet of the dispensation of the fullness of times; if localized at all he must be known as the 'American Prophet.' "[4]

---

journal, the "Scriptory Book," and the 1839 "Minute Book" of James Mulholland (Salt Lake City: Modern Microfilm). In 1984, Dean C. Jessee published the 1832 autobiographical sketch and the diaries and journals covering the years 1832 to 1836 in his edition of The Personal Writings of Joseph Smith (Salt Lake City: Deseret Book). Two years later, typescript photocopies of the 1843–44 journals surfaced in Provo, Utah, in an anonymously published four-volume set. In addition, lengthy excerpts from the Nauvoo journals were included in Andrew F. Ehat and Lyndon W. Cook, eds., The Words of Joseph (Provo, UT: Brigham Young University, Religious Studies Center, 1980).

[2] All or most of these books have been accepted by the various Mormon churches as official scripture. Joseph Smith also produced a "New Translation" of the King James Bible during the 1830s. This is currently published as The Holy Scriptures (Independence, MO: Herald Publishing House, 1976). See Richard P. Howard, Restoration Scriptures: A Study of Their Textual Development (Independence, MO: Department of Religious Education, Reorganized Church of Jesus Christ of Latter Day Saints, 1969); Robert J. Woodford, "The Historical Development of the Doctrine and Covenants," Ph.D. diss., Brigham Young University, 1974; Robert J. Matthews, "A Plainer Translation": Joseph Smith's Translation of the Bible: A History and Commentary (Provo, UT: Brigham Young University Press, 1978); Robert L. Millet and Kent P. Jackson, eds., Studies in Scriptures, Vol. 1: The Doctrine and Covenants (Sandy, UT: Randall Book Co., 1984); and Robert L. Millet and Kent P. Jackson, eds., Studies in Scriptures, Vol. 2: The Pearl of Great Price (Salt Lake City: Randall Book Co., 1985).

[3] Neal A. Maxwell, " 'A Choice Seer,' " Ensign 16 (Aug. 1986): 6.

[4] B[righam]. H. Roberts, Joseph Smith: The Prophet-Teacher, a Discourse (Salt Lake City: Deseret News, 1908), p. 66.

Though the diaries of other prominent Latter-day Saints are more comprehensive, none are as important to the history of early Mormonism — from Ohio to Missouri to Illinois — as those of its founder. Joseph Smith struggled throughout his adult life to document the story of his emerging church and the role he played in that drama. In so doing he was responding, in part, to a revelation recorded on 6 April 1830, the day his Church of Christ was formally organized: "Behold, there shall be a record kept among you; and in it thou shalt be called a seer, a translator, a prophet, an apostle of Jesus Christ, an elder of the church through the will of God the Father, and the grace of your Lord Jesus Christ" (D&C 21:1, LDS edition). In the documents that follow, the reader will discover a sincere and sometimes impassioned participant in the events described. The reader will not find evidence of pretext or deception, even though the documents may at times relate a story different from traditional accounts.

Mormon historians have identified ten extant manuscript volumes of Joseph Smith's personal diaries and journals. For the purposes of this book, the terms "diary" and "journal" have distinct, yet related meanings. A Joseph Smith "diary" contains entries written or dictated directly by Joseph Smith, whereas a Joseph Smith "journal" is made up of entries written or composed by a secretary, which Joseph Smith employed frequently. Several of the following documents have characteristics of both; but in either case, the entries were recorded daily, weekly, or more periodically. The ten manuscripts, except where noted, included in the present volume are:

1. "Joseph Smith, Jr. Record Book," diary and journal, 27 November 1832 to 5 December 1834, 105 manuscript pages, in the handwriting of Joseph Smith, Oliver Cowdery, Sidney Rigdon, Frederick G. Williams, Parley P. Pratt, and others;

2. "Sketch Book for the use of Joseph Smith, Jr.," diary and journal, 22 September 1835 to 3 April 1836, 194 manuscript pages, in the handwriting of Joseph Smith, Oliver Cowdery, Warren Parrish, William W. Phelps, Sylvester Smith, Frederick G. Williams, Warren A. Cowdery, and others;

3. "The Scriptory Book of Joseph Smith, Jr.," journal, 13 March 1838 to 10 September 1838, 69 manuscript pages, in the handwriting of George W. Robinson;

4. "Joseph Smith Journal," journal, 3 September 1838 to

6 October 1838 and 22 April 1839 to 20 October 1839, 12 manuscript pages, in the handwriting of James Mulholland;

    5. "Minute Book, 1839. J[oseph] Smith Journal," journal, 16 April 1839 to 15 October 1839, 13 manuscript pages, in the handwriting of James Mulholland;

    6. "The Book of the Law of the Lord," some journal entries, ca. 1841–43, more than 500 manuscript pages, in the handwriting of William Clayton, Robert B. Thompson, Willard Richards, and possibly Thomas Bullock;

    7. "President Joseph Smith's Journal, 1843," journal, 21 December 1842 to 10 March 1843, 283 manuscript pages, in the handwriting of Willard Richards;

    8. Untitled journal, 10 March 1843 to 14 July 1843, 309 manuscript pages, in the handwriting of Willard Richards;

    9. Untitled journal, 15 July 1843 to 29 February 1844, 278 manuscript pages, in the handwriting of Willard Richards; and finally

    10. "President Joseph Smith['s] Journal, Kept by W[illard] Richards, Vol. 4," journal, 1 March 1844 to 22 June 1844, 171 manuscript pages, in the handwriting of Willard Richards.[5]

    In addition to the complete texts of nine of the above diaries and journals, the present compilation contains the earliest autobiographical sketch composed by Joseph Smith. Written and dictated by Joseph Smith in 1832, the same year his first diary begins, this document provides supplementary details about Joseph's formative years, 1805–29.[6]

    Of the above texts, only previously published excerpts from "The Book of the Law of the Lord" are included in the present volume. Access to the original manuscript, which is in the custody of the First Presidency of The Church of Jesus Christ of Latter-day Saints, Salt Lake City, Utah, is generally restricted and was denied to me. In addition to Joseph Smith journal en-

---

[5] This final volume actually has more pages than noted, but only the first 171 pages are devoted to Joseph Smith's activities. The remaining pages were used by his secretary after his death in June 1844.

[6] This 1832 autobiography is one of at least four histories of early Mormonism known to have been written or dictated by Joseph Smith. Three other accounts date from 1835, 1838, and 1842. The 1835 sketch comprises the 9 November 1835 entry in Joseph Smith's 1835–36 diary. For the 1838 and 1842 histories, see Jessee, *Personal Writings*, pp. 196–220.

tries written during the early 1840s, "The Book of the Law of the Lord" is known to contain minutes of meetings, a record of financial contributions to the church, letters, revelations, and biographical sketches.

I have transcribed these documents, except for the excerpts from "The Book of the Law of the Lord," which were obtained from published sources, from microfilm copies of the originals. I was not allowed access to the originals of any of the documents, all of which are currently housed in the archives of the Historical Department, Church of Jesus Christ of Latter-day Saints. But except for "The Book of the Law of the Lord," complete copies (microfilm or photographic) of the above documents are also available at various university libraries and research institutions in Utah as well as at the library of the Reorganized Church of Jesus Christ of Latter Day Saints in Independence, Missouri. All of the Joseph Smith diaries and journals have been used in various ways as primary sources in the officially published histories of the LDS, the RLDS, and many of the other churches basing their claims on Joseph Smith.[7]

In transcribing, editing, and annotating the manuscripts that follow, my intent has been to present them in a readable format without adversely affecting the meaning or spirit of the originals. I stress "readable format" because in the past many editors have attempted to reproduce Mormon historical documents with "photographic fidelity" to the original, relying on their readers to decipher the sometimes unintelligible writings of nineteenth-century diarists and scribes.[8] Such an approach has as its objec-

---

[7] Joseph Smith's diaries and journals were used extensively but not exclusively by the early historians and editors who compiled the "Manuscript History of the Church," first published serially in 1842–46 in the *Times and Season* (Nauvoo, Illinois) and in 1851–58 in the *Deseret News* (Salt Lake City). This multi-volume compilation was subsequently re-edited by B. H. Roberts and published from 1902 to 1912 as *The History of the Church of Jesus Christ of Latter-day Saints. Period I. History of Joseph Smith, the Prophet* (Salt Lake City: Deseret Press). For additional information on the compiling, writing, and editing of Joseph Smith's manuscript and published histories, see Dean C. Jessee, "The Writing of Joseph Smith's History," *Brigham Young University Studies* 11 (Summer 1971): 439–73; Dean C. Jessee, "The Reliability of Joseph Smith's History," *Journal of Mormon History* 3 (1976): 23–46; and especially Howard C. Searle, "Early Mormon Historiography: Writing the History of the Mormons, 1830–58," Ph.D. diss., University of California, Los Angeles, 1979, pp. 144–336.

[8] Representative examples include Robert Glass Cleland and Juanita Brooks,

tive to bring "to the reader the original as nearly as it is possible for the printed word to reproduce the written one"[9] — complete with unintentional misspellings, deletions, misplaced punctuation, blemishes in the paper, and even smeared ink. Given the justifiable criticism that in the past some of the editors of official LDS and RLDS publications have deliberately tampered with original documents, I share such concern for the integrity of the original. However, I also believe that historical editing has reached a point in Mormon historiography where the conscientious editor may be allowed to adopt uniform guidelines regarding consistency, standardization, moderation, and especially readability, including, where appropriate, modernization, to facilitate comprehension and appreciation of the original document.

Modern American historical editing traces its genesis to the early 1950s with the publication of the first volume of *The Papers of Thomas Jefferson*, edited by Julian P. Boyd. Since then, virtually all editors of American historical writings have adopted and modified the editorial philosophy developed and advocated by Boyd.[10] Prior to Boyd's revolutionary editorial methods, which

---

eds., *A Mormon Chronicle: The Diaries of John D. Lee, 1848-1876*, 2 vols. (San Marino, CA: Henry E. Huntington Library and Art Gallery, 1955); Juanita Brooks, ed., *On the Mormon Frontier: The Diary of Hosea Stout*, 2 vols. (Salt Lake City: University of Utah Press, Utah State Historical Society, 1964); Andrew F. Ehat and Lyndon W. Cook, eds., *The Words of Joseph Smith* (Provo, UT: Religious Studies Center, Brigham Young University, 1980); Donald Q. Cannon and Lyndon W. Cook, eds., *The Far West Record: Minutes of The Church of Jesus Christ of Latter-day Saints, 1830-1844* (Salt Lake City: Deseret Book Co., 1983); Jessee, *Personal Writings of Joseph Smith*; and Milton V. Backman, Jr., and Lyndon W. Cook, eds., *Kirtland Elders' Quorum Record, 1836-1841* (Provo, UT: Grandin Book Co., 1985). This is not to criticize any of the above, but to allow the reader to compare the present volume with some of its predecessors.

[9] Brooks, *On the Mormon Frontier*, 1:xix.

[10] Several informative essays on the development of American historical editing are G. Thomas Tanselle, "The Editing of Historical Documents," *Studies in Bibliography* 31 (1978): 1-56; Lester J. Cappon, "A Rationale for Historical Editing Past and Present," *William and Mary Quarterly*, 3rd series, 23 (Jan. 1966): 56-75; Lyman H. Butterfield, "Historical Editing in the United States: The Recent Past," *Proceedings of the American Antiquarian Society* 72 (16-17 Oct. 1962): 283-308; Julian P. Boyd, "Historical Editing in the United States: The Next Stage?" *Proceedings of the American Antiquarian Society* 72 (16-17 Oct. 1962): 309-28; *A National Program for the Publication of Historical Documents: A Report to the President*, prepared by the National Historical Publications Commission (Washington, D.C.: Government Printing Office, 1954); and Clarence E. Carter, "Historical Editing," *Bulletins of the National Archives* 7 (Aug. 1952): 5-51.

included modernization, where necessary, the procedures for editing historical documents were frequently of questionable dependability and accuracy in relation to the original sources. In the past, considerable liberties were sometimes taken by well-meaning editors and compilers who were concerned that the originals, if reproduced accurately, might not always shed only positive light on their authors or on others mentioned therein. Since the 1950s, however, scholars, publishers, and the reading public have all encouraged, even demanded, more professional, honest, and consistent approaches and methods regarding the editing of historical documents.

The following editorial policy and procedures, developed and justified by recent American editorial standards, as well as my own desire for readability, were used as guides in transcribing, editing, and annotating the Joseph Smith diaries and journals for this publication. While I trust that not every reader will agree with my interpretation in those instances where a subjective editorial decision was required, I hope that I have nonetheless been consistent in my application of these guidelines.

1. *Spelling.* Generally, original spelling is preserved. However, when precise spelling could not be determined, the modern usage is given.

2. *Punctuation.* Most of Joseph Smith's holographic material and that of his clerks and scribes is poorly, if at all, punctuated. Therefore, some minimal punctuation, necessary for readability and intelligibility, has been supplied. If needed, periods, commas, hyphens, quotation marks, colons, question marks, etc., have been silently inserted. Periods that should be commas and vice versa have been corrected or omitted as required. When the end of a sentence is uncertain or ambiguous, punctuation is not added and the material is left intact. Intrusive or redundant punctuation has been edited out.

3. *Symbols.* Symbols, drawings, and figures drawn in the manuscript are transcribed as an asterisk (*) and are accompanied by, if needed, a descriptive explanation in a footnote or in the text. Line-end hyphenated words (for example, West = field) in the original are silently brought together. Lines drawn at the termination of a line or paragraph are silently converted to periods or other relevant punctuation. Semicolons have been replaced

with periods unless the semicolon connects related thoughts or ideas; if so, they are retained.

Ampersands (&) have been changed to "and" except at the beginning of paragraphs and sentences where they have been silently omitted. The ampersand is retained in the form "&c" (for "etc."). Redundant and run-on uses of "and" and "but" have also been omitted where possible. Ditto marks (") and "do" have been retained where practical. In some cases the words the ditto marks represent have been provided in brackets.

4. *Paragraphing, Spacing, Quotation Marks, and Underlining.* Within some diary and journal entries, two or more paragraphs have been created out of one, especially where the subject matter within the original seems to justify the creation of shorter paragraphs. Otherwise paragraphing follows the original. I have silently introduced spacing between some manuscript entries and between some paragraphs within entries for increased readability. Blanks left in the manuscript are noted as: [*blank*], [*entry left blank*], [*several lines left blank*] (unruled page), [*three lines left blank*] (ruled page), or [*rest of page blank*]. In some instances, where context seems to justify their use for increased readability, quotation marks have been silently introduced into the text. Words that are underlined in the originals have been italicized.

5. *Capitalization.* Capitalization has been preserved as rendered in the original with the exception of proper nouns (such as personal names, geographic names, days of the week, months of the year, and holidays), which have been capitalized. Ambiguous capitalization is reproduced as capitals unless the style of the writer indicates definite lowercase intent.

6. *Shorthand, Insertions, Omissions, and Abbreviations.* All known shorthand entries in the manuscripts have been deciphered and placed within angled brackets (for example, <were married>).

Written material inserted above the line in the original has been inserted into the text and enclosed in right-angled slashes (for example, /my son/). Placement of added material will be at the point designated in the original manuscript or where placement has been determined by context. Addendum material, written to be inserted either earlier or later in the manuscript, has been positioned in its intended place along with an editorial comment or footnote. Editorial insertions are enclosed in brackets and italicized (for example, [*written sideways on page*]).

Inadvertent omissions of words or letters are enclosed in square brackets (for example, curse [them] and). Abbreviations and truncated words have been expanded with added material bracketed but not italicized (for example, J. Smith is given as J[oseph] Smith), except in the case of words with line-end omissions or additions which are silently supplied. Common abbreviations have, for the most part, been retained (for example, Dr., etc., Jr., Rd., rd., Sr., St., and st). In some instances, particularly in the Nauvoo journals, I have relied on Joseph Smith's *History of The Church* to complete sentences in which the meaning would have otherwise been completely lost to most readers. These editorial insertions are enclosed in brackets and are not italicized.

7. *Canceled and Indistinguishable Material.* Canceled matter, either scored-out or erased, has been disregarded barring stylistic, psychological, or historical value. When included, such words or passages are reproduced with dashes throughout (for example, ~~leaving the meeting before~~). Repetitive or unnecessary strikeout material has been silently omitted.

Material that I could not decipher has been transcribed using [-] or [. . . . .], the dash representing an indistinguishable word, dots noting the approximate number of undecipherable letters. Conjectural readings of missing or unintelligible words or letters are enclosed in brackets with a question mark after the word or words (for instance, [slavery?]).

8. *Page Numbering.* Manuscript page numbers are included for reference purposes and are enclosed in fancy brackets. For example, {page 34} indicates the end of page 34 in the original manuscript.

9. *Handwriting Identification.* Where possible, I have tried to identify the handwriting of the various scribes. This is specified in the footnotes. Following the example of Dean C. Jessee in his edition of Joseph Smith's holographs, *The Personal Writings of Joseph Smith,* Joseph Smith's handwriting is highlighted in **bold** type. A back slash with a superscript footnote number ($\backslash^9$) identifies the beginning of the handwriting of a different scribe or clerk writing for Joseph Smith.[11] Readers are urged to keep in

---

[11] Jessee's important compilation was also used to help identify many of Joseph Smith's scribes.

mind that the identification of some of the handwriting is only tentative.

    10. *Annotation.* Due to the volume of manuscript material presented herein and my own dislike for what can sometimes result as largely self-indulgent pedantry, I have chosen to supply only necessary textual annotations. In other words, I have only annotated the manuscript rather than include, in addition, explanatory notes, thereby reserving for the interested reader the task of providing supplementary historical and biographical context. This position, dictated by moderation, is, I feel, in harmony with the following policy statement issued by the National Historical Publications and Records Commission: "Closely associated with the problem of selectivity is the unfortunate tendency of some editions to display an inordinate, unwarranted amount of document annotation . . . The research involved in unearthing information on obscure individuals or insignificant events mentioned incidentally in documents is a laborious and expensive process with dubious value."[12]

    Where essential, brief textual footnotes will be found on the page to which they refer. In addition, I have provided a map of relevant geographic sites, a chronology of significant events in Joseph Smith's life, a list of biographical sketches for the major characters mentioned throughout the diaries and journals, and a selected bibliography of articles, books, and theses relating to Joseph Smith.

    Finally, readers should know that I am a member of The Church of Jesus Christ of Latter-day Saints and that I believe in its claims. As a Latter-day Saint, I revere Joseph Smith for his role in the restoration of the gospel of Jesus Christ. Besides affirming the historical and biographical importance of these diaries and journals, I also believe they witness the teachings Joseph Smith revealed and advocated.

---

[12]*Annotation* 4 (Oct. 1976). See also Charles T. Cullen, "Principles of Annotation in Editing Historical Documents; or, How to Avoid Breaking the Butterfly on the Wheel of Scholarship," in George L. Vogt and John Bush Jones, eds., *Literary and Historical Editing* (University of Kansas Libraries, 1981), pp. 81–95.

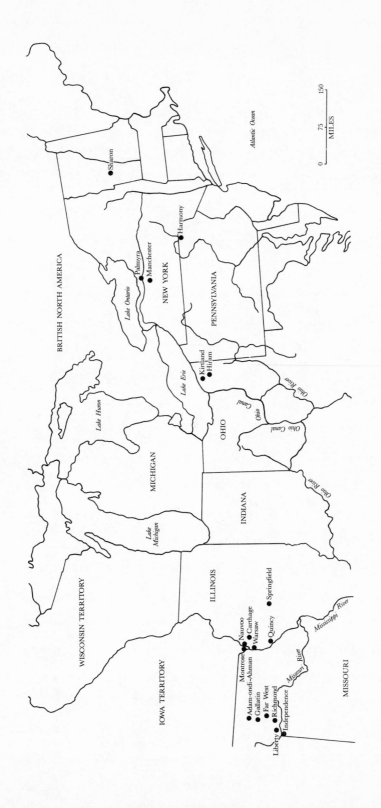

A
Joseph
Smith

CHRONOLOGY

1805		
	23 December	Born at Sharon, Windsor County, Vermont, fourth child of Joseph Smith and Lucy Mack.
1811		
		Family moves to Lebanon, New Hampshire.
1813		
		Contracts typhus fever. Undergoes leg operation.
1816		
		Family moves to Palmyra, Wayne County, New York.
1820		
	Spring	First vision.
1820–23		
		Falls into "transgressions" and sins in "many things."
ca. 1822		
		Acquires a seerstone while digging a well. Thereafter, occasionally acts as a treasure seer.
1823		
	21–22 September	First visitation of Moroni.
	19 November	Brother Alvin dies.

1825
October   Hired by Josiah Stowell (also Stoal)
                 to search for buried treasure in
                 Harmony, Pennsylvania. Stays at
                 Isaac Hale home.

1826
20 March   Tried and convicted as a
                 "glasslooker."

1827
18 January   Marries Emma Hale.
22 September   Obtains Book of Mormon plates.
Fall   Begins translation of Book of
                 Mormon.
December   Moves to Harmony, Pennsylvania.

1828
February   Martin Harris takes a transcript and
                 partial translation of Book of
                 Mormon to Samuel L. Mitchell and
                 Charles Anthon for verification.
April   Begins dictating Book of Mormon,
                 with Martin Harris as scribe.
June-July   Martin Harris loses first 116 pages
                 of dictation.
15 June   Son Alvin is born, dies the same day.

1829
7 April   Oliver Cowdery takes over as Book
                 of Mormon scribe.
15 May(-June?)   Receives priesthood.
17 June   Secures copyright for Book of
                 Mormon.
June-July   Finishes Book of Mormon at Peter
                 Whitmer home in Fayette, New York.
                 Performs some early baptisms.

1830
March   Publishes 5,000 copies of Book of
                 Mormon.
6 April   Organizes Church of Christ.
                 Sustained as first elder and as "seer,
                 prophet, translator, and apostle of
                 Jesus Christ."
June   Dictates and records Visions of
                 Moses; begins revision of the Bible.

	9 June	First conference of new church is held.
	30 June	Brother Samuel leaves for mission to East.
	October	Sidney Rigdon and other Campbellites join church.
1831		
	January	Moves church to Kirtland, Ohio.
	30 April	Twins, Thaddeus and Louisa, are born, live only three hours.
	9 May	Adopts twins, Joseph and Julia Murdock.
	19 June	Leaves for Jackson County, Missouri.
	July	Reveals site for City of Zion at Kaw Township (later Independence), Jackson County.
	2–3 August	With Sidney Rigdon, dedicates Land of Zion and temple site.
	1 September	Records revelation on tithing.
	12 September	Moves to Hiram, Ohio.
	December	Preaches in Ohio in response to anti-Mormon newspaper articles.
1832		
	25 January	Sustained as president of High Priesthood at conference of church in Amherst, Ohio.
	16 February	Reveals three degrees of post-mortal glory.
	24–25 March	Mobbed, tarred, and feathered.
	29 March	Adopted son Joseph dies.
	1 April	Leaves for church settlements in Missouri.
	June	Arrives back at Kirtland.
	1 June	*Evening and Morning Star*, first LDS periodical, appears in Independence.
	October	Travels to Albany, New York City, and Boston.
	6 November	Returns to Kirtland. Son Joseph III is born.

	8 November	Meets recent converts Brigham Young, Joseph Young, Heber C. Kimball, and others.
	25 December	Records revelation on war.
1833		
	27 February	Records Word of Wisdom.
	18 March	Re-organizes church (or first) presidency with two counselors, Sidney Rigdon and Frederick G. Williams.
	2 July	Finishes first phase of Bible revision.
	20 July	Mob destroys printing press in Zion (Independence), interrupting publication of Book of Command-ments, a compilation of revelations.
	23 July	Helps to lay cornerstones for Kirtland Temple. Mormons agree to leave Jackson County.
	5 October	Leaves Kirtland on mission to Canada.
	31 October	Armed mobs attack Mormons in Missouri.
	4 November	Returns to Kirtland.
	22 November	Learns of church's expulsion from Jackson County.
	Fall-Winter	Doctor Philastus Hurlbut, a Mormon apostate, collects affidavits from Palmyra neighbors and others to discredit Joseph Smith. Published following year by E. D. Howe in *Mormonism Unvailed* (sic).
1834		
	17 February	Organizes high council at Kirtland.
	26 February	Leaves Kirtland to find volunteers for Zion's Camp to aid Missouri Saints.
	28 March	Returns to Kirtland.
	1–3 April	Attends court in Doctor Philastus Hurlbut case.

	3 May	Name of church changed to Church of the Latter Day Saints.
	5 May	Leaves Kirtland for Missouri as leader of Zion's Camp.
	19 June	Arrives in Clay County, Missouri.
	3 July	Organizes Missouri high council.
	1 August	Returns to Kirtland.
	Fall	E. D. Howe publishes *Mormonism Unvailed*, an anti-Mormon expose.
	October	Visits church in Michigan. *LDS Messenger and Advocate* begins publication at Kirtland.
	November	Attends school of elders in Kirtland.
1835	14 February	Organizes Council of Twelve Apostles.
	28 February	Organizes Quorum of Seventy.
	28 March	Records revelation on priesthood.
	July	Church acquires Egyptian mummies and papyrus. Engaged in "translating" an Egyptian alphabet and grammar.
	August	Visits Saints in Michigan.
	23 August	Returns to Kirtland.
	September	Publishes Doctrine and Covenants, a compilation of revelations, including "Lectures on Faith."
	8–11 October	Father becomes ill.
	November	Studies Hebrew and Greek.
1836	27 March	Dedicates Kirtland Temple.
	3 April	With Oliver Cowdery, receives vision of Jesus Christ and other biblical personages in Kirtland temple.
	17 May	Meets grandmother at Fairport and accompanies her to Kirtland.
	20 June	Son Frederick is born.
	25 July	Leaves Kirtland for East.

	30 July	Visits New York City. Later, visits Salem, Massachusetts, in search of "much treasure."
	September	Returns to Kirtland.
	2 November	Establishes Kirtland Safety Society Bank.
1837	6 April	Holds solemn assembly in Kirtland Temple.
	May	Condemned by Kirtland dissenters.
	June	Is very ill.
	4 June	Sends Heber C. Kimball and others on mission to England.
	23 July	Records revelation to twelve apostles.
	August	Visits church in Canada.
	3 September	Holds conference in Kirtland. Three members of Council of Twelve Apostles rejected.
	27 September	Leaves for Missouri.
	October	*Elders' Journal* appears in Kirtland.
	7 November	Holds conference at Far West, Missouri.
	December	Returns to Kirtland. Encounters considerable dissension over financial matters. Martin Harris excommunicated.
1838	12 January	With Sidney Rigdon, leaves Kirtland to escape mob.
	14 March	Arrives with family at Far West.
	12–13 April	Oliver Cowdery excommunicated. David Whitmer withdraws from church fellowship.
	26 April	Name of church changed to The Church of Jesus Christ of Latter-day Saints.
	30 April	Commences dictating official history.
	19 May	Selects Adam-ondi-Ahman as new settlement site.

June-August	Vigilante Mormons organize as Danites.
2 June	Son Alexander is born.
6 August	Mormon/non-Mormon skirmish at Gallatin, Missouri.
4 September	Begins to study law.
11 October	Leads persecuted Saints from DeWitt to Far West.
27 October	Missouri governor Lilburn Boggs issues order to exterminate Mormons.
30 October	Mormons massacred at Haun's Mill.
31 October	Surrenders to Missouri militia at Far West and imprisoned.
4 November	Arrives under guard at Independence.
November	Attends hearing at Richmond.
1 December	Held at Liberty Jail while awaiting trial.

1839

6 April	Leaves Liberty Jail for Gallatin to attend trial.
15–16 April	Starts for Boone County on change of venue but escapes.
22 April	Reunites with family at Quincy, Illinois.
10 May	Moves to Commerce (later Nauvoo), Illinois.
June	Helps to resettle church members at Nauvoo.
11 June	Continues dictating and compiling official history.
29 October	Leaves Nauvoo to present grievances to federal government.
November	*Times and Seasons* begins publication in Nauvoo.
28 November	Arrives at Washington, D.C.
29 November	Visits United States president Martin Van Buren.
December	Visits church in Philadelphia and New Jersey.

1840

February	Leaves Washington, D.C., for Nauvoo.
4 March	Arrives at Nauvoo.
15 April	Sends Orson Hyde to dedicate Palestine for return of Jews.
14 September	Father dies.
16 December	Nauvoo Charter becomes law.

1841

30 January	Elected trustee-in-trust of church.
1 February	Elected to Nauvoo city council.
4 February	Elected lieutenant general of Nauvoo Legion.
5 April	Sealed polygynously to Louisa Beaman.
6 April	Lays cornerstone for Nauvoo Temple.
4 June	Arrested on "old Missouri charges."
9–10 June	Tried and acquitted at Monmouth, Illinois.
3 July	Delivers patriotic address to Nauvoo Legion.
7 August	Brother Don Carlos dies.
12 August	Addresses visiting Indians at Nauvoo.
14 September	Attends military parade at Montrose, Iowa.
27 October	Sealed polygynously to Zina D. (Huntington) Jacobs.
8 November	Dedicates baptism font in Nauvoo temple.
11 December	Sealed polygynously to Prescinda (Huntington) Buell.

1842

January	Makes polygynous proposal to Nancy Rigdon.
5 January	Begins selling merchandise at new store in Nauvoo.
February	Sealed polygynously to Mary Elizabeth (Rollins) Lightner.
1 March	Publishes Book of Abraham.

9 March	Sealed polygynously to Patty (Sessions) Sessions.
15–16 March	Officiates at installation of Nauvoo masonic lodge and receives first three degrees of masonry. Becomes editor of *Times and Seasons*.
17 March	Organizes Female Relief Society of Nauvoo.
27 March	Conducts baptisms for the dead in Mississippi River.
April	Applies for bankruptcy. Sealed polygynously to Marinda Nancy (Johnson) Hyde.
4 May	Introduces temple endowment, initiates called the Quorum of Anointed, or Holy Order. Conducts fifty-two meetings of Holy Order by 25 May 1844.
11 May	John C. Bennett disfellowshipped.
19 May	Elected mayor of Nauvoo.
Summer	Rumors of polygamy circulating. Sealed polygynously to Martha McBride.
29 June	Sealed polygynously to Eliza R. Snow.
8 July	John C. Bennett, previously a Mormon confidant, publishes the first in series of anti-Mormon newspaper articles.
27 July	Sealed polygynously to Sarah Ann Whitney.
8 August	Arrested for complicity in an attempt to assassinate Missouri governer Lilburn W. Boggs and forced into hiding.
26 December	Submits to arrest to test legality of extradition to Missouri.

1843

5 January	Writ of extradition ruled invalid by circuit court justice in Springfield, Illinois. Discharged from arrest.
20 January	Rebaptizes Orson Pratt after reconciliation regarding polygamy.
February	Sealed polygynously to Ruth (Vose) Sayers. Also, cares for mother during her illness.
4 March	Sealed polygynously to Emily Partridge.
8 March	Sealed polygynously to Eliza Partridge.
May	Sealed polygynously to Helen Mar Kimball.
1 May	Sealed polygynously to Lucy Walker.
3 May	*Nauvoo Neighbor*, a newspaper, begins publication.
16 May	Travels to Ramus, Illinois.
28 May	Sealed for time and eternity to first wife Emma.
1 June	Sealed polygynously to Elvira (Cowles) Holmes.
12 June	Sealed polygynously to Rhoda Richards.
13 June	Leaves Nauvoo to visit relatives at Dixon, Illinois.
23 June	Arrested at Dixon.
30 June	Arrives at Nauvoo.
July	Sealed polygynously to Desmodema Fullmer.
1 July	Discharged by Nauvoo court.
12 July	Dictates revelation on celestial marriage.
31 August	Moves into Nauvoo Mansion.
20 September	Sealed polygynously to Melissa Lott.
28 September	Introduces fullness of priesthood ordinance, or second anointing.
2 November	Sealed polygynously to Fanny (Young) Murray.

1844

29 January	Announces candidacy for United States presidency.
8 February	Publishes views on government.
20 February	Instructs twelve apostles to find new location for church in California or Oregon.
10–11 March	Organizes Council of Fifty.
18 March	Studies German.
3 April	Presides at Nauvoo court.
5 April	Attends dedication of Nauvoo masonic temple.
7 April	Delivers King Follett sermon on plurality of gods.
26 April	Life threatened by Nauvoo dissenters.
17 May	Nominated U.S. presidential candidate at Nauvoo convention.
7 June	First and only issue of *Nauvoo Expositor* newspaper, published by Mormon dissidents, appears.
10 June	Orders destruction of *Expositor* press.
12 June	Arrested for destroying press.
18 June	Places Nauvoo under martial law.
22 June	With brother Hyrum, crosses Mississippi River for the West.
25 June	Returns and surrenders at Carthage, Illinois.
27 June	With brother Hyrum, shot by mob at Carthage jail.

Prominent

CHARACTERS

JAMES ADAMS

(1783–1843). Born in Limsbury, Connecticut. Lawyer and justice of peace in Springfield, Illinois. Elected probate judge for Sangamon County in 1837 and 1841. Helped to found Springfield Masonic Lodge in 1839. Converted ca. 1840. Elected probate judge for Hancock County in 1843. Early participant in temple ceremonies and polygamy.

TRUMAN ANGELL

(1810–87). Born in Providence, Rhode Island. Living in China, New York, when converted. Moved to Kirtland in 1835 and worked on temple. Member of Second Quorum of Seventy. Migrated to Utah. Architect of Nauvoo and Salt Lake temples.

SAMPSON AVARD

(1809–?). Born in St. Peter, Isle of Guernsey. Baptized in 1835. Leader of Mormon vigiliante group during Missouri period called the Danites. Insisted the group was sanctioned by church leaders. Later excommunicated. Living in Illinois by 1850.

ALMON W. BABBITT

(1813–56). Born in Cheshire, Massachusetts. Baptized in 1833. Member of Zion's Camp. Ordained a seventy in 1835. President of the Kirtland Stake. Disaffected temporarily in 1836. Moved to

Missouri and later to Nauvoo. Disfellowshipped in 1841 but returned by 1842.

JACOB B. BACKENSTOS

(?-?). Non-Mormon clerk in circuit court for Hancock County, Illinois. Elected to Illinios state legislature in 1844. Elected Nauvoo sheriff in 1845. Friendly to Mormons in Nauvoo.

ALVAH (also Alva) BEAMAN (also Beeman and Beman)

(1775-1837). Born in New Marlboro, Massachusetts. Acquainted with Joseph Smith during translation of Book of Mormon. Acting member of Missouri high council in 1835. Ordained president of Kirtland elders' quorum in 1836.

JAMES A. BENNET

(?-1852). Born in Ireland. Proprietor of Arlington House, an educational institution on Long Island. Frequent correspondent of Joseph Smith. Proposed as vice-presidential running mate to Smith in 1844 but was ineligible.

JAMES G. BENNETT

(1795-1872). Born in Scotland. Conducted personal investigations into origins of Book of Mormon in 1831. Founded *New York Herald* in 1835. Visited Joseph Smith in Nauvoo and wrote about him afterward.

JOHN C. BENNETT

(1804-58). Converted in 1840. Confidant of Joseph Smith. Mayor of Nauvoo, major general of Nauvoo Legion, and assistant church president. Excommunicated in 1842. Authored anti-Mormon articles in *Sangamo Journal*, later published as *The History of the Saints*.

JOHN M. BERNHISEL

(1799-1881). Born in Loysville, Pennsylvania. A physician, graduating from University of Pennsylvania in 1827. Baptized in New York City in 1841. After 1844, copied Joseph Smith's revision of the Bible. Migrated to Utah. Later, acted as an LDS representative in Washington, D.C.

LILBURN W. BOGGS

(1798-1861). Born in Kentucky. Named governor of Missouri in 1836. Issued order to exterminate Mormons in 1838. Wounded in assassination attempt in 1842. Joseph Smith named as conspirator but never convicted.

JOHN F. BOYNTON

(1811–90). Born in Bradford, Massachusetts. Joined church in 1832. Member of Council of Twelve Apostles from 1835 to 1837, when he left the church.

JOSIAH BUTTERFIELD

(1795–1871). Born in Dunstable, Massachusetts. Baptized in 1833. Moved to Kirtland about 1834. Ordained president of First Quorum of Seventy in 1837. Member of Kirtland high council. Excommunicated in 1844. Rebaptized. Joined RLDS church in 1865.

JUSTIN BUTTERFIELD

(?–?). U.S. district attorney in Illinois. Offered opinion that the attempt to extradite Joseph Smith to Missouri would not stand up in an Illinois court.

REYNOLDS CAHOON

(1790–1862). Born in Cambridge, New York. Early Ohio convert. Called as counselor to Bishop Newell K. Whitney in Kirtland in 1832. Member of committee supervising construction of Kirtland temple. Migrated to Utah.

JOHN C. CALHOUN

(1782–1850). Born in South Carolina. Member, U.S. House of Representatives, 1811–17. U.S. secretary of war, 1817–25. U.S. vice-president, 1825–32. U.S. senator, 1832–43. U.S. secretary of state, 1844–45. U.S. senator, 1845–50. Champion of states' rights and slavery.

THOMAS CARLIN

(?–?). Governor of Illinois, 1838–42. Supported extradition of Joseph Smith to Missouri in 1840. Succeeded by Thomas Ford.

JARED CARTER

(1801–50). Born in Benson, Vermont. Converted and ordained elder in 1831. Member of Kirtland high council. Served on committee supervising Kirtland temple. Became disaffected in 1838.

SIMEON CARTER

(1794–1869). Born in Killingworth, Connecticut. Member of the Missouri high council.

HENRY CLAY

(1777–1852). Born in Virginia. U.S. senator, 1806–1807, 1810–11. Member, U.S. House of Representatives, 1811–14, 1815–21, 1823–25. U.S. secretary of state, 1825–29. U.S. senator, 1831–42. Whig candidate for U.S. president, 1832, 1844. U.S. senator, 1849–52.

WILLIAM CLAYTON

(1814–79). Born and converted in England. Arrived in Nauvoo in 1840. Secretary and clerk to Joseph Smith beginning in 1842. Witness to many of Joseph Smith's activities. Early polygamist. Migrated to Utah.

JOSEPH COE

(1785–?). Born in New Jersey. Ordained a high priest in 1831. Helped to lay the cornerstone to the Kirtland temple in 1833. Member of the Kirtland high council. Left the church in 1837.

ZEBEDEE COLTRIN

(1804–87). Born in Ovid, New York. Converted in 1830. Member of the Kirtland high council. Participated in Zion's camp. Member of First Quorum of Seventy from 1835 to 1837. Migrated to Utah.

LEMAN COPLEY

(1781–?). Born in Connecticut. Converted in 1831. Land owner in Ohio. Became disaffected. Disfellowshipped ca. 1834.

JOHN CORRILL

(1794–?). Born in Worcester County, Massachusetts. Converted in 1830. Second counselor to Bishop Edward Partridge from 1831 to 1837. Directed construction of Kirtland temple. Called as church historian in 1838 but excommunicated in 1839.

OLIVER COWDERY

(1806–50). Born in Wells, Vermont. Scribe to Joseph Smith during translation of Book of Mormon. One of the three witnesses to the Book of Mormon. Managed church printing office in Kirtland, Ohio. Called as "assistant president" to Joseph Smith in 1836. Excommunicated and left church in 1838. Returned ten years later.

WARREN COWDERY

(1788–1851). Born in Poultney, Vermont. Older brother of Oliver Cowdery. Presided over branch of church in Freedom, New York, in 1834. Moved to Kirtland the next year. Managed printing office, edited *Messenger and Advocate*, and clerked for Joseph Smith. Left church in 1838.

JONATHAN DUNHAM

(1800–45). Member of Danites in Missouri. Officer in Nauvoo Legion. Captain of the Nauvoo police.

KING FOLLETT

(1788–1844). Native of Vermont. Joined church in Ohio in 1831. Persecuted in Missouri, then settled in Nauvoo. Joseph Smith delivered important sermon on plurality and progression of gods at his funeral.

THOMAS FORD

(1800–50). Born in Pennsylvania. Moved to Illinois. Passed bar in 1823. Named to Illinois state supreme court in 1840. Elected governor of Illinois in 1842. Believed extradition attempts to remove Joseph Smith to Missouri in early 1840s were illegal. Promised protection to Joseph and Hyrum Smith, but both men were killed nonetheless. Wrote a history of Illinois.

ROBERT D. FOSTER

(?–?). Born in England. Converted to Mormonism in 1839–40. Physician to Sidney Rigdon and other church leaders in Nauvoo. Accompanied Joseph Smith and others to Washington, D.C. Owned much land in Nauvoo. Opposed polygamy. Denounced as traitor by Joseph Smith in 1844. Thereafter, strong opponent to Mormonism.

ISSAC GALLAND

(1791–1858). Born in Somerset County, Pennsylvania. Real estate speculator. Sold Mormons large tracts of land opposite from what would become Nauvoo. Baptized in 1839. Later became disaffected from church.

JESSE GAUSE

(1784?–1836?). Born Jesse Goss at East Marlborough, Pennsylvania. Served as counselor to Joseph Smith in church presidency from March 1832 until he left later that year.

SALMON GEE

(1792–1845). Born in Lyme, Connecticut. Living in Geauga County, Ohio, when converted in 1832. President of Seventy from 1837 to 1838. Member of Kirtland high council. Disfellowshipped in 1838.

ALGERNON SIDNEY GILBERT

(1789–1834). Born in New Haven, Connecticut. Business partner with Newel K. Whitney in Kirtland. Joined church in 1830. Driven from Jackson County, Missouri, in 1833. Died during Zion's Camp.

OLIVER GRANGER

(1794–1841). Born in Rutland, Vermont. Resident of Kirtland from 1835 to 1838. Member of Kirtland high council. Joseph Smith's attorney-in-fact in Ohio. Called as president of church in Kirtland, where he died.

JOHN P. GREENE

(1793–1844). Born in Herkimer, New York. Married Rhoda Young, sister of Brigham Young. Baptized in 1832 and moved to Kirtland. Moved to Far West in 1838 but returned to Illinois. Marshall in Nauvoo. Officer in charge of the destruction of the *Nauvoo Expositor*.

GEORGE W. HARRIS

(1780–1857[60?]). Born in Lanesborough, Massachusetts. Baptized in 1834. Member of the Far West and Nauvoo high councils. Active in Missouri Danites. Held many positions in Nauvoo. Did not migrate west. Excommunicated from LDS church before his death.

MARTIN HARRIS

(1783–1875). Born in Easttown, New York. Moved to Palmyra, New York, in 1827. Aided Joseph Smith financially during translation and printing of Book of Mormon. Lost first 116 pages of translation. One of the three witnesses of the Book of Mormon.

Excommunicated in late 1837. Rebaptized in 1842. Later, left church again and returned again before death.

ELIAS HIGBEE

(1795-1843). Born in Galloway, New Jersey. Living in Cincinnati, Ohio, when converted in 1832. Driven from Jackson County. Worked on Kirtland temple. Sons Chauncey L. and Francis helped to publish *Nauvoo Expositor*.

GEORGE M. HINKLE

(?-?). Called to Missouri high council in 1836. Commander of Mormon militia defending Far West. Became disaffected and turned Mormon leaders over to Missouri militia.

JESSE HITCHCOCK

(1801-?). Born in Ash County, North Carolina. Member of Missouri high council, 1836-37.

DIMICK B. HUNTINGTON

(1808-79). Born in Watertown, New York. Appointed Nauvoo city constable in 1841 and city coroner in 1842.

DOCTOR PHILASTUS HURLBUT

(1809-83). Born in Chittendon County, Vermont. Joined the church in 1833 but was shortly afterward excommunicated for immorality. Hired by group of Kirtland non-Mormons to collect information in New York critical of Joseph Smith and church.

ORSON HYDE

(1805-78). Campbellite pastor in Ohio when converted to Mormonism in 1831. Called as member of Council of Twelve Apostles in 1835. Disaffected from church temporarily in 1838-39. Sent on mission to Palestine in 1840. Migrated to Utah. Brother-in-law to Luke and Lyman Johnson.

BENJAMIN F. JOHNSON

(1818-1905). Born in Pomfret, New York. Moved to Kirtland in 1833. Baptized in 1835. Moved to Missouri in 1838. Settled at Adam-ondi-Ahman but forced to leave and was later arrested. Member of the Council of Fifty in Nauvoo. Migrated to Utah.

JOHN JOHNSON

(1779-1843). Born in Chesterfield, New Hampshire. Residing at Hiram, Ohio, when joined church in 1831. Member of

Kirtland high council. While revising the Bible, Joseph Smith stayed at the Johnson home.

LUKE JOHNSON

(1807-61). Born in Pomfret, Vermont. Son of John Johnson and older brother of Lyman. Member of Kirtland high council from 1834 to 1835. Member of Zion's Camp. Member of Council of Twelve Apostles from 1835 to 1837. Left church in 1838 but later returned.

LYMAN E. JOHNSON

(1811-56). Born in Pomfret, Vermont. Son of John Johnson. Joined church in 1831. Served as missionary in New England and Canada in 1832-33 with Orson Pratt. Businessman, lawyer, and member of Council of Twelve Apostles from 1835 until excommunication in 1838.

DAN JONES (called Captain)

(1811-62). Born in Flintshire, Wales. Emigrated to U.S. in 1840. Operated a steamboat on the Mississippi River called *Maid of Iowa*. Converted to Mormonism in 1843. Later, moved to Utah.

JOSHUA the Jewish Minister.

See Matthews, Robert.

HEBER C. KIMBALL

(1801-68). Born in Sheldon, Vermont. Employed as potter when converted in April 1832. Moved to Kirtland and was member of Zion's Camp. Called to Council of Twelve Apostles in 1835. Sent to open mission to England in 1837. Daughter sealed to Joseph Smith in 1843. Migrated to Utah.

JOSEPH KNIGHT

(1772-1847). Born in Oakham, Massachusetts. Early convert. Confidant and close friend of Joseph Smith in New York and Pennsylvania.

NEWEL KNIGHT

(1800-47). Born in Marlborough, Vermont. Son of Joseph Knight. Living in Colesville, New York, when converted. Moved to Ohio, then Missouri, in 1831. Driven from Jackson County in 1833. Worked on Kirtland temple. Member of Nauvoo high council.

VINSON KNIGHT

(1804–42). Born in Chester, New York. Called as counselor to Bishop Newel K. Whitney in Kirtland in 1836. Bishop in Nauvoo.

WILLIAM LAW

(1809–92). Born in northern Ireland. Converted in Canada in 1836. Moved to Nauvoo in 1839. Named counselor in First Presidency in 1841. Split with Joseph Smith over polygamy. Left church in 1844. Helped to publish *Nauvoo Expositor*.

WILSON LAW

(1807–77). Older brother of William Law. Charter member of Nauvoo city council. Elected brigadier general of Nauvoo Legion in 1841. Left church with brother. Helped to publish *Nauvoo Expositor*.

AMASA LYMAN

(1813–77). Born in Lyman, New Hampshire. Converted and moved to Kirtland in 1832. Moved from Iowa to Nauvoo in 1840. Named to Council of Twelve Apostles in 1842. Migrated to Utah. Later excommunicated.

WILLIAM E. MCLELLIN

(1806?–83). Joined church in Missouri in August 1831. Excommunicated following year but later rejoined. Schoolteacher and member of Council of Twelve Apostles from 1835 until he left church again in 1838.

WILLIAM MARKS

(1792–1872). Born in Rutland, Vermont. Served on Kirtland high council. Nauvoo stake president from 1839 to 1844. Opposed polygamy. President of Council of Fifty at time of Joseph Smith's death. Later joined RLDS church.

THOMAS B. MARSH

(1799–1866). Born in Acton, Massachusetts. Early convert. Moved to Kirtland in 1831 and to Jackson County in 1832. Member of Clay County high council in Missouri. Named member and president of Council of Twelve Apostles in 1835. Excommunicated in 1839 but later returned to the LDS church.

ROBERT MATTHEWS

(1800?-41?). Born in Cambridge, New York. Claimed to be God the Father reincarnated in body of Matthias, ancient apostle of Jesus Christ. Predicted destruction of Albany, New York, in 1830. Temporarily committed to asylum. Later tried for murder. Acquitted but held for three months on charges of brutality. Visited Joseph Smith in Kirtland in 1835.

ROBERT MATTHIAS

See MATTHEWS, Robert.

GEORGE MILLER

(1794-1856). Born in Virginia. Converted in Illinois in 1839. Called in 1841 to replace Edward Partridge as bishop and later Don Carlos Smith as president of high priests in Nauvoo. Left church after death of Joseph Smith.

ISSAC MORELY

(1786-1865). Born in Montague, Massachusetts. Among first Kirtland converts. Called as counselor to Bishop Edward Partridge in 1831. Driven from Jackson County in 1833. Named patriarch in 1837. Migrated to Utah in 1848.

JAMES MULHOLLAND

(1804-39). Scribe to Joseph Smith. Wrote early draft of official *History of the Church*.

ALEXANDER NEIBAUR

(1808-76). Born in England. Converted to Mormonism ca. 1840. Migrated to Nauvoo. Witness to much of Joseph Smith's activities. Accompanied main body of church to the west in 1846-47.

ELEAZER FREEMAN NICKERSON

(1806-62). Born in Cavendish, Vermont. Son of Freeman Nickerson. Living in Upper Canada when visited by father and Joseph Smith.

FREEMAN NICKERSON

(1779-1847). Born in South Dennis, Massachusetts. Baptized in 1833. Member of Zion's Camp. Missionary to Ohio and Canada in 1833 and 1835-36. Moved to Nauvoo.

JOSEPH B. NOBLE

(1810-1900). Born in Egremont, Massachusetts. Converted by Brigham Young in 1832. Member of Zion's Camp. Performed first known plural marriage, between his sister-in-law, Louisa Beman, and Joseph Smith in 1841. Migrated to Utah in 1847.

OLIVER OLNEY

(1800-?). Living at Shalesrville, in 1830. President of Kirtland teachers' quorum, 1836-38. Disaffected from church in Nauvoo.

JOHN E. PAGE

(1799-1867). Born in Trenton, New York. Converted in 1833. Moved to Kirtland in 1835. Member of Council of Twelve Apostles from 1838 to 1846, when he left the church.

WARREN PARRISH

(1800?-?). Brother-in-law of David Patten. Baptized by Brigham Young in May 1833. Member of Zion's Camp. Member of First Quorum of Seventy. Secretary to church's Kirtland bank in 1836. Resigned from church the following year.

EDWARD PARTRIDGE

(1793-1840). Born in Pittsfield, Massachusetts. Converted in Painesville, Ohio, in 1830. Appointed first bishop of church and called in 1831 to direct Saints to Jackson County. Named bishop in Nauvoo. Daughters sealed to Joseph Smith.

DAVID PATTEN

(1800?-38). Born in Theresa, near Indian River Falls, New York. Joined the church in Indiana in 1832. Served as member of Council of Twelve Apostles from 1835 to 1838. Killed near Crooked River, Missouri.

WILLIAM W. PHELPS

(1792-1872). Born in Hanover, New Jersey. Worked in church printing office in Kirtland. Edited *Evening and Morning Star*. Counselor to David Whitmer in Missouri stake presidency. Clerked for Joseph Smith. Excommunicated in 1838. Reinstated in 1841. Member of Nauvoo city council and Council of Fifty. Migrated to Utah.

DANIEL LEVY MADURA PIEXOTTO

(?-?). Graduate of Columbia College and Medical School. President of New York County Medical Society, 1830-32. Professor of Theory and Practice of Physics and Obstetrics at Willoughby Medical College.

ORSON PRATT

(1811-81). Born in Hartford, New York. Younger brother of Parley P. Pratt. Left Kirtland with Lyman Johnson in 1832 on mission to East. Called as member of Council of Twelve Apostles in 1835. Temporarily disaffected from Joseph Smith in 1842 because of differences over polygamy.

PARLEY P. PRATT

(1807-57). Born in Burlington, New York. Older brother of Orson Pratt. Converted in 1830 after reading Book of Mormon. Member of Council of Twelve Apostles from 1835. Critical of Joseph Smith during Kirtland Safety Society fiasco. Later served mission to England. Migrated to Utah.

THOMAS REYNOLDS

(?-?). Succeeded Lilburn Boggs as governor of Missouri. Pushed for extradition of Joseph Smith to Missouri in early 1840s.

LEVI RICHARDS

(1799-1845). Born in Hopkinton, Massachusetts. Older brother of Willard Richards. A physician practicing Thompsonian medicine. Baptized in Kirtland in 1836. Moved to Missouri.

WILLARD RICHARDS

(1804-54). Converted in 1837. Sent on mission to England and named to Council of Twelve Apostles in 1840. Member of Nauvoo city council in 1841. Church historian and private secretary to Joseph Smith. Present with Joseph and Hyrum and John Taylor in Carthage jail.

SIDNEY RIGDON

(1793-1876). Campbellite minister in Mentor, Ohio. Converted to Mormonism in fall 1830. Confidant of Joseph Smith. Called as counselor in church presidency in March 1832. Imprisoned in Liberty jail in Missouri with other Mormons. Disaffected from Joseph Smith in the 1840s. Excommunicated in 1844.

EBENEZER ROBINSON

(1816-91). Born in Rome, New York. Baptized in 1835 by Joseph Smith. Resided in Kirtland, Missouri, and Nauvoo. After death of Joseph Smith, joined RLDS church.

GEORGE W. ROBINSON

(1814-?). Born in Pawlet, Vermont. Lived in Kirtland from 1837 to 1838. Replaced Oliver Cowdery as church recorder in 1837. Scribe to Joseph Smith. Left church in Nauvoo in 1842.

ORRIN P. ROCKWELL

(1813-78). Early convert. Close friend and body guard of Joseph Smith. Member of Danites in Missouri. Accused in attempted assassination of Lilburn W. Boggs. Imprisoned for nine months but never tried.

KATHERINE (Smith) SALISBURY

(1813-1900). Born in Lebanon, New Hampshire. Younger sister to Joseph Smith. Married Wilkins Jenkins Salisbury on 8 January 1831.

JOSHUA SEIXAS

(1800?-1875?). Born in either Cuba or Virginia. Taught Hebrew and other languages in Andover, Massachusetts, and at Spanish and Portuguese Synagogue in New York City. Author of *Hebrew Grammar*, first appearing in 1833. Taught at Oberlin College in 1835.

LYMAN SHERMAN

(1804-39). Born in Monkton, Vermont. Baptized in 1832. Moved to Kirtland in 1833. Member of Zion's Camp. President of First Quorum of Seventy, 1835-37. Member of Kirtland and Far West high councils. Called to be an apostle but never ordained. Died at Far West.

HENRY G. SHERWOOD

(1785-1862). Member of Kirtland and Nauvoo high councils. Elected Nauvoo city marshal in 1841. Migrated to Utah.

ALVIN SMITH

(1798-1823). Oldest brother of Joseph Smith. Died from overdose of calomel.

DON CARLOS SMITH

(1816-1841). Born in Norwich, Vermont. Youngest brother of Joseph Smith. Edited *Elders' Journal* in Kirtland in 1837 and *Times and Seasons* in Nauvoo in 1839.

EMMA (Hale) SMITH

(1804-79). Born in Harmony, Pennsylvania. First wife of Joseph Smith. Compiled a selection of hymns for publication in 1835. Opposed polygamy. Did not accompany Brigham Young to the west. Remarried. Tacitly endorsed RLDS church by allowing oldest son, Joseph III, to be named president of reorganization.

GEORGE A. SMITH

(1817-75). Born in Potsdam, New York. Cousin of Joseph Smith. Converted in 1832. Moved to Kirtland in 1833. Member of Zion's Camp. Member of First Quorum of Seventy. Member of Council of Twelve Apostles from 1839 to 1875. Migrated to Utah.

HYRUM SMITH

(1800-44). Born in Tunbridge, Vermont. Older brother of Joseph Smith. One of the eight witnesses of the Book of Mormon. Member of committee supervising construction of Kirtland temple. Later, counselor in First Presidency and Presiding Church Patriarch.

JOHN SMITH

(1781-1854). Born in Derryfield, New Hampshire. Uncle to Joseph Smith. Coverted in 1832. Moved to Kirtland the following year. Presiding Patriarch in LDS church from 1849 to 1854. Migrated to Utah.

JOSEPH SMITH Sr.

(1771-1840). Born in Massachusetts. Married Lucy Mack in 1796. Father of Joseph Smith. One of the eight witnesses of the Book of Mormon. Ordained patriarch and president of high priests in Kirtland in 1833. Member of Kirtland high council.

LUCY (Mack) SMITH

(1775-1856). Born in New Hampshire. Mother of Joseph Smith. Survived husband and all sons except William. Did not travel west with Brigham Young. Spent last years with daughter-in-law Emma.

SAMUEL H. SMITH

(1808-44). Born in Tunbridge, Vermont. Younger brother of Joseph Smith. One of the eight witnesses of the Book of Mormon. Early missionary to New York and Ohio. Member of Kirtland high council from 1834 to 1838.

SYLVESTER SMITH

(1805?-?). Missionary to New England with Jared Carter in 1832. Participated in Zion's Camp. Member of Kirtland high council from 1835 to 1836. Member of First Quorum of Seventy form 1835 to 1837. Temporary scribe to Joseph Smith in 1836. Excommunicated in 1837.

WILLIAM SMITH

(1811-93). Born in Royalton, Vermont. Younger brother of Joseph Smith. Member of Council of Twelve Apostles from 1835. Dropped from, then re-instated to, council in 1839. Participated in Zion's Camp. Edited *Nauvoo Wasp*. Excommunicated in 1845.

ELIZA R. SNOW

(1804-87). Born in Massachusetts. Baptized in 1835. Educator, poet, author of several LDS hymns. First secretary of the Nauvoo Female Relief Society. Sealed polygynously to Joseph Smith in 1842. After 1844, married to Brigham Young. Moved to Utah.

ERASTUS SNOW

(1818-88). Born in St. Johnsbury, Vermont. Ordained LDS apostle in 1849 in Salt Lake City.

LORENZO SNOW

(1814-1901). Born in Mantua, Ohio. Brother of Eliza Snow. Baptized in 1835. Living at Kirtland from 1836 to 1838. Migrated to Utah. Ordained LDS apostle in 1849. Ordained president of LDS church in 1898.

ORSON SPENCER

(1802-55). Born in Massachusetts. Educated at Union College in Schenectady, New York, and at Theological College at Hamilton, New York. Converted to Mormonism and moved to Nauvoo in 1841. Served as alderman in Nauvoo. Later, migrated to Utah.

SOPHRONIA (Smith) STODDARD

(1803–76). Born in Tunbridge, Vermont. Oldest sister of Joseph Smith. Married Calvin W. Stoddard in Palmyra, New York, on 30 December 1827.

JOHN TAYLOR

(1808–87). Born in England. Converted in Canada in 1836. Named member of Council of Twelve Apostles in 1838. Served missions to England. Edited *Times and Seasons* and *Nauvoo Neighbor*. Seriously wounded in Carthage jail in 1844 when Joseph and Hyrum Smith were killed. Migrated to Utah. Later, president of LDS church.

ROBERT B. THOMPSON

(1811–41). Born in England. Converted in 1836. Moved to Kirtland and later to Missouri. Associate editor of *Times and Seasons*. Scribe to Joseph Smith.

THEODORE TURLEY

(1801–71). Born in England. Baptized in Ontario, Canada. Moved to Missouri and late to Nauvoo. Accompanied company of English Saints to Nauvoo in 1840. Operated a brewery in Nauvoo. Member of Council of Fifty. Migrated west after 1844.

MARTIN VAN BUREN

(1782–1862). Eighth U.S. president, 1837–41. Visited by Joseph Smith and others in attempt to solicit federal help in redressing Missouri persecutions. Told the Mormons he could not do anything.

DANIEL H. WELLS

(1814–91). Born in Trenton, New York. Baptized in Nauvoo. Before conversion, served in Nauvoo as alderman, regent of the university, and brigadier general in Nauvoo Legion. Migrated to Utah. Ordained LDS apostle, but never a member of Quorum of the Twelve, in 1857.

HARVEY WHITLOCK

(1809–?). Born in Massachusetts. Ordained a high priest and moved to Missouri in 1831. Disfellowshipped about 1834. Excommunicated in 1838.

DAVID WHITMER

(1805–88). Born near Harrisburg, Pennsylvania. Brother of John Whitmer. Met Joseph Smith in 1828. One of the three witnesses of the Book of Mormon. Baptized in 1829. Member of the Missouri high council. Left church in 1838.

JOHN WHITMER

(1802–78). Older brother of David Whitmer. One of earliest Mormon converts. Assisted Joseph Smith as clerk and scribe. Appointed church historian and called to preside over church in Missouri. Left church in 1838.

PETER WHITMER

(1809–36). Born in Fayette, New York. Early convert. One of the eight witnesses of the Book of Mormon. Member of Missouri high council.

NEWEL K.WHITNEY

(1795–1850). Born in Marlborough, Vermont. Baptized by Mormon missionaries in Kirtland in 1830. Appointed bishop the following year, a calling he retained until his death. Member of Council of Fifty.

LYMAN WIGHT

(1796–1858). Verteran of War of 1812. Converted with other Campbellites in Kirtland in 1830. Driven from Jackson County, Missouri, in 1833. Member of Council of Twelve Apostles from 1841 to 1848.

FREDERICK G. WILLIAMS

(1787–1842). Born in Suffield, Connecticut. Converted to Mormonism in Kirtland in 1830. Appointed clerk to Joseph Smith in July 1832. Became counselor in church presidency in 1833. Excommunicated ca. 1837 but rebaptized the following year. Excommunicated again in 1839.

WILFORD WOODRUFF

(1807–98). Converted in 1833. Moved to Kirtland in 1834. Member of Zion's Camp. Moved to Missouri and to Illinois. Called as member of Council of Twelve Apostles in 1839. Served mission to England. Migrated to Utah. Later, president of LDS church.

BRIGHAM YOUNG

(1801–77). Born in Whittingham, Vermont. Brother of Phineas Young. Carpenter, painter, and glazier in Mendon, New York. Converted in 1832. Moved to Kirtland in 1833. Member of Zion's Camp. Named a member of Council of Twelve Apostles in 1835. Migrated to Utah. President of LDS church, 1848 to 1877.

JOSEPH YOUNG

(1797–1881). Born in Hopkinton, Massachusetts. Older brother of Brigham Young, who baptized him in 1832. Member of Zion's Camp. One of the presidents of the Seventy from 1835 to 1881. Migrated to Utah.

PHINEAS H. YOUNG

(1799–1879). Brother of Brigham Young. Joined church in April 1832. Worked in church's printing office in Kirtland. Moved to Nauvoo but returned to Kirtland before 1845.

A
Joseph
Smith

BIBLIOGRAPHY

Alexander, Thomas G. "The Place of Joseph Smith in the Development of American Religion: A Historiographical Inquiry." *Journal of Mormon History* 5 (1978): 3-17.

Allen, James B. "The Significance of Joseph Smith's First Vision in Mormon Thought." *Dialogue: A Journal of Mormon Thought* 1 (Autumn 1966): 28-45.

————, and Glen M. Leonard. *The Story of the Latter-day Saints.* Salt Lake City: Deseret Book, 1976.

Anderson, Mary Audentia. *Ancestry and Posterity of Joseph Smith and Emma Hale.* Independence, MO: Herald Publishing House, 1929.

Anderson, Richard L. *Joseph Smith's New England Heritage.* Salt Lake City: Deseret Book, 1971.

————. *Investigating Book of Mormon Witnesses.* Salt Lake City: Deseret Book, 1981.

Arrington, Leonard J., Feramorz Y. Fox, and Dean L. May. *Building the City of God: Community and Cooperation Among the Mormons.* Salt Lake City: Deseret Book, 1976.

Arrington, Leonard J., and Davis Bitton. *The Mormon Experience.* New York: Alfred A. Knopf, 1979.

Bachman, Danel. "A Study of the Mormon Practice of PluralMarriage Before the Death of Joseph Smith." M.A. thesis, Purdue University, 1975.

Backman, Milton V., Jr. *Joseph Smith's First Vision*. 2nd ed. Salt Lake City: Bookcraft, 1980.

————. *The Heavens Resound: A History of the Latter-day Saints in Ohio, 1830–1838*. Salt Lake City: Deseret Book, 1983.

Bennett, John C. *The History of the Saints: An Expose of Joe Smith and Mormonism*. Boston: Leland and Whiting, 1842.

Book of Commandments, for the Government of the Church of Christ, Organized According to Law, on the 6th of April, 1830. Zion [Independence, MO]: W. W. Phelps & Co., 1833.

Book of Mormon. Salt Lake City: Church of Jesus Christ of Latter-day Saints, 1981. Independence, MO: Reorganized Church of Jesus Christ of Latter Day Saints, 1980.

Brodie, Fawn M. *No Man Knows My History: The Life of Joseph Smith, the Mormon Prophet*. New York: Alfred A. Knopf, 1945.

Bushman, Richard L. "The Character of Joseph Smith: Insights from his Holographs." *Ensign* 7 (April 1977): 11–13.

————. *Joseph Smith and the Beginnings of Mormonism*. Urbana: University of Illinois Press, 1984.

Conkling, J. Christopher. *A Joseph Smith Chronology*. Salt Lake City: Deseret Book, 1979.

Cook, Lyndon W. *The Revelations of the Prophet Joseph Smith — A Historical and Biographical Commentary of the Doctrine and Covenants*. Provo, UT: Seventy's Mission Bookstore, 1981.

Corrill, John. *Brief History of the Church of Jesus Christ of Latter Day Saints*. St. Louis: the Author, 1839.

Crawley, Peter, and Richard L. Anderson. "The Political and Social Realities of Zion's Camp." *Brigham Young University Studies* 14 (Summer 1974): 406–20.

Doctrine and Covenants. Salt Lake City: Church of Jesus Christ of Latter-day Saints, 1981. Independence, MO: Reorganized Church of Jesus Christ of Latter Day Saints, 1980.

Durham, G. Homer. *Joseph Smith: Prophet Statesman*. Salt Lake City: Bookcraft, 1944.

Edwards, F. Henry, ed. *History of the Reorganized Church of Jesus Christ of Latter Day Saints*. Independence, MO: Herald Publishing House, 1967.

Ehat, Andrew F. "Joseph Smith's Introduction of Temple Ordinances and the 1844 Mormon Succession Question." M.A. thesis, Brigham Young University, 1982.

————, and Lyndon W. Cook, eds. *The Words of Joseph Smith*. Provo, UT: Religious Studies Center, Brigham Young University, 1980.

Elder's Journal of the Church of Latter Day Saints, 1837–38. Kirtland, OH [Far West, MO].

Esplin, Ronald K. "The Emergence of Brigham Young and the Twelve to Mormon Leadership, 1830–1841." Ph.D. diss., Brigham Young University, 1981.

Evans, John Henry. *Joseph Smith: An American Prophet*. New York: Macmillan, 1933.

Evening and Morning Star, 1832–34. Independence, MO, and Kirtland, OH.

Flanders, Robert. *Nauvoo: Kingdom on the Mississippi*. Urbana: University of Illinois Press, 1965.

Ford, Thomas. *History of Illinois from Its Commencement as a State in 1814 to 1847*. Chicago: S. C. Griggs, 1854.

Foster, Lawrence. *Religion and Sexuality: Three American Communal Experiments of the Nineteenth Century*. New York: Oxford University Press, 1981.

Gentry, Leland H. "A History of the Latter-day Saints in Northern Missouri from 1836–1839." Ph.D. diss., Brigham Young University, 1965.

————. "The Danite Band of 1838." *Brigham Young University Studies* 14 (Summer 1974): 421–50.

Godfrey, Kenneth W. "Causes of Mormon-Non-Mormon Conflict in Hancock County, Illinois, 1839–1846." Ph.D. diss., Brigham Young University, 1967.

Gregg, Thomas. *The Prophet of Palmyra*. New York: John B. Allen, 1890.

Hansen, Klaus. *Quest for Empire: The Political Kingdom of God and the Council of Fifty in Mormon History*. East Lansing: Michigan State University Press, 1967.

Hill, Donna. *Joseph Smith: The First Mormon*. Garden City, NY: Doubleday, 1977.

Hill, Marvin S. "The Role of Christian Primitivism in the Origin and Development of the Mormon Kingdom, 1830-1845." Ph.D. diss., University of Chicago, 1968.

————, Keith Rooker, and Larry T. Wimmer. "The Kirtland Economy Revisited: A Market Critique of Sectarian Economics." *Brigham Young University Studies* 17 (Summer 1977): 391–475.

Holy Scriptures. Independence, MO: Reorganized Church of Jesus Christ of Latter Day Saints, 1944.

Howard, Richard P. *Restoration Scriptures: A Study of Their Textual Development*. Independence, MO: Herald House Publishing, 1969.

Howe, E. D. *Mormonism Unvailed* (sic). Painesville, OH: the Author, 1834.

Jenson, Andrew. *Encyclopedic History of the Church of Jesus Christ of Latter-day Saints*. Salt Lake City, 1941.

————. *Latter-day Saint Biographical Encyclopedia*. 4 vols. Salt Lake City: Andrew Jenson History Co., 1901.

Jessee, Dean C. "The Writing of Joseph Smith's History." *Brigham Young University Studies* 11 (Spring 1971): 439–73.

————. "The Reliability of Joseph Smith's History." *Journal of Mormon History* 3 (1976): 23–46.

————. *The Personal Writings of Joseph Smith*. Salt Lake City: Deseret Book, 1984.

Latter Day Saints' Messenger and Advocate, 1834–37. Kirtland, OH.

LeSueur, Stephen C. *The 1838 Mormon War in Missouri*. Columbia: University of Missouri Press, 1987.

Linn, William Alexander. *The Story of the Mormons from the Date of their Origin to the Year 1901*. 1902; rept. New York: Macmillan, 1923.

Matthews, Robert J. *"A Plainer Translation"—Joseph Smith Translation of the Bible: A History and Commentary*. Provo, UT: Brigham Young University Press, 1975.

Miller, David, and Della Miller. *Nauvoo: The City of Joseph*. Santa Barbara: Peregrine Smith, 1974.

Newell, Linda K., and Valeen Tippetts Avery. *Mormon Enigma: Emma Hale Smith*. Garden City, NY: Doubleday, 1984.

Oaks, Dallin H. "The Suppression of the *Nauvoo Expositor*." *Utah Law Review* 9 (Winter 1965): 862–903.

————, and Marvin S. Hill. *Carthage Conspiracy: The Trial of the Accused Assassins of Joseph Smith*. Urbana: University of Illinois Press, 1975.

Parkin, Max. *Conflict at Kirtland: A Study of the Nature and Causes of External and Internal Conflict of the Mormons in Ohio between 1830 and 1838*. Salt Lake City: Max H. Parkin, 1966.

————. "A History of the Latter-day Saints in Clay County, Missouri, from 1833 to 1837." Ph.D. diss., Brigham Young University, 1976.

Pearl of Great Price. Salt Lake City: Church of Jesus Christ of Latter-day Saints, 1981.

Porter, Larry. "A Study of the Origins of The Church of Jesus Christ of Latter-day Saints in the States of New York and Pennsylvania, 1816–1831." Ph.D. diss., Brigham Young University, 1971.

Pratt, Parley P. *The Autobiography of Parley Parker Pratt*. 1874; 3rd ed. Salt Lake City: Deseret Book, 1938.

Quinn, D. Michael. "Organizational Development and Social Origins of the Mormon Hierarchy, 1832–1932: A Prosopographical Study." M.A. thesis, University of Utah, 1973.

————. "The Mormon Hierarchy, 1832–1932: An American Elite." Ph.D. diss., Yale University, 1976.

————. *Early Mormonism and the Magic World View*. Salt Lake City: Signature Books, 1987.

Riley, Isaac Woodbridge. *The Founder of Mormonism: A Psychological Study of Joseph Smith, Jr*. New York: Dodd, Mead and Co., 1902.

Roberts, B. H. *A Comprehensive History of The Church of Jesus Christ of Latter-day Saints, Century I.* 6 vols. Salt Lake City: Church of Jesus Christ of Latter-day Saints, 1930. 2nd ed. rev. 1964.

Searle, Howard C. "Early Mormon Historiography: Writing the History of the Mormons, 1830–1858." Ph.D. diss., University of California at Los Angeles, 1979.

Shipps, Jan. "The Prophet Puzzle: Suggestions Leading Toward a More Comprehensive Interpretation of Joseph Smith." *Journal of Mormon History* 1 (1974): 3–20.

Smith, Joseph, et al. *History of the Church of Jesus Christ of Latter-day Saints.* B. H. Roberts, ed. 7 vols. 2nd ed. rev. Salt Lake City, 1964.

Smith, Joseph, III. *The Memoirs of President Joseph Smith III (1832–1914): A Photo-Reprint Edition of the Original Serial Publication as edited by Mary Audentia Smith Anderson and Appearing in The Saints' Herald (November 6, 1934–July 31, 1937).* Richard P. Howard, ed. Independence, MO: Herald Publishing House, 1979.

Smith, Joseph Fielding, comp. *Teachings of the Prophet Joseph Smith.* Salt Lake City: Deseret Book, 1938.

Smith, Lucy Mack. *Biographical Sketches of Joseph Smith the Prophet and His Progenitors for Many Generations.* Liverpool, England: S. W. Richards, 1853.

Smith, William. *William Smith on Mormonism.* Lamoni, IA: Herald Steam Book and Job Office, 1883.

Times and Seasons, 1839–46. Nauvoo, IL.

Van Wagoner, Richard S. *Mormon Polygamy: A History.* Salt Lake City: Signature Books, 1986.

Walker, John Phillip, ed. *Dale Morgan on Early Mormonism: Correspondence and a New History.* Salt Lake City: Signature Books, 1986.

The
DOCUMENTS

Autobiographical
Sketch

1832

T*he following document was evidently written sometime between 20 July and 27 November 1832[1] and is in the handwriting of Frederick G. Williams and Joseph Smith (in* **bold***). It represents Joseph Smith's first and, so far as is known, only attempt to record the events of his first vision ca. 1820 in his own hand. This sketch was written on the first three leaves, subsequently removed, of what would later be used as a letterbook. The original is housed in the archives of the Historical Department, Church of Jesus Christ of Latter-day Saints, Salt Lake City, Utah.*

A History of the life
of Joseph Smith, Jr.

An account of his marvelous experience and of all the mighty acts which he doeth in the name of Jesus Ch[r]ist the Son of the Living God of whom he beareth record. Also an account of the rise of the Church of Christ in the eve of time according as the Lord

---

[1] This is according to Dean C. Jessee, ed., *The Personal Writings of Joseph Smith* (Salt Lake City: Deseret Book, 1984), p. 640n6.

brought forth and established by his hand. /Firstly,/ he receiving the testamony from on high. Seccondly, the ministering of Angels. Thirdly, the reception of the Holy Priesthood by the ministring of Angels to admin[i]ster the letter of the Gospel /the Law and commandments as they were given unto him/ and the ordinenc[e]s. Fo[u]rthly, a confirmation and reception of the High Priesthood after the Holy Order of the Son of the Living God [with] power and ordinence[s] from on high to preach the Gospel in the administration and demonstration of the spirit, **the Kees of the Kingdom of God confered upon him and the continuation of the blessings of God to him &c.**

I was born in the town of Charon [Sharon] in the /State/ of Vermont, North America on the twenty third day of December AD 1805 of goodly parents who spared no pains to instruct/ing/ me in /the/ Christian religion.

At the age of about ten years my Father Joseph Smith, Siegnior [Senior] moved to Palmyra, Ontario County in the State of New York. And being in indigent circumstances [we] were obliged to labour hard for the support of a large Family having nine chilldren. As it required the exertions of all that were able to render any assistance for the support of the Family, therefore we were deprived of the bennifit of an education. Suffice it to say I was mearly instructid in reading, writing, and the ground /rules/ of Arithmatic which const[it]uted my whole literary acquirements.

At about the age of twelve years my mind become seriously imprest {page 1} with regard to the all important concerns for the wellfare of my immortal Soul which led me to searching the scriptures believeing, as I was taught, that they contained the word of God. Thus applying myself to them and my intimate acquaintance with those of differant denominations led me to marvel excedingly. For I discovered that /they did not ~~adorn~~/ ~~instead~~ of adorning their profession by a holy walk and Godly coversation agreeable to what I found contained in that sacred depository. This was a grief to my Soul.

Thus from the age of twelve years to fifteen I pondered many things in my heart concerning the sittuation of the world of mankind, the contentions and divi/si/ons, the wicke/d/ness and abominations, and the darkness which per-

4

vaded the minds of mankind. My mind become excedingly distressed for I become convicted of my sins and by searching the scriptures I found that ~~mand~~ /mankind/ did not come unto the Lord but that they had apostatised from the true and living faith. There was no society or denomination that built upon the gospel of Jesus Christ as recorded in the New Testament and I felt to mourn for my own sins and for the sins of the world.

For I learned in the scriptures that God was the same yesterday, to day, and forever. That he was no respecter to [of] persons, for he was God. For I looked upon the sun, the glorious luminary of the earth. And also the moon rolling in their magesty through the heavens. Also the stars, shining in their courses. And the earth also upon which I stood. And the beast of the field and the fowls of heaven and the fish of the waters. And also man walking forth upon the face of the earth in magesty and in the strength of beauty whose power and intiligence in governing the things which are so exceding great and {page 2} marvilous even in the likeness of him who created ~~him~~ /them/.

When I considered upon these things my heart exclaimed, "Well hath the wise man said ~~the~~ /it is a/ fool /that/ saith in his heart, 'there is no God.'" My heart exclaimed, "All these bear testimony and bespeak an omnipotent and omnipreasant power. A being who makith Laws and decreeeth and bindeth all things in their bounds. Who filleth Eternity. Who was, is, and will be from all Eternity to Eternity." When I considered all these things and that /that/ being seeketh such to worship him as worship him in spirit and in truth. Therefore I cried unto the Lord for mercy for there was none else to whom I could go and obtain mercy. The Lord heard my cry in the wilderness and while in /the/ attitude of calling upon the Lord /in the 16th year of my age/ a pillar of ~~fire~~ light above the brightness of the sun at noon day come down from above and rested upon me. I was filled with the spirit of God and the /Lord/ opened the heavens upon me and I saw the Lord.

He spake unto me saying, "Joseph /my son/ thy sins are forgiven thee. Go thy way, walk in my statutes and keep my commandments. Behold I am the Lord of Glory. I was

5

crucifyed for the world that all those who believe on my name may have Eternal life. /Behold/ the world lieth in sin at this time and none doeth good, no not one. They have turned asside from the gospel and keep not /my/ commandments. They draw near to me with their lips while their hearts are far from me and mine anger is kindling against the inhabitants of the earth to visit them acording to th/e/ir ungodliness and to bring to pass that which /hath/ been spoken by the mouth of the prophets and Ap/o/stles. Behold and lo, I come quickly as it [is] written of me, in the cloud /clothed/ in the glory of my Father."

My soul was filled with love and for many days I could rejoice with great Joy and the Lord was with me. But [I] could find none that would believe the he[a]venly vision. Nevertheless, I pondered these things in my heart. ~~about that time my mother and~~ But after many days {page 3} I fell into transgression and sinned in many things which brought a wound upon my soul. There were many things which transpired that cannot be writ[t]en and my Father's family have suffered many persicutions and afflictions.

And it came to pass when I was seventeen years of age, I called again upon the Lord and he shewed unto me a heavenly vision. For behold an angel of the Lord came and stood before me. It was by night and he called me by name and he said the Lord had forgiven me my sins. He revealed unto me that in the Town of Manchester, Ontario County, N[ew] Y[ork] there was plates of gold upon which there was engravings which was engraven by Maroni [Moroni] and his fathers, the servants of the living God in ancient days, deposited by the commandments of God and kept by the power thereof and that I should go and get them. He revealed unto me many things concerning the inhabitants of the earth which since have been revealed in commandments and revelations.

It was on the 22d day of Sept[ember] AD 1822 [1823]. Thus he appeared unto me three times in one night and once on the next day. Then I immediately went to the place and found where the plates was deposited as the angel of the Lord had commanded me and straightway made three attempts to get them. Then being excedingly frightened I supposed it had been a dreem of Vision, but when I consid[e]red I knew that it was not. Therefore I cried unto the Lord in the agony of my soul, "Why can I not obtain them?"

Behold the angel appeared unto me again and said unto me, "You have not kept the commandments of the Lord which I gave unto you. Therefore you cannot now obtain them, for the time is not yet fulfilled. Therefore thou wast left unto temptation that thou mightest be made acquainted with the power of the advisary. Therefore repent and call on the Lord [and] thou shalt be forgiven. And in his own due time thou shalt obtain them."
{page 4}

For now I had been tempted of the advisary and saught the Plates to obtain riches and kept not the commandment that I should have a eye single to the glory of God. Therefore I was chastened and saught dilegently to obtain the plates and obtained them not untill I was twenty one years of age.

In this year, I was married to Emma Hale, Daughter of Isaach Hale, who lived in Harmony, Susquehana County, Pen[n]-sylvania on the 18th [of] January AD 1827. On the 22d day of Sept[ember] of this same year I obtained the plates.

In December following, we mooved to Susquehana [Harmony] by the assistence of a man by the name of Martin Harris who became convinced of the visions and gave me fifty Dollars to bare my expences. Because of his faith and this rightheous deed the Lord appeared unto him in a vision and shewed unto him his marvilous work which he was about to do.

/He/ imediately came to Su/s/quehannah and said the Lord had shown him that he must go to New York City /with/ some of the c/h/aracters, so we proceeded to coppy some of them. He took his Journ[e]y to the Eastern Cittys and to the Learned /saying/, "Read this I pray thee" and the learned said, "I cannot," but if he would bring the plates they would read it but the Lord had fo/r/bid it. He returned to me and gave them to /me to/ translate and I said, "I cannot for I am not learned," but the Lord had prepared ~~speetticke~~ spectacles for to read the Book. Therefore I commenced translating the characters. Thus the Propicy [prophecy] of Is/ia/ah was fulfilled which is writ[t]en in the 29[th] chapter concerning the book.

And it came to pass that after we had translated 116 pages that he desired to carry them to read to his friends that per-adventure [preadventure] he might convince them of the truth.

7

Therefore, I inquired of the Lord and the Lord said unto me that he must not take them. I spoke unto him (Martin) the word of the Lord {page 5} and he said inquire again. I inquired again and also a third time and the Lord said unto me, "Let him go with them, only he shall covenant with me that he will not shew them to only but four persons." He covenented with the Lord that he would do according to the word of the Lord.

Therefore he took them and took his journey unto his friends to [in] Palmira, Wayne County, State of N[ew] York. He brake the covenent which he made before the Lord and the Lord suffered the writings to fall into the hands of wicked men. Martin was chastened for his transgression and I also was chastened also for my transgression for asking the Lord the third time. Wherefore the Plates was taken from me by the power of God and I was not able to obtain them for a season.

And it came to pass after much humility and affliction of soul, I obtained them again when [the] Lord appeared unto a young man by the name of Oliver Cowdery and shewed unto him the plates in a vision, also the truth of the work, and what the Lord was about to do through me his unworthy servant. Therefore, he was desirous to come and write for me and translate. Now my wife had writ[t]en some for me to translate and also my Brother Samuel H. Smith but we had be come reduced in property and my wive's father was about to turn me out of doors. I had not where [nowhere] to go and I cried unto the Lord that he would provide for me to accomplish the work whereunto he had commanded me. [*rest of page blank*] {page 6}

8

Diary and
Journal

1832-34

S*hortly after having dictated and writ-ten the preceding autobiographical sketch, Joseph Smith purchased in late November 1832 his first diary in efforts to keep a full and accurate record of his experiences. Unlike later diaries and journals, particularly those dating from the 1840s, the following was either written by Joseph Smith (in* **bold***) or dictated by him to secretaries and reveals an intimate portrait of a man struggling with the responsibility of leading a new church. The original manuscript is housed in the archives of the Historical Department, Church of Jesus Christ of Latter-day Saints, Salt Lake City, Utah.*

**Joseph Smith, Jr. Record Book
Baught for to note all the minute
circumstances that comes under my
observation**

Joseph Smith, Jr.'s Book for Record Baught on the 27th of November 1832 for the purpose to keep a minute ac[c]ount of all things that come under my obse[r]vation &c.

Oh may God grant that I may be directed in all my thaughts. Oh bless thy servent. Amen. {page 1}

November 28th [1832] This day I have [spent] in reading and writing. This Evening my mind is calm and serene for which I thank the Lord.

November 29th This day [I] road from Kirtland to Chardon to see my Sister Sop[h]ronia and also ca[lled?] to see my Sister Catherine [and found?] them [well?].

This Evening Brother Frederic[k G. Williams] Prophecyed that next spring I should go to the city of Pittsburg to establish a Bishopwrick and within one year I should go to the City of New York. The Lord spare the life of thy servent. Amen. {page 2}

November 30th 1830 [1832] This day retu[r]ned home to Kirtland [and] found all well to the joy and satisfaction of my soul. On my return home stopped at Mr. King's [and] bore testimony to him and Family &c.

December 1th [1st] /[I] bore testimony to Mr. Gilmore/ [I] wrote and corrected revelations &c.

December 2th [2nd] The Sabath, [I] went to meeting &c.

December 3d Ordained Brother Packherd with my own hand[s]. Also Brother Umfiry [Humphery who] came to see me from the East and braught news from Brother Lyman Johnson and Orson Pratt &c.

Also held a conference in the Evening. Br[others] Jes[s]e [Gause] and Mogan [Morgan?] and William McLel[l]en was excommunicated from the Church &c. {page 3}

December 4th This day I [have] been unwell [and] done but lit[t]le, been at home all day. Regulated some things this Evening. [I] feel better in my mind then I have for a few days back. Oh Lord deliver thy servent out of tem[p]tations and fill his heart with wisdom and understanding.

December 5th This day wrote let[t]ers, copying letters, and translating. In [the] evening held a council to advise with Brother Solomon Humphry. It was ordered by the council that he should be a companion with Brother Noah Packard in the work of the ministry.

December 6th Translating and received a revelation

explaining the Parable [of] the wheat and the tears [tares] &c. {page 4}

October 4th [1833] Makeing preperation to go East with Freeman Nickerson. A request of Brother David Elliott to call on his Brother in Law Peter Worrin, St. Kath[e]rine, Upper Cannada. Colburg [Colborne, Norfolk District, Upper Canada], Richard Lyman request of Uncle John.

5th This day started on a Journ[e]y to the East. Came to Ashtibuly [Ashtabula, Ohio, and] /stayed/ [at] Lamb's tavern.

6th Arrived at Springfield [Erie County, Pennsylvania] on the Sabbath. Found the Brotheren in meeting. Brother Sidney spoke to the people &c. In the {page 5} /Evening/ [we] held a meeting at Brother Reed's. Had a great congregation, [they] paid good attention. Oh God Seal our te[s]timony to their hearts. Amen.

\¹ Continued at Springfield untill Tuesday the 8th. Journeyed that day to Br[other] Rounday's at Elk Creek [Erie County, Pennsylvania and] taried there over night. Came the next day to a tavern.

The next day Thursday the 10th we ar[ri]ved at Br[other] Job Lewises at Westfield. The breatheren [brethren] by a previous appointment met there for [a] meeting. We spoke to them as the spirite gave {page 6} utterence. They were greatly gratifyed. They appeared to be strong in the faith.

Left there Friday the 11th and came to the house of an infidel by the Name of Nash. Reason[e]d with him but to no effect.

Came Saturday the 12th [to] the house of Father Nicke[r]son. I feel very well in my mind. The Lord is with us but [I] have much anxiety about my family &c.

Sunday the 13th Held a meeting at Freeman Nickerson's. Had a large congregation. Brother Sidney preached and I bear [bore] record to the people. The Lord gave his spirit in [a] {page 7} marvilous man[n]er for which I am thankful to the God of Ab[r]aham. Lord bless my family and preserve them.

---

¹ In the handwriting of Sidney Rigdon.

Monday, 14th At the same place this day. [We] expect to start for Canada [soon]. Lord be with us on our Journey. Amen &c.

\\[2] Monday evening ar[r]ived at Lodi [Cattaraugus County, New York]. Had an appointment. Preached to a small congregation [and] made an appointment for Tuesday at 10 oclock the 15th. The meeting was appointed to be held in the Presbeterian meeting house {page 8} but when the hour ar[r]ived the man who kept the key to the house refused to open the door. The meeting was thus prevented. We came immedeately away and left the people in great confusion. Journeyed till Friday [the] 17[th] [18 October 1833].

Ar[r]ived at Freeman Nickerson's in Upper Canada having after we came into Canada passed through a very fine Country and well cultivated and had many peculiar feelings in relation to both the country and people. We were kindly received at Freeman Nickerson's. {page 9}

On Sunday the 19th [20 October 1833] held [a] meeting at Brantford on Sunday at 10 o'clock to a very at[t]entive congregation. At candle lighting the same evening held [a] meeting at Mount Ple[a]sent where Freeman Nickerson lived to [address] a very large congregation which gave good heed to the things which were spoken. What may be the result we cannot tell but the p[r]ospect is flattering.

This morning, Monday the 20[th] [21 October 1833] enjoy pretty good {page 10} health with good prospects of doing good. [We] calculate to stay in Canada till the Monday of next week then the Lord willing [we] will start for home.

Left Mount Ple[a]sent Tuesday [22 October 1833] and ar[r]ived at the Village of Coulburn. Held [a] meeting at candle lighting. The evening was very bad, snowing vehemently. We were publickly opposed by a Wesleyen Methodist. He was very tumultious but destitute of reason or knowledge. He would not {page 11} give us an oppertunity to reply. This was on the 22nd.

We find that conviction is resting on the minds of some. We hope that great good may yet be done in Canada which O Lord grant for thy name's sake.

---

[2] In the handwriting of Sidney Rigdon.

During our stay at Mount Ple[a]sent, we [had] an interview with a Mr. Wilkeson of the Methodist order being a leader in that sect. He could not stand against our words. Whether he will receive the truth the Lord only knows. He seemed to [be] honest. {page 12} Written at Coulburn, Wednesday morning the 23[rd] [of October 1833] at the house of a Mr. Bemer.

Left Mr. Bemer's on Thursday [the] 24[th] [and] came to Watterford [Ontario]. Held [a] meeting at 1 o'clock. Spoke to a small congregation. Being a very wet day after meeting returned to Mount Ple[a]sent and held [a] meeting at candle lighting to a large congregation. One man, Freeman Nickerson, declared his full belief in the truth of the work. [He] is with his wife who is also convinced to be baptised on Sunday.

Great excitement {page 13} prevailes in every place where we have been. The result we leave in the hand of God. Written at the house of Freeman Nickerson in Mount Ple[a]sent on Friday morning the 24th [25 October 1833].

This afternoon [was spent] **at Mr. Pattrick's. [We] expect to hold a meeting this Evening &c. [The] people [are] very superstitious. Oh God esta[b]lish thy word among this people. [We] held a meeting this evening** [and] **had an attentive congregation. The spirit gave utterance.** {page 14}

Saterday, 25th [26 October 1833] **Held a meeting at Mount Pl[e]asant. The people** [were] **very tender.**

\[3] Sunday, 26[th] [27 October 1833] Held a meeting in Mount Ple[a]sent to a large congregation. Twelve [people] came forward and was baptised and many more were deeply impressed.

Appointed a meeting for this day Monday the 27[th] [28 October 1833] at the request of some who desires to be baptized. At candle lighting [we] held a meeting for confirmation. We broke bread [and] laid on hands for the gift of the Holy Spirit. [We] had a good {page 15} meeting. The spirit was given in great power to some and the rest had great peace. May God carry on his work in this place till all shall know him. Amen.

Held [a] meeting yesterday at 10 o'clock. After [the] meeting two [people] came forward and were baptised. [We] confirmed them at the watter's edge.

---

[3] In the handwriting of Sidney Rigdon.

Held [a] meeting last evening [and] ordained Br[other] E[leazer] F[reeman] Nickerson to the office of Elder. [We] had a good meeting. One of the sisters got the {page 16} gift of toungues which made the Saints rejoice. May God incre[a]se the gifts among them for his Son's sake.

This morning [28 October 1833] we bend our course for home. May the Lord prosper our journey. Amen.

Tuesday the **29th Left Mount Pleasant for home.**

30th continued on our Journ[e]y We[d]n[e]sday and on Thirsday [the] 31st [we] arrived at Buffalo [New York].

~~Friday 32th Started from Buffalo~~ {page 17}

\[4] Friday, November 1[st] Left Buffalo, N[ew] Y[ork] at 8 o'clock A.M. Arrived at home Monday, the 4th at 10 A.M. [and] found my family all well according to the promise of the Lord, for which blessing I feel to thank his holy name. Amen.

November 13th Nothing of note transpired from the 4th of Nove[m]ber u[n]til this day. In the morning at 4 Oh clock I was awoke by Brother Davis knocking at /my/ door saying "Brother Joseph {page 18} come git /up/ and see the signs in the heavens." I arrose and beheld to my great Joy the stars fall from heaven. Yea they fell like hail stones. A litteral fullfillment of the word of God as recorded in the holy scriptures and a sure sign that the coming of Christ is clost [close] at hand.

Oh how marvellous are thy works Oh Lord and I thank thee for thy me[r]cy u/n/to me thy servent. Oh Lord save me in thy kingdom for Christ['s] sake. Amen. {page 19}

November 19th /AD 1833/ From the 13th u[n]till this date nothing of note has transpired since the great sign in the heavins. This day my /h[e]art/ is somewhat sorrowfull but [I] feel to trust in the Lord the God of Jacob. I have learned in my travels that man is treche[r]ous and selfish but few excepted.

Brother /Sidney/ [Rigdon] is a man whom I love but [he] is not capa[b]le of that pure and ste[a]dfast love for those who are his benefactors as should p/o/sess the breast of a man /a/ President of the Chu/r/ch of Christ. {page 20} This with

---

[4] In the handwriting of Oliver Cowdery.

some other little things such as a selfish and indipendance of mind which to[o] often manifest distroys the confidence of those who would lay down their lives for him. But notwithstanding these things he is /a/ very great and good man. A man of great power of words and [he] can /gain/ the friendship of his hearrers very quick. He is a man whom God will uphold if he will continue faithful to his calling. O God grant that he may for the Lord's sake. Amen. {page 21}

The man who willeth to do well we should extoll his virtues and speak not of his faults behind his back. A man who willfuly turneth away from his friend without a cause is not ~~lightly to be forgiven~~/easily forgiven/. The kindness of a man ~~is~~ /should/ never to be forgotten. That person who never forsaketh his trust should ever have the highest place for regard in our hearts and our love should never fail but increase more and more. This [is] my disposition and sentiment &c. Amen. {page 22}

Brother Frederick [G. Williams] ~~is a man who~~ /is one of those men/ in whom I place the greatest confidence and trust. For I have found him ever full of love and Brotherly kindness. He is not a man of many words, but is ever wining because of his constant mind. He shall ever have place in my heart and is ever intitled to my confidence. \\[5] He is perfectly honest and upright, and seeks with all his heart to magnify his presidency in the Church of Ch[r]ist, but fails in many instances in consequence of a ~~lack~~ /want/ of confidence in himself. God grant that he may {page 23} overcome all evil. Blessed be Brother Frederick, for he shall never want a friend and his generation after him shall flourish. The Lord hath appointed him an inheritance upon the land of Zion. Yea, and his head shall blossom. /And he shall be/ as an olive branch that is bowed down with fruit. Even so. Amen.

And again, blessed be Brother Sidney, also notwithstanding he shall be high and lifted up, yet he shall bow down under the yoke like unto an ass that {page 24} coucheth beneath his burthen [burden], that learneth his master's /will/ by the stroke of the rod, Thus saith the Lord. Yet the Lord will have mercy on

---

[5] In the handwriting of Oliver Cowdery.

him and he shall bring forth much fruit. Even as the ~~vun~~ /vine/
of the choice grape when her clusters are /is/ ripe, before the time
of the gleaning of the vintage. The Lord shall make his heart
merry as with sweet wine because of him who putteth forth his
hand and lifteth him up ~~from~~ /out of/ [a] deep mire, and pointeth
him out the way, and guideth his {page 25} feet when he stum-
bles and humbleth him in his pride. Blessed are his generations.
Nevertheless, one shall hunt after them as a man hunteth after an
ass that hath strayed in the wilderness, and straitway findeth him
and bringeth him into the fold. Thus shall the Lord watch over
his generation that they may be saved. Even so. Amen.

\\[6] On the 13th and 14th days of October [1833],[7] I bap-
tized the following person[s] in Mount Pleasant, viz: {page 26}

> Moses Chapman Nickerson
> Eleser [Eleazer] Freeman Nickerson
> Prechard Ramon Stowbridge
> Andrew Rose
> Harvey John Cooper
> Samuel McAlester
> Eliza Nickerson
> Mary Gates
> Mary Birch
> Lidia Bailey [Lydia Baily]
> Elisabeth Gibbs
> Phebe Cook
> Margritt Birch
> Esther Birch

25th Nove[mber] Brother[s] Orson Hyde and John Gould
{page 27} returned from Zion and brough[t] the melencholly
intelegen[ce] of the riot in Zion with the inhabitants in pers[ec]ut-
ing the brethren.

[On] the 4th [of] Dec[ember 1833] [we] commenced dis-
tributing the type and commenced setting on the 6[th of Decem-
ber]. Being prepared to commence our Labours in the printing
buisness I ask God in the {page 28} name of Jesus to establish

---

[6] In the handwriting of Frederick G. Williams.
[7] These dates should be 27 and 28 October, according to Dean C. Jessee, ed.,
The Personal Writings of Joseph Smith (Salt Lake City: Deseret Book, 1984), p. 642n35.

it for ever and cause that his word may speedily go for[th] [to] the
Nations of the earth to the accomplishing of his great work in
bringing about the restoration of the house of Israel.

Nov[ember] 22d 1833 My brother [Don] Carlos Smith
came to live with me and also learn the printing art. {page 29}

On the 9th of Dec[ember] Bro[ther] Phi[neas] Young
came to board with me to board rent and Lodge at one dollar and
twenty five cents p[er] week.

Bro[ther] Wilbor Denton came to board [on] 11 Dec[ember] at one Dollar and twenty five cents per week.

Dec[ember] 18[th] /1833/ This day the Elders assembled
togeth[er] in the printing office. {page 30} Then [we] proce[e]ded
to bow down before the Lord and dedicate the printing press and
all that pertains thereunto to God by mine own hand and confirmed by Bro[thers] Sidney Rigdon and Hyrum Smith. [We]
then proceded to take the first proof sheet of the [Evening and
Morning] Star, edited by Oliv[er] Cowd[er]y.

Blessed of the Lord is Bro[ther] Oliver. Nevertheless there
are {page 31} are two evils in him that he must needs forsake or
he cannot altogeth[er] escape the buffettings of the adver[sar]y. If
he shall forsak[e] these evils he shall be forgiven and shall be
made like unto the bow which the Lord hath set in the heavens.
He shall be a sign and an ensign unto the nations. Behold he is
blessed of the Lord for his constancy {page 32} and steadfastness
in the work of the Lord. Wherefore he shall be blessed in his
generation and they shall never be cut off. He shall be helped out
of many troubles and if he keep[s] the commandments and harken
unto the /council of the/ Lord his rest shall be glorious.

Again blessed of the Lord is my father and also my mother
and my brothers and my sisters. For they shall {page 33} yet find
redemption in the House of the Lord and their of[f]springs shall
be a blessing, a Joy, and a comfort unto them.

Blessed is my mother for her soul is ever fill[ed] with benevolence and phylanthropy and notwithstanding her age yet she
shall receive strength and shall be comferted in the midst of her
house. She shall have eternal life.

Blessed is my father. For the hand of the Lord shall be
{page 34} over him. For he shall see the affliction /of his chil-
dren/ pass away when his head is fully ripe. He shall behold him-

17

self as an olive tree whose branches are bowed down with much fruit. He shall also possess a mansion on high.

Blessed of the Lord is my brother Hyrum for the integrity of his heart. He shall be girt about with truth and faithfulness shall be the strength of his loins {page 35} from generation to generation. He shall be a shaft in the hand of his God to exicute Judgement upon his enemies. He shall be hid by the hand of the Lord that none of his secret parts shall be discovered unto his hu[r]t. His name shall be accounted a blessing among men. When he is in trouble and great tribulation hath come upon him {page 36} he shall remember the God of Jacob and he will shield him from the power of Satan. He shall receive ~~counel~~ /councel/ in the House of the Most High that he may be streng[t]hened in hope that the going /of his feet/ may be established for eve[r].

Blessed of the Lord is [my] bro[ther] Samuel because the Lord shall say unto him, "Sam[ue]l, Sam[ue]l." Therefore he shall be made a teacher in {page 37} the House of the Lord and the Lord shall mature his mind in Judgement. Thereby he shall obtain the esteem and fellowship of his brethren. His soul shall be established and he shall benefit [from] the House of the Lord because he shall obtain answer[s] to [his] prayer[s] in his faithfulness.

[My] Bro[ther] William is as the fi[e]rce Lion {page 38} who divideth not the spoil because of his strength. In the pride of his heart he will neglect the more weighty matters until his soul is bowed down in sorrow. Then he shall return and call on the name of his God and shall find forgiveness and shall wax valient. Therefor[e] he shall be saved unto the utter most. As the {page 39} roaring Lion of the forest in the midst of his prey so shall the hand of his generation be lifted up against those who are set on high that fight against the God of Israel. Fearless and unda[u]nted shall they be in battle in avenging the [w]rongs of the innocent and relieving the oppressed. Ther[e]for[e] the blessings of the God of Jacob {page 40} shall be in the midst of his house notwithstanding his rebelious heart.

And /now/ O God let the residue of my father's house ever come up in remembrance before thee. That thou mayest save them from the hand of the oppressor and establish their feet upon the rock of ages. That they may have place in thy house and be saved in thy Kingdom. {page 41} Let all these things be even as I have said for Christ's sake. Amen.[8]

Dec[ember] 19th This day Bro[thers] William Pratt and David Pattin took their Journey to the Land of Zion for the purpose of bearing dispatches to the Brethren in that place from Kirtland, O[hio]. May God grant it a blessing for Zion as a kind Angel from heaven. Amen. {page 42}

January 16th 1834 This night at Brother Jinkins Salisbury came from home. Oh Lord keep us and my family safe untill I can return to them again. Oh my God have mercy on my Bretheren in Zion for Christ['s] Sake. Amen.

\\[9] January 11th 1834 This evening Joseph Smith, Jr., Frederick G. Williams, Newel K. Whitney, John Johnson, Oliver Cowdery, and Orson Hyd[e] united in prayer and asked the Lord to grant the following petition: {page 43}

Firstly, That the Lord would grant that our lives might be precious in his sight. That he would watch over our persons and give his angels charge concerning us and our families that no evil nor unseen hand might be permitted to harm us.

Secondly, That the Lord would also hold the lives of all the United Firm and not suffer that any of them shall be taken.

Thirdly, That the Lord would grant that our Brother Joseph [Smith] might prevail over {page 44} his enemy, even Doctor P[hilastus] Hurlbut, who has threatened his life. Whom Brother Joseph has /caused to be/ taken with a precept. That the Lord would fill the heart of the court with a spirit to do justice, and cause that the law of the land may be magnified in bringing him to justice.

Fourthly, That the Lord would provide, in the order of his Providence, the Bishop of this Church with means sufficient to discharge every debt that the [United] Firm owes, in due sea-

---

[8] In September 1835, Oliver Cowdery recorded Joseph Smith's blessings to members of his immediate family into what would become the first volume, pp. 8-20, of the Patriarchal Blessing books, located in the archives of the Historical Department, Church of Jesus Christ of Latter-day Saints. In so doing, however, Cowdery greatly expanded the blessings beyond their contents as initially recorded above.

[9] In the handwriting of Oliver Cowdery.

son. That {page 45} the Church may not be braught into disrepute, and the Saints be afflicted by the hands of their enemies.

Fifthly, That the Lord would protect our printing press from the hands of evil men, and give us means to send forth his word. Even his gospel that the ears of all may hear it. Also that we may print his scriptures. Also that he would give those who were appointed to conduct the press, wisdom sufficient that the cause {page 46} may not be hindered, but that men's eyes may thereby be opened to see the truth.

Sixthly, That the Lord would deliver Zion, and gather in his scattered people, to possess it in peace. Also, while in their dispersion, that he would provide for them that they perish not with hunger nor cold. And finally, that God in the name of Jesus would gather his elect speedily, and unveil his face that his Saints {page 47} might behold his glory and dwell with him. Amen.

On the 13th of March A.D. 1833, Doctor P[hilastus] Hurlbut came to my house. I conversed with him considerably about the Book of Mormon. He was ordained to the office of an Elder in this Church under the hand[s] of Sidney Rigdon on the **18th**[10] of March in the same year above written. According to my best recollection, I heard him say, in the {page 48} course of conversing with him, that if he ever became convinced that the Book of Mormon was false, he would be the cause of my destruction &c. He was tried before a counsel of High Priests on the 21st day of June 1833, and his license restored to him again. it /He/ previously having been ~~taken by the Church at~~ /cut off from the/ Church by the Bishop's court. He was finally cut off from the Church {page 49} a few days after having his license restored on the 21st of June. \[11] Then [he] saught the destruction of the Saints in this place and more particularly myself and family. As the Lord has in his mercy Delivered me out of his hand till the present and also the Church that he has not prevailed viz the 28[th] day Jan[uar]y {page 50} 1834 for which I offer the gratitud[e] of my heart to Allmighty God for the same.

On this night Bro[ther] Oliv[er] and Bro[ther] Frederick

---

[10] Oliver Cowdery left the date blank. It was later inserted by Joseph Smith.
[11] In the handwriting of Frederick G. Williams.

and my self bowed before the Lord. Being agre[e]d, [we] united in prayer that God would continue to deliver me and my brethren from /him/ [and] that he may not prevail again[st] us in the law suit that is pending. {page 51}

Also that God would soften down the hearts of E[lijah] Smith, J[osiah] Jones, [Austin] Lowd, and [Azariah] Lyman and also [Andrew] Bardsly that they might obey the gospel. Or if they would not repent that the Lord would send faithful Saints to purchase their farms that this stake may be strengthened and ~~the~~ /its/ borders [be] enlarged. **O Lord grant it for Christ['s] Sake. Amen.** {page 52}

\\[12] 31 Janu[ar]y 1834 It is my prayer to the Lord that three thousand subscriber[s] may be added to the [Evening and Morning] Star in the term of three years.

We[d]n[e]sd[a]y, /Feb[r]uary/ 26th Started from home to obtain volenteers for Zion['s Camp].

Thursday, 27th Stayed at Br[other] Rounday's.

28th Stayed at a stranger's who entertained us very kindly /in/ Westleville [Wesleyville, Erie County, Pennsylvania].

March 1th [1st 1833] **Ar[r]ived at Br[other] Lewis and on the 2d the Sabath. Brother Barly** [Parely P. Pratt] **preached in this place and I preached in the evening.** [We] **had a good** {page 53} **meeting. There is a small Church in this place that seem[s] to be strong in the faith. Oh may God keep them in the faith and save them and lead them to Zion.**

March 3d This morning [we] **intend to start on our Journ[e]y to /the/ east.** \\[13] /But did not start/ **O may God bless us with the gift of utterance to accomplish the Journ[e]y and the Errand on which we are sent and return soon to the land of Kirtland** {page 54} **and /find/ my Family all well. O Lord bless my little children with health and long life to do good in th[is] generation for Christ's sake. Amen.**

\\[14] Kirtland, Geauger [Geauga County], Ohio
Thom[p]son [Geauga County, Ohio]
Springfield, Erie [County, Pennsylvania]

---

[12] In the handwriting of Frederick G. Williams.
[13] In the handwriting of Parley P. Pratt.
[14] In the handwriting of an unidentified scribe.

Elkcrick [Elk Creek, Erie County] Pensy[l]vania
Westfield [Chautauqua County, New York]
Laona, Chautauque, N[ew] York
Silver Creek [Chautauqua County, New York]
Perrysburgh, Cateragus [Cattaraugus County, New York]
Collins, Genesee [County, New York]
China [Genesee County, New York] {page 55}
Warsaw [Genesee County, New York]
Geneseeo, Levingston [Geneseeo, Livingston County, New York]
Sentervill [Centerville, Allegany County, New York]
Cattlin, Alleghany [County, New York]
Spafford, Onondaga [County, New York]

John Gould payed me on papers $1.50.

\\[15] Journal of P[arley P. Pratt] and J[oseph Smith]

March 4th [1834] Took our Journ[e]y from Westfield [Chatauqua County, New York] /accompanyed by Br[other] Gould/ [and] rode 33 miles. Arrived in **Vilanova** [and] \\[16] s/t/aid all night with a Brother McBride. [The] next morning [we] went 4 m[iles] to Br[other] Nicisons [Nickerson's], found him and {page 56} his house hold full of faith and of the Holy Spirit.

We cal[le]d the Church together and Related unto them what had hap[p]ened to our Brethren in Zion. [We] opened to them the prophesyes and revelations concerning the order of the gathering of Zion and the means of her Redem[p]tion.

Brother Joseph Prophesyed to them and the spirit of the Lord came mightily upon them and with all re[a]dyness the yo[u]ng and mid[d]le aged volenteered for Zion['s Camp]. {page 57} [The] same evening [we] held 2 meetings 3 or 4 miles Apart.

[The] next day, March 6th, [we] held another Meeting at Bro[ther] Nicisons [Nickerson's]. The few un Believers that attended were outragious and the meeting ended in compleet confusion.

March 7[th] Started on our Journ[e]y accompanyed By

---

[15] In the handwriting of Parley P. Pratt.
[16] In the handwriting of Parley P. Pratt.

Br[other] Nicison [Nickerson] Leaving Br[other]s Goold [John Gould] and Mathews to prepare /and gather up/ the companys in the Churches in that region and meet us in Ohio, Re[a]ddy [to depart] for Zion the first of May.

We arrived after dark to the {page 58} county seat of Cataraugus cal[le]d Elicutville [Ellicottville]. Tryed every tavern in the place But Being Court time we found no room But were compeled to ride on in a dark, muddy, rainy night. We found shelter in rideing 1 mile, [but] Paid higher for our fare than tavern price.

March 8th Continued our Journ[e]y. Came to Palmersville [Farmersville] to the house of Elder McGown. Were Invited to go to Esq[uire] **Walker's** \[17] to spend the evening. {page 59} We found them verry friendly and somewhat Believeing. [We] tarryed [there] all night.

Sunday, 9[th] Held [a] meeting in a school house [and] had great attentian. Found a few desyples who were firm in [the] faith. After [the] meeting [we] found many Believeing and could hardly get away from them. We apointed A meeting in Freedom [Cattaraugus County, New York] for Monday [the] 10th. [We] are now at Mr. Cowdery'es in the full Enjoyment of /all/ the Blessings Both temporal and spiritual {page 60} of which we stand in need or are found worthy to recieve.

[10 March 1834] Held [a] meeting on Monday. Moved. Preached to [a] crowd[ed] /congregat[ion]/. At eve[ning] preacht again to a hous[e] crowded full to overflowing. After meeting I proposed if any wished to obey if they would make it manifest we would stay to administer. At another meeting a young man of the Methodist order arose and testified [of] his faith in the fulness of /the/ gospel and desired to Be Baptised. We Appointed another me[e]ting.

The next {page 61} day, Tuesday 11th, held [a] meeting and Baptised Heman Hide after which we rode 9 m[iles]. Put up with [*blank*] /**Steward's tavern**/. [The] \[18] next day rode 36 m[ile]s to farther [Father] Bosley's.

13[th] [March 1834], Thursday Held a me[e]ting [and] I Preached.

---

[17] In the handwriting of Parley P. Pratt.
[18] In the handwriting of Parley P. Pratt.

Friday, 14th **In F**[ather] **Beaman's.**

March 15th At Father Beaman's. Brother[s] **Sidn**[e]**y** [Rigdon] **and Lyman** [Wight] **ar**[r]**ived at his house to** /**the**/ **Joy of our Souls in Lyvona** [Livonia, Livingstone County, New York].

Sunday, 16th Brother Sidney preached to a very large congregation /**in Geneseo**/.

Monday, 17th Brother {page 62} **Parl**[e]**y** [P. Pratt] **preached in the afternoon.**

Tuesd[a]**y, 18th Stayed at Father Bosl**[e]**y's all day.**

We[d]**n**[e]**sday, 19th Started for home, arrived at Brother Whithey's** [and] **tarried all night &c.**

Thursday, 20th Started on /**our**/ **Journ**[e]**y at noon. Took dinner at Brother Joseph Holbrook's.** [At] **night we tryed three times to git keept in the name of Deciples and could not be kept.** {page 63} **After night we found a man who would keep us for mon**[e]**y. Thus we see that there** /**is**/ **more place for mon**[e]**y than for Jesus'** /**Deciples or**/ **the Lamb of God. The name of the man is** ~~Wilson Rauben Wilson~~ **Reuben Wilson that would not keep us without mon**[e]**y &c.** /[He] **lived in China**/ [Genesee County, New York]

March 21th Came to a man by the name of Starks, 6th miles East of Springville [Erie County, New York]. {page 64}

22d Came and tarri[e]**d with Vincen Night's** [Vinson Knight] **in Perrysburg, Co**[ounty] **of Cattaraugus.**

23d Came to Father Nickerson's, Perrysburg, the same Co[unty], **N**[ew] **Y**[ork and we] **held a meeting &c.**

24th This /**day**/ [I] **am not able to start for home but feel determined to go on the morrow morning.**

25th Came from Father Nickerson's to Father Leweses' [Job Lewis] **in** {page 65} **Westfield** [Chautaugua County, New York]. **Father Nickerson came with me.**

26th Came from Westfield to Elk Kreek [Erie County, Pennsylvania, and] **stayed with Elder Hunt on free cost.**

27th Came to Springfield [and] **found Brother Sidney.** [We] **came to within 16 miles from Painsville** [Ohio].

28th Came home. Found my Family all well and the Lord be praised for this blessing.

29th At home had much {page 66} Joy with /my/ Family.

30th Sabb/a/th at home and went to hear Brother Sidney Preach the word of life &c.

31th [31st], **Monday This day came to Sharden** [Chardon, Geauga County, Ohio] **to tend the Court against Docter P**[hilastus] **Hurlbut &c.**

~~32d~~ [1 April 1834], Tu[e]sday [I spent] **this day at Brother Rider's.** The Court has not braught on our tryal yet we are ingaged in makeing out some supenies [subpoenas] for witnesses &c. {page 67}

April 1st, Tu[e]sday **My soul delighteth in the Law of the Lord for he forgiveth my sins and /will/ confound mine Enimies. The Lord shall destroy him who has lifted his heel against me, even that wicked man Docter P**[hilastus] **H**[u]**rlbut. He /will/ deliver him to the fowls of heaven and his bones shall be cast to the blast of the wind /for/ he lifted his /arm/ against the Almi**[gh]**ty. Therefore** {page 68} **the Lord shall destroy him.**

\¹⁹ [2 April 1834] Wednesday Attended court at Chardon.

[3 April 1834] Thursday. The same.

[4 April 1834] Friday morning. Returned home.

[5 April 1834] Saturday Returned to Chardon /as witness for Fath[er] Johnson/. In the evening [I] returned home. Mr. Bussle [Benjamin Bissell], the State's Att[orne]y for Portage County, called on me this evening. He is a gentlemanly appearing man and treated me with respect.

\²⁰ On the 7th day of April Bro[ther]s Newel [K. Whitney], Oliver [Cowdery], Frederick [G. Williams], Heber [C. Kimball], and myself meet {page 69} in the counsel room and bowed down befor[e] the Lord and prayed that he would furnish the means to deliver the [United] Firm from debt and /be/ set at liberty. Also that I may prevail against that wicked [Philastus] Hurlbut and that he be put to shame.

Accordingly on the 9th after an impartial trial the court decided that the said Hurlbut was bound over under 200 dollars {page 70} bond to keep the peace for six month[s] and pay the

---

¹⁹ In the handwriting of Oliver Cowdery.
²⁰ In the handwriting of Frederick G. Williams.

[court] cost[s] which amounted to near three hundred dollars. All of which was in answer to our prayer for which I thank my Heavenly Father.

Remember to carry the bond between A[lgernon] S[idney] Gilbert and N[ewel] K. Whitney and have them exchang[e]/d/ when I go to Zion.[21]

On /Thursday/ the 10th had a concel [council] {page 71} of the United Firm at which it was agreed that the Firm should be desolv[ed] and each one have their stewardship set off to them.

Fryday, 11th Attended meeting and restored Father Tyler to the Church.

Satterday, 12[th] Went to the lake [Lake Erie] and spent the day in fishing and visiting the brethren in that place. Took my horse from Father [John] Johnson and let Brother Frederick [G. Williams] have him to keep.

13[th], Sunday Was sick and could not attend meeting. {page 72}

Monday, 14[th] Purch[as]ed some hay and oats and got them home.

Tuesday, 15[th] Drawed [drew] a load of hay.

/On We[d]n[e]sday [the] 16[th]/ [I] plowed and sowed oats for Brother Frederick [G. Williams].

On Thursday the 17[th] attended meeting agreeable to appoint[ment]. At which time the important subjects of the deliverence of Zion and the building of the Lord's House in {page 73} Kirtland [were discussed] by Bro[ther] Sidney. After which Bro[ther] Joseph arose [and] requested the brethren and sisters to contr[i]bute all the money they could for the deliverence of Zion. [We] received twenty nine dollars and sixty eight c[en]ts.

\[22] April 18[th] Left Kirtland in company with Brothers Sidney Rigdon, Oliver Cowdery, /and/ Zebedee Coltrin for New Portage to attend a conference. Travelled to W. W. Williams in {page 74} Newburgh [Cuyahoga County, Ohio] and took dinner, after which we travelled on.

After dark were hailed by a man who desired to ride. We were checked by the Spirit and refused. He professed to be sick,

---

[21] This material is enclosed in a pen-drawn box in the original.
[22] In the handwriting of Oliver Cowdery.

but in a few minutes was joined by two others who followed us hard, cursing and swearing. We were successful in escaping their hands through the providence of the Lord, and stayed at a tavern where we were treated with civility.

Next morning, 19 [April 1834] [we] started and arrived at Brother Joseph Bozworth's /in/ {page 75} Copley, Medina County, [Ohio?] where we took dinner. Bro[ther] J[oseph] Bozworth was strong in the faith. He is a good man and may, if faithful, do much good. After resting awhile, we left, and soon arrived at Brother Johnathan Tayler's, in Norton, where we were received with kindness.

We soon retired to the wilderness where we united in prayer and sup[p]lication for the blessings of the Lord to be given unto his Church. We called upon the Father in the name of Jesus to go with the breth[r]en who were {page 76} going up to the land of Zion. To give Brother Joseph strength and wisdom, and understanding sufficient to lead the people of the Lord, and to gather back and establish the Saints upon the land of their inheritances, and [to] organize them according to the will of heaven, that they be no more cast down forever.

We then united and laid on hands. Brothers Sidney, Oliver, and Zebedee laid hands upon Bro[ther] Joseph and confirmed upon him all the blessings necessary to qualify him to do /stand/ before the Lord in his high calling. {page 77} He return[ed] again in peace and triumph to enjoy the society of his breth[r]en.

Brothers Joseph, Sidney, and Zebedee then laid hands upon Bro[ther] Oliver and confirmed upon him the blessings of wisdom and understanding sufficient for his station. That he be qualified to assist Brother Sidney in arranging the Church Covenants [Doctrine and Covenants] which are to be soon published and to have intelligence in all things to do the work of printing.

Brother[s] Joseph, Oliver, [and] Zebedee then laid {page 78} hands upon Bro[ther] Sidney and confirmed upon him the blessings of wisdom and knowledge to preside over the Church in the abscence of Brother Joseph. To have the spirit to assist Bro[ther] Oliver in conducting the [Evening and Morning] Star, and to arrange the Church covenants [Doctrine and Covenants], and the blessing of old age and peace, till Zion is built up and Kirtland established, till all his enemies are under his feet, and of a crown of eternal life at the /in the/ Kingdom of God with us. {page 79}

27

We, Joseph, Sidney, and Oliver then laid hands upon Bro[ther] Zebedee and confirmed the blessing of wisdom to preach the gospel, even till it spreads to the islands of the sea, and to be spared to see three score years and ten, and see Zion built up and Kirtland established forever, and even at last to recieve a crown of life.

Our hearts rejoiced and we were {page 80} comforted with the Holy Spirit. Amen.

18 /20th/, Sunday Brother Sidney Rigdon entertained a large congregation of Saints with an interesting discourse upon the "Dispensation of the fulness of times," &c.

21[st] Attended conference and had a glorious time. Some few volunteered to go to Zion, and others donated $66.37 for the benefit of the scattered breth[r]en in Zion.

Returned to Kirtland on the 22d and found all well. {page 81}

23[rd] Assembled in council with the breth[r]en. Sidney, Frederick, Newel, John Johnson, and Oliver united in asking the Lord to give Bro[ther] Zebedee Coltrin influence over our Bro[ther] Jacob Myre, and obtain from him the money which he has gone to borrow for us. Or cause him to come to this place and give it himself.

\[23] April 30th This day paid the ~~amount~~ /Sum/ of fifty dollars on the following memorandom to the {page 82} following persons viz:

Milton Holmes	$15.00
Henry Herriman	7.00
Sylvester Smith	10.00
W[illia]m Smith	5.00
Harvey Stanl[e]y	5.00
William Smith	5.00
N[ewel] K Whitn[e]y	3.00
	$50.00

—

[23] In the handwriting of Frederick G. Williams.

Money received of the following brethren consecrated for the deliver[ance] of Zion:

By letter from East	$10.00
Do	50.00
Do	100.00 {page 83}
By letter	$7.00
W[illia]m Smith	5.00
W[illia]m Cahoon	5.00
Harvey Stanley	5.00
Received of Martin Harris	47.00
\24 Received of Dexter Stillman	10.00
Do of Lyman Johnson	5.00
Do of Sophia Howe	7.60

[*rest of page blank*] {page 84}

\25 August 21st 1834 This day Brother Frederick Williams returned from Cleveland and told us concerning the plague. After much consultation we agreed that Bro[ther] Frederick should go to Cleveland and commence administering to the sick, for the purpose of obtaing ~~means~~ /blessings for them, and/ for the ~~work of~~ /glory of/ the Lord.

Accordingly we, Joseph, Frederick, and Oliver united in prayer before the Lord for this thing. {page 85} Now, O Lord, grant unto us this blessing, in the name of Jesus Christ, and thy name shall have the glory forever. Amen.

—

August 30th 1834 Received of the Church by the hand of Jared Carter from the east of consecrated money $3.00.

—

Sept[ember] 4th 1834 This day Edward [Edmund] Bosley said that if he could obtain the management of his property in one year he would put it in for the printing of the word of the Lord. {page 86}

---

24 In the handwriting of an unidentified scribe.
25 In the handwriting of Oliver Cowdery.

November 29th 1834 This evening Joseph and Oliver united in prayer for the continuance of blessings. After giving thanks for the relief which the Lord had lately sent us by opening the hearts of certain brethren from the east to loan us $430.

After conversing and rejoicing before the Lord on this occasion we agreed to enter into the following covenant with the Lord, viz:

That if the Lord will {page 87} prosper us in our business, and open the way before /us/ that we may obtain means to pay our debts. That we be not troubled nor brought into disrepute before the world nor his people. That after that of all that he shall give us we will give a tenth to be bestowed upon the poor in his Church, or as he shall command. And that we will be faithful over that which he has entrusted to our care. That we {page 88} may obtain much and that our children after us shall remember to observe this sacred and holy covenant ~~after us~~. And that our children and our children's [children] may know of the same, we here subscribe our names with our own hands before the Lord:

Joseph Smith, Jr.
\\[26] Oliver Cowdery

And now, O Father, as thou didst prosper our father Jacob and bless {page 89} him with protection and prosperity wherever he went from the time he made a like covenant before and with thee. And as thou didst, even the same night, open the heavens unto him and manifest great mercy and favor and give him promises, so wilt thou do by us his sons; and as his blessings prevailed above the blessings of his Progenitors unto the utmost bounds of the {page 90} everlasting hills, even so may our blessings prevail ~~above~~ /like/ his.

May thy servants be preserved from the power and influence of wicked and unrighteous men. May every weapon formed against us fall upon the head of him who shall form it. May we be blessed with a name and a place among thy Saints here and [may] th[e]y [be] sanctified when they shall rest. Amen. {page 91}

Sabbath evening, November 30[th] 1834 While reflecting

---

[26] In the handwriting of Oliver Cowdery.

upon the goodness and mercy of the Lord, this evening, a prophecy was put into our hearts, that in a short time the Lord would
arrange his providences in a merciful manner and send us assistance to deliver us from debt and bondage. {page 92}

Friday Evening, December 5[th] 1834 According to the
direction of the Holy Spirit, Breth[r]en Joseph Smith, Jr., Sidney
[Rigdon], Frederick G. Williams, and Oliver Cowdery assembled
to converse upon the welfare of the Church, when Brother Oliver
Cowdery was ordained an Assistant President of the High and
Holy Priesthood under the hands of Brother Joseph Smith, Jr.
saying, "My brother, in the name of Jesus Christ who was crucified for the sins of the world, I lay my hands upon thee, and
ordain thee an Assistant President of the High and Holy Priesthood in the Church of the Latter Day Saints." {page 93}

[*pages 94 through 102 left blank*]

\²⁷ Please [remember] to send the Paper that Has formerly Been sent to John C[..]p[..]ton send it Now to Nathan
Chase at West Lodi, Cataraugus County, N[ew] Y[ork].

—

Received of Elisha C. Hubbard one Dollar for Papers,
Per[r]ysburgh. {page 103}

—

[Send] Hazard Andr[e]ws 1 paper [to] Fairview Post of-
fi[ce], Cattaragus County.

—

I have sent the money 25 cents by David Mo[. . . .] as
he was to send the paper to Mis[s] Taylor to Rushford but I wish
to have it come in my name as above.

—

---

²⁷ In the handwriting of an unidentified scribe.

Direct Samuel McBride and James McBride['s] Papers to Nashville Post office, Shitauqua [Chautauqua] County.

—

I wish you to send me one more Paper monthly and send one Monthly Paper to Eleazer and Samuel and Richard Nickerson, South Dennis in the County of Barnsta[ble], Massachusetts.

J[ohn] Nickerson {page 104}

—

\[28] The voice of the Spirit is that Brother Sidney [should] speak to the congregation this day first, Brother Joseph next, Bro[ther] Oliver [next?] and if time [permits] Bro[ther] Zebedee [Coltrin].

Joseph Smith, Jr.
Oliver Cowdery {page 105}

---

[28] In the handwriting of Oliver Cowdery.

Diary and
Journal

1 8 3 5 - 3 6

Perhaps *the most detailed of any of
Joseph Smith's diaries and journals,
the following document begins more than nine months after the preceding
diary/journal ends. Again, it contains original holographic entries in Joseph
Smith's hand (in* **bold***), in addition to that of his scribes. The original
document is housed in the archives of the Historical Department, Church of
Jesus Christ of Latter-day Saints, Salt Lake City, Utah.*

\\¹Sketch Book for the use of
Joseph Smith, Jr.

September 22nd 1835 This day Joseph Smith, Jr., labored with
Oliver Cowdery in obtaining and writing blessings. We were
thronged a part of the time with company, so that our labor in
this thing was hindered; but we obtained many precious things
and our souls were blessed. O Lord, may thy Holy Spirit be with
they servants forever. Amen.

September 23th [23rd] This day Joseph Smith, Jr.,

---

¹ In the handwriting of Oliver Cowdery.

was at home writing blessings for my most beloved Brotheren. /I/ have been hindered by a multitude of visitors, but the Lord has blessed our Souls this day. May Godd grant /to/ continue his mercies unto my house this /night/ day for Christ's sake. This day my Soul has desired the salvation of Brother Ezra Thay[e]r.

Also Brother Noah Packard came to my house and let the Chappel [Kirtland Temple] Committee have one thousand dollers by loan for the building [of] the House of the Lord. Oh may God bless him with an hundred fold! Even of the /things of [the]/ Earth, for this ri[gh]tious act.

My heart is full of desire to day, to /be/ blessed of the God of Abraham with prosperity untill I will be able to pay all my depts [debts]. For it is /the/ delight of my soul to /be/ honest. Oh Lord that thou knowes[t] right well! Help me and I will give to the poor.

September 23d 1835 This day Brothers William Tibbets, John, and Joseph Tibbits Started for Mosoura [Missouri] the place designated for Zion or the Saints' gathering. They came to bid us farewell. The Brotheren came in to pray with them and Brother David Whitmer acted as spokesman. He prayed in the spirit. A glorious time succeded his prayer. Joy filled our hearts and we {page 1} blessed them and bid them God speed. [I] promiced them a safe Journ[e]y and took them /by them hand/ and bid them farewell for /a/ season. Oh! may God grant them long life and good days. These blessings I ask /upon them/ for Christ's sake. Amen.

September 24th 1835 This day the High Council met at my house to take into consid[e]ration the redeem[p]tion of Zion. It was the voice of the spirit of the Lord that we petition to the Governer [of Missouri]. That is those who have been driven out /should/ to do so to be set back on their Lands next spring. We [should] go next season to live or dy [die] to this end so the dy is cast in Jackson County.

We truly had a good time and Covena[n]ted to strug-[g]le for this thing u[n]till death shall desolve [dissolve] this union. And if one falls that the rest be not discouraged but pe[r]sue this object untill it is ac[c]omplished. Which may God grant u[n]to us in the name of Christ our Lord.

September 24th 1835 This day drew up an Arti/c/le of

inrollment for the redem[p]tion of Zion that we may obtain volunteers to go next spring /to M[iss]o[uri]/. I ask God in the name of Jesus that we may obtain Eight hundred men /or one thousand/ well armed [men] and that they may ac[c]omplish this great work. Even so. Amen. {page 2}

\² Friday, 25th September This day I remained at home. Nothing of note transpired. ~~The Twelve [Apostles] all returned from the east to day.~~

26th This evening, the Twelve [Apostles] having returned from the east this morning, we met them and conversed upon some matters of difficulty which ware existing between some of them and President Rigdon. All things were settled satisfactorily.

27th, Sunday Attended meeting. Brethren Thomas B. Marsh, David W. Patten, Brigham Young, and Heber C. Kimball preached and broke bread. The Lord poured out his Spirit and my soul was edified.

28th High Council met and tried Brother Gladden Bishop. He was reproved, repented, and was reordained. The next was Lorenzo L. Lewis for fornication. He was cut off from the Church.

29th High Council met today and tried Brother Allen Avery. He was acquit[t]ed from any charge. Also Brother Phineas H. Young who was also acquit[t]ed. Also Bro[ther] Lorenzo Young, who confessed his error and was forgiven. In all these I acted on the part of the defence for the accused to plead for mercy. The Lord blessed my soul and the Council was greatly blessed also. Much good will no doubt result from our labors during the two days in which we were occupied on the business of the Church.

30th Stayed at home and visited [with] many who came to enquire after the work of the Lord.

October 1[st] 1835 This after noon labored on the Egyptian alphabet in company with Br[other]s O[liver] Cowdery and W[illiam] W. Phelps. The system of astronomy was unfolded [to us].

2nd Today [I] wrote a letter to be published in the Messenger and Advocate. {page 3}

\³ Saturday, 3d Oct[ober] Held a High Council on the case of Elder John Gould for giving credence to false and slander-

---

² In the handwriting of Oliver Cowdery.
³ In the handwriting of Frederick G. Williams.

ous reports instigated to Injure Bro[ther] Sidney Rigdon. Also
Dean Gould for thre[a]tning Bro[ther] Sidney Rigdon and others
in authority of the Elders. After due deliberation the[y] both confessed and wer[e] acquit[t]ed.

In the afternoon waited on the Twelve [Apostles], most of
them at my house. [I] exhibited to them the ancient reccords in
my possession and gave explanation of the same. Thus the day
passed off with the blessings of the Lord.

Sunday, 4[th] Started early in the mornin[g] with Brother
J. Carrell [John Corrill] to hold a meeting in Perry [Geauga
County, Ohio]. When about a mile from home we saw two Dears
playing in the field which diverted our minds by giving an impatus
to our thoughts upon the subject of the creation of God. We conversed upon many topicks and the day passed off in a very agreeable manner. The Lord blessed our souls. When we ar[r]ived at
Perry, we were disappointed of a meeting through misar[r]ange-
ments but conversed freely with Bro[ther] John Correl's relatives
which allayed much prejudice as we trust. May the Lord have
mercy on their souls.

Monday, 5th Returned home. Being much fatiegued [fa-
tigued] riding in the rain, [I] spent the remainder of the day in
reading and meditation &c. {page 4} In the evening attend[ed] a
High Councel of the Twelve Apostles. Had a glorious time and
gave them many instruction[s] concerning their duties for time to
come. Told them that it was the will of God they should take their
families to Missouri next season.

Also [told them to] attend this fall the Solemn Assembly
of the first Elders for the organization of the School of the Prophets and attend to the ordinence of the washing of feet and to prepare the[i]r hearts in all humility for an endowment with power
from on high. To which they all agreed with one accord and
seamed to be greatly rejoiced. May God spare the lives of the
Twelve [Apostles] with one accord to a good old age for Christ
the Redeemer's sake. Amen.

Tuesday, 6[th] At home. Father or Elder Stevens came to
my house and loaned F[rederick] G. Williams and Co[mpany]
six hundred Dollars which greatly releaved us out of our present
difficulties. May God bless and preserve his soul for ever.

[In the] Afternoon [I] called to visit my Father who was

very sick with a fever. [He was] some better towards evening. [I] spent the rest of the day in reading and meditation.

Wednesday, 7th Went to visit my Fathe[r]. Find [found] him very low. Administered some mild herbs agreeable to the commandment. May God grant to restore him immediately to health for Christ the Redeemer's sake. Amen.

This day Bro[ther] N[ewel] K. Whitney and Bro[ther] Hyrum Smith started for Buffalo [New York] to purchase good[s] to replenish the committe[e] store by land in the stage. May God grant in the name of Jesus that their lives may {page 5} be spared and they have a safe Journey and no accident or sickness of the least kind befall them. That they may return in health and in safety to the bosom of their families.

Blessed of the Lord is Bro[ther] [Newel K.] Whitney, even the Bishop of the Church of the Latter Day Saints, for the bishoprick shall never be taken away from him while he liveth. The time cometh that he shall overcome all the narrow mindedness of his heart and all his covetous desires that so easily besetteth him. And /he/ shall deal with a liberal hand to the poor and the needy, the sick and the afflicted, [and] the widow and the fatherless. And marviously [marvelously] and miraculously shall the Lord his God provid[e] for him. Even that he shall be blessed with a /all the/ fullness of the good thing[s] of this earth and his seed after him from generation to generation.

And it shall come to pass that according to the measure that he meeteth out with a liberal hand unto the poor, so shall it be measured to him again by the hand of his God, even an hundred fold. Angels shall guard /his/ house and shall guard the lives of his posterity. They shall become very great and very numerous on the earth.

Whomsoever he blesseth, they shall be blessed. Whomsoever he curseth, they shall be cursed. And when his enemies seek him unto his hurt and distruction, let him rise up and curse [them] and the hand of God shall be upon his enemies in Judgment. {page 6} They shall be utterly confounded and brought to dessolation. Therefor[e] he shall be preserved unto the utmost and his day /life/ shall be precious in the sight of the Lord. He shall rise up and shake himself as a lion riseth out of his nest and roareth untill he shaketh the hills. And as a lion goeth forth among the lesser beasts, so shall the goings forth of him /be/ whom the Lord

37

hath anointed to exalt the poor and to humble the rich, therefore his name shall be on high and his rest among the sanctified.

This afternoon recommenced translating the ancient reccords.

\⁴ Thursday, 8th At home. Nothing of note transpired as we now recollect. I attended on my Father with feelings of great anxiety.

Friday, 9th At home. Nothing worthy of note transpired on this day. Waited on /my Father/.

Saturday, 10th At home. Visited the house of my Father [and] found /him failing very fast/.

Sunday, 11th Visited my Father /again/ who was verry sick. /In secret prayer in the morning the Lord said, "My servant thy Father shall live."/ I waited on him all this day with my heart raised to God in the name of Jesus Christ that he would restore him to health again, that I might be blessed with his company and advise. Esteeming it one of the greatest earthly blessings, to be blessed with the society of Parents, whose mature years and experience renders them capable of administering the most whol[e]-some advice.

At Evening Bro[ther] David Whitmer came in. We called on the Lord in mighty prayer in the name of Jesus Christ, laid our hands on him [Joseph Smith, Sr.], and rebuked the diseas[e]. God heard and answered our prayers to the great Joy and satisfaction of our souls. Our aged Father arose and dressed himself, shouted, and praised the Lord. [I] called {page 7} Br[other] W[illia]m Smith who had retired to rest that he might praise the Lord with us by joining in Songs of praise to the Most High.

Monday, 12th Rode to Willoughby in company with my wife to purchase some goods at W[illiam] Lyon's Store. On our return we found a Mr. Bradl[e]y lying across the road. He had been thrown from his waggon [and] was much injured by the fall.

Tuesday, 13th Visited my Father who was verry much recovered from his sickness indeed, which caused us to marvel at the might[y] power and condes[c]ension of our Heavenly Father in answering our prayers in his behalf.

Wednesday, 14th At home.

⁴In the handwriting of Warren Parrish.

Thursday, 15th Laboured in Father's orchard gathering apples.

Friday, 16th Was called into the printing /office/ to settle some difficulties in that department. At evening on the same day I baptised Ebenezer Robinson. The Lord poured out his spirit on us and we had a good time.

Saturday, 17th Called my family together and ar[r]anged my domestick concerns and dismissed my boarders.

Sunday, 18th Attended meeting in the Chapel [Kirtland Temple]. Confirmed several who had been baptised and blessed several children with the blessings of the new and everlasting covenant. Elder Parley P. Pratt preach[e]d in the forenoon and Elder John F. Boynton in the after noon. We had an interesting time.

Monday, 19th At home. Ex[h]ibited the records of antiquuity to a number who called to see them.

Tuesday, 20th At home. Preached at night in the Schoolhouse.

Wednesday, 21st At home. Nothing {page 8} of note transpired.

Thursday, 22d At home. Attending to my domestick concerns.

Friday, 23d At home. ~~Attended the prayer meeting~~ /see page 50/ [*material inserted from page 50 begins here*] Copy of a prayer offered up on the 23d day of Oct[ober] 1835 by the following individuals at 4 o'clock P.M., viz Joseph Smith, J[u]n[ior], Oliver Cowdery, David Whitmer, Hiram Smith, John Whitmer, Sidn[e]y Rigdon, Samuel H. Smith, Frederick G. Williams and W[illia]m W. Phelps assembled and united in prayer with one voice before the Lord for the following blessings:

That the Lord will give us means sufficient to deliver us from all our afflictions and difficulties wherein we are placed by means of our debts.

That he will open the way and deliver Zion in the appointed {page 50} time and that without the shedding of blood.

That he will hold our lives precious and grant that we may live to the common age of man and never fall into the hands, nor power of the mob in Missourie, nor in any other place.

That he will also preserve our posterity that none of them fall even to the end of time.

That he will give us the blessings of the earth sufficient to carry us to Zion and that we may purchase inheritances in that land. Even enough to carry on /and accomplish/ the work unto which he was [has] appointed us.

Also that he will assist all others who desire, according to his commandments, to go up and purchase inheritances and all this easily and without perplexity and trouble.

And finally, that in the end he will save us in his Celestial Kingdom. Amen.

Oliver Cowdery, Clerk

[*end of inserted material*]

Saturday, 24th Mr. Goodrich and his lady called to see the antient [ancient] Records. [They] also called at Doct[or] F[rederick] G. Williams to see the mummies. Br[other]s Hawks and Carpenter from Michigan visited us and tar[r]ied over Sunday and attended meeting.

Sunday, 25th [I] attended meeting. President Rigdon preached in the fore noon [and] Elder Lyman Johnson in the after noon. After which Elder S[eymour] Bronson [Brunson] joined Br[other] W[illia]m Perry and Sister Eliza Brown in matrimony and I blessed them with long life and prosperity in the name of Jesus Christ.

At evening I attended prayer meeting. Opened it and ex-[h]orted the brethren and Sister[s] about one hour. The Lord pour[e]d out his spirit and some glorious things were spoken in the gift of toungs [tongues] and interp[r]eted concerning the redemption of Zion.

Monday, 26th Went to Chardon to attend the County Court in company with [my] Br[other]s Hyrum, Samuel, and [Don] Carloss Smith. Br[other] Samuel was called in question before this Court for not doing military duty, and was fined because we had not our conference minutes with us for testimony to prove that F[rederick] G. Williams was clerk of the conference.

This testimony we should have carried with us had it not been for the neglect of our Council, or Lawyer, who did not put us in possession of this information. This we feel was a want of fidelity to his client, and we concider it a base insult /practised/ upon us on the account of our faith, that the ungodly might have unlawful power over us and trample us under their unhallowed feet.

In consequence of this neglect, a fine was imposed on Br[other] Samuel {page 9} of $20 including costs, for which ~~Lawsuit~~ he was obliged to sell his cow to defray the expenses of the same.

I say in the name of Jesus Christ that the money that they have thus unjustly taken shall be a testimony against them and canker and eat their flesh as fire.

Tuesday, 27th In the morning I was called to visit at Br[other] Samuel Smith's. His wife was confined an[d] in a verry dangerous situation. Br[other] Carloss took one of my horses and went to Chardon after Doct[or] [Frederick G.] Williams. I went out into the field and bowed before the Lord and called upon him in mighty prayer in her behalf. The word of the Lord came unto me saying, "My Servant Frederick shall come and shall have wisdom given him to deal prudently and my handma[i]den shall be delivered of a living child and be spared." He [Frederick G. Williams] come in a bout one hour after that and in the course of about 2 hours she was delivered. Thus what God had manifested to me was fulfilled every whit. On the night of the same day, I preached in the School house to a crowded congregation.

Wednesday, 28th At holm [home] attending to my family concerns &c.

Thursday, 29th Br[other] W[arren] Par[r]ish commenced writing for me. Father and Mother Smith visit[ed] us. While we set writing Bishop Partri[d]ge passed our window. [He has] just returned from the East.

Br[other] Par[r]ish commenced writing for me at $15.00 per month. I paid him $16.00 in advance out of the committee Store. Br[other] Parrish agrees to board himself, for which I agree to /allow him/ four Dollars more p[e]r month making $19.00.

I was then called to appear before the High Council which was {page 10} setting to give my testimony in an action brought against Br[other] David El[l]iot for whip[p]ing his Daughter unreasonably. My testimony was in his favour.

41

Returned to our writing room. [We] went to Dr. [Frederick G.] William's after my large Journal[5] [and I] made some observations to my Scribe Concerning the plan of the City which is to be built up hereafter on this ground consecrated for a Stake of Zion.

While at the Doct[or's], Bishop E[dward] Partri[d]ge came in in company with President Phelps. I was much rejoiced to see him. We examined the mum[m]ies, returned home, and my scribe commenced writing in /my/ Journal a history of my life, concluding President [Oliver] Cowdery['s] 2d letter to W[illiam] W. Phelps, which President Williams had begun.

Bishop Whitney and his wife, with his Father and Mother, called to visit us. His parents having lately ar[r]ived here from the East, called to make enquiry concerning the coming forth of the Book of Mormon. Bishop Partri[d]ge and some others came in [and] I then set down and ~~taught~~ /related to/ them the history of the coming forth of the book, the administration of the Angel to me, the rudiments of the gospel of Christ &c. They appeared well satisfyed and I expect to baptise them in a few days, or this is my feelings upon the subject altho[ugh] they have not made any request of this Kind at present.

Went to the Council, the Presidency arose and adjourned. On my return Elder Boynton observed that long debates were bad. I replyed that it was generally the case that to[o] much altercation was ~~generally~~ indulged in on both sides and their debates protracted to an unprofitable length.

We were called to sup[p]er. After being seated around the table, Bishop Whitney observed to Bishop Partri[d]ge that /the/ thought had just occur[r]ed to his mind that perhaps in about one yea[r] from this time they might be seated together around a table on the land of Zion. {page 11} ~~Sister Emma~~ /My wife/ observed that she hoped it might be the case that not only they but the rest of the company present might be seated around her table in the land of promise. The same sentiment was recip-

---

[5] This is Book A-1 of the "Manuscript History of the Church," which contains some of Joseph Smith's and his scribes' earliest attempts to write a detailed history of the church and which was later used to prepare the published *History of Joseph Smith*. The original manuscript is housed in the archives of the Historical Department, Church of Jesus Christ of Latter-day Saints.

rocated from the company round the table and my heart responded, "Amen!" God grant it, I ask in the name of Jesus Christ.

After sup[p]er I went to the High Council in company with my wife and some others that belong to my house hold. I was solicited to take a seat with the Presidency and preside in a case of Sister El[l]iot's. I did so.

My Mother was called as testimony and began to relate circumstances that had been brought before the Church and settled. I objected against such testimony. The complainant, Br[other] William Smith, arose and accused me of invalidating or doubting my Mother's testimony, which I had not done, nor did I desire to do. I told him he was out of place and asked him to set down. He refused [so] I repeated my request. He become enraged. I finally ordered him to set down. He said he would not unless I knocked him down. I was agitated in my feeling on the account of his stubournness and was about to leave the house, but my Father requ[e]sted me not to /do so/. I complyed.

The house was brought to order after much debate upon the subject and we proce[e]ded to business. Br[other] El[l]iot and his wife were both cleared from the charges prefer[r]ed against them.

Friday, 30th At home. Mr. Fransis Porter from Jefferson Co[unty], New York, a member of the Methodist Church, called to make some enquiry about lands in this place [Kirtland]. [He wanted to know] whether there is any farmes for sale that are valuable and whether {page 12} a member of our Church could move into this vicinity and purchase lands and enjoy his own possessions and property without making it common Stock. He had been requested to do so by some brethren who live in the town of Leroy, Jeff[erson] Co[unty], N[ew] Y[ork]. I replyed that I had a valuable farm joining the Temple Lot that I would sell and that there is other lands for sale in this place. [I told him] that we have no common stock business among us. That every man enjoys his own property, or can, if he is disposed, consecrate liberally or illiberally to the support of the poor and needy, or the building up of Zion. He also enquired how many members there are in this Church. I told him that there is about five or six hundred who commune at our Chapel [Kirtland Temple] and perhaps a thousand in this vicinity.

At evening I was presented with a letter from Br[other]

W[illia]m Smith, the purport of which is, that he is censured by the brethren on the account of what took place at the Council last night and wishes to have the matter settled to the understanding of all, that he may not be censured unjustly, concidering that his cause was a just one, and that he had been materially injured. I replied that I thought we parted with the best of feelings, that I am not to blame on the account of the dissatisfaction of others. I invited him to call and talk with me, and that I would ~~give~~ /talk with/ him in the spirit of meekness and give him all the satisfaction I could. This reply was by letter [with a] copy retained

Saturday, 31st In the morning Br[other] Hyram Smith came in and said he had been much troubled all night and had not slept any, {page 13} that something was wrong. While talking Br[other] W[illia]m Smith came in according to my requ[e]st last night. Br[other] Hyram observed that he must go to the Store. I invited him to stay. He said he would go and do his business and return. He did so [and] while he was gone Br[other] William introduced the subject of our difficulty at the Council. I told him I did not want to converse upon the subject untill Hyrum returned. He [Hyrum] soon came in.

I then proposed to relate the occur[r]ences of the Council before named, and wherein I had been out of the way I would confess it, and ask forgiv[e]ness. Then he should relate his story, and make confession wherein he had done wrong ~~he said he had not done wrong~~ and then leave it to Br[other] Hyrum Smith and Br[other] Par[r]ish to decide the matter between us and I would agree to the decision and be satisfyed there with.

He observed that he had not done wrong, and that I was always determined to carry my points whether right or wrong, and there fore he would not stand an equal chance with me. This was an insult, but I did not reply to him in a harsh manner, knowing his inflam[m]atory disposition, but tryed to reason with him and show him the propriety of a complyance with my request. I finally succeeded with the assistance of Br[other] Hyrum, in obtaining his assent to the proposition that I had made. I then related my story, and wherein I had been wrong, I confessed it, and asked his forgiv[e]ness.

After I got through he made his statements, jus[t]ifying himself throughout in transgressing the order of the Council, and treating the authority of the Presidency with contempt.

After he had got through, Br[other] Hyrum began to make {page 14} some remarks in the spirit of meekness, he [William] became enraged. I joined my brother [Hyrum] in trying to calm his stormy feelings, but to no purpose. He insisted that we intended to add abuse to injury, his passion increased. He arose abruptly, declared that he wanted no more to do with us or the Church and said we might take his licence for he would have nothing to do with us. He rushed out at the door. We tryed to prevail on him to stop, but all to no purpose. He went away in a passion, and soon sent his licence to me. He went home and spread the levvin [leaven] of iniquity among my brethren and especially prejudiced the mind of Br[other] Samuel [Smith] as I soon learned [and] that he was in the street exclaiming against me, which no doubt our enemys rejoice at.

Where the matter will end I know not, but I p[r]ay God to forgive him and th[e]m, and give them humility and repentance. The feelings of my heart I cannot express on this occasion. I can only pray my Heavenly Father to open their eyes that they may discover where they stand, that they may extricate themselves from the snare they have fallen into.

After dinner I rode out in company with my wife and children, Br[other] [Don] Carloss and some others. We went to visit Br[other] [Shadrach] Roundy and family who live near Willoughby. We had an interesting visit at Br[other] Roundy[']s].

As soon as I returned I was called upon to baptise Samuel Whitney and his Wife and Daughter. After [the] baptism we returned to their house and offered our thanks in prayer. I obtained a testimony that [my] Br[other] William would return to the Church and repair the wrong he had done. {page 15}

Sunday morning, November 1st 1835 Verily thus Saith the Lord unto me, his servant, Joseph Smith, Jr., min[e] anger is kindle[d] against my servant Reynolds Cahoon because of his iniquities, his covetous and dishonest principles in himself and family and he doth not purge them away and set his house in order. Therefore, if he repent not, chastis[e]ment awaiteth him, even as it seemeth good in my sight, therefore go and declare unto him these words.

I went im[m]ediately and delivired this message according as the Lord commanded me. I called him in and read what

45

the Lord had said concerning him. He acknowledged that it was verily so and expressed much humility.

I then went to meeting. Elder Carrill [John Corrill] preached a fine discourse. In the after noon President Phelps continued the servises of the day by reading the 5th chapt[er] of Mat[t]hew, also the laws regulating the High Council, and made some remarks upon them, after which [the] Sacrament was administered.

I then confirmed a number who had been baptised and blessed a number of children in the name of Jesus Christ with the blessings of the new and everlasting covenant. Notice was then given that the Elders' School wou[l]d commence on the morrow. I then dismissed the meeting.

Monday morning, 2d [I] was engaged in regulating the affairs of the School. I then had my team prepared and Sidney, Oliver, Frederick, my scribe, and a number of others went to Willoughby to Hear Doct[or] Piexotto deliver a lecture on the theory and practice of Physic. {page 16} We called at Mr. Cushman's, had our horses put in the Stable, took dinner, [and] attended the lecture. [We were] was treated with great respect throughout [and] returned home.

Lyman Wight came from Zion to day. George and Lyman Smith also [arrived] from the East.

The question was agitated whether Frederick G. Williams or Oliver Cowdery Should go to New York to make ar[r]angements respecting a book bindery. They refer[r]ed to me for a decision, and thus cam[e] the word of the Lord unto me saying: It is not my will that my servant Frederick Should go to New York. But inasmuch as he wishes to go and visit his relatives, that he may warn them to flee the wrath to come, let him go and see them for that purpose, and let that be his only business. And behold in this thing, he shall be blessed with power to overcome their prejudices. Verily thus saith the Lord. Amen.

Tuesday, 3d Thus came the word of the Lord unto me concerning the Twelve [Apostles] /saying/: Behold they are under condemnation because they have not been sufficiently humble in my sight, and in consequence of their covetous desires, in that they have not dealt equally with each other in the division of moneys which came into their hands. Never/the/less, some of them dealt equally, therefore they shall be rewarded. But verily I say unto you, they must all humble themselves before me before they will be accounted worthy to receive an endowment to go forth in my name unto all nations.

As for my Servant William [Smith], let the Eleven humble themselves in prayer and in faith, {page 17} and wait on me in patience, and my servant William shall return. I will yet make him a polished shaft in my quiver, in bringing down the wickedness and abominations of men and there shall be none mightier than he in his day and generation. Nevertheless, if he repent not spe[e]dily, he shall be brought low and shall be chastened sorely for all his iniquities he has commit[t]ed against me. Nevertheless, the sin which he hath sin[n]ed against me is not even now more grevious [grievous] then the sin with which my servant David W. Patten, and my servant Orson Hyde, and my servant William E. McLellen have sinded [sinned] against me, and the residue are not sufficiently humble before me.

Behold the parable which I spake concerning a man having twelve Sons: For what man amon[g] you having twelve Sons and is no respecter to [of] them and they serve him obediantly, he saith unto the one, Be thou clothed in robes and sit thou here, and to the other, Be thou clothed in rages [rags] and sit thou there, and looketh upon his sons and saith I am just. Ye will answer and say, no man, and ye answer truly.

Therefore, Verely thus saith the Lord your God, I appointed these Twelve [Apostles] that they should be equal in their ministry, and in their portion, and in their evangelical rights. Wherefore they have sin[n]ed a verry grevious [grievous] sin in as much as they have made themselves unequal and have not heark[e]ned unto my voice. Therfor[e], let them repent speedily and prepare their hearts for the Solem[n] Assembly {page 18} and for the great day which is to come. Verely thus saith the Lord. Amen.

I then went to assist in organizing the Elders' School. [It was] called to order and I made some remarks upon the object of this School and the great necessity there is of our rightly improving our time and reigning up our minds to a sense of the great object that lies before us, viz, that glorious endowment that God has in store for the faithful. I then dedicated the School in the name of the Lord Jesus Christ. After the School was dismissed, I attended a patriarchal meeting at Br[other] Samuel Smith's, his

47

wifeses [wife's] parents were blessed. Also his child named Susan-[n]ah.

At evening I preach[e]d at the School house to a crowded congregation.

Wednesday, 4th In morning at home. Attended school during the school hours. [We] made rapid progress in our studies. In the evening lectured on grammar at home. On this day King Follet[t] ar[r]ived at this place from Zion.

Thursday, 5th Attended School. Isaac Morley came in from the east this morning. I was called to visit Thomas Burdick who was sick. I took my scribe with me and we p[r]ayed for and laid our hands on him in the /name/ of the Lord Jesus and rebuked his affliction.

W[illia]m E. McLellen and Orson Hyde came in and desired to hear the revelation concerning the Twelve [Apostles]. My scribe read [the revelation] to them. They expressed some little dissatisfaction, but after examining their own hearts, they accknowledged it to be the word of the Lord {page 19} and said they were satisfied.

After School, Brigham Young came in and desired also to hear it read. After hearing it, he appeared perfectly satisfied. In the evening [I] lectured on Grammar.

Friday morning, 6th At home. Attended School during the school hours. Returned and spent the evening at home. I was this morning introduced to a man from the east. After hearing my name, he remarked that I was nothing but a man, indicating by this expression, that he had supposed that a person /to/ whom the Lord should see fit to reveal his will must be something more than a man. He seems to have forgotten the saying that fell from the lips of St. James, that Elias was a man of like passions like unto us, yet he had such power with God, that He, in answer to his prayer, shut the heavens that they gave no rain for the space of three years and six months. Again in answer to his prayer the heavens gave forth rain and the earth brought forth fruit. Indeed such is the darkness and ignorance of this generation that they look upon it as incredible that a man should have any intercourse with his Maker.

Saturday, 7th Spent the day at home attending to my domestic concerns. The word /of the Lord/ came to me saying: Behold I am well pleased with my servant Isaac Morley, and my servant Edward Partridge, because of the integrity of their h[e]arts in laboring in my vin[e]yard for the salvation of the souls of men. Verely I say unto you, their sins are {page 20} forgiven them. Therefore say unto them in my name, that it is my will that they should tarry for a little season, and attend the school, and also the Solem[n] Assembly for a wise purpose in me. Even so. Amen.

Sunday, 8th [I] went to meeting in the morning at the us[u]al hour. Z[erubbabel] Snow preached a verry interesting discourse. In the after noon J[oseph] Young preached.

After preaching, Isaac Hill came forward to make some remarks by way of confession. He had been previously excommunicated from the Church for lying and for an attempt to seduce a female. His confission [confession] was not satisfactory to my mind. /Uncle/ John Smith arose and made some remarks respecting the dealings of the High Council on the case of said Hill. That is, that he should make a public confession of his crime and have it published in the Messenger and Advocate. He proposed that Mr. Hill should now make his confession before the congregation and then immediately observed that he had forgiven Mr. Hill which was in contradiction to the sentiment he first advanced. This I attributed to an error in Judgment not in design.

President Rigdon then arose, and verry abruptly militated against /the sentiment of/ Uncle John, which had a direct tendency to destroy his influence and bring him into disrepute in the eyes of the Church, which was not right. He also misrepresented Mr. Hill's case and spread darkness rather than light upon the subject.

A vote of the Church was then called on his case. He was restored without any further confession [and] that he should {page 21} be received into the Church by baptism which was administered ac[c]ordingly.

After I came home, I took up a labour with Uncle John and convinced him that he was wrong and he made his confession to my satisfaction. I then went and laboured with President Rigdon and succe[e]ded in convincing him also of his error which he confessed to my satisfaction.

The word of the Lord cam[e] unto me saying that President Phelps and President J[ohn] Whitmer are under condemnation before the Lord for their errors. \⁶ /For which they made satisfaction the same day/

\⁷ I also took up labour with J[ohn] Carrill [Corrill] for leaving the meeting before /not partaking of the/ Sacrament. He made his confession. Also my wife for leaving the meeting before Sacrament. She made no reply, but manifested contrition by weeping.

Monday morning, 9th After breckfast Sister /Mary/ Whitcher came in and wished to see me. I granted her request. She gave a relation of her grieveances, which were unfathomable at present, and if true, sore indeed. I pray my Heavenly Father to bring the truth of her case to light, that the reward due to evil doers may be given them, and /that/ the afflicted and oppressed may be delivered.

While setting in my house, between the hours of ten and 11 this morning, a man came in and introduced himself to me, calling /himself/ by the name of Joshua the Jewish minister. His appearance was some thing singular, having a beard about 3 inches in length which is quite grey. Also his hair is long and considerably silvered with age. {page 22} I should think he is about 50 or 55 years old, tall and strait, slender built, of thin visage, blue eyes, and fair complexion. He wears a sea green frock coat and pantaloons of the same [color], black fur hat with narrow brim, and while speaking [he] frequently shuts his eyes with a scowl on his countinance.

I made some enquiry after his name but received no definite answer. We soon commenced talking upon the subject of religion and, after I had made some remarks concerning the Bible, I commenced giving him a relation of the circumstances connected with the coming forth of the Book of Mormon, as follows:

Being wrought up in my mind respecting the subject of religion and looking at the different systems taught the children of men, I knew not who was right or who was wrong. I considered it of the first importance that I should be right in matters that involve eternal consequ[e]nces.

Being thus perplexed in mind I retired to the silent grove and bow[e]d down before the Lord, under a realising sense that

---

⁶ In the handwriting of William W. Phelps.
⁷ In the handwriting of Warren Parrish.

he had said (if the Bible be true), "Ask and you shall receive, knock and it shall be opened. Seek and you shall find." Again, "If any man lack wisdom, let him ask of God, who giveth to all men libarally and upbraideth not."

Information was what I most desired at this time and with a fixed determination to obtain it, I called upon the Lord for the first time in the place above stated. Or in other words, I made a fruitless attempt to p[r]ay. My toung [tongue] seemed to be swol[l]en in my mouth, so that I could not utter. I heard a noise behind me like some person walking towards me. I strove again to pray but could not. The noise of walking seemed to draw nearer. I sprung up on my feet {page 23} and looked around, but saw no person or thing that was calculated to produce the noise of walking. I kneeled again. My mouth was open and my toung [tongue] liberated and I called on the Lord in mighty prayer.

A pillar of fire appeared above my head. It presently rested down upon ~~my head~~ /me/ and filled me with Joy unspeakable. A personage appear[e]d in the midst of this pillar of flame which was spread all around and yet nothing consumed. Another personage soon appear[e]d like unto the first. He said unto me, "Thy sins are forgiven thee." He testifyed unto me that Jesus Christ is the Son of God. /I saw many angels in this vision/ I was about 14 years old when I received this first communication.

When I was about 17 years old, I saw another vision of angels in the night season, after I had retired to bed. I had not been a sleep but was meditating upon my past life and experience. I was verry con[s]cious that I had not kept the commandments. I repented h[e]artily for all my sins and transgression and humbled myself before Him /whose eyes are over all things/. All at once the room was il[l]uminated above the brightness of the sun. An angel appeared before me. His hands and feet were naked, pure and white. He stood between the floors of the room, clothed with purity inexpressible. He said unto me, "I am a messenger sent from God. Be faithful and keep his commandments in all things."

He told me of a sacred record which was written on plates of gold. I saw in the vision the place where they were deposited. He said the Indians were the literal descendants of Abraham. He explained many of the prophesies to {page 24} me. One I will mention which is in Malachi 4[th] chapt[er]: "Behold the day of the Lord cometh" &c. Also that the Urim and Thum[m]im was hid up with the record and that God would give me power to translate it with the assistance of this instrument. He then gradually vanished out of my sight, or the vision closed.

While meditating on what I had seen, the angel appeared to me again and related the same things and much more. Also the third time bearing the same tidings and departed.

During the time I was in this vision I did not realize any thing else around me except what was shown me in this communication. After the vision had all passed, I found that it was nearly daylight. The family soon arose, I got up also.

On that day while in the field at work with my Father he asked me if I was sick. I replyed I had but little strength. He told me to go to the house. I started and went part way and was finally deprived of my strength and fell, but how long I remained I do not know.

The Angel came to me again and commanded me to go and tell my Father what I had seen and heard. I did so. He wept and told me that it was a vision from God [and] to attend to it. I went and found the place where the plates were according to the direction of the Angel. Also saw them and the angel as before. The powers of darkness strove hard against me. I called upon God. The Angel told me that the reason why I could not obtain the plates at this time was because I was under transgression, but to come again in one year from that time. I did so, but did not obtain them. {page 25} Also the third and the fourth year, at which time I obtained them and translated them into the English language by the gift and power of God. [I] have been preaching it ever since.

While I was relating this brief history of the establishment of the Church of Christ in these last days, Joshua seemed to be highly entertained. After I had got through, I observed that the hour of worship and time to dine had now ar[r]ived and invited him to tarry which he concented to.

After dinner the conversation was resumed and Joshua proce[e]ded to make some remarks on the prophesies as follows. He observed that he was aware that I could bear stronger meat than many others. Therefore he should open his mind the more freely.

[Joshua said,] "Daniel has told us that he is to stand in

his proper lot, in the latter days according to his vision. He had a right to shut it up and also to open it again after many days, or in the latter times. Daniel's image whose head was gold and body, armes, legs, and feet was composed of the different materials described in his vision represents different governments.

"The golden head was /to represent/ Nebuchadnaz[z]er King of Babylon. The other parts, other kings and forms of government which I shall not now mention in detail, but confine my remarks more particularly to the feet of the Image. The policy of the wicked spirit is to separate what God had joined togather and unite what He has separated, which he has succe[e]ded in doing to admiration. In the present state of society, which is like unto Iron and clay, there is confusion in all things, {page 26} both Political and religious. And notwithstanding all the efforts that are made to bring about a union, society remains disunited and all attempts to /unite her/ are as fruitless as to attemp[t] to unite Iron and Clay.

"The feet of the Image is the government of these United States. Other Nations and Kingdoms are looking up to her for an example of union, fre[e]dom and equal rights and therefore worship her like as Daniel saw in the vision, although they are begin[n]ing to loose confidence in her, seeing the broils and discord that distract her political and religious horizon. This Image is characteristic of all governments and institutions or most of them as they begin with a head of gold and terminate in the contemp[t]ible feet of Iron and clay making a splendid appearance at first proposing to do much more than the[y] can perform and finally end in degradation and sink in infamy. We should not only start to com[e] out of Babylon, but leav[e] it entirely lest we are overthrown in her ruins. We should keep improving and reforming. Twenty-four hours for improvement now is worth as much as a year a hundred years ago.

"The spirit of the Fathers that was cut down, or those that were under the altar, are now rising. This is the first resur[r]ection. The Elder that falls first will rise last. We should not form any opinion only for the present and leave the result of futurity with God. I have risen up out of obscurity, but was looked up to when but a youth in temporal things. It is not necessary that God should give us all things at first or in his first commission to us, but in his second. John saw the angel deliver the gospel in the last

53

days which would not be necessary if {page 27} it was already in the world. This expression would be inconsistent. The small lights that God has given is sufficient to lead us out of Babylon. When we get out we shall have the greater light."

I told Jo[s]hua that I did not understand him concerning the resur[r]ection and wish[e]d him to be more explanitory on the subject. He replied that he did not feel impressed by the spirit to unfold it further at present, but perhaps he might at some other time.

I then withdr[e]w to do some business with another gentleman that called to see me.

He [Joshua] informed my Scribe that he was born in Washington County, Town of Cambridge, New York. He says that all the railroads, canals and other improvements are performed by spirits of the resur[r]ection. The silence spoken of by John the Revelator which is to be in heaven for the space of half an hour is between 1830 and 1851, during which time the judgments of God will be poured out. After that time there will be peace.

Curiosity to see a man that was reputed to be a Jew caused many to call during the day and more particularly at evening. Suspicions were entertained that said Joshua was the noted [Robert] Mat[t]hias of New York, spoken so much of in public prints on account of the trials he underwent in that place before a court of justice for murder, manslaughter, contempt of court, whip[p]ing his Daughter, &c. For the two last crimes he was imprisoned and came out about 4 months {page 28} since. After some equivocating he confessed that he was real[l]y Mat[t]hias.

After supper, I proposed that he should deliver a lecture to us. He did so sitting in his chair. He commenced by saying "God said, 'Let there be light and there was light,'" which he dwelt upon through his discource. He made some verry ex[c]el-[l]ent remarks but his mind was evidently filled with darkness.

After he dismissed his meeting and the congregation disperced, he conversed freely upon the circumstances that transpired in New York. His name is Robert Mat[t]hias. He say[s] that Joshua is his priestly name. During all this time I did not contradict his sentiments wishing to draw out all that I could concerning his faith.

The next morning, Tuesday, [November] 10th, I resumed the conversation and desired him to enlighten my mind more on his views respecting the resur[r]ection. He says that he posses[es] the spirit of his fathers. That he is a litteral de[s]cendant of Mat[t]hias the Apostle that was chosen in the place of Judas that fell and that his spirit is resur[r]ected in him. That this is the way or schem[e] of eternal life, this transmigration of soul or spirit from Father to Son.

I told him that his doctrine was of the Devil that he was in reality in possession of [a] wicked and depraved spirit although he professed to be the spirit of truth itself. /And he said/ also that he possesses the soul of Christ.

He tarried until Wednesday [the] 11th. After breckfast I told him that my God told me that his God is the Devil and I could not keep him any longer and he must depart. So I for once cast out the Devil in bodily shape and I believe [him to be] a murderer. {page 29}

On Monday th[e] 9th, Mr. [Alvah] Beeman of N[ew] Y[ork] came here to ask advice of me concerning purchasing lands. Whether it is best for him to purchase in this vicinity and move into this Church or not. He says that he cannot arrange his buisness [business] so as to go to the Missouri next spring. I advised him to come here and settle untill he could move to Zion.

Wednesday morning, 11th At home. Attended School during school Hours. [I] returned home and spent the evening around my fire side teaching my family the science of grammar. It commensed snowing this afterno[o]n [and] the wind is verry heavy indeed.

Thursday, 12th Attended School again during School Hours. Rain and Snow is still falling. It is about one inch in dept[h]. The wind is verry heavy and the weather extrem[e]ly unpleasant.

The labour[er]s who commenced finishing the out side of the ~~house~~ Chappel [Kirtland Temple] were oblieged to brake off from their buisness [business] at the commenc[e]ment of this storm viz on the 11th. They commenced plasturing and finishing the out side on Monday the 2[nd] inst[ant].

This job is let to A[rtemus] Millet and L[orenzo] Young /at $1,000/. They have progressed rapidly since they commenced. J[acob] Bump has the job of plastering the inside of the house through out at $1,500. He commenced on Monday the 9th and is continueing it notwithstanding the inclemency of the weather.

55

This evening, viz the 12th, at 6 o'clock meet [met] with the Council of 12 [Apostles] by their request; 9 of them were present. {page 30} [The] Council opened by singing and prayer. I made some remarks as follows: "I am happy in the enjoyment of this oppertunity of meeting with this Council on this occasion. I am satisfyed that the spirit of the Lord is here. I am satisfied with all the breth[r]en present. I need not say that you have my utmost confidence and that I intend to uphold you to the uttermost. For I am well aware that you have to sustain my character against the vile calumnies and reproaches of this ungodly generation and that you delight in so doing. Darkness prevails at this time as it was at the time Jesus Christ was about to be crucified. The powers of darkness strove to obscure the glorious sun of righteousness that began to dawn upon the world and was soon to burst in great blessings upon the heads of the faithful.

"Let me tell you brethren that great blessings awate [await] us at this time and will soon be poured out upon us if we are faithful in all things. For we are even entitled to greater blessings than they were because the[y] had the person of Christ with them to instruct them in the great plan of salvation. His personal presence we have not, therefore we need great faith on account of our peculiar circumstances. I am determined to do all that I can to uphold you. Although I may do many things /invertanbly/ [inadvertently] that are not right in the sight of God.

"You want to know many things that are before you that you may know how to prepare your selves for the {page 31} great things that God is about to bring to pass. But there is on[e] great deficiency or obstruction in the way that deprives us of the greater blessings. And in order to make the foundation of this Church complete and permanent, we must remove this obstruction which is to attend to certain duties that we have not as yet attended to. .

"I supposed I had established this Church on a permanent foundation when I went to the Missouri. Indeed I did so, for if I had been taken away it would have been enough, but I yet live. Therefore God requires more at my hands.

"The item to which I wish the more particularly to call your attention to night is the ordinance of washing of feet. This we have not done as yet, but it is necessary now as much as it was in the days of the Saviour. We must have a place prepared that we may attend to this ordinance aside from the world. We have not desired much from the hand of the Lord with that faith and obediance that we ought. Yet we have enjoyed great blessings and we are not so sensible of this as we should be.

"When or wher[e] has God suffered one of the witnesses or first Elders of this Church to fall? Never nor nowhere amidst all the calamities and judgments that have befallen the inhabitants of the earth. His almighty arm had sustained us. Men and Devils have raged and spent the[ir] malice in vain. {page 32}

"We must have all things prepared and call our Solem[n] Assembly as the Lord has commanded us that we may be able to accomplish his great work. It must be done in God's own way. The House of the Lord must be prepared and the Solem[n] Assembly called and organized in it according to the order of the House of God. In it we must attend to the ordinance of washing of feet. It was never intended for any but official members. It is calculated to unite our hearts that we may be one in feeling and sentiment and that our faith may be strong so that Satan cannot over throw us, nor have any power over us.

"The Endowment you are so anxious about you cannot comprehend now. Nor could Gabriel explain it to the understanding of your dark minds, but strive to be prepared in your hearts. Be faithful in all things that when we meet in the Solem[n] Assembly that is such as God shall name out of all the official members will meet and we must be clean ev[e]ry whit. Let us be faithful and silent brethren /and/ if God gives you a manifestation keep it to yourselves. Be watchful and prayerful and you shall have a prelude of those joys that God will pour out on that day. Do not watch for iniquity in each other. If you do you will not get an endowment, for God will not bestow it on such. But if we are faithful and live by every word that proce[e]des forth from the mouth of God I will venture to prophesy that we shall get a {page 33} blessing that will be worth remembering if we should live as long as John the Revelator. Our blessings will be such as we have not realized before, nor in this generation.

"The order of the House of God has and ever will be the same. Even after Christ comes and after the termination of the thousand years it will be the same and we shall finally roll into the Celestial Kingdom of God and enjoy it forever. You need an Endowment brethren in order that you may be prepared and able to over come all things. Those that reject your testimony will be

57

damned. The sick will be healed, the lame made to walk, the deaf to hear and the blind to see through your instrumentality. But let me tell you that you will not have power after the Endowment to heal those who have not faith, nor to benifit them. For you might as well expect to benefit a devil in hell as such an one who is possessed of his spirit and are willing to keep it. For they are habitations for the devils and only fit for his society.

"But when you are endowed and prepared to preach the gospel to all nations, kindred and toungs [tongues] in there own languages you must faithfully warn all and bind up the testimony and seal up the law. The destroying angel will follow close at your heels and execute his tremendeous mission upon the children of disobediance and destroy {page 34} the workers of iniquity, while the Saints will be gathered out from among them and stand in holy places ready to meet the bride groom when he comes.

"I feel disposed to speak a few words more to you my brethren concerning the Endowment. All who are prepared and are sufficiently pure to abide the presence of the Saviour will see him in the Solem[n] Assembly."

The brethren expressed their gratifycation for the instruction I had given them. We then closed by prayer. I then returned home and retired to rest.

Friday, 13th Attended School during School hours [and] returned home after School. Mr. Messenger of Bainbridge, Chenango Co[unty], N[ew] Y[ork] came in to make some enquiry about H[ezekiah] Peck's family. He is a Universalian Minister. We entered into conversation upon religious subjects. We went to President Rigdon's and spent the evening in conversation. We preach[e]d the gospel to him and bore testimony to him of what we had seen and heard. He attempted to raise some objections, but the force of the truth bore him down and he was silent, although unbelieving. Returned home and retired to rest.

Saturday morning, 14th Thus came the word of the Lord unto me saying: "Verily thus saith the Lord unto my servant Joseph concerning my servant Warren [Parrish]. Behold {page 35} his sins are forgiven him because of his desires to do the works of righteousness. Therefore in as much as he will continue to hearken unto my voice he shall be blessed with wisdom and with a sound mind even above his fellows. Behold it shall come to pass in his day that he shall /see/ great things shew forth themselves unto my people. He shall see much of my ancient records and shall know of hid[d]en things and shall be endowed with a knowledge of hid[d]en languages. And if he desires and shall seek it at my hand, he shall be privileged with writing much of my word as a scribe unto me for the benefit of my people. Therefore this shall be his calling until I shall order it otherwise in my wisdom. It shall be said of him in a time to come, 'Behold Warren the Lord's Scribe, for [it is] the Lord's Seer whom he hath appointed in Israel.' Therefore /if he will/ keep my commandments he shall be lifted up at the last day. Even so. Amen."

A Gentleman called this after noon by the name of Erastus Holmes of Newbury, Clemon [Clermont] Co[unty], Ohio. He called to make enquiry about the establishment of the Church of the Latter-day Saints and to be instructed more perfectly in our doctrine &c.

I commenced and gave him a brief relation of my experience while in my {page 36} juvenile years, say from 6 years old up to the time I received the first visitation of Angels which was when I was about 14 years old. Also the visitations that I received afterward concerning the Book of Mormon and a short account of the rise and progress of the Church up to this date.

He listened verry attentively and seemed highly gratified and intends to unite with the Church. He is a verry candid man indeed and I am much pleased with him.

On Sab[b]ath morning the 15th He [Erastus Holmes] went with me to meeting which was held in the Schoolhouse on account of the Chappel [Kirtland Temple] not being finished plastering. President Rigdon preached on the subject of men's being called to preach the gospel and their qualifications &c. We had a fine discourse. It was verry interesting indeed. Mr. Holmes was well satisfied. He came home with me and dined.

Said Holmes has been a member of the Methodist Church and was excommunicated for receiving the Elders of the Church of the Latter-day Saints into his house.

Went to meeting in the afterno[o]n. Before partaking of the Sacrament, Isaac Hill's case was agitated again and settled after much controversy. He [was] retained in the Church by making an humble acknowled[g]ement before the Church and concenting to have his confession published in the Messenger and Advo-

59

cate. After which the ordinance of the Lord's Supper was administered and the meeting closed verry late. Returned home and spent the evening. {page 37}

Monday the 16th At home. Dictated a letter for the [Messenger and] Advocate, also one to Harvey Whitlock. Father [Alvah] Beeman called to council with me, Elder Strong, and some others.

\8 Copy of the Letter from Harvey Whitloc[k]

[28 September 1835]

Dear Sir,

Having a few leisure moment[s] I have at last concluded to do what my own Judgement has long dictated would be right, but the allurements of many vices has long retarded the hand that would wield the pen to make intellegent the communication that I wish to send to you; And even now that ambition which is a prevailing and predominent principles among the great mass of natural men even now forbids that plainness of sentiment with which I wish to write. For know assuredly sir to you I wish to unbosom my feelings and unravil [unravel] the secrets of my heart as before the omni[s]cient Judge of all the earth.

Be not surprised when I declare unto you as the spirit will bear record that my faith is firm and unshaken in the things of the everlasting gospel as it is proclaimed by the servants of the Latter-day Saints.

Dear Brother Joseph (If I may be allowed the expression), when I considder the happy times and peaseful moments and pleasant seasons I have enjoyed with you and this people, contrasted with my now degraded state, together with the high and important station I have held before {page 38} God and the abyss into which I have fallen is a subject that swell \9 my heart to[o] big for utterance and language is

---

[8] In the handwriting of Frederick G. Williams.
[9] In the handwriting of Warren Parrish.

overwhelmed with feeling and looses its power of description.

And as I desire to know the will of God concerning me, believing it is my duty to make known unto you my real situation, I shall therefore dispas[s]ionately proce[e]de to give a true and untarnished relation. I need not tell you that in former times I have preached the word and endeavored to be instant in season, out of season, to reprove, rebuke, exhort and faithfully to discharge that trust reposed in me. But oh! with what grief and lamentable sorrow and anguish do I have to relate that I have fallen from that princely station where unto our God has called me. Reasons why are un[n]ecessary, may the fact suffice.

Believe me when I tell you that I have sunk myself (since my last separation from this boddy) in crimes of the deepest dye and that I may the better enable you to understand what my real sins are I will mention (although pride forbids it) some that I am not guilty of. My /hands/ have not been stained with in[n]ocent blood, neither have I lain couched around the cottages of my fellow men to seize and carry off the booty. Nor have I slandered my neighbor, nor bourn fals[e] testimony, nor taken unlawful hire, nor oppressed the widdow, nor the fatherless. Neither have I persecuted the Saints. But my hands are swift to do iniquity and my feet are fast running in the paths of vice and folly and my heart {page 39} quick to devise wicked imaginations. Nevertheless I am impressed with the sure thought that I am fast hast[e]ning into a ~~whole~~ world of disembodied beings without God and with but one hope in the world which is to know that to er[r] is human, but to forgive is divine.

Much I might say in relation to myself and the original difficulties with the Church which I will forbear and in asmuch as I have been charged with things that I was not guilty of I am now more than doubly guilty. [I] am now willing to forgive and forget. Only let me know that I am within the reach of mercy. If I am not I have no reflections to cast, but say that I have

sealed my own doom and pronounced my own
sentence. If the day is passed by with me may I here
beg leave to entreat of those who are still toiling up the
rug[g]ed assent to make their way to the realms of endless felicity and delight to stop not for anchors here below. Follow not my example, but steer your course on-
ward in spite of all the combined powers of earth and
hell. For know that one miss step here is only retriev-
able by a thousand groans and tears before God.

Dear Brother Joseph, let me entreat you on the reception of this letter as you regard the salvation of my
soul to enquire at the hand of the Lord in my behalf.
For I this day in the presence of God do covenant to
abide the word that may be given; for I am willing to
receive any {page 40} chastisement that the Lord sees I
deserve.

Now hear my prayer and suffer me to break forth
in the agony of my soul. O ye Angels! that surround
the throne /of God/, Princes of heaven that excell in
strength. Ye who are clothed with transcendant brightness, plead O plead for one of the most wre[t]ched of
the Sons of Men. O ye heavens! whose azure arches rise
immensely high and stre[t]ch immeasurably wide,
grand amp[h]itheater of nature, throne of the Eternal
God bow to hear the prayer of a poor wretched bewil-
dered way wanderer to eternity. O thou great Omni-
[s]cient and omnipresent Jehovah, thou who sit[t]eth
upon the throne, before whom all things are present,
thou maker, moulder and fashioner of all things visible
and invisible breath[e] O breath[e] into the ears of thy
servant the Prophet words su[i]tably adapted to my case
and situation. Speak once more. Make known thy will
concerning me. Which favours I ask in the name of the
Son of God. Amen.

N.B. I hope you will not let any business prevent
you from answering this letter. In hast[e],

Yours Respectfully,
Harvey Whitlock

To Joseph Smith {page 41}

—

Copy of a Letter sent [to] Harvey Whitlock in answer to his

Kirtland, Nov[ember] 16th 1835

Bro[ther] Harvey Whitlock,

I have received your letter of the 28th [of] Sept[em-
ber] 1835 and I have read it twice. It gave me sensa-
tions that are better imagined than discribed. Let it suffice that I say the verry flood-gates of my heart were
broken up. I could not refrain from weeping. I thank
God that it has entered into your heart to try to return
to the Lord and to his people, if it so be that he will
have mercy upon you.

I have inquired of the Lord concerning your case
[and] these words came to me: Verily thus saith the
Lord unto you. Let him who was my servant Harvey
return unto me and unto the bosom of my Church.
[Let him] forsake all the sins wherewith he has offended
against me and persue from hence forth a virtuous and
upright life and remain under the direction of those
whom I have appointed to be pillars and heads of my
Church.

Behold saith the Lord your God, his sins shall be
blotted out from under heaven and shall be forgotten
from among men and shall not come up in mine ears,
nor be recorded as /a/ memorial against him. But I will
lift {page 41} him up as out of [a] deep mire and he
shall be exalted upon the high places and shall be
counted worthy to stand ammong princes and shall yet
be made a polished shaft in my quiver of bringing
down the strong holds of wickedness among those who
set themselves up on high that they may take council
against me and against [my] annointed ones in the last
days.

Therefore let him prepare himself speedily and
come unto you, even to Kirtland. And inasmuch as he
shall harken unto all your council from henceforth he
shall be restored unto his former state and shall be

63

saved unto the uttermost, even as the Lord your God livith. Amen.

Thus you see my dear Brother the willingness of our Heavenly Father to forgive sins and restore to favour all those who are willing to humble themselves before him and confess their sins and forsake them and return to him with full purpose of heart (acting no hypocrisy) to serve him to the end.

Marvel not that the Lord has condescended to speak from the heavens and give you instructions whereby you may learn your duty. He has heard your prayers and witnessed your humility and holds forth the hand of paternal affection for your return. The angels rejoice over you, while the Saints are willing to receive you again into fellowship.

I hope on the rece[i]pt of this you will ~~not~~ loose ~~any~~ no time in coming to {page 43} Kirtland. For if you get here in season you will have the privilege of attending the School of the Prophets which has already commenced and also receive instruction in doctrine and principle from those whom God has appointed whereby you may be qualified to go forth and declare the true doctrines of the Kingdom according to the mind and will of God. And when you come to Kirtland it will be explained to you why God has condescended to give you a revelation according to your request.

Please give my respects to you[r] family and bee [be] assured I am yours in the bonds of the New and Everlasting Covenant.

Joseph Smith, Jun[ior]

On this evening, viz the 16th, a Council was called at my house to council with Father Alva Beeman on the subject of his mooving to the Missourie. I had previously told him that the Lord had said that he had better go to the Missourie next Spring. However he wished a council called. The Council met. President D[avid] Whitmer arose and said the spirit manifested to him that it was his duty to go. Also others bore the same testimony.

The same night I received the word of the Lord on Mr. Holmes case, he had desired that I would enquire at the hand of the Lord whether it was {page 44} his duty to be baptised here or wait until he returned home. The word of the Lord came to me saying, that Mr. Holmes had better not be baptised here and that he had better not return by water. Also that there were three men that were seeking his destruction to be ware of his ene[m]ys.

Tuesday, 17th Ex[h]ibited ~~some~~ /the Alphabet/ of the ancient records to Mr. Holmes and some others. Went with him to F[rederick] G. Williams to see the Mum[m]ies. We then took the parting hand and he started for home being strong in the faith of the gospel of Christ and determined to obey the requirements of the same.

I returned home and spent the day dictating and comparing letters.

This has been a fine pleasant day, although cool. This Evening at early candlelight I pr[e]ached at the School house, returned home and retired to rest.

Wednesday, 18th At home in the fore noon untill about 11 o'clock. I then went to Preserved Harris's to preach his father's Funeral Sermon by the request of the family. I preached on the subject of the resur[r]ection. The congregation were verry attentive. My wife, my mother, and my scribe went with me to the funeral. We rode in a waggon [and] had a pleasant ride. The weather was pleasant when we went, but cloudy and cool when we returned. {page 45}

At evening Bishop Whitney, his wife, Father and Mother, and Sister in law came in and invited me and my wife to go with them and visit Father Smith and family. My wife was unwell and could not go; however I and my Scribe went. When we got there we found that some of the young Elders were about engaging in a debate upon the subject of miracles. The q[u]estion was this: was or was it not the design of Christ to Establish his gospel by miracles?

After an interesting debate of three hours or more, during which time much talent was displayed, it was desided by the presidents of the debate in the negative, which was a righteous decision.

I discovered in this debate, much warmth displayed, to[o] much zeal for mastery, to[o] much of that enthusiasm that characterizes a lawyer at the bar who is determined to defend his cause right or wrong. I therefore availed myself of this favorable

65

opportunity to drop a few words upon this subject by way of advise that they might improve their minds and cultivate their powers of intellect in a proper manner. That they should handle sacred things verry sacredly and with due deference to the opinions of others and with an eye single to the glory of God. {page 46}

Thursday, 19th Went in company with Doct[or] Williams and my scribe to see how the workmen prospered in finishing the House [Kirtland Temple]. The masons on the inside had commenced put[t]ing on the finishing coat of plastureing.

On my return I met L[l]oyd and Lorenzo Lewis and conversed with them upon the subject of their being disaffected. I found that they were not so as touching the faith of the Church but with some of the members.

I returned home and spent the day in translating the Egyptian records. This has been a warm and pleasant day.

Friday, 20th In morning at home. The weather is warm but rainy. We spent the day in translating and made rapid progress.

At evening, President [Oliver] Cowdery returned from New York bringing with him a quantity of Hebrew books for the benefit of the school. He presented me with a Hebrew Bible, lexicon and grammar, also a Greek Lexicon and Webster's English Lexicon.

President Cowdery had a prosperous journey according to the prayers of the Saints in Kirtland.

Saturday, 21st At home. Spent the day in examining my books and studying ~~my~~ /the/ Hebrew alphabet. At evening met with our Hebrew class to make some arrang[e]ments about a Teacher. It was decided by the voice of the School to send {page 47} to N[ew] York for a Jew to teach us the language, if we could get released from the engagement we had made with Doct[or] Piexotto to teach the language, having as[c]ertained that he was not qualified to give us the knowledge we wish to acquire.

Sunday, 22d Went to meeting at the us[u]al hour. Simeon Ca[r]ter preached from the 7th Chapt[er] of Mat[t]hew. President Rigdon's brother in Law and Some other relatives were at [the] meeting. In the after noon the meeting was held in the School-house. Also in the evening [we] had a meeting and Elder [Andrew Jackson] Squires who had withdrawn from the Church made application to return. After giving him a severe chastisement he was recieved and his licence restored to him.

When the case of Elder Squires was introduced we organized into a regular Council. Sylvester Smith was chosen Clerk.
After conciderable altercation upon the subject and keen rebuke
he was restored by the voice of the Council and Church and the
clerk [was] ordered to give him his licence as above stated. On
this night we had a snow storm.

Monday, 23d Several brethren called to converse with
me and see the [Egyptian] records. Rec[eive]d a letter from Jared
Carter. Spent the day in conversing and in studying the Hebrew
language. This has been a stormy day. {page 48}

Tuesday, 24th At home. Spent the fore noon instructing
those that called to inquire concerning the things of God, in the
last days. In the after noon we translated some of the Egyptian
records.

I had an invitation to attend a wedding at Br[other] Hiram
Smith's in the evening. Also to solemnize the matrimonial ceremony /between Newel Knight and Lydia Goldthwaite/. I and my
wife went. When we arrived a conciderable company had collected. The bridegroom and bride came in and took their seats
which gave me to understand that they were ready. I requested
them to arise and join hands. I then remarked that marriage was
an institution of h[e]aven institude [instituted] in the Garden of
Eden. That it was necessary that it should be Solemnized by the
authority of the everlasting priesthood. Before joining hands however we attended [to] prayers. I then made the remarks above
stated.

The ceremony was original /with me/. It was in substance
as follows: "You covenant to be each others companions through
life and discharge the duties of husband and wife in every respect,"
to which they assented. I then p[r]onounced them husband and
Wife in the name of God and also ~~pronounced~~ the blessings that
the Lord confer[r]ed upon Adam and Eve in the Garden of Eden,
that is to multiply and replenish the earth, with the addition of
long life and prosperity. [I] dismissed them and returned home.
The weather is freezing cold, some snow on the ground. {page
49}

Wednesday, 25th Spent the day in Translating. To day
Harvey Redfield and Jesse Hitchcock ar[r]ived here from Missourie. The latter says that he has no doubt but that a dose of

poison was administered to him in a boll [bowl] of milk, but God
deli/vered him/.

Thursday, 26th At home. We spent the day in transcribing Egyptian characters from the papyrus. I am severely afflicted
with a cold. Today Robert Rathbone and George Morey arrived
from Zion.

Friday, 27th Much afflicted with my cold, yet able to be
about. I am determined to overcom[e] in the name of the Lord
Jesus Christ. Spent the day in reading Hebrew at home.

The weather continues cold and unpleasant. Br[other] Parrish my scribe being afflicted with a cold asked me to lay my
hands on him. In the name of the Lord I did so and in return I
asked him to lay his hands on me. We were both relieved.

/See page 9th/ [*material inserted on page 9 of the manuscript
appears here*]

Saturday, 28th At home. Spent the morning in compareing
our journal. Elder Josiah Clark called this morning to see me. He
lives in Cam[pb]ell County, K[entucky] about three miles above
[below] Cincinate [Cincinnati].

I am conciderably recovered from my cold. I think I shall
be able in a few days to translate again with the blessing of God.
The weather is still cold and stormy. The snow is falling and winter seems to be closing in ~~verry fast~~. All nature shrinks before the
chilling blasts of [a] [f]rigid winter.

Elder Clark above mentioned has been bit[t]en by a mad
dog some three or four {page 51} years since. Has [been] doctered
much and received some benefit by so doing, but is much afflicted. Notwithstanding, he came here that he might be benefited by the prayers of the Church. Accordingly we prayed for
and layed our hands on him in the name of the Lord Jesus Christ
and anointed him with oil and rebuked his affliction, praying our
Heavenly Father to hear and answer our prayers according to our
faith.

Sunday morning, 29th Went to meeting at the us[u]al
hour. Elder Morley preached and Bishop Partridge in the after
noon. Their discourses were well adapted to the times in which
we live and the circumstances under which we are placed. Their
words were words of wisdom, like apples of gold in pictures [pitch-
ers] of silver, spoken in the simple accents of a child, yet sublime
as the voice of an angels. The Saints appeared to be much pleased

with the beautiful discourses of these two fathers in Israel. After these servises closed, three of the Zion brethren came forward and received their blessing.

Solon Foster was ordained to the office of an Elder. The Lord's Supper was then administered and the meeting closed. Returned home and spent the evening. The storm continues. The weather is verry cold. {page 52}

Monday morning, 30th Yet the snow is falling and is sufficiently deep for sleighing. This is an uncommon storm for this country at this season of the year. Spent the day in writing a letter for the Messenger and Advocate on the Subject of the Gathering. This afternoon Henry Capron called to see me. He is an old a[c]quaintance of mine from Manchester, New York. [I] shewed him the Egyptian records.

Tuesday, December 1st 1835 At home. Spent the day in writing for the M[essenger] and Advocate. The snow is falling and we have fine Sleighing.

Wednesday, 2nd A fine morning. I made preparation to ride to Pain[e]svill[e] with my wife and family, also my Scribe. We had our sleigh and horses prepared and set out. When we were passing through Mentor Street we overtook a team with two men on the sleigh. I politely asked them to let me pass. They granted my request and as we passed them they bawled out, "Do you get any revelation lately," with an ad[d]ition of blackguard that I did not understand.

This is a fair sample of the character of Mentor Street inhabitants who are ready to abuse and scandalize men who never laid a straw in their way. In fact those whose faces they never saw and cannot bring an ac[c]usation against either {page 53} of a temporal or spir[i]tual nature, except our firm belief in the fulness of the gospel.

I was led to marvel at the long suffering and condescention of our Heavenly Father in permitting these ungodly wretches to possess this goodly land which is indeed as beautifully situated and its soil as fertile as any in this region of country, its inhabitance [inhabitants] wealthy even blessed above measure in temporal things and fain would God bless them with spiritual blessings, even eternal life, were it not for their evil hearts of unbelief.

We are led to ~~cry in our hearts~~ mingle our prayers with those Saints that have suffered the like treatment before us. Whose souls are under the altar crying to the Lord for veng[e]ance upon those that dwell upon the earth. We rejoice that the time is at hand when the wicked who will not repent will be swept /from the earth/ with the besom of destruction and the earth become an inheritance for the poor and the meek.

When we ar[r]ived at Pain[e]svill[e] we called at Sister Harriet How[e]'s and left my wife and family to visit her while we rode into Town to do some business. Called and visited H[enry] Kingsbury, returned and dined with Sister How[e] and returned home. Had a fine ride. The sleighing is ~~fine~~ /good/ and weather pleasant. {page 54}

Thursday the 3rd At home. Wrote a letter to David Dort, Rochester, Michigan. Another to Almyra Scoby, Liberty, Clay Co[unty], M[issouri]. At home all day.

At evening was invited with my wife to attend at Thomas Caricoe's to join W[arren] Parrish and Martha H. Raymond in mattrimony. We found a verry pleasant and respectable company waiting when we ar[r]ived. We opened our interview with singing and prayer, after which I delivered an address upon the subject of matrimony. I then invited the ~~couple~~ /parties/ to arise who were to be joined in wedlock and solemnized the institution in a brief manner and pronounced them husband and wife in the name of God according to the Articles and Covenants of the /Church of the/ Latter Day Saints. Closed by singing and prayer. Took some refreshment and retired having spent the evening agreeably.

Friday, 4th To day in company with Vinson Knights we drew three hundred and fifty Dollars out of Pain[e]svill[e] Bank on three months credit for which we gave the names of F[rederick] G. Williams and Co[mpany], N[ewel] K. Whitney, John Johnson, and Vinson Knights. I also settled with Br[other] Hiram Smith and V[inson] Knights and paid said [K]nights two hundred and forty five dollars. I also paid or have it in my power to pay J. Lewis for which blessing I feel h[e]artily to thank my Heavenly Father and ask him in the name of Jesus Christ to enable us to extricate {page 55} ourselves from all the embar[r]as[s]ments whatever that we may not be brought into disrepute in any respect that our enemys may not have any power over us.

Spent the day at home [and] devoted some time in studying /the/ Hebrew language. This has been a warm day with some rain; our snow is melting verry fast.

This evening, a Mr. John Holister of Portage County, Ohio called to see me on the subject of religion. He is a member of the Close Communion Baptise [Baptist] Church. He said he had come to enquire concerning the faith of our church having heard many reports of the worst character about us. He seemed to be an honest enquirer after truth. I spent the evening in talking with him. I found him to be an honest, candid man and no particular peculiarities about him only his simplisity. He tarried over night with me and acknowledged in the /morning/ that although he had thought he knew something about religion he was now sensible that he knew but little which was the greatest trait of wisdom that I could discover in him.

Saturday, 5th The weather is cold and freezing and the snow is falling moderately. There is a prospect of sleighing again. Spent the forenoon in studying Hebrew with Doct[or] Williams and President Cowdery. I am labouring under some indisposition of health. Laid down and slept a while and {page 56} arose feeling tolerable well through the blessings of God.

I received a letter to day from Reuben McBride, Vilanova [Chautauque County], N[ew] Y[ork]. Also another from Parley Pratt's mother in law from Herkimer Co[unty], N[ew] Y[ork] of no consequence as to what it contained, but cost me 25 cents for postage.

I mention this as it is a common occur[r]ence and I am subjected to a great deal of expence in this way by those who I know nothing about, only that they are destitute of good manners. For if people wish to be benefited with information from me, common respect and good breeding wou[l]d dictate them to pay the postage on their letters.

Sunday, [December] 6th 1835 Went to meeting at the us[u]al hour. G[ideon] Carter preached a splendid discourse. In the after /noon/ we had an ex[h]ortation and communion. Br[other] Draper insisted on leaving the meeting some 2 or 3 weeks since before communion and would not be prevailed upon to tarry a few moments although we invited him to do so as we did not wish to have the house thrown into confusion. He observed that he would not if we excluded him from the Church. To day he attempted to make a confession, but it was not satisfactory to me. I was constrained by the Spirit to deliver him over to the buf[f]etings

71

of Satan untill he should humble himself and repent of his sins and make satisfactory confession before the Church. {page 57}

Monday, 7th Received a letter from Milton Holmes and was much rejoiced to hear from him and of his prosperity in proclaiming the gospel. Wrote him a letter requesting him to return to this place.

Spent the day in reading the Hebrew. Mr. John Hollister called to take the parting hand with me and remarked that he had been in darkness all his days, but had now found the light and intended to obey it; also a number of brethren called this Evening to see the records. I ex[h]ibited and explained them to their satisfaction. We have fine sleighing.

Tuesday morning the 8th At holm [home]. Spent the day in reading Hebrew in company with President Cowdery, Doct[or] Williams, Br[other] H[yrum] Smith, and O[rson] Pratt.

In the evening I preached as us[u]al at the School House [and] had great liberty in speaking. The congregation were attentive. After the servises closed the brethren proposed to come and draw wood for me.

Wednesday, 9th At home. The wind is strong and chilly from the south and their is a prospect of a storm. Elder [Noah] Packard came in this morning and made me a present of 12 dollars which he held in a note against me. May God bless him for his liberality. Also James Aldrich sent me my note by the hand of Jesse Hitchcock on which {page 58} there was 12 dollars due. May God bless him for his kindness to me.

Also the brethren whose names are written below opened the[ir] hearts in great liberality and payed me at the committee Store the sums set op[p]osite their respective names:

John Corrill	$5.00
Levi Jackman	3.25
Elijah Fordham	5.25
James Emett	5.00
Newel Knight	2.00
Truman Angel	3.00
W[illia]m Felshaw	3.00
Emer Harris	1.00
Truman Jackson	1.00
Samuel Rolph	1.25

Elias Higbee	1.00
Albert Brown	3.00
W[illia]m F. Cahoon	1.00
Harlow Crosier	.50
Salmon Gee	.75
Harvey Stanley	1.00
Zemira Draper	1.00
George Morey	1.00
John Rudd	.50
Alexander Badlam	1.00
	$40.50

—

With the ad[d]ition of the 2 notes above $24.00

My heart swells with gratitude inexpressible w/h/en I realize the great condescention of my Heavenly Fathers in opening
the hearts of these my beloved brethren {page 59} to administer
so liberally to my wants. I ask God in the name of Jesus Christ to
multiply blessings without number upon their heads. Bless me
with much wisdom and understanding and dispose of me to the
best advantage for my brethren and the advancement of thy cause
and Kingdom. Whether my days are many or few, whether in life
or in death, I say in my heart O Lord let me enjoy the society of
such brethren.

To day Elder Tanner brought me the half of a fat[te]ned
hog for the be[ne]fit of my family. And a few days since Elder
S[hadrach] Roundy brought me a quarter of beef. May all the
blessings that are named above be poured upon their heads for
their kindness toward[s] me.

Thursday morning, 10th A beautiful morning indeed and
fine sleighing. This day my brethren meet according to previous
ar[r]angement to chop and haul wood for me. They have been
verry industrious and I think they have supplyed me with my
winters wood for which I am sincerely grateful to each and every
one of them for this expression of their goodness towards me.

In the name of Jesus Christ I envoke the rich benediction
of heav[e]n to rest upon them even all and their families. I ask
my Heavenly Father {page 60} to preserve their health's and those
of their wives and children that they may have strength of body

73

to perform their labours in their several oc[c]upations in life and the use and activity of their limbs. Also powers of intellect and understanding hearts that they may treasure up wisdom, understanding and intel[l]igence above measure and be preserved from plagues, pestilence and famine and from the power of the adversary and the hands of evil designing men and have power over all their enemys. And [may] the way be prepared before them that they may journey to the land of Zion and be established on their inheritances to enjoy undisturbe[d] peace and happiness for ever and ultimately to be crowned with everlasting life in the Celestial Kingdom of God. Which blessings I ask in the name of Jesus of Nazareth. Amen.

I would remember Elder Leonard Rich who was the first one that proposed to the brethren to assist me in obtaining wood for the use of my family, for which I pray my Heavenly Father to bless /him/ with all the blessings named above. I shall ever remember him with much gratitude, for this testimony of benovolence and respect and thank the Great I Am for put[t]ing into his heart to do me this kindness. I say in my heart, I will trust in thy goodness and mercy forever, for thy wisdom and benevolence /O Lord/ is unbounded and beyond the comprehension of men and all of thy ways cannot be found out. {page 61}

This afternoon, I was called in company with President David Whitmer to visit Sister Angeline Works who lives at Elder Booth's. We found her verry sick and so much deranged that She did not recognize her friends and intimate acquaintences. We prayed for and layed hands on her in the name of Jesus Christ and commanded her in his name to receive he[r] senses which was immediately restored to her. We also asked a healing blessing prayed that she might be restored to health. She said she was better.

On our return we found the brethren engaged in putting out the board kiln which had taken fire. After labouring for about one hour against this distructive element they succe[e]ded in conquering it and probably will save about one fourth part of the lumber that was in it. How much loss the committee have [has] sustained by this fire I do not know but it is conciderable. There was much lumber in the kiln. There was about 200 brethren engaged on this occasion and displayed much activity and interest for which they deserve much credit.

This evening I spent at hom[e]. A number of brethren called to see the [Egyptian] records which I ex[h]ibited to them. They were much pleased with their interview. {page 62}

Friday morning the 11th A fire broke out in a shoe-maker's shop owned by Orson Johnson but was soon extinguished by the active exertions of the brethren. The family were much alarmed, the shop being connected with their dwelling house. They carryed their furniture into the street, but not much damage was sustained.

This is a pleasant morning and their is a prospect of a thaw. Spent the day at home in reading and instructing those who called for advise. To day Elder Dayly and his wife left for home.

Saturday morning, 12th At home. Spent the fore noon in reading. At about 12 o'clock a number of young person[s] called to see the Egyptian records. I requested my Scribe [Warren Parrish] to ex[h]ibit them. He did so. One of the young ladies who had been examining them was asked if they had the appearance of Antiquity. She observed with an air of contempt that they did not. On hearing this I was surprised at the ignorance she displayed and I observed to her that she was an anomaly in creation for all the wise and learned that had ever examined them without hesitation pronounced them antient [ancient]. I further remarked that it was downright wickedness, ignorance, bigotry, and superstition that caused her to make the remark and that I would put it on record. I have done so because it is a fair sample of the prevailing spirit of the times {page 63} showing that the victims of priestcraft and superstition would not believe though one should rise from the dead.

At evening attended a debate at Br[other] W[illia]m Smith's. The question proposed to debate upon was as follows: Was it necessary for God to reveal himself to man in order for their happiness. I was on the affirmitive and the last one to speak on that side of the question, but while list[e]ning with interest to the ingenuity displayed on both Sides of the qu[e]stion, I was called away to visit Sister Angeline Work[s], who was sup[p]osed to be dangerously sick. Elder Corrill and myself went and prayed for and layed hands on her in the name of Jesus Christ. She appear[e]d to be better. Returned home.

Sunday morning the 13th At the us[u]al hour for meeting

viz. at 10 o'cl[oc]k attended meeting at the School house on the flats. Elder J[esse] Hitchcock preached a verry feeling discourse indeed. In the afternoon Elder Peter Whitmer related his experience, after which President F[rederick] G. Williams related his also. They both spoke of many things connected with the rise and progress of this Church which were interesting and the Saints listened with much attention.

After these serv[ic]es closed, the sacrament of the Lord's Supper was administered under the superintendance of President D[avid] Whitmer who presided over the meeting during the day. I then made some remarks respecting {page 64} prayer meetings and our meeting was brought to a close by invoking the blessings of heaven.

We then returned home. I ordered my horse saddled and myself and Scribe rode to Mr. E[benezer] Jennings where I joined Eb[e]nezer Robinson and Angeline Works in matrimony according to previous ar[r]angements. Miss /Works/ had so far recovered from her illness that she was able to sit in her easy chair while I pronounced the marriage ceremony.

We then rode to Mr. [Isaac] McWithy's a distance of about 3 miles from Town where I had been Solicited to attend and Solemnize the matrimonial covenant between Mr. E. Webb and Miss E. A. McWithy. The parents and many of the connections of both parties were present with a large and respectable company of friends who were invited as guests.

After making the necessary ar[r]angements the company come to order and the Groom and bride with the attendants politely came forward and took their seats. Having been requested to make some preliminary remarks upon the subject of matrimony, touching the design of the Almighty in this institution, also the duties of husbands and wives towards each other and after opening our interview with singing and prayer, I delivered a lecture of about 40 minuits [minutes] in length.

During this time all seemed to be interested, except one or two individuals who manifested a spirit of grov[e]ling contempt which I was constrained to reprove and rebuke sharply. After I had closed my remarks, I sealed the matrimonial {page 65} ceremony in the name of God and pronounced the blessings of heaven upon the heads of the young married couple. We then closed by returning thanks.

A sumptuous feast was then spread and the company were invited to seat themselves at the table by pairs, male and female, commencing with the oldest. I can only say that the interview was conducted in propriety and decorum and our hearts were made to rejoice while together and cheerfulness prevailed.

After spending the evening agreeably untill 9 o'clock, we pronounced a blessing upon the company and withdrew and returned home.

To day the board kiln took fire again.

Monday, 14th This morning a number of brethren from New York call[ed] to visit me and see the Egyptian records. Elder [Martin] Harris also returned this morning from Palmyra, N[ew] York. Br[other] Frazier Eaton of the same place called to pay us a visit. A verry fine man. Also Sister Harriet How[e] called to pay us a visit.

After dinner we went to attend the funeral of Sylvester Smith's youngest child. In the evening meet [met] according to notice previously given to make ar[r]angements to guard against fire and organized a company for this purpose. Counciled also on other affairs of a temporal nature.

To day Samuel Branum came to my house much afflicted with a swelling on his left arm which was occasioned by a bruise {page 66} on his elbow. We had been called to pray for him and anoint him with oil, but his faith was not sufficient to effect a cure. My wife prepared a poultice of herbs and applyed to it and he tarryed with me over night.

Spent the day at home reading Hebrew and visiting friends who called to see me. To day I received a letter from Elder Orson Hyde from his own hand.

Tuesday, 15th Spent the day at home and as us[u]al was blessed with much company, some of which called to see the records. Samuel Brannum is verry sick in consequence of his arm, it being much inflamed.

This afterno[o]n Elder Orson Hyde handed me a Letter, the purport of which is that he is dissatisfyed with the committee in their dealings with him in temporal affairs — that is that they do not deal as liberally in /with/ him as they do with Elder William Smith. [He] also requested me to reconcile the revelation given to the 12 [Apostles] since their return from the East. That unless these things and others named in the letter could be recon-

77

ciled to his mind his honour would not stand united with them.
This I believe is the amount of the contents of the letter although
much was written.

My feelings on this occasion were much laserated knowing that I had dealt in righteousness with him in all things and
endeavoured to promote his happiness and well being as much as
lay in my power. I feel that these reflection[s] are {page 67} ungrateful and founded in jealousy, that the adversary is striving
with all his subtle devises and influence to destroy him by causing a division amon[g] the Twelve [Apostles] that God has chosen
to open the gospel Kingdom in all nations.

I pray my Heavenly Father in the name of Jesus of
Nazareth that he may be delivered from the power of the destroyer
that his faith fail not in this hour of temptation and prepare him
and all the Elders to receive an endument [endowment] in thy
House [Kirtland Temple]. Even according to thine own order from
time to time as thou seest them worthy to be called into thy Solemn Assembly. [*rest of page blank*] {page 68}

Wednesday morning the 16th The weather is extremely
cold. This morning I went to the council room to lay before the
Presidency the letter that I received yester day from Elder O[rson]
Hyde, but when I ar[r]ived I found that I had lost said letter. I
laid the substance of it as far as I could recollect before the Council, but they had not time to attend to it on the account of other
buisness. Accordingly we adjourned untill Monday Evening the
20th Inst[ant].

Returned home, Elder McLellen, Elder B[righam] Young
and Elder J[ared] Carter called and paid me a visit with which I
was much gratified. I ex[h]ibited and explained the Egyptian
Records to them and explained many things to them concerning
the dealings of God with the ancients and the formation of the
planetary System. They seemed much pleased with the interview.

This evening according to adjournment I went to Br[other]
W[illia]m Smith's to take part in the debate that was commenced
on Saturday evening last. After the debate was concluded and a
desision given in favour of the affirmative of the question some
altercation took place upon the impropr[i]ety of continueing the
School fearing that it would not result in good.

Br[other] W[illia]m opposed these measures and insisted
on having another question proposed and at length become much

enraged particularly at me. [He] used {page 69} violence upon my person and also upo[n] Elder J[ared] Carter and some others for which I am grieved beyond expression and can only pray God to forgive him inasmuch as he repents of his wickedness and humbles himself before the Lord.

Thursday morning, 17th At home. [I am] quite unwell. This morning Elder Orson Hyde called to see me and presented me with a copy of the letter that he handed me on Tuesday last which I had lost. The following is a copy:

Dec[ember] 15th 1835

President Smith,

Sir, you may esteem it a novel circumstance to receive a written communication from me at this time. My reasons for writing are the following. I have some things which I wish to communicate to you and feeling a greater liberty to do it by writing alone by myself, I take this method. It is generally the case that you are thronged with buisness and not convenient to spend much time in conversing upon subjects of the following nature. Therefore let these excuses pal[l]iate the novelty of the circumstance and patiently hear my recital.

After the committee had received their stock of fall and winter goods, I went to Elder [Reynolds] Cahoon and told him that I was destitute of a cloak and wanted him to trust me until Spring for materials to make one. He told me that {page 70} he would trust me until January, but must then have his pay as the payments for the goods become due at that time. I told him that I know not from whence the money would come and I could not promise it so soon, but in a few weeks after I unexpectedly obtained the money to buy a cloak and applyed immediately to Elder C[ahoon] for one. [I] told him that I had the cash to pay for it, but he said that the materials for cloaks were all sold and that he could not accommodate me. I will here venture a guess that he has not realized the cash for one cloak pattern.

A few weeks after this I called on Elder Cahoon again and told him that I wanted cloth for some shirts to the amount of 4 or 5 Dollars. I told him that I would

79

pay him in the spring and sooner if I could. He let me
have it. Not long after my school was established and
some of the hands who laboured on the House [Kirtland
Temple] attended and wished to pay me at the Committee Store for their tuition. I called at the Store to see if
any nego/ti/ation could be made and they take me off
where I owe them, but no such negotiation could be
made. These with some other circumstances of like
character called forth the following reflections.

In the first place I gave the committee $275 in cash
besides some more. During the last season have traveled
thro[ugh] the Middle and Eastern states to sup[p]ort
and uphold the Store and in so doing have reduced myself to nothing in a pecuniary point. Under {page 71}
these circumstances this establishment refused to render
me that accom[m]odation which a worldlings [worldly]
establishment would have gladly done and one too
which never /received/ a donation from me, nor in
whose favour I never raised my voice or exerted my influence.

But after all this, thought I, it may be right and I
will be still. Un[t]il not long since I as[c]ertained that
Elder W[illia]m Smith could go to the store and get
whatever he pleased and no one to say why do ye so,
until his account has amounted to seven Hundred Dollars or there abouts and that he was a silent partner in
the concern, yet not acknowledged /as/ such, fearing
that his creditors would make a hawl upon the Store.

While we were abroad this last season we strained
every nerve to obtain a little Something for our familys
and regularly divided the monies equally for ought that
I know, not knowing that William had such a fountain
at home from whence he drew his support. I then called
to mind the revelation in which myself, [William E.]
McLellen and [David W.] Patten were chastened and
also the quotation in that revelation of the parable of
the twelve sons. As if the original meaning refer[e]d
directly to the Twelve Apostles of the Church of the
Latter Day Saints.

I would now ask if each one of the Twelve [Apos-

tles] has not an equal right to the same accom[m]oda-
tions from that Store provided they are alike faithful. If
not, with such a combination {page 72} mine honor be
not thou united.

If each one has the same right, take the baskets off
from our noses or put one to William's nose or if this
cannot be done, reconcile the parable of the twelve sons
with the superior privileges that William has.

Pardon me if I speak in parables or parody. A certain shepherd had twelve sons and he sent them out one
day to go and gather his flock which were scattered
upon the mountains and in the vallies afar off. They
were all obedient to their father's mandate. At Evening
they returned with the flock and one son received wool
enough to make him warm and comfortable and also
rec[eive]d of the flesh and milk of the flock. The other
eleven received not so much as one kid to make merry
with their friends.

These facts with some others have disqualified my
mind for studying the Hebrew Language at present.
Believing, as I do, that I must sink or swim, or in other
words take care of myself, I have thought that I should
take the most efficient means in my power to get out of
debt. To this end I proposed taking the school, but if I
am not thought competent to take the charge of it, or
worthy to be placed in that station, I must devise some
other means to help myself. Altho[ugh] having been
ordained to that office under your own hand with a
p[r]omise that it should not be taken from me. {page
73}

Conclusion of the whole matter is sutch [such]: I
am willing to continue and do all I can, provided we
can share equal benefits, one with the other and upon
no other principle whatever. If one has sup[p]ort from
the "publick crib," let them all have it; but if one is
pinched, I am willing to be, provided we are all alike.
If the principle of impartiality and equality can be observed by all, I think that I will not peep again. /If I
am damned, it will be for doing what I think is right./

There have been two applications made to me to go

into business since I talked of taking the school, but it is in the world and I had rather remain in Kirtland if I can consistently.

All I ask is Right. I Am Sir with Respect Your Ob[edien]t serv[an]t,

Orson Hyde

To President J[oseph] Smith, J[unior] Kirtland, Geauga Co[unty], Ohio {page 74}

Elder O[rson] Hyde called and read the foregoing letter himself. I explained upon the objections he had set forth in it and satisfyed his mind upon every point perfectly. He observed, after I had got through, that he was more than satisfyed and would attend the Hebrew school. [He] took the parting hand with me with every expression of friendship that a gentleman and a Christian could manifest, which I felt to reciprocate with cheerfulness.

[I] entertain the best of feeling[s] for him and most cheerfully forgive him the ingratitude which was manifested in his letter, knowing that it was for want of cor[r]ect information that his mind was disturbed as far as his reflections related to me. But on the part of the committee, he was not treated right in all thing[s]. However all things are settled amicably and no hardness exists between us or them.

My Father and Mother called this evening to see me upon the subject of the difficulty that transpired at their house on Wednesd[a]y evening between me and my Br[other] William. They were sorely afflicted in mind on the account of that occur[r]ance. I conversed with them and convinced them that I was not to blame in taking the course that I did, but had acted in righteousness in all thing[s] on that occasion. I invited them to come and live with me. They concented to do so as soon as it is practicable. {page 75}

Friday morning, 18th inst[ant] At home. Br[other] Hyrum Smith called to see me and read a letter to me that he received from William, in which he asked Hyrum for /his/ forgiveness for the abuse he offered to him at the debate. He tarried most of the fore noon and conversed freely with me upon the subject of the difficulty existing between me and Br[other] William. He said that he was perfectly satisfied with the course I had taken with

82

him in rebuking him in his wickedness, but he is wounded to the verry soul ~~with~~ /because of/ the conduct of William. Although he feels the tender feelings of a brother toward him yet he can but look upon his conduct as an abomination in the sight of God.

And I could pray in my heart that all my brethren were like unto my beloved brother Hyrum, who posses[s]es the mildness of a lamb and the integrity of a Job and in short the meekness and humility of Christ. I love him with that love that is stronger than death, for I never had occasion to rebuke him, nor he me which he declared when he left me to day.{page 76}

Copy of a letter from Br[other] William Smith

18th Inst[ant] [December 1835]

Br[other] Joseph,

Though I do not know but I have forfeited all right and title to the word brother, in consequence of what I have done. For I concider myself, that I am unworthy to be called one. After coming to myself and concidering upon what I have done I feel as though it was a duty to make a humble confession to you for what I have done or what took place the other evening, but leave this part of the subject at present.

I was called to an account by the 12 [Apostles] yesterday for my conduct or they desire to know my mind or determination and what I was going to do. I told them that on reflection upon the many difficulties that I had had with the Church and the much disgrace I had brought upon myself in consequence of these things. Also that my health would not permit me to go to school to /make/ any preperations for the endument [endowment]. That my health was such that I was not able to travel, ~~I told them~~ that it would be better for them to appoint one in the office that would be better able to fill it. By doing this they would throw me into the hands of the Church and leave me where I was before I was chosen.

83

Then I would not be in a situation {page 77} to bring so much disgrace upon the cause when I fell into temptation. Perhaps by this I might obtain Salvation. You know my passions and the danger of falling from so high a station, and thus by withdrawing from the office of the apostleship while their [there] is salvation for me and remaining a member in the Church. I feel afraid if I do'nt do this it will be worse for me, some other day.

And again my health is poor and I am not able to travel and it is necessary that the office should not be idle. And again I say you know my passions and I am afraid it will be worse for me, by and by.

Do so if the Lord will have mercy on me and let me remain as a member in the Church, and then I can travel and preach, when I am able. Do not think that I am your enemy for what I have done. Perhaps you may say or ask why I have not remembered the good that you have done to me. When I reflect upon the ingury [injury] I have done you I must confess that I do not know what I have been ~~sorry~~ about. I feel sorry for what I have done and humbly ask your forgiveness. I have not confidence as yet to come and see you for I feel ashamed of what I have done. As I feel now I feel as though {page 78} all the confessions that I could make verbally or by writing would not be sufficient to atone for the transgression. Be this as it may I am willing to make all the restitution you shall require. If I can stay in the Church as a member I will try to make all the satisfaction possible.

> Yours with respect,
> William Smith

[P.S.] Do not cast me off for what I have done, but strive to save me in the Church as a member. I do repent of what I have done to you and ask your forgiveness. I concider the transgression the other evening of small magnitude, but it is done and I cannot help it now. I know Brother Joseph you are always willing to forgive, but I sometimes think when I reflect upon the

many inguries [injuries] I have done you I feel as
though a confession was not hardly sufficient, but have
mercy on me this once and I will try to do so no more.

The 12 [Apostles] called a Council yester day and
sent over after me and I went over. This Council re-
m[em]ber was called together by themselves and not by
me.

W[illia]m S[mith] {page 79}

—

Answer to the foregoing Letter from Br[other] William Smith
A Copy

Kirtland, Friday, Dec[ember] 18th 1835

Br[other] William,

Having received your letter I now proce[e]de to answer it. [I] shall first proce[e]de to give a brief nar[r]a-
tion of my feelings and motives since the night I first
came to the knowledge of your having a debating
School, which was at the time I happened in with
Bishop Whitney, his Father, and Mother &c. which was
the first that I knew any thing about it. From that time
I took an interest in them and was delighted with it and
formed a determination to attend the School for the purpose of obtaining information with the idea of impart-
ing the same through the assistance of the spirit of the
Lord, if by any means I should have faith to do so.
With this intent I went to the school on /last/ Wednesday night. Not with the idea of braking up the school,
neither did it enter into my heart that there was any
wrangling or jealousy's in your heart against me.

Notwithstanding previous to my leaving home there
were feelings of solemnity rolling across my breast
which were unaccountable to me. Also these feelings
continued by spells to depress my ~~feelings~~ /spirit/ and
seemed to manifest that all was not right even after the

85

~~debate~~ school commenced and during the debate, yet I strove to believe that all would work together for good.

I was pleased with the power of the arguments that were ad[d]uced and did {page 80} not feel to cast any reflections upon any one that had spoken. But I felt that it was ~~my~~ /the/ duty of old men that set as presidents to be as grave at least as young men. That it was our duty to smile at solid arguments and sound reasoning and be impressed with solemnity which should be manifest in our countanance when folly and that which militates against truth and righteousness rears its head.

Therefore in the spirit of my calling and in view of the authority of the priesthood that has been confer[r]ed upon me, it would be my duty to reprove whatever I esteemed to be wrong. Fondly hoping in my heart that all parties would concider it right and therefore humble themselves that Satan might not take the advantage of us and hinder the progress of our School.

Now Br[other] William, I want you should bear with me notwithstanding my plainness. I would say to you that my feelings were grieved at the inter[r]uption you made upon Elder McLellen. I thought you should have concidered your relation with him in your apostle ship and not manifest any division of sentiment between you and him for a surrounding multitude to take the advantage of you. Therefore by way of entreaty on the account of the anxiety I had for your influence and wellfare, I said unto you, do not have any feeling, or something to that amount. Why I am thus particular is that if you have misconstrued my feelings toward you, you may be corrected. {page 81}

But to proce[e]de. After the school was closed, Br[other] Hyrum requested the privilege of speaking, you objected. However, you said if he would not abuse the school he might speak, that you would not allow any man to abuse the school in your house. Now you had no reason to suspect that Hyrum would abuse the school. Therefore my feelings were mortifyed at those unnecessary observations. I undertook to reason with you, but you manifested an inconciderate and

stub[b]ourn spirit. I then dispared [despaired] of bene-
fiting you on the account of the spirit you manifested
which drew from me the expression that you was as
ugly as the Devil.

Father then commanded silence. I formed a determination to obey his mandate and was about to leave
the house with the impression that you was under the
influence of a wicked spirit [when] you replyed that you
would say what you pleased in your own house. Father
replyed, "Say what you please, but let the rest hold their
toungs [tongues]."

Then a reflection rushed through my mind of the
anxiety and care I had had for you and your family in
doing what I did in finishing your house and provid-
in[g] flour for your family &c. Also father had possession in the house as well as your self. When at any time
have I transgressed the commandments of my father?
Or sold my birthright that I should not have the privilege of speaking in my father's house, or in other words,
in my father's family, or in your house {page 82} (for so
we will call it and so it shall be) that I should not have
the privilege of reproving a younger brother.

Therefore I said "I will speak, for I built the house,
and it is as much mine as yours," or something to that
effect (I should have said that I helped finish the
house). I said it merely to show that it could not be the
right spirit that would rise up for trifling matters, and
undertake to put me to silence. I saw that your indignation was kindled against me, and you made [movement]
towards me. I was not then to be moved and I thought
to pull off my loose coat least it should tangle me, and
you be left to hurt me, but not with the intention of
hurting You. But you was to[o] soon for me, and having
once fallen into the hands of a mob, and now been
wounded in my side and now into the hands of a
brother my side gave way.

After having been rescued from your grasp, I left
your house with feelings that were indescriba[b]le. The
scenery had changed and all those expectations that I
had cherished when going to your house of brotherly

87

kindness, charity, forbearance and natural affection,
that in duty binds us not to make each others offenders
for a word.

But alass! Abuse, anger, malice, hatred, and rage
/with a lame side/ with marks of violence /heaped/ upon
~~my body~~ me by a brother, were the reflections of my
disap[p]ointment, and with these I returned home not
able to sit down, or rise up, without help, but through
the blessings of God I am now better. {page 83}

I have received your letter and purused it with care.
I have not entertained a feeling of malice against you. I
am older than you and have endured more suffering. [I]
have been mar[r]ed by mobs, the labours of my calling,
a series of persecution, and injuries, continually heaped
upon me, all serve to debilitate my body, and it may
/be/ that I cannot boast of being stronger than you. If I
could, or could not, would this be an honor or dishonor
to me. If I could boast like David of slaying Goliath,
who defied the armies of the living God, or like Paul of
contending with Peter face to face, with sound arguments, it might be an honor. But to mangle the flesh or
seek revenge upon one who never done you any wrong,
can not be a source of sweet reflection to you, nor to
me, neither to an honorable father and mother, brothers
and sisters.

When we reflect with what care and with what un-
remit[t]ing diligence our parents have strove to watch
over us, and how many hours of sorrow and anxiety
they have spent over our cradles and bedsides in times
of sickness, how careful we ought to be of their feelings
in their old age. It cannot be a source of swe[e]t reflection to us to say or do any thing that will bring their
grey hairs down with sorrow to the grave.

In your letter you asked my forgiv[e]ness, which I
readily grant, but it seems to me that you still retain an
idea that I have given you reasons to be angry or disaffected with me. Grant me the privilege of saying then
{page 84} that however hasty or harsh I may have spoken at any time to you, it has been done for the express
purpose of endeavouring to warn, exhort, admonish,

and rescue you from falling into difficulties, and sorrows which I foresaw you plunging into by giving way to that wicked spirit, which you call your passions, which you should curbe and break down and put under your feet. Which if you do not you never can be saved, in my view, in the Kingdom of God. God requires the will of his creatures to be swallowed up in his will.

You desire to remain in the Church, but forsake your apostleship. This is a stratigem of the evil one. When he has gained one advantage he lays a plan for another, but by maintaining your apostleship in rising up and making one tremendious effort, you may overcome your passions and please God. By forsaking your apostleship is not to be willing to make that sacrifice that God requires at your hands and is to incur his displeasure. And without pleasing God do not think that it will be any better for you. When a man falls one step he must regain that step again, or fall another. He has still more to gain or eventually all is lost.

I desire Brother William that you will humble yourself. I freely forgive you and you know my unshaken and unchang[e]able disposition. I know in whom I trust. I stand upon {page 85} the rock. The floods cannot, no they shall not overthrow me. You know the doctrine I teach is true and you know that God has blessed me. I brought salvation to my father's house, as an instrument in the hand of God, when they were in a miserable situation. You know that it is my duty to admonish you when you do wrong. This liberty I shall always take and you shall have the same privilege. I take the privilege to admonish you because of my birthright. I grant you the privilege because it is my duty to be humble and to receive rebuke and instruction from a brother or a friend.

As it regards what course you shall persue hereafter, I do not pretend to say. I leave you in the hands of God and his Church. Make your own desision, I will do you good altho[ugh] you mar me, or slay me, by so doing my garments shall be clear of your sins. If at any time you should concider me to be an imposter, for heaven's sake leave me in the hands of God and not think to take veng[e]ance on me your self.

Tyran[n]y, usurpation, and to take men's rights ever has and ever shall be banished from my heart. David sought not to kill Saul, although he was guilty of crimes that never entered my heart.

And now may God have mercy upon my father's house. May God take {page 86} away enmity from be-twe[e]n me and thee. And may all blessings be restored and the past be forgotten forever. May humble repentance bring us both to thee /O God/ and to thy power and protection and a crown to enjoy the society of Father, Mother, Alvin, Hyrum, Sophron[i]a, Samuel, Catharine, Carloss, Lucy, the Saints and all the sanctified in peace forever, is the prayer of

This from Your brother,
Joseph Smith, Jun[ior]

To William Smith

—

Saturday morning the 19th At home. Wrote the /above/ letter to Br[other] William Smith. **I have had many sollam /solemn/ feelings this day Concerning my Brothe[r] William and have prayed in my heart to fervently that the Lord will not him /cast him/ off, but he may return to the God of Jacob and magnify his apostleship and calling. May this be his happy lot for the Lord of Glory's Sake. Amen.**

Sunday the 20th At home all day. Took solled [solid] Comfort with my Family [and] had many serious reflections. Also Brothers Palmer and Tailor Came to see me. I showed them the sacred record to their Joy and sati[s]faction. O may God have mercy upon these men and keep them in the way of Everlasting life in the name of Jesus. Amen. {page 87}

Monday morni[n]g, 21st At home. Spent this [day] in indeavering to treasure up know[l]edge for the be[n]ifit of my Calling. The /day/ pas[s]ed of[f] very pleasantly for which I thank the Lord for his blessings to my soul [and] his great

mercy over my Family in sparing our lives. O Continue thy Care over me and mine for Christ['s] sake.

Tu[e]sday, 22d At home ~~this~~. Continued my studys. O may God give me learning even Language and indo[w] me with qualifycations to magnify his name while I live. I also deliv[er]ed an address to the Church this Evening. The Lord blessed my Soul.

My scribe also is unwell. O m[a]y God heal him and for his kindness to me O my soul be thou greatful to him and bless him and he shall be blessed of God forever. I believe him to be a faithful friend to me therefore my soul delighteth in him. Amen.

Joseph Smith, Jr.

[10]Wednesday, 23d In the forenoon at home stud[y]ing the Greek Language. Also waited upon the brethren who came in and exhibiting to them the papirus. In the afternoon visited Brother Leonard Rich with the relatives of Bro[ther] Oliver Cowdery. Had not a very agreeable visit for I found them {page 88} filled with prejudice against the work of the Lord and their minds blinded with superstition and ignorance &c.

Thirsday, 24th At home in the forenoon. In the afternoon assisted in running /out/ a road across my farm by the commissionor who were appoint[e]d by the court for the same.

Fryday, 25th At home all this day. Enjoyed myself with my family, it being Chris/t/mas day, the only time I have had this privilege so satisfactorily for a long time.

Saturday, 26[th] Commenced studeing the Hebrew Language in company with Bro[ther]s Parrish and Williams. In the mean time Bro[ther] Lyman Sherman came in and requested to have the word of the Lord through me. For said he, "I have been wrought upon to make known to you my feelings and desires and was promised ~~to have~~ that I should have a revelation which should make known my duty."

Last evening a Brother from the east called upon me for instruction whose name is Jonathan Crosby. Also in the course of the day two gentlemen called upon me while I was cutting wood

---

[10] In the handwriting of Frederick G. Williams.

at the door and requested an interview with the head of the Church which I agreed to grant them on Sunday morning the 27th inst[ant]. {page 89}

The following is a revelation given to Lyman Sherman this day Dec[ember] 26th 1835:

"Verily thus saith the Lord unto you, my servant Lyman. Your sins are forgiven you because you have obeyed my voice in coming up hither this morning to receive councel of him whom I have appointed. Therefore, let your soul be at rest concerning your spiritual standing, and resist no more my voice. And arise up and be more careful henceforth in observing your vows which you have made and do make, and you shall be blessed with exce[e]ding great blessings. Wait patiently untill the time when the Solemn Assembly shall be called of my servants, then you shall be numbered with the first of mine elders and receive right by ordination with the rest of mine elders whom I have chosen. Behold, this is the promise of the Father unto you if you continue faithful. And it shall be fulfilled upon you in that day that you shall have right to preach my gospel wheresoever I shall send you, from henceforth from that time. Therefore strengthen your brethren in all your conversation, in all your prayers, and in all your exhortations, and in all your doings. And behold, and lo, I am with you to bless you and deliver you forever. Amen."

\\[11] Sunday morning, 27th At the us[u]al hour attended meeting at the School house. President Cowdery delivered a verry able and interesting discourse. In the after part of the day Br[other] {page 90} Hyrum Smith and Bishop Partri[d]ge delivered each a short and /interesting/ lecture, after which the Sacrament of the Lord's supper /was administered/ and dismissed our meeting.

Those Gentlemen that proposed to have an interview with me on this morning did not come and I conclude they were trifling characters.

Monday morning the 28th Having prefer[r]ed a charge against Elder Almon Babbit for traducing my character, he was this morning called before the High Council. I attended, with my witnesses, and substantiated my charge against him. He in part acknowledged his fault, but not satisfactory to the Council. After

---

[11] In the handwriting of Warren Parrish.

parleying with him a long time and granting him every indulgence that righ[t]eousness require, the Council adjourned without obtaining a full confession from him.

On this day the Council of the Seventy meet to render an account of their travels and ministry since they were ordained to that apostleship. The meeting was interesting indeed, and my heart was made glad while list[e]ning to the relations of those that had been labouring in the vin[e]yard of the Lord with such marvelous success. I pray God to bless them with an increas[e] of faith and power and keep them {page 91} all with the indurance of faith in the name of Jesus Christ to the end.

Tuesday morning the 29th At home untill about 10 o'clock. I then went to attend a blessing meeting at Oliver Olney's, in company with my wife and Father and Mother who had come to live with me. Also my scribe went with us.

A large company assembled and Father Smith arose and made some preliminary remarks, which were verry applicable on occasions of this kind, after which a hymn was sung. He opened the meeting by prayer. About 15 persons then received a patriarchal blessing under his hands. The servises were then dismissed as they commenced, viz. by singing and prayer.

A table was then spread and crowned with the bounties of nature, and after invoking the benediction of heaven upon the rich repast, we fared sumptuously. Suffice it to say that we had a glorious meeting through out and I was much pleased with the harmony and decorum that existed among the brethren and sisters.

We returned home and at early candlelight I went and pr[e]ach[e]d at the school house to a crowded congregation, who listened {page 92} with attention, while I delivered a lecture of about 3 hours in length. I had liberty in speaking. Some Presbyterians were present, as I after learned, and I expect that some of my sayings set like a garment that was well fit[t]ed, as I exposed their abominations in the language of the scriptures. I pray God that it may be like a nail in a sure place, driven by the master of assemblies. /Col[onel] Chamberlain's Son called to day/

Wednesday, 30[th] Spent the day in reading Hebrew at the council room in company with my scribe which gave me much sattisfaction on the account of his returning health, for I delight in his company.

93

Friday morning, Jany 1st 1836

Thursday morning, 31st At home. After attending to the duties of my family, [I] retired to the Council room to persue my studies. The Council of the 12 [Apostles] convened in the /upper/ room in the printing office directly over the room wher[e] we were convened in our studies. They sent for me and the Presidency (or part of them) to receive council from us on the subject of the council which is to be held on Saturday next.

In the after noon I attended at the Chapel [Kirtland Temple] to give directions concerning {page 93} the upper rooms and more especially the west room which I intend oc[c]upying for a translating room which will be prepared this week.

Friday morning, Jan[uar]y 1st 1836 This being the beginning of a new year, my heart is filled with gratitude to God that he has preserved my life and the lives of my family while another year has rolled away. We have been sustained and upheld in the midst of a wicked and preverse [perverse] generation, and exposed to all the afflictions, temptations and misery that are incident to human life. For which I feel to humble myself in dust and ashes as it were before the Lord. But notwithstanding the gratitude that fills my heart on retrospecting the past year and the multiplyed blessings that have crowned our heads, my heart is pained within me because of the difficulty that exists in my father's family.

The Devil has made a violent attack on [my] Br[other] William and Br[other-in-law] Calvin [Stoddard]. The powers of darkness seem lower[ed] over their minds. Not only theirs, but cast a gloomy shade over the minds of my parents and some of my brothers and sisters, which prevents them from seeing things as they real[l]y are and the powers of Earth and hell seem combined to overthrow us and the Church by {page 94} causing a division in the family. Indeed the adversary is bring[ing] into requisition all his subtlety to prevent the Saints from being endowed by causing division among the 12 [Apostles] also among the 70 and bickerings and jealousies among the Elders and official members of the Church. So the leaven of iniquity foments and spreads among the members of the Church.

But I am determined that nothing on my part shall be lacking to adjust and amicably dispose of and settle all family difficulties on this day, that the ensueing year and years, be they many or few, may be spent in righteousness before God. I know that the cloud will burst and Satan's kingdom be laid in ruins with all his black designs. The Saints [will] come forth like gold seven times tried in the fire being made perfect throug[h] sufferings and temptations and the blessings of heaven and earth multiplyed upon our heads, which may God grant for Christ['s] sake. Amen.

Br[other] William came to my house and Br[other] Hyrum, also Uncle John Smith. We went into a room in company with Father and Elder Martin Harris. Father Smith then opened our interview by prayer. After which he expressed his feelings on the oc[c]asion in a verry feeling and pathetic manner. Even with all the sympathy of a father whose feeling[s] were wounded deeply on the {page 95} account of the difficulty that was existing in the family. While he addressed us the spirit of God rested down upon us in mighty power and our hearts were melted.

Br[other] William made an humble confession and asked ~~our~~ my forgiveness for the abuse he had offered me. And wherein I had been out of the way I asked his forgiveness. The spirit of confession and forgiveness was mutual among us all and we covenanted with each other in the Sight of God and holy angels and the brethren to strive from hence fo[r]ward to build each other up in righteousness in all things and not listen to evil reports concerning each other, but like brethren, indeed, go to each other with our grievances in the spirit of meekness and be reconciled and thereby promote our own happiness and the happiness of the family and in short the happiness and well being of all.

My wife, mother, and my scribe was then called in and we repeated the covenant to them that we had entered into. And while gratitude swelled our bosoms [and] tears flowed from our ey[e]s, I was then requested to close our interview which I did with prayer. It was truly a jubilee and time of rejoiceing. {page 96}

Saturday morning, 2nd Ac[c]ording to previous ar[r]angement, I went to Council at 9 o'clock. This Council was called to set in judgment on a complaint preferred against Br[other] William [Smith] by Elder Orson Johnson. The Council organized and opened by prayer and proce[e]ded to business, but before entering on the trial Br[other] William arose and humbly confessed the charges prefer[r]ed against him and asked the forgiv[e]-

ness of the Council and the whole congregation. A vote was then called to know whether his confession was satisfactory and whether the brethren would extend the hand of fellowship to him again. With cheerfulness, the whole congregation raised their hands to receive him.

Elder Almon Babbit also confessed the charges which I prefer[r]ed against him in a previous Council and was received into fellowship. Some other buisness was transacted in union and fellowship. The best of feelings seemed to prevail among the brethren and our hearts were made glad on the occasion. There was joy in heaven. My soul doth magnify the Lord for his goodness and mercy [which] endureth forever. Council adjourned with prayer as us[u]al.

Sunday morning, 3d Went to meeting at the us[u]al hour. President Rigdon delivered a fine lecture upon the subject of revelation. In the afternoon I confirmed about 10 or 12 persons who {page 97} had been baptised, among whom was M[alcham] C. Davis who was baptized at the intermission to day.

Br[other] William Smith made his confession to the Church to their satisfaction and was cordially received into fellowship again. The Lord's Supper was administered. Br[other] William gave out an appointment to preach in the evening at early candlelight and preach[e]d a fine discourse.

This day has been a day of rejoicing to me. The cloud that has been hanging over us has burst with blessings on our heads. Satan has been foiled in his attempts to destroy me and the Church by causing jealousies to arise in the hearts of some of the brethren. I thank my Heavenly Father for the union and harmony which now prevails in the Church.

Monday morning, 4th Meet [met] and organized our Hebrew School according to the ar[r]angements that were made on Saturday last. We had engaged Doct[or] Piexotto to teach us in the Hebrew language when we had our room prepared. We informed him that we were ready and our room prepared. He agreed to wait on us this day and deliver his introductory lecture. Yesterday he sent us word that he {page 98} could not come untill Wednesday next.

A vote was called to know whether we would submit to such treatment or not and carried in the negative. Elder Sylvester Smith [was] appointed as clerk to write him on the subject and

inform him that his servises were not wanted. Elders W[illia]m
E. McLellen and Orson ~~Johnson~~ /Hyde/ despa[t]ched to Hudson
Semenary to hire a teacher. They were appointed by the voice of
the School to act in their behalf. However, we concluded to go on
with our school and do the best we can untill we can obtain a
teacher. By the voice of the School I concented to render them all
the assistance I am able to for the time being. We are oc[c]upying
the translating room for the use of the School untill another room
can be prepared.

This is the first day that we have oc[c]upied ~~this room~~ /it/
which is the west room in the upper part of the Chappel [Kirtland
Temple], which was concecrated this morning by prayer offered
up by Father Smith.

This is a rainy time and the roads are extremely mud[d]y.
Meet [met] this evening at the Chapel [Kirtland Temple] to make
ar[r]angements for a Singing School. After some altercation, a
judicious ar[r]angement was made. A com[m]ittee of 6 was chosen to take charge of the singing department. {page 99}

Tuesday, 5th Attended the Hebrew School [and] divided
them into classes. Had some debate with Elder Orson Pratt. He
manifested a stub[b]ourn spirit, which I was much grieved at.

Wednesday, 6th Attended School again and Spent most
of the fore noon in set[t]ling the unple[a]sant feelings that existed
in the breast of Elder O[rson] Pratt. After much controversy, he
confessed his fault and asked the forgiv[e]ness of the whol[e] school
and was cheerfully forgiven by all.

Elder McLellen returned from Hudson [Seminary] and
reported to the school that he had hired a Teacher [Joshua Seixas]
to teach us [for] the term of 7 weeks for $320.00. That is 40
Schollars for that amount, to commence in about 15 days hence.
He is highly celebrated as a Hebrew Schollar and proposes to
give us sufficient knowledge in the above term of time to read
and translate the language. {page 100}

Conference Minuits [Minutes]

At a conference held at the School house on Saturday the
2d [of] Jan[uary] 1836 the following individuals were appointed
by the voice of the conference to be ordained to the office of Elders in the Church of the Latter Day Saints under the hands of
President Joseph Smith, Jr., [and] Sidney Rigdon, Clerk.

Vincent [Vinson] Knight
Thomas Grover
Elisha [Elijah] Fordham   Eld[e]rs
Hyram Dayton
Samuel James
John Herrott

Thursday, 7th Attended a sumptuous feast at Bishop N[ewel] K. Whitney's. This feast was after the order of the Son of God. The lame, the halt and blind wer[e] invited according to the in[s]truction of the Saviour.

Our meeting was opened by singing and prayer offered up by Father Smith. After which Bishop Whitney's father and mother were bless[ed] and a number of others with a patriarchal blessing. We then received a bountiful refreshment furnished by the liberality of the Bishop. The company was large. Before we parted we had some of the Songs of Zion sung, and our hearts were made glad while partaking of an antipast [antepast] of those {page 101} Joys that will be poured upon the head of the Saints w[h]en they are gathered together on Mount Zion to enjoy each other's society forever more. Even all the blessings of heaven and earth, where there will be none to molest nor make us afraid. Returned home and spent the evening.

Friday, 8th Spent the day in the Hebrew School and made rapid progress in our studies.

[*Written sideways on page*] /Finished P[lastering] outside Temple. See P[age] 30./

Saturday, 9th Attended School in the fore noon. At about 11 o'clock received the following note:

> Thus saith the voice of the Spirit to me, if thy Brother
> Joseph Smith, J[unio]r will attend the feast at thy house
> this day (at 12 o'cl[ock]) the poor and lame will rejoice
> at his presence and also think themselves honored.
>
>   Yours in friendship and Love,
>   N[ewel] K. W[hitney]

9th Jan[uar]y 1836

I dismissed the School in order to attend to this polite invitation with my wife, father and mother. We attended the feast.

A large congregation assembled. A number was blessed under the hands of Father Smith and we had a good {page 102} time. Returned home and spent the evening.

Sunday, 10th Went to the meeting at the us[u]al hour. Elder Wilber Denton and Elder J[enkins] Salisbury preached in the fore noon. In the after noon Br[other] Samuel [Smith] and Br[other] Carloss Smith [preached]. They all did well concidering their youth and bid fair to make useful men in the vin[e]yard of the Lord. Administered the Sacrament and dismissed.

At the intermission to day 3 were baptised by Elder Martin Harris. Returned home and spent the evening.

Monday morning, 11th At home. There being no school I spent the day at home. Many brethren called to see me, among whom was Alva Beamon from New York, Jenesee [Genesee] Co[unty]. He has come to attend the Solemn Assembly. I delight in the society of my friends and brethren and pray that the blessings of heaven and earth may be multiplyed upon their heads.

Tuesday morning, 12th At home. This /day/ I called on the Presidency of the Church and made ar[r]angements to meet tomorrow at 10 o'clock A.M. {page 103} to take into concideration the subject of the Solemn Assembly.

This after noon a young man called to see the Egyptian manuscripts and I ex[h]ibited them to him. He expressed great satisfaction and appeared verry anxious to obtain a knowledge of the translation.

Also a man was introduced to me by the name of Russel[l] We[a]ver from Cambray, Niagary [Cambria, Niagara] Co[unty], N[ew] Y[ork]. This man is a preacher in the church that is called Christian or Unitarian. He remarked that he had but few minuits [minutes] to spend with me. We entered into conversation and had som[e] little controversy upon the subject of prejudice, but soon come to an understanding. He spoke of the gospel and said he believed it, adding that it was good tidings of great joy. I replyed that it was one thing to proclaim good tidings and another to tell what those tidings are. He waived the conversation and withdrew. He was introduced by Joseph Rose.

Wednesday morning the 13th At 10 o'clock A.M. meet in Council with all the Presidency of Kirtland and Zion together with /all/ their councilors that could be found in this place. However some of the councellors were absent, both of Kirtland and

99

Zion. The Presidency of the Seventy were also present and many more {page 104} of the Elders of the Church of the Latter Day Saints. [We] come to order, sung Adam-ondi-Ahman, and opened by prayer offered up by Joseph Smith, Sen[ior]. ~~President John Smith~~ /I/ presided on the occasion.

After the Council was organized and opened, I made some ~~verry pertinent~~ remarks in my introductory lecture before the authority [authorities] of the Church this morning, in general terms laying before them the buisness of the day which was to sup[p]ly some deficiencies in the Bishop['s] coun[c]il in this place, /also in the High Council/.

After some altercation upon the most proper manner of proce[e]ding, Elder Vinson Knight was nominated by the Bishop and seconded by the Presidency. Vote called of that body and car[r]ied. Vote was then called from the High Council of Zion and carried. Vote was then called from the Twelve [Apostles] and carried. Vote then called from the Council of the Seventy and carried. Vote then called from the Bishop and his Council from Zion and carried.

Elder Knight was received by the universal voice and concent of all the authority of the Church as a councilor in the Bishop's Council /in/ this place to fill the place of Elder Hyrum Smith who is ordained to the {page 105} Presidency of the High Council of Kirtland. He was then ordained under the hands of Bishop N[ewel] K. Whitney to the office of a councillor. Also to that [the office] of High Priest.

Council adjourned for one hour by singing the song, Come let us rejoice in the day of Salvation.

Council assembled at one o'clock P.M. organized, and proce[e]ded to buisness. The first buisness this afternoon was to supply some deficiencies in the High Council in Kirtland the Stake of Zion. John P. Greene was nominated and seconded by the Presidency. Vote taken and carried in his favour by the unanimous voice of all the authority of the Church. He supplyes the place of President O[liver] Cowdery who is elected to the Presidency of the High Council in this place.

Elder Thomas Grover was nominated to supply the place of Luke Johnson who is chosen and ordained one of the Twelve Apostles. The nomination was seconded and vote carried in his favour by all the authority present. He is received as a councilor in the High Council in Kirtland.

Elder Noah Packard was next nominated and seconded to supply the place of Sylvester Smith who is ordained to the Presidency of the Seventy. Vote called and carried {page 106} in his favour. Elder Packard was received by the unanimous vote of all the authority present as a High Councilor in Kirtland.

Elder John Page was nominated, but was not present and his name drop[p]ed.

Elder Joseph Kingsbury was nominated and seconded to fill the place of Orson Hyde, who is chosen and ordained one of the Twelve [Apostles]. Vote called and carried unanimously. Elder Kingsbury was received as a Hi[g]h Councilor in Kirtland.

Elder Samuel James was nominated and seconded to fill the place of Joseph Smith, Sen[ior]. Vote called and carried unanimously in his favour. Elder James was received as a High Councilor in Kirtland.

The new elected councilors were then called forward in order as they were elected and ordained under the hands of Presidents Rigdon, Joseph Smith, Sen[ior] and Hyrum Smith to the office of High Priests and councilors in this place, viz, Kirtland the Stake of Zion. Many great and glorious blessings were pronounced upon the heads of thes[e] councilors by President S[idney] Rigdon who was spokesman of the occasion.

Next proce[e]ded to supply the deficiencies in the Zion High Council {page 107} which were two viz Elders John Murdock and Solomon Hancock who were absent. Elders Alva Be[a]mon and Isaac McWithy were nominated and seconded to s[u]pply their place for the time being. Vote taken of the whole assembly and carried in their favour to serve as councilors in the High Council of Zion for the present.

Elder Nathaniel Mileken and Thomas Carrico were nominated and seconded to officiate as doorkeepers in the House of the Lord. Vote called and carried by the unanimous voice of the assembly.

Presidents Joseph Smith, J[unior], S[idney] Rigdon, W[illiam] W. Phelps, D[avid] Whitmer, [and] H[yrum] Smith were nominated and seconded to draft rules and regulation[s] to govern the House of the Lord. Vote called and carried by the unanimous voice of the whole assembly.

The question was agitate[d] whether whispering should be allowed in our councils and assemblys. A vote was called from the whole assembly and carried in the negative, that no whispering shall be allowed, nor any one allowed (except he is called upon or asks permission) to speak {page 108} loud in our councils or assemblies upon any concideration whatever. No man shall be inter[r]upted while speaking unless he is speaking out of place and every man shall be allowed to speak in his turn.

Elder Mileken objected to officiate in the House of the Lord as doorkeeper on account of his health and /was/ released by the voice of the assembly.

The minuits [minutes] of the Council were then read and Council adjourned untill Friday the 15th inst[ant] at 9 o'cl[ock] A.M. at the /west/ School room in the upper part of the Chapel [Kirtland Temple].

President S[idney] Rigdon made a request to have some of the Presidency lay their hands upon him and rebuke a severe affliction in his face which troubles him most at night. Eld[e]rs H[yrum] Smith and D[avid] Whitmer by my request laid their hands upon him and prayed for him and rebuked his disease in the name of the Lord Jesus Christ. The whole assembly responded, "Amen."

Elder D[avid] W. Patten also made a request in behalf of his wife for our prayers for her that she might be healed. I offered up a pray[er] for her recovery. The assembly responded, "Amen." {page 109}

President Rigdon then arose and made some verry appropriate remarks touching the enduement [Endowment] and dismissed the assembly by prayer.

W[arren] Parrish, Scribe

This has been one of the best days that I ever Spent. There has been an entire unison of feeling expressed in all our p[r]oceedings this day. The Spirit of the God of Israel has rested upon us in mighty power. It has /been/ good for us to be here in this heavenly place in Christ Jesus. Altho[ugh] much fatiegued with the labours of the day, yet my spiritual reward has been verry great indeed. Returned home and spent the evening.

Thursday morning the 14th At 9 o'clock, meet the Hebrew class at the School room in the Chapel [Kirtland Temple] and made some ar[r]angements about our anticipated Teacher Mr. J[oshua] Sexias [Seixas] of Hudson, Ohio.

I then retired to the council room in the printing office to me[e]t my colleagues who were appointed with my self to draft rules and regulations to be observed in the House of the Lord in Kirtland built by the Church of the Latter Day Saints, [beginning] in the year of our Lord 1834 /which are as follows:/ {page 110}.

1st It is according to the rules and regulations of all regular and legal organized bodies to have a President to keep order.

2nd The body thus organized are under obligation to be in subjection to that authority.

3d When a congregation assembles in this house they shall submit to the following rules, that due respect may be payed to the order of worship, viz:

1st No man shall be inter[r]upted who is appointed to speak by the Presidency of the Church, by any disorderly person or persons in the congregation, by whispering, by laughing, by talking, by menacing Jestures, by getting up and running out in a disorderly manner. Or by offering indignity to the manner of worship or the religion or to any officer of said Church while officiating in his office in any wise whatever by any display of ill manners or ill breeding from old or young, rich or poor, male or female, bond or free, black or white, believer or unbeliever. If any of the above insults are offered, such measures will be taken as are lawful to punish the ag[g]ressor or ag[g]ressors and eject them out of the house.

2nd An insult offered to the presiding Elder of said Church shall be concidered an insult to the whole {page 111} body. Also an insult offered to any of the officers of said Church while officiating shall be concidered an insult to the whole body.

3d All persons are prohibited from going up the stairs in times of worship.

4th All persons are prohibited from exploring the house except waited upon by a person appointed for that purpose.

103

5th All persons are prohibited from going into the several pulpits except the officers who are appointed to officiate in the same.

6th All persons are prohibited from cutting, marking, or mar[r]ing the inside or outside of the house with a knife, pencil, or any other instrument whatever under pain of such penalty as the law shall inflict.

7th All children are prohibited from assembling in the house above or below or [in] any part of it to play or for recreation at any time, and all parents, guardians or masters shall be ameneable [amenable, i.e., responsible] for all damage that shall accrue in consequence of their children.

8th All persons whether believers or unbelievers shall be treated with due respect by the authorities of the Church. {page 112}

9th No imposition shall be practiced upon any member of the Church by depriving them of their /rights/ in the house.

Council adjourned sini di [sine die]. Returned home and spent the after no[o]n.

Towards evening President Cowdery returned from Columbus the capital of this State. I could not spent much time with him being under obligation to attend at Mrs. Wilcox's to join Mr. John Webb and Mrs. Catharine Wilcox in matrimony. Also [joined] Mr. Tho[ma]s Carrier and Miss Elizabeth Baker at the same place. I found a large company assembled. The house was filled to overflowing. We opened our interview by singing and prayer suited to the occasion after which I made some remarks in relation to the duties that are incumbent on husbands and wives. In particular the great importance there is in cultivating the pure principles of the institution, in all its bearings and connexions with each other and Society in general.

I then invited them to arise and join hands and pronounced the ceremony according to the rules and regulations of the Church of the Latter Day Saints. After which I pronounced such blessings upon their heads as the Lord put into my heart, even the blessings of Abraham, Isaac, and Jacob. Dismissed by singing and prayer.

We then took some refreshment {page 113} and our hearts were made glad with the fruit of the vine. This is according to pattern Set by our Saviour himself and we feel disposed to patronize all the institutions of heaven. I took leave of the congregation and retired.

Friday the 15th, at 9 o'clock A.M. meet [met] in Council agreeably to the adjournment at the council room in the Chapel [Kirtland Temple] [and] organized the authorities of the Church agreeably to their respective offices in the Same. I then made some observation respecting the order of the day and the great responsibility we are under to transact all our buisness in righteousness before God inasmuch as our desisions will have a bearing upon all mankind and upon all generations to come.

Sung the song Adam-Ondi-Ahman and open[ed] by prayer and proceeded to buisness by reading the rules and regulations to govern the House of the Lord in Kirtland. The vote of the Presidency was called upon these rules and ~~carried~~ passed by the unanimous voice of this Presidency /viz/ of the High Council. Some objections were raised by President Cowdery, but waived on an explination.

The privilege of remarking upon the rules above named was next granted {page 114} to /the/ High Councillors of Kirtland. After much altercation, their vote was called and unanimously passed in favour of them. The investigation was then thrown before the /High/ Council of Zion. Some objections or inquiry was made upon some particular items which were soon settled and their vote called and passed unanimously in favour of them.

The Twelve [Apostles] next investigated the subject of these rules and their vote called and passed unanimously in favour of them. Counsel adjourned for one hour.

1 o'clock P.M. in cou[n]cil, come to order, and proce[e]ded to buisness. The subject of the rules to govern the House of the Lord come next in order before the Counsel of the Seventy. Their vote [was] called and carried unanimously. The vote of the Bishop /of Zion/ and his counsillors was then called and after some debate was passed unanimously. The question was then thrown before the Bishop in Kirtland and his counsellors. Their vote [was] called and carried in their favour.

The above rules hav[e] now passed through the several quorums, in their order, and passed by the unanimous vote of the

105

whole and are therefore received and established as a law to govern the House of the Lord in this place.

In the investigati[o]n of this subject, I found that many who had deliberated upon this subject {page 115} were darkened in their minds, which drew forth some remarks from me, respecting the privileges of the authorities of the Church, that they should each speak in his turn, and in his place, and in his time and season, that their may be perfect order in all things. That every man, before he makes an objection to any item that is thrown before them for their concideration should be sure that they can throw light upon the subject rather than spread darkness. That his objections be founded in righteousness which may be done by applying ourselves closely to study the mind and will of the Lord, whose Spirit always makes manifest and demonstrates to the understanding of all who are in possession of his Spirit.

Elder [Don] Carloss Smith was nominated and seconded to be ordained to the High Priesthood. Also to officiate as President to preside over that body in Kirtland. The vote was called of the respective quorums in their order and passed through the whole house by their unanimous voice.

Eld[e]r Alva Beamon was nominated and seconded to officiate as President of the Elders in Kirtland. Elder Beemon arose and asked permission to speak and made the following remarks: "Brethren you {page 116} know that I am young and I am old and ignorant and kneed much instructions, but I wish to do the will of the Lord." The vote of the several authorities was then called and carried unanimously.

William Cowdery was nominated and seconded to officiate as President over the Priests of the Aaronic Priesthood in Kirtland. The vote of the assembly was called, beginning at the Bishop's Council and passing through the several authorities untill it come to the Presidency of the High Counsel in Kirtland and received their sanction having /been/ carried unanimously in all the departments below.

Oliver Olney was nominated and Seconded to preside over the Teachers in Kirtland. The vote of the assembly was called and passed unanimously.

Ira Bond was nominated and seconded to preside over the Deacons in Kirtland. Vote [was] called and passed unanimously.

Eld[e]r [Don] Carloss Smith was called forward to the seat of the Presidency and ordained to the offices whereunto he was elected. Many blessings [were] pronounced {page 117} upon his head by Joseph Smith, Jr., S[idney] Rigdon, and Hyrum Smith who were appointed to ordain him.

Also Eld[e]r Beamon received his ordination under the hands of the same to the office whereunto he had been elected and many blessings [were] pronounced upon his head.

Bishop Whitney /and his counselors/ then proce[e]ded to ordain W[illia]m Cowdery to the office whereunto he had been called, viz to preside over the Priests of the Aaronic Priesthood in Kirtland. Many blessings were sealed upon his head.

Also Oliver Olney [was ordained] to preside over the Teachers in Kirtland with many blessings. Also Ira Bond [was ordained] to preside over the Deacons in Kirtland with many blessings [sealed] upon his head.

[We] next proceeded to nominate doorkeepers in the House of the Lord. The officers of the several quorums were nominated and seconded and carried that each Should Serve in their turn as doorkeepers. Also Nathaniel Miliken, Thomas Carrico, Samuel Rolph, and Amos R. Orton were elected to the office of doorkeepers. {page 118}

Nominated and seconded that the Presidency of the High Counsel hold the keys of the outer and inner courts of the Lord's House in Kirtland, except one of the vestries /keys/ which is to be held by the Bishopric of the Aaronic Priesthood.

The vote of the assembly [was] called and carried unanimously. Nominated and seconded that John Carrill [Corrill] be appointed to take charge of the House of the Lord in Kirtland immediately. The vote of the assembly [was] called and passed unanimously.

President Rigdon then arose and delivered his charge to the assembly. His remarks were few and appropriate. Adjourned by ~~singing and~~ prayer.

W[arren] Parrish, *Scribe*

Saturday morning the 16th By request I meet with the Council of the 12 [Apostles] in company with my colleagues F[rederick] G. Williams and S[idney] Rigdon. Council [was] organized and opened by singing and prayer offered up by Thomas B. Marsh, President of the 12 [Apostles]. He [Thomas B. Marsh] arose and requested the privilege in behalf of his colleagues of speaking, each in his turn without being inter[r]upted, which was granted them. Elder Marsh proceeded {page 119} to unbosom his feelings touching the mission of the 12 [Apostles] and more particularly respecting a certain letter which they received from the Presidency of the High Council in Kirtland, while attending a conference in the East State of Maine. [He] also spoke of being placed in our Council, on Friday last, below the Council's of Kirtland and Zion, having been previously placed next [to] the Presidency in our assemblies. [He] also observed that they were hurt on account of some remarks made by President H[yrum] Smith on the trial of Gladden Bishop who had been previously tried before the Council of the 12 [Apostles], while on their mission in the east, who had, by their request, thrown his case before the High Council in Kirtland for investigation. The 12 [Apostles] concidered that their proceedings with him were in some degree discountenanced.

Elder Marsh then gave way to his brethren. They arose and spoke in turn untill they had all spoken acquiessing in the observations of Elder Marsh and mad[e] some additions to his remarks which are as follows: That the letter in question [was the one] which they received from the Presidency, in which two of their members were suspended and the rest severely chastened, and that [the accusations rested] too [much] upon testimony which was unwar[r]antable.

Particularly stress was laid upon a certain letter which the Presidency had received from Dr. {page 120} W[arren] A. Cowdery of Freedom, New Yorke in which he prefer[r]ed charges against them which were false. Upon which they /we/ (the Presiden[cy]) had acted in chast[e]ning them. Therefore the 12 [Apostles] had concluded that the Presidency had lost confidence in them and that whereas the Church in this place had carressed them at the time of their appointment to the appostleship, they now treated them coolly and appear to have lost confidence in them also.

They spoke of their having been in this work from the beginning almost and had born[e] the burden in the heat of the day and passed through many trials and that the Presidency ought not to suspect their fidelity, nor loose confidence in them, neither [should] have chastised them upon such testimony as was lying before them. Also urged the necessity of an explanation upon the letter which they received from the Presidency, and the propriety of their having information as it respects their duties, authority &c. that they might come to /an/ understanding in all things, that they migh[t] act in perfect unison and harmony before the Lord and be prepared for the endument [Endowment].

Also that they had prefer[r]ed a charge against Dr. [Warren] Cowdery for his unchristian conduct which the Presidency had disregarded. Also that President O[liver] Cowdery on a certain occasion had made use of language to one of the {page 121} Twelve [Apostles] that was unchristian and unbecoming any man, and that they would not Submit to such treatment.

The remarks of all the 12 [Apostles] were made in a verry forcible and explicit manner, yet cool and deliberate.

\12 I observed that we had heard them paietiently [patiently] and in turn should expect to be heard patiently also. First, I remarked that it was necessary that the 12 [Apostles] should state whether they were determined to persevere in the work of the Lord, whether the Presidency are able to satisfy them or not. Vote [was] called and carried in the affirmative unam/in/ously [unanimously]. I then said to them that I had not lost confidence in them, that they had no reason to suspect my confidence, that I would be willing to be weighed in the scale of truth today in this matter and risk it in the day of judgement.

As it respects the chast[e]ning contained in the letter in question which I acknowledge might have been expressed in too harsh language, which was not intentional, and I ask your forgiveness in as much as I have hurt your feelings. But nevertheless, the letter that Elder McLellen wrote back to Kirtland while the Twelve [Apostles] were at the east was harsh also and I was willing to set the one against the other.

I next proceeded to explain the subject of the duty of the Twelve [Apostles], and their authority which is next to the present Presidency, and that the ar[r]angement of the assembly in this place on the 15[th] inst[ant] \13in placing the High Councils of Kirtland ~~and~~ next [to] the Presidency was because the buisness [business] to be transacted was buisness [business] that related to

---

12 Possibly in the handwriting of Jesse Hitchcock.
13 In the handwriting of Warren Parrish.

that body in particular, which was to {page 122} fill the several quorum's in Kirtland. Not beca[u]se they were first in office, and that the ar[r]angement was most judicious that could be made on the occassion. Also the 12 [Apostles] are not subject to any other than the First Presidency, viz, myself, S[idney] Rigdon, and F[rederick] G. Williams.

I also stated to the 12 [Apostles] that I do not countinanc[e] the harsh language of President [Oliver] Cowdery to them, neither in myself nor any other man. Although I have sometimes spoken to[o] harsh from the impulse of the moment. And inasmuch as I have wounded your feelings brethren, I ask your forgiv[e]ness, for I love you and will hold you up with all my heart in all righteousness before the Lord and before all men. For be assured brethren, I am willing to stem the torrent of all opposition in storms, in tempests, in thunders and lightning, by Sea and by land, in the wilderness, or among fals[e] brethren or mobs, or wherever God in his providence may call us. I am determined that neither hights nor depths, principalities nor powers, things present or to come, nor any other creature shall separate me from you.

I will now covenant with you before God that I will not listen too [to] nor credit any derogatory report against any of you nor condemn you upon any testimony beneath the heavens, short of that testimony which is infal[l]ible, untill I can see you face to face and know of a surity. {page 123} I do place unlimited confidence in your word for I believe you to be men of truth. I ask the same of you [so that] when I tell you any thing that you [may] place equal confidence in my word. For I will not tell you I know anything which I do not know. But I have already consumed more time than I intended to when I commenced. I will now give way to my colleagues.

President Rigdon arose next and acquiessed in what I had said and acknowledged to the 12 [Apostles] that he had not done as he ought, in not citing Dr. [Warren] Cowdery to trial on the charges that were put into his hands by the 12 [Apostles]. That he had neglected his duty in this thing, for which he asked their forgiveness and would now attend to it if they desired him to do so.

~~Elder~~ /Pres[i]d[en]t/ Rigdon also observed to the 12 [Apostles] ~~that he might~~ /if he/ had spoken or reproved too harshly at any time and had injured their feelings by so doing he asked their forgiv[e]ness.

President Williams arose and acquiessed in the above sentiments expressed by myself and President Rigdon in full and said many goods things.

The President of the 12 [Apostles] [Thomas B. Marsh] then called a vote of that body to know whether they were perfectly satisfied with the {page 124} explenation which we had given them. And whether they would enter into the covenant we had proposed to them, which was most readily manifested in the affirmative by raising their hands to heaven in testimony of their willingness and desire to enter into this covenant and their entire satisfaction with our explanation upon all the difficulties that were on their minds.

We then took each others by the hand in confirmation of our covenant. Their was a perfect unison of feeling on this occasion and our hearts over flowed with blessings which were pronounced upon each other's heads as the Spirit gave us utterance. My scribe is included in this covenant and blessings with us, for I love him for /the/ truth and integrity that dwelleth in him.

May God enable us all to perform our vows and covenants with each other in all fidelity and righteousness before Him that our influence may be felt among the nations of the earth in mighty power. Even to rend the Kingdom of darkness in sunder and triumph over priest craft and spiritual wickedness in high places, and brake in pieces all ~~other~~ Kingdoms that are opposed to the Kingdom of Christ and spread the light and truth of the everlasting gospel from the rivers to the ends of the earth.

Elder Beamon call[ed] for council upon the subject of his returning home. He wished to know whether it was best for him to return before the Solemn Assembly {page 125} or not. After taking it into concideration the Council advised him to tarry. We dismissed by singing and prayer and retired.

W[arren] Parrish, *Scribe*

Sunday morning the 17th \14 Attended meeting at the schoolhouse at the usual hour. A large congregation assembled. I proceeded to organize the several quorums present. First the Pres-

---

14 Possibly in the handwriting of Jesse Hitchcock.

idency, then the Twelve [Apostles], and the Seventy, all who were present. Also the Counsellers of Kirtland and Zion.

President Rigdon then arose \[15] and observed that instead of preaching the time would be occupied by the Presidency and Twelve [Apostles] in speaking each in their turn untill they had all spoken. The Lord poured out his spirit upon us and the brethren began to confess their faults one to the other. The congregation were soon overwhelmed in tears and some of our hearts were too big for utterance. The gift of toungs [tongues] come upon us also like the rushing of a mighty wind and my soul was filled with the glory of God.

In the after noon I joined three couple[s] in matrimony, in the publick congregation, whose names are as follows: W[illia]m F. Cahoon and Maranda Gibbs, Harv[e]y Stanl[e]y and Larona Cahoon, also Tunis Rapleye and Louisa Cutler. We then administered the Lord['s] Supper and dismissed the congregation, /which/ was so dense that it was {page 126} verry unpleasant for all.

We were then invited to Elder Cahoon's to a feast which was prepared on the occasion, and had a good time while partaking of the rich repast that was spread before us. I verily realized that it was good for brethren to dwell together in unity like the dew upon the mountains of Israel, where the Lord commands blessings, even life for ever more. Spent the evening at home.

Monday the 18th Attended the Hebrew School. This day the Elders' School was removed into the Chapel [Kirtland Temple] in the room adjoining ours. Nothing very special transpired.

—

Copy of a Letter

Willoughby, January 5th 1836

To Elder W[arren] Parrish
Sir, I have received an open note from Mr. Sylvester Smith informing me that your School concidered itself dissolved from all ingagements with

---

[15] In the handwriting of Warren Parrish.

me. For this I was not unprepared, But he adds that I must excuse him for saying that I appear to be willing to trifle with you in regard to appointments, time, &c.

This insinuation is unworthy of me, beneath my sence of honour, and I {page 127} could hope unwar-[r]anted by any mean suspicion of your whole body. I wrote for books to New York by Mr. [Oliver] Cowdery not but [because] I could not have taught the rudiments without them but because I wished to make my instruction philosophically availing as well as mere elementary. In this object I thought myself confirmed by you. My books have not come as yet and are probably lost, of the pecuniary value I seek not. I bor[r]owed a book of Elder [John F.] Boynton and told him, believing him to be responsible, that Wednesday would be best for me to deliver a publick lecture owing to my engagements here. I here was officially informed when the School was to be opened by me.

The addition of insult to wrong may be gratifying to small minds, mine is above it, scorns and repud[i]-ates it.

> I am verry respectfully,
> Your verry ob[edient] Serv[ant],
> Daniel L. M. Piexotto

———

\\[16] The Answer

Kirtland, Jan[uary] 11th 1836

Dr. Piexotto,

Sir, I received yours of the 5th Inst[ant] in which you manifested much indignation and considered your hounour highly insulted by us as a body, if not by me as an individual, and deprecated our conduct because we informed you that you appeared willing to trifle with

---

[16] Possibly in the handwriting of Jesse Hitchcock.

us as it {page 128} respects our engagement with you
to teach our Hebrew class. I have acted in this matter as
agent for the School. The time agreed upon for you to
commence was not to be protracted at farthest later
than Dec[ember] 15th. The class have ever till now,
considered themselves bound by the engagement I made
with you.

When Elder Cowdery and myself called, you set a
time that you would come over to Kirtland and have
our agreement committed to writing, but did not come,
some were displeased. I excused you. Some days passed
without our hearing from you. At length Dr. Williams
called and you specified another time that you would
come (which is some 2 or 3 weeks since) [and] the class
were disappointed. I again plead an excuse for you.

On last Saturday week, or in other words on the
2nd Inst[ant], our class met and agreed to organize on
Monday morning the 4 Inst[ant] at 9 o'clock A.M. By
the voice of the school, I was appointed to wait on you
and advertize your honour that we were ready, and
should expect you to attend at that hour. Presuming
that you would be ready at this late period to fulfill
your engagement if you ever intended to. Accordingly, I
called and informed you of the ar[r]ang/e/ments we had
made, but on account of your ar[r]ang/e/ments at the
Medical University I was willing to exceed my instructions and let you name the hour that you would wait on
us on that day, which was at 4 o'clock P.M.

Sunday the 3[rd] inst[ant], I learned from Elder
Boyanton [Boynton] that it would be most convenient
for you to call on Wednesday. The school knew nothing
of this as a body [and] on Monday morning we met. I
was called upon to report which I did. I also stated
what I had {page 129} heard from Elder Boyanton
[Boynton]. The voice of the class was called to know
whether they considered themselves any longer under
obligation to you and whether they would wait any
longer for you. [The vote was] carried in the negative.

Now sir, what could I say in your behalf? I answer,
nothing! I should have considered it an insult to have

asked 40 men who had laid by every other consideration to attend this school to lay upon their oars 3 days longer with the impression on their minds (and justly too) that it would be altogether uncertain whether you would come then or not.

With these things lying before us, we are told by your honour that it may be gratifying to small minds to add insult to wrong. You also informed me in your note that you was not unprepared for the intel[l]igence it contained, which is vertually saying that you intended the abuse you have heaped upon us.

I assure you sir that I have ever entertained the best of feelings towards you and have recognized you as a friend in whom I could repose unlimited confidence and whith [with] whom I have acted in good faith. I am not a little surprized on this occasion that you should treat us with such marked contem/pt/ and then upbraid us with adding insult to wrong. Small as you may consider our minds, we have sufficient discernment to discover this insult, although offered by your honour, and suffi-cient good manners not to insult or wrong any man.

Respectfully your most obedient, humble servant,

Warren Parrish

P.S. The note that we sent you was well sealed when it was put into the hands of the messenger which you informed me you recieved open.

Yours,

W[arren] P[arrish] {page 130}

\\[17] ~~Monday morning the 18th At 9 o'clock attended the Hebrew school. Nothing special transpir[e]d on this day. Spent the evening at home with my family~~.

Tuesday the 19th Spent the day at School. The Lord blessed us in our Studies. This day we commenced reading in our Hebrew Bibles with much success. It seems as if the Lord opens our minds in a marvelous manner to understand his word in the original language. My prayer is that God will speedily indu [en-dow] us with a knowledge of all languages and toungs [tongues]

---

[17] In the handwriting of Warren Parrish.

that his servants may go forth for the last time to bind up the law and seal up the testimony.

—

Form of Marriage Certificate

I hereby certify that agreeably to the rules and regulations of the Church of Christ of Latter-Day Saints on matrimony, were joined in marriage Mr. William F. Cahoon and Miss Nancy M. Gibbs, both of this place, on Sabbath the 17th instant.

Joseph Smith, Jun[ior]
Presiding Elder of said Church

Kirtland, Ohio, Jan[uary] 18th 1836 {page 131}

—

Wednesday morning 20th Attended school at the us[u]al hour. Spent the day in reading and lecturing. [We] made Some advancement in our studies.

At evening I attended at John Johnson's with my family, on a matrimonial occasion, having been invited to do so, to Join President John F. Boynton and Miss Susan Lowell in marriage. A large and respectable company assembled and were seated by Eld[e]r's O[rson] Hyde and W[arren] Parrish in the following order: The Presidency and their companions in the first Seats, the Twelve Apostles in the second, the 70 in the third and the remainder of the congregation seated with their companions.

After the above ar[r]angments were made, Eld[e]r Boynton and his Lady with their attendants, came in and were seated in front of the Presidency. A hymn was sung, after which I ad[d]ressed a throne of grace. I then arose and read aloud a licence granting any minister of the gospel the priviledge of Solemnizing the rights of matrimony. After calling for objection if any there were against the anticipated alliance between Eld[e]r Boynton and Miss Lowell and waiting sufficient time, I observed that all forever after this must hold their peace.

I then envited them to Join hands and I pronounced the ceremony according to the rules and regulations of the Church of the Latter-day Saints. In the name of {page 132} God and in the

116

name of Jesus Christ, I pronounced upon them the blessings of Abraham, Isaac, and Jacob and such other blessings as the Lord put into my heart. Being much under the influence of a cold I then gave way and President S[idney] Rigdon arose and delivered a verry forcible address suited to the occasion and closed the Services of the evening by prayer.

Eld[e]r O[rson] Hyde, Eld[e]r L[uke] Johnson, and Eld[e]r W[arren] Parrish who served on the occasion then presented the Presidency with three Servers filled with glasses of wine to bless. It fell to my lot to attend to this duty, which I cheerfully discharged. It was then passed round in order, then the cake in the Same order. Suffise it to say our hearts were made cheerful and glad, while partaking of the bounty of the earth which was presented untill we had taken our fill.

Joy filled every bosom and the countenances of old and young alike seemed to bloom with the cheerfulness and Smiles of youth and an entire unison of feeling seemed to pervade the congregation. Indeed, I doubt whether the pages of history can boast of a more Splendid and in[n]ocent wedding and feast than this. For it was conducted after the order of heaven, who has a time for all thing[s]. This being a time of rejoicing, we hartily embraced it and conducted ourselves accordingly. Took leave of the {page 133} company and returned home.

Thursday morning the 21st This morning a minister from Conne[c]ticut by the name of John W. Olived called at my house and enquired of my father if Smith the pro[p]het lives here. He replied that he did not understand him. Mr. Olived asked the same question again and again and received the same answer. He finally asked if Mr. Smith lives here. Father replied "O yes Sir, I understand you now." Father then stept [stepped] into my room and informed me that a gentleman had called to See me. I went into the room where he was and the first question he asked me, after passing a compliment, was to know how many members we have in our Church. I replyed to him that we hav[e] between 15 hundred and 2,000 in this branch.

He then asked me wherein we differ from other Christian denomination[s]. I replyed that we believe the Bible and they do not. However he affirmed that he believed the Bible. I told him then to be baptised. He replied that he did not realize it to be his duty. But when laid before him the principles of the gospel, viz,

117

faith, repentance, baptism for the remission /of sins/, and the laying on of hands for the reseption of the Holy Ghost /he manifested much surprise/. I then observed that the {page 134} hour for school had ar[r]ived and I must attend. The man seemed astonished at our doctrine, but by no means hostile.

At about 3 o'clock P.M I dismissed the School. The Presidency retired to the loft of the printing office, where we attended to the ordinance of washing our bodies in pure water. We also perfumed our bodies and our heads in the name of the Lord.

At early candlelight, I meet with the Presidency at the west school room in the Chapel [Kirtland Temple] to attend to the ordinance of annointing our heads with holy oil. Also the Councils of Kirtland and Zion meet in the two adjoining rooms, who waited in prayer while we attended to the ordinance.

I took the oil in my ~~right~~ /left/ hand, Father Smith being seated before me and the rest of the Presidency encircled him roundabout. We then stretched our right hands to heaven and blessed the oil and concecrated it in the name of Jesus Christ. We then laid our hands on our aged Fath[er] Smith and invoked the blessings of heaven. I then annointed his head with the concecrated oil and sealed many blessings upon his/m/ [him] ~~head~~.

The Presidency then in turn laid their hands upon his head, beginning at the eldest, untill they had all laid their hands on him and pronounced such blessings upon his head as the Lord put into their hearts. All blessing him to be our patraark [patriarch] ~~and~~ /to/ annoint our {page 135} heads and attend to all duties that pertain to that office.

I then took the Seat and [my] Father annoint[ed] my head and sealed upon me the blessings of Moses to lead Israel in the latter days, even as Moses led him in days of old. Also the blessings of Abraham, Isaac, and Jacob. All of the Presidency laid their hands upon me and pronounced upon my head many prophesies and blessings. Many of which I shall not notice at this time, but as Paul said, so say I, let us come to vissions and revelations.

The heavens were opened upon us and I beheld the Celestial Kingdom of God and the glory thereof, whether in the body or out I cannot tell. I saw the transcendant beauty of the gate through which the heirs of that Kingdom will enter, which was like unto circling flames of fire. Also the blasing throne of

God whereon was Seated the Father and the Son. I Saw the beautiful streets of that Kingdom which had the appearance of being paved with gold.

I saw Father Adam, Abraham, and Michael and my father and mother, [and] my brother Alvin that has long since slept. [I] marveled how it was that he had obtained an inheritance /in/ that Kingdom Seeing that he had departed this life before the Lord /had/ Set his hand to gather Israel /the second time/ and had not been baptised for the remission of sins.

Thus came the voice /of the Lord/ unto me saying: "All who have {page 136} died with[out] a knowledge of this gospel, who would have received it, if they had been permitted to tarry, shall be heirs of the Celestial Kingdom of God.

"Also all that shall die henseforth, with/out/ a knowledge of it, who would have received it, with all their hearts, shall be heirs of that Kingdom, for I the Lord /will/ Judge all men according to their works according to the desires of their hearts." And ~~again I also beheld the Terrestial Kingdom~~ I also beheld that all children who die before they ar[r]ive to [at] the years of accountability are saved in the Celestial Kingdom of heaven.

I saw the 12 Apostles of the Lamb, who are now upon the earth who hold the keys of this last ministry, in foreign lands standing together in a circle much fatiegued, with their clothes tattered and feet swol[l]en, with their eyes cast downward, and Jesus /standing/ in their midst, and they did not behold him. The Saviour looked upon them and wept. I also beheld Elder McLellen in the South standing upon a hill surrounded with a vast multitude preaching to them and a lame man standing before him supported by his crutches. He threw them down at his word and leaped as an heart [hart] by the mighty power of God.

Also [I saw] Eld[e]r Brigham Young standing in a strange land in the far southwest, in a desert place, upon a rock in the midst of about a dozen men of colour who appeared hostile. {page 137} He was preaching to them in their own toung [tongue] and the angel of God standing above his head with a drawn sword in his hand protec[t]ing him, but he did not see it.

And I finally saw the 12 [Apostles] in the Celestial Kingdom of God. I also beheld the redemption of Zion and many things which the toung [tongue] of man cannot discribe in full.

Many of my brethren who received this ordinance with

me saw glorious visions also. Angels ministered unto them, as well as my self, and the power of the Highest rested upon us. The House [Kirtland Temple] was filled with the glory of God and we shouted Hosanah to ~~the~~ God and the Lamb.

I am mistaken concerning my receiving the holy anointing first after Father Smith. We received /it/ in turn according to our age (that is the Presidency). My scribe also recieved his anointing /with us/ and saw in a vision the armies of heaven protecting the Saints in their return to Zion /and many things that I saw/.

The Bishop of Kirtland with his counsellors and the Bishop of Zion with his counsellors were present with us and received their annointing under the hands of Father Smith and confirmed by the Presidency. The glories of heaven was unfolded to them also.

We then invited the [High] Counsellors of Kirtland and Zion into our room and President Hyrum {page 138} Smith annointed the head of the President of the [High] Counsellors in Kirtland and President D[avid] Whitmer the head of the President of the [High] Counsellors of Zion. The President of each quorum then annointed the heads of his colleagues, each in his turn beginning at the eldest.

The vision of heaven was opened to these also. Some of them Saw the face of the Saviour and others were ministered unto by holy angels. The spirit of prop[h]esy and revelation was poured out in mighty power and loud hosan[n]ahs and glory to God in the highest saluted the heavens for we all communed with the h[e]avenly hosts. I saw in my vision all of the Presidency in the Celestial Kingdom of God and many others who were present.

Our meeting was opened by singing and prayer offered up by the head of each quorum and closed by singing and invoking the benediction of heaven with uplifted hands. Retired between one and 2 o'clock in the morning. {page 139}

Friday morning the 22nd Attended at the school room at the us[u]al hour. But inste[a]d of persuing our studies \\[18] we spent the time in rehearsing to each other the glorious scenes that transpired on the preceding evening while attending to the ordinance of [the] holy anointing.

---

[18] Possibly in the handwriting of Jesse Hitchcock.

At evening we met at the same place with the Council of the 12 [Apostles] and the Presidency of the 70 who were to receive this ordinance. The High Councils of Kirtland and Zion were present also.

We called [the meeting] to order and organized. The Presidency then proceeded to consecrate the oil. We then laid our hands upon Elder Thomas B. Marsh who is the President of the 12 [Apostles] and ordained him to the authority of anointing his brethren. I then pour[e]d the consecrated oil upon his head in the name of Jesus Christ and sealed such blessings upon him as the Lord put into my heart. The rest of the Presidency then laid their hands upon him and blessed him each in their turn beginning at the eldest. He [Elder Marsh] then anointed /and blessed/ his brethren from the oldest to the youngest. I also laid my hands upon them and pronounced many great and glorious [blessings] upon their heads. The heavens were opened and angels ministered unto us.

The 12 [Apostles] then proceeded to anoint and bless the Presidency of the 70 and seal upon their heads power and authority to anoint their brethren. The heavens were opened upon Elder Sylvester Smith and he leaping up exclaimed, "The Horsemen of Israel and the chariots thereof." \[19] Br[other] [Don] Carloss Smith was also annointed and blessed to preside over the High Priesthood.

President Rigdon arose to conclude the servises of the evening {page 140} by invoking the benediction of heaven upon the Lord's anointed /which he did/ in an eloquent manner. The congregation shouted a loud hosannah.

The gift of toungs [tongues] fell upon us in mighty pow[e]r, angels mingled their voices with ours, while their presence was in our midst and unseasing pra[i]ses swelled our bosoms for the space of half an hour.

I then observed to the brethren that it was time to retire. We accordingly /closed/ our interview and returned home at about 2 o'clock in the morning. \[20] The spirit and visions of God attended me through the night.

Saturday, 23rd Attended at the school room as usual. We

---

[19] In the handwriting of Warren Parrish.
[20] In the handwriting of Sylvester Smith.

came together filled with the spirit as on the past evening and did not fe[e]l like studying, but commenced conversing upon heavenly things. The day was spent agre[e]ably and profitably. ~~Father~~ /Elder/ Alvah Beeman had been tempted to doubt the things which we rec[eive]d on Saturday evening. He made an humble confession and asked forgiveness of the school whi[c]h was joyfully given and he said he would try to resist Satan in [the] future.

Sunday, Jan[uar]y 24[th] Met the several quorems in the room under the printing office. After organizing and op[e]ning by prayer, called upon the High Council of Kirtland to proceede and confess their sins as th[e]y might be directed by the spirit. They occupied the first part of the day and confessed and exhorted as the spirit led. P.M. attended again and saw /the/ Bread and wine administered to the quorems and brethren who were present.

In the evening met the Presidency in the room over the printing room and counseled on the subject of [the] Endowment and the preperation necessary for {page 141} the Solemn Assembly which is to be called when the House of the Lord is finished.

Jan[uar]y 25[th], Monday Rec[eive]d a line from my scribe informing me of his ill health as follows:

Brother Joseph,
My great desire to be in your company and in the Assembly of the Saints where God opens the heavens and exhibits the treasures of eternity is the only thing that has stimulated me for a number of days past to leave my house. For be assured, dear brother, my bodily affliction is severe. I have a violent /cough/ more especially nights, which deprives me of my appetite, and my strength fails. Writing has a particular tendacy [tendency] to injure my lungs while I am under the influence of such a cough. I therefore, with reluctance, send your journal to you untill my health improves.

Yours in heart,
Warren Par/r/ish

P.S. Brother Joseph, pray for me and ask the prayers of the class on my account also.

—

Appointed Elder Sylvester Smith acting Scribe for the time being or till Eld[e]r Parrish shall recover his health. Spent the day at home receiving visiters &c.

Tuesday, 26[th] Mr. Seixas ar[r]ived from Hudson to teach the Hebrew Langu[a]ge. I attended upon the organizing of the class for the purpose of receiving his lectures on Hebrew grammar. His hours of instruction are from ten to eleven A.M. and from two to three P.M. His introduction pleased me much. I think he will be a help to the class in learning the Hebrew.

Wednesday [27 January 1836] Attended school as usual and other matters which came before me to attend to. {page 142}

Thursday, /28[th]/ Attended school at the usual hours. In the evening met the quorems of High Priests in the west room of the upper loft of the Lord's House. In company with my Council of the Presidency concecrated and anointed cou[n]sellors of the President of the High Priesthood. Having instructed them and set the quorem in order I left them to perform the holy anointing and went to the quorem of Elders in the other end of the room. I assisted in anointing the Counsellors of the President of the Elders and gave them the instruction necessary for the occasion. [I] left the President and his council to anoint the Elders while I should go to the adjoining room and attend to organizing and instructing of the quorem of the Seventy.

I found the Twelve Apostles assembled with this quorem. I proceeded with the quorem of the Presidency to instruct them and also the seven presidents of the Seventy Elders to call upon God with uplifted hands to seal the blessings which had been promised to them by the holy anointing.

As I organized this quorem with the Presidency in this room, Pres[ident] Sylvester Smith saw a pillar of fire rest down and abide upon the heads of the quorem as we stood in the midst of the Twelve [Apostles].

When the Twelve [Apostles] and the seven [presidents] were through with their sealing prayers, I called upon Pres[ident] S[idney] Rigdon to seal them with uplifted hands. When he had done this and cried hossannah [so] that all [the] congregation should join him and shout hosannah to God and the Lamb and glory to God in the highest. It was done so and Eld[er] Roger

123

{page 143} Orton saw a ~~flaming~~ /mighty/ Angel riding upon a horse of fire with a flaming sword in his hand followed by five others encircle the house and protect the Saints, even the Lord's anointed from the power of Satan and a host of evil spirits which were striving to disturb the Saints.

Pres[ident] W[illia]m Smith, one of the Twelve [Apostles], saw the heavens op[e]ned and the Lord's host protecting the Lord's anointed. Pres[ident] Z[ebedee] Coltrin, one of the seven [presidents of the Seventy], saw the Saviour extended before him as upon the cross and [a] little after crowned with a glory upon his head above the brightness of the sun.

After these things were over and a glorious vision which I saw had passed, I instructed the seven presidents to proceed and anoint the Seventy. Returned to the room of the High Priests and Elders and attended to the sealing of what they had done with uplifted hands. The Lord had assisted my bro[ther] [Don] Carloss the Pres[ident] of the High Priests to go forward with the anointing of the High Priests so that he had performed it to the acceptance of the Lord, notwithstanding he was verry young and inexperienced in such duties.

I f[e]lt to praise God with a loud hossannah for His goodness to me and my father's family and to all the children of men. Praise the Lord all ye His Saints, Praise His Holy Name. After these quorems were dismissed I retired to my home filled with the spirit and my soul cried hossannah to God and the Lamb through /the/ silent watches of the night and while my eyes were closed in sleep the visions of the Lord were sweet unto me and his glory was round about me. Praise the Lord. {page 144}

Friday, 29[th] Attended school and read Hebrew. [I] rec[eive]d the following line from the Presidency of the Elders:

Kirtland, Jan[uar]y 29[th] AD 1836

To the Presidents of the Church of Latter Day Saints,

Beloved Bret[hren], feeling ourselves amenable to you for our proceedings as the Presidency of the First Quorem of Elders in Kirtland, and believing that we are to be governed by you, we desire to know if we are to receive all those who are recommended to us by Elders for ordination, or shall we receive none only those who have written recommendations from you. Please answer our request.

Alvah Be[a]man Pres[ident]
[Evan] M. Green Cl[er]k
Reuben Hadlock [Hedlock]
John Morton Counsel

Answered the above verbally and attended to various duties. P.M. I called in all my family and made a feast /and related my feelings towards them/.

My Father pronounced the following Patriarchal blessings:

Henry Garrett, born in Deerfield, Onieda Co[unty], N[ew] Y[ork] [on] Sept[ember] 5[th] AD 1814. Bro[ther] [Garrett], I bless thee by the authority of the Priesthood. [The] Lord had [an] eye upon thee. Satan seek destruction [upon thee and thy] relatives also. I seal thee unto [eternal] life [with] power to tread the adversa[r]y under thy feet and be useful [to] reclaim [thy] friends, [to] Be a son of God, an heir jointly with Jesus Christ. [You shall] stand on the earth if faithful till thou hast rec[eive]d all the desires of thy heart which are in righteousness. The Lord shall bless thy chil[dren] after thee with the blessings of Abraham, Isaac, and Jacob. [Thou] shall walk with [thy] companion to the {page 145} House of God and see his glory fill the house and thou shalt receive all the blessings which thy heart can desire. I seal these blessings upon thee in the name of Jesus. Amen.

Charles H. Smith born in Potsdam, St. Lawrence Co[unty], N[ew] Y[ork] [on] April 16th 1817. Thou art in thy youth. Satan will lay many snares for thee but I secure thee by the power of the Holy Priesthood from his grasp. Thou hast no father. [Thou art] an orphan. The Lord shall watch over thee and keep thee. Thou shalt receive the Priesthood and be mighty in word. Save [thy] father's house [and] receive all the blessings of the Earth even of A[braham], I[saac], and Jacob. [Thou shalt] stand on earth till [thy] Redeamer com[es]. Do all that the power of the Holy Priesthood can qualify thee for. I seal these blessings upon thee in the name of Jesus. Amen.

Marietta Carter born in Benson, Rutland Co[unty], V[ermon]t [on] April 1st AD 1818. Thou art an orphan and the

Lord shall bless thee more than thy own father could do if he had not been taken from thee. Thy name is written in the Book of life. [Thou shalt] become a companion and a mother. [The] Lord [will] bless thy children and some of them shall prophecy. Thy father laid down his life for the redemption of Zion [and] his spirit watches over thee. Thy heart shall be filled with light [and shall] not sleep in the dust. [Thou shalt] see thy Redeamer come in the clouds of heaven and be caught up to meet him and be ever with him. These blessings I seal upon thee in the name of Jesus. Amen. {page 146}

Angeline Carter born in Benson, Rutland Co[unty], V[ermon]t [on] Aug[u]st 26[th] /1823/. Thou art a child [and] thy heart is pure. Satan shall have no power over thee because of thy blessing. God shall be thy father [and thou shalt be] an heir with Jesus. Observe the words of thy friends who care for thee and seek to please them. The Lord will give thee children and wisdom to teach them righteousness. They shall be blest of the Lord and call thee blessed, a daughter of Abraham. [Thou shalt] live till satisfied with life. I sealed the[e] up unto eternal life in the name of Jesus. Amen.

Joanna Carter born in Putnam, N[ew] Y[ork] [on] No-v[ember] 26th AD 1824. I seal the blessings of a father [since] thy father is no more. [I seal the] Blessings of Abraham, Isaac, and Jacob [upon thee]. [Thou shalt receive] strength [and] health [and be] healed of all infirmities. Satan [shall] have no power to afflict [thee]. [The] Lord [shall] guard thee by his holy Angels. [Thy] name [shall be] written in heaven [and thine] eyes opened to see visions. Angels [shall] minister unto thee. A companion [shall] lead thee to the House of God. [Thou shalt] see the glory of God fill the house. [Thou shalt] see the end of this generation. [Thou shalt] have power to stand against all the power of Satan and overcome through the faith which is in Jesus. I seal thee up unto eternal life in the name of the Lord Jesus. Amen.

Nancy Carter born in Benson, Rutland Co[unty], V[ermon]t [on] Feb[ruar]y 26[th] AD 1827. Thou art a child [and] the Lord loves thee. Satan shall seek in vain to destroy thee [but the] Lord [shall] raise friends for thee which shall guard thee from the destroyer. Thy name is written in heaven [and thou

shalt] live to see the winding up of this generation. {page 147}
Angels shall watch over thee in thy youth. [Thine] Eyes [shall be]
op[e]ned [and thou shalt] see thy God. Raise [thy] children in
righteousness and they shall be blest and call thee blessed because of thy diligence in teaching them the doctrine of the kingdom. I seal all these blessings upon thee in the name of Jesus.
Amen.

Written and recorded by Sylvester Smith, scribe

—

This was a good time to me and all the family rejoiced
together. We continued the meeting till about eight o'clock in the
evening and related the goodness of God to us in op[e]ning our
eyes to see the visions of heaven and in sending his holy Angels to
minister unto us the word of life. We sang the praise of God in
animated strains and the power of love and union was felt and
enjoyed.

Saturday, 30[th] Attended school as usual, and waited
upon several visiters and showed them the record of Abraham.
Mr. Seixas our Hebrew teacher examined them with deep interest and pronounced them to be original beyound all doubt. He is
a man of excellent understanding and has a knowledge of many
languages which were spoken by the Antints [ancients]. He is an
honorable man so far as I can judge as yet.

In the evening went to the upper rooms of the Lord's
House and set the different quorems in order. Instructed the Presidents of the Seventy concerning the order of their anointing and
requested them to proceed and anoint the Seventy. Having set all
the quorems in order, I {page 148} returned to my house being
weary with continual anxiety and labour in put[t]ing all the Authorities in and in striving to purify them for the Solemn Assembly according to the commandment of the Lord.

Sunday, 31 [January] 1836 Attended divine service in the
schoolhouse. Organized the several quorems of the Authoraties of
the Church [and] appointed door keepers to keep order about the
door because of the croud [crowd] and to prevent the House from
being excessively crowded. The High Council of Zion occupied

127

the first part of the day in speaking as they were led and relating experi[e]ncies, trials, &c.

P.M. House came to order as usual and Pres[ident] Sidney Rigdon delivered a short discours[e] and we attended to the breaking of bread. The season was as interesting as usual. In the evening my father attended to the blessing of three Brethren at Pres[ident] O[liver] Cowderies. Spent the evening at home.

Monday, Feb[r]uary 1[st] Attended school as usual. In company with the other committe[e] [members, I] organized another class of 30 [students] to receive Mr. Seixas' Lectures on the Hebrew. In the evening attended to the organizing of the quorems of High Priests, Elders, Seventy, and Bishops in the up[p]er rooms of the House of the Lord. After blessing each quorem in the name of the Lord, I left them and returned home.

Had an other interview with Mr. Seixas our Hebrew teacher and related to him some of the dealings of God to me and gave him some of the evidences of the work of the latter days. He list[e]ned candidly and did not appose. {page 149}

Tuesday, February 2[nd] A.D. 1836 Attended school as usual and various duties. Went to the schoolhouse in the evening and heard an animated discourse delivered by Pres[ident] S[idney] Rigdon. He touched the outlines of our faith. [He] showed the scattering and gathering of Israel from the scriptures and the stick of Joseph in the hands of Eaphraim and The law of Eaphraim aside from that of Moses. It was an interesting meeting. The spirit bore record that the Lord was well pleased!

Wednesday, 3[rd] Attended our Hebrew lecture A.M. and studied with O[liver] Cowdery and Sylvester Smith. P.M. received many visiters and showed the records of Abraham. My father blest three with a patriarchal blessing. Eld[er] A[lvah] Be[e]man handed in the names of seventy of his quorem, designed for another seventy if God will.

Thursday, 4[th] Attended school and assisted in forming a class of 22 [students] to read at 3 o'clock P.M. The other 23 [students] reads at 11 o'clock. The first class recites at a quarter before 10 /A.M./ and the second at a quarter before 2 P.M. We have a great want of books, but are determined to do the best we can. May the Lord help us to obtain this language that we may read the scriptures in the language in which they were given.

Friday, 5[th] Attended school and assisted the committe[e] to make ar[r]angements for supplying the third and fourth classes with books. Concluded to divide a Bible into several parts for the benefit of said classes. Continued my studies in the Hebrew, rec[eive]d several visiters and attended [to] various duties. {page 150}

Saturday, 6[th] Called the anointed together to receive the seal of all their blessings. The High Priests and Elders [met] in the council room as usual. The Seventy [met] with the Twelve [Apostles] in the second room and the Bishop in the 3rd. I laboured with each of these quorems for some time to bring [them] to the order which God had shown /to/ me which is as follows:

[The] first part to be spent in solemn prayer before God without any talking or confusion and the conclusion with a sealing prayer by Pres[ident] Sidney Rigdon when all the quorems are to shout with one accord a solemn hosannah to God and the Lamb with an Amen, Amen, and Amen. Then all take [their] seats and lift up their hearts in silent prayer to God and if any obtain a prophecy or vision to rise and speak that all may be edified and rejoice together.

I had considerable trouble to get all the quorems united in this order. I went from room to room repeatedly and charged each separately, assuring them that it was according to the mind of God. Yet notwithstanding all my labour, while I was in the east room with the Bishops' quorems, I felt by the spirit that something was wrong in the quorem of Elders in the west room.

I immediately requested Pres[ident] O[liver] Cowdery and H[yrum] Smith to go in and see what was the matter. The quorem of Elders had not observed the order which I had given them. [They] were reminded of it by Pres[ident] [Don] Carloss Smith and mildly requested to observe order and continue in prayer and [as] requested. Some of them replied that they had a teacher of their own and did not wish to be troubled by others. This caused the spirit of the Lord to withdraw. {page 151} This interrupted the meeting and this quorem lost th[e]ir blessing in a great measure.

The other quorems were more careful and the quorem of the Seventy enjoyed a great flow of the Holy Spirit. Many arose and spok[e], testifying that they were filled with the Holy Spirit which was like fire in their bones, so that they could not hold

129

their peace, but were constrained to cry hosannah to God and the Lamb and glory in the highest.

Pres[ident] W[illia]m Smith, one of the Twelve [Apostles], saw a vision of the Twelve and Seven[ties] in council together in old England. [He] prophecied that a great work would be done by them in the old co[u]ntries and God already beginning the work in the hearts of the p[e]ople. Pres[ident] Z[ebedee] Coltrin, one of the seven [Presidents of the Seventy], saw a vision of the Lord's Host. Others were filled with the spirit and spoke in tongues and prophecied. This was a time of rejoicing long to be remembered! Praise the Lord.

\\[21] Sunday, Feb[ruar]y 7[th] Attended meeting at the us[u]al hour. The quorums were seated according to their official standing in the Church. The Bishop of Zion and his counsellors oc[c]upied the fore noon in confession and ex[h]ortation. The Bishop of Kirtland and his counsellors occupied the stand in the after noon. The discourses of these two quorums were verry interesting.

A number of letters of commendation were presented and read. A vote [was] called and all [were] received into the Church in Kirtland. Bread was broken and blessed and while it was passing President Rigdon commenced speaking from Acts 2d [chapter] and continued [for] about 15 minuits [minutes]. His {page 151}[22] reasoning was cogent. The wine was then blessed and passed after which [the] meeting [was] dismissed.

At evening meet [met] with the Presidency in the loft of the Printing office, in company with the Presidency of the 70 to chose other 70 also. Blessed one of the Zion brethren. [The meeting was] dismissed and [I] retired.

Monday morning the 8th Attended School at the us[u]al hour. Nothing worthy of note transpired. In the afternoon lectured in upper room of the printing office with some of the brethren. At evening visited Mr. Seixas in company with Presidents Rigdon and Cowdery. He converses freely [and] is an interesting man.

This day Elder Parrish my scribe received my journal

---

[21] In the handwriting of Warren Parrish.
[22] Due to a clerical error, two pages are numbered 151 in the original.

again. His health is so much improved that he thinks he will be able, with the blessing of God, to perform this duty.

Tuesday the 9th Spent the day in studying the Hebrew language. We have pleasant weather and fine sleighing. Spent the evening at home.

Wednesday morning the 10th At home. At 10 o'clock met at [the] School room to read Hebrew. In the afternoon, read in the upper room of the printing office. At 4 o'clock called at the School room in the Chapel [Kirtland Temple] to make some arrang[e]ments concerning the classes.

On my return home I was informed that Br[other] Hyrum Smith had cut himself. {page 152} I immediately repaired to his house and found him badly wounded in his /left/ arm. He had fallen on his axe which caused a wound about 4 or 5 inches in length. Dr. Williams was sent for immediately, who, when he came in, sewed it up and dressed it. I feel to thank God that it is no worse. I ask my Heavenly Father in the name of Jesus Christ to heal my brother Hyrum ~~Smith~~ of his wound and bless my father's family one and all with peace and plenty and ultimately eternal life.

\\[23] Feb[ruary] 8th 1836 Met in council. Meeting opened with prayer by President Hyrum Smith. Levi Jackson supplied the place of Joseph Coe.

Sister [*blank*] entered a complaint against Joseph Keeler. After hearing the testimony, the Councillors proceeded to give their council after which Pres[ident] Hyrum Smith arose and made some remarks. The same was agreed to by President David Whitmer after which the Presidency gave room for the parties to speak. Both of which made a few remarks. The Pres[ident] then decided that Joseph Keeler be acquit[t]ed. A vote of the council was called [and] the council agreed to the decision of the Presidency.

Jesse Hitchcock, Clerk

\\[24] Thursday mornin[g], 11th Feb[ruar]y 1836 At home. Attended the School and read Hebrew with the morning Class. Spent the afternoon in reading and ex[h]ibiting the Egy[p]tian

[23] Possibly in the handwriting of Jesse Hitchcock.
[24] In the handwriting of Warren Parrish.

records to those who called to see me. Heaven's blessings have attended me. {page 153}

Friday, 12th Spent the day in reading Hebrew and attending to the duties of my family and the duties of the Church. Nothing very special transpired. /Meet [met] this evening to make ar[r]angements concerning ordinations/

Saturday, 13th Spent the fore noon in reading Hebrew. At noon I prepared a horse and sleigh for Professer Seixas to go to Hudson to visit his family.

Sunday, 14th Attended to the ordinance of baptism before meeting. At the us[u]al hour attended meeting. The Presidents of the 70 expressed their feelings on the occasion and their faith in the Book of Mormon and the revelations. Also their entire confidence in /all/ the quorums that are organized in the Church of Latter Day Saints. Had a good time [and] the Spirit of God rested upon the congregation. Administered the Sacrament and confirmed a number who had been baptised and dismissed [the meeting].

Kirtland, Feb[ruary] 12th 1836 I met in the School room in the Chapel [Kirtland Temple] in company with the several quorums to take into concideration the subject of ordinations, as mentioned at the top of this page.

Opened by singing and prayer. I then arose and made some remarks upon the object of our meeting, which were as follows:

First, that many are desiring to be ordained to the ministry who are {page 154} not called and consequently the Lord is displeased.

Secondly, many already have been ordained who ought [not] to hold official stations in the Church because they dishonour themselves and the Church and bring persecution swiftly upon us in consequence of their zeal without k[n]owledge.

I requested the quorums to take some measures to regulate the same. I proposed some resolutions and remarked to the brethren that the subject was now before them and open for discussion. The subject was taken up and discussed by Presidents S[idney] Rigdon, O[liver] Cowdery, Eld[e]r M[artin] Harris, and some others and some resolutions drafted by my scribe who served as clerk on the occasion. Read and rejected.

It was then proposed that I should indite resolutions which I did as follows:

1st Resolved that no one be ordained to any office in the Church in this Stake of Zion at Kirtland without the unanimous voice of the several bodies that constitute this quorum who are appointed to do Church buisness in the name of said Church, viz, the Presidency of the Church and council [of] the 12 Apostles of the Lamb and 12 High Counsellors of Kirtland, the 12 High Counsellors of Zion, the Bishop of Kirtland and his counsellors, the Bishop of Zion and his counsellors, [and] the 7 Presidents of the Seventies untill otherwise ordered by the said quorums. {page 155}

2nd And further resolved that no one be ordained in the branches of said Church abroad unless they are recommended by the voice of the respective branches of the Church to which they belong to a general conference appointed by the heads of the Church, and from that conference receive their ordination.

Monday the 15th Attended the Hebrew School at the usual hour. Spent the afternoon in reading Hebrew and receiving and waiting upon visitors. On this day we commenced translating the Hebrew language under the instruction of Professor Seixas. He acknowledg[e]'s that we are the most forward of any class he ever taught the same length of time.

Tuesday the 16th Attended School at the usual hour and resumed our translating and made rapid progress. Many called to day to see the House of the Lord and to visit me and see the Egy[p]tian manuscripts. We have {page 156} extremely cold weather and fine sleighing.

Wednesday the 17th Attend[ed] the School and read and translated with my class as usual. My Soul delights in reading the word of the Lord in the original and I am determined to persue the study of languages untill I shall become master of them if I am permitted to live long enough. [Or] at any rate, so long as I do live, I am determined to make this my object and with the blessing of God I shall succe[e]d to my sattisfaction.

This evening Elder [Joseph] Coe called to make some ar-

[r]angements about the Egyptian records and the mummies. He proposes to hire a room at J[ohn] Johnson's Inn and ex[h]ibit them there from day to day at certain hours, that some benefit may be derived from them. I complied with his request and only observed that they must be managed with prudence and care, especially the manuscripts.

Thursday the 18th Spent the day as usual in attending to my family concerns, receiving and waiting upon those who called for instruction and attending to my studies.

Friday the 19th Attended with the morning class and translated. Professor Seixas {page 157} handed me the names of a few whom he had selected from the first class, and requested us to meet together this afternoon and lecture, which we did in the upperroom of the printing office. The names are as follows: Presidents S[idney] Rigdon, O[liver] Cowdery, W[illiam] W. Phelps, Bishop E[dward] Partridge, Eld[e]rs [William] E. McLellen, O[rson] Hyde, O[rson] Pratt, Sylvester Smith, myself, and Scribe [Warren Parrish]. These Professor Seixas requested to meet one hour earlyer on the following morning.

I conversed with Mr. Seixas upon the subject of religion at my house this after noon. He listened with attention and appeared interested with my remarks. I believe the Lord is striving with him by his Holy Spirit and that he will eventually embrace the new and everlasting covenant, for he is a chosen vessel unto the Lord to do his people good. But I forbear lest I get to prophesying upon his head.

This evening President Rigdon and myself called at Mr. Seixas lodgings and conversed with him upon the subject of the School. Had a pleasant interview.

Saturday morning the 20th At home attending to my domestick concerns. At 9 o'clock attended the School and translated with the morning class. Spent the after noon with my class in the printing office. Spent the evening at home. {page 158}

Sunday the 21st Feb[ruary] 1836 Spent the day at home in reading, meditation, and prayer. I reviewed my lessons in Hebrew. On this day some 3 or 4 persons were baptised and the powers of darkness seem to be giving way on all sides. Many who have been enemies to the work of the Lord are beginning to enquire in to the faith of the Latter day Saints and are friendly.

Monday the 22nd Translated Hebrew with the 1st class

in the morning. Returned home and made out my returns to the county clerk on 11 marriages which I have Solemnized within 3 months past, 8 by license from the clerk of the Court of Common Pleas in Geauga County, Ohio and 3 by publishment. Sent them to Chardon by Elijah Fuller. I baptised John O. Waterman.

I spent the afternoon translating with my scribe, Eld[e]r W[arren] Parrish, at his house. At 4 o'clock meet [met] Professor Seixas and the school committee at [the] printing office to make some ar[r]angements for the advancement of the several classes.

The lower room of the Chapel [Kirtland Temple] is now prepared for painting. This afternoon the Sisters met to make the veil of the Temple. Father Smith presided over them and gave them much good instruction. Closed by Singing and prayer. {page 159}

Tuesday the 23d Read and translated Hebrew. This after noon the Sisters met again at the Chapel [Kirtland Temple] to work on the veil. Toward the close of the day I met with the Presidency and many of the brethren in the House of the Lord. I made Some remarks from the pulpit upon the rise and progress of the Church of Christ of Latter day Saints and pronounced a blessing upon the Sisters for the liberality in giving their servises so cheerfully to make the veil for the Lord's House, also [pronounced a blessing] upon the congregation and dismissed.

Wednesday the 24th Attended to my studies as us/u/al. At evening met the quorums at the school room in the Chapel [Kirtland Temple] to take into concideration the propriety or impropriety of ordaining a large number of individuals who wish to be ordained to official stations in the Church. Each individual's name was presented and the voice of the assembly called and all of them except 7 were rejected. Their ordinations defer[r]ed untill another time.

O[rson] Hyde, O[liver] Cowdery, and Sylvester Smith were nominated and seconded to draft and /make/ regulations concerning licenses. Vote of the assembly called and unanimously passed.

Thomas Burdick nominated and seconded to officiate as clerk to record licenses and receive pay for his servises. Accordingly [a] {page 160} vote [was] called and passed unanimously.

Also nominated and seconded that the 12 [Apostles] and Presidents of the 70 see that the calls for preaching in the region

135

round about Kirtland be attended to and filled by judicious Elders of this Church. Adjourned and closed by singing and prayer.

Thursday the 25th of Feb[ruary] 1836 Attended to my studies as usual and made some proficiency. In the afternoon I was called upon by President Rigdon to go and visit my wife who was verry sick. I did so in company with my scribe. We prayed for and annointed her in the name of the Lord and she began to recover from that verry hour. Returned home and spent the evening.

Friday the 26th Attended and read Hebrew with the first class in the morning. Spent the afternoon in the printing office. Settled som[e] misunderstanding between Br[other] W[illia]m Smith and Professor Seixas.

Saturday morning the 27th I prepared my horse and sleigh for Mr. Seixas to ride to Hudson to visit his family. He is to return on Monday next. Attended with my class at the printing office {page 161} both in the fore and after noon and lectured /on/ and translated Hebrew. We have cold weather and fine sleighing.

Sunday the 28th This morning two gentlemen, late from Scotland, called to see me to make inquiry about the work of the Lord in these last days. They treated me with respect and the interview was pleasing to me and I presume interesting to them. They attended our meeting with me and expressed a satisfaction in what they heard. They spoke of Irvin the oriental reformer and his prop[h]esies. After meeting, I returned home and spent the after part of the day and evening in reading and translating the Hebrew.

Monday the 29th Spent the day in studying as usual. A man called to see the House of the Lord in company with another gentleman. On entering the door they were politely invited by the gent[l]eman who has charge of the House to take off their hats. One of them complyed with the request unhesitatingly while the other observed that he would not take of[f] his hat, nor bow to Jo[e] Smith, but that he had made Jo[e] bow to him at a certain time. He was immediately informed by Eld[e]r Morey, the keeper of the House, that his first buisness was to leave for when {page 162} a man imposed upon me [Joseph Smith] he was imposed upon himself [Elder Morey]. The man manifested much anger but left the house.

For this independence and resolution of Eld[e]r Morey, I respect him and for the love he manifests toward me may Israel's God bless him and give him an ascendency over all his enemies.

This after noon Professor Seixas returned from Hudson and brought a few more Bibles and one grammar of his 2d edition. The weather is warm and our Sleighing is failing fast.

Tuesday, March the 1st 1836 Attended School in the fore noon. In the afternoon [attended school] at the printing office and read and translated with my class untill 4 o'clock. Returned home and attended to my domestic concerns. We have fine sleighing which is uncommon in this country at this season of the Year.

Wednesday the 2nd Persued my studies as usual. At 7 o'clock in the evening, the first class met agreeably to the request of Mr. Seixas at Eld[e]r O[rson] Hyde's to spend one hour in translating. Dismissed and returned home.

Thursday the 3d Attended to my studies in the Hebrew. Some misunderstanding took place between {page 163} Professor Seixas and some of the schollars respecting the sale of some Bibles. His feelings were much hurt. Appearantly he made some remarks concerning it to each class. At noon he called on the School committee with his feelings much depressed. We gave him all the Satisfaction we could in righteousness and his feelings were measur[a]bly allayed.

\[25] This evening the several quorums met agreeably to adjour[n]ment and were organized according to their official standing in the Church.

I then arose and made some remarks on the object of our meeting which are as follows:

1st To receive or reject certain resolutions that were drafted by a commit[t]ee chosen for that purpose at a preceeding meeting respecting licenses for Elders and other official members.

2nd To sanction by the united voice of the quorum[s] certain resolutions respecting ordaining members that had passed through each quorum separately without any alteration or amendment except/ing/ in the Quorum of the Twelve [Apostles].

The council opened by singing and prayer. President

---

[25] Possibly in the handwriting of Jesse Hitchcock.

O[liver] Cowdery then arose and read the resolutions respecting licenses three times. The third time he read the ~~article~~ /resolutions/ he gave time and oppertunity after reading each article for objections to be made if any there were. No objections were made.

I then observed that these resolutions must needs pass through each quorum separately begin[n]ing at the Presidency \26 and concequently it must first be thrown into the hands of the President of the Deacon[s] and his council as equal rights and privileges are my motto and one {page 164} man is as good as another, if he behaves as well, that all men should be esteemed alike without regard to distinctions of an official nature. The resolutions passed through the quorum of the Deacons by their unanimous voice.

It was then thrown before the President of the Teachers and his council and passed unanimously. Next into the hands of the President of the Priests and his council and passed unanimously. Then into the hands of the Bishop's council of Kirtland and passed unanimously.

From them to the Bishop of Zion and his council and passed unanimously. Next into the hands of the President of the ~~High Priests and his~~ Elders and his council and passed unanimously.

From them into the hands of the President of the High Priests and his council and passed unanimously. Next into the hands of the Presidents of the 70 and passed unanimously.

From them to the High Council of ~~Kirtland~~ /Zion/ and passed unanimously. From them to the High Council of Kirtland and passed unanimously. And then into the hands of the 12 [Apostles] and passed unanimously.

And lastly into the hands of the Presidency of the Church and all the quorums and rec[eive]d their Sanction. Having now passed through all the quorums, the resolutions are received as a Law to govern the Church. {page 165}

I was nominated and seconded for a standing chairman, F[rederick] G. Williams for clerk to is[s]ue licenses to the official members of the Church, S[idney] Rigdon for chairman pro tem

---

26 In the handwriting of Warren Parrish.

and O[liver] Cowdery [for] clerk. Vote called from the several quorums in their order and passed unanimously.

I then made some remarks on the amendment of the 12 [Apostles] upon the resolutions recorded on pages 155 and 156. President T[homas] B. Marsh made some observations after me and then called a vote of his quorum to as[c]ertain whether they would repeal their amendment or not. Nine of the 12 [Apostles] vote[d] in the affirmative and 3 in the negative and the original bill was passed, which is recorded on the pages above named. Dismissed by prayer and retired 1/2 past 9 o'clock.

Friday the 4th ~~Feby~~ /March/ 1836 Attended school as usual. The sleighing is failing fast. The icy chains of winter seem to be giving way under the influence of the returning Sun and spring will soon open to us with all his charms.

Saturday the 5th Attended School. In the after noon the board kiln to[ok] fire and the lumber principally consumed. This is the 5[th] or 6[th] time it has burnt this winter if my memory serves me cor[r]ectly.

Sunday the 6th Spent the day at home in the enjoyment /of the society/ of my family around the social fireside. {page 166}

Monday, March 7th 1836 Spent the day in attending to my studies. At evening met with my class at Professor Seixas' Room and translated the 17th chapter of Genesis.

After the class was dismissed I was requested to tarry with the rest of the School committee to make some ar[r]angements about paying Mr. Seixas for his instruction and to engage him for another q[uarte]r. We did not ar[r]ive at any thing definite upon this point, however Mr. Seixas has agreed to ~~stay~~ /teach us/ 3 weeks longer after having a vacation of 2 weeks at the expiration of this course and perhaps a q[uarte]r.

Tuesday the 8th Attended school and translated most of the 22[nd] chapter of Gen[esis]. After my class were dismissed, retired to the printing office and translated 10 verses of Ex[odus] 3d [chapter] which with the 1st and 2nd Psalms are our next lesson.

Wednesday the 9th Attended School as usual. ~~This day the snow is falling.~~

Thursday, 10th Attended School in the morning. In the after noon read Hebrew in the office. At evening went down to

[the] Professor['s] room to be instructed by him in the language. On the account of the Storm the class did not meet. {Page 167}

Friday the 11th Meet [met] with the morning class at 9 o'clock. At 10 o'clock went into the office and made a divission of our class for private studies for our better accommodation and advancement in the language we are persuing. Presidents Rigdon, Phelps, Cowdery, and myself meet [met] at the printing office. Eld[e]rs O[rson] Pratt, Sylvester Smith, and Bishop Partri[d]ge at L[uke] Johnson's. Eld[e]rs McLellen, O[rson] Hyde, and W[arren] Parrish on the flats.

This evening our class met at Mr. Seixas' room and spent an hour in our Studies. Class dismissed and retired except the school committee who tarried and made some ar[r]angements with Mr. Seixas about continuing longer with us and bringing his family to this place.

This has been a very stormy day and the Snow is still falling fast and the prospect is fair for another run of Sleighing which is uncommon for this country at this Season of the Year.

Saturday the 12th Engaged a team to go to Hudson after Mr. Seixas' family /and goods/, also a Horse and cutter for himself and wife. We have cold weather and fine Sleighing.

I was informed to day that a man by the name of Clark froze to death last night near this place, who was under the influence of ardent Spirits. O my God, how long will this monster intemperance {page 168} find its victims on the earth, me thinks until the earth is swept with the wrath and indignation of God and Christ's Kingdom becomes universal. O come Lord Jesus and cut short thy work in rightieousness.

Eld[e]r Solomon Hancock received a letter to day from Missouri bearing the painful intelligence of the death of his wife. May the Lord bless him and comfort him in this hour of affliction.

Sunday the 13th of March 1836 Met with the Presidency and some of the 12 [Apostles] and counseled with them upon the subject of removing to Zion this Spring. We conversed freely upon the importance of her redemption and the necessity of the Presidency removing to that place, that their influence might be more effectually used in gathering the Saints to that country. We finally come to the resolution to emigrate on or before the 15th of

May next if kind providence Smiles upon us and opens the way before us.

Monday the 14th Attended School as usual. Professor Seixas returned from Hudson with his family.

Tuesday the 15[th] At School in the forenoon. In the afternoon met in the printing office rec[eive]d and waited upon those who called to see me and attended to my domestick concerns. At evening met in the printing office and rec[eive]d a lecture on grammar. {page 169}

Wednesday the 16th Persued my Studies in the Hebrew language. At evening met the quorum of Singers in the Chapel [Kirtland Temple]. They performed admirably concidering the advantages they have had.

Thursday the 17th At School in the morning. In the afternoon in the office. In the evening met with the quorums in the west School room of the Lord's House to receive or reject certain individuals whose names were presented for ordinations. A number were received by the united voice of the assembly.

Friday the 18th Attended School with the morning class. At 10 o'clock went to the School house to attend the funeral of Susan Johnson, daughter of Esekiel Johnson. She is a member of the Church of Latter day Saints and remained strong in the faith untill her spirit took its exit from time to eternity. May God bless and comfort her afflicted parents, family connexions, and friends. President Rigdon delivered a fine discourse on the occasion and much solemnity prevailed.

Saturday the 19th Read Hebrew with the morning class. Spent the day in attending {page 170} to my domestick concerns and the affairs of the Church.

Sunday the 20th March 1836 Attended the house of worship as usual. The quorum of High Priests delivered short addresses to the congregation in a very feeling and impressive manner. At the intermission at noon one individual was baptised. In the afternoon, administered the Lord's Supper, as we are wont to do on every Sab[b]ath. The Lord blessed our Souls with the out pouring of His Spirit and we were made to rejoice in his goodness.

Monday the 21st At school in the morning. After school went to the printing office and prepared a number of Elders licences to Send by Elder Palmer to the court [in] Medina County

141

in order to obtain licenses to marry as the court in this county will not greant [grant] to us this privilege. To day 10 persons were baptized in this place.

Tuesday the 22nd Read Hebrew with the morning class. To day 5 young men were received into the Church by baptism in this place. This is a stormy day. The snow is nearly a foot deep. An uncommon Storm for this Season of the year. {page 171}

Wednesday the 23rd /M[ar]ch/ 1836 Attended School. This is a pleasant day and fine Sleighing. Two more were received into the Church by baptism.

Thursday the 24th Attended School as usual. In the evening, met with my class at the printing office and rec[eive]d a lecture from Professor Seixas upon the Hebrew language.

After we were dismissed, we called at the School room to hear the ~~quire~~ /choir/ of Singers perform, which they did admirably. On this day 5 more were rec[eive]d into the Church by baptism.

Friday the 25th Attend[ed] School with the morning class, also at 5 o'clock P.M. and rec[eive]d a lecture upon the Hebrew Grammar. We have pleasant weather and good Sleighing.

Saturday the 26th At home attending to my domestick concerns in the morning. After bre[a]kfast met with the Presidency to make ar[r]angements for the Solemn Assembly which occupied the remainder of the day.

Sunday morning the 27th The congregation began to assemble /at the Chapel [Kirtland Temple]/ at about 7 o'clock, one hour earlier than the doors were to be opened. Many brethren had come in from the regions {page 172} round about to witness the dedication of the Lord's House and Share in His blessings. Such was the anxiety on this occasion that Some hundreds (probably five or six) assembled ~~collected~~ before the doors were opened.

The Presidency entered with the door ke[e]pers and ar[r]anged them at the inner and outer doors, also placed our stewards to receiv[e] donations from those who should feel disposed to contribute something to defray the expenses of building the House of the Lord. /We also dedicated the pulpits and concecrated them to the Lord/ The doors were then opened.

President Rigdon, President Cowdery, and myself Seated the congregation as they came in. According to the best calculations we could make we received between 9 /hundred/ and 1,000 which is as many as can be comfortably situated. We then informed the door keepers that we could receive no more and a multitude were deprived of the benefits of the meeting on account of the House not being sufficiently capacious [spacious] to receive them.

I felt to regret that any of my brethren and sisters should be deprived of the meeting. I recommended them to repair to the School house and hold a meeting which they did and filled that house /also/ and yet many were left out.

The assembly were then organized in the following manner, viz:

~~President F. G. Williams, Presdt Joseph Smith, Sen father and Presdt W. W. Phelps occupied the first pulpit /in the west end of the house/ for the Melchisedec priesthood. Presdt S. Rigdon, myself, and Prest Hyrum Smith the 2nd. Presdt D. Whitmer, Presdt O. Cowdery, and Presdt John Whitmer the 3rd. The 4th was~~ {page 173} ~~occupied by the president of the high priests and his counselors and 2 choristers, 12 apostles on the right, the high council of Kirtland on the left. The pulpits /in the east end of the house/ for the Aaronic priesthood were occupied in the following manner: The Bishop of Kirtland and his counsellors in the first pulpit, the Bishop of Zion and his counsellors in the 2nd, the presdt of the priest and his counsellors in the 3rd, the presdt of the Teachers and his counsellors in the 4th, the 7 presdt of the seventies. The high council of Zion on the right, the 7 presdt of the Seventies on the left.~~

West end of the House

Pres[i]d[en]t F[rederick] G. Williams, Pres[i]d[en]t Joseph Smith, Sen[ior], and President W[illiam] W. Phelps occupied the 1st pulpit for the Melchisedic Priesthood. Pres[i]d[en]t S[idney] Rigdon, myself, and Pres[i]d[en]t Hyrum Smith in the 2nd [pulpit]. Pres[i]d[ent] D[avid] Whitmer, Pres[i]d[en]t O[liver] Cowdery, and Pres[i]d[en]t J[ohn] Whitmer in the 3d [pulpit]. The 4th [pulpit] was occipied by the President of the High Priests and his counsellors, and 2 choiresters. The 12 Apostles on the right in the 3 highest seats, the Pres[i]d[en]t of the Eld[e]rs, his clerk, and counsellors in the seat immediately below the 12 [Apostles]. The High Council of Kirtland consisting of 12 [counsellors] on the left in the 3 first seats. The 4th seat below them was occupied by

143

Eld[e]rs W[arren] A. Cowdery and W[arren] Parrish who served as scribes.

The pulpits in the east end of the House for the Aaronic Priesthood were occupied as follows: The Bishop of Kirtland and his counsellors in the 1st pulpit. The Bishop of Zion and his counsillors in the 2nd. The Pres[i]d[en]t of the Priests and his counsellors in the 3d. The Pres[i]d[en]t of the Teachers and his counsellors /and one choirester/ in the 4th. The High Council of Zion consisting of {page 174} 12 counsellors on the right. The Pres[i]d[en]t of the Deacons and his counsillors in the seat below them. The 7 Pres[i]d[en]ts of the Seventies on the left. The choir of singers were seated in the 4 corners of the room in seats prepared for that purpose.

/Rec[eive]d by contribution $960.00/

9 o'clock A.M. the servises of the day were opened by Pres[i]d[en]t S[idney] Rigdon by reading 1st the 96[th] Psalm [and] secondly the 24th Psalm. The choir then Sung hymn on the 29th page of Latter day Saints' collection of hymns ["Ere long the veil will rend in twain," by Parley P. Pratt]. Prayer by Pres[i]d[en]t Rigdon. Choir then sung hymn on 14th page ["O happy souls, who pray," William W. Phelps]. Pres[i]d[en]t Rigdon then /read/ the 18[th], 19[th] and 20[th] verses of the 8th Chapter of Mat[t]hew and preached more particularly from the 20th verse. His prayer and address were very forcible and sublime, and well adapted to the occasion.

After he close his sermon, he called upon the several quorums commenceing with the Presidency to manifest by rising up their willingness to acknowledge me as a prophet and seer and uphold me as such by their p[r]ayers of faith. All the quorums in their turn cheerfully complyed with this request. He then called upon all the congregation of Saints also to give their assent by rising on their feet which they did unanimously.

After [an] intermission of 20 minutes the servises of the day were resumed by singing Adam-ondi-Ahman. \\[27] I then made a short address and called upon the several quorums and all the congregation of Saints to acknowledge the Presidency as Prophets

[27] Possibly in the handwriting of Jesse Hitchcock.

and Seers and uphold them by their prayers. They all covenanted to do so by rising.

I then called upon the quorums and congregation of Saints to acknowledge the 12 {page 175} Apostles who were present as Prophets and Seers and special witnesses to all the nations of the earth, holding the keys of the kingdom to unlock it or cause it to be done among all nations them and [to] uphold them by their prayers, which they assented to by rising. *[see note bottom of manuscript page 176]

I then called upon the quorums and congregation of Saints to acknowledge the High Council of Kirtland in all the authorities of the Melchisedec Priesthood and uphold them by their prayers which they assented to by rising.

I then called upon the quorums and congregation of Saints to acknowledge and uphold by their prayers the Bishops of Kirtland and Zion and their counsellors, the Presidents of the Priests in all the authority of the Aaronic Priesthood which they did by rising.

I then called upon the quorums and congregation of Saints to acknowledge the High Council of Zion and uphold them by their prayers in all authority of the High Priesthood which they did by rising.

I next called upon the quorums and congregation of Saints to acknowledge the Presidents of the Seventys who act as their represent[at]ives as /Apostles and/ special witnesses to the nations to assist the 12 [Apostles] in opening the gospel kingdom among all people and to uphold them by their prayers which they did by rising.

I then called upon the quorums and all the Saints to acknowledge [the] President of Elders and his counsellors and uphold them by their prayers which they did by rising.

The quorums and congregation of Saints were then called upon to acknowledge and uphold by their prayers the Presidents of the Priests, Teachers, and Deacons and their counsellors which they did by rising.

* N.B. The Presidents of the Seventys were acknowledged first after the 12 Apostles. {page 176}

The hymn on the hundred and 14 page ["How pleased and blessed was I," by Isaac Watts] was then sung, after which I offered to God the following dedication prayer:

145

[Dedicatory] Prayer

At the dedication of the Lord's House in Kirtland, Ohio, March 27th 1836 by Joseph Smith, Jr., President of the Church of the Latter Day Saints.

Thanks be to thy name, O Lord God of Israel, who keepest covenant and shewest mercy unto thy servants, who walk uprightly before thee with all their hearts. Thou who hast commanded thy servants to build an house to thy name in this place (Kirtland). And now thou beholdest, O Lord, that so thy servants have done according to thy commandment. And now we ask the[e], Holy Father, in the name of Jesus Christ, the Son of thy bosom, in whose name alone salvation can be administered to the children of men, we ask the[e], O Lord, to accept of this house, the workmanship of the hands of us, thy servants, which thou didst command us to build; for thou knowest that we have done this work through great tribulation; and out of our poverty we have given of our substance to build a house to thy name, that the Son of Man might have a place to manifest himself to his people.

And as thou hast said, in a revelation given unto us, calling us thy friends, saying, "Call your Solemn Assembly, as I have commanded you; and as all have not faith, seek ye diligently and teach one another words of wisdom; yea, seek ye out of the best books words of wisdom; Seek learning; even by study, and also by faith. Organize yourselves; prepare every needful thing, and establish a house, even a house of prayer, a house [of] fasting, a house of faith, a house of learning, {page 177} a house of glory, a house of order, a house of God; that your incomings may be in the name of the Lord, that your outgoings may be in the name of the Lord: that all your salutations may be in the name of the Lord, with uplifted hands to the Most High."

And now, Holy Father, we ask thee to assist us, thy people with thy grace in calling our Solemn Assembly, that it may be done to thy honor, and to thy divine acceptance, and in a manner that we may be found worthy in thy sight to secure a fulfil[l]ment of the promises which thou hast made unto us thy people, in the revelatio[n]s given unto us; that thy glory may rest down upon thy people, and upon this thy house, which we now dedicate to thee; that it may be sanctified and consecrated to be holy, and that thy holy presence may be continually in this house; and that all people who shall enter upon the threshold of the Lord's House may feel thy power and be constrained to acknowledge that thou hast sanctified it, and that it is thy house, a place of thy holiness.

And do thou grant, Holy Father, that all those who shall worship in this house, may be taught words of wisdom out of the best books, and that they may seek learning, even by study, and also by faith, as thou hast said; and that they may grow up in thee and receive a fulness of the Holy Ghost, and be organized according to thy laws, and be prepared to obtain every needful thing and that this house may be a house of prayer, a house of fasting, a house of faith, a house of glory and of God, even thy house; that all the incomings of thy people, into this house, may be in the name of the Lord; that all their outgoings, from this house, may be in the name of the Lord; that all their salutations may be in the name of {page 178} [the] Lord, with holy hands uplifted to the Most High; and that no unclean thing shall be permitted to come into thy house to pollute it.

And when thy people transgress, any of them, they may speedily repent and return to thee, and find favour in thy sight, and be restored to the blessings which thou hast ordained, to be poured out upon those who shall reverance thee in this thy house.

And we ask, Holy Father, that thy servants may go forth from this house, armed with thy power, and that thy name may be upon them and thy glory be round about them, and thine angels have charge over them, and from this place they may bear exceeding great and glorious tidings, in truth, unto the ends of the earth, that they may know that this is thy work, and that thou hast put forth thy hand, to fulfil that which thou hast spoken by the mouths of thy prophets concerning the last days.

We ask the[e], Holy Father, to establish the people that shall worship and honorably hold a name and standing in this thy house, to all generations, and for eterni/ty/ that no weapon formed against them shall prosper; that he who diggeth a pit for them shall fall into the same himself; that no combination of wickedness shall have power to rise up and prevail over thy people, upon whom thy name shall be put in this house: and if any people shall rise against this people, that thine anger be kindled against them: and if they shall smite this people, thou wilt smite them, thou wilt fight for thy people as thou didst in the day of battle, that they may be delivered from the hands of all their enemies.

147

We ask thee, Holy Father, to confound and astonish, and bring to shame and confusion, all those who have {page 178} spread lying reports abroad over the world against thy servant or servants, if they will not repent when the everlasting gospel shall be proclaimed in their ears, and that all their works may be brought to nought, and be swept away by the hail, and by the judgements, which thou wilt send upon them in thine anger, that their may be an end to lyings and slanders against thy people: for thou knowest, O Lord, that thy servants have been innocent before thee in bearing record of thy name for which they have suffered these things, therefore we plead before thee a full and complete deliverance from under this yoke. Break it off O Lord; break it off from the necks of thy servants, by thy power, that we may rise up in the midst of this generation and do thy work!

O Jehovah, have mercy upon this people, and as all men sin, forgive the transgressions of thy people, and let them be blotted out forever. Let the anointing of thy ministers be sealed upon them with power from on high. Let it be fulfilled upon them as upon those on the day of Pentacost. Let the gift of tongues be poured out upon thy people, even cloven tongues as of fire, and the interpretation thereof. And let thy house be filled, as with a rushing mighty wind, with thy glory.

Put upon thy servants the testimony of the covenant that where they go out and proclaim thy word, they may seal up the law, and prepare the hearts of thy Saints for all those judg/e/-ments thou art about to send, in thy wrath, upon the inhabitants of the earth because of their transgressions, that thy people may not faint in the day of trouble. {page 179}

And whatever city thy servants shall enter, and the people of that city receive their testimony let thy peace and thy salvation be upon that city, that they may gather out from that city the righteous, that they may come forth to Zion or to her stakes, the places of thine appointment, with songs of everlasting joy, and until this be ac[c]omplished let not thy judgements fall upon that city.

And whatever city thy servants shall enter, and the people of that city receive not their testimony of thy servants, and thy servants warn them to save themselves from this untoward generation let it be upon that city according to that which thou hast spoken, by the mouths of thy prophets; but deliver thou, O Jehovah, we beseech thee, thy servants from their hands, and cleanse them from their blood. O Lord, we delight not in the destruction of our fellow men; their souls are precious before thee, but thy word must be fulfilled. Help thy servants to say, with thy grace assisting them, thy will be done, O Lord, and not ours.

We know that thou hast spoken by the mouth of thy prophets, terrible things concerning the wicked in the last days, that thou wilt pour out thy judgements, without measure. Therefore, O Lord, deliver thy people from the calamity of the wicked. Enable thy servants to seal up the law and bind up the testimony, that they may be prepared against the day of burning.

We ask thee, Holy Father, to remember those who have been driven by the inhabitants of Jackson County, Missouri, from the lands of their inheritance, and break off, O Lord, this yoke of affliction {page 180} that has been put upon them. Thou knowest, O Lord, that they have been greatly oppressed and afflicted, by wicked men, and our hearts flow out in sorrow because of their grevious [grievous] burdens. O Lord, how long wilt thou suffer this people to bear this affliction and the cries of the innocent ones to ascend up in thine ears, and their blood to come up in testimony before thee and not make a display of thy power in their behalf?

Have mercy, O Lord, upon that wicked mob, who have driven thy people, that they may cease to spoil, that they may repent of their sins, if repentance is to be found; but if they will not, make bare thine arm, O Lord, and redeem that which thou didst appoint a Zion unto thy people. And if it cannot be otherwise, [grant] that the cause of thy people may not fail before thee. May thine anger be kindled and thine indignation fall upon them that they may be wasted away, both root and branch from under heaven; but inasmuch as they will repent, thou art gracious and merciful, and will turn away thy wrath, when thou lookest upon the face of thine anointed.

Have mercy, O Lord, upon all the nations of the earth. Have mercy upon the rulers of our land. May those principles which were so honorably and nobly defended: viz, the Constitution of our land, by our fathers, be established forever. Remember the Kings, the princes, the nobles, and the great ones of the earth, and all people, and the Churches, all the poor, the needy, and the afflicted ones of the earth; that their hearts may be soft-

149

ened when thy servants shall go out from thy house, O {page 181} Jehovah, to bear testimony of thy name, /that/ their prejudices may give way before the truth, and thy people may obtain favour in the sight of all, that all the ends of the earth may know that we thy servants have heard thy voice, and that thou hast sent us, that from among all these thy servants, the sons of Jacob, may gather out the righteous to build a holy city to thy name, as thou hast commanded them.

We ask thee to appoint unto Zion other stakes besides this one, which thou hast appointed, that the gathering of thy people may roll on in great power and majesty, that thy work may be cut short in righteousness.

Now these words, O Lord, we have spoken before thee, concerning the revelations and commandments which thou hast given unto us, who are i[de]ntified with the Gentiles. But thou knowest that we have a great love for the children of Jacob who have been scattered upon the mountains, for a long time in a cloudy and dark day.

We therefore ask thee to have mercy upon the children of Jacob, that Jerusalem, from this hour, may begin to be redeemed, and the yoke of bondage may begin to be broken off from the house of David, and the children of Judah may begin to return to the lands which thou didst give to Abraham, their father, and cause that the remnants of Jacob, who have been cursed and smitten, because of their transgression, to be converted from their wild and savage condition, to the fulness of the everlasting gospel, that they may lay down their weapons of bloodshed and cease their rebellions. And may {page 182} all the scattered remnants of Israel, who have been driven to the ends of the earth, come to a knowledge of the truth, believe in the Messiah, and be redeemed from oppression, and rejoice before thee.

O Lord, remember thy servant Joseph Smith, Jun[ior], and all his afflictions and persecutions, how he has covenanted with Jehovah and vowed to thee O mighty God of Jacob, and the commandments which thou hast given unto him, and that he hath sincerely strove to do thy will. Have mercy, O Lord, upon his wife and children, that they may be exalted in thy presence, and preserved by thy fostering hand. Have mercy upon all their immediate connexions, that their prejudices may be broken up, and swept away as with a flood, that they may be converted and redeemed with Israel and know that thou art God.

Remember, O Lord, the Presidents, even all the Presidents of thy Church, that thy right hand may exalt them with all their families, and their immediate connexions, that their names may be perpetuated and had in everlasting rememberance from generation to generation.

Remember all thy Church, O Lord, with all their families, and all their immediate connexions, with all their sick and afflicted ones, with all the poor and meek of the earth, that the kingdom which thou hast set up without hands, may become a great mountain and fill the whole earth, that thy Church may come forth out of the wilderness of darkness, and shine forth fair as the moon, clear as the sun, and terrible as an army with banners, and be adorned as a bride for that day when {page 183} thou shalt unveil the heavens, and cause the mountains to flow down at thy presence, and the valleys to be exalted, the rough places made smooth, that thy glory may fill the earth. That when the trump shall sound for the dead, we shall be caught up in the cloud to meet thee, that we may ever be with the Lord, that our garments may be pure, that we may [be] clothed upon with robes of righteousness, with palms in our hands, and crowns of glory upon our heads, and reap eternal joy for all our sufferings.

O Lord, God Almighty, hear us in these our petitions, and answer us from heaven, thy holy habitation, where thou sittest enthroned with glory, honour, power, majesty, might, dominion, truth, justice, judgement, mercy, and an infinity of fulness, from everlasting to everlasting.

O hear, O hear, O hear us, O Lord, and answer these petitions, and accept the dedication of this house unto thee, the work of our hands, which we have built unto thy name; and also this Church to put upon it thy name. And help us by the power of thy spirit, that we may mingle our voices with those bright shining seruphs, around thy throne with acclamation of praise, singing hosanna to God and the Lamb! And let these thine anointed ones be clothed with salvation, and thy Saints shout aloud for joy. Amen and Amen.

151

\\[28] Sung "Hosanah to God and the Lamb," after which the Lord's Supper was administered.

I then bore testimony of the administering of angels. Pres[i]d[en]t Williams also arose and testified that while Pres[i]d[en]t Rigdon was making {page 184} his first prayer an angel entered the window and /took his/ [position] seated between Father Smith and himself, and remained their during his prayer. Pres[i]d[en]t David Whitmer also saw angels in the House.

We then sealed the proceedings of the day by shouting hosanah to God and the Lamb 3 times, sealing it each time with Amen, Amen, and Amen and after requesting all the official members to meet again in the evening we retired. Met in the evening and instructed the quorums respecting the ordinance of washing of feet which we were to attend to on Wednesday following.

Monday the 28[th] M[ar]ch 1836 Attended school. Nothing worthy of note transpired.

Tuesday the 29th Attended school, which was the last day of our course of lectures in Hebrew by Professor Seixas. ~~After we dismissed made some ar[r]angements for our meeting on the morrow. Attended to my domestick concirns, nothing very special transpired.~~

~~At evening I met with the Presidency in the Temple of the Lord. The Lord commanded us to tarry and san[c]tify our selves by washing our feet.~~

At 11 o'clock A.M. Presidents Joseph Smith, Jun[ior], Frederick G. Williams, Sidney Rigdon, Hyrum Smith, and Oliver Cowdery met in the Most Holy Place in the Lord's House and sought for a revelation from Him to teach us concerning our going to Zion and other {page 185} important matter[s]. After uniting in prayer, the voice of the Spirit was that we should come into this place three times, and also call the other Presidents, the two Bishops and their councils (each to stand in his place) and fast through the day and also the night and that during this, if we would humble ourselves, we should receive further communication from Him.

After this word was received, we immediately sent for the

[28] In the handwriting of Warren Parrish.

other brethren who came. The Presidency proceeded to ordain George Boosinger to the High Priesthood and annoint him. This was in consequence of his having administered unto us in temporal things in our distress. And also because he left the place just previous to the dedication ot the Lord's House to bring us the temporal means previously named.

Soon after this, the word of the Lord came to us through Pres[i]d[en]t J[oseph] Smith, Jun[ior], that those who had entered the Holy Place must not leave the House untill morning, but send for such things as were necessary, and also that during our stay we must cleans[e] our feet and partake of the sacrament that we might be made holy before Him, and thereby be qualified to officiate in our calling upon the morrow in washing the feet of the Elders.

Accordingly we proceeded and cleansed our faces and our feet, and then proceeded to wash each other's feet. President S[idney] Rigdon first washed Pres[i]d[en]t J[oseph] Smith, Jun-[ior], and then in {page 186} turn was washed by him. After which President Rigdon washed Pres[i]d[en]t J[oseph] Smith, Sen[ior], and Hyrum Smith. /Pres[i]d[en]t/ J[oseph] Smith, Jun-[ior], washed Pres[i]d[en]t F[rederick] G. Williams, and then Pres-[iden]t Hyrum Smith washed President David Whitmer's feet and President Oliver Cowdery's. Then Pres[ident] D[avid] Whitmer washed Pres[ident] W[illiam] W. Phelps' feet and in turn Pres[ident] Phelps washed Pres[ident] John Whitmer's feet.

The Bishops and their councils were then washed, after which we partook of the bread and wine. The Holy S[p]irit rested down upon us and we continued in the Lord's House all night prophesying and giving glory to God.

\\[29] Wednesday morning, 8 o'clock, March 30th 1836 According to appointment the Presidency, the 12 [Apostles], the Seventies, the High Councils, the Bishops and their entire quorums, the Elders, and all the official members in this Stake of Zion amounting to about 300 met in the Temple of the Lord to attend to the ordinance of washing feet.

I ascended the pulpit and remarked to the congregation that we had passed through many trials and afflictions since the

---

[29] Possibly in the handwriting of Jesse Hitchcock.

organization of this Church and that this is a year of jubilee to us and a time of rejoicing, and that it was expedient for us to prepare bread and wine sufficient to make our hearts glad, as we should not probably leave this house until morning. To this end we should call on the brethren to make a contribution; the stewards passed round and took up a liberal contribution and messengers were dispatched for bread and wine.

Tubs, water, and towels were prepared and I called the House to order and the Presidency preceeded to wash the feet of the 12 [Apostles], pronouncing many prophecys and blessings upon them in the name of the Lord Jesus. The brethren began to prophesy {page 187} upon each others' heads and cursings upon the enimies of Christ who inhabit Jackson County, Missouri. Continued prophesying, blessing, and sealing them with Hosanna and Amen until nearly 7 o'clock P.M.

The bread /and wine/ was then brought in and I observed that we had fasted all the day, and lest we faint as the Saviour did so shall we do on this occasion. We shall bless the bread and give it to the 12 [Apostles] and they to the multitude, after which we shall bless the wine and do likewise.

While waiting for the wine I made the following remarks: that the time that we were required to tarry in Kirtland to be endued [endowed] would be fulfilled in a few days, and then the Elders would go forth and each must stand for himself, that it was not necessary for them to be sent out two by two as in former times; but to go in all meekness, in sobriety and preach Jesus Christ and him crucified, not to contend with others on the account of their faith or systems of religion but persue a steady course.

This I delivered by way of commandment, and all that observe them not will pull down persecution upon your /their/ heads, while those who do shall always be filled with the Holy Ghost. This I pronounced as a prophesy sealed with a Hosanna and Amen.

Also that the Seventies are not called to serve tables or preside over Churches to settle difficulties, but to preach the gospel and build them up, and set others who do not belong to these quorums to preside over them who are High Priests. The Twelve [Apostles] also are not to serve tables, but to bear the keys of the kingdom to all nations and unlock them and call upon the Seventies to follow after them and assist them. The 12 [Apostles] are at liberty to go wheresoever they will {page 188} and if one shall say, I wish to go to such a place let all the rest say Amen.

The Seventies are at liberty to go to Zion if they please or go wheresoever they will and preach the gospel and let the redem[p]tion of Zion be our object, and strive to affect it by sending up all the strength of the Lord's House wherever we find them. I want to enter into the following covenant, that if any more of our brethren are slain or driven from their lands in Missouri by the mob that we will give ourselves no rest until we are avenged of our enimies to the uttermost. This covenant was sealed unaminously [unanimously] by a hosanna and Amen.

I then observed to the quorums that I had now completed the organization of the Church and we had passed through all the necessary ceremonies. That I had given them all the instruction they needed and that they now were at liberty after obtaining their lisences to go forth and build up the kingdom of God. That it was expedient for me and the Presidency to retire, having spent the night previous in waiting upon the Lord in his Temple, and having to attend another dedication on the morrow, or conclude the one commenced on the last Sabbath for the benefit of those of my brethren and sisters who could not get into the House on the former occasion, but that it was expedient for the brethren to tarry all night and worship before the Lord in his house. I left the meeting in charge of the 12 [Apostles] and retired at about 9 o'clock in the evening.

The brethren continued exhorting, prophesying, and speaking in tongues until 5 o'clock in the morning. The Saviour made his appearance to some, while angels minestered unto others, and it was a penticost and enduement [endowment] indeed, long to be remembered. For the sound shall go forth from this place into all the {page 189} world and the occurrences of this day shall be hande[d] down upon the pages of sacred history to all generations as the day of Pentecost. So shall this day be numbered and celebrated as a year of Jubilee and time of rejoicing to the Saints of the Most High God.

Thursday morning, 8 o'clock, March 31st This day being set apart to perform again the ceremonies of the dedication for the benifit of those who could not get into the house on the preceeding Sabbath. I repaired to the Temple at 8 o'clock A.M. in company with the Presidency and arranged our doorkeepers and stewards as on the former occasion. We then opened the doors and a large congregation entered the House and were comfortably seated. The authorities of the Church were seated in their respective order and the services of the day were commenced, prosecuted, and terminated in the same manner as at the former dedication and the Spirit of God rested upon the congregation and great solemnity prevailed.

\³⁰ Friday th[e] 1st day of April 1836 At home most of the day. Many brethren called to see me, some on temporal and some on spiritual buisiness [business]. Among the number was Leeman Copley who testified against me in a suit I brought against Doctor P[hilastus] Hurlbut for threat[e]ning my life. He confessed that he bore a fals[e] testimony against me in that suit, but verily thought at the time that he was right, but on calling to mind all the circumstances connected with the things that transpired at the time he was {page 190} convinced that he was wrong, and humbly confessed it and asked my forgiveness, which was readily granted. He also wished to be received into the Church again by baptism and was received according to his desire. He gave me his confession in writing.

\³¹ Saturday, April 2d Transacted business (although of a temporal nature) in company with S[idney] Rigdon, O[liver] Cowdery, J[ohn] Whitmer, F[rederick] G. Williams, D[avid] Whitmer, and W[illiam] W. Phelps which was to have a bearing upon the redemption of Zion. The positive manner in which he [Joseph Smith] expressed himself on this, /his/ favorite theme, was directly calculated to produce conviction in the minds of those who heard him, that his whole soul was engaged in it, notwithstanding on a superficial view of the same subject they might differ from him in judgement.

It was determined in council, after mature deliberation, that he and O[liver] Cowdery should act in concert in raising funds for the accomplishment of the aforesaid object. As soon as the above plan was settled, he and O[liver] Cowdery set out together, and their success was such in one half day as to give them

---

³⁰ In the handwriting of Warren Parrish.
³¹ In the handwriting of Warren A. Cowdery.

pleasing anticipations assuring them that they were doing the will of God and that his work prospered in their hands.

Sabbath, April 3d He attended meeting in the Lord's House and assisted the other Presidents of the Church in seating the congregation and then became an attentive listener to the preaching from the stand. T[homas] B. Marsh and D[avid] W. Patten spoke in the A.M. to an attentive audience of about 1,000 persons.

In the P.M. he assisted the other Presidents in distributing the elements of the Lord's Supper to the Church receiving them from the Twelve [Apostles] whose privilige it was to officiate in the sacred desk this day. After having performed this service to his brethren, he retired to the pulpit, the vails being dropped, {page 191} and bowed himself, with O[liver] Cowdery, in solemn but silent prayer to the Most High.

After rising from prayer the following vision was opened to both of them. The vail was taken from their minds and the eyes of their understandings were opened. They saw the Lord standing upon the breast work of the pulpit before them and under his feet was a paved work of pure gold, in color like amber. His eyes were as a flame of fire; the hair of his head was like the pure snow. His countenance shone above the brightness of the sun, and his voice was as the sound of the rushing of great waters, even the Voice of Jehovah, saying, "I am the first and the last. I am he who liveth. I am he who was slain. I am your Advocate with the Father. Behold your sins are forgiven you. You are clean before me. Therefore lift up your heads and rejoice. Let the hearts of all my ~~brethren~~ /people/ rejoice, who have, with their might, built this house to my name.

"For behold I have accepted this house and my name shall be here; and I will manifest myself to my people, in mercy, in this House. Yea, I will appear unto my servants and speak unto them with mine own voice, if my people will keep my commandments and do not pollute this Holy House. Yea, the hearts of thousands and tens of thousands shall greatly rejoice in consequence of the blessings which shall be poured out and the endowment with which my servants have already been endowed and shall hereafter be endowed in this House. And the fame of this House shall spread to foreign lands, and this is the beginning of

157

the blessing, which shall {page 192} be poured out upon the heads of my people. Even so. Amen."

After this vision closed, the Heavens were again opened unto them and Moses appeared before them and committed unto them the keys of the gathering of Israel from the four parts of the Earth and the leading of the ten tribes from the Land of the North. After this Elias appeared and committed the dispensation of the gospel of Abraham, saying, that in them and their seed all generations after them should be blessed.

After this vision had closed, another great and glorious vision burst upon them, for Elijah the Prophet, who was taken to Heaven without tasting death, also stood before them, and said, "Behold the time has fully come which was spoken of by the mouth of Malachi, testifying, that he should be sent before the great and dreadful day of the Lord come, to turn the hearts of the Fathers to the children, and the children to the fathers, lest the whole earth be smitten with a curse. Therefore, the keys of this dispensation are committed into your hands; and by this ye may know that the great and the dreadful day of the Lord is near, even at the doors." [*rest of page blank*] {page 193}

1 8 3 8

One month following the arrival of his family in Missouri, Joseph Smith began dictating to George W. Robinson, who had recently been appointed one of the prophet's scribes, the third of his extant diaries and journals. Besides daily third-person journal entries, the following document, which, unless otherwise noted, is in Robinson's handwriting, also contains copies of revelations, letters, and other historically important documents. Robinson's record book was later used by scribes to record patriarchal blessings, and the original is currently identified as volume 9 of the patriarchal blessing books in the archives of the Historical Department, Church of Jesus Christ of Latter-day Saints, Salt Lake City, Utah.

The Scriptory Book
of Joseph Smith, Jr.
President of The Church of
Jesus Christ of Latter-day Saints
In all the world
Far West, April 12th 1838
/Kept by Geo[rge] W. Robinson

Recorder of the Church of [Jesus] Christ
of Latter Day Saints/

/The following is a letter from Pres[iden]t Smith/ {page 15}[1]

On the 13th day of March [1838], I with my family
and some others arrived within 8 milds [miles] of Far West [Missouri] and put up at Brother Barnerd's to tarry for the night.
Here we ware meet by an escort of brethren from the town who
came to make us welcome to their little Zion.

[14 March 1838] On the next day as we ware about entering the town many of the bretheren came out to meet us who
also with open armes welcomed us to their boosoms. We were
immediately received under the hospitable roof of George W. Harris who treated us with all kindness possible. Here we refreshed
ourselves with much satisfaction after our long and tedious Journey and the bretheren brought in such necessaries as we stood in
need of for our present comfort and necessities.

After being here two or three days my Brother Samuel
arrived with his family an[d] shortly after his arrival while walking with him and certain other bretheren the following sentiments
occur[r]ed to my mind:

Motto of the Church of [Jesus] Christ of Latter-day Saints

The Constitution of our country formed by the Fathers of
Liberty. Peace and good order in society. Love to God and good
will to man. All good and wholesome Laws, And virtue and truth
above all things, And Aristarchy live forever!!! But Wo to tyrants,
Mobs, Aristocracy, Anarchy and Toryism, And all those who invent or seek out unrighteous and vexatious lawsuits under the
pretext or color of law or office, either religious or political.

Exalt the standard of Democracy! Down {page 16} with
that of Priestcraft, and let all the people say Amen! That the
blood of our Fathers may not cry from the ground against us.

---

[1] According to a scrap of paper over the first page of the original, the first
fourteen pages of the "Scriptory Book" contain an extensive list of the "Names of the
members of the Church in Missouri, then situated most[ly] in Caldwell County,
commencing in June 1838."

Sacred is the Memory of that Blood which bought for us our liberty.

Signed: Joseph Smith, Jr.
Thomas B. Marsh
D[avid] W. Patten
Brigham Young
Samuel H. Smith
George M. Hinkle
John Corrill
Geo[rge] W. Robinson

—

Quest[ions] on Scripture

1st Who is the stem of Jesse spoken of in the 1st, 2d, 3d, 4th and 5th verses of the 11th Chap[ter] of Isaiah?

Ans[wer] Verily thus saith the Lord, It is Christ.

Q[uestion] 2d What is the Rod spoken of in the 1st verse of the 11th Chap[ter] that should come of the stem of Jessee?

Ans[wer] Behold thus saith /the Lord/, it is a servant in the hands of Christ, who is partly a de[s]cendant of Jessee as well as of Ephraim or of the house of Joseph, on whome thare is laid much power.

Q[u]est[ion] 3d What is the Root of Jessee spoken of in the 10th verse of the 11th Chap[ter]?

Ans[wer] Behold thus saith the Lord, it is a de[s]cendant of Jessee as well as of Joseph unto whom rightly belongs the Priesthood and the kees of the Kingdom for an ensign and for the geathering of my people in the Last days. {page 17}

Questions by Elias Higby

1st Q[uestion] What is me[a]nt by the command in Isaiah 52d Chap[ter], 1st verse which saith, "Put on thy strength O ZION," and what people has I[sa]iah referance to?

A[nswer] He had reference to those whome God should call in the last days who should hold the power of Priesthood to bring again Zion and the redemption of Israel. And to put on her strength is to put on the authority of the priesthood which She

161

(Zion) has a right to by lineage. Also to return to that power which she had lost.

Ques[tion] 2d What are we to understand by Zions loosing herself from the bands of her neck, 2d verse?

A[nswer] We are to understand that the scattered remnants are ex[h]orted to return to the Lord from whence they have fal[l]en which if they do the promise of the Lord is that he will speak to them or give them revelation. See 6th, 7th, and 8th verses. The bands of her neck are the curses of God upon her or the remnants of Israel in their scattered condition among the Gentiles.

———

The following letter I wrote previous to my leaving Kirtland and Sent by the hand of T[homas] B. Marsh:

Sept[ember] 4th A.D. 1837
Kirtland, Geauga Co[unty], Ohio

Joseph Smith, Jr., Pres[iden]t of the Church /of [Jesus] Christ/ of Latter Day Saints in all the world.

To John Corroll [Corrill] and the whole Church of Zion, {page 18}

Sendeth Greeting, Blessed be the God and father of our Lord Jesus Christ Who has blessed you with many blessings in Christ. Who has delivered you many times from the hands of your enemies And planted you many times in an heavenly or holy place.

My respects and love to you all, and my blessings upon all the faithful and true h[e]arted in the new and everlasting covenant. For as much as I have desired for a long time to See your faces and Converse with you and instruct you in those things which have been revealed to me pertaining to the Kingdom of God in the last days, I now write unto you offering an appology, My being bound with bonds of affliction by the workers of iniquity And by the labours of the Church endeaveroring in all things to do the will of God for the

Salvation of the Church both in temporal as well as spiritual things.

Bretheren, we have waided through a Scene of affliction and Sorrow thus far for the will of God that language is inadequate to describe. Pray ye therefore with more earnestness for our redemption. You have undoubtedly been informed by letter and otherwise of our difficulties in Kirtland which are now about being Settled and that you may have a Knowledge of the same I Subscribe to you the following minuits [minutes] of the com[m]ittee of the whole Church of Kirtland, the authorities &c., refer[r]ing you to my Brother Hyrum and Br[other] T[homas] B. Marsh for further particulars. Also that you {page 19} may know how to proceed to Set in order and regulate the affairs of the Church in Zion whenever they became disorganized. The minuts [minutes] are as follows:

Minuts [minutes] of a Conference assembled in committee of the whole Church on the 3rd of Sept[ember] 1837, 9 o'clock A.M. G[eorge] W. Robinson was called upon to take the minuts [minutes] of the conference. S[idney] Rigdon then presented Joseph Smith, Jr., to the Church to know if they Still looked upon and would Still receive and uphold him as the Pres[iden]t of the Whole Church. The vote was unanimous in the affirmative. Pres[iden]t Smith then presented S[idney] Rigdon and F[rederick] G. Williams for his councilors and to constitute with himself the three first Pres[iden]t of the Church. Vote unanymous in the affirmative.

Pres[iden]t Smith then introduced O[liver] Cowdery, J[oseph] Smith, Sen[ior], Hiram Smith, and John Smith for assistant Councilors. These last four together with the three first are to be concidred the heads of the Church. Carried unanimously. Vot[e] that N[ewel] K. Whitn[e]y hold his office as Bishop and continue to act as Such in Kirtland and that R[eynolds] Cahoon and V[inson] Knight continue to act as councilors to the Bishop.

The Twelve Apostles were then presented one by one. When T[homas] B. Marsh, D[avid] W. Patten,

B[righam] Young, H[eber] C. Kimball, O[rson] Hyde,
P[arley] P. Pratt, O[rson] Prat[t], W[illia]m Smith,
[and] W[illia]m E. McLellin were received unanymously in their Apostleship. Luke and Lyman Johnson
and J[ohn] F. Boynton were rejected and cut off though
privileged with Conffesing and making Sattisfaction.

Elder Boynton (which was the only one present at
the time) arose and endeavoured to Confess, Justifying
himself in his former conduct by reason of the failure of
the Bank &c. His conduct was Strongly protested by
Elder {page 20} Brigham Young in a plain and ener-
getic manner, Stating various reasons why he would or
could not receive him into fellowship until a hearty
conffession and repentance was manifested. He was followed by Elder Marsh who acquiesed in testimony and
resolutions.

Elder Boynton again arose and Still attributed his
difficulties to the failure of the Bank. Stating that he
had understood the Bank was instituted by the will of
God and he had been told that it never should fail let
men do what they would.

Pres[iden]t Smith then arose and Stated that if this
had been declared, no one had authority from him for
So doing. For he had allways Said unl[e]ss the institution was conducted on richeous [righteous] principals it
would not Stand. A Vote was then taken to know if the
congregation was satisfied with [Elder] Boynton's Confession. Voted in the nagative. Conf[erence] Adjourned
for one hour.

Conference assembled at 2 o'clock P.M. Opened by
reading, Singing and prayer. The Pres[iden]t then
arose and said he would call upon the Church to know
if they were Sattisfied with their High Council and
Should proceed to name them individually. John
Johnson, Joseph Coe, Joseph Kingsbury, and Martin *
Harris were objected to. Also John P. Green, but his
case put over untill he Should be present. Noah
Packard, Jared Carter, Samuel H. Smith, these were
Voted to retain their office. Oliver Granger, Henry G.
Sh[e]rwood, W[illia]m Marks, Mahw [Mayhew] Hill-

man, Harlow Readfield, Asael Smith, Phinehas
Richards, and David Dort were chosen to fill the place
of those objected to.

The Pres[iden]t then called upon the congregation
to know if the recent appointed Presidents of the Seventies Should Stand in their Calling. Voted that John
Gaylord, James Foster, Solmon Gee, Daniel S. Miles,
Joseph Youngs, Josiah Butterfield, {page 21} and Levi
Handcock Should retain their office as Pres[iden]ts of
the Seventies. John Gould was objected.

The Pres[ident] then arose and made some remarks
concerning the formers Pres[iden]ts of the Seventies, the
callings and authorities of their Priesthood &c. &c.
Voted that the old Presidents of the Seventies be refer[r]ed to the quorum of High Priests. Also that if any
of the members of the quorum of the Seventies Should
be dissattisfied and would not submit to the Present
order and receive these last Presidents that they Should
have power to demand their lisence and they should no
longer be concidered members of the church.

Conference closed by Prayer by the President

G[eorge] W. Robinson, Cl[er]k   *Joseph Smith, Pres[iden]t*

Dear Brotheren,
Oliver Cowdery has been in transgression, but as
he is now chosen as one of the Presidents or Councilors
I trust that he will yet humble himself and magnify his
calling but if he Should not, the Church will Soon be
under the necessaty of raising their hands against him.
Therefore pray for him.

David Whitmer, Leonard Rich, and others have
been in transgression, but we hope that they may be
humble and ere long make Sattisfaction to the Church
otherwise they cannot retain their Standing.

Therefore, we Say unto you beware of all
disaffected Characters for they came not to build up but
to destroy and Scatter abroad. Though we or an Angel
from Heaven preach any other gospel or introduce
[any] order of things than those things which ye have
received and are authorized to receive from the First

165

Pr[e]sidency let him be accursed. May God Almighty
Bless you all and keep you unto the coming and Kingdom of our Lord and Savior Jesus Christ.

Yours in the Bonds of the new
/covenant/,
J[oseph] Smith, Jr.

over* {page 22}

*Samu[e]l James was objected to by reason of his ab-
sence on a mission and circumstances Such that it is
impossible for him to attend to the duties of this office.
~~Joseph Smith, Prest~~   ~~George W. Robinson~~
Revelation to Joseph Smith, Jr., Given in Kirtland,
Geauga Co[unty], Ohio, Sept[ember] 4th 1837 Making
known the transgression of John Whitmer [and] W[il-
liam] W. Phelps.

Verily thus saith the Lord unto you my Servant
Joseph. My servants John Whitmer and William W.
Phelps have done those things which are not pleasing in
my Sight. Therefore if they repent not they Shall be
removed out of their places. Amen.

J[oseph] Smith, Jr.

—

The above letter and revelation relative to the transgression and removal from office D[avid] Whitmer, O[liver] Cowdery,
J[ohn] Whitmer, and W[illiam] W. Phelps Has been fulfiled as
will be Seen in the following Sequence.

—

Far West, March 29th A.D. 1838

To the ~~first~~ Presidency of the Church of Jesus
Christ of Latter Day Saints in Kirtland,
Dear and well beloved brotheren, Through the
grace and mercy of our God, after a long and tedious
journey of two months and one day, I and my family
arrived in the City of Far West Having been met at
Huntsville 120 Miles from this by brotheren with teams

and money to forward us on our journey. When within eight miles of the City of Far West We were met by an {page 23} escort of bretheren from the city Who were T[homas] B. Marsh, John Corril[l], Elias Higby, and several others of the faithful of the West Who received us with open arms and warm hearts and welcomed us to the bosom of their Society. On our arrival in the City we were greeted on every hand by the Saints who bid us welcome. Welcome to the land of their inheritance.

Dear bretheren, you may be assured that so friendly a meeting and reception paid us well for our long Seven years of Servictude, persecution, and affliction in the midst of our enemies in the land Kirtland. Yea verrily our hearts were full and we feel greatfull to Almighty God for his kindness unto us.

The particulars of our journey brotheren cannot weell [well] be writ[t]en, but we trust that the same God who has protected us will protect you also, and will sooner or later grant us the privilege of seeing each other face/to/face and of rehe[a]rsing all our sufferings. We have he[a]rd of the destruction of the printing office which we presume to believe must hav[e] been occasioned by the Parrishity [i.e., Parrishites] or more properly the Aristocrats and Anarchys as we believe.

The Saints here have provided a room for us and daily necessary's which is brought in from all parts of the Co[unty] to make us comfortable. So that I have nothing to do but to attend to my spiritual concerns on the spiritual affairs of the Church.

The difficulties of the Church had been A[d]justed before arrival here by a Judicious High Council with T[homas] B. Marsh and D[avid] W. Patten who acted as Pres[ident] Pro Tem of the Church of Zion being appointed by the voice of the Council and Church. W[illiam] W. Phelps and John Whitmer having been cut off from the Church, D[avid] Whitmer remaining as yet.

The Saints at this time are in union and peace and love prevails throughout. In a word, Heaven smiles

upon the Saints in Caldwell. Various and many have
been the fals[e]hoods writ[t]en from thence {page 24}
to this place, but have prevailed nothing. We have no
uneasiness about the power of our enemies in this place
to do us harm.

Br[other] Samuel H. Smith and family arrived here
soon after we did in go[o]d health. Br[other] B[righam]
Young, Br[other] D[aniel] S. Miles, and Br[other]
L[evi] Richards arrived here when we did. They were
with us on the last of our journey which ad[d]ed much
to our sattisfaction. They also are well. They have provided places for their families and are now about to
break the ground for seed.

Being under the hand of wicked, vex/at/ious Lawsuits for Seven years past, my buisness was so dangerous that I was not able to leave it in as good a Situation
as I had antisipated, but if there are any wrongs They
shall all be noticed so far as the Lord g[iv]es me ability
and power to do so.

Say to all the brotheren that I have not forgotten
them, but remember them in my prayers. Say to
Mother Beaman that I rememb[e]r her, Also Br[other]
Daniel Carter, Br[other] St[r]ong and family, [and]
Br[other] Granger and family. Finally I cannot
innumerate them all for the want of room. I will just
name Br[other] Knights the Bishop &c. My best respects to them all and I commend them and the
Church of God in Kirtland to our Heavenly Father and
the word of his grace, which is able to make you wise
unto Salvation.

I would just say to Br[other] Marks that I Saw in a
vision while on the road that whereas he was closely
persued by an innumerable concource of enemies and
as they pressed upon him hard as if they were about to
devour him and had seemingly attained some degre[e]
of advantage over him, But about this time a chariot of
fire came near the place and the Angel of the Lord put
forth his hand unto Br[other] Marks and said {page 25}
unto him, "Thou art my son come here." And immediately he was caught up in the Chariot and rode away

triumphantly out of their midst and again the Lord
Said, "I will raise the[e] up for a blessing unto many
people."

Now the particulars of this whole matter cannot be
writ[t]en at this time, but the vision was evidently given
to me that I might know that the hand of the Lord
would be on his behalf.

J[oseph] Smith, Jr.

[P.S.] I transmit to you the following motto of the
Church of Jesus Christ of Latter day Saints Recorded
on Pages 16 and 17 of J[oseph] Smith, Jr., Scriptory
Record Book A.

We left Pres[ident] Rigdon 30 miles this side of
Parris, Illinois in consequence of the sickness of
Br[other] G[eorge] W. Robinson's wife. On yesterday
Br[other] Robinson arrived here who informed us that
his father in Law (S[idney] Rigdon) was at Huntsville
detained there on account of the ill health of his wife.
They will probably be here soon.

Choice seeds of all kinds of fruit also Choice breed
of Cattle would be in much demand also best blood of
horses, garden seeds of every description, also hay seed
of all sorts. All of these are much needed in this place.

Verry respectfully I subscribe myself your Servent
in Christ our Lord and Savior,

Joseph Smith, Jr.
Pres[iden]t of the Church of
Jesus Christ of Latter-day
Saints

—

Pleasent Park, M[iss]o[uri], March 31st 1838

Respected Sir,

Permit me to introduce to your acquaintance Mr.
Henry Root of Dewit near this Place on [the] Misso/u/ri
River. His business I am unacquainted with, Though
any thing he may Say to you; you may put the most

implisit confidence in, as I have allways found him to
be a man of truth and honor, neither have I ever {page
26} known him to give a misrepresentation of any part.
He is a merchant and I suppose doing a moderate business. His place is now, only laid out a year Since, a
beautifull sight to the river and a first rate landing.

Sir, permit me to Say to you, if you could make it
convenient or for your advantage to settle in this
County, I would let you have part of my land. There is
yet to enter adjoining my land, as good [a piece of]
land [as] is in the world. I have no doubt you can do as
weell here in forming a settlement and probably better
than any place in the State. The facilities of the river
will be of great servise in settling this up[p]er country.
Besid[e]s some of the knowing ones have ar[r]ived to
uproot you, but here you can break them down in turn.

I will join you in the speculation if necessary and if
possible the Church. I will have after paying for *1,000*
acres of land $4,000, If they pay me in Far West.
Enough, give my respects to Mrs. Smith and accept for
yourself a friend's respect.

David Thomas

Elder Joseph Smith, Jr.

N.B. P.S. Further I own a Section of land in
Monroe near the forks of [the] Salt River, and if necessary [can] Sell or make a Settlement there. I know of no
man in the world I would rather entertain than yourself.
I would be glad if you would find whether my debt is
secure in that place and let me know. Please to help me
if you can do so without being oppressive to your feelings or interest then I do not wish you violate[d] for me.
Mr. Root is my confidential friend anything [you] may
say to him is Safe. If you cannot come {page 27} a line
from you at any time will be thankfully Received
through the mail or otherwise. D[avid] T[homas]

I expect Mr. Root is on the buisness which I have
named to you in this. We have consulted on this buisness by others.

David Thomas

—

Letter Sent to John Whitmer in consequence of [his] with-
[h]olding the records of the Church in the City of Far West when
called for by the Clerk &c.

Far West, April 9th 1838

Mr. J[ohn] Whitmer,
    Sir, We were desireous of hononoring you by giving
publicity to your notes on the history of the Church of
Latter-day Saints After Such corrections as we thought
would be necessary. Knowing your incompetency as a
historian and that your writings coming from your pen
could not be put to the press without our correcting
them, or elce [else] the Church must Suffer reproach.
    Indeed Sir, we never Supposed you capable of writ-
ing a history, but were willing to let it come out under
your name notwithstanding it would real[l]y not be
yours but ours. We are still willing to honour you if you
can be made to know your own interest and give up
your notes, so that they can be corrected, and made fit
for the press. But if not, we have all the materials for
another, which we Shall commence this week to write.

Your humble Servents,
Joseph Smith, Jr.
Sidney Rigdon
Presidents of the whole
Church of Latter-day Saints

Attest[ed by]
E[benezer] Robinson, Clerk
N.B.* over {page 28}
*The preceding letter to John Whitmer was entered
through a mistake occupying a space not belonging to it ~~notwith-
standing in its place~~.

Minut[e]s of a Conf[erence] of the authorities of the Church
of Latter-day Saints Assembled at their first quarterly conference

171

in the City of Far West, April 6th 1838 for the aniveseary [anniversary] of the organization of the Church. Also to transact Church buisness. Presidents Joseph Smith, J[u]n[ior] and Sidney Rigdon Presidency.

2nd[2] George Morey and Demick Huntington were appointed Sexton and door Keepers. John Corril[l] and Elias Higbee [were appointed] /Historians/.

3rd T[homas] B. Marsh, D[avid] W. Patten, and B[righam] Young of the Twelve [Apostles] were appointed Presidents Pro Tem of the ~~City of Far West~~ /Church of Christ of L[atter] D[ay] Saints in Missouri/ as the former Pres[idency] D[avid] Whitmer, W[illiam] W. Phelps, [and] John Whitmer had been put out of their office.

4th George W. Robinson was elected as general Church Clerk and Recorder to Keep a record of the whole Church, also as Scribe for the First Presidency.

5th Ebinezer Robinson was Chosen Clerk and Recorder for the ~~City Far West~~ /~~High Council~~ Church in M[iss]o[uri]/, also for the High Council.

The remainder of the proceedings will be seen in the record kept by E[benezer] Robinson. Also the trial of the ex-Presidents as will be seen by the following abridgement.

Charge[s] prefer[r]ed against O[liver] Cowdery before the High Council in Far West, M[iss]o[uri] by Elder Seymour Brounson.

To the Bishop and Council of the Church of Jesus Christ of Latter Day Saints, {page 29} I do hereby prefer the following Charges against Oliver Cowdery, which consists of nine in number.

1st For persecuting the bretheren by urging on vexatious lawsuits against the Bretheren and thus distressing the in[n]ocent.

[2] There is no item number one. The list begins with number two.

2nd For seeking to destroy the Character of Pres[ident] Joseph Smith, Jr., by fals[e]ly insinuating that he was guilty of Adultery &c.

3rd By treating the Church with contempt by not attending meeting.

4th For virtually denying the faith by declaring that he would not be governed by any eclesiasticle authority nor revelation whatever in his temporal affairs.

5th For selling his lands in Jackson Co[unty] Contrary to the revelations.

6th For writing and sending an insulting letter to Pres[ident] T[homas] B. Marsh while on the High Council attending to the duties of his office as President of the Council and by insulting the High Council with the contents of Said letter.

7th For leaving his Calling in which God had appointed him by revelation for the sake of filthy lucre and turning to the practice of Law.

8th For disgrasing the Church by being Connected in the Bogus buisness as common report says.

9th For dishonestly retaining Notes after they had been Paid and finally for lea/v/ing or forsaking the cause of God and returning to the beg[g]erly elements of the world, neglecting his high and holy calling Contrary to his profession.

April 11th 1838

The Bishop and High Council assembled at the Bishop's office in trial of the above Charges.

April 12th 1838 After the organization of the Council the above Charges were read. Also a letter from O[liver] Cowdery as will be found recorded in the Church record of the City of Far West, Book A [Far West Record]. The 1st, 2nd, 3rd, 7th, 8th, and 9th Charges were Sustained. {page 30} The 4th and 5th Charges were rejected and the 6th withdrawn. Consequently he (O[liver] Cowdery) was concidered no longer a member of the Church of Jesus Christ of Latter-day Saints. Voted by the High

Council that Oliver Cowdery be no longer a Committee [member] to select locations for the gathering of the Saints.

The following Charges were prefer[r]ed against David Whi[t]mer before the High Council which assembled on the 13th of April 1838 for the purpose of attending to such Charges, which Charges are as follows:

1st For not observing the words of wisdom.

2nd For unchristianlike conduct in neglecting to attend to meetings [and] in uniting with and possessing the same spirit of the desenters.

3rd In writing letters to the desenters in Kirtland unfaivorable to the Cause and to the Character of Joseph Smith, Jr.

4th In neglecting the duties of his calling and Sepperating himself from the Church while he has a name among us.

5th For Signing himself Pres[ident] of the Church of Christ after he had been cut off, in an insulting letter to the High Council.

After reading the above Charges together with a letter Sent to the Pr[e]s[ident] of Said Council (a copy of which may be found recorded in [the] Far West Record, Book A). The Council considered the Charges Sustained and Consequently considred him no longer a member of the Church of Jesus Christ of Latter-day Saints.

Also the same day and date a Charge was prefer[r]ed against Lyman E. Johnson Consisting of 3 Charges which were read together with a letter from him in answer to them in which will be /found/recorded in Far West Record, {page 31} Book A. The charges were sustained and he was consequently cut off from the Church.

—

Revelation to D[avid] W. Patten, given April 17th 1838

"Verily thus Saith the Lord, it is wisdom in my Servant D[avid] W. Patten that he settle up all his buisness, as soon as he possibly can, and make a disposition of his merchandise, that he may perform a mission unto me next spring, in company with others even [the] Twelve [Apostles] including himself, to testify of my name and bear glad tidings unto all the world.

"For verrily thus Saith the Lord that inasmuch as there are those among you who deny my name, others shall be planted in their stead and receive their bishoprick. Amen."

—

Revelation given to Brigham Young at Far West, April 17th 1838

"Verily thus Saith the Lord, Let my Servant Brigham Young go unto the place which he has bought on Mill Creek and there provide for his family until an effectual door is op[e]ned for the sup[p]ort of his family untill I Shall command [him] to go hence, and not to leave his family untill they are amply provided for. Amen."

—

Revelation given in Far West, April 26th 1838[3]

Making known the will of God concerning the building up of this place and of the Lord's House &c. "Verrily thus Saith the Lord unto you my servant Joseph Smith, Jr. and also my Servant Sidney Rigdon, and also my servant Hyrum Smith and your counselors who are and who shall be hereafter appointed and also unto my Servant Edward Partridge and his Councilors, and also unto my faithfull Servants, who are of the High Council of my Church in Zion (for thus it shall be called) and unto all the Elders and people of my Church of Jesus Christ of Latter Day Saints Scattered abroad {page 32} in all the world. For thus Shall my Church be called in the Last days even the Church of Jesus Christ of Latter Day Saints.

"Verrily I say unto you all, arise and Shine forth that thy light may be a standard for the nations and that thy gathering

---

[3] The original manuscript for the next several pages is written in very light, faded ink. Words that are difficult to read or that are contextually determined are enclosed in brackets.

together upon the land of Zion and upon her stakes may be for a defence and for a reffuge from the storm and from wrath when it Shall be poured out without mixture upon the whole earth. Let the City [of] Far West be a holy and consecrated land unto me, and /it shall/ be called most holy, for the ground upon which thou Standest is holy.

"Therefore I command you to build an house [temple] unto me for the gathering together of my Saints that they may worship me. And let there be a begin[n]ing of this work; and a foundation and a preparatory work this following Summer; and let the begin[n]ing be made on the 4th day of July next; and from that time forth let my people labour diligently to build an house unto my name, And in one year from this day, let them recommence laying the foundation of my house. Thus let them from that time forth labour diligently untill it Shall be finished from the Corner Stone thereof unto the top thereof, untill there Shall not any thing remain that is not finished.

"Verrily I Say unto you let not my Servant Joseph, neither my Servant Sidney, neither my servant Hyrum, get in debt any more for the building of an house [temple] unto my name. But let my house be built unto my name according to the pattern which I will Shew unto them, and if my people build it not according to the pattern which I Shall Shew unto their Presidency, I will not accept it at their hands. But if my people do build it according to the pattern which I Shall Shew unto their Presidency even my Servant Joseph and his Councilors then I will accept it at {page 33} the hands of my people.

"And again verrily I say unto you it is my will that the City Far West Should be built up spe[e]dily by the gathering of my Saints and also that other places Should be appointed for Stakes in the regions round about as they shall be manifested unto my Servant Joseph from time to time. For behold I will be with him and I will Sanctify him before the people for unto him have I given the Keys of this Kingdom and ministry. Even so. Amen."

Friday, April the 27th 1838 This day was chiefly spent writing a history of this Church from the earliest period of its existance up to this date, By Presidents Joseph Smith, Jr., Sidney

Rigdon, [and] myself [George W. Robinson] also engaged in keeping this record.

Saturday, 28th This morning Pres[iden]ts Smith and Rigdon and myself were invited to attend the High Council and accordingly attended. The business before the High Council wasthe trial of a case appealed from the branch of the Church near Gymany Horse Mill. Whereas [*blank*] Jackson was plan[tiff] and Aaron Lyon defendant. Council called to order. T[homas] B. Marsh and D[avid] W. Patten Presiding.

It appeared in calling the Council to order that some of the seats were vacated. The council then proceeded to fill those seats eligible to that office. Presidents Smith and Rigdon were strongly solisited to act as councilors [or to] Preside and let the three presiding officers Sit on the council &c. They accepted of the former proposal and accordingly Pres[iden]t Smith was chosen to act on the part of the defence and to speak upon the case, togeth[er] with Geo[rge] W. Harris. Pres[iden]t Rigdon was chosen to act on the part of the prossecution and to speak upon the case together with Geo[rge] M. Hinkle.

After the counsil was organized and op[e]ned by prayer, the notorious case of Aaron Lyon was called in question. After some Arbitrarious Speeches to know whether witnesses should be admitted to testify against A[aron] Lyon or whether he should have the privilege [of] confessing his own Sins, It was desided that witnesses Should be admit[t]ed and also the writ[t]en testimony {page 34} of the wife of Said Jackson.

Now as to this man Lyon, it is a well known fact and without contradiction that he has been in transgression /ever/ since he first came into Kirtland, which is some four or five years Since, as appeared this day by different witnesses which are unimpeachable.

Witnesses against the man Lyon were these: 1st Sarah Jackson, wife of Said plantiff Jackson, one Br[other] Best, also Br[other] Roundy, Br[other] John P. Barnard, also Br[other] Thomas Gaimon, also Br[other] Benjamin and the plantiff. Which testimony Says, Whereas, the plantiff had Some time last Season Sent his wife from Alton, Illinois, to this country as he himself could not come at that time. Accordingly his wife, Mrs. Jackson, came and Settled in the branch first above mentioned.

Now this man Lyon had settled in this branch also and

was their presiding High Priest and had gained to himself great influence in and over that branch. It also appears that this man had great possessions and (if we may judge from testimony given this day) calculates to keep them let the Saints' necessities be what they may. And it also appears that this man was in want of a wife (if actions bespeak the desires of any man) [and] consequently set his wits to work to get one. He commences by getting (as he Said) revelations from God that he must marry Mrs. Jackson, or that She was the woman to make his wife. It appeared that these revelations were frequently received by him and Shortly introdused to Mrs. Jackson. It also was manifested that the old man had Sagasity enough to know that unless he used his priestly office to assi[s]t him in accomplishing his designs /he would fail in the attempt/.

He therefore told Mrs. Jackson that he had had a revelation from God that her husband was dead &c. and that she must concent to marry him, or She would be forever miserable; for he had seen her future State of existance and that She must remember, that whoom soever he blessed, would be blessed, and whom soever he cursed, would be cursed, {page 35} influencing her mind if possible to believe his power was sufficient to make her forever miserable provided she complied not with his request &c. Accordingly they came to an agreement and were soon to be married, but fortunately, or unfortunately for both parties, previous to the arrival of the nuptial day, Behold! to the asstonishment of our defendant, the husband of Mrs. Jackson arrived at home and consequently, disan[n]ul[l]ed the proceedings of the above alluded parties.

The old gentleman Lyon at this time (if not before) knew verry well that his God who gave these revelations (if revelations he had) must of course be no less than the devil and in order to pal[l]iate the justice of his crime, Sad[d]led the whole burden upon the devil, that in scourging the person who had previously befriended him and counseled him in his former days, peradventure he might extricate himself from the Snare of his own setting and dictation. But alass to[o] late for the old man, the testimony being closed and the sword of justice began to be unsheathed which fell upon the old man like a scourge of ten thousand lashes wielded by the hand of President S[idney] Rigdon and George M. Hinkle, inspired by the spirit of justice, accompanied with a flow of elequence, which searched for the feelings like the Sting of so many scorpions, which served to atone for past iniquity there were no feelings that were not felt after, there were no sores that were not probed, there were no excuses rendered that were not exceptionable.

After justice had ceased to weild /its/ sword, Mercy than advanced to rescue its victom, which inspired the heart of President J[oseph] Smith, Jr., and George W. Harris who, with profound elequence with /a/ deep and sublime thought, with clemency of feeling, spoke in faivour of the defendant, but in length of time, while mercy appeared to be doing her utmost, in contending against justice, the latter at last gained the ascendency, and took full /possession of/ the mind of {page 36} the speaker, who leveled a vol[l]ey of darts which came upon the old man like a hur[r]icane upon the mountain tops, which seemingly, was about to sweap the victor entirely out of the reach of mercy, but amidst the clashing of the sword of justice, mercy still claimed the victom and saved him Still in the Church of Jesus Christ of Latter Day Saints, and in this last Kingdom.

Happy is it for those whose sins (like this man's) goes before them to judgement, that they may yet repent and be saved in the Kingdom of our God. Council desided that inasmuch as this man had confessed his sins and asked for forgiveness and promised to mark well the path of his feet and do (inasmuch as lay in his power) what God Should require at his hands. Accordingly, it was decided that he give up his license as High Priest and Stand as a member in the Church. This in consequence of his being concidered not capable of dignifying that office &c. Council Adjourned.

Geo[rge] W. Robinson, Scribe

Sunday the 29th This day was spent chiefly in meeting with the Saints in this place and in administering unto them the word of Life.

Monday, the 30th This day was Spent by the First Presidency in writing the history of the Church and in resitation of grammer lessions [lessons] which resitations is attended to in the /each/ morning previous to writing.

Tuesday, 1st May 1838 This day was Also spent in writing Church History by the First Presidency.

Wednesday, 2nd This day was also spent in writing history and /receiving/ lectures on grammer by President Rigdon. {page 37}

Thursday the 3rd This day also was spent in Writing and Gram[m]er and in administering to the sick.

Friday, 4th This day also was spent in Studying and writing history by the Presidency. Also [received] /a/ letter from J[ohn] E. Page.

Saturday, 5th This day was spent by the Presidency in writing for the Elders Journal. Also received intelligence from Cannada by one Br[other] Bailey who called upon Pres[ident] Smith and Stated that two hundred Wagons with families would probably be here in three weeks. The Presidency also attended an address delivered by Gen[eral] Willson upon Political /matters/. General Willson is a candidate for Congress (a Federalist).

Sunday, 6th This day President Smith delivered a discourse to the people Showing or setting forth the evils that existed, and would exist, by reason of hasty judgement or dessesions [decisions] upon any subject given by any people, or in judging before they heard both sides of the question.

He also cautioned them against men who should come here whining and grouling about their money because they had helped the Saints and bore some of the burden with others and thus thinking that others (who are Still poorer and who have Still bore greater burden than themselves) aught to make up their loss &c. Thus he cautioned them to beware of them for here and there they through [throw] out foul insinuations to level as it were a dart to /the/ best interests of the Church, and if possible to destroy the Characters of its Presidency.

He also instructed the Church in the mistories [mysteries]of the Kingdom of God giving them a history of the Plannets &c. and of Abraham's writings upon the Plannettary System &c. In the after part of the day Pres[ident] Smith spoke upon different Subjects. He dwelt Some upon the Subject of wisdom and upon the word of wisdom &c. {page 38}

Monday, 7th This day was spent in company with Judge Morain one of our neighbouring County judges, also the Democratic candidate for the State Senate. In company with Elder [Reynolds] C/a/hoon and P[arley] P. Pratt, who this day arrived in this place, the former from Kirtland and the latter from the

City of New York, where he had been preaching for Some time past. Our hearts were made glad with the pleasing intel[l]igence of /the/ gathering of the Saints flocking from all parts of the world to this land to avoid the destructions which are coming upon this generation as spoken by all the Holy Prophets Since the world began.

Tuesday, 8th This day Presidents J[oseph] Smith, J[u]n-[ior] and S[idney] Rigdon spent the day with Elder Cahoon in the visiting the place he had selected to live. Also in some private buisness of their own. Also in the after part of the day in answering the questions proposed in the Elders' Journal, Vol. 1st, No. 2nd, Pages 28 and 29th.

On yesterday Thomas B. Marsh lost his Son James who died near the close of the day. This brother though young, [and. . . . .?] his profession as a Saint of God and died in the faith of the everlasting gospel.

Wednesday, 9th This day the Presidency attended the funeral of James Marsh. Pres[iden]t Smith was requested to preach the funeral discourse and accordingly complied and we were greatly edified upon the occassion.

Thursday, 10th This day President S[idney] Rigdon delivered an address in the Schoolhouse in the South west quarter of the City upon the subject of the Political policy of our Nation to a large concourse of People from all quarters of the County and even from other Count[i]es. {page 39} Although he being verry hoarse with a /Severe/ cold yet being assisted by the Spirit and power of Allmighty God was enabled to elucidate The policy to the understanding of all present, Both of the Federal party and also of the Democratic party, from the time of their first appearance in our country, endeavering to give an impartial hearing on both Sides of the question, In consequence of One Gen[eral] Willson['s] speech delivered upon Politics in the Same place a short time previous to this, Who touched upon one side of the matter only; He being a Federalist and knowing that for the good of his cause and for the safety of his electionereing campaign it would be policy for him to dwell on one side of the question only. But the Politics of this Church (with but few exceptions only) is that of Democracy; which is the feelings of the speaker /who spoke/ this day and /all/ of the First Presidency. It is my principles also.

Pres[iden]t Smith and myself attended the Delivery of Said speech and were highly edified.

Friday, 11th This day the Presidency attended the Council of the Bishop in case of the trial of W[illia]m E. McLellin and Doctor McCord, Who were found in transgression. Mr. McCord arose and Said he was sorry to troubl[e] the council on his account for he had intended to withdraw from the Church before he left the place. He also Stated he had no confidence in the work of God, neither in his Prophet which he /has/ raised up in these last days and consequently should go his own way. He accordingly gave up his License and departed.

W[illia]m E. McLellin also said the Same. He further said he had no confidence in the heads of the Church, believing they had transgressed and got out of the way. Consequently he left of[f] praying and keeping the commandments of God and went his own way and indulged himself in his lustfull desires, But when he he/a/rd that {page 40} the First Presidency had made a general Settlement and acknowledged their Sins, he then began to pray again and to keep the commandments of God. Though when inter[r]ogated by Pres[iden]t Smith, he said he had seen nothing out of the way himself but it was heresay.

Thus he judg[e]d from heresay, But we are constrained to Say, O! foolish Man! What excuse is that [this] thou renderest for thy sins, that because thou hast heard of some man's transgression that thou Shouldest leave thy God and forsake thy prayers and turn to those things that thou Knowest to be contrary to the will of God. We say unto thee, and to all Such, beware! beware! for God will bring the[e] into judgement for thy Sins.

Saturday, 12th This day Pres[iden]ts Smith and Rigdon, together with myself, attended the High Council to Say before it Some buisness pertaining to themselves directly and individually.

The Presidency laid before the High Council their Situation as to maintaining their families in the situation and relation they stood to the Church, spending as they have for eight years their time, tallents, and property in the service of the Church and now reduced as it were to absolute beg[g]ery and still were detained in service of the Church. It now become necessary that something should be done for their support, either by the Church or else they must do it themselves of their own labours. If the Church said, "Help yourselves," they would thank them and immediately do so, but if the Church said, "Serve us," then some provisions must be made for them.

The subject was taken into concideration by the Council (who acts for the Church) And throuroughly [thoroughly] investigated. Whereupon {page 41} the Council voted to authorize the Bishop to give or to make over to Pres[iden]ts Joseph Smith, Jr., and Sidney Rigdon each an eighty [acre lot] of land situate[d] adjacent to the city Corporation which land is the property of the Church.

Also voted that a committee of three be appointed of the Council to contract with said Presidency to their sattisfaction for their services this present year, not for preaching or for receiving the word of God by revelation, neither for instructing the Saints in richteousness, but for Services rendered in the Printing establishment, in translating the ancient records, &c. &c.

The committee, which consisted of Geo[rge] W. Harris, Elias Higbee, and Simeon Carter, who agreed that Pres[iden]ts Smith and Rigdon Should be entitled to and receive for this year [*blank* [$1,100 each]] as a just remuneration for their services.

Sunday, 13th Today Pres[iden]t R[eynolds] Cahoon (late Pres[iden]t of Kirtland) delivered a discourse to the Saints in the former part of the day. Pres[iden]t Rigdon preached the funeral Sermon of Swain Williams, Son of F[rederick] G. Williams in the after part of the day.

Monday, 14th Pres[iden]t Smith spent this day in ploughing for himself in his garden. Pres[iden]t Rigdon spent the day in correcting and prepareing matter for the press and also /spent a short time/ in Company with Elder Harlow Readfield who arrived this day from Kirtland, Ohio. I have spent this day in helping Pre[siden]t Smith and also in writing.

Friday, 18th To day Presidents J[oseph] Smith, Jr., S[idney] Rigdon, T[homas] B. Marsh, D[avid] W. Patten, Bishop E[dward] Partridge, E[lias] Higbee, S[imeon] Carter, A[lanson] Ripley, myself, and many others left Far West to visit the north countries for the purpose of Laying off Stakes of Zion, making Locations, and laying claims for the gathering of the Saints for the benefit of the poor and for the upbuilding of the Church of God.

We traveled this day to the mouth of Honey Creek, which {page 42} is a tribuitory to Grand River, where we camped for

183

the night. We passed this day a beautifull country of land, a majority of which is Pra[i]rie which signifies untimbered land and thickly covered with grass and weeds. There is a plenty of wild game in this land such as Deer, Turkey, Hens, Elk, &c. We saw a large black wolf.

Pres[iden]t Smith put on his dog after the wolf and /we/ followed on after, but the wolf out run us and we lost. We have nothing to fear in camping out except Rattle Sknakes which are ~~peculiar~~ natural to this country, though not verry numerous. We turned our horses loose and let them feed in the prairie.

/19th, Sat[urday]/ The next morning we struck our tents and marched crossed Grand River at the mouth of Honey Creek at a place called Nelson's Ferry. Grand River is a large, beautifull, deep, and rapid stream and will undoubtedly admit of [a] Steam Boat and other water craft navigation. At the mouth of Honey Creek is a splended harbour for the safety of such crafts and also for landing freight.

We next kept [traveling] up the river mostly in the timber for ten miles, untill we came to Col[onel] Lyman Wight's who lives at the foot of Tower Hill. A name appropriated by Pres[iden]t Smith in consequence of the remains of an old Nephitish Alter an[d] Tower where we camped for the Sab[b]ath.

In the after part of the day, Pre[siden]ts Smith and Rigdon and myself went to Wight's Ferry about a half mile from this place up the river for the purpose of selecting and laying claims to City plott near said Ferry in Davis County, Township 60, Range 27 and 28, and Sections 25, 36, 31, 30 which was called Spring Hill. A name appropriated by the bretheren present, But afterwards named by the mouth of [the] Lord and was called Adam Ondi Awmen, because Said he, "It {page 43} is the place where Adam Shall come to visit his people, or the Ancient of Days shall sit as spoken of by Daniel the Prophet."

/20th/ Sunday was spent principally at Adam Ondi Awmen, but at the close of the day we struck our tents and traveled about six miles north and camped for the Knight. We had in company at this place Judge Morain and company traveling also to the north.

/21st, M[onday]/ In the morning after making some Locations in this place which is in Township 61, Range 27 and 28, we next returned to Robinson's Grove about two miles in order to secure some land near Grand River which we passed the day previous. Finding a mistake in the /former/ survey [we] Concluded to send the surveyor south 5 or 6 miles to obtain correct survey. We did so and some of us tar[r]ied to obtain water from the camp.

In the evening we held a council to consult the bretheren upon the subject of our journey to Know whether it is wisdom to go immediately into the north country or to tar[r]y here and about here to secure the land on Grand River &c. The Bretheren spoke their minds verry freely upon the subject.

Pre[siden]t Smith Said he felt impressed to tarry and Secure the land near by, all that is not secured between this and Far West, especially on Grand River. Pre[siden]t Rigdon Said if they Should go to [the] north in this expedition he thought it best to go immediately to that place, but thought it best by all means to secure the land near by on the river &c. The question was put by Pres[iden]t Smith and carried unanymously in favour of having the land secured on the river and between this place and Far West.

/22[nd]/ The next day Pres[iden]t Rigdon with a company went to the east of the camp and selected some of the best locations in the county and returned with news of good locations in that vicinity yet {page 44} to be secured ~~notwithstanding~~.

Pre[siden]t Smith and myself followed on in their course, but could not find them and consequently returned to the camp in Robinson's Grove. We next scouted west in order to obtain some game to sup[p]ly our necessities but found or Killed none. We [found] some ancient antiquities about one mile west of the camp, which consisted of stone mounds, appearently laid up in squire [square] piles, though somewhat decayed and obliterated by the almost continual rains. Undoubtedly these were made to seclude some valuable treasures deposited by the aborigionees of this land.

/23[rd]/ The next day we all traveled and located lands east on Grove Creek and near the city of Adam Ondi Awman. Towards Knight Pres[iden]ts Smith and S[idney] Rigdon went to Col[onel] Wight's and the remainder returned to the tents.

/24[th]/ The next morning the company returned to Grove Creek to finish the survey. Pres[iden]t Rigdon and Col[onel] Wight also returned to the surveying and Pres[iden]t Smith returned to Far West.

/25[th]/, Friday This day our company Went up the river and made some locations. In the after part of the day we struck our tents and moved to Col[onel] Wight's.

/26[th]/ The next day we surveyed land across the river opposite *Adam-Ondi-Awmen.*

/27[th]/ Sunday was spent principally at Col[onel] Wight's.

/28[th]/ The next morning we started for home (Far West). About noon we met /Pres[iden]ts/ J[oseph] Smith, Jr., and Hyram Smith and some 15 or 20 others who were going to seek locations in the *north.* We continued our way home where we ar[r]ived Monday evening and found our families well &c.

/30[th]/ The 30[th] Pres[iden]t Hyram Smith returned /to/ Far West.

Friday, 1st of June Pres[iden]t J[oseph] Smith, Jr., returned on account of his wife's sickness, who was delivered of a son [on the 2nd of June].

Monday, 4th Pr[e]s[iden]t J[oseph] Smith, Jr., S[idney] Rigdon, {page 45} Hyram Smith, and myself and others left this place for Adam Ondi Awman. We stayed this knight at Br[other] Moses Dailey's.

[5 June 1838] The next morning we went to Col[onel] Wight's. It rained and was somewhat wet. We continued surveying and building houses &c. for some time day after day. The surveyors run out the City plat and we returned to Far West.

This day was spent in diverse labors for the Church together with a greater share of this month and the ensuing one.

July 4th 1838 This day was spent in Cellabrating the 4th of July in commemoration of the decleration of the Independance of the United States of America. And also to make our decleration of Independance from all mobs and persecutions which have been inflicted upon us time after time /un/till we could bear it no longer being driven by ruthless mobs and enimies of the truth from our homes, our property confiscated, our lives exposed and our all Jeopardized by such conduct.

We therefore met on this day in Far West, M[iss]o[uri] to make our decleration of independance and to Lay the corner Stones of the House of the Lord agreeably to the commandment of the

Lord unto us given April 26th 1838 as recorded on Pages 32, 33, and 34 Book A [i.e., the "Scriptory Book"].

An address was delivered by Pres[iden]t S[idney] Rigdon. Pres[iden]t J[oseph] Smith, Jr., [was] Pres[iden]t of the day, Pres-[iden]t H[yrum] Smith Vice Pres[iden]t, and Pres[iden]t S[idney] Rigdon Orator. R[eynolds] Cahoon [was] Chief Marshial, G[eorge] M. Hinkle and J[efferson] Hunt ass[istan]t Marshail and myself commanded the Regiment.

The order of the day was most splendid and beautifull. Several thousands of spectators were present to witness the same. The address was delivered on the public square under the hoisted flagg representing the Liberty and Independence {page 46} of these United States of America.

Shortly after Pres[iden]ts J[oseph] Smith, Jr., S[idney] Rigdon, H[yrum] Smith, and myself left this place for Adam Ondi Awman, we saw a deer or two on the way. Pre[siden]t Smith set his dogs after them, one of which was a grayhound which cau[gh]t the deer but could not hold him, although he ~~through~~ /threw/ him down, yet he injoured the dog so badly that he let him go and we lost him. The race was quite amusing indeed.

/June/ [1838] I would mention or notice something about O[liver] Cowdery, David Whitmer, Lyman E. Johnson, and John Whitmer who being guilty of bace [base] iniquities and that to[o], manifest in the ages of all men, and being often entreated would continue in their course seeking the lives of the First Presidency and to overthrow the Kingdom of God which they once testified off [of].

Pres[iden]t Rigdon preached one Sabbath upon the salt that had lost its savour that it is henceforth good for nothing but to be cast out and trod[d]en under foot of men, and the wicked flee when no man pursueth. These men took warning and soon they were seen bounding over the prairie like the scape Goat to carry of[f] their own sins. We have not seen them since. Their influence is gone and they are in a miserable condition. So also it [is] with all who turn from the truth to Lying, Cheating, defrauding, and Swindeling.

Some time past was spent in trying to obtain pay from these men who are named above who have absconded and endeavered to defraud their creditors. {page 47}

July 6th This day received a letter from Orson Hyde and Heber C. Kimball, Two of the Twelve Apostles of the Lamb in these last Days, who having been on a mission to England just returned to Kirtland, Ohio and dated same place, Directed to Pre[siden]t J[oseph] Smith, Jr.

Dear Brother Joseph,

In health, peace, and saf[e]ty we arrived in this place on Monday last from the time of our labor during the past year after a passage of 31 days. We cannot give a full account of our labors now, but suffise it to say, the standard of truth is reared on the other side of the great waters and hundreds are now fi[gh]ting the good fight of faith beneath the shade of its glorious banner. We have fought in the name of the Lord Jesus and under the shadow of the cross we have conquered. Not an enimy has risen up against us, but that has fallen for our sakes. Every thing we have done has prospered. The God of the Holy Prophets has been with us [and] to him belongs the praise.

Our bretheren in the east are poor, yet rich in faith and the peace of our God abides upon them. We have not interfeared with the priests at all except when we have been assa[u]lted by them. We have preached repentance and baptism and baptism and repentance. We have strictly attended to our buisness and have let others alone. We have experienced the truth of Solomon's words which are as follows: "When a man's ways pleaze the Lord he maketh his enimies that they are at peace with him." Our enimies have seen their entire insufficiency to stand against the power of truth manifest through us and have gone away and left us in pe[a]cefull possession of {page 48} the feild [field].

Concerning the Nicholatine Band [heretics] of which you warned us against, We would say God is not there and we are not there. They deal in sandstone and bogus, but we in faith, hope, and Charity. We have not means to situate our families in Far West at present and as we have not been charg[e]able to the Church hitherto, we do not like to be/c/ome a burthen [burden] to them in the extreme state of poverty to which they are reduced. We can preach the gospel when the Lord is with us and by it we can live. The time will come when we Shall have means to settle with the Saints.

Kirtland is not our home, it looks dolefull here, we shall go westward as soon as we can. The folks here [exchange gossip] like money [and spread] dark and pittifull notes about yourself and others, but the faults of our bretheren is poor entertainment for us. We have no accusation to bring, for the Lord has shown us that he has taken the matter into his own hands and every secret shall be brought to light and every man chastened for his sins untill he confess and forsake them and then he shall find mercy. Therefore, we can say we are at peace with God and with all mankind. And if any creature has ought against us, we have naught against him, and we say forgive us for Christ['s] sake.

We should be glad to see all our bretheren of the Twelve [Apostles] and we s[h]all as we can consistantly. Our good wishes and best respects to them, To yourself, Bro[ther] Sidney, and families, and to all the faithful bretheren and sisters in Christ Jesus our Lord.

Will you or some other of the bretheren write us soon and let us know the true state of things in Far West. We have been gone allmost a year and have heard but very little, but we now hear much. We would like to know if a spirit of union prevails &c. &c.

We are as ever your bretheren in the bonds of the everlasting covenant.

H[eber] C. Kimball
Orson Hyde
We are one
To Pres[iden]t J[oseph] Smith, Jr. {page 49}

The following is a letter from Don C[arlos] Smith

Nine Miles from Terre Haute, Ind[iana]   189

Bro[ther] Joseph,

I sit down to inform you of our situation at the
present time. I started from Norton, Ohio [on] the 7th
of May in company with Father, W[illia]m, [Wilkins]
Jenkins Salsbury, W[illia]m McClerry, and Lewis Rob-
ins and families. Also Sister Singly is one of our number.

We started with 15 horses, seven wagons, and two
cows. We have left two horses by the way sick, one with
a swelling on his shoulder, a 3rd horse (as it were our
dependance) was taken lame, last evening and is not
able to travel. We have stop[p]ed to docter him.

We were disappointed on every hand before we
started in getting money. We got no assistance whatever
only as we have taken in Sister Singly and she has assisted us as far as her means extends. We had when we
started $75 dollars in money. We sold the 2 cows for
$13.50 per cow. We have sold of[f] your goods to the
amount of $45.74 and now we have only $25 dollars to
carry 28 souls and 13 horses 500 Miles.

We have lived very close and camped out [at]
knight, notwithstanding the rain and cold, and my babe
[was] only 2 weeks old when we started. Agness is very
feeble. Father and Mother are not well, but verry much
fatigued. Mother has a severe cold. It is nothing in fact
but the prayer of faith and the power of God that will
sustain them and bring them through. Our carriage is
good and I think we shall be brought through.

I leave it with you and Hyrum to devise some way
to assist us to [with] some more expence money. We
have had unaccountable bad roads, had our horses
down in the mud, and broke of[f] one waggon tongue
{page 50} and fills, and broke down the carriage twice.
Yet we are all alive and camped on a dry place for allmost the first time. Poverty is a heavy load, but we are
all obliged to welter under it. It is now dark and I
close. May the Lord bless you all and bring us together
is my prayer. Amen.

All the arrangements that Bro[ther] Hyram left for
getting money failed, they did not gain us one cent.

Don C[arlos] Smith

To J[oseph] Smith, Jr.

—

The following Revelations were read in the congregation this day, which was given in Ohio.[4]

Revelation Given at the French Farm in Kirtland, ~~Geagua~~ /Geauga/ Co[unty], Ohio In the presence of J[oseph] Smith, Jr., S[idney] Rigdon, V[inson] Knight, and Geo[rge] W. Robinson, January 12th 1838.

When inquiry was made of the Lord relative to the trial of the First Presidency of the Church of Christ of Latter Day Saints, For transgressions according to the item of law found in the Book of [Doctrine and] Covenants, 3rd Section, 37th Verse [1835 ed.], Whether the descesion [decision] of such an Council of one Stake Shall be conclusive for Zion and all her stakes.

"Thus Saith the Lord, Let the First Presidency of my Church be held in full fellowship in Zion and all her Stakes untill they Shall be found transgressors by Such an High Council as is named in the above alluded Section in Zion by three witnesses standing against each member of Said Presidency. And these witnesses Shall be of long and faithfull standing and Such also as cannot {page 51} be impeached by other witnesses before such Council.

"And when a descision is had by such an Council in Zion, it shall only be for Zion. It shall not a/n/swer for her stakes, but if such descision be acknowledged by the Council of her Stakes, then it shall answer for her Stakes, But if it is not acknowledged by the stakes, then such Stake may have the privilege of hearing for themselves or if such descision shall be acknowlededged by a majority of the stakes, then it shall answer for all her Stakes.

"And again, The Presidency of my Church may be tried by the Voice of the whole body of the Church in Zion and the voice of a majority of all her Stakes.

"And again, Except a majority is had by the Voice of the

---

[4] Written sideways along the left hand margin on pages 51-53 of the original manuscript is the notation, "Over looked in its place."

Church of Zion and a majority of all her Stakes, The Charges will be concidered not sustained. And in order to sustain such Charge or Charges, before such Church of Zion or her Stakes, such witnesses must be had as is named above, that is the witnesses to each President, who are of long and faithfull standing, that cannot be immpeached by other witnesses before the Church of Zion or her Stakes.

"And all this saith the Lord because of wicked and asspiring men. Let all your doings be in meekness and in humility before me. Even so. Amen."

—

Revelation Given the same day, January 12th 1838

Upon an inquiry being made of the Lord whether any branch of the Church of Christ of Latter Day Saints can be concidered a Stake of Zion untill they have acknowledged the authority of the First Presidency by a vote of such Church.

"Thus saith the Lord, Verrily I Say unto {page 52} You, Nay. No Stake shall be appointed except by the First Presidency and this Presidency be acknowledged by the voice of the same, otherwise it shall not be counted as a Stake of Zion.

"And again, except it be dedicated by this Presidency, it cannot be acknowledged as a Stake of Zion. For unto this End have I appointed them in Laying the foundation of and establishing my Kingdom. Even so. Amen."

—

Revelation Given the same day, January 12th 1838

"Thus Saith the Lord, let the Presidency of my Church take their families as soon as it is practicable and a door is open for them and moove to the west as fast as the way is made plain before their faces. And let their hearts be comforted for I will be with them.

"Verrily I Say unto you, the time has come that your labors are finished in this place for a season. Therefore arise and get yourselves into a land which I Shall Show unto you, Even a land flowing with milk and honey. You are clean from the blood of this people. And wo unto those who have become your enimies, who have professed my name, Saith the Lord, for their Judgement lingereth not and their damnation Slumbereth not. Let all your faithfull friends arise with their families also and get out of this place and gather themselves together unto Zion and be at peace among yourselves O ye inhabitants of Zion, or their shall be no saf[e]ty for you. Even so. Amen." {page 53}

It hap[pe]ned about these times that some excitement was raised in the adjoining Counties, that is Ray and Clay, against us in consequence of the sud[d]en departure of these wicked character[s] of the apostates from this Church into that vicinity repor[t]ing false stories and statements, but when they come to hear the other side of the question their feeling[s] were all allayed upon that subject especially.

The emigration to this land is verry extensive and numerous. Some few are troubled with the *ague and fever*. The First Presidency are chiefly engaged in counciling and settling the emigrants to this land. The Prophets' [prophecies] are fulfilling very fast upon our heads and in our day and generation. They are gathering from the North, and from the South, from the East, and from [the] West unto Zion for safety against the day of wrath which Is to be poured out without mixture upon this generation according to the prophets.

—

The following Revelation was given in Far West, M[iss]o[uri], July 8th 1838 and read this day in the congregation of the Saints.

Revelation Given to the Twelve Apostles, July 8th 1838, in Far West, M[iss]o[uri] in the presence of J[oseph] Smith, J[unio]r, S[idney] Rigdon, H[yrum] Smith, E[dward] Partridge, I[saac] Morl[e]y, J[ared] Carter, S[amson] Avard, T[homas] B. Marsh, and G[eorge] W. Robinson Making known the will of the Lord concerning the Twelve [Apostles]. Show unto us thy will O Lord Concerning the Twelve.

"Verily thus saith the Lord, Let a conference be held immediately. Let the Twelve [Apostles] be organized. Let men be appointed to supply the place/s/ of those who [have] fallen. Let

193

my servant Thomas [B. Marsh] remain for a season in the land
of Zion to publish my word. Let the residue continue to preach
from that hour. And if they will do this in all Lowliness of Heart,
in meekness and pureness and long suffering, I the Lord God
give unto them a promise that {page 54}[5] I will provide for their
families and an effectual door shall be op[e]ned for them
fromhenceforth. And next spring let them depart to go over the
great waters and there promulg[at]e my gospel in the fullness
thereof and to bear record of my name. Let them take l[e]ave of
my Saints in the City [of] Far West on the Twenty sixth day of
April next on the building spot of mine house saith the Lord.

"Let my servent *John Taylor*, and also my servent *John E.
Page*, and also my servent *Willford Woodruff*, and also my servent
Willard Richards be appointed to fill the places of those who have
fallen and be officially Notified of their appointment. *Even so.
Amen.*"

—

Revelation Given the same day and at th[e] same pla[c]e
and read the same day in the congregations of the Saints Making
known the duty of *F[rederick] G. Williams and W[illia]m W. Phelps.*

"Verrily thus Saith the Lord, in consequence of their Transgressions their former standing has been taken away from them
and now if they will be saved Let them be ordained as Elders in
my Church, to preach my gospel and travel abroad from land to
land and from place to place to gather mine Elect unto me saith
the Lord, and let this be their labors from henceforth. *Even so.
Amen.*" {page 55}

—

Revelation Given the same day and read at the same time
of [as] the prece[e]ding ones, July 8th 1838.

O Lord show unto thy servent how much thou requirest
of the properties of thy people for a Tithing?

---

[5] The leaf containing pages 54-55 has been removed from the original
manuscript and placed in the Revelations Collection, under section 118 of the
Doctrine and Covenants, at the archives of the Historical Department, Church of
Jesus Christ of Latter-day Saints.

Answer: "Verrily thus saith the Lord, I require all their surpluss property to be put into the hands of the Bishop of my Church of Zion for the building of mine house and for the Laying the foundation of Zion and for the priesthood and for the debts of the Presidency of my Church.

"And this shall be the begin[n]ing of the tithing of my people and after that those who have thus been tithed Shall pay one tenth of all their interest an[n]ually and this Shall be a Standing Law unto them forever For my Holy Pri/e/sthood Saith the Lord.

"Verrily I say unto you, it shall come to pass that all those who gather unto the land of Zion shall be tithed of their surpluss properties and shall observe this Law or they shall not be found worthy to abide among you. And I say unto you, If my people observe not this Law to keep it holy and by this law Sanctify the Land of Zion unto me that my Statutes and my Judgements may be kept thereon that it may be most holy, behold verrily I say unto you, it shall not be a land of Zion unto you and this shall be an ensample unto all the Stakes of Zion. Even so. Amen." {page 56}

—

Revelation Given the same day, July 8th 1838, Making known the disposition of the properties tithed as named in the preceeding revelation.

"Verrily thus saith the Lord, the time has now come that it shall be disposed of by a council composed of the First Presidency of my Church and of the Bishop and his Council and by /my/ High Council and /by/ mine own voice unto them saith the Lord. Even so. Amen."

—

Revelation Given to W[illia]m Marks, N[ewel] K. Whitney, Oliver Granger, and others /Given/ in Zion, July 8th 1838.

"Verrily thus saith the Lord unto my Servent W[illia]m Marks, and also unto my Servent N[ewel] K. Whitney, Let them settle up their buisness spe[e]dily, and Journ[e]y from the land of Kirtland before I the Lord Sendeth the Snows again upon the ground. Let them awake and arise and come Forth and not tarry for I the Lord command it. Therefore if they tarry, it shall not be well with them. Let them repent of all their sins and of all their covetous desires before me saith the Lord. For what is property unto me saith the Lord?

"Let the properties of Kirtland be turned out for debts saith the Lord. Let them go, saith the Lord, and whatsoever remaineth let it remain in your hands saith the Lord, for have I not the fowls of heaven, and also the fish of the sea, and the bea[s]ts of the Mountains, have I not made the earth, do I not hold the destinies of all the armies of the Nations of the earth. Therefore will I not make the solitary places to bud and to blossom {page 57} and to bring forth in abundence Saith the Lord. Is there not room enough upon the mountains of Adam Ondi Awmen and upon the plains of Olah Shinehah, or in the land where Adam dwelt, that you should not covet that which is but the dross and neglect the more weighty matters. Therefore come up hither unto the Land of my people, even Zion.

"Let my Servant W[illia]m Marks be faithfull over a few things and he shall be a ruler over many. Let him preside in the midst of my people in the City [of] Far West and let him be blessed with the blessings of my people.

"Let my Servant N[ewel] K. Whitney be ashamed of the Nicholatine band and of all their secret abominations, and of all his littleness of soul before me saith the Lord and come up unto the land of Adam Ondi Awman, and be a Bishop unto my people Saith the Lord, not in name but in deed saith the Lord.

"And again Verrily I say unto you, I remember my Servent Oliver Granger. Behold verrily I say unto him that his name shall be had in sacred rememberance from Generation to Generation for ever and ever saith the Lord. Therefore let him contend e[a]rnestly for the redemption of the First Presidency of my Church saith the Lord. And when he falls he shall rise again, for his sacrifice shall be more sacred unto me than his increase saith the Lord. Therefore let him come up hither spe[e]dily unto the land of Zion and in due time he shall be made a merchent unto my name Saith the Lord for the benefit of my people.

"Therefore let no man despise my Servent Oliver {page 58} Granger, but let the blessings of my people be upon him forever and ever. And again verily I say unto you, let all my

Servents in the Land of Kirtland rem[em]ber the Lord their God and mine house also, to keep and preser[v]e it holy and to overthrow the money Changers in mine own due time Saith the Lord. Even so. Amen."

July 26th 1838 This day the First Presidency, High Council, and Bishop's Court met to take into concideration the disposing of the publick properties in the hands of the Bishop in Zion, for the people of Zion have commenced liberally to consecrate agreeably to the revelations and commandments of the Great I Am of their surpluss properties &c.

It was agreed that the First Presidency keep all their properties that they can dispose of to their advantage and Support and the remainder be put into the hands of the Bishop or Bishops agreeably to the commandments and revelations.

1st Mooved, Seconded, and carried unanimously That the First Presidency shall have their expences defrayed in going to Adam Ondi Awman and also returning therefrom. That the Bishop of Zion pay one half and the Bishop of Adam Ondi Awman the other half.

2nd Mooved, Seconded, and carried unanimously that all the traveling expences of the First Presidency Shall be defrayed in traveling at any time or place. {page 59}

3rd Mooved, Seconded, and carried unanimously That the Bishop be authorised to pay orders coming from the east inasmuch as they will consecrate liberally, but this to be done under the inspection of the First Presidency.

4th That the First Presidency Shall have the prerogative to say to the Bishop whose orders shall or may be paid by him in this place or in his Jurisdiction. Carried unanimously.

5th Mooved, Seconded and carried That the Bishop of Zion receive all consecrations, east, west, and south, who are not in the Jurisdiction of a Bishop of any other Stake.

6th Mooved and carried that we use our influence to put a stop to the selling of Liquiors in the City [of] Far West or in our midst, That our streets may not be filled with drunk[e]ness. And that we use our influence to bring down the price of provisions.

197

7th Mooved, Seconded and carried unanymously that *Br[other] W[illia]m W. Phelps* be requested to draw up a petition to remove the county seat to Far West.

July 27th [For] Some time past the bretheren or Saints have come up day after day to consecrate and to bring their offerings into the store house of the Lord to prove him now herewith and se[e] if he will not pour us out a blessings that there will not be room enough to contain it. They have come up hither. {page 60}

Thus far, according to the order /revelation/ of the Danites. We have a company of Danites in these times, to put to right physically that which is not right, and to clense the Church of every [very?] great evil[s?] which has hitherto existed among us inasmuch as they cannot be put to right by teachings and persuasyons. This company or a part of them exhibited on the fourth day of July [-] They come up to consecrate, by companies of tens, commanded by their captain over ten[6]

28th President Smith and Pres[iden]t Rigdon left Far West for Adam Ondi Awman to transact some important buisness and to settle some Cannadian bretheren in that place, as they are emegrating numerously to this land from all parts of the Country. Elder [Almon W.] Bab[b]it from Cannada with his company has arrived. Brother [Theodore] Turley is with him.

29th This day Elder Orson Hyde and Heber C. Kimball Preached. They have just returned from England from a mission of som[e]thing over a year's duration. They bring glad tidings of great joy from that people. They baptised between one and two thousand and left Greater prospects than they had ever before seen. [They] Ord[a]ined a large number of Elders, Prie[s]ts, Teachers, and Deacons. Thus the word is spreading rappedly throug[h] the country.

A large majority of the Saints in Kirtland have and are arriving here every day. Kirtland has been broken up by those who have professed the name of Latter Day Saints and have denied the faith {page 61} which they once preached and by their

---

6 Reconstructed, in part, from the transcript in Dean C. Jessee and David J. Whittaker, "The Last Months of Mormonism in Missouri: The Albert Perry Rockwood Journal," *Brigham Young University Studies* 28 (Winter 1988), 1:14.

preaching gathered many Saints into this land, and now have betrayed them. O Justice where hast thou fled And thou administrations whither hast thou concealed thyself.

30th, Monday This day the circuit court of our circuit Sits in this place commencing today. Judge [Austin A.] King [is the] presiding Judge [and] quite a number of Lawyers were here from Liberty and Richmond &c. They have just returned from Davis County session. Pr[e]s[iden]t Hyram Smith and myself attended court.

Tuesday, 31st This day was spent principaly in Court by most of the Presidency. Judge King waited upon President J[oseph] Smith, Jr., and spent a short time with him. Counselor Burch, who is also the Circuit Attorney, called upon Pres[iden]t Rigdon this day and had a short interv[i]ew with him, solisiting him verry hard to preach this evening as he said those gentlemen of his profession wished to hear him, as also did Judge King. But being quite fatigued in consequence of his absence and labors, returning last evening with Pres[iden]t Smith from Adam Ondi Awman. Court adjourned for its regular sessions.

Wendnessday [Wednesday, Thursday, and Friday], August 1st, 2nd, [and] 3rd [These days] were all spent by the First Presidency at home being somewhat fatigued in consequence of nisesant [incessant] labors, therefore nothing of importance transpired during this time.

We saw the publication of the Oration delivered by {page 62} Pres[iden]t Rigdon on the 4th day [of] July 1838. It was published in the Far West, a paper published in Liberty, Clay County, M[iss]o[uri].

Sunday the 5th The First Presidency attended meeting this day at the usual place of worship. Erastus Snow preached a discourse. Pres[iden]t Smith made some observations immediately after by way of instructions to the Elders in particular relative [to] wisdom &c. Pres[iden]t Rigdon delivered a short discourse in the after part of the day.

At the close thereof, Elder Simeon Carter and Myself were called upon to administer unto severall by the laying on of hands for their confermation and the giving of the Holy Ghost. Br[other] F[rederick] G. Williams was among the number, who being rebaptized a few days since was this day confermed.

Monday the 6th This day is the day for General Election

199

throughout the State for officers. Office seekers from without the Church who depend verry much on our help begin to flatter us with smooth Stories, but we understand them verry well through the wisdom of God given unto us. They cannot deceive us for God is with us and very near us. For he speaks often unto us through the means he has appointed.

Met in the morning in Council with the First Presidency at Pres[iden]t Smith's house to take into concideration the conduct of certain Cannada [Canadian] bretheren, who had gone contrary to council and settled at the forks of Grand River. Whereupon it was agreed that they must return to Adam Ondi Awman according to the Council of God or they Would not be concidered one among us {page 63} just as the Lord has said in a revelation to us Given July 8th 1838.

In the after part of the day a meeting was held in the school house as follous [follows]:

At [a] meeting of the Citizens of Caldwell County assembled in the City [of] Far West, The meeting was called to order by Calling Judge Elias Higbee to the Chair and appointing Geo[rge] W. Robinson Secretary.

After some remarks made by the Chairman relative to the object of this meeting — the resignation of the present Post Master W[illia]m W. Phelps and in appointing his successor. Mr. S[idney] Rigdon was nominated, seconded, and carried unanymously to succeed W[illia]m W. Phelps in the post office department and that he be recommended to the Post Master Gen[eral] as the person of our choice as citizens of this City and also worthy of our Sufferage, Dated Far West, M[iss]o[uri], August 6th 1838.

> Elias Higbee, Chairman
> Geo[rge] W. Robinson,
> Secretary

———

August 6th 1838 This afternoon the Citizens of Far West assembled in the school house in the S[outh] W[est] gr[ove?] of the Town. The meeting was opened by Calling Judge Elias Higbee to the Chair and appointing Geo[rge] W. Robinson Secretary.

200   1st Whereupon it was unanymously agreed that the Cit-

izens of the counties of Caldwell and Davis {page 64} ought and [s]hould have a Weekly News paper published for their information upon the news of the day. Pres[iden]t Smith said the time had come when it was necessary that we should have som[e] thing of this nature to unite the people and aid in giving us the News of the day &c. Whereupon it was unanimously agreed that Pres[iden]t S[idney] Rigdon should Edit the same.

2nd That a petition be drawn up to remove the County seat to this place. Some remarks were made by Pres[iden]t Rigdon upon the subject showing the great necessity of so doing.

3rd And that [it] is the duty of the bretheren to come into Cities to build and live and Carry on their farms out of the City. Pres[iden]t Smith spoke upon the same subject of mooving into Cities to live according to the order of God. He spoke quite lengthy and then Pres[iden]t H[yrum] Smith spoke and endeavoured to impress it upon the minds of the saints.

Tuesday the 7th This morning an alarm come from Galliton, the County Seat of Davis County, that during the Election on yesterday at that place some two or three of our bretheren were killed in consequence of the Malignity of the Missourians.

It was reported that the citizens of Daviess County who were opposed to our religion did endeavor to prohibit the bretheren from voting at the election in that place. And that the men who were killed were left upon the ground and not suffered to be inter[r]ed. And that the majority of that County were determined to drive the {page 65} bretheren from the County under these conciderations.

Quite a number of us volunteered to go to the assistance of our bretheren in that place. Accordingly some 15 or 20 men started from this place armed and equipt for our defence. The bretheren from all parts of the County followed after and continued to come and join us and before we arrived at Col[onel] Wight's we had quite a large company.

Pres[iden]ts Smith, Rigdon, and H[yrum] Smith, alll [all] the First Presidency, Genera[l] Higbee, Gen[eral] Avard, myself, and ma/n/y others to[o] tedious to mention at this time or in this record were in the company.

It was put upon me [George Robinson]to take the com-

201

mand in consequence of my holding the office of *Colonel* whose duty it is to command one regiment. We marched without much intermission untill we reached Col[onel Lyman] Wight's. However some of our small parties were attacked, I think on twice in going over, but no serious injury done.

We reached Col[onel] Wight's that same evening. Found some of the bretheren assembled for to receive council upon what to do as a number of the men who were at the battle the day before were there and I beleive all of them were threatened with vengence by some of their enemies. Some of the bretheren were wounded badly but none killed. Quite a number of the Missourians were badly wounded, some with their sculs [skulls] cracked. As reported about 150 Missourians fau[gh]t ~~against~~ from 6 to 12 of our bretheren.

Our bretheren fau[gh]t like tigers. They cl[e]ared the ground at that time in knocking down and drag[g]ing out. The principal men who faught so bravely were John S. Butler [and] Hyrum Nelson, {page 66} whose names aught to be immortalized from [for] the courage they possessed and their determination in this thing and for the victory they gained.

We tarried all knight at that place and in the morning we called to se[e] Squire Adam Black who was mainfstly [manifestly] an enimy of ours. For the evidences were before us that he did last summer unite himself to a band of mob[b]ers to drive our brethern from the County and to prohibit them from settleing in the County and that [he] personally warned many of said bretheren to leave in a certain given time or they should be further de[a]lt with.

He was obliged to confess this when interrogated upon the subject. And in consequences of the violation of his oath as a magistrate in the County of Daviess, we required him to give us some sattisfaction so that we might know whether he was our friend or enimy and whether he would administer the laws of our country or not in Justice for people. We presented him with a paper to sign which was an article of peace, but he being Jealous of us would not sign it. But said he would draw one himself and sign it to our sattisfaction. He did so and we left him in peace.

The same evening some of the citizens of the County came to visit us to sue for peace. We told them we would [meet] their principal men in a committee on the next day at that place

at twelve o'clock. Accordingly we did so and entered into a covenant of peace with their principal men of said County. For inst[ance,] Judge Morin, Mr. Williams, Mr. Turner, Mr. Rogers,
and many others. {page 67}

The covenant of peace was to preserve each other's rights
and [to] stand in their defence. That if men should do wrong
they, neither party, should uphold them or endeavour to secret
them from Justice, but they shall be delivered up even all offenders to be de[a]lt with according to law and Justice. Upon these
terms, we parted in peace and soon every man left the ground
and returned to his habitation. We came home the same knight
arrived at home about 12 o'clock at knight and found all well in
Far West.

Friday, 10th Nothing of importance transpired this day.
The Presidency were at home [and] being somewhat fatigued [they]
did not leave their houses to transact much buisness.

Saturday, 11th This morning the First Presidency left this
place for the forks of Grand River in company with Elder Almon
Babbit to visit Elder Babbit's company who come on with him
from Cannada and settled contra[r]y to council on the forks of
Grand River to give such council as is needed.

This afternoon a committe[e] from Ray County Come
into this place to inquire into the proce[e]dings of our society in
going armed into the County of Daviess as [a] complaint had
been entered by Adam Black and others in said county of Ray
and said committee desired to confer with a committee that might
be appointed by our Citizens.

Accordingly a meeting was called of the Citizens of
Caldwell County to meet in the City Hall in the City [of] Far
West At 6 o'clock P.M. The following are the minut[e]s of a
meeting held in Far West in the City Hall: {page 68}

At a meeting of the Citizens of Caldwell County, Mett
[met] in the City Hall in Far West, August 11th 1838, To take
into concideration certain movements on the part /of the Citizens/
of the County [of] Ray. Wherein they have accused the people of
our sosciety [society] of breaking the peace, Even in defending
our rights and those of our bretheren of late in the County of
Daviess.

Meeting called to order by calling Bishop E[dward] Par-   203 tridge to the *Chair* and appointing Geo[rge] W. Robinson *Secretary*.

1st Resolved That a committee of seven be appointed on the part of the Citizens of Caldwell to confer with and wait on the Committee on the part of the Citizens of the County of Ray.

2nd Resolved That this committe[e] with their Secretary have power to answer such questions and interrogat[i]ons as shall be put by the committee of the County of Ray and as are named in the document presented to this meeting purporting to be the preamble and resolutions and resolves of said meeting of said Citizens of Ray.

3rd Resolved That whereas the document presented, as above named, had no date or signiture either as Chairman or secretary That this committee Shall sattisfy themselves of the fact or reasons given and act accordingly.

4th Resolved That this committee report again to this meeting as soon as may be together with all information received.

> Edward Partridge, Chair[man]
> Geo[rge] W. Robinson,
> Secretary {page 69}

—

Sunday, 12th This day the First Presidency were in the north country not having returned from the forks of Grand River, to which place they went with Elder Babbit. I remained in Far West during this Journey taken by them.

Monday, 13th This day was spent as usual. The First Presidency returned at Evening all sound and well, though some what fatigued with the Journey. They were chased some 10 or 12 miles by some Evil designing persons but escaped out of their hands.

Men were sent to notify them that a writ had been ishued [issued] by Judge [Austin] King the circuit Judge to ap[p]rehend Pres[iden]t Joseph Smith, Jr., and Lyman Wight for defending their rights &c. They met the Presidency about 8 miles from this place and all returned /safe/ to this place.

Tuesday, 14th This day was spent by the Presidency in secular buisness [business] of their own.

The 15th was also spent in the same manner.

The 16th was spent principally at home. The sherriff of Daivess [Daviess] County ac[c]ompanied by Judge Morin called on Pres[iden]t Smith and notified him that he had a writ for [to] take him into Daviess County and try him for visiting that County as before stated.

Pres[iden]t Smith did not refuse to be taken as some people had reported that he would not be taken nor submit to the Law, but he said he would or calculated always to Submit to the Laws of our Country. But he told the Sheriff that he wished to be tried in his own County as the Citizens of Daviess County were {page 70} highly exasperated toward him. He further stated that the Laws of our Country gave him this privilege.

The Sheriff did not serve his writ upon hearing this and Said he would go to Richmond and see Judge King upon the subject. Pres[iden]t Smith told him he would remain at home untill he should return, etc. The Sheriff accordingly returned and found Pres[iden]t Smith at home where he had been during his absence. The Sheriff informed him very gravely that he (Pres[iden]t Smith) was out of his Jurisdiction and that he (Said Sheriff) could not act in this County. He therefore returned as light as he came.

20th This day the inhabitants of the different parts of the Town or County met to organize themselves into Companies called agricultural Companies. The Presidency were there and took a part in the same. One Company was established Called the Western Agricultural Com[pan]y who voted to take in one field for grain Containing twelve Sections which is Seven thousands Six hundred and Eighty Acres of land. Another Company was organised Called the Eastern Agricultural Company. The number of acres is not yet as[c]ertained.

[21 August 1838] The next day another Company was organised Called the Southern Agri[cultural] Company. [Their] field to be as large as the first one.

22nd This day was spent part of the time in counciling with several bretheren upon different Subjects. Bretheren continue to gather into Zion daily.

23rd This day was spent in such labors as they Saw was necessary in this place.

205

Friday the 24th This day was spent at home by the First Presidency, as also was the 25th, 26th, 27th, 28th, 29th, and 30th. \7 /See page 74/ {page 71}

—

\8 A Revelation given [in] Kirtland, July 23rd 1837

The word of the Lord unto Thomas B. Marsh concerning the Twelve Apostles of the Lamb.

"Verily thus saith the Lord unto you my servant Thomas, I have heard thy prayers and thine alms have come up as a memorial before me in behalf of those thy brethren who were chosen to bear testimony of my name and to send it abroad among all nations, kindreds, tongues, and people and ordained through the instrumentality of my servants.

"/2/9 Verily I say unto you, there have been some few things in thine heart and with thee with which I the Lord was not well pleased. Nevertheless inasmuch as thou hast abased thyself thou shalt be exalted. Therefore all thy sins are forgiven thee. Let thy heart be of good cheer before my face and thou shalt bear record of my name, not only unto the Gentiles but also unto the Jews and thou shalt send forth my word unto the ends of the earth.

"/3/ Contend thou therefore morning by morning and day after day. Let thy warning voice go forth and when the night cometh let not the inhabitants of the earth slumber because of thy speech.

"/4/ Let thy habitation be known in Zion and remove not thy house for I the Lord have a great work for ~~you~~ /thee/ to do in publishing my name among the Children of men. Therefore gird up ~~your~~ /thy/ loins for the work. Let ~~your~~ /thy/ feet be shod also

---

7 In the handwriting of Thomas Bullock.
8 In the handwriting of an unidentified scribe.
9 Inserted versification appears throughout the following revelation. Presumably, these numbers were added when the revelation was prepared for publication in the second edition of the Doctrine and Covenants published in 1844 in Nauvoo, Illinois.

for thou art Chosen and thy path*[10] lyeth among the mountains and among many nations. And by thy word many high ones shall be brought low and by thy word many low ones shall be exalted. Thy voice shall be a rebuke unto the transgressor and at thy rebuke let the tongue of the slanderer cease its perverseness.

"[5] Be thou humble and the Lord thy God shall lead thee by the hand and give thee an answer to thy prayers. I know thy heart and have heard thy prayers concerning thy brethren. Be not partial towards them in love above many others but let your /thy/ love be for them as for your/thy/self and let your /thy/ love abound unto all men and unto all who love my name. And pray for your /thy/ brethren of the Twelve [Apostles]. Admonish them sharply for my name's sake and let them be admonished for all their sins and be ye faithful before me unto my name. And after their temptations and much tribulation, behold I the Lord will feel after them. And if they harden not their hearts and stiffen not their necks against me they shall be converted and I will heal them.

" [6] Now I say unto you, and what I say {page 72} unto you I say unto all the Twelve [Apostles]. Arise and gird up your loins, take up your cross, follow me and feed my sheep. Exalt not yourselves, rebel not against my servant Joseph; for verily I say unto you, I am with him and my hand shall be over him and the keys which I have given him and also to youward shall not be taken from him until I come.

" [7] Verily I say unto my servant Thomas, thou art the man [whom] I have chosen to*[11] hold the keys of my Kingdom (as pertaining to the Twelve [Apostles]) abroad among all nations that thou mayest be thy my servant to unlock the door of the Kingdom in all places where my servant Joseph, and my servant Sidney, and my servant Hyrum cannot come for on them have I laid the burden of all the Churches for a little season. Wherefore whithersoever they shall send you, go ye, and I will be with you.

---

[10] This is a printer's "take" mark used by the typesetter to mark his or her place. It marks the end of page 414 in the 1844 edition of the Doctrine and Covenants.

[11] This is a second printer's "take" mark. It marks the end of page 415 in the 1844 edition of the Doctrine and Covenants.

And in whatsoever place ye shall proclaim my name an effectual door shall be opened unto you that they may receive my word. Whosoever receiveth my word receiveth me and whosoever receiveth me receiveth those (the First Presidency) whom I have sent, whom I have made counsellors for my name's sake unto you.

"/8/ And again I say unto you that whosoever ye shall send in my name by the voice of your brethren the Twelve [Apostles] duly recommended and authorized by you shall have power to open the door of my Kingdom unto any nation whithersoever ye shall send them inasmuch as they shall humble themselves before me and abide in my word and hearken to the voice of my spirit.

"/9/ Verily! Verily! I say unto you, darkness covereth the earth and gross darkness the minds of the people and all flesh has become corrupt before my face. Behold vengeance cometh speedily upon the inhabitants of the earth. A day of wrath! A day of burning! A day of desolation! Of weeping! Of mourning and of lamentation! And as a whirlwind it shall come upon all the face of the earth, Saith the Lord.

"/10/ And upon my house shall it begin and from my house shall it go forth, Saith the Lord. First among those among you Saith the Lord who have professed to know my name and have not known me and have blasphemed against me in the midst of my house, Saith the Lord.

"[11] Therefore, see to it that you trouble not yourselves concerning the affairs of my Church in this place, Saith the Lord, but purify your hearts before me and then go ye into all the world and preach my gospel unto every creature who have not received it and he that believeth and is baptised shall be saved and he that believeth not and is not baptised {page 73} shall be damned.

"/12/ For unto you (the Twelve [Apostles]) and those (the First Presidency) who are appointed with you to be your counsellors and your leaders is the power of this priesthood given for the last days and for the last times, in the which is the dispensation of the fulness of times which power you hold in connection with all those who have received a dispensation at any time from the beginning of the Creation. For verily I say unto you, the keys of the dispensation which ye have received have come down from the fathers and last of all being sent down from heaven unto you.

"/13/ Verily I say unto you, Behold how great is your calling. Cleanse your hearts and your garments lest the blood of this generation be required at your hands. Be faithful untill I come for I come quickly and my reward is with me to recompense every man according as his work shall be. I am Alpha and Omega. Amen.*"12

\13 The above revelation was given in Kirtland, and was not here in time to insert in its proper sequence.

G[eorge] W. R[obinson], Recorder

Friday the 31st Pres[iden]t Joseph spent some considerable time this day in conversation with Br[other] John Corril[l], in consequence of some expressions made by him in [the] pressence of some considerable number of bretheren present, who might perhaps be weak in the faith, as they had not been long in the place. Therefore [his expressions] consequently were made verry unwisely.

Br[other] Corril[l]'s conduct for some time past has been verry unbecoming indeed, especially a man in whoom so much confidence has been placed. He has been difficulted to keep track and walk step by step with the great wheel which is propelled by the arm of the great Jehovah. He says he will not yeald [yield] his Judgement to any thing proposed by the Church, or any individuals of the Church, or even the voice of the great I Am given through the appointed organ as revelation, but will always act upon his Judgement. {page 74} Let him believe in whatever religion he may.

He says he will always say what he pleases. For he says he is a Republican and as such he will do, say, act, and believe what he pleases. Let the reader mark such Republicanism as this — That a man should [not?] oppose his own Judgement to the Judgement of God and at the same time profess to believe in the same God, when that God has said, the wisdom of God is foolishness

---

12 This is a third printer's "take" mark.
13 In the handwriting of George W. Robinson.

with men, and wisdom of Judgement of men is foolishness with God.

Pres[iden]t Rigdon also made some observations to Br[other] Corril[l], which he afterwards acknowledged were correct and that he understood things different after the interview from what he did before.

Saturday, 1st [of] Sept[ember] 1838 The First Presidency [with] Judge Higbee (as surveyor) Started this morning for the halfway house (as it is called) kept [by] Br[other] Littlefield, some 14 or 15 miles from Far West directly north, For the purpose of appointing a City of Zion for the gathering of the Saints in that place for safety and from the Storm which will soon come upon this genneration. That the bretheren may be together in the hour of the coming of the Son of Man and that they may receive instructions to prepare them for that great day which will come upon this generation as a thief in the knight.

There is great ex[c]itement at present among the Mis-[s]ourians seeking, if possible, an occasion against us. They are continually chafing us, and provoking us to anger if possible, one sine [sign] of threatening after another but we do not fear them {page 75} For the Lord God the Eternal Father is our God and Jesus the mediator is our Saviour, and in the great I Am is our strength and confidence.

We have been driven time after time and that without cause and smitten again and again, and that without provocation untill we have pre[a]ched the [word?] with kindness, and the world proved us that we have no designs against any man or set of men, That we injure no man, That we are peasible [peaceable] with all men, minding our own buisness and our buisness only.

We have Suffered our rights and our liberties to be taken from us. We have not avenged ourselves of those wrongs. We have appealed to magistrates, to Sheriffs, to Judges, to Govonours, and to the President of the United States, all in vain. Yet we have yealded peacibly to all these things. We have not complained at the Great God, we murmured not, but peacibly left all and retired into the back Country, in the broad and wild prairie, in the barren and desolate plains, and there commenced anew. We made the desolate places to bud and blos[s]om as the rose, and now the fiend-like rose [and] are disposed to give us no rest.

Their Father (the Devil) is hourly calling upon them to

be up and doing, and they like willing and obedient Children need not the second admonition. But in the name of Jesus Christ the Son of the Living God we will endure it no longer, if the Great God will arm us with courage, with strength and with power, to resist them in their persecutions. We will not act on the offensive but always on the defensive.

Our rights and {page 76} our liberties shall not be taken from us, and we peacibly submit to it as we have done heretofore, but we will avenge ourselves of our enemies, inasmuch as they will not let us alone.

But to return again to our subject. We found the place for the city and the bretheren were instructed to gather immediately into it and soon they should be organised according to the Laws of God.*

*A more particular history of this city will /may/ be given /expected/ hereafter, perhaps at the /at its/ organisation and dedication.

We found a new route home saving, I should think, 3 or 4 miles. We arrived at Far West about Day light down.

Sunday, 2nd The First Presidency attended worship as usual the fore part of the day. Pres[iden]t [-]¹⁴ /Smith/ did not attend in the after part of the day, but retired to Pres[iden]t Smith's to examin[e] the Church records. Br[other] Joseph spent some considerable part of the afternoon in company with a gentleman from Livingston County who had become considerable ex[c]ited on account of a large collection of people saying [conspiring] /as they say/ to take Joseph Smith, Jr., and Lyman Wight for going to one Adam Black's /in Daviess County/ as has been previously stated and recorded in this record.

They said Pres[iden]t Smith and Col[onel] Wight had resisted the officer who had endeavoured to take them, etc. Accordingly these men were /are/ assembling to take them (as they said). They are collecting from every part of the Country to Daviess County. Report says they are collecting from Eleven Counties to help take two men {page 77} who had never resisted the Law or officer, neither thought of doing so. This they knew at the same time, or many of them at least. This looks a little to[o] much like

¹⁴A name, possibly that of Sidney Rigdon, has been crossed out at this point in the original manuscript.

mobocracy. It foretells some evil intentions. The whole up[p]er Missouri is all in an uproar and confusion.

This evening ~~we~~ /I/ sent for General Atchison of Liberty, Clay County, who is the Major General of this division ~~we sent for him~~ to come and counsil with us to see if he could not put a stop to this collec[t]ion of people, and to put a stop to hostilities in Daviess County. ~~We~~ /I/ also sent a letter to Judge King containing a petition for him to assist in putting down and scattering the mob which are collecting at Daviess.

Monday, Sept[ember] 3rd Nothing of importance transpired this day, only reports concerning the collection of the mob in Daviess County which has been collecting and collected ever since the election in Daviess ~~which was~~ on the sixth of August last ~~as has been heretofore mentioned~~. /I [Joseph Smith] was at home most of the day/ This evening General Atchison arrived ~~in Town~~ /at Far West/.

Tuesday, 4th This day was spent in council with the Gen[eral] /Atchison/. He says he will do all in his power to disperce the mob &c. We employed him and Doniphan (his partner) as our Lawyers and counselors in Law. They are concidered the first Lawyers in the Up[p]er Missouri.

Pres[iden]t Rigdon and myself [Joseph Smith?] commenced this day the Studay of Law under /the instruction of/ General Atchison and Doniphan. {page 78} They think by diligent application we can be admitted to the bar in twelve months.

The result of the council was that Pres[iden]t Smith and Col[onel] Wight Volunteer and be tried by Judge King in Daviess County. Col[onel] Wight being present being previously notified to attend the council. Accordingly Thursday next was appointed for the trial and word to that amount was sent to Judge King (who had previously agreed to volunteer and try the case) to meet all at Br[other] Littlefield's near the county line ~~South~~ /in the southern part/ of Daviess [County].

Wendnessday, 5th Judge King came to town on his way to Daviess to meet the above named engagement. Gen[eral] Atchison had gone before Judge King arrived. The Judge stayed all Knight.

Thursday the 6th Pres[iden]t Smith repaired to Br[other] Littlefield's to stand trial. He was accompanied by several of the bretheren among whoom was Pres[iden]t Hyram Smith, Judge E[lias] Higbee, and myself &c. &c.

Pres[iden]t Smith thought it not wisdom to make his appearance before the public in consequence of the many threats made against him and the high state of ex[c]itement in that place. The trial could not go on in consequence of the absence of the Plaintiff and lack of testimony. Consequently the court adjourned till tomorrow at 10 o'clock at a Mr. Raglin's some 6 or 8 miles farther south. Also he is a real mob character. He lives within {page 79} one half mile of Caldwell County line. We all returned this evening to Far West.

Friday the 7th We all met at Raglin's agreeable to adjournment. We did not know but there would be a distirbane [disturbance] among the mob characters today. We accordingly had an army of men placed at the county line so as to be ready at a minuits [minute's] warning if there should be any difficulty at the trial.

The trial commenced. W[illia]m P. Penningston who was the prossecutor had no witnesses, but Adam Black who contrived to swear a great ma[n]y things that never had an exista[n]ce untill he swore them and I presume never entered the heart of any man. And in fine I think he swore by the Job (or /that/ he was employed so to do by Penningston). The witnesses on the part of the defence was Dimick B. Huntington, Gideon Carter, Adam Lightner, and ~~myself~~ /Geo[rge] W. Robinson/.

The Judge bound ~~Prest Smith and~~ Col[onel] Wight /and myself [Joseph Smith]/ over to court in a five hundred dollar bond. There was no proof against ~~them criminaly~~ /us to [in]criminate us/, but it is supposed he did it to pacify as much as possible the feelings of the mob[b]ers. The Judge stated after/wards/ in ~~my~~ /Geo[rge] W. Robinson's/ presence that there was nothing proven against them worthy of bonds, but ~~they~~ /we/ submitted without murmuring a word, gave the bonds with sufficient securities and all returned home the same evening.

We found two persons in Daviess at the trial which Gentlemen were sent from Charriton County as a committe to enquire into all this matter as the mob[b]ers had sent {page 80} to that place for assistance. They said [they were] to take Smith and Wight, but their object was to drive the bretheren from the County of Daviess as was done in Jackson County. They said the people in Charriton did not se[e] proper to send help without knowing for what purpose they were doing it, and this they said was their errand. They ~~came home with us~~ /accompanied us to Far West/ to hold a council with us in order to learn the facts of this great ex[c]itement, which is as it were, turning the world up side down.

Saturday the 8th [of] Sept[ember] The Presidency met in council with the committe ~~above named~~ from Charriton County, together with General Atchison, where a relation was given of this whole matter, the present state of ex[c]itement and the cause of all this confusion. These Gentlemen expressed their fullest sattisfaction upon ~~this matter~~ /the subject/ considering they had been outragiously imposed upon in this matter. They left this afternoon apparently perfectly sattisfied with the interview. News came this evening that the mob were to attack Adam Ondi Awman /and a few of the brethren from Far West started to assist the brethren to defend themselves/.

Sunday the 9th This morning a company in addition to what went last evening went to Adam Ondi Awman to assist the bretheren there in their defence against the mob. Capt[ain] W[illia]m Alred took a company of ten men, all mounted, and went to entercept a team with guns and am[m]unition from Richmond for the mob in Daviess. They found the wagon broke down and the boxes of guns drawn into the high grass near by the wagon. {page 81} No one [was] present that could be discovered.

In a short time, two men /on/ horse back came from towards the camp of the mob and immediately behind them was a man with a wagon. They all came up and were taken by virtue of a writ supposing them to be the men who were abetting the mob in carrying the guns and am[m]unition to those murderors. Yea and murderers to[o] in cold blood.

The men were taken together with the guns to Far West. The guns were distributed among the bretheren for their defence and the prissoners were held in custosday.

This was a glorious day indeed, the plans of the mob were frustrated in loosing their guns and all their efforts appeared to be blasted ~~or blast before carried into effect~~. The mob continue[d] to take prisioners at their pleasure. Some they keep [kept] and some they let go. They try [tried] all in their power to make us commit the first act of violence. They frequently send [sent] in word that they are tor[t]ureing the prisioners to death in the most ag[g]rauvating manner. But we understand all their ways and their cunning and wisdom is not past finding out.

Monday, 10th Today we proceeded to trial of those prisioners. They said they wished for an opportunity of getting bail so as to obtain counsil. They were given to understand that no bail could be taken for this purpose, but that [t]he[y] could have a sufficient time to send for counsil if [t]he[y] wished. The court accordingly adjourned untill Wendnessday {page 82} following. The Prisioners names were: John B. Comer, Alem Miller, [and] W[illia]m L. McHoney. They were brought before Albert Petty a Justice of the Peace in Far West.

Tuesday, 11th [of] Sept[ember] [*entry left blank, journal ends*] {page 83}

[*Pages 84 through 100 are blank in the original manuscript.*]

\\[15] Liberty Jail, Missouri
16th December 1838

To the Church of Latter day Saints in Caldwell County, and all the Saints who are scattered abroad, [who] are persecuted and made desolate, and are afflicted in divers manners for Christ's sake and the Gospel's and whose perils are greatly augmented by the wickedness and corruption of false brethren.

May grace, mercy, and the peace of God be and abide with you and notwithstanding all your sufferings we assure you that you have our prayers and fervent desires for your welfare and salvation both day and night. We believe that that God who seeth us in this solitary place will hear our prayers and reward you openly.

Know assuredly Dear Brethren that it is for the testimony of Jesus that we are in bonds and in prison. But we say unto you that we consider that our condition is better, (notwithstanding our suffering) than those who have persecuted us and smitten us and borne false witness against us, and we most assuredly believe that those

---

[15] In the handwriting of an unidentified scribe.

who bear false witness against us do seem to have a great triumph over us for the present.

We want you to remember Haman and Mordecai. You know that Haman could not be satisfied so long as he saw Mordecai at the King's gate. He sought the life of Mordecai and the people of the Jews, But God so ordered that Haman was hanged upon his own gallows. So shall it come to pass with poor Haman in the last days. Those who have sought by their unbelief and wickedness and by the principle of mobocracy to destroy us and the people of God by killing and scattering them abroad and wilfully and maliciously delivering us into the hands of murderers desiring us to be put to death thereby having us dragged about in chains and cast into prison, and for what cause? It is because we were honest men and were determined to defend the lives of the Saints at the expense of our own.

I say unto you that those who have thus vilely treated us like Haman shall be hanged upon their own gallows, or in other words, shall fall into their own gin and snare and ditch and trap which they have prepared for us and shall go backwards {page 101} and stumble and fall, and /their/ names shall be blotted out, and God shall reward them according to all their abominations.

Dear Brethren, do not think that our hearts faint as though some strange thing had happened unto us for we have seen and been assured of all these things beforehand, and have had an assurance of a better hope than that of our persecutors, therefore God hath made broad our shoulders for the burden.

We glory in our tribulations because we know that God is with us, that he is our friend and that he will save our souls. We do not care for them that kill the body; they cannot harm our souls; we ask no favors at the hands of mobs, nor of the world, nor of the Devil, nor of his emissaries the Dissenters, and those who love and make and swear falsehoods, to take away our lives.

We have never dissembled, nor will we for the sake of our lives, forasmuch then as we know that we have been endeavoring with all our minds, mights, and strength to do the will of God and all things whatsoever he has commanded us. And as to our light observations from time to time they have nothing to do with the fixed purposes of our hearts.

Therefore it sufficeth us to say that our souls were vexed from day to day. We refer you to Isai[a]h who considers those who make a man an offender for a word and lay a snare for him that reproveth in the gate. We believe that the old Prophet verily told the truth, we have no retraction to make, we have reproved in the gate and men have laid snares for us, we have spoken words and men have made us offenders, and notwithstanding all this our minds are not yet darkened but feel strong in the Lord. But behold the words of the Saviour, "If the light which is in you become darkness, behold how great is that darkness."

Look at the dissenters. Again if you were of the world, the world would love its own. Look at Mr. Hinkle [who negotiated the surrender at Far West]. A wolf in sheep's clothing. Look at his Brother John Corrill. Look at the beloved Reed Peck who aided him by /in/ leading us, as the Saviour was led, into the camp as a lamb prepared for the slaughter and a sheep dumb before his shearer so we opened not our mouths. But these men like Balaam being greedy for [a] reward sold us into the hands of those who loved them, for the world loves his own.

I would remember W[illiam] W. Phelps who comes up before us as one of Job's destroyers. God suffered such {page 102} kind of beings to afflict Job, but it never entered into their hearts that Job would get out of it all. This poor man who professes to be much of a Prophet has no other dumb ass to ride only David Whitmer to forbid his madness when he goes up to curse Israel. And this ass, not being of the same kind of Balaam's, therefore the angel notwithstanding he appeared unto him yet he could /not/ penetrate his understanding sufficiently so but what he brays out cursings instead of blessings. Poor Ass whoever lives to see it will

217

see him and his rider perish like those who perished in the gain saying of Core, or after the same condemnation.

Now as for these and the rest of their company we will not presume to say that the world loves them but we presume to say that they love the world and we classify them in the error of Balaam and in the gainsaying of Core and with the company of Cora, Dathan, and Abiram. Perhaps our brethren may say because we thus write that we are offended at those Characters! If we are, it is not for a word neither because they reproved in the gate, but because they have been the means of shedding innocent blood. Are they not murderers then at heart? Are not their consciences seared as with a hot iron?

We confess that we are offended, but the Saviour said, "It must needs be that offences come but woe unto them by whom they come, and again blessed are ye when men shall revile you and persecute you and shall say all manner of evil fals[e]ly for my sake. Rejoice and be exceeding glad for great is your reward in heaven for so persecuted they the Prophets which were before you."

Now brethren, if any men ever had reason to claim this promise we are the men, for we know that the world not only hates us but they speak all manner of evil of us falsely for no other reason than that we have been endeavoring to teach the fulness of the gospel of Jesus Christ. After we were bartered away by Hinkle and were taken into the militia camp, we had all the evidence we could have asked for that the world hated us. If there were Priests among them of all the different sects they hated us and that most cordially too. If there [were] Generals they hated us, if there were Colonels they hated us, and the soldiers and officers of all classes hated us, and the most profane blasphemers and drunkards and whoremongers hated us. They all hated us most cordially.

And now what did they hate us for? Purely because of the testimony of Jesus Christ. Was it because we ar[e] liars? We know that it is reported {page 103} by

218

some but it is reported falsely. Was it because we have committed treason against the state in Daviess County or of burglary, or of larceny or arson, or any other unlawful act in Daviess county?

We know that Priests and certain lawyers and certain judges who are the instigators, aiders, and abettors of a certain gang of murderers and robbers who have been carrying on a scheme of mobocracy to uphold their priestcraft against the saints of the last days for a number of years. Who have by a well contemplated and premedi[t]ated scheme to put /down/ by physical operation a system of religion that all the world by all their mutual attainments and any fair means whatever were not able to resist.

Hence, mobbers were encouraged by Priests and Levites, by the Pharisees and the Sadducees, and Essenees, and the Herodians, and every other [-] and -ite egging on the most ruthless, abandoned, and debauched and lawless, inhuman, and beastly set of men that the earth can boast of. Indeed, a parallel cannot be found any where else, to gather together to drive, to steal, to plunder, to starve, and to exterminate and burn the houses of the Mormons.

These are the characters that by their treasonable and overt acts have desolated and laid waste Daviess County. These are the characters that would fain make all the world believe that we are guilty of the above-named acts, but they represent us falsely. We stood in our defence and we believe that no man of us acted only in a just, a lawful, and righteous retaliation against such marauders.

We say unto you that we have not committed treason, neither any other unlawful act in Daviess County. Was it for murder in Ray County against Mob Militia? Who was a wolf in [the] first instance, Hide and hair, teeth, legs, and tail, who afterwards put on a Militia sheepskin well tanned with the wool on, who could sally forth in the day time into the flock and snarl and show his teeth, and scatter and devour the flock and satiate himself upon his prey, and then sneak back into the

219

brambles in order that he might conceal himself in his well tryed skin with the wool on?

We are well aware that there is a certain set of Priests and satellites and mobbers that would fain make all the world believe that we are the dogs that barked at this howling wolf that made such havoc among the sheep. Who when he retreated he howled and bl[e]ated at such a desperate rate that if one could have been there he would have thought that all the wolves whether wrapped up in sheep skins or in goat skins or in any other skins and {page 104} in fine all the beast[s] of the forest were awfully alarmed and catching the scent of innocent blood, they sallied forth with a tremendous howl and crying of all sort[s] and such a howling and such a tremenduous havoc never was known. Such a piece of inhumanity and relentless cruelty and barbarity cannot be found in all the annals of history.

These are the characters that would make the world believe that we had committed murder by making an attack upon this howling wolf while we were at home and in our beds and asleep and knew nothing of the transaction any more than we know what is going on in China while we are within these walls.

Therefore we say again unto you in these things they have represented us falsely. Was it for committing adultery? We are aware that false slander has gone abroad for it has been reiterated in our ears. These are falsehoods also. Renegade Mormon dissenters run abroad into the world and spread various false and libelous reports against us thinking thereby to gain the friendship of the world because they know that we are not of the world and that the world hates us; therefore they make a toast of these characters [and] by them try to do all the injury they can and after that they hate them worse than they do us because they find them to be base traitors and sycophants. Such characters God hates; we cannot love them. The world hates them and we sometimes think that even Satan ought to be ashamed of them.

We have heard that it is reported by some that some

of us should have said that we not only dedicated our property but our families also to the Lord; and Satan taking advantage of this has transfigured it into licentiousness such as a community of wives which is an abomination in the sight of God.

When we consecrate our property to the Lord it is to administer to the poor and the needy, for this is the law of God. It is not for the purpose of the rich, those who have no need. And when a man consecrates or dedicates his wife and children, he does not give them to his neighbour, nor to his brother, for there is no such law. For the law of God is that thou shalt not commit adultery. Thou shalt /not/ covet thy neighbor's wife. He that looketh on a woman to lust after her has committed adultery /already/ in his heart.

Now for a man to consecrate his property and his wife and children to the Lord is nothing more or less than to feed the hungry, clothe the naked, visit the widow and the fatherless, the sick, and the afflicted, and do {page 105} all he can to administer to their relief in their afflictions, and for him and his house to serve the Lord. In order to do this, he and all his house must be virtuous and must shun the very appearance of evil.

Now if any person has represented anything other wise than what we now write he or she is a liar and has represented us falsely and this is another manner of evil which is spoken against us falsely.

We have learned also, since we have been prisoners, that many /false/ and pernicious things, which were calculated to lead the saints far astray and to do them great injury as coming from the Presidency, [were] taught by Dr. [Sampson] Avard. We have reason to fear many other designing and corrupt characters like unto himself which the Presidency never knew of being taught in the Church by any body untill after they were made prisoners, which if they had known of they woud have spurned them and their authors from them as they would the very gates of hell.

Thus we find there have been frauds and secret

221

abominations and evil works going on leading the
minds of the weak and unwary into confusion and dis-
traction, and pawning it all the while upon the Presidency, while mean time the Presidency were ignorant,
as well as innocent of these things, which were practicing [being practiced] in the church in their name.
[This, while the members of the Presidency] were attending to their own secular and family concerns,
weighed down with sorrow, in debt, in poverty, in hunger assaying to be fed. Yet finding themselves receiving
deeds of charity, but inadequate to their subsistence,
and because they /we/ received those deeds they were
envied and hated by those who professed to be [our]
own friends.

But notwithstanding we thus speak, we honor the
church when we speak of the church, as a church, for
their liberality, kindness, patience, and long suffering,
and their continued kindness towards us. And now
brethren, we say unto you, what more can we enumer-
ate? Is not all manner of evil of every description spoken of us falsely? Yea, we say unto you, falsely we have
been misrepresented and misunderstood and belied.
And the purity and integrity and uprightness of our
hearts have not been known. And it is through
ignornace, yea,the very depth of ignorance is the cause
of it, and not only ignorance but on the part of some
gross wickedness and hypocracy also who by a long face
and sanctimonious prayers and very pious sermons had
power to lead the minds of the ignorant and unwary
and thereby obtain such influence that when we ap-
proached their {page 106} iniquities the Devil gained
great advantage [and] would bring great sorrow and
trouble on our heads.

In fine, we have waded through an ocean of tribulation, and mean abuse practice[d] upon us by the
illbred and the ignorant such as [George] Hinkle,
[John] Corrill, [William W.] Phelps, [Sampson] Avard,
Reed Peck, [John] Cleminson, and various others who
are so very ignorant that they cannot appear respectable

in any decent and civilized society, and whose eyes are full of adultery and cannot cease from sin.

Such characters as [William] McLellin, John Whitmer, D[avid] Whitmer, O[liver] Cowdery, and Martin Harris, who are too mean to mention and we had liked to have forgotten. [Thomas] Marsh and [Orson] Hyde whose hearts are full of corruption, whose cloak of hypocrisy was not sufficient to shield them or to bear them up in the hour of trouble, who after having escaped the pollutions of the world through the knowledge of our Lord and Saviour Jesus Christ became again entangled and overcame. Their latter end is worse than the beginning. But it has happened /unto them/ according to the words of the Saviour, "The dog has returned to his vomit, and the sow that was washed to her wallowing in the mire."

Again, if we sin wilfully after we have received the knowledge of the truth, there remaineth no more sacrifice for sin, but rather a certain fearful looking of judgement and fiery indignation to come which shall devour these adversaries. For [if] he who despiseth Moses' Law died without mercy under two or three witnesses, of how much sorer punishment suppose ye shall he be thought worthy who hath sold his brother and denied the new and everlasting covenant by which he was santified calling it an unholy thing and doing [evil] despite [his claim] unto the spirit of grace.

And again we say unto you, inasmuch as there be virtue in us and the Holy Priesthood hath been conferred upon us, and the keys of the kingdom have not been taken from us. For verily thus saith the Lord, "Fear not, but be of good cheer. For the keys which I gave unto you are yet with you!"

Therefore we say unto you, Dear Brethren in the name of the Lord Jesus Christ, we deliver these Characters unto the buffetings of Satan, until the day of redemption, that they may be dealt with according to their works, and from henceforth their works shall be made manifest.

And now Dear and Well-beloved Brethren and

when we say Brethren, we mean those who have continued faithful in Christ — Men, Women, and Children, we
feel to exhort you in the name of the Lord Jesus to be
strong in the faith of the new and {page 107} everlasting covenant, and nothing fright[en]ed at your enemies.
For what has happened unto us is an evident token to
them of damnation but unto us of Salvation and that of
God. Therefore hold on even unto death, "For he that
seeks to save his life shall loose it, but he that looseth
his life for my sake and the Gospel's shall find it,"
sayeth Jesus Christ.

Brethren, from henceforth let truth and righteousness abound in you; and in all things be temperate, ab-
stain from drunkeness and from swearing and from all
profane language, and from every thing which is
unrighteous or unholy; also from enmity and hatred,
and covetousness, and from every unholy desire. Be
honest one with another, for it seemeth that some have
come short of these things, and some have been uncharitable and have manifested greediness because of their
debts towards those who have been persecuted and
dragged about in chains without cause and imprisoned.
Such characters God hates and shall have their turn of
sorrow in the rolling of the great wheel for it rolleth and
none can hinder. Zion shall yet live, though she
seemeth to be dead. Remember that whatsoever measure you meet out to others it shall be measured unto
you again. We say unto you Brethren be not afraid of
your adversaries. Contend earnestly against mobs, and
the unlawful works of dissenters and of darkness. And
the very God of peace shall be with you and make a
way for your escape from the adversary of your souls.

We commend you to God and the word of His
grace which is able to make us wise unto Salvation.
Amen.

Joseph Smith, Jr. {page 108}[16]

---

[16] The remainder of the "Scriptory Book" was used to record patriarchal blessings.

Journal

1 8 3 8 - 3 9

*T*he following journal, written by James
Mulholland, describes Joseph Smith's
activities in the third person and is actually more of a Mulholland than a
Smith journal. It is included in this compilation because it was intended to
record Smith's activities and does contain details, however superficial, re-
garding Smith from one of his scribes. The original is housed in the archives
of the Historical Department, Church of Jesus Christ of Latter-day Saints,
Salt Lake City, Utah.

Sept[ember] 3[rd] 1838

James Mulholland
M'
Joseph Smith['s]
Jour[n]al

[*wrapper notation, written sideways on page*] James Mulholland ~~vs~~ /for/
Joseph Smith, 1838 {cover page}

—

Page 175[1] Withdrew my Spirit and I [Jesus Christ] do his [God's] will

Page 177 His [Joseph Smith's] word ye shall receive as if from mine [Jesus Christ's] own mouth

—

Be patient in afflictions for thou [Joseph Smith] shalt have many Page 111

According to this pattern [of not requiring miracles] 112 page

—

The Song of the righteous [is a prayer unto me] Page 179

—

Thou [Oliver Cowdery] shalt not command him who is at thy head Page 181

—

Contrary to Church Covenants [Hiram Page's claiming revelations for the church] [page] 182

—

His [God's] glory [bestowed upon the original twelve apostles] even as I [Jesus Christ] am   Page 113

And none else [than those who keep the commandements]   Do.

Because of their agency [the third of the hosts of heaven deceived by the devil]   P[age] 115

Even that same death [as Adam's and Eve's]   Do. Do.

---

[1] This and subsequent page references on the first page of the original manuscript probably refer to the 1835 edition of the Doctrine and Covenants (Kirtland, Ohio), a compilation of revelations, policy guidelines, and teachings governing the church.

Even as many as would believe [will receive immortality]
Do. Do.
{page 1}

—

Ideas &c. &c. &c.

When Juda[h] is gathered, the Lord will also bring again
the Assyrian captivity viz. Israel. The Spirit poured out upon all
flesh, but your Sons and daughters shall prophecy. Joel promice,
Book of Mormon, pages 541 and 34. No imposter would attempt
to make such for instance the promise of the Holy Ghost.

—

Another angel — a falling away come. Saviou[r] did not
come untill his time came. So also the Book of Mormon. Proof
that Gentiles were not the other sheep that is [mentioned]. The
Saviour Said, "I am not sent save to the lost sheep of the house of
Israel."

Jealousy of the Chinese, hid up 6 million children of Israel. In England 1,000 souls [baptized] in 9 months. Unbelief
close[s] the way to knowledge. Ephraimites to be the hunters and
fishers. Testimony of the Spirit will seal the destiny of men.

The difference between [the] Saints and [the] world is
that Saints know [the truth], the world do[es] not. {page 2}

Commenced to write for President Joseph Smith Jun[io]r
on Monday the 3rd [of] September 1838.

Memorandum &c. &c.

Monday, Sept[embe]r 3rd [1838] At home all or greater
part of day.

Tuesday, 4th Breakfast with him 1/2 past 7 o'clock, ~~dined~~
at home for dinner a little before noon and again in the evening
between 5 and 6 o'clock.

Wednesday, 5th At home for breakfast at 1/2 past 7. Also
for dinner from 1 to 2 o'clock. At home in the evening about 6
o'clock.

Thursday, 6th ~~He rode out on Horseback~~ He left home

227

on horseback 1/2 past 7 [this] morning. At home again in the evening before dark.

Friday, 7th Saw him leave home about sun rising and heard and saw him at home between 10 and 11 o'clock same night.

Saturday, 8th At home about 8 o'clock [this] morn[ing]. At home between 2 and 3 o'clock [this] Afternoon.

No memorandum from 8th to 14[th]

Friday, 14th At home about 3 P.M. and all this evening.

Saturday, 15th At home early in mor[n]ing for breakfast say 9 and 2 o'clock.

Sunday, 16th At home all day.

Monday, 17th Saw him early [this] morning, again at 9 o'clock forenoon, [and] also [this] afternoon.

Tuesday, 18[th] At home all day and unwell, in better health towards evening. {page 3}

Wednesday, 19th At home in the morning for breakfast about 8 o'clock. Also for dinner about 1 o'clock and in the evening before bed time.

Thursday, 20th At home from morning untill about 10 o'clock. Went out on horseback and returned at about sunset or rather before it. At home all evening.

Friday, 21st Saw him at home at breakfast.

Saturday, 22nd At home early in the morning and at breakfast about 1/2 past 7 o'clock. Saw him ride out a horseback about 9 o'clock.

Sunday, 23rd At home and at meeting all the day. Also saw [him] /at home/ in evening about 9 o'clock.

Monday, 24th At home at breakfast and before. Saw him ride out on horseback about 1/2 past 8 o'clock morning. Returned home about 5 o'clock evening.

Tuesday, 25th At home for breakfast. About 8 o'clock saw him go out on horseback. Saw him again between 11 and 12 o'clock at which he was [occupied] untill about 1/2 past 5 ev[eni]ng. Saw him at home in evening about 1/2 past 6.

Wednesday, 26th At home morning early also at b[r]eakfast between 7 and 8 o'clock. Saw him ride out between 10 and eleven o'clock. And saw him at home again [at] 9 o'clock [in the] evening.

Thursday, 27th At home before and at breakfast 8 o'clock.

Saw him again at 4 o'clock in the evening and between 5 and 6 o'clock in the City. {page 4}

Friday, 28th At home for breakfast about 8 o'clock. Saw him walk out about nine. Saw him again between one and two. At home all afternoon. Saw him ride out about sunset.

Saturday, 29th Did not see him untill about 3 o'clock afternoon. Saw him then come home on horseback. At home all evening.

Sunday, 30th At home for breakfast and u[n]till ten o'clock. Went from home at that time.

Monday, 1st October [1838] Not at home untill about 5 o'clock afternoon. At home all the evening.

Tuesday, 2nd At home for breakfast about 1/2 past 7 o'clock. Saw him again in the evening about 1/2 past four o'clock. Again at supper about 1/2 past 6 o'clock.

Wednesday, 3rd At home before and at breakfast. Also about one o'clock afternoon.

Thursday, 4th Saw him at home about sunrise, all the forenoon, and at noon. In the evening again about 8 o'clock.

Friday, 5th Saw him early in the morning say 7 o'clock. Again about 10 o'clock, did not see him all the afternoon, understood that he went from home.

Saturday, 6th [*entry left blank*][2]

[*written upside down at the bottom of page*] On acc[oun]t of my labors last fall I have received pay for 2 month[s] at $20 per-$40. {page 5}

Contra Acc[oun]t

April 22nd /1839/	Laid out for Pen, ink and paper	$0.50
May 5th	Do.　　Do.　　paper	0.25
14th	Quills and ink powder	0.37½
		$1.12½

—

[2] When Mulholland began to write regularly again on 22 April 1839, he also started a second journal for Joseph Smith, which he called a minute book (and which follows next in the present compilation). Entries in the two Mulholland journals thus overlap, this one serving more as a personal memoranda book than as a journal.

July 16th	T[w]o Stell[steel] pens	$1.25
Do	Sand and Caster	~~0.75~~
		/0.50/ {page 6}

[*written sideways on page*] Mulholland, James Journal kept for Joseph Smith, Jun[ior], 1839 /A.J.[3]{page 7}

Commenced again to write for the Church on Monday the 22nd [of] April 1839.

April 22nd	Received in money from	$0.12½
	Elder Green	
May 4th	Do from Bishop Knights	0.50
4th	Do from President Smith	0.50
		$1.12½
	Do from Do	.75

All this time bussy for Church.

May 9th Accompanied President Smith to Commerce, Illinois. Returned on the 14th and again returned with my wife to Commerce on Sunday evening the 19th.

[20 May 1839] On Monday spent part of the day assisting Br[other] Ripley to survey.

[21 May 1839] Tuesday Spent in same manner.

[22 May 1839] Wednesday /Sick/

[23-24 May 1839] Thursday and Friday Writing.

[25 May 1839] Saturday At Council.

Committe[e] &c. [Certificate] on account of late Services By Sundries as per account $5.64 c[en]ts

Monday, 27th Writing all day for Church.

[28 May 1839] Tuesday Writing /&c./ about 3/4 of the time.

[29 May 1839] Wednesday /Do/ about 1/3 of the day, rest unwell.

[30 May 1839] Thursday Writing and examining papers &c. Six o'clock evening commenced to work on Lot.

30th Received of Br[other] Knight on acc[oun]t $1.00.

[1-2 June 1839] Friday and Saturday Writing.

---

[3] These are the initials of Andrew Jensen (1850-1941), an assistant LDS church historian at the turn of the twentieth century. This line is in Jensen's handwriting.

Monday, 3rd June & Tuesday [4 June 1839] Writing for Church.

[5-6 June 1839] Wednesday and Thursday Writing and working for myself.

[7-8 June 1839] Friday and Saturday [Writing] for Church.

[10-13 June 1839] Monday 10th, Tuesday, Wednesday, and Thursday 13th /Writing &c. for Church history/. Received cash $10.00.

[14-15 June 1839] Friday and Saturday [Writing] for Church.

[16 June 1839] Sunday at meeting [at] Br[other] Bosier's. {page 8}

Monday 17th and Tuesday [18 June 1839] Writing history.

[19 June 1839] Wednesday Forenoon unwell, afternoon writing history.

[20 June 1839] Thursday Forenoon Study/ing/ /for/ history. Afternoon unwell.

[21 June 1839] Friday Unwell.

[22 June 1839] Saturday Copying in Letter book.

[23 June 1839] Sunday At home.

Monday, 24th All this week Copying Letters &c. &c.

[30 June 1839] Sunday At home.

Monday, July 1rst Writing letters &c.

[2 July 1839] Tuesday To myself [and went] across the river.

[3 July 1839] Wednesday Forenoon to myself. Afternoon writing history.

[4-6 July 1839] Thursday, Friday, and Saturday Forenoon writing for the Church. Afternoon to myself.

Sunday, 7th At Meeting.

[8 July 1839] Monday Forenoon writing. Afternoon unwell.

[9-10 July 1839] Tuesday and Wednesday Writing.

[11 July 1839] Thursday Went to Quincy. Received on acc[oun]t cash of Br[other] S[mith] $3.00. Left Quincy on Tuesday 16th and arrived home at Commerce on Wednesday noon.

[18 July 1839] Thursday Moved to Brother Turley's.

[19-20 July 1839] Friday and Saturday Unwell.

[21 July 1839] Sunday At home rather unwell.

/End of first Quarter/

Monday, 22nd Commenced again to write.

[22-24 July 1839] Monday, Tuesday, and Wednesday Writing.

[25 July 1839] Thursday Idle from the extreme heat and sultriness. {page 9}

[26 July 1839] Friday Writing and recording history.

[27 July 1839] Saturday For myself. [At home, wife ill?]

Sunday, 28th At meeting, home &c.

Monday, 29th and all the week working and writing for myself.

> Received cash $20.00
> Pantaloons,
> Paper at sundries white and blue 2 quire
> Sewing silk .12
> Potatoes 1/2 bushel .25

Sunday, 4th August At meeting &c.

Monday, 5th and all the week writing and working for myself.

Sunday, 11th At meeting also.

[12-17 August 1839] Monday and all the week for myself.

Sunday the 18th At meeting also.

Monday, 19th and all the week at home attending my wife who was sick.

Sunday, 25th And all the week at home my wife still sick.

Saturday, 31rst Rec[eive]d 1 Box pills $1.50.

Sunday, 1rst Sept[embe]r and all the week at home. Wife recovering.

27 lbs pork at 8 c[en]ts $2.16

1/2 bushel corn 0.25

Sunday, 8th At home. Wife much better.

[9-13 September 1839] Monday, Tuesday, Wednesday, Thursday, and Friday Writing &c. &c. for Church. {page 10}

[13 September 1839] Friday Received cash of J[oseph] S[mith] $1.00.

[14 September 1839] Saturday At home.

Sunday, 15th At home.

Monday, 16th At home.

4-3/4 lbs hog's lard at [*blank*] per ℔

[17-18 September 1839] Tuesday and Wednesday Writing.

[19 September 1839] Thursday Doing business for T[heodore] Turley.

Received 12 lbs pork at [*blank*] c[en]ts per [lb]

Ferriage across river .25

[20-21 September 1839] Friday and Saturday Writing

Sunday, 22nd At meeting with wife.

Flour per Br[other] Markam 41 lbs at 3.50 per hundred $1.43

All this week writing &c. for J[oseph] S[mith], Jr.

Sunday, 29th At meeting at Br[other] J[oseph's].

[30 September-1 October 1839] Monday and Tuesday Writing &c.

[2 October 1839] Wednesday Forenoon at home. Afternoon writing.

[3 October 1839] Thursday Forenoon writing.

Received 12 lbs meat at [*blank*] per

Do.   1/2 bushel corn   [$].25

House logs p[e]r J. Holman   [$]30.00

[4 October 1839] Friday 3 hours work of 2 men.

[5 October 1839] Saturday Unwell.

Sunday, 5th [6th] October Unwell.

[7 October 1839] Monday Ditto.

[8 October 1839] Tuesday Forenoon writing. Afternoon writing. Also Wednesday.

[10-12 October 1839] Thursday, Friday, and Saturday Do. Do.

1 Bowel [bowl] full of Honey

First payment on lot $30.00

Sunday, 13th At meeting in grace.

Monday, 14th and all the week Writing &c. {page 11}

Received 10 lbs beef at 4 per lb $00.45

1/2 bushel Corn

Sunday, 20th At meeting in the evening.

[21-23 October 1839] Monday, Tuesday, and Wednesday about half time unwell. {page 12}

Journal

1839

L ike the preceding journal, the following manuscript was written entirely
by James Mulholland. Although not as insightful as might be hoped for, it
is nonetheless reasonably detailed and comprehensive in describing some of
Joseph Smith's activities during this period. References to Joseph Smith are
in the third person until mid-June when Mulholland becomes an invisible
scribe. At this point, references to Joseph Smith shift to the first person. The
original of this document is housed in the archives of the Historical Department, Church of Jesus Christ of Latter-day Saints, Salt Lake City, Utah.

Minute Book, 1839
J[oseph] Smith's Journal
Escape from Prison {cover page}

Escaped April 16th 1839

[22 April 1839] President Smith and his fellow prisoners
arrived safe at Quincy, Ill[inois] on ~~Tuesday~~ /Monday/ the ~~23rd~~
/22nd/ of April And spent all [the] next day greeting and receiving visits from his brethren and friends.

234 [24 April-3 May 1839] In the evening of the 24th met in

council with the Church, when a committee was appointed to go to Ioway [Iowa] &c. of which he was one. Went to Ioway, made purchases and returned on Friday the 3rd [of] May.

Saturday, 4th [of] May Presided at General Conference near Quincy, Ill[inois].

[5 May 1839] Sunday Do. Continued.

Monday, 6th Met in Council with the Twelve [Apostles] and others [at] Quincy, Ill[inois].

[7 May 1839] Tuesday Do. Do. Do.

May 10th Moved with his family to Commerce, Hancock Co[unty], Ill[inois].

Monday, 13th Transacted various business with Br[other] Oliver] Granger &c. At home attending to general business.

[14-19 May 1839] Tuesday Do. ~~Wednesday~~ Do. On the 14th I returned to Quincy so kept no ~~record~~ /Minute[s]/ of Course. I got back here Sunday evening the 19th [of] May. {page 1}

Monday, 20th This week at home and employed dictating letters and attending to the various business of the Church.

On Saturday [May] 25th Met in Conference with the Twelve [Apostles] and others of the Church. W[illia]m Smith['s] case disposed of.

[26 May 1839] Sunday At home. Elder O[rson] Pratt and John Taylor preached.

Monday, 27th &c. and beginning of the week at home. Latter part of [the] week he (President Smith) went to Quincy with others of the Presidency and returned on Wednesday [the] 5th [of] June. ~~Spent greater part of latter part study we~~ Latter part [of the week] at home.

Sunday, 9th At meeting with wife and family at Brother Bosier's. Elder [John E.] Page preached.

Monday, 10th Began to Study and Elder Page baptised one woman. Prepare[d] to dictate history.

[11 June 1839] Tuesday [Joseph] commenced to dictate and I to write [Church] history.

[12-14 June 1839] Wednesday, Thursday, and Friday Generally so employed.

Saturday, 15th June [Joseph] left here with his family on a visit. {page 2}

Sunday, 16th Meeting held [at] Br[other] Bosier's [with] Br[other]s Rose and Turley presiding. I was present and considered that Br[other] Rose /spoke/ not /in/ accordance with the doctrines of the Church, nor with the Spirit of God. Others thought so too. President Rigdon preached at Montrose. Bishop Whitney arrived here.

Monday, 17th Bishop Knight arrived [and] returned to Quincy on Tuesday evening. Br[other] Rose baptised one man named [*blank*] at P[re]s[iden]t Rigdon's place.

15th June [Joseph Smith] Started on Saturday morning with my [his] family on a visit to Br[other] [Don] Carlos [Smith]. Met Br[other] W[illia]m on the prairie [and] found him in good spirits. Went to his house /in Plymonth/ [and] found his family all well. Staid over night and had a very satisfactory visit.

[16-17 June 1839] Next day went on to Br[other] Don C. Smith's [in] McDonough Co[unty] near /the village of/ McComb. Staid there untill Monday and there met with Br[other] Sam[ue]l Smith, who I had not before seen since our deliverance from prison.

Tuesday, 18th Went to a house of a man by the name of Mathews. During the {page 3} evening the neighbors came in and I gave them a short discourse.

[20 June 1839] Thursday following went to Elder Zebedee Coulter's [Coltrin's]. From there were invited to visit a Brother [Vi?] Vance's which we did. And there [I] gave to the brethren and friends of the Neig[h]borhood a brief history or account of the coming forth of the Book of Mormon.

Saturday, 22nd We returned to Don C. S[mith's] place.

[23 June 1839] On Sunday went to Br[other] Wilcox's and there preached to a very Crowded Congregation. So eager were they to hear that a part of them stood out in the rain during the Sermon and /in/ general they all expressed good satisfaction as to what they had heard.

Monday, 24th [We] started for home and got as far as Br[other] Parkin's near Fountain Green, Hancock Co[unty] when they insisted that we should tarry.

[25 June 1839] On Tuesday we held [a] meeting and Spoke with considerable liberty to a large congregation.

Wednesday, 26th [We] arrived all safe and sound at home [in] Commerce, Ill[inois].

[27 June 1839] Thursday Attended a Conference {page

4} of the Twelve [Apostles] at which time Br[other] Orson Hyde made his confession and was restored to the Priesthood again.

[28 June 1839] Friday [Spent] transacting business of various Kinds [and] Counseling [with] the Brethren &c. &c.

[29 June 1839] Saturday At home principally.

[30 June 1839] Sunday At meeting at Br[other] Bosier's. Bore testimony to a crowded audience concerning the truth of this work and also of the truth[fulness] of the Book of Mormon &c. &c.

Monday, 1rst July Spent the day principally counseling with the Brethren.

[2 July 1839] Tuesday Spent this day on the Iowa side of the river. Forenoon went in company with Elders Rigdon and H[yrum] Smith, Bishops Whitney and Knights and others to visit a purchase lately made by Bro/ther/ Knights as a location for a town. Advised that a town be built there.

Afternoon met with the Twelve [Apostles] and Some of the Seventies who are about to proceed on their mission to Europe, the nations of the earth, and the Islands of the Sea. The meeting was {page 5} opened by singing and prayer after which The Presidency proceeded to bless two of the Twelve [Apostles], who had lately been ordained into that quorum viz: Wilford Woodruff and George /A./ Smith and one of the Seventies viz Theodore Turley. After which blessings were also pronounced by them on the heads of the wives of /Some of/ those about to /go/ abroad.

The meeting was then addressed by President Hyrum Smith by way of advice to the Twelve [Apostles] &c. &c. Chiefly Concerning the nature of their mission, their practicing prudence, ~~Charity~~, and humility in their plans /or subjects/ for preaching, the necessity of their not trifling with their office, and of holding on strictly to the importance of their mission and the authority of the priesthood.

I (President Joseph Smith, Jr.) then addressed them and gave much instruction calculated to guard them against self-sufficiency, self-righteousness, and self-importance touching upon many subjects of importance and value to all who wish to walk humbly before the Lord, but especially teaching them {page 6} to observe charity, wisdom, and fellow feeling with Love one towards another in all things and under all circumstances.

237

Wednesday, July 3rd Baptised Dr. Isaac Galland and confirmed him by the water edge, [and] about two hours afterwards ordained him to the office of an Elder. Afternoon [spent] dictating History.

[4-5 July 1839] Thursday and Friday (Assisted by Br[other] Newel Knight) dictating History.

[6 July 1839] Saturday Also at home Studying Church records &c. &c.

Sunday, July 7th Meeting held in the open air as a large assemblage was expected to ~~witness~~ /Listen/ [to] the farewell addresses of the 12 [Apostles] who were then about to take their departure on this most important mission viz. to the nations of the earth and the Islands of the sea.

Elder John E. Page, being the first of the 12 [Apostles] present, opened the meeting by addressing a few words /of an/ introductory nature. After which singing and prayer were observed, when Elder Page delivered a very interesting discource on the subject of the Book of Mormon, recapitulating in short terms the Subjects of a former discource on the same subject. {page 7} [He] afterwards proceeded to read portion[s] from the Bible and Book of Mormon concerning the best Criterions whereby to judge of its authenticity. [He] then went on to show that no imposter would ever attempt to make such promises as are contained pages 541 and 34th which he did in a very satisfactory manner. [He] then bore testimony after which the meeting adjourned for one hour.

Afternoon, the meeting was again opened by prayer &c. Elder John Taylor spoke on the subject of this dispensation, the other Angel which John saw having the Everlasting gospel to preach &c. &c. He then bore testimony /of the truth[fulness] of the Book of Mormon &c. &c./.

Elder Woodruff's address went chiefly to exhortation to the Saints to preserverance after which he bore his testimony also.

Elder Orson Hyde next came forward and having alluded to his own late fall exhorted all to perserverance in the things of God [and] expressed himself one with his brethren and bore testimony to his knowledge of the truth and the misery of falling from it.

Elder Brigham Young made some very appropriate remarks and also bore his testimony to the truth of these {page 8} things. [He] gave an invitation to come forward and be baptised when three manifested their determination to renounce the world and take upon themselves the name of Jesus Christ.

One brother was then confirmed after which President S[idney] Rigdon addressed the meeting in a very feeling manner, showing that it must be no small matter which /could/ induce men to leave their families and their homes to travel over all the earth amidst persecutions and trials such as always followed the preaching of this gospel. He then addressed himself to the Twelve [Apostles] and gave them some cou[n]sel and consolation as far as in his power.

After which I (J[oseph] S[mith]) requested their prayers and promised to pray for them. The meeting was large and respectable. A large number were present who did not belong to our Church. The most perfect order prevailed throughout. The meeting dismissed about 1/2 past five o'clock when we repaired to the water and the three candidates were baptised and confirmed. {page 9}

Sunday, [August] 11th At meeting forenoon a Sermon by P[arley] P. Pratt. Afternoon /there was/ 1 baptized and 4 confirmed viz. Br[other] Hibbard, his wife, and little son and daughter and [the] Sacrament [was] administered.

[12-17 August 1839] This week [was] chiefly spent visiting the sick. [The] sickness [was] much decreased.

News from Kirtland by D[imick B.] Huntington. [*several lines left blank*]

Sunday, 18th Not at meeting. Self and wife rode out. Forenoon Sermon by Orson Pratt on the order and plan of [the] creation. Three baptized. Afternoon three confirmed and one ordained an Elder.

[19-24 August 1839] This week [was] chiefly spent among the sick also. New purchase made.

Sunday, 25th At meeting. Sickness [among us] decreasing.

Sunday, 1rst Sept[embe]r At meeting also. [I] Spoke concerning some errors {page 10} in Br[other] P[arley] P. Pratt's works &c. &c. &c.

[2-7 September 1839] This week sickness [was] much decreased.

Sunday, 8th Sept[embe]r [*entry left blank*]

[9-12 September 1839] Monday and greater part of [the]

239

week [was spent] visiting the sick and attending to business of the new town &c. &c.

[13-14 September 1839] Friday At noon left home for Brother W[illia]m Smith's place. Returned home Saturday evening.

Sunday, 15th Visiting the sick.

Monday, 16th ~~and greater part of the Went to Burlington and returned.~~ A greater part of the week [was spent] arranging business of town lots &c.

[18-19 September 1839] Wednesday Went to Burlington, I[owa] T[erritory] and returned on Thursday evening.

[20-21 September 1839] Friday and Saturday At home.

Sunday, 22nd Attended and presided at meeting. Spoke Concerning the /other/ Comforter &c. &c. &c.

[23-28 September 1839] This week [was spent] transacting various business. At home greater part of time except when visiting the sick. All in general recovering, but some very slowly.

Sunday, 29th Meeting at own house. After others had spoken, I Spoke and explained concerning [the] uselessness of preaching {page 11} to the world about great judgements, but rather to preach the simple gospel. Explained concerning the Coming of the Son of Man &c. that all will be raised to meet him. The righteous will remain with him in the cloud whilst all the proud and all that do wickedly will have to return to the earth and suffer his vengeance which he will take upon them. This is the second death &c. &c. Also that it is a false idea that the Saints will escape all the judgements whilst the wicked suffer. For all flesh is subject to suffer and "the righteous shall hardly escape." Still many of the Saints will escape. For the just shall live by faith. Yet many of the righteous shall fall a prey to disease, to pestilence, &c. by reasen [reason] of the weakness of the flesh and yet be saved in the Kingdom of God. So that it is an unhallowed principle to say that such and such have transgressed because they have been preyed upon by disease or death for all flesh is subject to death and the Saviour has Said, "Judge not, lest ye be judged."

[30 September-3 October 1839] All the fore part of this week [was spent] at home and preparing for Conference.

[4 October 1839] Thursday Met in Council.

Saturday, 5th [6th] October 1839 Met in General Conference which Continued [through] Saturday and Sunday. The assemblage {page 12} was very large. A great deal of business was transacted and great instructions given. See Conference Minutes.

[7-12 October 1839] Week beginning Sunday 6th [7th] October After Conference busied in attending to general affairs of the Church, principally about home.

Sunday, 13th At meeting in the Grove. Meeting small on account of cold weather.

Tuesday, 15th Oct[obe]r Afternoon went to Quincy in company with Br[other] Hiram, J[ohn] S. Fulmer, and Bishop Knight. Quite a number of families moving in. {page 13}

Journal, ca.

1841-43

"The Book of the Law of the Lord" —
Excerpts

The Book of the Law of the Lord,"
from which the following excerpts[1]
are taken, was begun in Nauvoo, Illinois, sometime between 19 January
and 7 April 1841. It is a large leather-bound record book, more than 500
pages long, and contains copies of letters, revelations, minutes of meetings,
and a record of donations to the church (especially to the construction of the
Nauvoo temple), as well as some Joseph Smith journal entries. Scribes in-

---

[1] All of these excerpts have previously appeared in Joseph Smith et al., *History of the Church of Jesus Christ of Latter-day Saints*, B. H. Roberts, ed., 7 vols., 2nd rev. ed. (Salt Lake City: Deseret Book, 1964), 5:106-109, 124-28, 421; Andrew F. Ehat and Lyndon W. Cook, eds., *The Words of Joseph Smith* (Provo, UT: Religious Studies Center, Brigham Young University, 1980), pp. 75-76, 103, 105-106, 114, 119-20, 122, 125-29, 131-32, 225; or Dean C. Jessee, ed., *The Personal Writings of Joseph Smith* (Salt Lake City: Deseret Book, 1984), pp. 530-37. Material that comes directly from "The Book of the Law of the Lord," according to Ehat, Cook, or Jessee, is not enclosed in brackets. Entries that, according to Ehat and Cook, "most probably" come from "The Book of the Law of the Lord" are enclosed in brackets, with additional editorial expansions enclosed in double brackets. The direct source for the material in the bracketed entries, "most probably" from "The Book of the Law of the Lord," is the "Manuscript History of the Church," located in the archives of the Historical Department, Church of Jesus Christ of Latter-day Saints, Salt Lake City, Utah. Where possible, page numbers to "The Book of the Law of the Lord" are also provided. Access to the original manuscript was denied.

clude *Robert B. Thompson, Willard Richards, William Clayton. and Thomas Bullock.*

"The Book of the Law of the Lord" is one of the original sources used in compiling Joseph Smith's published History of the Church. *Its first entry is the revelation currently identified as section 124 in LDS editions of the Doctrine and Covenants and as section 107 in RLDS editions. Subsequent entries cover "the most important transactions of the First Presidency and of the Twelve Apostles, important correspondence with Governor [Thomas] Carlin, Henry Clay, John C. Calhoun, James Arlington Bennett, and other distinguished characters. His [Joseph Smith's] letters on baptism for the dead [written] while in seculsion, now contained in the Doctrine and Covenants [sections 127 and 128 in LDS editions; sections 109 and 110 in RLDS editions], laying [the] cornerstones of the Nauvoo House and temple, the dedication of the font, [the] organization of the Relief Society, the Nauvoo Legion and City of Nauvoo, in short all the most important events that transpired with him [Joseph Smith] and the Church so long as he had his liberty." [2] The original manuscript is currently under the control of the First Presidency of The Church of Jesus Christ of Latter-day Saints, Salt Lake City, Utah, and is generally restricted from access, hence my reliance on only previously published excerpts in what follows.*

. . . . .

[25 July 1841] [I followed him [[Sidney Rigdon]], illustrating the subject of the resurrection by some familiar figures.]

[22 August 1841] [I preached at the Stand on Wars and desolations that await the nations.]

[5 September 1841] [I preached to a large congregation at the Stand, on the Science and practice of Medicine, desiring to persuade the Saints to trust in God when sick, and not in an arm of flesh, and live by faith and not by medicine, or poison, and when they were sick, and had called for the Elders to pray for them, and they were not healed, to use herbs and mild food.]

---

[2] Franklin D. Richards to John Taylor, 26 December 1883, archives, Historical Department, Church of Jesus Christ of Latter-day Saints.

[16 January 1842] [I preached at my own house morning and evening, illustrating the nature of Sin, and shewing that it is not right to sin that grace may abound.]

[30 January 1842] [I preached at my house morning and evening, concerning the different Spirits, their operations, designs — &c.]

[27 February 1842] [Engaged in Counselling the Saints.]

[6 March 1842] [I preached at Elder Orson Spencer's near the Temple. {page 89}]

[17 March 1842] [I assisted in commencing the organization of "The Female] Relief Society of Nauvoo" in the "Lodge Room." Sister Emma Smith, President, and Sisters Elizabeth Ann Whitney and Sarah M. Cleveland Counsellors. I gave much instruction, read in the New Testament [2 John 1], and Book of Doctrine and Covenants [25:16, in LDS editions] concerning the Elect Lady, and shewed that the elect meant to be elected to a certain work &c and that the revelation was then fulfilled by Sister Emma's election to the Presidency of the Society, she having previously been ordained to expound Scriptures. {page 91} [Emma was blessed, and her counselors were ordained by Elder John Taylor.][3]

[10 April 1842] [I preached in the grove, and pronounced a curse] upon all adulterers and Fornicators, and unvirtuous persons and those who have made use of my name to carry on their iniquitous designs. {page 93}

[24 April 1842] [Preached] on the hill, near the Temple, concerning the building of the temple, and pronounced a curse on the Merchants and the rich, who would not assist in building it. {page 94}

[28 April 1842] [At two o'clock P.M. I met] the members of the "Female Relief Society" and after presiding at the admission of many new members gave a lecture on the Priesthood shewing how the sisters would come in possession of the privileges, blessings, and gifts of the Priesthood, and that the signs should follow them, such as healing the sick, casting out devils &c and that they might attain unto these blessings by a virtuous life and con-

[3] See also Ehat and Cook, pp. 104-105.

versation and diligence in keeping all the commandments. {page 94}

[1 May 1842] I preached in the grove on the keys of the Kingdom, Charity &c The keys are certain signs and words by which false spirits and personages may be detected from true, which cannot be revealed to the Elders till the Temple is completed — The rich can only get them in the Temple — the poor may get them on the Mountain top as did Moses. The rich cannot be saved without Charity, giving to feed the poor when and how God requires as well as building. There are signs in heaven, earth, and hell. The Elders must know them all to be endowed with power, to finish their work and prevent imposition. The devil knows many signs but does not know the sign of the Son of Man, or Jesus. No one can truly say he knows God until he has handled something, and this can only be in the Holiest of Holies. {page 94}

[1 June 1842] [I attended a political meeting in the Grove, for the nomination of County officers, for the County at large, in which I concurred, with the exception of the Candidate for the Sheriffalty [[William Backenstos]] and spoke in favor of the proceedings.]

[15 July 1842] [It was reported early in the morning that Elder Orson Pratt was missing. I caused the Temple hands and the principle men of the city to make a search for him. After which a meeting was called at the Grove, and I gave the public a general outline of John C. Bennett's conduct.]

[24 July 1842] [This morning at home sick — Attended meeting at the Grove in the afternoon and spoke of brother [[George]] Miller's having returned with the good news that [[John C.]] Bennett could not be able to accomplish his designs.]

[27 July 1842] [Attended meeting at the Grove and listened to the Electioneering Candidates, and spoke at the close of the meeting.]

[16 August 1842] Brother Erastus H. Derby is one among the number of the faithful souls, who have taken as yet the greatest interest that possibly could have been imagined for the welfare of President Joseph [Smith]. I [William Clayton] record the following from the mouth of the President himself:

Blessed is Brother Erastus H. Derby, and he shall be blessed of the Lord. He possesses a sober mind, and a faithful heart. The snares therefore that are subsequent to befall other men, who are treacherous and rotten-hearted, shall not come nigh unto his doors, but shall be far from the path of his feet. He loveth wisdom, and shall be found possessed of her. Let there be a crown of glory, and a diadem upon his head. Let the light of eternal Truth shine forth upon his understanding, let his name be had in everlasting remembrance, let the blessings of Jehovah be crowned upon his posterity after him, for he rendered me consolation, in the lonely places of my retreat.

How good and glorious, it has seemed unto me, to find pure and holy friends, who are faithful, just and true, and whose hearts fail not, and whose knees are confirmed and do not faulter, while they wait upon the Lord, in administering to my necessities, {page 135} in the day when the wrath of mine enemies was poured out upon me. In the name of the Lord, I feel in my heart to bless them, and to say in the name of Jesus Christ of Nazareth that these are the ones that shall inherit eternal life. I say it by virtue of the Holy Priesthood, and by the ministering of Holy Angels, and by the gift and power of the Holy Ghost.

How glorious were my feelings when I met that faithful and friendly band, on the night of the eleventh on thursday, on the Island, at the mouth of the slough, between Zarahemla and Nauvoo. With what unspeakable delight, and what transports of joy swelled my bosom, when I took by the hand on that night, my beloved Emma, she that was my wife, even the wife of my youth, and the choice of my heart. Many were the reviberations [reverberations] of my mind when I contemplated for a moment the many ~~passt~~ scenes we had been called to pass through. The fatigues, and the toils, the sorrows, and sufferings, and the joys and consolations from time to time [which] had strewed our paths and crowned our board. Oh! what a comingling of thought filled my mind for the moment. Again she is here, even in the seventh trouble, undaunted, firm and unwavering, unchangeable, affectionate Emma.

There was Brother Hyrum who next took me by the hand. A natural brother, thought I to myself, brother Hyrum, what a faithful heart you have got. Oh, may the eternal Jehovah crown eternal blessings upon your head, as a reward for the care you have had for my soul. O how many are the sorrows we have shared together, and again we find outselves shackled with the unrelenting hand of oppression. Hyrum, thy name shall be written in the Book of the Law of the Lord, for those who come after thee to look upon, that they may pattern [themselves] after thy works.

Said I to myself here is brother Newel K. Whitney also. How many scenes of sorrow, have strewed our paths together, and yet we meet once more to share again. Thou art a faithful friend in whom the afflicted sons of men can confide, with the most perfect safety. Let the blessings of the eternal be crowned also upon his head. How warm that heart! How anxious that soul! For the welfare of one who has been cast out, and hated of almost all men. Brother Whitney, thou knowest not how strong those ties are, that bind my soul and heart to thee.

My heart was overjoyed, as I took the faithful band by [the] hand, that stood upon the shore one by one. W[illia]m. Law, W[illia]m. Clayton, Dimick B. Huntington, George Miller, were there. The above names constituted the little group. I do not think to mention the particulars of the history of that sacred night, which shall forever be remembered by me. But the names of the faithful are what I wish to record in this place. These I have met in prosperity and they were my friends. I now meet them in adversity, and they are still my warmer friends. These love the God that I serve. They love the truths that I promulg[at]e. They love those virtuous, and those holy doctrines that I cherish in my bosom with the warmest feelings of my heart, and with that zeal which cannot be denied. I love friendship and truth. I love virtue {page 164} and Law. I love the God of Abraham and of Isaac and of Jacob, and they are my brethren, and I shall live. And because I shall live, they shall live also.

These are not the only ones, who have administered to my necessity, whom the Lord will bless. There is Brother John D. Parker, and Brother Amasa Lyman, and Brother Wilson Law, and Brother Henry G. Sherwood. My heart feels to reciprocate the unweried kindness that have been bestowed upon me by these men. They are men of noble stature, of noble hands, and of noble deeds, possessing noble and daring, and giant hearts and souls. There is Brother Joseph B. Nobles also, I would call up in remembrance before the Lord. There is brother Samuel Smith, a natural brother; he is, even as Hyrum. There is Brother Arthur

Millikin also, who married by [my] youngest sister, Lucy. He is a faithful, an honest, and an upright man.

While I call up in remembrance before the Lord these men, I would be doing injustice to those who rowed me in the skiff up the river that night, after I parted with the lovely group, who brought me to this my safe and lonely and private retreat, brother Jonathan Dunham and the other whose name I do not know. Many were the thoughts that swelled my aching heart, while they were toiling faithfully with their oars. They complained not of hardship and fatigue to secure my safety. My heart would have been harder than an adamantine stone, if I had not have prayed for them with anxious and fervent desire. I did so, and the still small voice whispered to my soul, these that share your toils with such faithful hearts, shall reign with you in the kingdom of their God. But I parted with them in silence and came to my retreat. I hope I shall see them again that I may toil for them and administer to their comfort also. They shall not want a friend while I live. My heart shall love those, and my hands shall toil for those, who love and toil for me, and shall ever be found faithful to my friends. Shall I be ungrateful? Verily no! God forbid!

The above are the words, and sentiments, that escaped the lips of President Joseph Smith on the 16th day of August AD 1842, in relation to his friends, and has now quit speaking for the moment, but will continue the subject again.

W[illia]m Clayton, Clerk. {page 165}

[23 August 1842] This day President Joseph [Smith] has renewed the subject of conversation, in relation to his faithful brethren, and friends in his own words, which I now proceed to record as follows:

While I contemplate the virtues and the good qualifications and characteristics of the faithful few, which I am now recording in the Book of the Law of the Lord, of such as have stood by me in every hour of peril, for these fifteen long years past, say, for instance, my aged and beloved brother Joseph Knight, Sen[io]r., who was among the number of the first to administer to my necessities, while I was laboring, in the commencement of the bringing forth of the work of the Lord, and of laying the foundation of the Church of Jesus Christ of Latter Day Saints. For fifteen years has he been faithful and true, and even handed, and exemplary and virtuous, and kind, never deviating to the right hand or to the left. Behold he is a righteous man. May God Almighty lengthen out the old man's days, and may his trembling, tortured and broken body be renewed, and in the vigor of health turn upon him, if it can be thy will, consistently, O God. And it shall be said of him, by the sons of Zion, while there is one of them remaining, that this man, was a faithful man in Israel. Therefore his name shall never be forgotten. There are his son[s] Newel Knight and Joseph Knight whose names I record in the Book of the Law of the Lord, with unspeakable delight, for they are my friends.

There is a numerous host of faithful souls, whose names I could wish to record in the Book of the Law of the Lord, but time and chance would fail. I will mention therefore only a few of them as emblematical of those who are to[o] numerous to be written.

But there is one man I would mention namely [Orrin] Porter Rockwell, who is now a fellow-wanderer with myself, an exile from his home because of the murderous deeds and infernal disposition of the indefatigable and unrelenting hand of the Missourians. He is an innocent and a noble boy. May God Almighty deliver him from the hands of his pursuers. He was an innocent and a noble child, and my soul loves him. Let this be recorded for ever and ever. Let the blessings of salvation and honor be his portion.

But as I said before, so say I again while I remember the faithful few who are now living, I would remember also the faithful of my friends who are now dead, for they are many. And many are the acts of kindness, and paternal and brotherly kindnesses which they have bestowed upon me. And since I have been hunted by the Missourians many are the scenes which have been called to my mind. Many thoughts have rolled through my head, and across my breast.

I have remembered the scenes of my childhood. I have thought of my father who is dead, who died by disease which was brought upon him through suffering by the hand of ruthless mobs. He was a great and a good man. The envy of knaves and fools was heaped upon him, and this was his lot and portion all the days of his life. He was of noble stature, and possessed a high, and holy, and exalted, and a virtuous mind. His soul soared above

249

all those mean {page 179} and groveling principles that are so subsequent to the human heart. I now say, that he never did a mean act that might be said was ungenerous, in his life, to my knowledge. I love my father and his memory, and the memory of his noble deeds, rest with ponderous weight upon my mind; and many of his kind and parental words to me, are written on the tablet of my heart. Sacred to me, are the thoughts which I cherish of the history of his life, that have rolled through my mind and have been implanted there, by my own observation since I was born. Sacred to me is his dust, and the spot where he is laid. Let the memory of my father eternally live. ~~Let the faults and the follies~~ Let his soul, or the spirit my follies forgive. With him may I reign one day, in the mansions above, and tune up the Lyre of anthems, of the eternal Jove. May the God that I love look down from above, and save me from my enemies here, and take me by the hand, that on Mount Zion I may stand and with my father crown me eternally there. Words and language, is inadequate to express the gratitude that I owe to God for having given me so honorable a parentage.

My mother also is one of the noblest, and the best of all women. May God grant to prolong her days, and mine, that we may live to enjoy each other's society long yet in the enjoyment of liberty, and to breathe the free air.

Alvin my oldest brother, I remember well the pangs of sorrow that swelled my youthful bosom and almost burst my tender heart, when he died. He was the oldest, and the noblest of my father's family. He was one of the noblest sons of men. Shall his name not be recorded in this book? Yes, Alvin. Let it be had here, and be handed down upon these sacred pages, forever and ever. In him there was no guile. He lived without spot from the time he was a child. From the time of his birth, he never knew mirth. He was candid and sober and never would play, and minded his father, and mother, in toiling all day. He was one of the soberest of men and when he died the angel of the Lord visited him in his last moments. These childish lines I record in remembrance of my childhood scenes.

My Brother Don Carlos Smith, whose name I desire to record also, was a noble boy. I never knew any fault in him. I never saw the first immoral act, or the first irreligious, or ignoble disposition in the child. From the time that he was born, till the time of his death, he was a lovely, a goodnatured, and a kind-hearted, and a virtuous and a faithful upright child. And where his soul goes let mine go also. He lays by the side of my father. Let my father, Don Carlos, and Alvin, and children that I have buried be brought and laid in the tomb I have built. Let my mother, and my brethren, and my sisters be laid there also, and let it be called the Tomb of Joseph, a descendant of Jacob. And when I die, let me be gathered into the tomb of my father. There are many souls, whom I have loved stronger than death. To them I have proved faithful. To them I {page 180} am determined to prove faithful, untill God calls me to resign up my breath.

O, thou who seeeth, and knoweth the hearts of all men, thou eternal omnipotent, omnicient, and omnipresent Jehovah, God, thou Eloheem, that sitteth, as saith the psalmist, enthroned in heaven, look down upon thy servant Joseph, at this time, and let faith on the name of thy Son Jesus Christ, to a greater degree than thy servant ever yet has enjoyed, be conferred upon him, even the faith of Elijah. And let the Lamp of eternal life, be lit up in his heart, never to be taken away, and the words of eternal life, be poured upon the soul of thy servant, that he may know thy will, thy statutes, and thy commandments, and thy judgments to do them. As the dews upon Mount Hermon, may the distillations of thy divine grace, glory and honor in the plenitude of thy mercy, and power and goodness be poured down upon the head of thy servant.

O Lord God, my heavenly Father, shall it be in vain, that thy servant must needs be exiled from the midst of his friends, or be dragged from their bosoms, to clank in cold and iron chains, to be thrust within dreary prison walls, to spend days of sorrow, and of grief and misery there, by the hand of an infuriated, insensed and infatuated foe, to glut their infernal and insatiable desire upon innocent blood, and for no other cause on the part of thy servant, than for the defence of innocence, and thou a just God will not hear his cry?

Oh, no, thou wilt hear me, a child of woe, pertaining to this mortal life, because of sufferings here, but not for condemnation that shall come upon him in eternity. For thou knowest O God, the integrity of his heart. Thou hearest me, and I knew that thou wouldst hear me, and mine enemies shall not prevail. They all shall melt like wax before thy face, and as the mighty floods,

251

and waters roar, or as the billowing earthquake's, devouring gulf, or rolling thunder's loudest peal, or vivid, forked lightnings flash, or sound of the Arch-Angels trump, or voice of the Eternal God, shall the souls of my enemies be made to feel in an instant, suddenly, and shall be taken, and ensnared, and fall backwards, and stumble in the ditch they have dug for my feet, and the feet of my friends, and perish in their own infamy and shame, be thrust down to an eternal hell, for their murderous and hellish deeds.

After writing so much President Joseph left off speaking for the present but will continue the subject again.[4]

W[illia]m Clayton, Clerk. {page 181}

[29 August 1842] [Near the close of Hyrum's remarks I went upon the Stand. I was rejoiced to look upon the Saints once more, whom I have not seen for about three weeks. They also were rejoiced to see me, and we all rejoiced together. My sudden appearance on the Stand under the circumstances which surrounded us, caused great animation and cheerfulness in the Assembly. Some had supposed that I had gone to Washington, and some that I had gone to Europe, while some thought I was in the City; but whatever difference of opinion had prevailed on this point, we were now all filled with thanksgiving and rejoicing.

When Hyrum had done speaking I arose and congratulated the brethren and Sisters on the victory I had once more gained over the Missourians. I had told them] formerly about fighting the Missourians, and about fighting alone. I had not fought them with the Sword, or by carnal weapons. I had done it by strategem, by outwitting them, and there had been no lives lost, and there would be no lives lost if they would hearken to my Council. Up to this day God had given me wisdom to save the people who took Council. None had ever been killed who abode by my Council. At Hauns Mill the brethren went contrary to my Council. If they had not, their lives would have been spared. I had been in Nauvoo all the while, and outwitted [John C.] Bennett's associates, and attended to my own business in the City all the time.

---

[4] According to Dean C. Jessee (*Personal Writings*, p. 530), nothing else was added on the subject of Joseph Smith's persecutions and his feelings towards his supporters and enemies.

We want to whip the world mentally and they will whip themselves physically. The brethren cannot have the tricks played on them that were done at Kirtland and Far West, they have seen enough of the tricks of their enemies and know better. Orson Pratt has attempted to destroy himself and caused all the city almost to go in search of him. Is it not enough to put down all the infernal influence of the devil, what we have felt and seen, handled and evidenced of this work of God? But the Devil had influence among the Jews after all the great things they had witnessed to cause the death of Jesus Christ by hanging him between heaven and earth. O. Pratt and others of the same class caused trouble by telling stories to people who would betray me, and they must believe those stories because his Wife [Sarah Marinda Bates] told him so? I will live to trample on their ashes with the souls of my feet. I prophecy in the name of Jesus Christ that such shall not prosper, they shall be cut down in their plans. They would deliver me up Judas like, but a small band of us shall overcome.

We don't want or mean to fight with the sword of the flesh, but we will fight with the broad Sword of the Spirit. Our enemies say our [Nauvoo City] Charter and writs of Habeas Corpus are worth nothing. We say they came from the highest authority in the State and we will hold to them. They cannot be disannulled or taken away.

I then told the brethren I was going to send all the Elders away, and when the Mob came there would only be women and children to fight and they would be ashamed. I dont want you to fight but to go and gather tens, hundreds, and thousands to fight for you. If oppression comes, I will then shew them that there is a Moses and a Joshua amongst us; and I will fight them, if they dont take off oppression from me. I will do as I have done this time. I will run into the woods. I will fight them in my own way. I will send brother Hyrum to call conferences everywhere throughout the States and let documents be taken along and show to the world the corrupt and oppressive conduct of [Lilburn W.] Boggs, [Thomas] Carlin, and others, that the public may have the truth laid before them. Let the Twelve [Apostles] send all who will support the character of the Prophet, the Lord's anointed, and if all who go will support my character, I prophecy in the name of the Lord Jesus, whose servant I am, that you will prosper in your missions. I have the whole plan of the kingdom before me, and no

253

other person has. And as to all that Orson Pratt, Sidney Rigdon, or George W. Robinson can do to prevent me, I can kick them off my heels, as many as you can name, I know what will become of them. I concluded my remarks by saying I have the best of feelings towards my brethren, since this last trouble began, but to the Apostates and enemies, I will give a lashing every opportunity and I will curse them. {pages 183-84}

[25 September 1842] [At the Grove. Spoke more than two hours, chiefly on the subject of my persecution.]

[29 October 1842] In the forenoon [about 10 a.m.] I rode up and viewed the Temple. I expressed my satisfaction at the arrangements, and was pleased with the progress made in that sacred edifice. After conversing with several of the brethren and shaking hands with numbers who were very much rejoiced to see their Prophet again, I returned home, but soon afterwards went over to the Store, where a number of brethren and Sisters were assembled who had arrived this morning from the neighborhood of New York, Long Island &c. After Elders [John] Taylor, [Wilford] Woodruff, and Samuel Bennett, had addressed the brethren and Sisters, I spoke to them at considerable length, shewing them the proper course to pursue, and how to act in regard to making purchases of land &c.

I shewed them that it was generally in consequence of the brethren disregarding or disobeying counsel that they became dissatisfied and murmured; and many when they arrived here were dissatisfied with the conduct of some of the Saints because every thing was [not] done perfectly right, and they get mad and thus the devil gets advantage over them to destroy them. I told them I was but a man, and they must not expect me to be perfect; if they expected perfection from me, I should expect it from them; but if they would bear with my infirmities and the infirmities of the brethren, I would likewise bear with their infirmities. I told them it was likely I would have again to hide up in the woods but they must not be discouraged but build up the city, the Temple &c. When my enemies take away my rights, I will bear it and keep out of the way, but if they take away your rights, I will fight for you. I blessed them and departed. {page 208}

[8 June 1843] He [Elias Higbee] has been sick only five days of cholera morbus and inflammation, which produced mortification, and his death was unexpected by all. His loss will be universally lamented, not only by his family, but by a large circle of brethren who have long witnessed his integrity and uprightness, as well as a life of devotedness to the cause of truth. He has endured a great share of persecution and tribulation for the cause of Christ, both during the Missouri troubles and other times. On the 6th day of October, 1840, he was appointed one of the committee to build the Temple in Nauvoo, which office he maintained during his life. In that station he has shown a disposition to do right at all times, and always manifested a great anxiety for the prosperity of the Temple as well as the work at large. He has left a large family to mourn his departure; but he is gone to his rest for a little season, even until the morning of the resurrection, when he will again come forth and strike hands with the faithful, and share the glory of the kingdom of God for ever and ever. {page 315}

[2 July 1843] [About 6 p.m. The Maid of Iowa returned to her landing at the Nauvoo House, the company who had been on the expedition on board of her, formed in a procession and walked up to my office, where they formed a hollow square and sent in a deputation to me, as soon as I had bid them welcome I opened the window of my office and requested that no man would leave the ground until I had spoken to them. My Brother Hyrum and I went into the hollow square and directed them not to allow their ranks to be broken. I then shook hands with each man, blessing them and welcoming them home.

I then took off my hat and related to them how I was brought home to the midst of my friends, and how I regained by liberty. "I feel by the Spirit of the Lord that if I had fallen into your hands that you would either have brought me safe home, or that we should all have died in a heap together." At this time, a well dressed man, a stranger, who had a cloak around him, broke through the South line of the ranks when the orderly sergeant took the strange man by the nape of the neck and kicked him outside the ranks telling him not to come in again; as soon as quiet was resumed I continued my address to the company . . .

About dusk I dismissed the company, blessing them in the name of the Lord.]

1 8 4 2 - 4 3

So far as is known, no diary or journal, other than the "Book of the Law of the Lord," covers Joseph Smith's life from October 1839 to December 1842, when Willard Richards, the prophet's private secretary, began to keep the following journal.[1] Although conscientious, Richards could be frustratingly concise, and none of the four Nauvoo journals he kept for Joseph Smith contains the introspection that characterizes Joseph's Kirtland diaries and journals. Richards is also the only one of Joseph's scribes to have employed shorthand in recording entries.[2] Whereas Richards refers to Joseph Smith in

---

[1] Evidently, LDS church historians in the 1850s considered that two of William Clayton's three Nauvoo diaries, those covering the years 1842-45 and 1843-44, should be classified as Joseph Smith journals, much like those kept by Willard Richards, because of Clayton's having clerked for Joseph Smith beginning in 1842. These two Clayton diaries were identified as such in an official inventory of the "Contents of the Church Historian and Recorder's Office" prepared in July 1858 (see Church Records, Historical Department, Church of Jesus Christ of Latter-day Saints). However, during the early 1840s, Clayton was also recording journal entries for Joseph Smith in the "Book of the Law of the Lord," which would seem to qualify more as a Joseph Smith journal than do Clayton's own personal diaries, just as Willard Richards kept his own diaries separate from the journals he kept for Joseph Smith.

[2] In those rare instances where Richards resorted to shorthand, he used an early form developed in the late 1700s in England by Samuel Taylor. Taylor's

both the first person and third person, all entries, including those in ambig-
uous voice, describe Joseph's, rather than Richards's, activities. The original
of the following journal, which is entirely in Richards's handwriting, is in
the archives of the Historical Department, Church of Jesus Christ of Latter-
day Saints, Salt Lake City, Utah.

President Joseph Smith's
Journal 1843
/As kept by Willard Richards/
{cover page}

December 21st 1842 President Joseph at his own house
attending a variety of business. Gave instructions about a communication to [General James] A[rlington] Bennet and made a
particular request that W[illard] Richards would act as his private se[c]retary and historian.

22[nd] Heard his correspondence with Gov[ernor] Carlin
as prepared for Gen[eral] Bennet. Recited in German to Elder
Hyde.

Bro[ther] Shearer asked the meaning of the little leaven
in 3 measures of meal. Joseph said, "It alludes expressly to the
last days when there should be little faith on the earth and it
{page 1} leaven the whole world. Thare shall be safity [safety] in
Zion and Jerusalem and the remnants whom the Lord shall call.
It refers to the Priesthood. Truth springing up on a fix[e]d principle. Three measures refers to the 3 in the grand Presidency,
confining the oracles to a certain head on the principle of 3."

23[rd] I [Joseph] visited with Franklin [D. Richards] and
his wife.

24[th] P.M. Read and revised history. [Joseph] Walked
with Sec[retary Richards] to see Sister Lyons who was sick. Her
babe died 30 minutes before he arrived. Thence to Bro[ther]
Sabin['s] to get some money for expences to [go to] Springfield,
having just borrowed $100 of Nehemiah Hatch.

In reply to the {page 2} question, "Do you want a wicked

---

innovation later gave way to the more popular versions created by Pittman and
Gregg. See Andrew F. Ehat, "Joseph Smith's Introduction of Temple Ordinances
and the 1844 Mormon Succession Question," M.A. thesis, Brigham Young
University, 1982, pp. 61-63.

man to pray for you?" [Joseph answered,] "Yes, if the fervent, effectual prayer of the righteous availeth much, a wicked man may avail a little when praying for a righteous man. There is none good but one. The better a man is the more his prayer will prevail like the publican and pharisee, one was justified rather than the other showing that both were justified in a degree. The prayer of the wicked man may do a righteous man good when it does the one who prays no good."

Sunday, 25th [*entry left blank*] {page 3}

Dec[ember] 26th Held court. Sis[ter] Morey [was the] defendant. [Joseph] had consultation with [Nauvoo Legion] Gen[eral] W[ilson] W. Law and was arrested by him on Proclamation of Gov[ernor] Carlin [for extradition to Missouri]. Elders [Henry G.] Sherwood and [William] Clayton started for Carthage after Habeus Corpus to carry him to Springfield.

Visited Sis[ter] Morey in custody of Sec[retary Richards] and prescribed for her afflictions. Spoke very highly of Lobelia [an herb], good in its place, was one of the works of God. But like the power of God or any good, it become an evil when improperly used. Had lear[ne]d the use and value [of Lobelia] by his own experience.

[At] Home. Sister Emma sick, had another chill. Had a consultation concerning her with Secretary [Richards]. While walking up {page 4} Main St[reet], Joseph asked Bro[ther] Tully if he had ought against him? He replied, "I have not." Bro[ther] Morey gave Joseph a walking stick consisting of whole ivory top and sperm-whale tooth body with mahogany interstice.

27th 9 A.M. Started in custody of Gen[eral] Wilson W. Law for Springfield, in co[mpany] with Hiram Smith, John Taylor, William Marks, [Levi] Moffitt, Peter Hawes, Lorin Walker, W[illard] Richards, and Orson Hyde. When 1/2 way to Carthage met Bro[thers] Sherwood and Clayton who had obtained an order from the Master of Chancery for Habeus Corpus, but the court {page 5} clerk had been elected Senator. Therefore they could not obtain the writ but joined the party and watering at the public well in Carthage.

Arrived at Bro[ther] Samuel Smith's in Plymouth about sunset. /35 mi[les]/ (Sister Durphy and daughte[r] rode in the carri[a]ge) One hour after, Edward Hunter, Theodore Turly, Dr.

[*blank*] Tate, and Shadra[c]h Roundy arrived and joined the party. Supped with W[illia]m's wife.

28[th] Slept with sec[retary Richards] on buffalo [skin]. After retiring I [Joseph] stated that the purifying of the sons of Levi was by giving unto them intel[l]igence that we are not capable of meditating /on/ and receiving all the intel[l]igence which belongs {page 6} to an immortal state. It is to[o] powerful for our faculties.

Started at 8 o'clock. (Sis[ter] Durphy's daughter tarried and Bro[ther] W[illia]m Smith, wife, and little daughter accompanied). Before starting Joseph related his [dream]. Was by a beautiful stream of water. Saw a noble handsome fish. Threw it out. Soon after saw more, threw them out and soon a great many and threw them out a great abundance, and sent for salt to salt them down and salted them.

Arrived at Rushville Bell Tavern by Mrs. Stevenson 3 P.M. 20 miles. After supper Joseph with a part of the co[mpany] spent the eve[ning] with Mrs. Brown. Joseph stated that to touch the Nauvoo Charter was no better than highway robbery. That since the {page 7} creation there never had been a repeal of a perpetual charter by God, angels, or man and that he never would submit to lowering our charter but they might bring others up to it. After returning to the tavern, Joseph was measured 6 feet, Hiram 6 [feet], Hunter 6 [feet], Wilson Law 6 [feet], 3/4 in[ches], and Moffit 6 [feet], 1/2 [inches].

29th Started 20 [minutes past] 9. Arrived [at] Capt[ain] Dutches [at] 4 P.M., Lomour 32 mi[les]. After supper Gen[eral] Law asked why the Sun was masculine and /Moon/ feminine? /Joseph/ [said], "The root of Masculine is stronger and of feminine weaker. [The] Sun is a governing planet to certain planets, while the moon borrows her light from the sun {page 8} and is less or weaker &c.

"Let the Government of M[iss]o[uri] redress the wrongs she has don[e] to the Mormons or let the curse follow them from generation to generation till they do.

"When /I [Joseph]/ was going up to Missouri in co[mpany] with Elder [Sidney] Rigdon and our families we arrived at Paris, Illinois on a[n] extreme cold day. To go forward was 14 mil[e]s to a house and backward nearly as far. We applied to all the taverns for admission in vain. We were Mormons and could not be received. Such was the cold that in one hour we must have perished. We plead for our women and children in vain. We councelled together and the brethren agreed to stand by me. We concluded {page 9} we might as well die fighting as freeze to death.

"I [Joseph] went into a tavern and plead our cause to get admission. The Landlord said he could not keep us for love or money. I told him we must and would stay. Let the consequen[c]e be what it might. For we must stay or perish. The Landlord said they had heard the Mormons were very bad people and the inhabitants of Paris had combined not to have any thing to do with them but we might stay. I told him we would stay, but no thanks to him ~~and we went in and all~~ {page 10} ~~the taverns~~ I have men enough to take the town and if we must freeze we will freeze by the burning of there [their] houses. The taverns were then opened and we were accommodated and received ma/n/y apologies in the morning from the inhabitants for their abusive treatment."

(It was reported through the county that a camp of the Mormons stole an acre of corn of one man in the neighborhood of Terra Haut [Terre Haute, Indiana]).

[We had] Much good music on the piano with singing in the evening. {page 11}

Dec[ember] 30th Started at 8 [A.M.]. Broke one of the carriages and were detained awhile. Arrived [in Springfield] at Judge [James] Adams [at] 2 1/2 o'clock. Joseph said he had decided that he would not vote for a Slave holder. It is giving them power and if they could obtain sufficient power and get a religious peak against any religionists they would subdue them and compel our children to mix with their Slaves.

[Question] By Elder [Orson] Hyde, "What would you advice a man to do who come in the [Church] having a hundred slaves?" Joseph [replied], "I have always advised such to bring their slaves {page 12} into a free country, set them free, Educate them and give them their equal rights. Should the slaves be organized into an independent government, they would become quarrelsome. It would not be wisdom."

(The remainder of the co[mpany] arrived 3 1/2 P.M.) All the party supped at Judge Adams. Justin Butterfield, Esqu[ire], District Att[orne]y of the United States for Illinois, was introduced by Judge Adams.

Bro[ther] W[illia]m Smith stated that [James M.] Pittman, Sheriff of Adams county had been here some days but whither he had the writ against Joseph or not, tis supposed he has it. Conversation {page 13} continued on the writ and proclamation. Butterfield said that Judge Pope would close the court on the morrow. Had continued it 2 or 3 days on account of Joseph's case and [said] he should try the case on its merits and not on any technicality. When Pittman entered the Secretary's office, Trumbull asked him if he had the writ. He replied with a smile, "It will be forth coming."

It was decided by the council that the old writ should be had if possible in the morning by some one beside Pittman [and] Joseph be arrested thereon and by Habeus Corpus brought {page 14} before Judge Pope in the morning and he would go clear, and Said Joseph, "Let me have a happy new years."

Conversation then turned on Missouri. Joseph stated that he never had done military duty in his life, was taken prisoner of war at Far West in his own door yard. The man who took me thrust my little boy (who was clinging to my garments) from me by his sword saying, "God Damn you, get away you little rascal or I will run you through."

I [Joseph] was condem[ne]d by court martial to be shot at 8 o'clock in the Morning. There were 18 Priests in the court martial. Gen[eral Alexander] Donithan [Doniphan] said it was cold blooded murder [and] would have nothing to do with it and marched {page 15} of[f]. His Brigade were marched to Jackson Co[unty]. The soldiers refused to obey orders and we were returned and thrust in Prison by Gen[eral] Clark's orders.

[We were] kept 6 mo[nths] and 5 days with little food and no bed except a little straw, suffered much with cold, without [due] p[r]ocess on charge of Treason, Larceny, and Stealing. [We] had [a] mock trial. Witnesses sworn at the point of [a] bayonet. King sent summons by Bogard, [a] Methodist Priest. [They] took 50 of our witnesses and put them in Prisons and then 20 more. We got one witness by beckoning through the window. He was thrust out of court and 2 or 3 soldiers [were sent] after to kill him. King was expostulated with. {page 16} He replied, "Gentlemen you are Mormons and I have pledged myself to exterminate you from the state [in] 1839."

[We were] afterwards tried by Jury who were our guards

at night, 2 sober at a time. [They swore,] "God damn God and Methodist[s] &c. and God damn Mormons."

When we escaped I was the worst off. Hiram got one of my boots and I jumped into the mud, put on my boots without working and when I got to water after going over 15 mi[les] [of] Prarie, my boots are full of blood. When I arrived at shore opposite Quincy, I saw a man talking with Gov[ernor] Carlin who said, "God damn Joe Smith, if I could get my eyes on him I'd fix him." A ferry beckoned me and I put off immediately.

[George M.] Hinkle ordered a retreat. I rode through and ordered them to stand, 300 against 3,000. A truce came and [they] said, "We want Clemenson and wife and [*blank*]. We will protect them. We will massacre all the rest." They refused to go. I said, "Go tell the army to retreat in 5 minutes or we'll give them hell" and they run.

Ex-Gov[ernor] Carlin told Butterfield a few days since at Springfield he thought Joseph Smith had left Nauvoo. He was there 3 weeks ago with long beard and slouch hat to bye [buy] a Bowie knife and some one present knew him and he had gone off.

Joseph said to Judge Adams {page 18} that Christ and the resurrected Saints will reign over the earth, but not dwell on the earth. [They will] visit it when they please or when necessary to govern it. There will be wicked men /on/ the earth during the 1,000 years. The heathen nations who will not come up to worship will be destroyed.

Joseph gave a lecture on medicine. [He said,] "Salt, vinegar and pepper given internally and plunging in the river when the paroxysms begin will cure the cholora." {page 19}

Dec[ember] 31st 1842 9 A.M. Esqu[ire] Butterfield came in [and] said [Sherriff] Pittman told Sec[retary] of State that King had the writ and he had shewed his [Butterfield's] letter to King. /He/ said he [King] was coming up some time and he would bring it. Joseph Signed a pitition to Gov[ernor] Ford for a new writ that his case might be tried ther[e]on.

11 A.M. Esq[ui]r[e] Butterfield called with Deputy Jerold Maxey having the Gov[ernor]'s writ ~~and Habeus Corpus~~. The parties repaired immediately to Messr. Edwards and Butterfield's office where Butterfield read a Petition to Judge [Nathaniel] Pope of the U[nited] S[tates] C[ircuit] C[ourt] and Joseph Signed it.

Present W[illia]m F. Elkin, Sheriff of Sangomo Co[unty], {page 20} entered court Room before Judge Pope.

11 1/2 A.M. Heard several decisions in Bankruptcy, when Esq[ui]r[e] Butterfield read the pititions of Joseph. [He] next stated that the writ and warrant was different from the requisition of the Gov[ernor] [of] M[iss]o[uri]. [He] then read Gov[ernor] Ford's Warrant, then Watson's affidavit, next Gov[ernor] Reynold's Requisition on Gov[ernor] of Illinois, next Proclamation of Gov[ernor] Carlin shewing that Reynolds (with all defference to the Gov[ernor] of M[iss]o[uri]) has made a false statement as nothing appears in the affidavit to show that said Smith ever was in M[iss]o[uri during the attempt on Governor Boggs's life or that Joseph had attempted to flee justice].

Esqu[i]r[e] B[utterfield] said all the authority for transportation of prisoners from one state to another {page 21} rests on the Constitution and the Law of Congress. We ask for Habeus Corpus because the papers are false and because we can prove that Joseph Smith was in this State at the time of the commission of the crime. Writ is granted, when will it be returned? Esq[uire] B[utterfield] instant[iat]e[d]. It was returned in one minute and served and Joseph walked up to the bar.

After a few minut[e]s delay, Esq[ui]r[e] B[utterfield] read the Habeus Corbus and moved the court take bail till the court hear the case. Judge [asked], "Is the prisoner in custody of court or officers?" Butterfield [replied], "Of the court" and [then] read the Law. Court thought proper to take bail {page 22} though it was only a misdemeanor.

Gen[eral] Adams and Gen[eral] Law were bailed in the sum of $4,000 [and] $2,000 each. Monday was set for Trial. Court rose and as the co[mpany] dispersed (for the room was crowded) and came to the bottom [of the stairs] a row commenced [with] swearing &c. which was quelled by interference of the Marshall after we had tarried above a few minutes.

/One or two rowdies - See Note A, page 74/ [*Note A from page 74 is included here and follows:*] /See page 23/ Note A[:] As Gen[eral] Law came to the head of the stairs, Some men observed, "There goes [Joseph] Smith the Prophet and a great looking man he is." And (said another) "As damned a rascal as ever lived." Then Hyrum replied, "And a good many Ditto." "Yes," said the man, "Ditto, D[itt]o. God Damn you and any one that takes his part is as damned a rascal as he is." Then at the foot of the stairs, [General] Law says, "I am the man and I take his part." "You are a damned rascal to[o]." "/You are/ a Liying /schondrel/," said ~~the man~~ /Law/. /The man/ began to take of[f] his clothes and went out {page 74} in the street and the Marshall interfered. Much credit is due to Mr. Prentice the Marshall for his diligence in quelling the mob. [*End of Note A.*]

Twenty /mi[nutes]/ [past] one, Esq[ui]r[e] B[utterfield] accompanied Joseph to the Governor's room who was sick. Said he had a requisition for renewal of Prosecution in the old case of Treason against Missouri, but I [Joseph] happended to know it was all dead.

Dined with Esq[ui]r[e] Butterfield at American House. Returned to Gov[ernor]'s Room. Present Mr. Scommon {page 23} and Mr. Shields. [We had] conversation about Nauvoo and /Gov[ernor] said he was not a regionist/. Joseph said to the Governor, "I have no creed to circumscribe my mind. Therefore the people do not like me because I do not, cannot circumscribe my mind to their creeds."

"Well," said the Gov[ernor], "from reports we had reason to think the Mormons were a peculiar people. Different from other people having horns or something of the kind, but I find they look like other people. Indeed I think Mr. Smith is a very good looking man."

Mr. Scommon enquired about the Terible sign[s] &c. Mr. Shields proposed a question about the [Nauvoo] Legion. [He wanted to know] /if it was to subdue the state Janisarly [janissary]?/ Joseph replied, "We have raised up a Legion to defend the {page 24} state."

2 P.M. Returned to Judge Adams. Mr. W[illia]m Prentice [the] Marshall was very friendly and expressed much sorrow that he could not have the care of Gen[eral] Smith. Joseph appointed Elders Hyde and Tayler to preach on the Morrow. Dr. Gray called for an introduction and Mr. Taylor also.

After supper conversation was had on the Nauvoo Charter. Joseph Prophecied that before 5 years rol[l]ed [a]round Judge [Stephen A.] D[o]uglass will acknowledge that it would have been better for him to have followed his [Joseph's] council. D[o]uglass had been stating to Gen[eral] Law and El[der] Taylor that it was possible to revoke political charters but not co/mpany/ charters. {page 25}

Joseph argued, "If a legislature has power to grant a charter for 10 years and has no power to revoke it till the expiration thereof, the same principle will hold good for 20 years and for 100 years and also for a perpetual charter. It cannot be revoked in time."

John Darby came in, said he was going to California. Joseph Said, "I will say as the prophet said to Hezekiah go and prosper, but ye shall not return in peace. [James C.] Brewster [leader of a Mormon schismatic group] may set out for California but he will not get there unless some body shall pick him up by the way [and] feed him &c. Brewster showed me [Joseph] the Manuscripts [of his revelations]. {page 26} He /I/ enquired of the Lord and the Lord told me the book was not true. It was not of him. If God ever cal[l]ed me, or spoke by my mouth, or gave me a revelation, he never gave revelations to that Brewster Boy or any of the Brewster race."

In the P.M. a team ran away and went past the State house, when the cry was raised, "Joe Smith is running away," which produced great excitement and produced a sudden adjournment of the House of Rep[resentative]s. {page 27}

January 1st 1843, Sunday Speaker of the House of Representatives called to inform us we could have the Hall for preaching this day.

Esq[ui]r[e] Butterfield called with Esq[ui]r[e] Gilaspie, Judge Douglass, [and] Mr. Rusk. Joseph explained the nature of a Prophet, "[The] spirit of Prophecy, which is the testimony of Jesus, is necessary to constitute a witness or a preacher or a prophet."

Three Gent[lemen] called, One from Cass County (Esq[ui]r[e] Pratt).

11 8/11 A.M. Repaired to House of Representatives. 11 1/2 [A.M.] Elder [Orson] Hyde read the Hymn "Rejoice Ye Saints of Latter Days." Elder {page 28} [John] Taylor followed in prayer. The Saints then sung "The Spirit of God like a Fire is Burning" &c. 3 verses. Elder Hyde then read a portion of the 3d Chapter of Malichi commencing at the beginning 6 verses.

[Elder Hyde said,] "Although strangers permit me to wish you all a happy new year. Though aware /of/ the difficulties and

265

prejudices yet we let it all pass by like the summer threshing floors. 'For what is chaff to the wheat.' saith the Lord. Lord whom ye seek and supposed to be John [the] Baptist. It was not fulfilled at [the] coming [of] Christ. After [the] Jews return from Babylon in a short time the prophets were killed. Malachi about 500 years before Christ. Lost Record. Hosea [was] sawn asunder in the valley of Jehosophet. {page 29}

"From Malachi to John [the] Baptist [the] voice of Revelation was not heard. John came to prepare the way. [He] baptized many of the different sects. Lawyers &c. were the ones who could not be baptized. [They] were the first to pers[e]cute and rec[e]ive the curses of the Savior [who] died in Jerusalem and ascended from Mount Olivet. [The] Temple [was] built by the commandment of God [and] received the heavenly messenger. It became polluted. Took a whip of small cords &c., not one stone shall not be thrown down. German Bible says, 'which shall not be broken.' Temple [is a] Type of the church. Spirit of God is mind of God.

"When a lad I went out to find poultry. Where the corn was done every one went his own way and sung his own {page 30} song. When inspiration ceased every one sung his own song. Gross darkness covered the people. Let us have this temple purified. How shall I educ[a]te my son? God no longer speaks then is prima facie Evidence he never spoke to you. Will send his messengers and Lord shall come suddenly, objected Angels no more come? Four angels &c. in Rev[elation] when servants of God are sealed have a mark by which God knows them, send his angels &c.

"The Lord has sent his angel in these last days. If the Christian church will not be cleansed, God will put his finger on this and on that nation, and nation will rise against nation. We are neither Catholic [n]or P[r]otestant, but like the Temple {page 31} we have not passed under the polishing of any denomination and the people think to throw down the Latter Day Saint under the rubbish, but they cannot do without them." /Elder Hyde [concluded his remarks and] returned thanks./

Quarter [past] 1, I retired for dinner /to Judge Adams/. 2 1/2 [P.M.] returned to the Representatives Hall. 3.3[0 P.M.] Elder Hyd[e] read Hymn 154 page and followed in prayer. Elder Taylor Read Rev[elation] 14 ch[apter] 6 and 7 verses. [Elder Taylor said,] "Some object to my text in Rev[elation] because it is so mysterious. Whatever is revealed is not a mystery. Blessed is he that readeth and might refer to the ministering of angels to Noah, Abraham, Ezekial, Paul, Peter, past.

"Old and New Testament is not the gospel, as a map is not the country it represents. It tells {page 32} what the gospel is. Gospel is good news a savor of life to them that receive or the sabor [saber] of Death unto death to those who reject. Gospel is the power of God unto Salvation. Go ye into all the world and preach the Gospel &c. These signs shall follow them &c., faith, Repenta[n]ce, Baptism, Laying on of Hands, certain officers, enough that we have it in the Bible can read of those things which were tong[u]es, dreams, &c. A man has a history of a feast in his pocket can read it in the wilderness to keep from starving." 4 1/2 [P.M.] Elder Taylor returned thanks to the audience and the Lord and meeting dispersed. {page 33}

Went to Bro[ther] Bowman's to supper. His wife /Julia Stringham/ was baptiz[e]d at Colesville, [New York] one of the first fruits. Many Saints called to see the President.

While supper was preparing Joseph related an anecdote. While young, his father had a fine large watch dog which bit off an ear from David Stafford's hog, which Stafford had turned into Smith['s] corn field. Stafford /shot the dog and/ with six other fellows pitched upon him [Joseph] unawares. Joseph whipped the whole of them and escaped unhurt /which they swore to as recorded in Hurlburt's or Howe's Book [*Mormonism Unvailed*]/.

[Joseph also related,] While in Kirtland a Baptist Priest came in my house and abused my family. I turned him out of doors. He raised his cane to strike me {page 34} and continued to abuse me. I whipped him till he begged. He threatened to prosecute me. I sent Luke Johnson the constable after him and he run him out of the County into Mentor. 7 [P.M.] returned to Judge Adams.

January 2nd, Monday After breakfast Joseph prophesied in the name of the Lord God, "I shall not /go/ to Missouri dead or alive." Mr. Jonas from Adams called [and] conversed on the policy of modifying the City charters.

9 1/2 A.M. Repaired to the court house. 10 [A.M.] court opened. Judge Pope present. Docket read by the clerk in matter of Joseph Smith and then of various Bankrupts. {page 35} When

the court opened Joseph was with his attorney in his office [and] rested while the Docket was reading. At the close of the reading The Marshall waited on 7 ladies who took their seats beside the Judge [at his request to witness the proceedings]. The state Attorney [General] /Esqu[i]r[e] Lamborn/ requested the case to be continued till tomorrow morning out of respect to the officers of State and of the Gov[enor] of Missouri. Wednesday morning was set for trial.

Esqu[i]r[e] Butterfield moved to file some objections to facts set forth in the Habeus Corpus. Joseph Smith is not a fugitive from justice. [He] was not in M[iss]o[uri] {page 36} at that time, has not been for 3 years &c. but was in Nauvoo when the attack was made on Lilborn W. Boggs. Filed. Ladies retired.

10 1/2 [A.M.] Repaired to the Senate Lobby had conversation with Senator Davis, Mr. Webber (Resolution lost to make up the deficit of the failure of the State Bank to public office), [and] Mayor Baker of Sangamon. Senator appears much like an African Monkey. At /one/ moment standing by one stove, the next by another on the opposite side of the chamber, setting down in every Senator's chair in his way. He never goes out of his way, for his way is every where and his nose in every man's face. Eating apples, staring at and pointing and staring at every one. Next moment in the Galery pointing the Ladies to Old Joe whom he once drilled his regiment to go against and slaughter him or give him up to Missouri. An eavesdropper, a monkey without a monkey's wit. {page 37}

J[acob] B. Backenstos wishing to return to Carthage gave the names of Witnesses who dined with Joseph on the 7th day of May, [the day in question, as] James H. Ralston, J. N. Morris,/ [who] can[n]ot com[e, and] Almeron/ Wheat.

Rep[rentative] Geo[rge] C. Dixon at the /Mrs. Eno's/ brick Hotel. Several Senators came and conversed with Joseph /viz. Chief Justice Wilson of Illinois court/.

A discussion arose in the Senate on the propriety of Taxing the rich for repair of Roads. [Senator] Davis spoke in faver. Bill laid on the Table till 4 July. Repaired 12 A.M. to Senator Davis' private room. Mr. Nye called. Dined at the American opposite Judge Pope and Brown. As we arose from the table Judge Brown invited Joseph to his room. I [Joseph] Told him [I knew] he was about publishing a history of Illinois and wished him {page

38} to [allow me to] furnish a history of the rise and faith of the Church of Latter Day Saints to add to his history. 1 1/2 [P.M.] returned to Jud[g]e Adams'.

A gentleman from St. Louis told General /Law/ that the "General Impression was that Joseph was innocent and it would be a kind of murder to give him up. They thought he ought to be whipt alittle and let go." It is evident that prejudice is giving way and good feeling is gaining ascendency in the public mind.

4 o'clock Esq[ui]r[e] Lamborn [the] state's attorney [general], the marshall, and some 1/2 dozen others called. The Marshall said it was the first time in {page 39} his administration that the Ladies had attended court on trial.

Mr. McCoy of Missouri told the Marshall that he tried to pacify the people and keep the peace. It was false, he headed a co[mpany] and was a leader in the mob.

Esq[ui]r[e] Lamborn remarked "Mr. Smith is a very good looking, jovial man." "Examine his head," said Laconly, "I think he is not particulary given to burglary, rape, and Murder."

Esq[ui]r[e] Lindsay had much conversation. Marshall was very Jovial and {page 40} pleasant. A peculiarly pleasant and conciliatory feeling pervailed through the company and the Marshall invited Joseph to a family dinner when he was freed.

5 o'clock went to Mr. W[illia]m Sollar's. Mr. Bridewood visited in the eve. Elder Hyde was present and after Supper asked, "What is the situation of the Negro?" [Joseph replied,] "They come into the world slaves, mentally and physically. Change their situation with the white and they would be like them. They have souls and are subjects of salvation. Go into Cincinati and find one educated [and who] rid[e]s in his carriage. He has {page 41} risen by the power of his mind to his exalted state of respectability. Slaves in Washington [are] more refined than the president. Boys will take the shine off those they brush and wait on."

Says Elder Hyde, "Put them on the [same] level and they will rise above me." Joseph [said], "If I raised you to be my equal and then attempt to oppress you would you not be indignant and try to rise above me? Did not Oliver Cowdery and Peter Whitmer and many others say I was fallen and they were capable of Leading the people. {page 42} Had I any thing to do with the Negro I would confine them by strict Laws to their own Species [and] put them on a national Equalization.

269

"Because faith is wanting the fruits [of faith] are not [evident]. No man since the world was, ever had faith without having something along with it. The ancients quen[c]hed the violence of [nature and] escaped the edged of the sword. Women received their Dead &c. By faith the worlds were made. A man who has none of the gifts has no faith. He deceives himself if he supposes it. Faith has been wanting not only among the brethren but professed Christendom also, that Tongues and healings {page 43} and prophecy and prophets and apostles and all these gifts and blessings have been wanting." Joseph spoke at great length and edification to the little co[mpany].

/Objections being made to the Prophet's [lack of] meekness/ "I am meek and lowly in heart. I will personify Jesus for a moment to illustrate and [for] you inquirers. 'Wo unto you ye Doctors. Wo unto you ye scribes, pharisees, and Hypocrit[e]s.'

"You cannot find the place where I ever went that I found fault with their food, their drink, their board, or their Lodging. No never. This is what is meant by the meekness and Lowliness of Jesus." {page 44}

Mr. Sollars stated that James Mullone, carpenter, of Springfield told him he had been to Nauvoo and seen Joe Smith the Prophet. He had a grey horse and I [Mullone] asked him where he got it and the Prophet said, "you see that white cloud?" "Yes." "Well as it came along I got the horse from that cloud." Joseph replied, "It was a lie. I never told him so."

/In reference to preparing Generally/, what is it inspires with a hope of Salvation? It is that smooth sophisticated influence of the Devil by which he deceives the whole world. Mr. Sollars says, "May I not Repent and be baptized and not pay any attention to dreams and visions &c?" Joseph said, "Suppose I am Travelling and I am hungry and meet {page 45} a man and tell him I am hungry. He tells me to go yonder, there is a house for Entertainment, go knock, and you must conform to all the rules of the house or you cannot satisfy your hunger. Knock, call for food and set down and eat, and I go and knock and ask for food and set down to the table but do not eat shall I satisfy my hunger? No! I must eat. The Gifts are the food. The graces of the spirit are the Gifts of the spirit."

Joseph [said], "When I first commenced this work and had got 2 or 3 individuals to believe I went about 30 miles with

270

Oliver Cowdery, one horse between us, to see {page 46} them. When we arrived, a mob of a hundred come upon us before we had time to eat, and chased us all night and we arrived back again about 60 miles in all, and without food, a little after Day light. I have often travelled all night to see the brethren and often been turned away without food."

Evening closed by singing and prayer per El[der] Hyde. Posted the bed on the floor [for] Joseph, Orson, [and] Willard.

Tuesday, 3d Jan[uary] 1843 8 [A.M.] Called after breakfast on Sister Crane and blessed the boy. Joseph Smith returned to Judge Adams. Present Mr. Trobridge, Mr. Beers, Mr. Jonas, and Esqu[i]r[e] Browning. [We] conversed on the old Missouri case. {page 47} /Esqu[i]r[e] Browning expressed the best of feeling/

9 1/2 [A.M.] Repaired to court Room. Present Mr. Butterfield, Owen, Pope, Prentice. Mr. Prentice told a very interesting story concerning Bro[ther] Eddy's debate with Mr. Slocum the Presbyterian Priest on the Steam boat "Nonpariel" in August last. Present at that time [were] Rev. Mr. Wells and McCoy. Affidavits prepared during the P.M. Joseph at Judge Adams'.

At Dusk the Marshall, Mr. Prentice, called with subpoenas and sat some time and retold the story about Rev. Mr. Slocum &c. After he retired Joseph prophecied in the name of the Lord that no very formidable {page 48} opposition would be raised at the trial on the morrow.

Evening spent in a very social manner. The most harmonious feeling prevailed. Closed by Singing and Prayer by Elder Hyde. Joseph Lodged on the soffa as he has every night but one since he has been in Springfield. {page 49}

Mr. Butterfield wrote drafts of Affidavits. 12 retired to Judge Adams.

Jan[uary] 4th, Wednesday 9 A.M. Repaired to court room in Butterfield's office a few moments [before] court opened. While docket was reading the Ladies come in and took their seats by the side of the Judge, 6 Ladies.

By court: "Gentlemen of the Bar any motions this morning?"

Sworn [were] Wilson Law, H[enry] G. Sherwood, Theodore Turl[e]y, Shadrach Roundy, William Clayton, John

Taylor, William Marks, Lorin Walker, [and] Willard Richards. {page 50}

Matter of Joseph Smith. Mr. Butterfield [present.] (2 Ladies come in) [Enters Josiah Lamborn,] Att[or]ny Gen[eral of Illinois] motion to [dismiss the proceedings by] J[osiah] Lamborn [because court has] no jurisdiction.

(Motion of Mr. Lamborn) No Jurisdiction to enquire into any facts behind the writ by the court. Court will [otherwise] take up the case entire [which would be improper].

Butterfield: Joseph Smith is in custody under order of authority of the United States [charged with being an] accesory to the Shooting of Gov[ernor] {page 51} Boggs on the 6th of May. Read the affidavit of 10 witnesses. /Stephen A./ Douglas and/ J[acob] B./ Backenstos sworn to affidavit. Affidavit read.

Esqu[i]r[e] Lamborn: I am much at a loss how I got into this case as prosecuting attorney. I don't know /why the/ district attorney /should bring this case in this court which I contend/ admitted has no Jurisdiction /except of common Law/.

[Butterfield: It is] Of common Law Jurisdiction. [Lamborn cited] 2d condensed report 37 page Ballman vs Courts of U[nited] States [to show that courts] have no authority where there is no law evident on the face of the {page 52} papers that he [Joseph] is not arrested under of the authority of the /United/ State[s] but of our state. Statute of our own state /has Jurisdiction/ not contradictory to United States Powers. /Read/ Gales Statute 315 page [on] fugitives from Justice. [If a fugitive is arrested upon request of the governor of another state, neither state nor federal court may question the merits of extradition.]

[Lamborn:] Whole proceedings illegal untill they can show that this law is unconstitutional, [and that] compliance on the part of the Gov[ernor] with State Law [was not required]. /Read/ Conklin's Treaties 51 page. There is no general jurisdiction in this case. The only authority of this court [is] in the Digest read Conklins Treaties 85. If Sheriff refuses to give up a prisoner {page 53} he has all the power /of the State/ to back him. /Read/ 2d condensed 55 Washington reports &c.

The party [has] attempt[ed] to prove an allibi. Can such a defence be made here? Can the court try this part of the case that Smith was in this State? No court is competent to try the case. If we go behind the papers then we can try the whole case, we are trying the guilt or innocence. Court /said the/ question is not the guilt or innocence, but is he a fugitive? /Lamborn said/ if the court could understand me.

/Court/: *The court does understand you perfectly.* {page 54}

L/amborn/: If the papers are sufficient you abandon the papers and go into the case. The whole case, guilt or innocence. Did he flee from M[issouri]? Is he a fugitive from justice? [If so, then the] Gov[enor] is bound to surrender him as a fugitive. [Butterfield:] Gov[ernor] has complied with the statutes by the court /so you say the/ Judge of the S[upreme] C[ourt] of Ill[inois] could not issue a Habeus corpus?

L/amborn/: [I] Don't deny H/abeus/ Corpus. [But the] Party brought up has no right to go into trial on any of the facts behind Record. /Read/ Gordon Digest, Charles 2d Grant Habeus Corpus /Act/. Large Majority of English Judges submitted to the 12 by Parliament. 9th Wendell {page 55} 212 page if he prophesied that Boggs should be shot, where should he be tried? In M[issouri]. [As in] Some instances in N[ew] York &c. and Maine &c. on account of Slaves &c. One independant state equals another independent state. Decision made for political effect in those cases. Positively I take it this court has no Jurisdiction, no disrespect to court. Party not held by United States Laws, but of Illinois subject /to the jurisdiction of/ our own Government if they had a right. It would be only to try the papers. Our own statutes cover the ground and no other courts have authority. The lawyers agree with me {page 56} with few Exceptions, No jurisdiction. No court has power to try the papers.

/Esqu[i]r[e] Lamborn is/ in the dark. [said] Esqu[i]r[e] Edward /[who] does not know/ why /he [Lamborn] is made the/ prosecutor. He /is/ not a prosecutor, but /is permitted to come in here/ [as] a matter of courtesy. Fugitives /must be taken by/ virtue of the Constitution of the United /States/. Kent's Commentaries 2d vol[ume] 32 in the notes. Judicial powers extends in all cases where the action arises under U[nited] S[tates] Laws. Tremendous power of the executive to deliver up an affidavit [is granted] to enquire into the fact. Greater than any Emperor ever used [for the extradition of a suspect] to be transplanted from his home. Transplanting of Individuals from the colonies {page 57} to Great Britain. Seven years was [framers?] of Constitution [debating whether they] would vest the Governors of the States with

273

the same powers of oppression. /Suppose he is guilty in view of the retributive justice due on the murders/ [according to the] Boggs affidavit. That Joe Smith has been accessory /to the shooting of [Boggs] himself/. This people whom he has compelled to flee from Missouri. /Which does the fleeing refer to?/ From the shooting of Boggs or the fleeing of the people from the M[iss]o[uri] mob.

Mr. Butterfield asked question by Att[orne]y Gen[eral if Butterfield does not concur] /that this court has/ no jurisdiction to relieve and says that this is [also] the opinion of the bar. [Butterfield:] /I have a/ great respect for the bar /but a/ contempt for out door /and bar room [justice] without thought [of the Constitution] according [to previous]/ opinion; this court has exclusive jurisdiction. Prisoner is {page 58} arrested under Con[stitution] of U[nited] S[tates] and Law arising under the Constitution['s] Power. 2nd section 4th Art[icle] Constitution delivered up on demand made by demand made under color of U[nited] S[tates] Law. Any executive of the Union shall demand, and produce copy [of] indictment or affidavit, [and] /the fugitive shall be/ arrested and secured.

Was Jose[ph] Smith arrested by law of this state. No /most/ untruly has it been stated here. Does Gov[ernor] Reynolds call /for him/ by authority of the Laws of M[iss]o[uri] or Ill[inois]? No! By Constitution and laws of the United States, /Governor Carlin/ being a good Gov[ernor] and good Lawyer and says [upon], Requisition from Gov[ernor] Reynolds, Gov[ernor] General [of Illinois] was [then] requested [and was happy] to issue {page 59} this copy /because the original writ was out of our reach. Constitution and Laws of/ United States and of this state. Law of this state is a furtherance if the United States is null and void.

/The Prisoner looks to/ this C[ourt] for redress. /He is/ a prisoner of U[nited] S[tates] /and the/ Gov[ernmen]t one in issuing [the] Requisition [and in] the other in [issuing a] Warrant. [Officials] Acted as appointees of the U[nited] States, bound by oath to Support the constitution of U[nited] States. Have done so, Gov[ernor] in issuing the warrant acts as agent in carrying into effect the laws of the U[nited] S[tates], [Joseph is] in Custody under U[nited] States. Can he apply to state's courts? Would not conflicts ensue which have {page 60} been anticipated by opposite Council. 12th Wendall 311. A fugitive slave /in/ New York,

Jack [a] negro man vs. Mary Martin, fled from Lou[i]s[i]ana to N[ew] York. [He was] pursued, /arrested, and taken on/ writ of H[abeus] Corpus.

Action of Congress is exclusive on actions. Being under law of Congress. Decision of the court was they /(State)/ had no jurisdiction. He's not my client. [Does] Joseph Smith [have] the Rights of a negro? He has been arrested under a Law of Congress and must seek redress before the federal court. A war /between the slave/ and non-slave holding states /and the non-slave holding states/ [has been avoided even though the states] have passed laws, and juries have had [their say]. Virginia passed {page 61} laws to require bon[d]s of masters of vessels by retaliation.

Priggs [vs.] Com[mon]wealth of P[ennsylvani]a fugitives from justice and [from] slavery are the same [facting?]. Congress having passed laws, the state laws are void. 5 Wheeten where Congress has legislated it is not competent for States to legislate. All power /is/ in Congress in relation to fugitive Slaves

(Story) [During] last January['s] terms S[upreme] C[ourt] of U[nited] States [ruled that the] aid of States is not wanted. They cannot intrude themselves. Federal Government is competent.

The court has not only jurisdiction {page 62} but it is the only court [where] I [Butterfield] could bring this case. Judicial power shall extend to all cases arising [from] or [based] on the Constitution /and laws/ of the U[nited] States. I hope the Gent[lemen] of the bar will not give their opinion without reading the books. There [Their] out door opinions /are a disgrace to the profession/.

Has this court power to issue Habeus Corpus? It has! Is the return sufficient to hold the prisoner in custody without further testimony? Unless it appears on the testimony that he is a fugitive, it is not sufficient.

Affidavit read. It does not state he ever was in M[iss]o[uri] that he ever was in the {page 63} state of /M[iss]o[uri]. It/ states nothing that would bring him within the Law of the United S[tates]. He must have fled. Shall Flee. Boggs knew what he was about. He knew that Joe Smith had not been in M[iss]o[uri] since the Mormons were murdered. He dare not purjur[e] himself. He thought his Gov[ernor] would certify to a lie and save him from perjury.

[Was it] Represented /to him [Reynolds]/ who made the false and foul statement that Jo[seph] Smith had fled? No body would swear to it! But the citizens of Illinois are not to be {page 64} imprisoned on representation to Gov[ernor] Reynolds, sent over the great father of waters to Gov[ernor] Carlin by some necromancy of /a jurisdiction/ beyond our control. /Boggs affidavit says he [Joseph] was in Ill[inois]. Reynolds [says] that it was [reported?] to him who reported it./

Copy the progress of Error. Little beyond Requisition. Carlin [prepares] a writ [which] appears [necessary] from [the] affidavit, spread before Carlin, while writing. No man ought to flee from the justice of M[iss]o[uri].

1st position /is for/ the court /to/ examine all the papers /there is not/ a particle of testimony that Joseph has fled from M[iss]o[uri]. Gov[ernor] Carlin would not have given up his dog on such a requisition. /The/ Gov[ernmen]t says /it is/ not {page 65} necessary it should appear /that he had fled/. The Gov[ernor] thought it necessary or why insert the falsehood? He is not subject to be transported till /it is proved that he is a fugitive/. They must prove he has fled. If he is guilty can this court deliver him up? No! He must have fled.

The question is whether he will be transported to another state or tried on his own soil? Transported to Botany Bay of Missouri and very indifferent which [people should try him].

We have shown we were not in M[iss]o[uri]. /He is/ not a fugitive {page 66} from Justice. He was at officers' drill on 6 [May 1842] and /in the/ Lodge /from/ 6 to 9 /o'clock/ 7th day 300 miles off /in uniform/ reviewing the Nauvoo /Legion/. Instead of running away from Boggs [he dressed] in uniform [and] Judge Douglass partook of the hospitality of Gen[eral] Smith. /Instead of/ fleeing from Justice /he/ [was] dining on [the attention of] courts, the highest courts in our land.

Have I a right to try him. Power of Habeus Corpus is pretty well settled. /There is/ no proof in /the/ writ that he is a fugitive from justice. {page 67}

3rd Peters 193 Tobias Watkins, convicted of embezzling money. Cannot go behind the Judgement where Judgement is not issued. Can go behind the writ. /Some/ notice of writ of Error body of Prisoner and cause of commitment, 3rd Crenshaw 447.

3d Bacon's abridgment to question [as] proposed to 12

Judges. Since a person is so informed that the court cannot discharge yet unjustly, manifestly to unwarrantable means, clear on Habeus Corpus, [the] most clear and undoubted testimony [regarding] this man are not {page 68} manifestly against law and Justice. /Is the/ Habeus Corpus a civil or criminal [matter]? [If] Not criminal, [then a] civil proceding[, and] whether the law of this state on Habeus Corpus [or another] Statute of this /state/[, it is clear] that [even if this is a state issue, a] prisoner may make allegations and court shall hear. In H[abeus] Corpus the Laws of the State shall be regarded by the courts where they are held. Statute of this state, prisoner shall be allowed to controvert on trial [of] this as well as [post a] promissory note. Not only [to] contravene the return but [to establish] that he is not to be surrendered or discharged. {page 69}

/Gent[leman Lamborn] read/ 9th Wendell 212. When a person is brought on Habeus C[orpus] court is not to enquire into the /guilt or innocence/. Authority is against it, 9th Wendell previous to 12th Wendell and /is/ all set aside. Has he fled? and not is he guilty? If Smith was in this state, says Attorney General, constructing [a crime] in that state [then he has fled]. [Butterfield:] /I/ don't wish to go into a spiritual disquisition. /The words/ "shall flee" occurs 3 times /in the Constitution/. The removal is not spiritually, but bodily, look at it. States have passed laws to take effect out of the state where /they were passed/ but they were void. Suppose {page 70} Ill[inois] passed a law to prevent any person from speaking disrespectfully of his inability to pay his debts. We might have 1/2 the city of N[ew] York /before our courts/ for saying we could not pay our debts. [Lamborn:] Alabama ag[ain]st N[ew] York in case of Williams. W[illia]ms had been Spiritually there [and] had not fled from the Justice of that state. The Right to demand and power to give up co-extensive. [2/3?] Gov[ernor] Marcy's Message to above abolitionist./ [Butterfield:] Gov[ernor] Marcy was not an abolitionist as the court would intimate./

That an attempt should be made to deliver up a man who has never been out of the State strikes at all the liberty /of our institutions/. His fate to day may be yours tomorrow. {page 71} I do not think the defendant /ought/ under any circumstances to be delivered up to M[iss]o[uri].

It is a matter of history that he and his poeple have been

/murdered and driven from the state/. He had better been sent to the gallows. He is an innocent and unoffending man. The difference is this people believe in prophecy and others do not. Old prophets prophecied in poetry and the modern in Prose.

/Went into the Judge's room. Introduced to one senator and some Ladies, Mrs. Ford./ 1/2 Ladies retired.

Lamborn read from 12th Wendell case of Williams on the part of the Gov[ernor] to act. [Butterfield:] No court {page 72} could compel him to act. Difference of oppinion of the North and South.

Court adjourned till 9 [o'clock] tomorrow Morning for making up opinion. Retired to Judge Adams. After Dinner Joseph was with Hiram and Orson in the chamber and Bro[ther] T[heodore] Turl[e]y and mended the bellows and dug some horse raddish with Lorin.

5[th] h[our] evening Joseph, Gen[eral] Law, and Bro[ther] Hyde took their departure in Mr. Prentice's carriage to visit his house, and returned about 11 o'clock, giving a very interesting account of their visit with Mr. Prentice and family. Judge Douglass, /Esqu[i]r[e] Butterfield, and Edward,/ Judge Pope's Son, Esqu[i]r[e] Lamborn and many others. See page 76 {page 73}

[*Material from page 76 is included here and follows:*] Had a Most splendid Supper with many outstanding anedotes and every thing to render the visit agreeable. [*End of material added from page 76.*]

[*Note A appears at this point in the original manuscript but is placed with material on manuscript page 23.*]

Jan[uary] 4[th] The court Room was crowded the whole of the Trial and the utmost decorum and good feeling prevailed. Much prejudice was allayed. Esqu[ire] Butterfield managed the case very learned and Judiciously. [He was] prece[e]ded by Esqu[i]r[e] Edwards who made some very pathetic allusions to our sufferings in Missouri. Esqu[i]r[e] Lamborn was not severe, apparently saying little more than the nature of his situation required, and no more than would be usefull in satisfying the public mind, that there had been a fair investigation of the whole matter. {page 75}

[*Material inserted on manuscript page 73 appeared here in the original.*]

278   January 5[th] 1843 8 1/2 [A.M.] repaired to Mr.

Butterfield's room. 9 [A.M.] entered Co[u]rt Room, the room was crowded before He entered with spectators. Mostly of a very respectable class in Society anxious to hear the decision although the public expression was decidedly in favor of an acquittal.

9 and 10 minut[e]s [after] the [hour] Judge Pope entered prece[e]ded by 2 ladies, court opened, Docket called. 4 more Ladies entered and took seat[s] beside the Judge while the docket was reading (four councillors sworn &c.) in matter of J[oseph] Smith /the court/ has taken occasion to examine.

Thanks to gentlemen of the bar. {page 77} More [thanks because] it is [perhaps] more [*blank* [important than]][3] any other case [*blank* [affecting the lives and liberties of our citizens, in that]] the found[ers] of the Constitution of the [*blank* [United States were also in anxious deliberation to see union among the]] states of this [*blank* [confederacy in preventing]] bloodshed caused by [border] collision. [*blank* [Wisely did the founders of the Constitution see that the]] national and political Government takes charge [*blank* [in the regulation of these matters and granted]] Congress power to regulate [interstate] commerce and fugitive [*blank* [justice]] {page 78}

[The] Quest[ion arising] from this provision of Constitution of the U[nited] S[tates] [*blank* [2nd Section, 4th Article, is whether a citizen of Illinois can be transported to Missouri for an alleged crime committed in Illinois. If the]] Crime was committed in M[iss]o[uri] if the P[risoner] had escaped from M[iss]o[uri] to Ill[inois] [*blank* [it would be the]] duty of [the state of Illinois to submit to] Congress [*blank* [and to]] Laws of its own creation [*blank* [and]] not partake of the Passions and [*blank* [rivalry over a]] power [that] should be [*blank* [mutually agreed to]] {page 79}

J[oseph] S[mith] applied to the court [*blank* [for a writ of habeas corpus, directed to the sheriff of]] Sangamon Co[unty] [*blank* [to try the]] Requisition [*blank* [of the]] Gov[ernor of] Ill[inois which] professes to [*blank* [be pursuant to the]] Laws of the U[nited] S[tates] and Ill[inois.] [*blank* [The]] court deemed it Re-

---

[3] Willard Richards, at this point, begins to take fragmentary notes of the court's proceedings, leaving several lines blank between entries. Bracketed editorial insertions are based on the text of Judge Pope's opinion, as it appears in Joseph Smith et al., *History of the Church of Jesus Christ of Latter-day Saints*, B. H. Roberts, ed., 7 vols., 2nd ed. rev. (Salt Lake City, 1964), 5:223-31, which, according to its editors, was copied from the *Sangamo Journal*.

spectful that the Gov[ernor] be informed [*blank* [of the action upon
the habeas corpus. According to the 12 February 1793 act of Congress, the]] Executive and Att[orne]y Gen[eral] were required [to
give proof to support the charges underlying the writ of extradition.] Att[orne]y Gen[eral] appeared {page 80} and objected [to
jurisdiction] when the prisoner was under [warrant to] return
[*blank* [to Missouri]] under authority of S[tate of] Ill[inois.] [*blank*
[But the]] Congress of U[nited] S[tates conferred the authority on
the state of Illinois and Illinois] had no power to confer the authority [or to countermand federal law either in Illinois or] in
M[iss]o[uri.] [*blank*] 2d sec[tion] 4 Art[icle of U.S. Constitution]
read [followed by a reading of Illinois law].

[It] Will be perceived this clause [in the Illinois statute
does not and] cannot [confer any additional power upon the] ex-
ecut[ive of the state than that conferred by federal law.] [*blank*
[The governor's warrant]] itself [is otherwise] what testimony shall
[*blank* [have supported its issuance, it containing more statements
of fact than the affidavit accompanying the governor of Missouri's
requisition.]] {page 81}

[*page left blank*] {page 82}
[*page left blank*] {page 83}

The power of Congress [is] to pass [*blank* [laws prescrib-
ing the means of fulfilling constitutional provisions.]] shortly after
[*blank* [the judicial act of 1789, regarding persons confined "under color of, or by the authority of the United States," the state]]
executive [was required by an act of Congress] to [*blank* [deter-
mine the support for a writ of extradition by examining the] testimony [provided in the form of a] copy of [an] indictment or [an]
affidavit. [*blank* [The]] Clause of [the relevant state statute does
not purport to go beyond the federal law and therefore examination of the] affidavit [is required.] complain[ts] [*blank* [of the attorney general considered. The attorney general]] claimed [one
may not inquire into the facts behind the writ. That if the writ is
issued] by [the] executive of the state [then the content of the]
Indictment or affi[davit] [*blank* [is irrelevant. But]] Where Congress has power to Legislate [*blank* [the governor must comply]]
{page 84} on [risk of] the peace of the state of Ill[inois.] [*blank*] in
order to maintain the position of the Att[orne]y Gen[eral] that
[this warrant was not issued under authority of] Congress of
[*blank* [the United States, he would have to show that Congress

did not confer this authority. But Congress did confer this authority.] the Law [of the state of Illinois never] had any effect [*blank* [but]] power only to carry into effect the Law [*blank* [of Congress. The state law had]] no power to carry the Constitution. [*blank* [It is the]] duty of the Governor to obey [*blank*] authority conferred by Con[gress] and laws of U[nited] S[tates]. {page 85}

Therefore this Court has Jurisdiction and power to issue Habeus Corpus. [*blank* [It has]] been contended by U[nited] S[tates] Att[orne]y Gen[eral that this court] has not [the] A[u]th[or]i[t]y, [that this] Court has no authority to try writs by Gov[ernor]. [*blank* [This is not true.]] Encroachment from the crowd. [*blank*]

It was not for petty crime but [for] those high {page 86} offences [against the crown that Englishmen were once arbitrarily imprisoned, until granted the right of habeas corpus, which was hailed as] Chap[ter] 2d [of the] Magna Charta. [As] Powerful it [the Magna Carta] may be it[']s without [protection without] Habeus Corpus. [This] act offered means to any man of enjoying that liberty [offered the sovereign] no matter how [great or] mean the prisoner. [All doors fly open at its command, no matter] How high the keeper, from Garret to Dungeon. [It is the] duty of every court [to look] into [the] full [details of every matter brought before it. By so] doing it does not [intend] to [play a legal] game [but to guarantee a government of laws. To assert that the executive officer of any state is exempt from this scrutiny] is ridiculous. {page 87} [It has] Be[e]n contended [that the] court cannot go behind the warrant [although it is] unnecessary to go ~~behind~~ into that point [in this case because of the deficiencies of the affidavit. But the issue is clear,] and if ever the importance of a scrutiny into the acts of the executive [*blank* [should be stressed, it is in the case of extradition of citizens to be tried by a foreign state. The] Constitution [provides that if one] flee [the suspect] may be [returned for trial] by Indictment or affidavit. [When] a crime [is committed] in the state of M[iss]o[uri a Missouri] court will [hear the case. The re]turn [of the suspect is based on the warrant, the indictment, the demand, and the affidavit.] [*blank* [Former governor]] Bogg[s] swears [*blank* [that]] {page 88} on 6 May 1842 [*blank* [he]] was shot and his life was dispaired [*blank* [of for several days and that he has]] good reason to believe [*blank* [that Joseph Smith was an accessory before the fact. He]] does not say that he was a fugitive from justice, does not say who he was accessory to. [*blank*] this is [the only] evidence [*blank* [presented.]] what does the Gov[ernor of] M[iss]o[uri] say? [The] Gov[ernor of] M[iss]o[uri] knew [of] no [evidence to promote in convincing this court of the need for] arresting [the suspect. We are] without [the aid of an inquiry by a grand jury or otherwise. Joseph Smith is to be arrested on the] principle [*blank* [of suspicion. The governor of Illinois assumed the suspect was]] accused [of being an] accessory to Mr. [Orrin Porter] Rockwell [*blank* [and that the crime was committed in Missouri. There is]] not a word of his fleeing from [Missouri in the affidavit. The] {page 89} Gov[ernor of] Ill[inois] acted on [an entirely incomplete] affidavit. [He assumed] Mr. Bogg[s] was shot by Mr. R[ockwell] [*blank* [and that Joseph]] Smith [was therefore an] accessory. [*blank*] How cautious Judges should be and how loosely Executive officers do act. [The court can alone regard the facts set forth in the affidavit and supported by oath as having any legal existence.] [*blank* [That]] Boggs was shot [we know. That Joseph] Smith [was an] accessory [is not a fact]. [We know he is a] Citizen of Illinois.

[The] Warrant issue[d] for Joseph S[mith] [*blank* [involves]] 2 parts Can a citizen of Ill[inois] be transported to M[iss]o[uri] to be {page 90} tried for an offence committed [in Illinois, and can one be extradited on suspicion only? Regarding the first point, Joseph Smith] Cannot violate a law he has not promised to obey. [He is a citizen of Illinois, not of Missouri.]

Man naturally is a sovereign but when he enters into a state of society [and] upon principle of consent that society shall [guarantee his] protect[ion]. Has that society a right to give him up. By tribunals [to which] He has [sworn his obedience, to be tried by peers who have] seen events [*blank* [of alleged wrongs against society, he has a right to be tried. If that society]] pu[s]hes him before tribunals [of another community to hear testimony] {page 91} from witnesses [*blank* [who are not his peers, this]] would violate every [social] contract. This is the principle. [There is] No man here but may he admitt [*blank* [it would be wrong to]] deliver up Jos[eph] Smith. Any individual [could otherwise be subjected to laws unknown to him, and punished by a foreign state to which he owes no allegiance]. [*blank* [It is]] True [that] every writer [on the laws of nations has maintained that] — every state should be [*blank*] responsible [to its neighbors for the conduct of its citizens and] shall [punish its citizens for violations of foreign laws on the principle of good neighborhood. Except for the consitutional provisions, Illinois and Missouri would stand in the same relation to each other as Spain and England.] no [citizen of Illinois could otherwise be tried in Missouri. Because of the Constitution] annyone [violating Missouri law in Missouri is tried in Missouri, although Missouri allows] for their neighbor Ill[inois] [*blank* [to protect its citizens against unreasonable charges originating in] M[iss]o[uri]. [*blank*] {page 92}

[This is the] Right of territorial boundary. [*blank* [A man's]] Home [is] his castle. When departed from Far West, M[iss]o[uri,] many complain of Ill[inois harboring fugitives, but] if their [there is evidence there] has been aggression [by Mormons against Missourians there, the Mormons should be tried there].

[The] United States [is] bound to see that no annoyance is suffered by any state. [A] Military Expedition [by U.S. citizens] against [a neighboring state] may bring notions [that the offended state may have the right to prosecute, but the aggressors are still] amenable [to U.S. law only].

If J[oseph] Smith aided and abetted Rockwell [it] might [have been in Illinois. It would] be the duty [of the Illinois legislature] to provide for acts of the kind that M[iss]o[uri] has [passed so that] nothing [could be construed] to [*blank* [deter justice]]. {page 93} J[oseph] S[mith] cannot be tried in M[iss]o[uri]. [*blank* [The]] Offence must be committed where? [In Missouri.] What would necessarily be the action [based on] Congress and Laws? The evidence should be so specific as to leave no doubt a crime was committed. Where the crime was committed — [and that the suspect fled] to [another state from] the state where the crime [*blank* [was committed]] The Gov[ernor] of the State where crime was committed[, the] Gov[ernor] M[iss]o[uri,] is the proper [*blank* [authority to request extradition.]] {page 94}

If ever there was a case when the Judge ought to scrutinize this is the case. [*blank* [The officers of Missouri must bear the responsibility of examining the]] case to correct [any omissions or errors before requesting custody of the suspect] so [that we may know if there is] any authority why he should be [delivered besides the opinion of the former] Gov[ernor]. [*blank* [The]] Affidavit [by] definition [must tell why] J[oseph] S[mith] is accessory before the fact.

Who constituted [that] Bogg[s was] competent to advise

this court. [As a] Question of Law — [the] facts [this] court has to do with must affirm [a] crime was {page 95} committed. [Mr. Boggs says he] Believes and has good reason to believe [Joseph Smith was an accomplice, and that this evidence is] now in his possession. [He should have incorporated this evidence into his affidavit to support his "belief."]

Who ever heard of a man[']s being arrested [on "belief"]? [The] Reasons may have been futile. [The] Court might not think them very good.

Another [legal] Question read — familiar principles, [the Supreme Court's] own opinion [that when one is] charged with Treason, [or some other] felony [there must be evidence f]or the crime [or the suspect] shall [not] be delivered. [Mr. Boggs only] Suspects J[oseph] S[mith] as [an] accessory [or he would have stated the facts]. {page 96} [One might think the] Court must put a construction where there is fear of escape. Issue a warrant to detain for examination. [The Supreme] Court don't concur.

[One must] Proceed on more [than] suspician. [If the] Motive [of Mr. Boggs were] fear that he [Joseph Smith] will escape [it] is done away — parties have time to collect testimony [and] submit it to [a] Grand Jury. [One may] Impeach Congress [on suspicion] — [this is] only an impeachment. [The word] Charged used in the Constitution [requires] positive [evidence] not suspicion. {page 97} Bogg[s] says he was shot on 6 May — (Ladies [*blank*]) and his affidavit [was] made 20 July following — shall [he] not [be required to] find [evidence for an] indictment befor[e rendering] Judg[e]ment[? He] had time to bring a serving [before a grand jury] of the Citizens of those U[nited] States — should [Joseph Smith] be transported unless on positive charge, not on [mere] Suspicion. Mature reflection [reveals an] Affidavit so imperfect [as to be a collection of mis-recitals and overstatements].

J[oseph] Smith [should] be discharged and the entry be made so that {page 98} /he shall be [free from any attempt]/ to secure him. ~~from any further arrests on this~~ /[He should be] trouble[d] no more ~~on this matter~~ in relation to the matter touching this/ prosecution. (Joseph arose and bowed to the court) Spectators retired and court adjourned to 10 o'clock tomorrow.

Joseph repaired to Judge Pope's room and spent 1 hour in conversation with his honor shewing that he did not profess to be a prophet [to aggrandize himself] then every man ought [to be a prophet] who professes to be a preacher of Righteousness. That the testimony of Jesus is the spirit of Prophecy and [he] preached to the Judge. Esqu[ire] Butterfield asked him to Prophecy how {page 99} many inhabitants would come to Nauvoo.

Joseph replied, "I will not tell you how many inhabitants will come to Nauvoo but I will tell you what I saw when I came to Commerce. I told them I could build up a city and the old inhabitants said We'll be damned if you can, so I prophesied that I could build up a city. The inhabitants prophesied I could not. We have now about 12,000 inhabitants. I will prophecy we will build a great city, for we have the stakes, and we have only to {page 100} fill up the insterstices."

Joseph came in the Clerk's office after he left the Judge, who by the bye was very attentive and agreeable, and said to the clerks that he had been disaffected in one thing which appeared to allay their pleasure for the moment. But said he, "I have met with less prejudice and better and more noble and liberal feelings on the part of the people generally than I expected before I come which lightened my countenance with joy."

After mailing letters to Liverpool, {page 101} Philadelphia, and St. Louis—retired to Gen[eral] Adams—when Secretary went to [inquire about] preparing the Judges Decision for the press on request of Judge Pope, per President Joseph.

Visited Mr. Butterfield with W[illia]m Clayton [and] had conversation concerning the abuse which had been received from M[iss]o[uri] and the officers. Joseph asked Butterfield if he or the assigned could sell the Lots on the Hotchkiss pu[r]chase in Nauvoo. Butterfield [said] neither can, see [since] all the assignee can sell is Joseph's Right. The conveyance {page 102} has not been made by Hotchkiss, therefore it reverts back again to him. Joseph has nothing to do with paying the remainder which is due Hotchkiss in the event he is discharged on bankruptcy.

Visited at Mr. M. Graves in the evening. [We] had a very social visit and had a disquisition on phrenology. Slept in the Guest Chamber with Secretary [Richards]. {page 103}

January 6th 1842 [1843] After finishing a copy of Judge Pope's decision, went with Joseph and presented the same to the Judge. We were in the court Room with Butterfield and the Clerk. Joseph gave Butterfield 2 notes of $230 each for his fees [and] bind [retainer] /note signed by Joseph Smith, Hyrum Smith, [Levi]

285

Moffat [Moffit], and [Edward] Hunter/. [Including the] $40 he had received [it made] $500 in the whole.

Took certified copies of the Affidavit, of Boggs-Reynolds Requisition, Carlin's Writ as reissued by Ford, Joseph's Petition, Carlin's Proclamation, Habeus Corpus, order of Court, Joseph's affidavit, and affidavits of Eleven others, and all the {page 104} doings of the court certified by the clerk and the order of the governor thereon showing that Joseph is discharged from all prosecution on the case of the arrest on Requisition from Missouri.

Joseph visited Judge Pope to request a copy of his decision for the Wasp [a Mormon newspaper] and not let Mr. [S.] Francis [editor of the *Sangamo Journal*] have the first chance. As he has published much against us and we have a little pride in being the first. Judge Pope said he could not well deny Mr. Francis but he would give Gen[eral James] Adams the first chance of copying the decision as soon as it should be written. {page 105}

After the Governor had certified the decision of court and the papers, he offered a little advice to Joseph that he refrain from all political electioneering. Joseph shewed him that he always had acted on that principle and proved it by Gen[eral William] Law and Sec[retar]y quite to the satisfaction of the governor. As it [was] affirmed that the Mormons were driven to union in their election by persecution and not by the influence of Joseph. Thus the Mormons acted on the most perfect principles of Liberty in all their Movements. {page 106}

In the court room Mr. Butterfield inquired the price of lots in Nauvoo. Said if he become a Mormon he should want to come to live with us. Had conversation on the subject of Religion. Judge Pope's son wished me well and hoped I should not be persecuted here any more. Jos[eph] blessed him. Conversed with Owens, [a] Catholic. When we retired the Lawyers were laughing at him saying that he would be a Mormon in 6 weeks if he would go to Nauvoo. Mr. Butterfield said Joseph must deposite his discharge and all the papers in the archives of {page 107} the [Nauvoo] Temple, when it was completed.

3 1/2 P.M. Retired to Judge Adams. Evening, W[illia]m Smith called [and] said Cochron Representatives from Union had brought charges or insinu[a]tions against the Mormons saying certain things false in the Mormon Bible. The Man[a]ger of the Theatre sent a ticket for /Gen[eral]/ Joseph Smith to attend the

theatre this eve[ning], but the action was dispensed with on account of the weather. {page 108}

[*page left blank*] {page 109}

January 7[th], Saturday 8 1/2 [A.M.] Left Judge Adams on our way to Nauvoo and arrived at Mr. Dutches [at] 4 P.M. Travelling very bad much of the way. Snow fell the ev[en]ing previous on the road which had not frozen, though extremely cold, so as to turn the horses white with frost. While riding Gen-[eral] Law sang the following hymn:

And are you sure the news is true?
And are you sure he's free?
Then let us join with one accord,
And have a Jubilee

Chorus
We'll have a Jubilee, My Friend {page 110}
We'll have a Jubilee
With heart and voice we'll all rejoice
~~Because~~ /In that/ our Prophet's free

2d
Success unto the Federal Court.
Judge Pope presiding there;
And also his associates too,
So lovely and so fair

3 Chorus
Also to our learned Councillors
We owe our gratitude
Because that they in freedom's cause
Like valiant men have stood

4 Chorus
In the defence of Innocence,
They made the truth to bear; {page 111}
Reynolds and Carlin's baseness both
Did fearlessly declare

5 Chorus see [1]13, 114 page[s]

/Edwards and Butterfield and Pope/
~~The names of Pope and Butterfield~~
We'll mention with applause
Because that they like champions bold
Support the Federal Law

7 chorus
One word in praise of Thomas Ford
That Democrat so true;
He understands the people's rights
And will protect them too.

8 chorus
There is one more we wish enrol'd
Upon the Book of fame
That master spirit in all jokes
And Prentice but in name {page 112}

8 chorus see P[age] 114
/12/ With warmest heart we bid good bye
to those we leave behind
The citizens of Springfield all
So courteous and so kind.

15 chorus
And now we're bound for home my friend
A bond of brothers true
To cheer the heart of those we love
In beautiful Nauvoo.

We'll have a Jubilee My friends
We'll have a Jubilee
With heart and voice we'll all rejoice
In that our Prophet's free {page 113}

Note 13, 6
The Attorney General of the State
His duty nobly did
And ably brought those errors forth
from which we now are freed.

9 c. Chorus
The sucker State we'll praise in song
She's succour'd us in deed
And we will succour her again
In every time of need.

10 chorus
Our Charter'd rights she has Maintained
Through opposition great
Long may her charter champions live
Still to protect the State.

chorus {page 114}
And Captain Dutch we cannot pass
Without a word of Praise
For he's the king of comic song
As well as comic ways

Chorus
And the fair Ladies of his house
/flowers of Morgan's plains/
~~to thank them we take pains~~
Who from the soft piano bring
Such soul enchanting strains

We'll have a Jubilee, My friends
We'll have a Jubilee
With heart and voice we'll all rejoice
In that our Prophet's free

11-We'll stand by her through sun and shade
Through calm and sunshine too
And when she need our Legion's aid
Tis ready at Nauvoo.

chorus {page 115}

Which was written and sung repeatedly during the evening
with many other songs and stories and the whole party were very

cheerful and had a rich entertainment. We retired at a late hour and rose early.

Sunday, Janu[a]ry 8[th] 1842 8 o['cloc]k rode through Geneva past Beardstown, crossed the Illinois River on the ice and arrived at Rushville 4 P.M. Soon after a man, Mr. Royalty {page 116} 6 1/2 feet high called to see us. After supper we repaired to Mr. [Uriah] Brown's and sung the Mormon Jubilee.

Mr. Brown repeated his incertion [assertion?] for national defence [but said there was] poor prospect of the nation adopting [*blank* [his invention. He elaborated on his]] vessel [and] investment. [*blank* [In his]] speech [be]fore [*blank* [he had showed the protection]] against the destruction instantly sealed [*blank* [in a rival design. He]] turned my attention to Land operation confection [liquid fire, invented] by him as steam engine [*blank* [to revolutionize war for the next]] 300 y[ea]rs. {page 117} Some plans and diagrams [showed forces] behind movable batteries [with] cutters and on wheels [driven] by steam if level.

[The] Confidence of an individual at St. Louis [*blank* [was obtained, and he]] made a proposition for operation in the Southern [and] Northern Provinces of Mexico with a small force if it was not connected with the United States. Some other power will avail itself. Vessel contain[s] Machine ball [where one] cannot get at it. Cannon ball will destroy {page 118} 300 ft by land [when protected] by breastworks. Account from Colt. N[ew] York proposed the same thing to Mr. Madison. Services of Rand. Expl[oded?] their Magazine by conduction.

To determine precisely Method of determining when the vessel comes over Magazine, [one can plan a] land explosion. Will not effect our shipping, but our enemy [cannot confront us on land]. Observation by telescope. Meet our army. Battery moved up touch off, approach our enemy under cover of sand bags. {page 119} engine for beseiging city defended by india Rubber &c.

Joseph said he had thought that the Lord had designed the apparatus for some more magnificent purpose than for the defense of nations. [*rest of page blank*] {page 120}

Monday, January 9th Started 8 1/2 o'clock for Plymouth. Roads pretty good but smooth an[d] icy. When 2 miles beyond Brooklynn at 12 1/2 noon while Bro[ther] Richards and Lorin Walker was in the covered carriage and descending a steep hill the horses bolted. The carriage slipped and capsized and fell off the side of the bridge, 5 feet descent. Broke the carriage, some on the top and the fore axletree which we soon spliced and w[h]itt[l]ed and went on no one being injured which we considered a special interposition {page 121} of Providence and agreed that Lilburn W. Boggs should pay the damage. [*blank*]

Arrived at Bro[ther Samuel] Smith's in Plymouth 4 P.M. After supper, Joseph went to see his sister Catharine Salisbury with Sister Durphy and Sec[retar]y [Richards]. The first time he had visited her in the state of Illinois.

While there Joseph spoke {page 122} of his friends particularly his father's family in general and particularly of his brother Alvin, that he was a very handsome man. Surpassed by none but Adam and Seth and of great strength. While 2 Irishmen were fighting and one was about to gouge the others eyes, Alvin took him by his collar and breeches and threw him over the ring which had been formed to witness the fight.

While there my heart was pained to witness a lovely wife and sister of Joseph almost barefoot and four lovely children entirely so in the middle of winter. {page 123} Ah! thought I, what has not Joseph and his father's family suffered to bring forth the work of the Lord? I [Willard Richards] sung the Mormon Jubilee to cheer our hearts and we returned to Bro[ther] Smith's Just before the close of the meeting in the school house where Bro[ther John] Taylor preached. Soon after as some had called to see the Prophet we all collected and sung the Jubilee and retired. {page 124}

January 10th, Tuesday 8 1/2 [A.M.] Started for Nauvoo. Had a prosperous journey stopping only to water our horses at the public well in Carthage. Arrived at [home of] Gen[eral Joseph] Smith at 2 1/2 P.M. when his family and friends assembled together and sung the /Mormon/ Jubilee. Soon after, his mother came in and got hold of his arm before he saw her which produced a very agreeable surprise on his part and the olde Lady was overjoyed to behold her son free once more. {page 125}

[January] 11th, Wednesday Joseph rode out in his sleigh with his wife. Started to go to Bro[ther] Russel[l']s to apologize about the broken carriage. Broke sleigh shoe and returned. Visited by a co[mpany] of Ladies and Gentlemen from Farmington on the DesMoin River [who] left at 2 1/2 P.M.

Directed /written/ Invitations to be given to Wilson Law,

W[illia]m Law, Hyrum Smith, Sam[ue]l Bennet[t], John Taylor, W[illia]m Marks, [Levi] Moffat, Peter Hawes, Orson Hyde, H[enry] G. Sherwood, W[illia]m Clayton, Jabez Durphy, H[arvey] Tate, Edward Hunter, Theodor[e] Turley, Shadrach Roundy, W[illard] {page 126} Richards, Arthur Milikin with their Ladies, and Mrs. Lucy Smith to a dinner party on Wednesday next at 10 A.M.

Brigham Young, Wilford Woodruff, Geo[rge] A. Smith, Eliza Snow, Mr. [Carlos] Granger, Sisters Ells [and] Partridge, Alpheus Cutler, Reynolds Cahoon, [and] H[eber] C. Kimball were afterwards added. [*rest of page blank*] {page 127}

Thursday, January 12th At home all day. [*rest of page blank*] {page 128}

January 13th, Friday At home till near sun set when Bro[ther] Russel[l] called to see if $20 had been received. Said he put it in his brother's bag where both their monies were deposited and his bro[ther] said if there was $20 due the Church he must make it good.

Then went to Bro[ther] W[illia]m Marks to see Sophia who was sick. Heard her relate the vision or dream of a visit from her two brothers who were dead — Touching the associations and relations of another world. {page 129}

[*seven lines left blank*]

January 14[th], Saturday Rode out with Emma in the fore noon. Evening in special council in the chamber — to pray for Sophia Marks. {page 130}

Sunday, Jan[uar]y 15[th] At home. [*rest of page blank*] {page 131}

Monday, January 16[th] [*entry left blank*] {page 132}

Tuesday, Janu[ua]ry 17[th] At home. Fast day. Meeting in the Court Room /with 6 others/. Reference on Dr. Foster's Land case. [*rest of page blank*] {page 133}

January 18th 1843 Party /began to/ assembled at the time appointed and before 12 o'clock the Jubilee songs — by Gen[eral] Law and Miss [Eliza R.] Snow were distributed by the governor of the feast to fifty individuals — the party invited except Mr. Moffat who were seated in the Court Room, who sung the same. Elder Taylor then read a vision from a New Orleans paper. Bro[ther] and Sister Marks came in.

Gen[era]l S[mith]: "I will call your attention to one of the most enticing cases you ever saw." He then arose and read a letter from John C. Bennet[t] to [Elders Orson] Pratt and [Sidney] Rigdon dated Springfield, January 10[th] 1843, Stating that [Jacob B.] Backenstows {page 134} was soon going to have Joseph arrested on the old score from M[iss]o[uri] and for Murder &c. Mr. Pratt shewed Joseph the Letter. Mr. Rigdon did not want to have it known that he had any hand in showing the letter. Joseph said he had sent word to Gov[ernor] Ford by Backensto[s] that before he would be troubled any more by M[iss]o[uri] he would fight first.

Dreamed that a sheriff came after me [Joseph]. A man put a musket in my hand and told me to keep him [the sheriff]. I took the musket and walked around him. When he went to go {page 135} away, I would push him back and if others came to trouble him I would keep them off.

Conversation continued fre[e]ly until 2 o'clock when 21 sat down to dinner. The Governor and Governess in waiting — while thus serving the table — Joseph stated that this was not only a Jubilee but commemoration of his marriage to Emma. Just 15 [16] years this day.

20 [people] sat at the 2d table, 18 at the 3d table including Joseph and Emma — with many jokes. /15 at the 4th table including children/

H[enry] G. Sherwood preached a Methodist Sermon {page 136} and received a vote of thanks from the company and he continued to tell story. /Elder Hyde told the Eddy Story/ [rest of page blank] {page 137}

[page left blank] {page 138}

Thursday, Jan[uary] 19th At home through the day except out in the city a little while in the fore noon. [rest of page blank] {page 139}

Friday, Jan[uary] 20[th] Visited President Marks. Returned at 10 o'clock and gave some instructions about [W. W.] Phelps and Richards uniting in writing the history of the church. Bro[ther] Phelps presented some po[e]try to Joseph Smith the Prophet — "Will you go with me in."

Joseph told his dream in council[:] I dreamed this morning that I was in the Lobby of the Representative House at Springfield when some of the members who did not like my being there began to mar and cut and pound my shins with pieces of Iron. I

293

bore {page 140} it as long as I could, then Jumped over the rail into the hall, caught a rod of Iron and went at them cursing and swearing at them in the most awful manner and drove them all out of the house. I went to the door and told them to send me a clerk and I ~~will~~ /would/ make some laws that would do good. There was quite a collection around the /State/ house trying to raise an army to take me and there were many horses tied around the square. I thought they would not have the privilege of getting me so I took a rod of Iron and mowed my way through their ~~way~~ /ranks/, {page 141} looking after their best race horrse thinking they might catch me when the[y] could find me when I was awoke.

To dream of flying signifies prosperity and deliverence from Enemies. Swimming in deep water signifies success among Many people. The word will be accompanied with power. Told Elder Hyde when he spoke in the name of the Lord, it should prove true, but do not curse the people.

Prop[h]ecy in the name of the Lord God. [Joseph said,] "As soon as we get the temple built so that {page 142} we will not be obliged to exhaust our means. Thereon we will have means to gather the saints by thousands and tens of thousands."

Elder Hyde told of the excellent white wine he drank in the east [Palestine]. Joseph prophesied in the name of the Lord that he would drink wine with him in that country. Joseph [said], "From the 6th day of April next, I go in for preparing with all present for a Mission through the United States and when we arrive {page 143} at Maine we will take ship for England and so on to all countries where we are a mind for to go." P[r]e[se]nt: H[yrum] Smith, B[righam] Young, H[eber] C. Kimball, Orson Hyde, Orson Pratt, John Taylor, W[ilford] Woodruff, Geo[rge] A. Smith, [and] W[illard] Richards.

[Joseph said,] "We must write for John E. Page. We must love the whole Quorum. We must send Kings and Queens to Nauvoo and we will do it. We must all start from this place. Let the 12 [Apostles] be called in on the {page 143} 6th of April and a notice be given for a special conference on the platform on [the] House of the Lord. We are sure to go as we live till spring. If I live I [will] take these b[r]ethren through these United States and through the world. I will make just as big a wake as God Almighty will let me."

/4 P.M./ Baptized Orson Pratt and wife and Lydia

Granger and confirmed them. Ordained Orson to all the authority of his former office. {page 144}

[*page left blank*] {page 145}

Saturday, January 21st Went out in the city with Elder Hyde to look at some Lots. [*six lines left blank*]

Sunday, January 22d Preached at the Temple on the setting up of the Kingdom [of God]. [*rest of page blank*] {page 146}

Monday, January 23rd Visited, with Emma, in the evening Bro[ther] Richards who is sick. Bro[ther] John Snider come home from England, where he had been sent by the Twelve [Apostles] according to Revelation to procure help for the Temple.

Tuesday, January 24th At home till P.M. Rode out with Emma. Eve[ning] at [the] Lodge for trial of Geo[rge] W. Robinson which was postponed &c. till Tuesday eve[ning] next. [*rest of page blank*] {page 147}

Wednesday, January 25th [*entry left blank*]

Thursday, January 26th [*entry left blank; rest of page blank*] {page 148}

Friday, January 27[th] [*entry left blank*]

Saturday, January 28th Played ball and rode round the city with Mr. Taylor [a] land agent from New York. Snowed some. Steamer went from Montrose over the falls to Keokuk. {page 149}

[*page left blank*] {page 150}

Sunday, Jan[uar]y 29[th] Meeting on floor of the Temple. Joseph Read the parable of the prodigal son after prayer by John Taylor then singing by the Quoir.

[Joseph remarked,] I feel thankful to Almighty God for the privilege of standing before you this morning. It is necessary that the hearers should have good and honest hearts as well as the speaker. I aim to address you on the important subject of the Prodigal Son.

2 Items I wish to notice. Last Sabbath, 2 questions [were posed about the] saying[s] of Jesus [concerning the] coming [of] John, [1st he was] a greater prophet that [than] Jer[emia]h {page 151} [and] 2[nd the] least in the kingdom of God [is] greater than he. Some so blind they won't see. I don't expect I can work Miracles enough to open [their eyes].

Greatest prophet. What constituted him [as such]. [Some

say] No prophet if do no miracles. John did no miracles. How is it John was considered one of the Greatest of Prophets? 3 things:

1st He was trusted with a divine mission of preparing the way before the face of the Lord. [Who has been so] Trust[ed] before or since? No man!

2d He was trusted and it was required at his hands to baptize the Son of Man. Who ever did that? Who {page 152} had so great a privilege and glory? Son of God into the waters of baptism and beholding the Holy Ghost in /in the sign/ the form of a dove — with the sign of the dove instituted before the creation. [The] Devil could not come in [the] sign of a dove. Holy Ghost is a personage in the form of a personage. Does not confine itself to form of a dove, but in sign of a dove. No man holds this book more sacred that [than] I do.

3d John at that time was the only legal administrator holding the keys of Power there was on Earth. The Keys of the Kingdom, the power, the Glory from the Jews, Son of Zachariah by the holy anointing [and] decree of heaven. {page 153}

These 3 constituted him the greatest born of woman.

He that is least in the Kingdom is greater than he? Who did Jesus have reference to? Jesus was looked upon as having the least claim in all God's Kingdom. He that is considered the least among you is greater than John! [Jesus said,] That is myself.

Another question, [the] Law and prophets were [preached] until John, since which time the kingdom of heaven is [the subject of] preaching and all men press into it. Additional proof to what I offered you on the last Sabbath that that even the beginning of the Kingdom. {page 154}

Prodigal Son. When you have heard, go and read your Bible if the thing[s] are not wring[ing] true.

Great deal of speculation. Subject I never dwelt upon. Understood by ma/n/y to be one of the intricate subjects [the] Elders in this church preach. No rule of interpretation. What is the rule of interpretation? *Just no interpretation at all.* Understood precisely as it read[s]. I have [a] Key by which I understand the scripture. I enquire what was the question which drew out the answer.

[This is not a] National [issue] — [regarding] Abraham &c. as some suppose. 1st place dig up the root. What drew out the saying out of Jesus? Pharisees and scribes murmurred! This man {page 155} receives sinners and eateth with them. This is the key word to answer their murmurrings and [the] questioning of Saducees and Pharisees. How is it this man as great as he pretends to be and eat with publicans and sinners. Jesus not put to it so but he could have found something of the kind [and] discerned it for nations. Men in an individual capacity, all straining on this point is a babbler [bubble?]. Boy /Boys/ say [I] ought to be hanged [but I] can tell it to you.

Big folks Presbyterians, Methodists, Baptists &c. [I] despise the ignorance and abomination of this world.

This man receiveth sinners. He spoke this parable. What man of you having an hundred sheep and 100 Saducees and Parisees. {page 156} If you Pharisees and Saducees are in the sheepfold. I have no mission for you. [I was] sent to look up sheep that are lost [and the father] will back him up and make joy in heaven. Hunting after a few individuals laying it on his Shoulder. One publican you despise. One piece of Silver, the piece which was lost. Joy in presence of the angels over one sinner that repenteth. [The others are] So righteous they will be damned any how. You cannot save them — [it is like catching] rain off from a goose's back. G[r]eat I, little you.

[A] Certain man had two sons &c. [I] Am a poor publican, a sinner — [they] humbled themselves — spending their bread and living &c. I'll return to my father's house to Jesus. You pharisees [are] so righteous you cannot {page 157} be touched. I will arise &c. claim not [to] be a pharisee or saducee. I claim not to be a son. Do not let me starve — nothing about Ephraim [or] Abraham — [it] is not mentioned. All that is meant is brought to bear upon the pharisee, saducee, the publicans, sinners, [and] Eld[e]st son. Pharisee and saducees murmuring and complaining because Jesus sat with publicans and sinners.

Joshu[a] came out and entreated. When John came [he] baptized all. When Jesus come they were angry and would not go in. Dealing of God with individuals men always Righteous always have access to throne of God, eats in his father's house. If we interpret this to national view where is the eldest son? {page 158}

Likened the kingdom to an old woman's milk pan. How

could Jesus take the kingdom from those who bore no fruit and give it to another. Is an apple tree no longer a tree because it has no apples? Parable of Prodigal son spoken to illustrate the sinner. From the moment John's voice was first heard he was the power on earth entitled to salvation on the earth.

Servants of God of the last days, myself and those I have ordained have the Priesthood and a mission to the publicans and sinners & if the Presbyterians and [*one and a half lines left blank* [Methodists and Baptists will investigate, they will see that we]] are in the kingdom. {page 159} If they are not righteous what is the result. They are sinners and if they reject our voice they shall be damned.

If a man was going to hell I would not let any man disturb him. While we will be the last to oppress, we will be the last to be driven from our post. Peace be still, bury the hatchet and the sword, the sound of war is dreadful in my ear. [But] Any man who will not fight for his wife and children is a coward and a bastard.

[Mohometons [Muslims,]] Presbyterians &c. if ye will {page 160} not embrace our religion embrace our hospitalities. [*rest of page blank*] {page 161}

Monday, January 30th At home. Evening [with] City council closing the old Election. Storm of snow. Mr. Taylor gave a Fractional Section of land near Alton. [*two lines left blank*]

Tuesday, January 31st Severe blowing of snow. At home all day. [*rest of page blank*] {page 162}

Wednesday, February 1st [*entry left blank*]

Thursday, Feb[ruary] 2nd At home. Towards evening went onto the hill to see about the caucus the previous evening. Davidson Hibbard presiding. [Benjamin] Clapp [was the] chief speaker reporting that Joseph and Hyrum had attempted to take away the rights of the citizens, referring to the slim Election on the last Council. Esqu[ire] Higbee, Dr. Foster &c. H. Kimball being concerned gave those present a blowing up. The spirit maketh inter[c]ission &c. better &c. "The spirit maketh intercession for us with striving which cannot be expressed." {page 163}

Friday, Feb[ruary] 3d At home attending to Lesson in German. 11 walked out a few mintutes. Returned 12 1/4 /o'clock/ and paid Mr. Peck $100 for W[illia]m Manhard. Read proof of Doctrin[e]s and Covenants. Bro[ther] John Mabery sent me a cow to assist [me] in bearing my expences to Springfield. 2 1/2 [P.M.] Rode out with Emma to purchase Trimming for a new carriage. Conversed with Elder Hyde and others. [*rest of page blank*] {page 164}

Saturday, Feb[ruary] 4th 1843 At home. 1 o'clock P.M. attended the General City election caucus at the Temple where all things were amicably settled and mutual good feelings were restored to all parties. Bro[ther] Clapp made a public confession for the speech which he made at a former caucus. /4 1/4 [P.M.]/ [Joseph] told Amasa Lyman he had restored Orson Pratt to his former standing [and] that he had concluded to make Amasa counciler to the First Presidency. (Municipal court in the eve[ning] on a case of assault and Battery) {page 165}

Sunday, Feb[ruary] 5th 1843 Home all day studying German. [*two lines left blank*]

Monday, Feb[ruary] 6[th] At the fore noon at the city election of Mayor, Alderman, and Council for next two years at Pres[iden]t Hiram's office. One o'clock dined at home. After dinner Thomas Mo[o]re came in and enquired about a home and received this blessing. "God bless you forever and ever. May the blessings of Abraham, Isaac, and Jacob rest upon you forever, and may you be set on thrones high and lifted up in the name of Jesus Christ Amen." Returned to city election. {page 166}

Tuesday, Feb[ruary] 7th 1843 [In the forenoon] At a council of the Twelve [Apostles] at B[righam] Young's. In the afternoon sent a warrant to Hiram Kimball's for the book of blessings given by Father Smith which was stolen from Far West. The ~~affidavit~~ /warrant/ was issued on affidavit of Johnathan Holmes and the book obtained. When Hiram Kimball came to Joseph's and heard a general expose of the frauding of Oliver Granger. [*rest of page blank*] {page 167}

Wednesday, Feb[ruary] 8th Lesson in German. Visited with brethren and Sisters from Michigan [and told them,] "A Prophet is not always a Prophet" only when he is acting as such. After dinner Bro[ther] Parley Pratt came in from England. Conversation [regarding] a bill [which] was reported in the Legislature to divorce a man or women. W[illia]m Smith said they could not repeal the Nauvoo Charter and the divorce [issue] had better be referred to the courts.

One Gentleman said he understood it was very fruitful at

299

Nauvoo. Two women from his neighborhood who had no children went to Nauvoo {page 168} and since have families. W[il-
lia]m Smith said he would explain the lives [or births? as originating?] in the gentlemen's neighborhood before they came to
Nauvoo.

John C. Bennett was like Jonah's gourd. He came up like
Jonah out of the whale's belly, but when the sun arose he with-
ered. 4 P.M. went out with Frederick [Smith] to slide on the ice.
[*rest of page blank*] {page 169}

Thursday, Feb[ruary] 9th 1843 Was at the Masonic Hall
some time in the forenoon. Conversing with Mr. Remick and trying to effect a Settlement. Remick promised to let Joseph have
some notes on a paper Maker in Louisville to pay him and then
went off contrary to promise.

/*Conversation with Martin Nye* and W[illiam] W. Phelps went
to Keokuk/ Read many letters, one from Judge Young. Gave a
relation of the Mob in Hyrum which was written for the History.
[*blank*] Parley Pratt and others came in.

Joseph explained the following: {page 170} "There are 3
administrater[s]: Angels, Spirits, [and] Devils. One [manner of]
dress in heaven. Angels [are] the spirits of Just men made perfect. Innumerable co[mpany] of angels and spirits of Just men
made perfect. [If] an Angel appears to you how will you prove
him? Ask him to shake hands. If he has flesh and bones he is an
angel. 'Spirit hath not flesh and bones.' Spirit of a Just man made
perfect. Person[age] in its tabernacle could [not] hide its glory.
{page 171} If David Patten or the Devil come how would you
determine? Should you take hold of his hand you would not feel
it. If it were a false administrater he would not do it. True spirit
will not give his hand. The Devil will. 3 keys.

"A man came to me in Kirtland and told me he had seen
an angel dressed so and so. I told him he had seen no angel.
There was no such dress in heaven. He got mad and went out in
the street and commanded fire to come down out of heaven and
consume me. {page 172} I laughed at him and told him he was
one of Baal's prophets. His God did not hear him. Jump up and
cut yourself and he commanded fire from heaven to consume my
house.

"When I was preaching in Philadelphia a Quaker wanted
a sign. I told him to be still. After sermon he wanted a sign. I

300

told the congregation the man was an adulterer. 'A wicked and adulterous generation' and the Lord to[ld] me in a revelation that any man who wanted a sign was [an] adulterous person. 'It is true' {page 173} said one 'for I caught him in the very act which he afterward confessed when he was baptized.' "

Parley Pratt asked for some council and tomorrow evening was appointed before the Quorum of the Twelve [Apostles]. [*rest of page blank*] {page 174}

Friday, February 10th 1842 [1843] Conversation with Strangers and others. Reviewed the History of the Mob in Hyrum and the first Journey to Missouri.

3 o'clock P.M. in court room with B[righam] Young, H[eber] C. Kimball, Orson Hyde, P[arley] P. Pratt, Orson Pratt, Wilford Woodruff, John Taylor, Geo[rge] A. Smith, and Willard Richards according to previous appointment by Pre[siden]t Joseph at 3 1/2 P.M. Let business be presented in short. No explaination.

Had an interview with Mr. Cowan this morning. He is a {page 175} delegate from the inhabitants 20 miles above this, opposite Burlington /viz. Shokokon/ to come to Nauvoo and petition that a talented Mormon preacher take up his residence with them [and] they would find him a good house and give him support with liberty to invite as many Mormons to settle in that place as they please to so to do. Decided that Bro[ther] [John] Bear go and preach to them.

Observation concerning theiving and the Post office and suggested that a general Meeting be called and that Elder Geo[rge] J. Adams be silenced and called to Nauvoo with his family. /Requested that all business be presented without comments/ {page 176}

5 o'clock P.M. Adjourned and immediately Oliver Olney and Newell Nurse were brought in by Sheriff J[ohn] D. Parker as prisoners for stealing goods from the Store of Moses Smith on the night of the 23d of January last. Olney confessed before the Mayor's court that he had been visited many times by the Ancient of Days.

[Mr. Olney stated,] "Sat with him on the 9th, 10th, and 11th days of June last and shall sit in council with ancient of days on Tuesday next. Have had a mission from him to the 4 Quarters of the world and have been [and] have established the

12 stakes of Zion. I have visited them all but one in the south. I have suffered much for 2 or 3 years, been without clothes and suffered much. I despise a thief, but to clothe myself I opened the store of Moses Smith on the eve[ning] of 23d of January by boring into a board window and took out the goods present (several Hundred peices) hid them in the cornfield and carried them home from time to time under the same roof with Smith. No one knows anything about the robbery but myself. [I] found the $50 bill among the goods. Mrs. had a piece of cloth to make some frocks."

Witnesses: Harriet Nurse, Mary Olney, Isaac Chase, Joseph Hadlock, Mr. Far, [and] Moses Smith. Decision of court: [that] Mr. Nurse be dischar[ge]d [and] Olney be remanded to prison for trial on bond under $5,000 bonds. {page 177}

Olney stated that the Church had never taught him to steal or any such thing. Olney was cut off from the Church some time since. [*rest of page blank*] {page 178}

Saturday, Feb[ruary] 11th 1843 City council assembled at 10 o'clock A.M. 7 new councillors sworn in, when the Mayor come in and said he had been doing a good deed. Had been conversing with Elder Rigdon and he and his family were willing to be saved. Good feelings prevailed and we have shaken hands together.

A general Election of Petty officers took place. Prophecied to James Sloan, Recorder, that it would be better for him 10 years hence not to say any thing more about [payment of] fees.

Mayor [Joseph Smith] made his Inaugural Address /in which he/ and urged the necessity of the city council acting upon the principle of liberality and of relieving {page 179} the city from all unnecessary expences and burthens [burdens]. Not to attempt to improve the city but enact such laws as will promote peace and good order and the people will improve the city. Capitalist[s] will come in from all quarters and Mills, factories, and machinery of all kind and buildings will arise on every hand [and] this will become a great city. [Joseph] prophecied that if the council would be liberal in their proceedings they would become rich.

[Joseph] spoke at considerable length against the principle of pay for every little service rendered and especially that of committees having extra pay {page 180} for services.

[Joseph] reproved the Judges of the late Election for not

holding the poll open after 6 o'clock when there were many wishing to vote. Judges were Geo[rge] W. Harris, Daniel Spencer,
and [*blank*] Warrington. Dr. Foster took an active part in electioneering for the written opposition ticket and obstructing the passage to the polls. Adjourned at 3 P.M. for one hour.

Assembled at 4 [P.M.] the subject of marketing was introduced when Alderman Harris spoke. B[righam] Young [and]
Harris again recommending 2 houses for Marketing. Hyrum Smith
advocating the same. Said he, "There is old Aunt Sabrey. She
comes to Market with {page 181} horse and carriage with her
butter and we can accomodate old Au/n/t Sabry."

Mayor said if we began too large we shall do nothing. If
the council will give me leave I will build a house, a small one at
once and the markitt ought to be holden by the corporation of the
house. When built [it] will support itself [and] then we can go on
the hill and build another or on[e] larger. Council should hold an
influence over the prices in market so that the poor shall not be
oppressed. The machanic should not oppress the farmer.

The upper part {page 182} of the town has no right to
rival us. Here on the bank of the river was where we first pitched
our tents, where the sickness and deaths occured. We have been
the making of the upper part of town. We have given them the
Temple. We began here and let the market go out from this part
of the city. Let the upper part of the town be marketed by the
waggon till they can build a Market.

Voted that a market house be built, that the committee
on public improvements be required to select a piece of ground
for Market and the rise of ground on Main St. [be] reported.
{page 183} Voted that it be left discretionary with the Mayor how
large the market shall be. [*nine lines left blank*]

Changing the furniture in the house to receive Mother
Smith in the family. [Brigham] Young and [Willard] Richards
wrote G[eorge] J. Adams to come to Nauvoo and silenced him.
{page 184}

Sunday, Feb[ruary] 12th 1843 Some 7 or 8 young men
called to see me, part of them from the city of N[ew] York. They
treated me with the greatest respect. I shewed them the fallacy of
Mr. Miller's data concerning the Millerism and preached them
quite a sermon. Shewed them that the error is in the Bible or
translation and that Miller is in want of information. The Proph-

ecies must be fulfilled; sun be turned into darkness, moon into black and many more things before Christ come. {page 185}

Monday, Feb[ruary] 13th 1843 Elder Rigdon came in early in the morning and gave a brief history [of] the 2d visit of the Presidency to Jackson Co[unty], Missouri.

Recited in German and walked out in the city with Elder Hyde. /Returned at 12 o'clock/ Elder Samuel Snider of Job /Creek/ Branch gave a bag of flour hearing [that] the President was in want. [He] also [gave] a dollar in cash from Sister Davis of the same place. John C. Annis come in for council about wood taken from Iowa and got it. The Marshall come in and stated that one Ralston was trying to get the Post office and Dr. Foster had {page 186} signed the Petition for the first one. Gave instruction concerning bonding 1/8 of the lot north of his dwelling to John Oakley for $500 dow[n] [and] $100 in 3 months.

1/4 [to] 4 P.M. [Joseph] said he would go to printing office with W[illiam] W. Phelps.

Evening at O[rson] Hyde's with Bro[ther] Dixon from Salem, M[a]ss[achusetts]. [Joseph] said that those who come here having money and purchased without the Church and without council must be cut of[f] and many observations which aroused Bro[ther] Dixon's feelings much.

Copy [of a petition] to the Hon[orable] Mr. Bryant, 2[nd] Ass[istan]t [to the] P[ost] M[aster] General.

> We, your petitioners, beg leave respectfully to submit
> that as an attempt is now, by certain individuals, being
> made to place the Post Office in this place into hands of
> William H. Rollison a stranger in our place, and one
> whose conduct since he came here, has been such as to
> forbid our having confidence in him, and we do hope
> and pray, both for our sakes, and that of the public,
> that he may not receive the appointment of Post Master
> in Nauvoo, Ill[inois] but that the present Post Master
> may continue to hold the office.
>
> Bro[ther] J[oseph] Smith, If the foregoing can have
> a number of respectable subscribers I believe Rollison
> cannot get the office. I should like to have it so as to
> send it out on Sunday's mail.

Res[pect]f[ul]ly,
Sidney Rigdon {page 187}

Tuesday, Feb[ruary] 14[th] 1843 Read proof of some of
the Book of [Doctrine and] Covenants with W[illiam] W. Phelps.
German Lesson from 9 1/2 to 11 A.M. Stove removed from the
Mayor's office to the smoke house which is designed for the Mayor's
office till a new one can be built. Mr. Cowan arrived from
Shokokon. Much conversation with various individuals. Sold Dr.
[Willard] Richards a cow. [*rest of page blank*] {page 188}

Wednesday, Feb[ruary] 15th 1843 Helped change the
top plate of the office stove. After reading in the Alton paper
about the Libellous letter written to Mr. Bassett of Quincy about
Judge Pope, Butterfield, and the Ladies attending the trial at
Springfield.

About ~~noon~~ /1 o'clock/ started for Shokokon with Cowan,
O[rson] Hyde, and P[arley] P. Pratt in sleighs. Previous to starting W[illia]m Law gave 1 barrel flour, 5 bushels Meal, and 10
bu[shels] of brann. When we come on the prairie it was so cold I
proposed {page 189} to Mr. Cowan and wait till the morrow, but
he chose to go forward. We arrived safely at Mr. Rose's, where
we had supper and gave long exposition of Millerism. Slept with
Mr. Cowan.

Thursday, Feb[ruary] 16th 1843 After breakfast I started
with Mr. Cowan and Bro[thers] Hyde and Pratt started from
Michael Crane's to go to Shokokon 5 miles.

On the way [Elders] Hyde and Pratt turned over and [El-
der] Hyde hurt his hand. Their horse ran away and we brought
him back. We dined at /Mr./ Quin[n]'s {page 190} Mills and
went to Shokokon and viewed the place which is very desirable
for a city.

When we returned to the place of dining, Elder Hyde
prayed [and] I preached to a large and attentive audience 2 hours
from 19 Rev[elation], 10 verse and shewed them that any man
who denied his being a prophet was not a preacher of righteousness. They opened their eyes and appeared well pleased and had
a good effect.

After meeting when we had returned as far as Mr. Quinn's
Mills, Mr. Cowan turned up to the fence and proposed to call.
While waiting a moment {page 191} Mr. Crane's horse (for he

305

went with our company) which was behind ran and jumped into our sleigh as we jumped out and thence over our horses and the fence sleigh and all, fence 8 rails high and both horses ran over lots and through the woods clearing themselves from the sleighs and had their frolic out without hurting themselves or riders. It was truly a wonderful feat and as wonderful a deliverance of the parties.

We took supper at Mr. Crane's and I staid at Mr. Rose's. Dr. Richards invited [the] brethren to come on Monday and pile up and chop wood for the President. {page 192}

Friday, Feb[ruary] 17th and 18th 1843 Mr. Cowan returned with me to my house where we arrived about noon. [I] enjoyed myself by my own fire side with many of my friends around me. Mr. Cowan proposed to give me 1/4 of city lots in Shokokon and 2 each to [Elders] Hyde and Pratt.

Saturday, Feb[ruary] 18th 1843 About house and office. Mostly some at High Council in store or Lodge Room. Ells on trial from Laharpe. Several called for council on Law. One /Christopher Dixon/ against Nauvoo house. Carlos Granger called. {page 193} Esqu[ire] Warren called; [he] had hurt his horse. Said it was not the first time he had missed it by not following Joseph's advice. At dinner Joseph said, "When the earth was sanctified and become like a sea of glass it would be one great Urim and Thummin [and] the Saints could look in it and see as they are seen."

The 12 [Apostles] wrote a letter to the Saints in Laharpe to call for food for the President. {page 194}

Sunday, Feb[ruary] 19th 1843 From 9 A.M. to 1 P.M. with /High Council/ listening to the proof of a great Big nothing in a case between Wilson Law and [*blank* [Uriel C.]] Nickerson who had been fighting some time previous. I explained the laws of the U[nited] S[tates and] the laws of Iowa and Illinois. Shewed them that Nickerson had the oldest claim and best right and left it for the law to say how much Nickerson should have. The parties shook hands in token of settlement of all difficulties. {page 195}

Monday morning, Feb[ruary] 20[th] About 70 of the brethren come together according to previous notice and drawed, sawed, chopped, split, moved, and piled a large lot of wood /for the

Prophet/. The day was spent by them in much pleasentry, good humor, and feeling. A white oak log 5 f[ee]t, 4 inches [in] diameter was cut through with a cross saw in 4 1/2 minutes by Hiram Daton and Bro[ther] Tidwell. /This tree was cut and drawed by Joseph/

From 9 to 11 [A.M.] reciting in German. From 11 to 12 [A.M.] {page 196} in court in brick store on assumpsit Charles R. Dana vs. W[illia]m B. Brink. Adjourned for ten days. /Snow melted away so as to destroy sl[e]ighing/

Last night Arthur Milikin had a quantity of books stolen and found them at 3 this P.M. in Hyrum Smith's Hayloft. Thomas Morgan and Robert Taylor (Morgan 15, Robert Taylor 13 years old next April) /both members of the Church/ were arrested on suspicion in the forenoon. On finding the books [they] immediately went to trial before the Mayor having had a brief examination about noon. Court adjourned till 10 [A.M.] tomorrow. {page 197}

While the court was in session 2 boys were seen fighting in the street by Mill's tavern. The Mayor [Joseph Smith] saw it and ran over immediately, caught one of the boys (who had began the fight with clubs) and stopped him and then the other. [Joseph] gave the bystanders a lecture for not interfering in such cases and returned to court. "No body is allowed to fight in this city but me," said the Mayor.

/This day John Q. Adams presented a petition to the House of Representatives signed by 51,863 citizens of Mass[achuset]ts praying Congress "to pass such acts and prepare such amendments to the Constitution as will seperate the petitioners from all connection with the institution of slavery."/

Evening called at <Kimballs>.

Tuesday, February 21[st] 1843 Mayor's court at the smoke house 10 A.M. City of Nauvoo vs. Robert Taylor and Thomas J. Morgan. [They both] pled guilty. Taylor for stealing and Morgan for receiving. [They were] sentenced [to] 6 months imprisonment in [the] Carthage Jail.

11 [o'clock] went to Temple [and] found Bro[ther] Hawes preaching about [the] Nauvoo {page 198} House. Mr. [Lucien] Woo[d]worth[, architect and foreman,] spoke say[ing] something in vindicating my [his] own character, [that the project] commenced under peculiar circumstances [i.e., as a joint stock ven-

ture, by revelation, not to receive church funds, and to be built on the flat land instead of on the hill where land was more valuable], [yet he, not a Mormon] have made all contracts for Nauvoo House, was employed to build from the commencement. Some brick on hand, most ready to start brick work. One says "can you give me something to eat?" "I'll try." Another says "I will have my pay." "Go to hell and get it." /said I [Woodworth]/. "I have set me down to a dry Johncake and cold water and the men who have worked with me. No man shall go into my poverty stricken foundation to build himself up for I began it and will finish it. Not that public spirit here [should be] as [any different than] in other cities [but I] don't deny revelation. If the Temple and Nauvoo {page 199} House are not finished you must run away.

"When I have had a pound of meat or quart of meal I have divided with the workmen." (Pretty good Doctrin[e] for paganism said Joseph.) "Have had about 300 men on the job, the best men in the world. Those that have not complained I want them to continue with me and them who hate Mormonism and every thing else that's good I want them to get their pay and run away."

Joseph say, Well the pagan prophet [Woodworth] has preached us a pretty good sermon this morning to break off the yoke of oppression. /I don't know as I can better it much/ and say what he is [of] a mind to. {page 200} That the pagans and the pagan prophets [should come] to feel more [intensely about] our prosperity is curious. I am almost converted to his doctrine. "He has prophecied if these buildings go down it will curse this place." I know verily it is true. Let us build the Temple. There may be some speculations about the Nauvoo House. Some say because we live on the hill we must build up this fort on the hill.

Does that coat fit you Dr. Foster? Pretty well! Put it on then. This is the way people swell like the ox or toad. They come down under the hill among little folks. Brother Joseph how I love you and get up opposition [to our building plan] and sings names to strangers and scoundrels &c. {page 201} I want all men to feel for me. When I have shook the bush & bare the burden, and if they do not, I speak in authority in the name of the Lord /God/. He shall be damned. People on the flats are aggrandizing themselves by the Nauvoo House [just as people on the hill are buying land because of the temple].

Who laid the foundation of the Temple? Bro[ther] Joseph in the name of the Lord, not for his aggrandizement but for the good of the whole. Our speculators say our poor folk on the flat are down and keep them down. How the Nauvoo House cheats this man and that man, say the speculators. They are fools [and] ought to hide their heads in a hollow pumkin and never take it out. {page 202} The first principle brought into consideration is aggrandizement, some think it unlawful — but it is lawful while he has a disposition to aggrandize all around him. False principle, to aggrandize at the expence of another. Every thing God does is to aggrandize his kingdom.

How does he lay the foundation? Build a temple to my great name and call the attention of the great. But where shall we lay our heads? An old log cabin? I will whip Hiram Kimball and Esq[uire] Wells and every body else over Dr. Foster's Head. Instead of building the Nauvoo House build a great many little skeletons [of houses]. See Dr. Foster's mammoth skeletons[, monuments] {page 203} of Dr. Foster rising all over town but there is no flesh on them.

Personal aggrandizement, [but I] don't care how many bones [there are,] somebody may come along and clothe them, [these] elephants, crocodiles, &c. [man]eaters such as grog shop[s], card shops, &c. Those who live in glass houses should not throw stones. The building of N[auvoo] House is just as sacred in my view as the Temple [and should not be left a skeleton].

I want the Nauvoo House built. It must be built. Our salvation depends on it. When men have done what they can or will for the Temple, let them do what they can for the Nauvoo House. We never can accomplish our work at the expense {page 204} of another.

There is a great deal of murmurring in the Church about me, but I don't care any thing about it. I like to hear it thunder, to hear the Saints grumbling. The growling dog get[s] the sorest head. If any man is poor and afflicted let him come and tell of it and not complain or grumble.

Finishing [the] Nauvoo House [is] like a man finishing a fight. If he give up he is killed. If he holds out a little longer he may live. A story, a man who will whip his wife is a coward. I fought with a man who had whipped [his] wife. [I was going to give in, but I] Still remembered he was whipped [whipping] his wife. I whipped him till he said enough.

Hang on to the {page 205} Nauvoo House thus and you will build it and you will be on [Mount] Pishagah. The great men who come will pile their gold and silver till you are weary of receiving them. If you are not careful [you] will be lifted up and fall and they will cover up and cloak all your former sins and hide a multitude of sins and shine forth fair as the sun &c.

Those who have labored and cannot get your pay be patient. If you take the means which are set apart [for the construction,] let him[, t]he[y] will destroy themselves. {page 206} If any man is hungry let him come to me and I will feed him at my table. If any are hungry or naked don't take away the brick &c. but come and tell. I will divide and then if he is not satisfied I will kick his back side.

There cannot be some fire without some smoke. Well if the stories about Jose[ph] Smith are true, then the stories of J. C. Bennet[t] are true about the Ladies of Nauvoo. Ladies that the Relief Society was organized of those who are to be wifes of Jos[eph] Smith. Ladies you know whether it is true, no use of living among hogs without a snout. This biting an[d] devouring each other {page 207} for God's sake stop it.

One thing more. Political economy. Our duty [is] to concentrate all our influence to make popular that which is sound and good and unpopular that which is unsound. Tis right /politically/ for a man who has influence to use it as well as for a man who has no influence to use his. From henceforth I will maintain all the influence I can get.

In relation to politics I will speak as a man in religion in authority. If a man lift[s] a dagger to kill me, I will lift my tongue. When I last preached, [I] heard such a {page 208} groaning I thought of the paddy[']s ell [eel] when he tried to kill him could not contrive any way so he put it [in] the water to drown him. As he began to come to—see said he what pain he is in how he wigles his tail.

The banks are failing and it is the [a] privilege to say what a currency we want[:] gold and silver to build the Temple and Nauvoo House. We want your old nose rings and finger rings and brass kettles no longer. If you have old raggs, watches, guns go and peddle them and bring the hard metal. If we will do this by popular opinion you will have a sound currency. {page 209} Send home bank notes and take no paper money. Let every man write his neighbor before he starts to get gold and silver. I have contemplated these things a long time, but the time has not come till now to speak till now.

I would not do as the Nauvoo House committee has done sell stock for an old stone house where all the people who live die and put that stock into a man's hand to go east and purchase to come here and build up Mammoth bones with.

As a political man in the {page 210} name of old Joe Smith I command the Nauvoo [House] committee not to sell a share in the N[auvoo] House without the gold or silver. Excuse Bro[ther] Snider he was in England when they sold stock for [a] stone house. I leave it. The meeting was got up by N[auvoo House] Committee.

The pagans, Roman Catholics, Methodists, and Baptist[s] shall have peace in Nauvoo only they must be ground in Joe Smith's mill. I have been in their mill. I was ground in Ohio and [New] York States—a Presbyterian smut machine—and [the] last machine was in Missouri and last of all I have been through [the] Illinois smut machine. {page 211} Those who come here must go through my smut machine and this is my tongue.

Dr. Foster remarked much good may grow out of a very little and much good may come out of this. If any man accuse me of exchanging N[auvoo House] Stock for Rags &c. I gave $1,000 to this house and $50 to [the] Relief Society and some to Fulmer to get stone to build Joseph['s] house. I mean to build Joseph a house and you may build this and I will help you. I mean to profit this. I will divide the mammoth bones with you. I am guilty of all {page 212} I have been charged. I have signed my name to a petition to have W[illia]m H. Rolinson to have the Post Office. I did not know [of] a petition for Joseph Smith.

Joseph[:] "I thought I would make a coat. It don't fit the D[octo]r /only in the P[ost] office. If it does fit any one let them put in on. The bones are skeleton and as old Ezekiel said I command the flesh and the sinnews to come upon them that they may be clothed." Blessing by Bro[ther] P[arley] P. Pratt. [*rest of page blank*] {page 213}

Wednesday, Feb[ruary] 22nd 1843 9 A.M. The President and Mr. Cowan come in the office and soon after, Abel

311

Owen presented a claim against Carter, Cahoon, and Company and notes of Oliver Granger of about 700 dollars for payment. Joseph told him to burn the papers and he would help him. He gave the papers to Joseph and Joseph gave him an order on Mr. Cowan for $15 for provisions. Rode out about the city with Mr. Cowan. Recited in German. {page 214}

Thursday, Feb[ruary] 23rd 1843 Recited in German. Rode out a few miles but did not get off my horse. P.M. Mr. Bagby called to collect taxes. Mr. [William] Clayton /was/ sent for and come to examine the books. Bro[ther] Dixon called to see the Mayor about some lost or stolen property.

3 1/2 P.M. the Mayor burned $23 of city scrip on the stove hearth and while burning said so may all uncurrent and unsound money go down as this burns. Said he would pay no taxes on Hotchkiss purchase. Amasa Lyman went to Shokokon to commence preaching this morning. {page 215}

Friday, Feb[ruary] 24th 1843 Rode out with Elder Young. Dined at Mr. [*blank*]. Rode to Dr. Foster's [and] had some conversation about the Post Office and other Similar matters. Foster had some feelings on the occasion. Returned to the office. Walked a way with Elder Young at about 3 P.M. [*rest of page blank*] {page 216}

Saturday, Feb[ruary] 25th 1843 Received a Gold watch. A.M. in city council. 3 o'clock P.M. met after adjournment. I have read the Constitution and find my doubts removed. The Constitution is not a law, but empowers the people to make laws. Constitution govern the lands of Iowa but is not a law for the people. Constitution tells what shall not be lawful tender. Constitution Section 10. This is not saying gold and silver shall be lawful tender. It only provides the states may make a law to make gold and silver lawful Tender. {page 217}

The Legislature have ceded up to us the privilege of enacting laws. We stand in the same relation as the State. This clause is for the Legislature, is not a law for the people [and is] diametrically contrary to the Constitution. This state have passed a stay law, making it lawful /to/ tender property and if we [do] not [say we want] no [such] law, we must be governed by them.

Shall we be such fools as to abide their laws which are unconstitutional? No! We will make a law for gold and silver. Then their law ceases and we can collect our debts. "Powers not delegated to the states or reserved from the states" is constitutional. {page 218} Congress or Constitution acknowledged that the people have all power not reserved to itself.

/I am a Lawyer/. I am big lawyer and comprehend heaven, earth, and hell to bring forth knowledge which shall cover up all Lawyers and doctors. This is the doctrine of the Constitution so help me God. The Constitution is not law to us, but provision to make laws. Where it provides that no one shall not be hindered from worshipping God according to his own conscience is [it] a law. No legislature can enact a law to prohibit. Constitution provides to regulate {page 219} bodies of men not individuals.

[Daniel H.] Wells objected to its taking effect immediately. O[rson] Pratt amended to 1st June. O[rson] Spencer said he could have wished Daniel Webster the Lion of the East had heard the Lion of the west in the choir. Unnecessary to wait, so said [Brigham] Young. Ordinance Regulating the currency before the council. [W. W.] Phelps and [Willard] Richards were invited to give an opinion (by the Mayor [Joseph]) and did in affirmative and left afterward the Mayor gave another speech.

[Oliver] Olney come to the Marshalls and was inm[ated].

Sunday, February 26th [Joseph was] At home with his Mother who was [sick] with an affection [infection] of the Lungs. Nursing [his mother] with his own hands. [*two and a half lines left blank*] [Oliver] Olney carried to Carthage. {page 220}

Monday, Feb[ruary] 27th 1843 In house. Mostly with his mother who was sick. Come in the office and signed a writ or search warrant for Bro[ther] Dixon to search Fidlers and John Eagles house for a box of shoes. [*three and a half lines left blank*]

Tuesday, Feb[ruary] 28th Mostly with his mother and family. Mr. John Brassfield who helped Joseph to escape from the Missourians came and spent the day and night. P.M. Mother [Smith] rather easier. To Elder Hydes to dinner at 4 o'clock P.M. [*blank*]

Notice in Chicago Express that Wm /Hiram/ Redding had seen sign of the son of man. Wrote Editor of Times and Seasons for no. 8 vol. 4 that Reding had not seen the sign of the son of man and he would not come in [18]43 &c. See Times and Seasons. {page 221}

Wednesday, March 1st 1843 Recited in German. In the office reviewing his valedictory published in Times and Seasons

No. 7 vol[ume] 4. Went with Marshall to Bro[ther] Laws to get provision for the prisoners—Morgan and Taylor.

Elder Hyde called to get a horse this afternoon. Joseph ordered Ira to get his best horse and put on the Lieut[enant] General's saddle and let Elder Hyde ride the Governor on the Lieutenant's saddle.

Signed a power of attorney dated 28 February to Amasa {page 222} Lyman to sell all the lands in Henderson County deeded to me by Elder McQuinn. Walked out.

Thursday, March 2d 1843 Adjourned case of Charles Dana vs. Dr. Brink in assumpsit come up at 10 A.M. Before the Mayor at Mason's Hall. Orson Spencer side [of] justice, Skinner Esqu[ire] for Plaintive. Claimed $99 failing to perform correctly as physician in treatment of Dana's wife, complaint read. Witnesses Dr. Foster, Dr. Wild, Dr. Bennett. [*blank* [and]] Mrs Sessions {page 223} Rigdon and Marsh Esqu[ire] for defendant.

Rigdon objected to certain witnesses viz. the [dispute among] physicians [which is] enough to alarm Nauvoo. [They argue] Enough to swear them selves into business and the other who is opposed out of business not the 20th time that attempt[s] have been made of this kind, Legislatures have taken it up. Come here professing [to be] Botonic[al] Physicia[ns]. The other Boerhevein Physicians, come here from /Germany/ [and] England to America to [align themselves for or against] Dr. Brink, antipod[e]s [whose] feet come together instead of /their/ heads. They have ever been crying out against Botonic and Botonic against the others for Payson. If they {page 224} are permitted to witness this court is to decide between the parties. The Legislature and no court has attempted to decide.

Let them bring physicians of the same school for witnesses. Mr. Dana knew what practice the Do[c]tor was of. Why not call physic[ian]s of the same school. Your Honor has once been tried on account of your religion. The physici[an]s must testify according to their practice believing the other to be wrong. If this order of things should prevail you would loose your head and I mine. {page 225}

Skinner replied, When a party claims interest he must establish his claim. Objection should be made before Placing vis a vis, to settle this grand question [of] interest no witness can be objected to on ground of interest unless the party must be a gainer or looser in the case. Bailor cannot be witness. No other /kind [of]/ interest can destroy testimony. If every witness was desirous to have the suit go on their testimony [it] would [still] be valid. Evidence Harrisus Digest /Page 1047/ immended intent in the suit only.

Philips on evidence 71. Rule of Int[erest] {page 226} and Teron Gilbert where there is a certain benefit at stake. Watsons reports 199 5 Wendall Report 55, 13 Mass 99 and 99. Swonns Tracts 59. We defy the gentlemen to present any defect [in this] rule of law.

Marsh[: Ojection] not on the ground of definite interest. We made the objection. We obje[c]t to witnesses on ground of incompetincy, of judging of a different practice. This state has not decided which practice. What makes them witnesses. From knowledge of facts or experts. Were they present? if so I have no objection. [It is wrong if] A should contract for building a [steam] boat [when B builds steam boats but]. C is called to examine (who is a [builder of] sail boat[s]) {page 227} or brick house judged by a carpenter. Those who are of the same school are competent. Those are experts who are of the practice with the defendant.

Judge Emmons[, for the plaintiff,] asked leave to reply. Objected [to] by Marsh. Opinion of the court [is that they] cannot tell whether they are competent or not till they give their testimony. What is the rule of competency? Mrs. Miles some deli-[c]acy to be heard alone. Rigdon requested that witness be examined alone. Skinner, we shall look to the court. Marsh produced the law[, it was] found [to be relevant, and the] court ordered the house cleared. Skinner—We design to shew certain {page 228} facts by witnesses present and then to physicians to know whether they consider the treatment correct.

Rigdon /it is/ [an] effort to secure to themselves the advantage we have conten[d]ed against. /Physician[s]/ to give testimony on testimony they have not heard—because the witness[es] are examined apart. Let us have this trial on the principle of common sense. Lady presented to witness certain things and physicians called to testify on that testimony as they are called one by one and we object to any other course. Ladies build a mud house and Doctors chink it.

Emmons—singular case, to request witness Doctors to withdraw, read section of Law {page 229} in Medical Men, and on science May witness — Philips on evidence 836.899.

Objected to witness for which this court was adjourned on the same principle. Corrected by Rigdon.

Marsh insisted on what the law of the state grants us. —

Court is of opinion it can do no harm to have witnesses present.

Mr. Miles present at Mrs. Dana's on her sickness. [She] Had been sick several weeks. Did not know what it was, was injured by a fright[, Miles] present when Dr. Brink came about noon. {page 230} Don't think she was in labor pains. [Brink] Did [not] discover any symptoms of labor pains, [Miles] did not stay but a minute or two, did not return till about 11 P.M. [Brink] said he had given her sweet rye. She said she was in pain. We expected they were labor pains. Brink said her water had discharged and she would be delivered in a short time. Child appeared to be pitched one side. Mrs. Dana did not know the waters had discharged. Brink staid till morning, [Miles was] There when he introduced his hand hurt her and [she] begged to let her alone and let [it] have its own operation, on the bed [he] used more violence than I thought was necessary but not enough to crowd her out of her position. I did not examine the woman don't know any thing about it.

By court {page 231} you have been at such cases and know what is usual? Yes— Mrs. Dana was not expecting it for 10 days. Don't recollect that Dr. Brink said it was necessary to deliver her of the child on account of Diarehea or fever. But was sent for Dr. to cure fever &c. Won't expe[c]ting to be confined [for weeks afterwards]. She was better when I went away in the morning. Got easier and did not know when it would be. Had not meddled with her since before day light.

Monday P.M. her water discharged she told me from Saturday. Went for sister [Patty] Sessions[, a midwife, when Mrs. Dana] was in labor pains, delivered some time Monday night. Had 4 living children. Since she was confined {page 232} she told me she had not been free from pain. Had had the piles 3 or 4 weeks ago.

Objection by Marsh to the [introduction of a] saying of the parties [to the plaintiff reported days] since the operation.

Rigdon objected to the [hearsay] testimony of parties concerned.

Court is of opinion any injury the woman may have received may be made to appear by patient or any other testimony [corroborating that she] had not been free from pain since her delivery 3 or 4 months ago. 11 o'clock I expected she was g[o]ing to be delivered soon. Mrs. Sessions said Mrs. Dana['s] water had not escaped. Don't know who told me. She did not expect to be confined for 10 days. {page 233}

Court adjourned for one hour. 3 o'clock, opened court. (Mary Duel [a midwife]) was present at Mrs. Dana's sickness 24th October. Was not there prior to Dr. Brink being there. Was present with them. She [Mrs. Dana] was lying on the bed appe[a]ring in considerable pain, not labor pains. I was called 11 at night, Dr. was there previous. Was at my house after the syringe to give her injection. Mr. Dana he thought the child had been dead 2 or 3 days. I told my sister she was not expecting to be sick in [bed] 2 or 3 weeks. I did not examine the patient. She [Mrs. Dana] said her period had not come yet.

Mr. Dana expected to have Mother Session when she was confined. Called Brink {page 234} to give fever powders. Dr. Brink thought it time for delivery. Needed to be hurried. She begged of him to let her alone, you'll kill me. Dr. s[a]id he hurt her as little as he could. The child was turned and must be turned back. He gave her sweet rye, pepper, and composition and so[a]ked her feet. He thought she would be delivered in 3 pains more. There was no such pain as I ever saw before. Dr. said he never was where he was so sick before. [I] Thought he was not fit to be there.

2 o'clock, 3 more mo[ve]ments before morning. His operation was unusual under the circumstances. I insisted she would not get through without some one of more experience. {page 235}

She was fixed on a seat for she could not lie so. But soon moved aright and the Dr. sat down and commenced operating by his hand. She begged him to let go and he said he could not something would go back. Next day she was perfectly cosy and went to sleep. Dr. was there [and] said nothing. Sister Session was present.

Since the birth she says it is the cause of all her difficulty and piles. Has [had] 5 or 6 children before had no such symptom. Dr. said it was necessary to keep up the irritation to create pain.

(Marr [a physician]) cross examination. 1st visit 11 Sat-[urday] night. I expressed disapprobation, in an 1 1/2 hour [visit], to Sister Mills. I think the pains were from the {page 236} medicine. It might have been a [result of] cutting her [that she had] pains, independant of Med[icine]. I did not examine a day or two before, she told me she did not expect to be confined for 3 or 4 [weeks]. Women may be dec[e]ived 2, 3, or even 4 weeks. Could not say he entered the os[tium]. Had no pains after Dr. Brink left. He was called away in the night between 2 o'clock and daylight. I prepar[e]d to have some one called. He opposed. He proposed to call Vienna. She appears to be weak, bearing down.

(By court) Was it unusal for physician to treat patient as Brink did?

I[t] is unusual. I have Dr. Bennett of this town operater and Botonic physicians in other places. {page 237} Have had no great experience say 50 or 60 cases. Never saw similar treatment from Botonic practice. If the child is born in 3 pains more it will be something I never experienced.

(Mrs. Session) Sunday morning I was called by Mr. Dana, say[ing] Dr. Brink is at my [Mr. Dana's] house. I [Mr. Dana] called him yesterday to cool the bowels and still the fever. He says she is going to be confined, and the women are dissatisfied. Went, Dr. Brink shook hands and held on. We have a difficult case. The membrane is broken; the waters have escaped; the child is turned. I sent for you to turn the child because my hand is swoll[en]. {page 238}

I prepared and sat down to her. I said D[octo]r. What have you give[n]? Novine raspbery Cayinene. I said Did I understand you the water had escaped? Yes, understand you the child was [w]rong and must be turned? [I said,] Yes, it was a fair presentation. [Then I said] Did I understand you the child was dead? Yes. I had my finger on the child's head and felt pulsation. The waters have not gathered tis a fair presentation your child is a live. As I run my finger round apex as large as a tea cup near the child's head /[I] reached the ear/. [and felt] A rupture.

When was you hurt? [I asked Mrs. Dana] With my last child, if ever. Had no labor pains, had no pains {page 239} but such as appeared [with] wind. I got up, sat down to talk with the

318

Dr. about a patient he had doctored and said it [the baby] had been dead 3 weeks when I took it the skin was fair and I think it had just died. Dr. went to Marsh. I asked Mrs. Dana what the Dr. gave her. She said Ergot. He came to me for it last week. When I moved her onto her bed I found mark of the ruptures on the under clothes. Fresh blood. Dr. returned and asked me what is the cause of her pain last night? That Ergot you gave her. Curse the Doctors. If a D[octo]r should do so by me I would kill him if I could. I gave him a figure. {page 240}

Never undertake to get a nut out of the burr till it is ripe and it will fall out. The Dr. went away. Now said I, we have delivered the Dr. I will go home and when you get ready send for me. I went home and when I got there I made a minute of my visit, that I found Dr. Brink had [not] operated according to nature right or reason.

Sunday P.M. I took [delivered] a living child and as I had told her the waters had broke when I got there. Mr Dana stated to Dr. Brink, I never had my feelings wrought up so in all my children as last night. Dr. you know I did not call you here to officiate in such a capacity. Dr. Brink said he only gave her 11 grains Ergot. {page 241}

(Duel) Not the same bed but bedding was the same. Blood was of different appearance than what is usual as though it came from the ruptures. 3 places she would twinge never said ouch [little] relaxation /as there/ was. Mouth of womb about as large as common size teacup. Bro[ther] Dana requested me to call. I did and she said she had not been well. I thought Brink hurt her, could not hold her water. /Brink/ gave her two injections himself which she thought was the cause of it. They were very hot [and she] could hardly get up stairs, weak in her back.

I have attend[ed] 30 years in the profession, never witnessed such an operation before. Child was {page 242} born after midnight. We called it Tuesday morning. I asked her if her true time had come? She said she thought 3 or 4 weeks but was certain 10 or 12 days.

On one garment where the blood was it appeared as though some one had wiped a hand or the fingers. It appeared of a fresh bloody texture as pubis was turned up towards the back said Dr. Brink.

(Mrs Dana) sworn.

319

(Mars[h]) Objected to the testimony of a wife in civil suit.

(Rigdon) Would not object if the defendant can be admitted. Poor rule if the will not work both ways. {page 243} Philips on evidence. Evidence admitted.

(Mrs Dana) In the morning as Dr. Brink was first called to give me something to allay my fever, steeped something and gave me [something] which increased my pain. [He] staid in the P.M. and got the syringe and administered which appeared to me all pepper. What [Why] he sta[i]d all night. What for I don't know. It was a mere imposition administered as other witnesses stated which created pain every time I took them. I refer to the injections of pepper in the first instance which gave me pain. Afterward the drinks.

I told him my time was not in 3 or 4 {page 244} weeks that every thing was wrong. [He said] That an inflamation had taken place in my bowels which killed the child and I must have help immediately or I could not live. There was nothing unnatural before he commenced and I so insisted to him. The fresh blood was from no[ne] other than his treatment. Easier after he desisted. No labor pains till Monday. 7 children, never suffered so. Wakup trembling, bearing down, never had those symptoms before. Not be[e]n able to do any thing since. Have not been free from pain since. {page 245} No other cause to attribute the pain but Brinks treatment.

/Court Did Brinks take an unusual course?/

Brink took an unusual course. Brink placed his head on my bowels and exerted his strength in other ways which gave me great pain.

(Mr Shoemaker) Mr Dana asked me to go down to Mr Brink. I went as a neighbor 3 times before we found him at home. Mr Dana made his proposition to leave it to men or 3 men. Mr Brink told him he would not make any settlement. What he had done he had done right. I [he] gave her Ergot and {page 246} cayenne pepper and other medicines mentioned. Said he had done nothing but what any physician would do. Acknowledged what they told him about her time.

(Dr. Bennett) to explain as Matter of science [in response to questions presented] on testimony already given. Philips on evidence 259. Court is willing to give its opinion [about which treatments Dr. Brink] is not bound to know [of]. Dr. Brink is a Botonical Dr. or to be [unlearned in] mineral [potions]. Court will hear more of good character.

When Dr. is called to a pregnant woman to administer for dysentry and she says her time is not for 3 or 4 {page 247} would [he] be justified in giving any thing to produce delivery? No difference in Labor pains and others? Under certain combinations Ergot is not good. From 15 to 30 grains [causes] a specific effect on the Uterus to expel the contents of the uterus to produce delivery.

Under the circumstances would a person be justified in inserting the hand? If every thing is natural /it/ would be considered fine. [But for] Such delivery from the impression I have [there were] no circumstances existing to warrant the preceding.

The introduction of the hand altogether unnecessarily. {page 248} Introduction of the hand is unnecessary to ascertain the situation of the featus, would be productive of great pain if done roughly or unskillfully. Prefered after labor pains have existed some time. Mouth of the womb will enlarge. In this case [it could only be done] by violence I would think. It would not be justifiable to force open the womb. Might be lascerated or ruptured such condition might be discovered, such treatment would be likely to produce the effects [noted]. No reason why physician should conclude the child was dead and use means to produce delivery. Could not be justified in [this] case.

Adjourned to 10 tomorrow morning. {page 249}

Evening in company with Phelps and Richards in the middle room looking out of Blackstone on evidence of wife for husband &c.

Friday, March 3d 1843 Court opened at 10 according to adjournment.

/Dr. Bennett/ Should there be an obliquity of the womb a gentle action may be justifiable. The exertion in this case I think the exertion [was] unjustifiable. Could not be a falling back of the womb at that stage of pregnancy and if there was a midwife [she] would easily detect it. {page 250} A delivery at such time would be calculated to injure the womb. Common cases require no help. What was done [was] unnecessary. Mouth of the womb will be open by Regular pain, not be opened as in this case without force. /Force/ would injure the parts. /Injuries/ reasonably refered to [as the result of] the force. If things were wrong as stated by the Dr. [the] woman would be likely to know it first. (Law read by Court, Swann Treatus 63)

(Court) What do you know Dr. Bennett about this case? [Bennett:] Mouth [of the] womb open before labor pains and lacerated. [I] Suppose it had been {page 251} hurt, [that] fresh blood and rupture by force [was] to combat the fever &c. /Woman/ would be the first to know if she was in labor. Medical men will never attempt examination without cause. Then not necessary to insert the hand to ascertain presentation.

(Cross[-examination]) Have known mouth [of the] womb to be elastic. So as easily to be prest [pressed] open. Ergot acts upon the womb to contract it [and expel the contents] so the child would [have] press[ed] open the mouth [of the womb]. At intervals of the pain there is a relaxation when the finger might be inserted. This [constant] dilation was from the intrusion of the hand. {page 252}

No uncommon thing to have blood pass in first stages of labor. When ostince [ostium] is dilated not [less than] 1/2 cases where blood passes. Much blood might or might not flow from the rupture. /Could not have accured before the fright/ A woman of Mrs Session['s] experience would know as well as a physician.

11 grains of Ergot would not produce any great effect in absence of labor pains where the womb was ruptured and the head of the child pressing [against the] mouth opened by force. Womb would not contract again. Parturition scarcely happens when acute disease is going on. Fresh wound, red blood is 1[st] stages parturition[, later] {page 253} darker.

(Dr. Wild) No necessity for physician to interfere at all. Highly criminal. Ruptu[r]es might have been made. Ruptures caused by violence, sometime duties of physician to let her alone. Force deleterious. What was done might produce lascerations of the os uteri and inflamation and various things such as wer[e] mentioned by witness. No precise time for womb to open, said nothing to justify the course persued. Much to condemn. Have conversed with Mrs Dana within a week.

(Philips on evidence 202) (Harrison's Digest 1037) {page 254} /1st [blank] 160 to 171/ (Philips on evidence 152) 361 Blackstone (Harrison digest 2d Vol[ume] 1031) (190 Phi[li]ps digest)

[Defense attorney:] I felt there was a little overbearance particularly because the [attorney for the plaintiff] was young. Young[er] perhaps in court matters than in knowledge. As Lawyers know a great deal and are very wise, I will put them to the trouble of finding the quotation, "any thing the wife may have said will be received in evidence."

(Wild) Would attribute the injuries to the violence used. Compliained of the bearing down of the womb. Never knew mouth of the womb to dilate without Labor pains. Ergot['s] specific effect is on the uterus to contract. {page 255} 15 to 20 grains common doses. Don't know as 11 grains would produce abortion. Never gave but in one case. Were I called in such a case I would wait and see what the consequences would be. Have [not] seen this appearance of blood without ho[a]rse treatment. Been in practice 7 years.

(Dr. Foster) Sayings of patient index to treatment. If things were wrong that would be first known to the mother. Duty of physician to let her alone. Ostince [ostium] dillated by ergot [in]-capable for to introduce even finger. Punching the woman by [with] the head might weaken some of the internal {page 256} organs. Causes that have been stated here before. If the hand had been pressed [against] the bone of the pelvis /the foetus [fetus]/ it would have been expelled before 24 or 48 hours if he had [not withdrawn his] hand[; the fetus] not [longer] forced. Do not consider the injury could have been sustained in the womb.

Ergot same as Dr. Wild. 11 grains would be inert. A free use of Ergot might destroy the tone of the womb. Do not consider it possible that the ostinse [ostium] should have been opened thus by inserting the hand and rupturing the womb, without producing birth sooner than it was.

10 o'clock adjourned for 1 1/2 hour. /Philips on Evidence 151/ {page 257}

3 o'clock court opened.

(Dr. Higby) effects unavoidably follow introducing the hand or any instrument in the mouth of the womb, so as to displace the membrane, would be birth in from 24 to 36 hours or more sometime.

(council for plaintive closed)

1st General character of the Defendant /defense/ as practitioner. 2d rebutting testimony.

(Dr. /Geo[rge] R/ Bostwich) practiced 24 years had 2300 cases of obstretics rather difficult to tell the amount of injury and when and by whom. Have known premature labor produced by Diahrrea when I had no other cause to attribute it to. Have seen Peter Wilson's wife {page 258} complete dilation of the os uteri. Have seen frequent dilations without pain then close and go their time and close again. If there is sufficient ~~contractile~~ /dilating/ powers in the neck of the womb ergot may be given as free as flour. Its effect is on the top of the womb. [It] also stops Hermerge [hemorrhage] of the womb. If dilated by force I should expect immediate delivery in a few hours, 5 or 6 hours. It might [take] 30 hours if a weak system.

If 3 ruptures so large I should think it would produce more blood. I look for a fontonells when the head is presented, never knew a finger [to be] inserted to the ear, in such cases presented to court uterus in {page 259} plate. Might wait 6 or 7 hours if there was nothing peculiar before giving Ergot. Bearing down from passage child hurt and fright produces abortion. I concur with Dr. Foster about inserting the finger would give some mild purgative in such cases.

In case of fever I have found the child dead when the mother did not know it. Have seen water discharge 3 times in one case 1 1/2 hours [later] I burst one myself. I would rather manage a dozen such Ladies to manage than to give my opinion in this case. Inserting finger as Mrs Sessions did is uncalled for and cruel. {page 260}

Court ruled that testimony to prove defendants general character was illegel and would not be heard.

Dr. Bennett said he had no interest in this suit. Had practiced medicine in this place but never charged a cent, received a cent nor have any book account.

(Dr. Tate) Objected by Court. Adjourned from 5 to 7 o'clock. 7 [P.M.] court open. In the interim called at Br[other] Durphy's, his wife sick. Also Bishop Whitney's with Dr. Rich. /5 loaded teams arrived with provision from Ramus/

Plea of Mr Skinner for Plaintiff {page 261}

1. Brink not called to her confinement
2. No business to undertake delivery
3. was told labor pains [had] not come on
4. said child was dead

5. pretended any thing was wrong
6. pronounced waters gathered and broke
7. injections so hot as to put her in g[rea]t pain
8. denied giving Ergot
9. used violence
10. introduced [t]he hand
11. made 3 ruptures
12. extreme violence when implored to let her alone
(Swans Treatise 429) Fraud) 4 minutes before 8 [P.M.], Mars[h] commenced his plea. (Statute of Illinois 405) amount of damage in $ and cents. {page 262}

22 minutes past 8 [P.M.], Esqu[ire] Rigdon commenced his plea (United States dispensatory). 28 minutes past 9 [P.M.], Esqu[ire] Emmons commenced his plea. (Swans Treaties 240 contract) 10 1/4 o'clock closed. Adjourned to next Friday 10 o'clock to give its decision from this stand.

Had 1 hours interview at home with W[illiam] W. Phelps after court concerning trial. /Mother Smith better. F./ [*Rest of page blank*] {page 263}

Saturday, March 4th 1843 9 A.M. Brother Benjamin Johnson and the brethren from Ramus who come for to bring provision /corn, pork, oats, flour, wheat, as per Bill/ at the house. Agreed to go with Hiram to Ramus one week [from] to day. Bro[ther] John wanted to know if they might build a meeting house in Ramus out of Church property. Joseph said the property of the Church should be disposed of as the church said. It was for them to decide not him.

There is a wheel. This is the Hub. We will drive the first spoke in Rome [Ramus], 2d Laharpe, 3d Shokokon [and] 4th Lima [Illinois settlements with Mormon populations]; that is 1/2 the wheel. The other half is over the river. We will let that {page 264} alone at present. We will call the Saints from Iowa to these spokes then send Elders over and convert the whole. It is like a bank, they will not discount because they have plenty of specie. We will draw this specie. Then they will discount our paper. (Call for our address).

9 1/2 called at the office and gave instructions concerning making out the decision of court.

10 o'clock, opened City Council. Prayer B[y] Geo[rge] A. Smith. Bill regulating currency read. The Legislature of Illi-

nois have long been trying to repeal the Charter of Nauvoo. Upon which the Mayor [Joseph Smith] made some [comments] {page 265} as he had done on former occasions to shew the council and others that the Legislature cannot repeal a charter where there is no repealing clause. Upon which he read a letter from James Arlington Bennet to confirm his decision. Letter dated Arlington House Feb[ruary] 1st 1843.

Spoke against [Alexander] Makenzie's murdering those boys Spencer &c. [for mutiny] as stated in Arlington's letter. Called it murder. The boys had the malary [malaria] on the coast of Africa and did not know what they did.

In debate on the bill, Geo[rge] A. Smith thought imprisonment better than hanging. Mayor said he was opposed to hanging. If a man kill another shoot him {page 266} or cut his throat spilling his blood on the ground and let the smoke thereof ascend up to God. If I ever have the privilege of Making a law on this point I will have it so.

In reply to councillors who thought it impolitic to stop circulating uncurrent Bank notes at once. Mayor said he would use a figure and talk like a father to his children. If you want to kill a serpent, don't cut off his head for fear he will bite you, but cut off his tail piece by piece and perhaps you won't get bit. So with this bill. If paper currency is an evil {page 267} put it down at once. Stop the circulation at once.

When councillors get up here let them talk sense. Great God where is common sense and reason? Is there none in the Earth? Why have the kanker lingering to sap our life? Get a 5 dollar bill can get nothing with it. Dare not touch it any one because it is a [-]. Shovel it out then.

I wish you had my soul long enough to know how good it feels. It is expedient when you strike at an enemy, strike the most deadly blow possible. (Hyde asked what the {page 268} editer would do)? Mayor said advertise in the next paper to your agents to send you gold and silver as we take no paper here.

Prisoners may be kept in the city as safe as in the Prison of the state by chaining to a block with a guard and labor in blacksmith shops or any where else and never have a prisoner sent out of the city for imprisonment.

Bills passed to stop circulation of paper currency in the city, punish counterfeiting &c. by unanimous vote. Dr. Samuel

Bennet[t] chosen Alderman, A[lbert] P. Rockwood fire warden for 1st ward. {page 269} Elijah Fordham fire warden 2d ward. Charles C. Rich fire warden 3d ward. /Voted/ [to] opened an alley north and south through block 126. 1 1/2 P.M., Adjourned to next regular meeting.

Dined about 3 P.M. Cold, clear. Repaired to office with O[rson] Spencer.

Proverb: For a man to be a great man, he must not dwell upon small things though he may enjoy them. Spoken while entering the office. Explanation a prophet cannot be a scribe &c.

Joseph said to Dr. [Willard] Richards there is one thing you fail in as historian the naming or noticing surrounding objects, {page 270} weather, &c.

The weather is extremely cold and freezing and has been almost continually since October. There was a breaking up of the ice in the River in February so that Boats passed from St. Louis to Quincy. The Falls were clear so that boats passed from Montrose to Keokuk, but the river has not been cleared yet from the Edwards Brick house and upwards.

The brethren have brought a multitude of wood on the ice from the opposite shore and the islands. Hundreds of cords per day. Ground clear except a little ice. {page 271}

Brought in by Hyrum Smith, "Christian Soldier Jan[uary] 7th 1843" "41st article of court Martial laws." "No such sentence (that of death) shall be carried into execution until *confirmed* by the President of the United Sates, or if the trial take place *out* of the United States, until it be *confirmed* by the *commander* of the *Fleet* or *Squadron*. Capt[ain] M[akenzie]. does not rank as commander of the two latter."

Joseph "They'll hang Makenzie, or imprison him, or break him of his office"

The battle of Gog and Magog is after the Millenium. The[y] {page 272} were command[ed] all to come up to Jerusalem to worship in the Millenium.

Continued to write on decision of court till 4 1/2 o'clock, then called at Bro[ther] Durphy's to see sick [*two words crossed out, unreadable*] /<Woodsworth>/ and Whitneys <and Kimballs> [*rest of page blank*] {page 273}

Sunday, March 5th 1843 Taking care of Mother all day. [*rest of page blank*] {page 274}

Monday, March 6th 1843 Read Elder Adam's letter in the "Bee" Boston. Also another communication showing the progress of truth in Boston.

9 o'clock called at office. Told Dr. Richards to answer or [write what he had] commented to the Bee. Recited in German at the house. Called at office for paper. After Dinner lay down to rest. Toward evening rode out. [*two and a half lines blank*]

This evening presented a grand display of burning prairie on the bank of the river opposite Nauvoo. East wind through the day, cold. Thawed a little ~~during~~ /in middle/ of the day. {page 275}

Tuesday, March 7th At the office at 9 A.M. Heard [and] read decision of court. Gave an order on Lot for corn to Bro[ther] Allen. Sister Sayres called to exchange notes, her's for Dr. Rust's. At office before dinner conversing on medicine. After signed several deeds. Bro[ther] Clayton present to settle.

Brother Manhard brought and gave 2 loads of corn and 1 hog to President from Iowa. Reconed with Theodore Turly, who enquired what was wisdom concerning a brewery in this place? Reconed with Dymic {page 276} Huntington. East Wind through the day.

3 [P.M.] o'clock rain commenced. Informed Phe[l]ps and Richards they might bond themselves at dinner. (Clayton began to settle with the brethren about Lots at Mayor's office)

Wednesday, March 8th 1843 Suddenly in the night wind changed to N.W. Extremely cold this morn[ing, now] very pleasant and calm. Much floating ice in the river. At the office 8 o'clock signed some writing concerning the [Nauvoo] Legion. After dinner in office /Mr Cowan came in/ wrote a letter to [-]. Conversed with the Pr[o]cession about Military tactics. Reconed with Ford. 5 o'clock cloudy. Rode out with Cowan. {page 277}

Thursday, March 9th 1843 This morning received another No of the Bee containing minutes of conference in Boston &c. Read decision of court in Dana vs Brink. Mr. Cowan took court papers and Butterfield's opinion to go to Gov[ernor] of Iowa to have him recall the M[iss]o[uri] writ.

12 o'clock called with a letter concerning land of Hotchkiss. Read decision, read papers. Bro[ther] Phelps you shall know law, and understand law and you shall be a lawyer in Israel and the

328

time shall come when I shall not need say thus is the law for you {page 278} shall know the law.

William O. Clark gave a load of corn, Bro[ther] Sanford Porter a hog. Issued attachment for Peter Haw[e]s agai[ns]t Artemus Johnson. Clayton in office. Sleet and rain through the day and evening.

Friday, March 10th 1843 Clear and cold. Read the decision in office with O[rson] Spencer. At 10 [A.M.] repaired to the Hall over the store and 10 [minutes later] /[we had?]/ commenced the decision in case of Dana vs. Brink that the Plaintiff recover his bill $99 and costs. The whole included 12 pages written matter. After decision {page 279} court referred to the threat of the Defendant['s] council ordering court, as attempting to intimidate &c. Council explained satisfactorily. Also court referred to what Dr. Brink had said since trial that he had not a fair chance. His witnesses were not allowed, repelled by court.

2 [o'clock] afternoon, Mayor came in office, when Daniel Sherwood 14 years old was brought up on suspicion of stealing a watch from the house of Geo[rge] Nelson. No positive testimony appearing against him [so] Mayor ordered his father to take him home and try him. If he found the boy guilty to whip him severely, for he is too young to imprison or whip. {page 280}

/Mayor ordered [Lucien] Woodworth to fix a room in the Nauvoo House with a large stone in the center to chain the boys to and chain them till their time is out./

As Thomas Morgan went out to speak with Mayor, said he had been told by several that Joseph had taught that it was right to steal viz. O. P. Rockwell, David B. Smith, and James Smith which was the means of drawing Thomas into the practice of stealing.

David Smith once attempted to shoot me. The gun did not go and he was so mad that he through down the gun and broke the stock. It was my gun. He was carrying to [ar]rest me. After the attempt we stopped to rest and refresh when unknown to him I removed the priming from the gun and pistols, wet the touch holes, and made him carry them all home with me and saw me across the river from {page 281} Montrose.

Joseph decided that he had no objection to having a brewery put up by Theodore Turley.

329

Proverb

As finest steel doth show a brighter polish
The more you rub the same;
E'en so, in love, rebuke will ne'er demolish
A wise man's goodly name.

Ordered a search warrant for W[illia]m Law for tools &c. stolen and believed to be in the house of Deal Sherwood.

When in Kirtland I saw Elder Cahoon's boy steal a cucumber, put it in his pocket. I told Cahoon of it. At the same time his boy came up and denied it saying he had an apple [and] let it fall {page 282} and picked it up. There said Cahoon I did not believe he stole it. [I said] His boys drove their cows among mine while the women were milking to endanger their safety. I rebuked him and threatened him and made him confess in public next day. This was about the time of the commencement of building Temple in Kirtland.

Signed the warrant, said he should not send decision of Court to press without a petition. Ordered an execution for Dana against Brink and signed. Dana swore he feared Brink would abscond or place his property out of reach. {page 283}

Journal

1843

The following journal, which is in the handwriting of Willard Richards except where noted, begins precisely where the preceding journal ends. The original is again housed in the archives of the Historical Department, Church of Jesus Christ of Latter-day Saints, Salt Lake City, Utah.

Friday, March 10th 1843 4 P.M. Bro[ther] Norton claimed 2 trying squares, W[illia]m Law 1 padlock, David Grant 1 shirt of property found by the Marshall on warrant just issued. A bit stock and smoothing plane and 3 or 4 other little tools were presented on this case. Mayor [Joseph Smith] present. Clear and cold.

[At] 10 minutes before 7, I, Willard W. Richards, discovered a stream of light in the South West quarter of the heavens. The pencil rays of light /were/ in the form of a broad sword with the hilt downward. The blade [was] raised, pointing from the west southwest {page 1} raised at an angle of 45 degrees from the horizon, and extending nearly /or within 2 or 3 degrees/ to the Zenith of the degree where the sign appeared. This sign gradually disappeared from 7 1/2 o'clock and at 9 had entirely disappeared.

Saturday, March 11th Too cold last night as to freeze wa-

331

ter in the warmest rooms in the city. River filled with anchor ice. 8 1/2 o'clock in the office, Joseph said he had tea with his breakfast. His wife asked him if [it] was good. He said if it was a little stronger he should like it better, when Mother Granger remarked, {page 2} "It is so strong and good I should think it would answer Both for drink and food."

A dream then related. Night before last I [Joseph] dreamed that an /old/ man came to me /and said/ there was a mob force coming upon him, and he was likely to loose his life, that I was Lieut[enant] General and had the command of a large force. I was also a patriot and disposed to protect the innocent and unoffending and wanted I should assist him. I told him I wanted some written documents to show the facts that they are the agressors, and I would raise a force sufficient for his protection, that I would call out the Legion. He turned to go from me, but turned again and {page 3} said to me. "I have any amount of men at my command and will put them under your command."

The words of Joseph: "While conversing about the sign in the heavens last evening, as sure as there is a God who sits enthroned in the heavens, and as sure as he ever spoke by me. So sure there will be a speedy and bloody war, and the broad sword seen last evening is the sure sign thereof."

About 9 A.M. Joseph and Brigham started for Ramus.

It is reported in the papers that the workman employed on the General {page 4} Pratt (which was burned and sunk last fall near Memphis in the Mississippi) with a diving bell on the third of January found the wreck in about 24 f[ee]t water. In that night [there] was an earth quake [and the] next day the wreck had disappeared. No trace could be found and the water was from 100 to 120 feet deep and for about 100 feet no bottom. A bar was discovered where previous was deep water.

Joseph and Brigham had a pleasant and delightful ride and arrived at Bro[ther] McClary's in Ramus 15 minutes before 4 P.M. at Benjamine Johnson's to lodge while they staid in Ramus. In the eve[ning] Joseph pulled up Bro[ther] Moses with one hand pulling sticks. {page 5}

Sunday, March 12th Joseph preached 14 John, "In my Father's house are many mansions." Found the brethren well and in good spirits. Had a very pleasant visit. P.M. Brigham preached.

Monday, March 13th Throwed the bully of Ramus wrestling. 2 P.M. held Church meeting. Appointed Almon Babbitt Presiding Elder of Ramus by unanimous voice of the Church. In the evening held a meeting for blessing children, 27 blessed. {page 6}

Mercury 3 degrees below zero at sunrise in Nauvoo. It is said by many the sword was seen in the heavens last eve again. It is said in the papers that iron filings and sulphur have fallen in form of snow storm in Missouri in five counties. This day heard that the Quincy Institute was burned last week. 3 or 4 tracks were followed in the light snow from the institute to the middle of the river which was frozen over.

Mr. Ivins arrived at Nauvoo and stated that [Orrin] Porter Rockwell came with him from New Jersey to St. Louis when Porter was taken by advertisement {page 7} Saturday, March 5th and put in St. Louis Jail.

New Meeting house lately dedicated for Quincy and the dedication sermon was all against the Mormons. Elder O[rson] Hyde has gone down there to preach and the Mormons say they ~~want their Meeting house~~ /would be glad to have their own meeting house/ &c. for Elder Hyde to preach in.

Tuesday, March 14th Joseph and Brigham returned about 4 P.M. had a severe cold ride. This evening appeared a large circle around the moon. Similar to what is frequently seen but larger. (See page 11) {page 8}

Wednesday, March 15th Dictated a letter to G[eorge] J. Adams [and] read letter from Butterfield and [James] Arlington Bennet. Signed deeds for Sister Granger and Smith and Alread.

Spent the day mostly in the office. Gave the following [new] name to the "Wasp" enlarged as is contemplated "The Nauvoo Neighbor", [with the following in the masthead:] "Our Motto, the Saints Singularity" "Is unity, liberty, charity".

Joseph prophecied in the name of the Lord Jesus Christ that [Orrin] Porter Rockwell will get away from the Missourians.

Told [Peter] Hawes he must curtail his boys or they will get into State Prison. {page 9}

Dream, last night dreamed of swimming in a river of pure water, clear as crystal, over a school of fish of the largest /size/ I ever saw. They were directly under my belly. I was astonished and felt afraid they might drown me or do me injury. They were the largest I ever saw.

333

Conversed much about Porter, wishing the boy well. [*rest of page blank*] {page 10}

Tuesday, March 14th 1843 * [*Richards includes at this point a drawing of five interconnecting circles and the following description of the three most prominent circles:*]

A. A large circle seen round the moon on the evening of this day dark shades within the circle surround the moon which is the fur[t]hest spot in the centre.

B. An additional circle seen about 9 o'c[loc]k by Joseph /and/ the whole diagram as then seen and discribed by the Prophet. This circle is a mistake.[1]

C. This circle was visible this evening about 8 o'clock and continuous through the evening. The Parhelion on this circle [at points] B. [and] B. were brightest as also the circle C. about 1/4 before 9 o'clock. The circle and Parhelion were very brilliant and grew paler by nine o'clock. Description of W[illiam] W. Phelps.

Dr. R[obert] D. Foster states that at 11 o'clock there were an innumerable number of circles interwoven as above around the moon. The whole design to represent as one of the signs of the times. "A Union of Powers and Combination of the Nations," says Joseph.

\\[2] Not correct. See page 17 [of the original manuscript]. {page 11}

\\[3] Thursday, March 16th 1843 9 A.M. in the office, read a piece on Mormonism in "Uncle Sam" Feb[ruary] 18th written by reporter of the paper and conversed with Hiram, Dr. Foster, and many others. [*several lines left blank*]

Friday, March 17th 1843 A part of the fore noon in the office and the remainder at home. P.M. Settled with Father Perry gave him a deed of 80 acres of land and city lot and prophecied that it would not be 6 mo[nths] before he could sell it for cash. {page 12}

4 o'clock P.M. N[ewel] K. Whitney brought in a letter from R. S. Blennarhassett, Esqu[ire], St. Louis concerning [Orrin] Porter Rockwell, dated March 7th saying Porter was arrested the day previous and wishing instruction. Read and dic-

---

[1] This sentence is enclosed in a rectangle in the original manuscript.
[2] In the handwriting of an unknown scribe.
[3] In the handwriting of Willard Richards.

tated answer. Heard read letters No. 1 Boston Bee by Viator and his own to [James] Arlington Bennet.

2 P.M. Walked out with 4 or 5 ladies towards the store. Went into Holmes. A report is circulated that the new indictments have been found in M[iss]o[uri] against Joseph, Hyrum, and some 100 others on the old subject and John C. Bennet[t] is going to do so and so. {page 13}

Saturday, March 18th 1843 Most of the fore noon in the office in cheerful conversation. Closed letter to [James] Arlington Bennet. Laid down on the writing table with /back of the/ head on Law Books saying write and tell the world I acknowlidge myself a very great lawyer. I am going study law and this is the way I study and [then I] fell asleep and went to snoring. This was about noon.

In the afternoon rode out and about 4 [o'clock] took a game of ball east of Main street. {page 14}

Sunday, March 19th Rode with Emma to the farm. Returned about 11 A.M. At home the remainder of the day.

D[imick] Huntington started for Chicago with letter to [Justin] Butterfield concerning O[rrin] P. Rockwell. [rest of page blank] {page 15}

Monday, March 20th 1843 Rode to Hiram Kimball's with Mrs. Butterfield about a deed.

Reconed with R[obert] D. Foster, and give Foster a note to balance all demands. Foster took the acknowledgement of about 20 deeds of the Trustee to sundry individuals and left the office about 3 o'clock.

This evening from 7 to 9 was seen /by Bro[ther] Hawes and others/ in the heavens a dark stripe of considerable width passing over our Zenith, dark as the darkest clouds. {page 16}

Tuesday, March 14th 1843 * [Richards includes at this point a second drawing of circles, this one of four circles attached to the circumference of a larger fifth one, and the following description:] This circle was similar to the one around the moon in appearance but larger. [Points] A. A. Parhelion visible from 8 to 9 o'clock P.M. when it was seen by Joseph and this diagram was drawn from his description.

This space [at the point between A. and A. inside the largest circle] was darker than other parts of the horizon. The outer part of parhelion was much more brilliant than the inner.

The above is a diagram of one of the signs of the times designed to represent "A union of power and combination of Nations," says Joseph.

Dr. R[obert] D. Foster says that at 11 o'clock the circle[s] interwoven around the moon were innumerable. {page 17}

Tuesday, March 21st 1843 Called at the office about 9 [A.M.] and wrote an order and took leave for Shokokon. Cold west wind as it has been for a week. Cold, freezing water in the houses. [*rest of page blank*] {page 18}

Wednesday, March 22d [*entry left blank*] {page 19}

Thursday, March 23d 7 1/2 A.M. Mercury 1 Deg[ree] below zero at sunrise. * Semicircle near the Zenith. [*Richards includes a third drawing of circles at this point.*] [*rest of page blank*] {page 20}

* [*Richard includes at this point a fourth drawing of circles, with the following written sideways on the page, along side the drawing:*] Parhelion. Appearance of the Sun. March 23d 1843 at 7 1/2 o'clock A.M. Parhelion. The colors of the circles were of the hue of the rainbow only brighter. [*rest of page blank*] {page 21}

[*page left blank*] {page 22}

Friday, March 24th 1843 [*several lines left blank*] Having been out west, arrived at home about one or two o'clock. [*several lines left blank*] I loaded team and came in from Augusta with provision[s] and two [arrived] from Lima this evening. [*rest of page blank*] {page 23}

Saturday, March 25th 1843 In the office at 8 o'clock, heard a report from Hyrum concerning thieves as given by J[ohn?]. <Wilson> and directed a proclamation to be published offering security to all who will devulge their secrets.

Received a letter from A. Jonas requesting the use of a cannon to celebrate /the creation of/ the New County of Marquetts and answered it that he might have it. Also rec[eive]d letter from Senator Young containing a bond for 1/4 section of land from Welch.

9 [A.M.] Baptized Esqu[ire] Mif[f]lin of Philadelphia. {page 24}

10 [A.M.] Ordered a writ against A. Fields for disorderly conduct. Gave E[benezer] Robinson an order on T[aylor] and Woodruff for papers $16.

A. Fields was brought in about noon drunk or pretending

to be so and was ordered to be put in irons till sober. He abused all present by his drunken appearance. Has been out in the city.

Dined at 2 o'clock.

"Awful gale" says St. Louis Gazette, within the last 6 weeks 154 vessels were wrecked on the coast of England and 190 lives lost; on the east of Ireland 5 vessels and 134 lives; on the coast of Scotland 17 vessels [and] 39 lives; on the coast of France 4 vessels and 100 lives. Value of vessel and cargoes roughly estimated 825,000. {page 26}

Sunday, March 26th At home all day. [*rest of page blank*] {page 27}

Monday, March 27th 1843 Dictated a letter to Esqui[re] Rigdon showing that he [Joseph] believed said Rigdon was concerned [connected] with J[ohn] C. Bennet[t], Geo[rge] W. Robinson, and Jared Carter and unless satisfaction was made should withdraw fellowship and bring him before conference. Letter was presented by W[illard] Richards.

11 [A.M.] Court assembled over the store to try A. Field for drunkenness and abusing his wife. [He was] fined $10 costs and bail $50 for 6 months to keep the peace. {page 28}

Tuesday, March 28th Removed the office from the smoke house to the President's office over the counting room in the Store. [*rest of page blank*] {page 29}

Wednesday, March 29th Sat on trial with Orson Spencer on case of Dr. Foster. Judgement against Foster. ~~Removed from Smoke house to office over the store also~~. [*rest of page blank*] {page 30}

Thursday, March 30th 1843 9 A.M. Came and gave instructions to have Brink's bond returned to him if it was delayed till after 10 o'clock. Called at 11 [A.M.] Brought in N[ew] York Herald reported March 11th that the Island of Antigua was destroyed by an earthquake on the 8th of Feb[ruary] and Nevis and Kitts were considerably injured.

Andrew L. Lamoreaux paid $73 for W[illia]m Henry on Temple.

Dr. Brink brought in a new Bond which the Mayor [Joseph] rejected as informal. Told Charles Ivins he might improve his share of the Ferry one year. {page 31} Told Charles Ivins unless he considered Dr. Brink good for heavy damages, he was foolish to go his bonds.

New York Herald of the 11th of March published the Vision in Poetry &c. and Miss Snow's festival song &c.

Brink's case /took/ appeal from Mayor's Court to the Municipal to be tried 10th April [at] 10 A.M.

1 1/2 P.M. was called to sit as Justice with Alderman Harris on case of Webb and Rigby for forcible entry and detainer. During trial Esqu[ire] Skinner [was fined] 10 dollars for contempt of court for insulting a witness and abused [abuse.] Said Skinner in his [final] plea [repeated the offense] and [was again abusive and the court] threatened to fine him $10 {page 32} more for contempt of court, but let him off on submission &c. Trial closed about one [o'clock A.M.] Friday Morning. Jury [consisted] of 12 men.

Elder Hyde returned from Quincy having delivered 10 Lectures and baptized 3 persons. [rest of page blank] {page 33}

Friday, March 31st 1843 10 A.M. Opened Mayor's Court for Trial of Amos Lower for assaulting John H. Burghardt. After hearing the testimony, fined Defendant $10. * [rest of page blank] {page 34}

Saturday, April 1st 1843 Called at the office with Mr. Clayton about 10 A.M. for the "[Book of the] Laws of the Lord." About noon heard read Truthiana No. 3. Very warm and pleasant.

2 P.M. Started with W[illia]m Clayton, O[rson] Hyde, and J[acob] B. Backenstos for Ramus. [We] arrived about 6 1/2 [P.M.] Very muddy. [We were] very joyfully received by Bro[ther] Benjamin F. Johnson. J[acob] B. Backenstos was with me continually. [rest of page blank] {page 35}

Sunday, April 2nd 1843 Missouri-St. Louis Republican, March 24[th] says at Point Petre, W[est] I[ndies] islands lava ran together in the public square, the earth opened and swallowed them whole mass.

Wind [from the] N[orth] E[ast]. Snow fell several inches but melted more or less. D[imick] Huntington returned from Chicago. After breakfast called on Si[s]ter Sophronia.

10 A.M. to meeting. Elder Hyde Preached 1[st] epistle [of] John, 1 chap[ter] 1st 3 verses, "When he shall appear we shall be like him &c. He will appear on a white horse as a warrior and maybe we shall have some of the same spirit. Our God is a

warrior." John 14:23 "It is our privilege to have the Father and Son dwelling in our hearts." {page 36}

Sunday, April 2d 1843 Cloudy, earth 1/2 covered with snow. Elder Hyde remarked that he read in one of the newspaper[s] concerning the passage of an act in one of the certain states to prohibit the citizens from killing crows because they eat up all the filth and carcuss from of[f] the earth, thereby tending to preserve the health of the people. But offer them a piece of clean fresh meat and a crow will not touch it for he has no appitite for it.

He had often thought that there was [a] very great resemblance between the priests of the day and these crows. For they were continually picking up all the dirt, filth, and meaness of the [Mormons?], feasting on it [as] if it was a precious morsel. But offer them any good and sobriety /from/ among the Mormons, they have no appetite and will turn away from it. I think for the same reason the Legislature lets the crows live. We ought to let the priest live, gather and eat up all the filth and rubbish from the Mormon people that they may be healthy. {page 37}

Dined at Sophrona's and soon as we arrived [I told] Elder Hyde, "I am going to offer some corrections to you." Elder H[yde] replied, "They shall be thankfully received."

[Joseph said,] "When he shall appear we shall see him as he is. We shall see that he is a Man like ourselves. And that same sociality which exists amongst us here will exist among us there only it will be coupled with eternal glory which glory we do not now enjoy."

14 John 23 "The appearing of the Father and of the Son in that verse is a personal appearance. To say that the Father and the Son dwells in {page 38} a man's heart is an old Sectarian notion and is not correct.

"There are no angels who administer to this earth but who belong or have belonged to this earth. The angels do not reside on a planet like this earth, but they reside in the presence of God, but on a Globe like a sea of glass and fire." 'Sea of glass before the throne &c.' where all things are manifest past, present, and to come. The place where God resides is a great Urim and Thummin. This earth in its sanctified and immortal state will be a Urim and Thummin for all things below it in the scale of creation, but not above it." {page 39}

Related the Dream written on page 3d, Book /B/. Interpretation by O[rson] Hyde: "Old man [is the] Government of these United States, who will be invaded by a foreign foe, probably England. U.S. Government will call on Gen[eral] Smith to defend probably all this western territory and offer him any amount of men he shall desire and put them under his command."

[Joseph said,] "I prophecy in the Name of the Lord God that the commencement of bloodshed as preparatory to the coming of the Son of Man will commence in South Carolina. (It probably may come through the slave trade) This the voice declared to me while I was praying earnestly on the subject 25 December 1832. {page 40}

"I earnestly desired to know concerning the coming of the Son of Man and prayed, when a voice Said to me, 'Joseph my son, if thou livest until thou art 85 years old thou shall see the face of the Son of Man. Therefore let this suffice and trouble me no more on this matter.'"

1 P.M. Attended meeting. Joseph read 5th Chapter of John's Revelation referring particularly to the 6th verse showing from that the actual existence of beasts in heaven. [It is] probable those were beast which had lived on another planet than ours. God never made use of the figure of a beast to represent the kingdom of heaven. Beast [with] 7 eyes [is the] Priesthood. {page 41}

This is the first time I have ever taken a text in Revelation. If the young Elders would let such things alone it would be far better. [I] then corrected Elder Hyde as in private.

Supped at Bro[ther] Johnson's. [We] expected to start for Carthage, but bad weather prevented [us]. [We] called another meeting by bell. [I] read Rev[elations] between Meetings with Elder Hyde and [was] expounding. During this time several come in and expressed fear that I had come in contact with the old serpent.

Meeting [at] 7 [o'clock] eve resumed the subject of the beast [and] showed very plainly that John's vision was very different from Daniel's Prophecy, [the] one referring to things existing in heaven. The other figure of things on /which/ be on the earth. {page 42}

Whatever principle of inteligence we attain unto in this life, it will rise with us in the revelation [resurrection]. If a person gains more knowledge and intelligence through his obedience and diligence than another he will have so much the advantage in the world to come.

There is a law irrevocably decreed in heaven before the foundation of the world upon which all blessings are predicated and when we obtain a blessing it is by obidience to the law upon which that blessing is predicated.

Again reverted to Elder Hyde's mistake &c. The Father has a body of flesh and bones as tangible as mans. {page 43} The Son also, but the Holy Ghost is a personage of spirit and a person cannot have the personage /of the H[oly] G[host]/ in his heart. He may receive the gift of the Holy Ghost. It may descend upon him but not to tarry with him.

What is the meaning of the scripture, "He that is faithful over a few things shall be made ruler over Many? And he that is faithful over many [things] shall be made ruler over many more?"

What is the meaning of the Parable of the 10 talents? Also conversation with Nicodemus, "Except a man be born of water and of the spirit." I shall not tell you?

[I] Closed by flagellating the audience {page 44} for their fears and called upon Elder Hyde to get up and fulfil his covenant to preach 3/4 of an hour, otherwise I will give you a good whipping.

Elder Hyde arose and said, "Brothers and Sister, I feel as though all had been said that can be said. I can say nothing but bless you."

To B[enjamin] F. Johnson, the 144,000 seal[e]d are the priests who are appointed to administer in the daily sacrifice. [*rest of page blank*] {page 45}

Monday, April 3d 1843 Miller's Day of Judgement has arrived, but tis too pleasent for false prophets.

Dined at Joel Johnson's on a *big Turkey*. 2 P.M. Started for Carthage, arrived at 4 P.M. Staid at J[acob] B. Backensto's. [Spent the] evening reading [the] /Book of/ Revelation with Elder Hyde and conversing with Esqu[ire] Backman. [*rest of page blank*] {page 46}

April 4th, Tuesday Spent 5 hours preaching to Esqu[ire] Backman, Chauncey Robinson, and the Backenstos. Backman said, "Almost thou persuadest me to be a Christian." 2 P.M. [We] left [and] arrived at Nauvoo [at] 5 P.M. [*rest of page blank*] {page 47}

Wednesday, April 5th 1843 Attended Municipal Courts

341

for People vs. Hoops on Habeas Corpus. After hearing the testimony they were discharged. Johnathan Hoops gave me receipt for $50 in lands in Iowa, dated Sept[ember] 2d 1840. [*rest of page blank*] {page 48}

Thursday, April 6th 1843 The first day of the Jubilee of the Church of Jesus Christ of Latter Day Saints. A special Conference assembled on the platform of the Temple, or /rough/ floor of the basement at 10 o'clock A.M. The sun shone clearly and was very warm and pleasent. Scarce[ly] a speck of snow is to be seen except on the north side of Zarahemla Hill [where there] is considerable, but the ice was about 2 feet deep in the river west of the Temple and north of that point and south /of that/. The channel is clear of ice. The walls of the Temple are from 4 to 12 feet above the floor of the conference.

President Joseph was detained by a court ~~Conversation between~~ {page 49} Widow Thompson vs. Sister and Bro[ther] Dixon (from Salem) in assumpsit.

President B[righam] Young had charge of the meeting during the absence of President Joseph. [The following members of the] Quorum of the Twelve [Apostles] [were] present: H[eber] C. Kimball, O[rson] Pratt, W[ilford] Woodruff, John Taylor, Geo[rge] A. Smith, [and] W[illard] Richards.

[At] 1/2 past 11 o'clock Amasa Lyman present prayed after a hymn was sung by the quire. O[rson] Pratt read the 3d chap[ter] of 2d Epistle of Peter and preached on the subject of the resurrection.

10 /mi[nutes]/ before 12, President Joseph Smith and Elder Rigdon and O[rson] Hyde arrived. The floor was about 3/4 covered with listeners. {page 50}

[At] 12 o'clock O[rson] Pratt gave way and Joseph [a]rose to state the object of the meeting. It is my object to ascertain the stan[d]ing of the First Presidency (as I have been instructed). I present myself for trial. I shall next present my councillors for trial. 3d to take into consideration the sending out of the Twelve [Apostles] /or some portion of them/ or somebody else to get means to build up [the] Nauvoo House and Temple.

4th Elders will have the privilege of appeals from the different conferences to this if there are any such cases. It is important that this conference {page 51} give importance to the

N[auvoo] House, as a prejudice exists against the Nauvoo House in favor of the Lord's House.

There is no place where men of wealth, character, and influence can go to repose themselfs and it is necessary we should have such a place.

Are you satisfied with the First Presidency, so far as I am concerned, or will you choose another? If I have done any thing to injure my character in the sight of men or angels, or men and women, come forward tell of it and if not ever after hold you[r] peace. {page 52}

President B[righam] Young [a]rose and nominated Joseph Smith to continue as the President /of the Church/. Orson Hyde 2d it. Voted unanimously. Such a show of hands was never seen before in the Church. Joseph returned his thanks to the assembly and said he would serve them according to the best of his ability.

/Next President Joseph/ Brought forward Elder Rigdon for trial. Br[other] Young nominated Elder Rigdon to continue. 2d by O[rson] Hyde.

Elder Rigdon spoke, "The last conference I have had privilege of attended was at the Laying of the corner stone of this house. I have had no health and been connected with circumstances {page 53} the most forbidding which doubtless has produced some feeling. I have never had a doubt of the work.

"My feelings concerning [John C.] Bennet[t] were always the same and [I] told my family to guard that fellow, for some time he will make a rupture among this people. [I] had so little confidence. I always felt myself at his difiance.

"I was one threatened by Warren Parrish /if I would not coincide with his views/. I have got such a threatening letter from J[ohn] C. Bennet[t] that if I did not turn my course I should feel the force of his power. This is an increase of my health and strength and I desire to serve you in any way it is possible for me to do. If any one has any feelings I hope they will express them." {page 54}

Dymick Huntington asked concerning Rigdon stating that Bennet[t] was a gentleman and had nothing against him. Some time since, Rigdon recollects nothing or little about the conversation. Thinks Dimick Mistaken. Dimick knows he was not. Rigdon /said/ Bennett never offered any abuse to my family and at that

343

time he had never been familiar with him. Dymick[:] I have no private pique against Elder Rigdon.

Voted (in general) /almost unanimous/ that Elder Rigdon retained his standing. /Joseph presented W[illia]m Law for trial/ Moved by B[righam] Young, 2d by Heber Kimball. Voted that W[illia]m Law retain his standing.

Voted unanimously that Hyrum Smith retain his office as Patriarch. &c. {page 55} Hyrum said the Lord bless the people and Elder Rigdon said so too. /Joseph said "I do not know any thing against the Twelve [Apostles]. If I did I would present them for trial."/

It is not right that all the burden of the Nauvoo House should rest on a few individuals and /we/ will now consider the propriety of sending the Twelve [Apostles] to collect names for the Nauvoo House. There has been too great latitude in individuals for the building of the Temple to the exclusion of the Nauvoo House. It has been reported that the Twelve have wages $200 per day for their services. I never heard this till recently and I do not believe I have ever known their having any thing. I go in for binding up the Twelve.

Let this conference institute an order to this end {page 56} and let no more pay money or stock into the hands of the Twelve except the payer transmit the account immediately to the Trustee in trust and no man else /but the Twelve [Apostles]/ have authority to act as agents for the Temple and Nauvoo House.

I will mention one case. He is a good man. That man's name is Russel. He had been in East on business for his brother and took money belonging to the Temple and put it in the bag with his brother' money. Two or 3 days after /his return/ he called on his brother for the money, but his brother thought he had paid out too much money and he would keep the {page 57} Church money /to make good his own/. I called to see Russel about the money and he treated me so politely I concluded he never meant to pay. Bro[ther] Russel[l] said /that/ his brother said he should not be out of money again. There was $20 of the Church money and some dried apple for the Pres[iden]ts.

I propose that you send moneys for the Temple by the Twelve [Apostles] some or all; or some agent of your chosing and if you send by others and the money is lost, tis lost to yourselves. I cannot be responsible for it.

It is wrong for the Church to make a bridge of my nose in appropriating Church funds. The incorporation required of me securities which were lodged in the proper hands. {page 58} Temple committee are bound to me in /the sum/ $2,000 and the Church is running to them /with funds/ every day and I am not responsible for it.

So long as you consider me worthy to hold this office, it is your duty to attend to the legal forms belonging to the business. My desire is /that/ the conference Minutes go forth to inform all branches of the order of doing business and the Twelve [Apostles] be appointed to this special mission of collecting funds for the Nauvoo House.

When I went to the White House at Washington /and/ presented Letters from Thomas Carlin. Van Buren said /Tho[ma]s Carlin, Tho[ma]s Carlin/. Who [is] Tho[ma]s Carlin? I erred in spirit and /I/ confess my mistake in being angry with Martin Van Buren {page 59} for saying Tho[ma]s Carlin is nobody. Let it be recorded on earth and in heaven that I am clear of this sin.

There has been complaint against the Temple Committee for appropriating the Church funds to the benefit of their own children, to the neglect of others who need assistance more than they do.

I have /the/ complaint by W[illia]m Clayton. W[illia]m Clayton called, says I have to say to the conference I am not so fully prepared to substantiate the proof as I could wish. I am able to prove that [property was] used to a great extent. {page 60} I am able to prove by the books that Cahoon and Higby have used property for their own families to the exclusion of others.

/Joseph said/ Let the trial of the committee be deferred to another day /then let/ the Lion and the unicorn come together, day after tomorrow. Mr. Clayton can have the privilege of bringing his books to the trial.

Moved, seconded, and voted that the Twelve [Apostles] be appointed a committee to receive and gather funds to build the Nauvoo House. With this provision, that the Twelve give bonds for good delivery to trustee in trustee and payer make immediate report to the trustee in trust. Bro[ther] W[illiam] W. Phelps proposed that the Twelve give duplicate receipts. {page 61}

President Young remarked he should never give receipts for cash /except such as he put in his own pocket for his own use/

345

but wished this speculation to stop and asked if any one knew any thing against any one of the Twelve, any dishonesty. I know of one who is not and referred to Muzzling the ox that treadeth out the corn.

Joseph said, "I will answer Bro[ther] Brigham. Let the Twelve [Apostles] spend the time belonging to the Temple for to collect funds and the remainder of the time they may labor for their support. The idea of not muzzling the ox that treadeth out the corn is a good old quaker songs. I have never taken the first farthing of Church funds for my {page 62} own use till I have first consulted the proper authorities and when there was no quorum of the Twelve or High Priests I have asked the Temple Committee who had no business with it. Elder Cutler said it was so. Let this conference stop all agents in collecting funds except the Twelve."

1 1/2 P.M. Hym[n] by Quoir. 12 [minutes before] 2 P.M. dismissed by prayer [given by] O[rson] Hyde. [Conference adjourned] for 1 hour.

3 [P.M.] Hyrum commenced by observing that he had some communication to make before Joseph came and would read from the Wasp, last number. A man who formerly belonged to the Church revealed to me there are a band of men and some {page 63} strong in the faith of the Doctrine of Latter Day Saints, and some who do not belong to the Church /were bound by secret oaths &c./ that it is right to steal from any one who does not belong to the Church if they gave 1/4 part to the Temple. If they did not remain stedfast they ripped open their bowels and gave them to the cat fish and they are the very Gadianton robbers of the last days.

Then /read/ his own affidavit as reprinted in the "Wasp" dated 26 Nov[ember] 1841 and the doings of the conference at Ramus and proclamation /or declaration of/ of the Twelve [Apostles] /and/ affidavit of Joseph. These said /11/ /the/ theives /have been compared to/ the little foxes. The presidency are the great foxes and they told me this was the interpretation given the preaching from the /stand by the theives/.

David Holman [and] James Dunn confessed {page 64} to me when they lived in my house that they had stolen from the world. I told him to get out of my house. The[n] David /Holman/ lifted his hand to heaven and swore if I would forgive him he would never do so again. He went to Montrose and stole and run away to Nauvoo, found a barrel of flour on the bank, just delivered from a Steam boat. Stole the flour went to Keokuk and sold it, saying he had picked up the barrel in the /river/ as it was likely a little damaged, he would take $2.00 got his pay and went his way. Made many observations to the Saints on stealing.

Joseph followed. I want the Elders to make hon[or]able proclamation abroad {page 65} what the feelings of the Presidency are. I despise a theif above ground. He would betray me, /if he could get the opportunity/ if I were the biggest rogue in the world, he would steal my horse when I wanted to run away, /then/ read proclamation of the Mayor on stealing. Dated 25th day [of] March 1843 "Wasp" No. 48. Many observation and confirmatory and said, enough said for this conference on this subject. Elders have a privilege to appeal from any decision of a branch to know if they shall retain their office or membership.

Necessary I explain concerning Keokuk. It is known that the Gov[erno]r of Iowa has posted a writ for me on affidavit {page 66} of Boggs. He still holds that writ as a cudgil over my head. (U.S. Attorney told me all writs issued thus were legally dead) I said that is a stumper and I will shew them a trick or the Devil never did /that is/ leave them. Every man who wishes to [win] out econimically with regard to futurity, let them come over here as soon as they can settle their affairs without sacrifice. Let them come and we will protect them and let that government know that we don't like to be imposed upon.

About the first of August 1842 Mr. Remick came to my house, put on a long face, said he was in distress, about to loose $1,400 from /a theft of/ 300 [dollars] at Sheriff's {page 67} Sale. Said he the sale takes place tomorrow. I have money in St. Louis. Next morning he called. I did not like the looks of him /but thought I/ he is a stranger. I have been a stranger and better loose 200 than be guilty of sin of ingratitude. Took his note on demand. /The/ day I was taken I asked him for the money. You ought to have it /said he but/ I have not got the money from St. Louis. I have a curious plan in my mind. I will give you a quit claim deed of the land you bought of Galland and /give notes to/ Gallands which I have as his agent.

"I," said Joseph, "have not asked you for your property and would not give a snap /for it/ but I will accept your offer, but

347

want my money (1/2 my land in the state) /said he I will give you deed and/ {page 68} he gave me deeds and I got them recorded. He called for some more favors and I let him have some clothes /to the amount/ of 6 or 7 hundred dollars. I have offered this land to many, if they would go to settle there but nobody will go. /I agreed/ if I found he owned as much as he pretended I would give my influence to build up Keokuk.

"J. G. Rem[m]ick /is his name. He has got/ most $1,100 per acre. He looks exactly like a woodchuck and talks like a wood-chuck on a stump with a chaw of tobacco /in his mouth/. He tried to get his hands to steal a stove from near my stove and carry it off on the raft. He is a theif. My advice is, {page 69} if they choose /to/ come away from Keokuk and not go there more. I am not so much of a christian as many suppose I am, when a man undertakes to ride me I am apt to kick him off and ride him. I wouldn't bye property in the Iowa. I considered it stooping to accept it as a gift.

/"I wish to speak of the/ 1/2 breed lands [Half Breed Tract] opposite this city [in Iowa]. 1/2 breed lands and every man there who is not 1/2 breed had better come away and in a little time we will call them all 1/2 breed. I wish we could swap some of our 1/2 breeds here for /the 1/2 breeds who/ lived there. I will give you a key, if any /one/ will growls tomorrow [about being called a 1/2 breed], you will know him to be a 1/2 breed. {page 70}

"My opinion is the Legislature have done well in giving the best tittle to settlers and squatters. Those who have deeds to those islands from the chancery of Iowa have as good tittle as any, but the settlers under /the/ laws of Iowa Legislature and chancery of Iowa are at variance. I believe it a fine [example] of swindling by court of Chancery.

"Dr. Galland said those Islands don't belong to any body. /They were/ thrown out of U.S. Survey. Hence no man had a claim /and it was/ so considered when I came here. My advice to the Mormons who have deeds and possessions /is/ fight it out. You who have no deeds or possessions let them {page 71} alone. Touch not a stick of their timber. Deeds given by court of chancery warrants and defend[s] against all unlawful claims. It is a 1/2 breed. It [is] an anomaly, without form and void, a nondescript. If they have your note, let them come here and sue you then you can carry up your case to the highest court so long as the Laws have a shadow of tittle. It is not right for the Mormons to go and carry away the wood. In the name of the Lord God, I forbid any man from using any observations of mine to rob the land of wood.

"Moses Martin has been tried and had fellowship withdrawn /by the Church/ at ~~Keokuk~~ /Nashville/. {page 72}

/"The question has been asked/ can a member not belonging to the Church bring a member before the High Council for trial? I answer No! I ask no Jurisdiction /in religious matters/. I merely give my opinion when asked. If there was any feelings at Nashville because I gave my opinion, there is no occasion for it. I only advice the brethren to come from Iowa and they may do as they please /about coming/. If I had not actually got into this work and been called of God, I would back out. But I cannot back out. I have no doubt of the truth. Were I going to prophecy I would prophecy the end will not come in 1844 or 5 or 6 or 40 years ~~more~~. {page 73}

"There are those of the rising generation who shall not taste death till Christ comes. I was once praying earnestly upon this subject and a voice said unto me, 'My son, if thou livest till thou art 85 years of age, thou shalt see the face of the Son of Man.' I was left to draw my own conclusions concerning this and I took the liberty to conclude that if I did live till that time ~~Jesus~~ /he/ would make his appearance but I do not say whether he will make his appearance or I shall go where he is. I prophecy in the name of the Lord God, and let it be written, that the Son of Man will not come in the heavens till I am 85 years old, 48 years hence or about 1890."

/Then read/ 14 Rev[elation] 6 verse another Angel {page 74} fly[ing] in the midst of heaven for the *hour* of his judgement is come to [begin] extermination from the commencement commence[d] when the angel commences preaching this gospel. /1 day [equals] 1,000 years/ 1,000 years as 1 day. 41 years, 8 months only 6 years from the voice saying, "If thou live till thou art 85 years old."

Hosea 6th chapter after 2 days &c. 2,520 years which brings it to 1890. Taylor says 45 years according to Bible reckoning. The coming of the Son of Man never will be, never can be, till the judgments spoken of for this /hour/ are poured out, which judgments are commenced. Paul says, "Ye are the children of the light and not of the darkness, that that day {page 75} should not overtake us as a theif in the night."

It is not the design of the Almighty to come upon the earth and crush it and grind it to powder. He will reveal it to his servants the prophets. Others [talk?] like an ass. /O what wonderous wise men there are going about and braying like [an ass] cry-[ing] O Lord, where is Joe Smith, Joe Smith? Whare /O/ away up on the top of the topless throne aha &c.

Jerusalem /must be/ rebuilt. /Judah returns, must return/ and the Temple water come out from under the temple. The /waters of the/ Dead Sea be healed. /It will take/ some time to build the walls and the Temple &c. All /this must be done before/ Son of Man /will make his appearance/. Wars and rumors of wars, signs in the Heavens above, on the earth beneath. Sun turned into {page 76} darkness, moon to blood. Earthquakes in divers places, oceans heaving beyond their bound. There one grand sign of the Son of Man in heaven, but what will the world do? They will say it is a planet, a comet, &c. Consequently the sun of man will come as a sign. [The] coming of the son of man is as the light of the morning cometh out of the East. 10 minutes before 6 [P.M.] singing. Prayer by W[illia]m W Phelps. Adjourned to 10 A.M. tomorow. Sister Richards requested prayer for her health. {page 77}

Friday, April 7th 1843 Assembled at 10 according to adjournment. President Marks presented the request of Sister Van Hymon, Milan Webb, [and] Sister Dodds /for/ the prayers of the conference. Singing by Quoir. President /Joseph/ rather hoarse from speaking so long yesterday said he would use the boys lungs to day.

Prayer by O[rson] Hyde. Appeals from the Elders were then called for. Elder Brown arose. Said Elder Winchester called for his license but he did not give it. Set down with the President, B[righam] Young presiding. Jedidiah M. Grant was voted should go to Philadelphia and preside there.

Also Joshua Grant go to Cincinati to preside. {page 78} Voted that Peletiah Brown go to the village of Palmyra in the state of N[ew] York and build up a church.

Bro[ther] Brown signified his willingness to go any where the conference shall direct. Singing by Quoir.

Temple committee were called up for trial at 11 o'clock. /W[illia]m Clayton said/ some many expect I am going to be a means of a downfall of the Temple committee. Tis not so, but I design to show they have been partial.

Elder Higby has over run the amount allowed by trustees about 1/4. P[r]etty much all Elder Higby's son has received [has been] in money and store pay. Higby's son has had nothing credited {page 79} for his tenth.

Elder Cahoon, W[illia]m S. Cahoon has paid all his tenth. The others of Cahoon's sons have had nothing to their credit in tenth. The committee have had a great amount of store pay. One man who is laboring continually wanted 25 c[en]ts in store when his family were sick. Higby said he could not have it.

W[illia]m S. Cahoon was never appointed a boss over the cutting shop, but was requested to keep an amount of labor in the shop. During the last 6 months very little has been brought into the committee. {page 80}

There are certain individuals in this city who are watching every man who has any thing to give the Temple, to get it from him and pay for the same in his labor.

Elder Cutler said he did not know of any wrong. If any one would shew it he would make it right. Voted, clear, unanimously.

Elder Cahoon said this is not an unexpected matter at all, to be called up. I do not want you to thing [think] I am perfect. Some how or other, since Elder Cutler went up into the pine country, I have, from some cause, been placed [in] very peculiar circumstances. I think I never was placed in so tight a screw since I was born. Been screwed to the back bone. {page 81}

The Marshall brought up a man for disorderly conduct. Mayor fined him $5.00 or go out of the crowd. The [*several lines blank*]

Cahoon said, the better people have known my proceedings, the better they have liked them. When President Smith had goods last summer we had better property. Goods would not bye corn without some cash. Instead of horses &c., we took store pay. I have dealt out meal and flour to the hands to the last ounce when I had not a morsel of bread, meal, or flour in my house. If the Trustee Bro[ther] Hyrum or the Twelve [Apostles] or /all/ will examine and see if I have too much it shall go freely. {page

82} I call upon all the brethren if they have anything to bring it forward and have it adjusted.

Hyrum said he felt it his duty to defend the committee so far as he could. He would as soon go to hell as be a committee, but to make a comparison for the Temple committee. A little boy came in and said he saw an elephant on a tree and the people did not believe it, and they looked and it was only an owl.

Cahoon said when Bro[ther] Cutler was gone, Higbee kept the books, and we have found as many mistakes against Bro[ther] Higby, as in his favor. Voted unanimously clear in his favor. {page 83}

Elder Higby said I am not afraid or ashamed to appear before you. When I kept the books I had much other business and made some mistakes. My house was built out of a lot I bo[ugh]t of Hiram Kimball &c., &c. Not much of it from the Temple. Voted in favor of Elder Higbee, unanimously.

President Joseph stated that the business of the conference had closed and the remainder of the conference would be devoted to instruction. It is an insult to the meeting to have people run out of meeting /just/ before we close. If they must go let them go 1/2 hour before. No gentleman will go out of meeting just at close. {page 84}

Singing by Choir. 12 1/2 [P.M.] adjourned till 2 o'clock. Prayer by B[righam] Young. [*rest of page blank*] {page 85}

2 1/2 /25 mi[nutes]/ P.M. singing and Prayer by B[righam] Young opened the conference. Elder O[rson] Pratt read 7 chapter Daniel, 9 verse &c.

[Elder Pratt remarked,] "The 2d advent of the Son of God is a subject which occupies the attention of the people of this day. The Latter day Saints believe he will come at least 1000 years before the final consummation. Millerites believe he will make his 2d advent in a few months, but they will find themselves mistaken.

"Mistaken as they are, good will come out of the investigation. It will arouse the attention of Multitudes to the facts as they exist or will open the minds of the people to the truth when it shall be proclaimed by the Elders of Israel. They believe that the stone is not to strike the image on {page 86} his feet till the 2d advent and a kingdom will come direct from heaven. We believe God will not destroy the kingdom of the earth till he has set /up/ his own kingdom.

"Do Millerites look for more revelation? No! They raise the midnight cry but does not tell the people what to do. Latter D[ay] S[aints] /are the/ most reasonable and the most inteligent of any people on the face of the whole earth. I have heard /them/ 13 years. /I had as/ [likely] worship a hors[e] or a stump as a God who gives no instructions to his people.

"Ancient of Days. One came to the Ancient of Days. Many suppose this was the son. After judgment [is] set Son of Man comes to Ancient of Days. {page 87} The most Ancient Man of God that lived in days. [Or] Else he could not have been called the Ancient of Days. Father Adam is to come and organize a great Council to prepare for the coming of the 2d advent. Jesus comes to the Ancient of Days. We believe in Miracl[e]s and they do not. Angels will come /a[nd]/ the heavens /will be/ opened [to] send forth angels to prepare the earth for Christ's 2d Coming.

"One man thinks he is authorized to call on men to repent &c. I defy any one to scorn the errors of any generation without revelations.

"Resurrection of the body is denied by many because it is contrary to the laws of nature, because flesh and bones are constantly changing, completely new in 7 or 10 years. If this is {page 88} true a man in 70 years would have matter enough for 10 different bodies. Objector says this resurrection cannot be true, for if so, men would be quarreling which body belong[s] to himself and others. Who shall have the best right to it.

"I do not believe that more than 3/4 of our bodies is comprised of animal organization, but is purely vegetable. Hence through all the 70 years a man will have one or two parts, which will be the same original. If he receives the matter he was in possession of 50 years before he died, he has the same body. The people living in the house are the occupants of the house and the house {page 89} though repaired all through its different parts from time to time even to new timbers throughout; yet it is said to be the same house still."

While the choir was singing, President Joseph remarked to Elder Rigdon this day is a Millenium. It is a millenium within these walls. There is nothing but peace (nothing to be seen from the stand but the heads and bodies of the congregation, as they stood on the walls and covered the walls and the floor it was one mass of Saints or people. To speak was literally speaking to the people for there was nothing else to be seen.)

25 [minutes] past 3 [P.M.] Elder W[illia]m Smith said he had no doubt but that many who were baptized by John enjoyed much of the religion of Jesus, but when he came there was more light, and unless they followed it the light that they had received became darkness. If the sects have any power it is only such as they have usurped from the Pope. {page 90} No man has authority except he be sent.

While bewildering clouds spread their glooming wings over our horizons and the Almighty sits in the heavens laughing at our ignorance, the Midnight cry /is raised and/ what shall I cry? All tables are become unclean. What shall I cry? They have changed transgressed /the laws, changed ordinances,/ broken the everlasting covenant! What [-] shall [I do to] retain my darling religion against this "new light" or Mormonism. I have about as much religion as others, but I have not got so much but what I might receive a little more. When I pray for more light and God bestows it, I will not say as the poor Negro {page 91} who prayed behind the Stone wall if what he said was not true, he hoped the stone wall would fall on him /when/ some one pushed a stone on his head, poor negro cried out I did not mean what I said.

So with sectarians about Rev[elations] and healings. Said had had a conversation with a Reverand Presbyterian who asked me what I believed. I told him we believed the gospel as preached by the ancient apostles and to leave the first principles and go on to perfection. O[h] said the Rev[erand] Presbyterian that means leaving their dead works, but said I how can I leave the first principles before I embrace them? O said /he/ these are some of the Mysteries of the kingdom. We know but little about them. Tis no more care to agree with you, it's a stump. {page 92} Unfurl the golden banner. We will stay in Sodom till we are burned. We will stay in Jerusalem till the Romans come and burn the temple of the great God. For if we escape the calamities it will prove we are not true. [*several line left blank*]

(The ice started down stream of considerable dimensions west of the stand or temple. Up nearly opposite the old Post office building.) {page 93}

354   4:45 [P.M.] Joseph said to complete the subject of

Bro[ther] Pratt's. "I thought it a glorious subject with one ~~additional idea~~ /addition/. Their is no fundamental principle belonging to a human System that "ever goes into another /in this world or the world to come/." The principle of Bro[ther] Pratt was correct. I care not what the theories of men are. We have the testimony that God will raise us up and he has power to do it. If any one supposes that any part of our bodies that is the fundamental parts thereof, ever goes into another body he is mistaken."

5:00 [P.M.] Choir sung and notice [given] that Bro[ther] Joseph will preach tomorrow morning at 10 [A.M.]. Prayer by Elder Taylor. {page 94}

[*page left blank*] {page 95}

8th April 1843 Prayer by Elder Taylor [followed by Joseph Smith's address]. /See Clayton copy/ Three requests:

1st That all who have faith will pray Lord to calm the wind, for as it is now I cannot speak.

2nd That the Lord will strengthen my Lungs.

3d That I may have the Holy Ghost.

The subject which I shall speak from is the beasts spoken of by John. I have seldom spoken from /the Revelations/ and I do it now to do away [with] divisions and not that the knowledge is so much needed.

Knowledge is necessary to prevent division although it may puff up it does away [with] suspence, in knowledge is power, hence {page 96} God knows how to subject all beings he has power over all.

Should not have called up this subject if it had not been for this old white head before [us] Father [Pelatiah] Brown. I did not like the old man being called up /before the High Council/ for erring in doctrine. Why I feel so good to have the privilege of thinking and believing as I please.

They undertook to correct him there. Whether they did or not I don't care. Rev[elation] 5 chap[ter] 8 vers[e]. Father Brown had been to work [interpreting scripture] and confounded all christendom. That these were figure[s] John saw in heaven to represent the different Kingdoms of God on Earth. {page 97} He put down sectarianism and so far so good, but I could not help laughing that God should take a figure of a beast to represent his

355

kingdom consisting of Men. To take a lessor figure to represent a greater, old white head you missed it that time. By figures of Beasts, God represented the kingdoms of the world. Bear, Lion, &c. represented the kingdoms of the world says Daniel. For I refer to the prophets to qualify my observations to keep out of the wasp nests of young Elders.

The things John saw had no allusion to the day of Adam, Enoch, Abraham, or Jesus, only as clearly specified and set forth to John. I saw that which {page 98} was lying in futurity. Rev[elation] 1:1. Read [this], [it] /is/ [the] key to the whole subject.

4 beasts and 24 Elders which was out of every nation. It is great stuffing, to stuff all nations into 4 beasts and 24 Elders. Things which /he/ saw had no allusions to what had been, but what must shortly come to pass. Rev[elation] is one of the plainest books God ever caused to be written. What John saw he saw in heaven /that which/ the Prophet saw in vision /was/ on earth. In Hebrew is a Latitude vs Longitude compared with English version.

They saw *figures* of beasts. Daniel did not see a lion and a bear. He saw an image like unto a bear in every {page 99} place. John saw the actual beast itself. /It was/ to let John know that beasts existed there and not to represent figures of things on the earth. /The/ prophets always had interpretations of their visions &c. God always holds himself responsible to give revelations of his visions and /if/ he does it not, we are not responsible.

Speculators read not, fear they shall be condemned [by what they read]. If God has given no Rev[elation]. How do you prove John saw creatures in heaven? /C[hapter]/ 5 /V[erse]/ 11 Revelation. 13 verse every creature which was in heaven and on the Earth. I John saw all beasts of /a/ 1,000 forms /from/ 1,000 worlds like this. The grand secret was to tell what {page 100} was in heaven. God will gratify himself with all these animals. Says one I cannot believe in salvation of beasts. I suppose God could understand the beasts &c. In certain worlds the 4 beasts were angels there. Don't know where they come from. /They were inteligent/ inteligent /but my/ Darling religion says /they/ meant something beside beast[s]. Then the 24 Elders must mean something else. 4 beasts meant Bonapart and Cyrus, &c. Then the 24 Elders meant the kingdoms of the beasts. It is all as flat as a pancake.

What do /you/ use such flat and vulgar /expressions for/

being a prophet? Because the old women understand it. They make {page 101} pancakes. The whole argument is flat and I don't know of anything better to represent the argument.

There is no revelation any where to show that the beasts meant any thing but beasts.

O ye Elders of Israel hearken to my voice and when ye are sent into the world to preach, tell them things you are sent to tell. Declare the first principles, and let mysteries alone lest you be overthrown.

Father Brown when you go to Palmyra say nothing about the 4 beasts.

Dan[iel] 1 /[Revelation] c[hapter]/ 13, 2 verse[s] /some say/ [the beast with the] Deadly wound /means/ Nebuchadnezzar. [or] Constantine and [others say it means] the Catholic[s]. {page 102} Now for the wasp nest. Priests and [others use the word] Dragon for Devil. They have translated [the scripture to represent a] beast in heaven. It was not to represent [a] beast in heaven. It was an angel in heaven who has power in the last days to do a work. All the world wondered after the beast, /and/ *if the beast was all the world, how could the world [have] wondered after the beast?* When the old devil shall give power to the beast to do all his mighty work, all the world will wonder.

"Who is able to make war with the beast?" says the inhabitants of the earth. If it means the kingdoms of the world, it don't mean the kingdoms {page 103} of the Saints. Who is able to make war with my great big self? The Dragon. We may interpret it and it is sometimes [translated] Alpelyel [Apollyon]. [Revelation] 9th verse, 12 chap[ter] [the] key word [is] independant beast. Abstract from the human family. (25 minutes past 11 lungs failed, the wind blew briskly) I said more than I /ever/ did before except once at Ramus and then the little /apostates stuffed me like a fellow/ cook[s] turkey /with the prophecies of Daniel/ and crammed it down my throat with their fingers.

After singing, [at] 27 [minutes] to 12, John Taylor commenced, saying "I did not know but I might say something but since the Prophet has got {page 104} through I find there is nothing left, but the toil." Elder Taylor says, "If you write it down we are all fools it will not be /very/ far from the mark." No man in the Church knows anything but what he has been told.

He had never said much about Beasts &c. in his preaching and when he had, he had done it to attract attention and keep the people from running after a greater fool than himself.

Daniel saw an image of Gold, Iron, Clay, &c. the profet [prophet] explained. Thou Nebuchadnezzar are the head &c. 12 minutes [to noon] choir sung. Elder Hyde prayed. Adjourned till 2 o'clock. {page 105}

12 o'clock noon. Strong west wind and the ice is floating down the Mississippi (Seen from the Stand).

2:26 minutes meeting open by singing. The wind was so high from the N[orth] West that the speaker changed his position from the stand on the East end of the temple walls to a temporary (and momentary) stand near the west end. The day was warm (and pleasant except strong wind). Prayer by Elder Cahoon. Singing 12 /m[inutes]/ [before] 3 [o'clock].

Elder Taylor resumed the subject where he adjourned in the forenoon. Little horn was the Pope some say. Pope of Rome prevailed against the saints or Church, whence the Church of England, {page 106} Presbyterian, Methodist, &c., put the Church of Rome in the place of the Devil and when they find out the old Lady is their mother, they don't like the relationship mentioned the 10 kingdoms or the toes.

While in the story, if these kings or some of them, the God of heaven should set up a kingdom which should never end. I am not going to say with regard to the little stone when this kingdom will be set up, but it will be a kingdom and the saints will take and possess it and it will be a kingdom on earth not in heaven, not Methodist, not Presbyterian or Baptist. I was going to say the Church of Rome comes the {page 107} nearest to a kingdom of any of them. Not Millerites. They expect the coming of Christ is like lightning, whereas the kingdom is like a little stone cut out of the mountain without hands. 3:20 [P.M.] Singing [by] choir.

Elder O[rson] Hyde said it was 3 years since I met with you and was set apart to a foreign mission by you. Mat[thew] 24 chapter in part read concerning the temple. Jesus acted very un-christian like and uncharitable and meddled with other people's property. Took a scourge of small cords and drove them out of the temple. The German Bible says there shall not be one stone left upon another that shall not be broken. {page 108} Compared the gifts in the Church to the gold/en/ vessels of the temple which

Nebuchadnezzar or some other nezzar took away. Where are they? In Babylon. Wrapped up in a napkin. Give me so much money and I will give you so much gospel say the Sectarian priests. There is now and then one, Like the gleaning of grapes when vintage is done.

He compared the Mormons to the rought stone, which could not be make to fit any where and would be thrown away. So with the Mormons the[y] will not fit any way or where, but must {page 109} be cast out by all soci[e]ties, and yet at last they will come out the head of the heap. The Saints shall possess the kingdom.

I have been in the four quarters of the world among 14 or 15 different languages and people and they all agree the [that] some great event is coming, close at hand is coming. What has produced this impression? The true light, that light that lighteth every man that cometh into the world. It is like the press that presses the paper on to the whole type at once and God is the pressman. When this gospel has been preached to all nations the hours of his judgment is come. Good-bye. 5:05 [P.M.] Singing and prayer [by Elder] Taylor. {page 110}

[*page left blank*] {page 111}

Sunday, April 9th 10:25 A.M. Meeting opened by singing /"Spirit of God &c."/ at Temple stand. Prayer by William Smith. Singing. Joseph remarked that some might have expected him to preach but his heart and lungs would not admit. Joshua Grant will occupy the stand awhile followed by Amasa Lyman. [*rest of page blank*] {page 112}

Monday, April 10th 1843 Elders Conference commenced at the Temple at 10 o'clock A.M. [*rest of page blank*] {page 113}

Tuesday, April 11th 1843 Called at office [at] 11 A.M. and 1 P.M. to give some instructions to have an order Made out for W[illiam] W. Phelp[s] to get a note out of the Bank at St. Louis and started after W[illia]m Clayton to find the date of the note. Some rain and wind. Conference adjourned till tomorrow [at] 10 A.M. [*rest of page blank*] {page 114}

Wednesday, April 12th 1843 9 A.M. In conversation with Mr. Gillet concerning [the] Hotchkiss purchase. Mr. Jackson present gave a certificate (written by Elder Hyde) to W[illia]m Weeks to carry out the designs and Architecture of the Temple in Nauvoo.

Conference of Elders commenced at 10 [A.M.] and closed at 12:20 having ordained about 22 Elders and appointed about 118 to different Missions in U[nited] S[tates] and Canida and restored Almon Babbitt to fellowship &c., &c. See Minutes of the Quorum of the Twelve [Apostles].

Before the Conference closed the Steamer Amarenth appeared in {page 115} sight of the Temple coming up the River and about noon landed her passengers at the wharf opposite the old Post office building. About 240 of the Saints from England in charge of Elder Lorenzo Snow who has been preaching in England 2 or 3 years. Joseph and Emma were present and a large company of the brethren and sister[s] ready to greet their friends on their arrival.

/Notice was given at Close of the conference for the emigrants to meet at the stand tomorrow morning [at] 10 to hear instructions./ After unloading /Saints/ the Amarenth proceeded up the river. This is the first boat up this season. Bro[ther] Snow and Co[mpany] left Liverpool in January. {page 116}

About 5 P.M. The Steamer "Maid of Iowa" hauled up at the Nauvoo House Landing and discharged about 200 Saints In charge of Elders P[arley] P. Pratt and Levi Richards. These had been detained at St. Louis, Alton, &c. through the Winter, having come out of Liverpool in the fall. Capt[ain] Jones of the "Maid of Iowa" was baptized a few weeks since. Joseph was present at the landing and the first to board the steamer and appeared Melted in tenderness when he met Sister Pratt (who had been to England with Parley) and her little daughter only 3 or 4 days old. The "Maid /of Iowa"/ was 11 days coming from St. Louis {page 117} detained by ice &c.

Joseph was very busy the P.M. and coming among the brethren shaking hands and conversing freely till about 9 o'clock and rejoiced to meet so many of the Saints and in such good health and fine spirits equal to any that had ever come in Nauvoo. [rest of page blank] {page 118}

[page left blank] {page 119}

[page left blank] {page 120}

Thursday, April 13th 1843 Trial of Brink vs Dana came up at 10 o'clock A.M. but was adjourned to Wednesday next, 9 A.M. At 10 /A.M./ the Emigrants and a great Multitude of others assembled at the Temple. When after singing by the Choir and prayer by Elder Kimball, Joseph addressed the assembly and said, [*rest of page blank*] {page 121} I most heartily congratulate you on your safe arrival at Nauvoo and your safe deliverance from all dangers and difficulties you have had to encounter but you must not think your tribulations are ended.

I shall not address you on doctrine but concerning your temporal welfare. Inasmuch as you have come up here assaying to keep the Commandments of God I pronounce the blessings of heaven /and earth/ upon you, and inasmuch as [you] will /follow/ counsel and act wisely and do right {page 122} these blessings shall rest upon you so far as I have power of /with/ God to seal them upon you. I am your servant and it is only through the Holy Ghost that I can do you good. God is able to do his own work.

We do not present ourselves /before you/ as any thing but your humble servants willing to be spend and be spent in your services. We shall dwell on your temporal welfare on this occasion. In the 1st place, where a crowd is flocking from all parts of the world of different minds, religions, &c. there /will be some/ who do not live up to the commandments. /There will be/ designing characters {page 123} who would turn you aside and lead you astray. Speculators who would get away your property. Therefore it is necessary we should have an order here and when emigrants arrive to instruct them concerning these things.

If the heads of the Church have laid the foundation /of this place, and have had the trouble/ of doing what has been done, are they not better qualified to tell you how to lay out your money than those who have had no interest &c?

Some start on the revelation to come here and get turned away and loose all, and then come and enter their complaints /to us/ when it is too late to do any thing for them. {page 124}

The object of this meeting is to tell you these things and then if you will pursue the same courses you must bear the consequence. There are several objects in your coming here. One object has been to bring you from Sectarian bondage. Another from National bondage, where you can be planted in a fertile soil. We have brought you into a free government. Not that you are to consider yourselves outlaws. By free governemt, we do not mean that a man has a right to steal, /rob/ &c., /but free/ from bondage, taxation, [and] oppression. Free in everything if he con-

361

duct[s] himself honestly and circumspectly with his neighbor. Free in Spiritual capacity. {page 125}

This is the place that is appointed for the oracles of God to be revealed. If you have any darkness you have only to ask and the darkness is removed. Tis not necessary that the miracles should be /wrought/ to remove darkness. Miracles are the fruits of faith. "How shall we believe on him of whom /&c./ i.e., inasmuch as I have resumed leading before I God may correct the scripture by me if he choose. Faith comes by hearing the word of God /and not faith by hearing and hearing by the word &c./ If a man has not faith Enough to do one thing he may do another. If he cannot remove a Mountain he may heal the sick. Where faith is, there will be some of the fruits. All the gifts and power /which/ poured out from heaven were poured out on {page 126} the heads of those who had faith.

You must have a oneness of heart in all things. You shall be satisfied one way or the other with us before you have done with us! There are a great many old huts here /but they/ are all new. Our city is not 6[00] or 700 years /old/ as /those/ you came from. It is only a 4 year old not a 4, but 3 year old. /We/ commenced building 3 years last fall. /There/ [are] few old settlers. I got away from my keepers /in Missouri/ and run and come on these shore[s] and found 4[00] or 500 families. /I/ went to work to get meat and flour. Folks were not afraid to trust me. I went to work and bought all this region of country. /I cried/ Lord what will thou have me to do? /And the answer was/ "build up a city {page 127} and call my saints to this place!" And our hearts leaped with joy to see you coming here. We have been praying for you all winter, from the bottom of our hearts. We are glad to see you. We are poor and cannot do by you as we would, but will do all we can.

'Tis not to be expected that all can locate in the city. There are some who have money and will /build and/ hire others. Those who cannot purchase lots can go out in the cou[n]try. The farmers wants your labor. No industrious man need suffer in this land.

The claims of the poor /on us/ are such that {page 128} we have claim on your good feelings for your money to help the poor. The Church debts /also have their demands to/ save the credit of the Church. This credit has been obtained to help the poor and keep them from starvation &c. Those who purchase Church lands and pay for it, this shall be their sacrifice.

[We have] Men of 50 and 100,000 dollars who were robbed /of every thing/ in the state of M[iss]o[uri and] are laboring in this city for a morsel /of bread and there are those/ who must have starved but for the providence of God through me. If any man say here is land or there is land, believe it not. We can beat all our competitors in lands, price, and every {page 129} thing. /We have the/ highest prices, best lands, and do the most good with the money /we get/. /Our system/ it is a real smut machine, a bolting machine, and all the /shorts/ brann and smut runs away and all the flour remains with us.

Suppose I sell you land for $10 per acre and I gave [$] 3.45 per acre then you are speculating /says one/. Yes, I will tell you how. I buy others lands and give them to the widow and the fatherless. If the specualtors run against me they run against the buckler of Jehovah. God did not send me up as he did Joshua in former days. God sent {Page 130} his servants to fight, but in the last days he has promised to fight the battle himself. God will deal with you himself and will bless or curse you as you do behave yourselves. I speak to you as one having authority that you may know when it comes and that you may have faith and know that God has sent me.

The lower part of the town is the most healthy. In /the/ upper part of the town the Merchants will say /I/ am partial &c., but the lower part of the town is much the most healthy. I tell you in the name of the Lord I have been out in all parts of the city at all times of night to learn these things. {Page 131}

The Doctors in this region don't know much and the lawyers /when I spoke about them/ began to say, "We will renounce you on the stand," but they don't come up and I take the liberty to say what I have a mind to about them.

Doctors won't tell you where to go to be well. They want to kill or cure you to get your money. Calomel Doctor will give you Calomel to cure a sliver in the big toe and does not stop to know whether the stomach is empty or not, and Calomel on an empty stomach will kill the patient and the Lobelia doctors will do the same. Point me out a patient and I will {page 132} tell you whether Calomel or Lobelia will kill him or not. If you give it [for washing], the [water from the] river Mississippi is healthy unless they drink it, and it is more healthy than the spring water. Dig wells from 15 to 30 feet and it will be healthy.

There are many sloughs on the islands from /where/ Miasma arises in the summer, and is flown over the upper part of the city, but it does not extend over the lower part of the city.

All those persons who are not used to living on a river or lake [or] a large pond of water, I do not want you should stay on the banks of the river. {page 133} Get away to the lower part of the city, back on the hill where you can get good well water. If you feel any inconvenience take some mild physic 2 or 3 times and then some good bitters.

If you can't get any thing else take a little salts and cyanne pepper. If you can't get salt take pecoria, or gnaw down a butternut tree, /eat some/ boreset /or/ hoarhound.

Those who have money come to me and I will let you have lands. Those who have not money if they look as well as I do I will give you advice that will do you good. 12 1/4 I bless you in the name of Jesus Christ. Amen. {page 134}

Hyrum made remarks concerning the prophets. Every report in circulation not congenial to good understanding is false. False as the dark regions of hell. Closed 12 25/60.

Joseph gave notice that Bro[ther] Gardner wanted 2[00] or 300 hands ditching, a good job.

Singing by choir, Bro[ther] Thompson requests prayer. Closed by prayer [given by] O[rson] Pratt.

After meeting many of the saints repaired to the landing of the Nauvoo House, as the "Maid of Iowa" arrived (during the meeting) from Keokuk where it went last night after the freight which it left to get over the rapids. Joseph was among them till about 3 o'clock and then when the boat left walked away with {page 135} Bro[ther] Kimball. [rest of page blank] {page 136}

Friday April 14th 1843 Went out to the farm and beyond and sold 20 acres of land and returned.

Started to go again and in the Side hill broke the carriage and returned home. [rest of page blank] {page 137}

[page left blank] {page 138}

Saturday, April 15th Attended court Martial at his house. Gave instructions to have an notice written to John F. Cowan of Shokokon appointing him his aiddecamp as L[i]eut[enant] Gen-

[eral]. 4.05 P.M. Rode out with Emma. [*rest of page blank*] {page 139}

Sunday morning, April 16th 1843 Meeting at the Temple. A.M. 10 o['cloc]k Joseph read Bro[ther] Pratt's letters to the Editor of "T[imes] and Seasons" concerning the death of Lorenzo Barn[e]s /and remarked he read it because it was so approriate to all who had died in the faith/. Almost all who have fallen in these last days in the Church have fallen in a strange land. This is a strange land to those who have come from a distance. We should cultivate sympathy for the afflicted among us.

If there is a place on earth where men should cultivate this spirit and pour in the oil and wine /in the bosom of the afflicted/, it is this place, and this spirit is manifest here. Although he is a stranger /and afflicted/ when he arrives, he finds a brother and friend already to administer to his necessities. {page 140}

Another remark, "I would esteem it one of the greatest blessings if I am to be afflicted in this world to have my lot cast where I can find brothers and friends all around me, /but/ this is not /thing referred to it is/ to have the privilege of having our dead buried on the land where God has appointed to gather his saints together. Where there will be nothing but saints. [It is] Where they may have the privilege of laying their bodies where the Son will make his appearance and where they may hear the sound of the trump that shall call them forth to behold him. That in the morn of the resurrection they may come forth in a body and come right up out of their graves and strike hands /immediately/ in eternal glory /and felicity rather/ than to be {page 141} scattered thousands of miles apart. There is something good and sacred to me /in this thing/. The place where a man is buried has been sacred to me. /This subject is made mention of/ in [t]he Book of Mormon and Scriptures to the aborigines. The burying places of their fathers is more sacred than any thing else.

"When I heard of the death of our beloved hero Barn[e]s it would not have affected me so much if I had the opportunity of burying him in the land of Zion. I believe those who have buried their friends here their condition is enviable. Look at Joseph in Egypt [and] how he required his friends to bury him in the tomb of his fathers. See the expence /and great company and/ which attended the embalming and the going up of the great company to his burial. It has always been considered a great curse not to

365

obtain an honorable buryal and one of the greatest curses the ancient prophets could put on any one was that a man should go without a burial. {page 142}

"I have said, 'Father, I desire to be buried here, and before I go home, but if /this is not thy will/ may I return or find some kind friend to bring me back. Gather my friends who have fallen in foreign lands and bring them up hither that we may all lie together.'

"I will tell you what I want. If to morrow I shall be called to lay in yonder tombs, in the morning of the resurrection let me strike hands with my father and cry, 'My father,' and he will say 'My son, my son.' As soon as the rock rends and before we come out of our graves, may we contemplate these things so? {page 143} Yes, if we learn how to live and how to die, when we lie down we contemplate how we may rise up in the morning. /It is/ pleasing for friends to lie down together locked in the arms of love, to sleep, and [awake] locked in each others embrace and renew their conversation.

"Would you think it strange that I relate what I have seen in vision in relation [to] this interesting theme. Those who have died in Jesus Christ, may expect to enter in to all that fruition of Joy when they come forth, which they have pursued here. {page 144}

"So plain was the vision I actually saw men before they had ascended from the tomb as though they were getting up slowly, they take each other by the hand. It was my father and my son, my Mother and my daughter, /my brother and my sister/. When the voice calls suppose I am laid by the side of my father. What would be the first joy of my heart? Where is my father, my mother, my sister? They are by my side. I embrace them and they me.

"It is my meditation all the day and more than my meat and drink to know how I shall make the Saints of God to comprehend the visions that roll like /an/ overflowing surge before my mind. {page 145}

"O how I wo[u]ld delight to bring before you things which you never thought of, but poverty and the cares of the world prevent. But I am glad I have the privilege of communicating to you some things which if grasped closely will be a help to you when the clouds /are/ gathering and the storms /are/ ready to burst upon you like peals of thunder. Lay hold of these things and let not your knees tremble, nor hearts faint. What can Earthquakes, wars and tornados do? Nothing, all your losses will be made up to you in the resurrection provided you continue faithful. By the vision of the Almighty I have seen it. {page 146} More painful to me [are] the thoughts of anhilitation [annihilation] than death. If I had no expectation of seeing my mother, brother[s], and Sisters and friends again my heart would burst in a moment and I should go down to my grave. The expectation of seeing my friends in the morning of the resurrection cheers my soul and make me bear up against the evils of life. It is like their taking a long journey and on their return we meet them with increased joy.

"God has revealed his Son from the heavens and the doctrine of the resurrection also. We have a knowledge that those we ~~lay~~ /bury/ here God [will] bring them up again, clothed upon and quickened by the spirit {page 147} of the Great God. What matteredth it whether we lay them down, or we lay down with them, when we can keep them no longer.

"Then let them sink down like a ship in the storm. The mighty anchor holds the storm so let these truths sink down in our hearts that we may even hear begin to enjoying that which shall be in full hereafter.

"Hosanna, Hosanna, Hosanna to Almighty God that rays of light begin to burst forth upon us even now. I cannot find words to express myself. I am not learned, but I have as good feelings as any man. O that I had the {page 148} language of the archangel to express my feelings once to my friends, but I never expect to. When others rejoice, I rejoice. When they mourn, I mourn.

"To Marcellus Bates, let me administer comfort, you shall soon have the company of your companion in a world of glory and the friend of Bro[ther] Barn[e]s and all the Saints who are mourning, this has been a warning voice to us all to be sober and diligent and lay aside mirth, vanity, and folly and be prepared to die tomorrow." (Preached about 2 hours) {page 149}

/Erastus/ Snow said he was a boarder with Pres[iden]t J[oseph] Smith [during] the first week he was in Nauvoo [and] helped carry the chains for the surveyor and lay out the first farms. [He] has been [absent from Nauvoo] about 2 1/2 years. 5 [minutes before] 12 [P.M.]. (P[reache]d about 1 h[our])

Prophet Joseph said "as President of this house I forbid

any man's leaving this house just as we are going to close the meeting. He is no gentleman who will do it. I don't care who it comes from, if it were from the King of England. *I forbid it.*"

Singing and prayer by Elder Taylor. [*rest of page blank*] {page 150}

[*page left blank*] {page 151}

Monday, April 17th 1843 [*entry left blank*] {page 152}

This day a letter was received at the Nauvoo Post office, Sidney Rigdon Post M[aster] of which the following is a copy:

Washington, D.C. April 1[st] 1843

Sir,

The government of the Un[ited] States need[s] your service no longer. You will deliver all your accounts to this office, Sealed and addressed to the Post Master General, as the Post Of[fice] at Nauvoo, Ill[inois] is hereby abolished. The President of the Uni[ted] St[ate]s having Directed it so.

Respectfully your Most Ob[edi-
en]t S[er]v[an]t,
Charles A. Wicliffe

[P.S.] You will receive your letters &c. at any P[ost] O[ffice] you direct. C.A.W. Superscription by order of J[ohn] Tyler, Pre[sident] of the U[nited] S[tates].
Nauvoo Post Office, Ill. {page 153}

/Rain last night/.

April 17[th], Monday /Green grass begins to be seen/. Walked out in the city with [William] Clayton. Called on Brother Taylor. Handed him the letter purporting to be from the Attorney Gen[eral] of the U[nited] State[s] and gave him instruction about it. Looked at several lots. Called at Samuel Bennets to make arrangements to leave that house above the old bur[y]ing ground. Returned home. Had conversation with Erastus Snow. Received 50 Gold Sovereigns of P[arley] P. Pratt for the Temple and Nauvoo House. 5 1/2 P.M. Called at the printing office. Returned home and listened to the reading of a synopsis of his sermon of last Sabbath. {page 154}

Tuesday Morning, April 18th 9 A.M. At home. Signed

an appointment to John F. Cowan as his aid /decamp/ in the Nauvoo Legion. Conversed with Cowan &c. and went onto the prairie.

(Twelve [Apostles] met at President's office). Sold 130 acres of land to the English Brethren. Signed a transcript of his Docket Thomson M. vs Dixon [at] 3 P.M.

In the Evening had a talk with the delegation [*blank*] Indians who complained of having their cattle and horses &c. stolen and they were much troubled and wanted to know what they should do. They had borne their grievances patiently. {page 155}

Wednesday, April 19th 1843 At the office at 9 o'clock waiting for the assembling of the Municipal Court in case of Dana Versus Brink or Brink vs Dana. Appealed case.

12 1/2 [P.M.] Mayor's Court opened. Original papers called for. Clerk [James] Sloan inquired of the execution [which] would issue from this court. "Sit down," said the Mayor, "and attend to your own business. If any thing is wanted I will tell you time enough."

Marr Esqu[ire] opened the case &c. Moved this case be dismissed for want of jurisdiction in the court below and read from pag[e] 400, Statutes [of] Ill[inois]. Case of Lat[e] not assumpsit. Mayor's court [has] no jurisdiction. Chittyes pleadings 88.138 what assumpsit in &c. Blackston[e] Com[mentary], {page 156} vol[ume] 2d, pages 122, 157, 161, 163. Defendant' council read Liegh Nisi Prices 199, 550 Morgan. Brink's council stated their appeal was contrary to their council. After the court had decided that the Mayor had jurisdiction, but this court had not, dismissed. Mayor stated that a legal bond was not presented till after the 20 days had expired.

After adjournment, while conversing with Dr. Brink and Esqu[ire] Marr, Joseph said he had been called to thousands of cases in sickness and he had never failed of administering comfort. Where the patient had thrown themself unreservedly on him [he had never done harm] and the reason was he never prescribed any[thing] that would injure the patient [even] if it did him no good.

I have lost a father, brother, {page 157} and child because in my anxiety I have depended more on the jud[g]ment of the other men than my own, while I have [myself] raised up others who were lower than they were. I will here remark (by the

369

bye I will say that man who stands there (pointing to Levi Richards) is the best physician I have ever been acquainted with and I say it honestly) people will seldom die with disease provided we know it seasonably and treat it mildly, patiently, and perserveringly and do not use harsh means.

It is like the Irishman digging down the mountain, he does not put his shoulder to it to push it over but puts it in his wheel barrow and carries it away day after day and day after day {page 158} and perseveres and the whole mountain is removed. So we should persevere in the case of simple remedies (and not push against the constitution of the patient) [and continue] day after day and the disease will be removed and the patient saved. It is better to save the life of a man than to raise one from the dead.

1 P.M. to dinner returned to the office soon after and had conversation with 3 gentlemen introduced by Geo[rge] A. Smith.

3 P.M. In the President's office [with] B[righam] Young, W[illia]m Smith, P[arley] P. Pratt, O[rson] Pratt, W[ilford] Woodruff, J[ohn] Taylor, Geo[rge] A. Smith, [and] W[illard] Richards.

Joseph said to the Twelve [Apostles] "go in the name of the Lord God and tell {page 159} Woodworth to put the hands onto the Nauvoo House and begin the work and be patient till means can be provided. Call on the inhabitants of Nauvoo and get them to bring in their means, then go to Laharpe and serve them the same.

"Thus commence your career and never stand still till the Master appear[s], for it is necessary the house should be done. Out of the stock that is handed me, you shall have as you have need for the laborer is worthy of his hire.

"I hereby command the hands to go to work on the house trusting in the Lord. Tell Woodworth to put them on and he shall be backed up with it. You must get cash, {page 160} property, lands, horses, cattle, flour, corn, wheat, &c. The grain can be ground at this mill. If you can get hands onto the house, it will give such an impetus to the work. It will never stop till it is completed.

"Let the Twelve [Apostles] keep together. You will do more good to keep together, not travel together, but meet in conference alternately from place to place and associate together and not be found more than 200 miles apart. Thus travel from Maine [to] here till they make a perfect highway for the Saints from here to Maine.

"It is better for you to be together for it is difficult for a man to have strength of lungs and health, to be instant in season and out of season, under all circumstances and you {page 161} can assist each other and when you go and spend a day or two in a place you will find it as it is with Miller. They will gather together in great companies. If 12 men cannot build that House they are poor tools."

President Young asked if the Twelve [Apostles] should go to England? Said Joseph, "No, I don't want the Twelve to go to England this year. I have sent them to England and they have broke the ice /and done well/ and now I want to send some of the Elders and try them. I will not designate who. Lorenzo Snow may stay at home till he gets rested.

"The Twelve must travel to save their lives. I feel all the veins and stratus [strata] necessary for {page 162} the Twelve to move in [are provided] to save their lives.

"You can never make any thing out of Benjamin Winchester if you take him out of the Channel he wants to be in.

"Send Samuel James to England, thus saith the Lord, also Reuben Hedlock. He's a heavenly Messenger wherever he goes. Need not be in a hurry, send these two and when you think of some one else send them.

"[Concerning] John Taylor, I believe you can do more good in the editorial department than preaching. He can write for thousands to read while he can preach to but few. We have no one else we can trust the paper with and hardly with you. You suffer the paper to come out with so many mistakes. {page 163} Parley [Pratt] may stay at home and build his house.

"Bro[ther] Geo[rge] A. Smith. I don't know how I can help him to a living, but to go put on a long face and make them dol[e] over to him. If he will go his lungs will hold out. The Lord will give him a good pair of lungs yet.

"[Wilford] Woodruff can be spared from the printing office. If you both stay you will die. Orson Pratt I want him to go."

Bro[ther] Brigham asked if he should go? "Yes, go! I want

John E. Page to be called away from Pittsburgh. Send a good Elder to take his place. Orson Hyde can go and travel.

"You will all go to Boston. I want Elder Richards to continue in the history {page 164} at present. Perhap[s] he will have to travel some to save his life. The History is going out by little and little in the papers and cutting its way. So that when it is completed it will not raise a persecution against us.

"When Lyman Wight comes home I intend to send him right back [out] again. W[illia]m Smith is going east with his sick wife.

"I want you to cast up a highway for the saints from here to Maine. [Heber C.] Kimball will travel. Don't be scared about the Temple. Don't say any thing against it, but make all men know your mission is to build the Nauvoo House. {page 165}

"It is not necessary that Joshua Grant should be ordained a High Priest. He is to[o] young. He is one of Zebedee Coltrin's children and has got into Zebedee's spirit and Jedediah also, and they clip 1/2 their words and I intend to heal them of it. If a High Priest comes along and goes to snub him, let him knock his teeth down his throat &c. &c.

"You shall make a monstrous wake as you go. Clayton, tell the temple committee to put hands on that house (Beyond corner from the brick store) to finish it right off. The Lord hath need of other houses as well as a temple.

"If I can sell $10,000 of property this spring. I will meet you at any conference in {page 166} Maine, or any conference where you are and stay as long as it is wisdom. Take [*blank*] Zundell and [*blank*] Messer and tell them never to drink a drop of ale or wine /or any spirit/ only that which flows right out from the presence of God. Send them to Germany and when you meet with an Arab send him to Arabia, when you find an Italian send him to Italy and a French man to France, or an Indian that is suitable, send him among the Indians and this and that man send them to the different places where they belong. Send som[e]body to Central America to Spanish {page 167} America and don't let a single corner of the earth go without a mission.

"Write to Oliver Cowdery and ask him if [he] has not eat[en] husks long enough. If he is not most ready to return and go up to Jerusalem, Orson Hyde hath need of him." (A letter was written and signed by the members of the Quorum present)

Joseph went home about 4 1/2 P.M. Voted that W[illard] Richards procure a good book for the records of the Twelve [Apostles].

Voted that O[rson] Hyde and W[illard] Richards take charge of the book and bring up the records. Ad[journed] [until] Monday next 1 P.M. {page 168}

[*page left blank*] {page 169}

Thursday, April 20th 1843 Out on the prairie with [Willam] Clayton. P.M. Settled with Manhard. Listened to the proof of the Elders conference. [*rest of page blank*] {page 170}

Friday, April [21st] Officer drill. [*rest of page blank*] {page 171}

[*page left blank*] {page 172}

Saturday, April 22nd The cohorts of the Legion were in exercise this day. L[i]eut[enant] Gen[eral] J[oseph] Smith's staff came out by his invitation and spent the day in riding, exercising, or organizing and in Council or court martial to ascertain to what staff the Robert D. Foster Surgeon Gen[eral], Hugh McFall Adjutant Gen[eral], Daniel H. Wells Commissary Gen[eral] and Leonard Soby Quarter Master General belonged. [*rest of page blank*] {page 173}

[*page left blank*] {page 174}

Sunday, April 23rd 1843 9 to 10 A.M. At home with Elder Hyde. Heard read Truthiana, No. 6 /objected to its being printed. It was too strong meat/ and /heard read/ minutes of special conference which were not explicit enough and said he would dictate them over again.

11 o'clock meeting at temple stand. [Present:] B[righam] Young, Parley and O[rson] Pratt, O[rson] Hyde, Geo[rge] A. Smith, W[illard] Richards. O[rson] Hyde prayed. B[righam] Young preached 24 past 11. Text [was] Salvation. Twelve [Apostles] commenced their mission to build the Nauvoo House /for the/ salvation of Church. It was necessary this public buildings should be erected &c.

P.M. P[arley] P. Pratt addressed the assembly concerning the city as it was 3 years ago and as it is, his disappointment at finding greater {page 175} improvements than he anticipated, more brick houses &c. Elder Haws spoke concerning the pine country and called for 25 hands to go up thither &c., and also the N[auvoo] House. Elder Hyde followed and Elder Brigham Young instructed the laborers on the N[auvoo] House to commence next morning. [that they should] Beg food of their neighbors to commence if necessary and requested families to board hands till means could be procured. [*rest of page blank*] {page 176}

[*page left blank*] {page 177}

April 24th, Monday A.M. Rode out with his children. The Twelve [Apostles] met at President J[oseph] Smith's at 1 P.M. See Minutes. [*rest of page blank*] {page 178}

Tuesday morning, April 25th 9 a.[m.] Called at the office a few moments and heard the report of the procedings of the 12 [Apostles] the day previous. [*several lines left blank*]

3 /o'clock/ and 15 minutes. Rain fell in torrents and wind blew, so dark for 15 minutes could not see to write. Considerable hail fell. Wind blew N[orth] W[est]. Land covered with water. {page 179}

Wednesday, April 26th [*several lines left blank*] Squally and cool, some rain. {page 180}

Thursday, April 27th 1843 Court. Johnathan Ford proved a stolen horse. See Mayor's Docket. [*several lines left blank*] Very pleasant but cool. {page 181}

Friday, April 28th 9 A.M. At his yard in front of the house, conversing with a gentleman and giving directions to the boys about removing the house banking. [*rest of page blank*] {page 182}

Saturday, April 29th 1843 [*entry left blank*] {page 183}

Sunday, April 30th 1843 10 A.M. Trial before the First Presidency. Present Joseph Smith, councillors W[illia]m Law and Sidney Rigdon. ~~Anson Matthews vs~~ Graham Coltrin /vs Anson Matthews/. [At] 12 noon adjourned 1 hour. ~~Bro John Taylor took minutes in the P.M.~~ /Appeal from the High Council/ On complaint:

1st For a Failure [or] in refusing to perform according to contract respecting the Sale of a piece of land by him sold to me.

2d For transferring his property in a way to enable him to bid defiance to the result and force of Law to compel him to evade the aforesaid contract {page 184} thereby wronging me out of my Just claim to the same and also for lying &c. &c. [dated] Nauvoo, March 20th 1843.

Adjourned from 12 to 1 1/2 o'clock P.M. Witnesses for Plaintiff: [Henry G.] Sherwood, N. G. Blodget, Zebedee Coltrin,

[and] Father Coltrin. Witnesses for Defendant: /2 affidavits of Geo[rge] Reads/, Mrs. Matthews, Bro[ther] Browitt, Samuel Thompson, [and] Richard Slater.

Decision of Court is that the charges are not sustained. (See Minutes on file) Adjourned to next Sunday 2 o'clock P.M. {page 185}

B[righam] Young, H[eber] C. Kimball, W[ilford] Woodruff, Geo[rge] A. Smith and Joseph Young were at Augusta, Iowa and held meeting. [*rest of page blank*] {page 186}

Monday, May 1st 1843 Rode out [in the] forenoon and afternoon. [*rest of page blank*] {page 187}

Tuesday, May 2d 1843 Rode out in the forenoon. P.M. "Maid of Iowa" arrived from St. Louis. Sister Emma and Lorin Walker returned. On the Bank of the river waiting their arrival 3 o'clock P.M. W[illiam] W. Phelps returned from Louisville. [*rest of page blank*] {page 188}

Wednesday, May 3d 1843 Called at the office. Drank a glass of wine with Sister Richards of her mother's make in England. Reviewed the conference minutes of the 1st half day [at] 10 o'clock. 2 P.M. held court. City vs A. Gay on complaint of William Law for unbecoming language and refusing to leave store when Law told him to leave. Fined $5 and costs.

[Joseph] directed a letter to be written to Gen[eral] James Adams of Springfield to have him meet the Maid of {page 189} Iowa on her return from St. Louis and arrange with the propri-[e]tors to turn her into a Nauvoo Ferry boat which was done same hour and sent out instructions by W[illard] R[ichards].

First No. of "Nauvoo Neighbor" was issued by Taylor and Woodruff in place of the "Wasp" which ceased. [*rest of page blank*] {page 190}

Thursday, May 4th 1843 4 P.M. called at the office and read a letter from [James] Arlington Bennet /shewing that he was sick and could not be at inspection of the Legion as had been expected/. After sup[p]er called again and left a letter from Woods and gave instructions about a deed from Geo[rge] W. Robi[n]son to Carlos Granger. 7 o'clock called at Elder Rigdon's and got the deed. Returned home and read it. [*rest of page blank*] {page 191}

Friday, May 5[th] 1843 [*entry left blank*] {page 192}

Saturday, May 6[th] 1843 Morning had an interview with a lecturer on Mesmerism [and] phrenology. [Joseph] objected to his performing in the city though[t] we had been imposed upon enough by such kind of things. Interview with a Methodist Minister about his God of no body or of parts.

9 1/2 [A.M.] mounted with staff, Band and about 12 ladies, led by Emma and proceeded to the General Parade of the Legion east of My farm on the Prairie and had a good day of it except very high wind. Marched the Legion down Main St[reet] and disbanded about 2 o'clock P.M. after a short speech on the {page 193} Prairie.

There were 2 United States officers Present and General Swazey from Iowa. In my remark[s] told the Legion when we have petitioned those in power for assistance they have always told us they had no power to help us. "Damn such powers! When they give me power to protect the innocent /I will never say I can do nothing/. I will ex[er]cise that power /for their good/. So help me God."

7 1/2 to 11 1/2 eve in the court room over the store. Attend on a Mr. Vicker's performance of wire dancing, Legerdemain Magic, &c. {page 194}

[*page left blank*] {page 195}

Sunday, May 7th 1843 Forenoon visited by several gentlemen concerning the plates which were dug out [of] a mound near Qunig [Kinderhook, Pike County, Illinois]. Sent by W[illia]m Smith to the office for Hebrew Bible and Lexicon. Mr. Vickers the wire dancer called.

A.M. Court of [the] 1st Presidency met and adjourned one week. 2 P.M. President not well, councillors acted. Evening preaching by Elder Hyde, text Luke 21st Chapter. {page 196}

Monday, May 8th Called at the office 7 A.M. with a supersedas to stay Suit Thompson vs Dixon. [*rest of page blank*] {page 197}

Tuesday, May 9th 1843 Went with Emma and the whole family, Sidney Rigdon, J[ohn] Taylor, P[arley] P. Pratt, W[ilford] Woodruff, and a large co[mpany] on the "Maid of Iowa." Started 10 minutes before 8 o'clock /from Nauvoo Dock with salute of cannon/ to go up Skunk River. [There were] more than 100 in this party. Dined on board. Called at Ft. Madison, Burlington, and Shokokon. Had a very pleas[an]t day and time. Returned [to Nauvoo] about 8 o'clock. [*rest of page blank*] {page 198}

Wednesday, May 10th 1833 [1843] 11 [A.M.] Court,

Alford vs Gurney. [Joseph] came in office and gave instructions to Richards never to let the court room be occupied till $2.00 is received in advance. About this time blossoms of the apples &c. began to shew. Little Nauvoo Boat started for the pinery expecting to receive provisions at Burlington. {page 199}

Thursday, ~~April~~ /May/ 11th 6 A.M. Baptized [*blank*] Snow, Louisa Beman, Sarah Alley, &c. Came out to see the new carriage made by Mo/o/re. [It's] ready for travelling (Emma went to Quincy in [the] new carriage) on the Prairiee.

10 A.M. [The] Twelve [Apostles] held a council in the President's office to send R[uben] Hedlock to England &c. (See Minutes) [*rest of page blank*] {page 200}

Friday, May 12th 1843 Purchased 1/2 of the Steamer "Maid of Iowa" of Moffatt and Capt[ain] Jones. Commenced running said boat between Nauvoo and Montrose as a ferry boat. Sunrise, Bishop George Miller arrived with a raft of 50,000 ft. of pine lumber from the north or pinery. Snow was about 2 1/2 feet deep in the winter. [*rest of page blank*] {page 201}

Saturday, May 13th Joseph [Smith], [Wilford] Woodruff, and Geo[rge] A. Smith went to Lima /to Yelmore/. Brigham [Young] to Laharpe, Heber C. [Kimball] /and O[rson] Pratt/ to Ramus to hold conferences concerning [the] Nauvoo House on the Morrow. Dr. Samuel Bennet[t]'s wife's mother died very suddenly. [*rest of page blank*] {page 202}

Sunday, May 14th 1843 [*blank*] [Edward Brazier] was drowned in the Mississippi River. The wind blew terribly from S[outh] W[est] all day. Almon Babbit preached all the P.M. and prevented [Heber C.] Kimball and O[rson] Pratt from executing their mission. [*rest of page blank*] {page 203}

Monday, May 15th Joseph and the brethren and Emma returned towards night. [*rest of page blank*] {page 204}

Tuesday, May 16th 1843 To Carthage. The Twelve [Apostles] met at the office to see Mr. Brown but he did not appear and the Twelve voted that John E. Page be requested to repair immediately to Cincinati and preach till they arrived. [*rest of page blank*] {page 205}

~~Wednesday, May 17th~~ [*entry left blank*] {page 206}

Wednesday, May 17th Wrote Bro[ther] Page in behalf of the Quorum [of the Twelve Apostles]. [*rest of page blank*] {page 207}

Thursday, May 18th 1843 [Joseph] returned home in the P.M. Mr. Jackson, [a] Catholic Priest was at his house and called at the office with, for [James] Arlington Bennet's letter [at] 6 P.M. [*rest of page blank*] {page 208}

Friday, May 19th 1843 Told Bro[ther] Phelps a dream that the history must go ahead before any thing. 5 P.M. gave a warrant against Samuel Fuller for running a boat on the Ferry. [*rest of page blank*] {page 209}

Saturday, May 20th 10 A.M. called at court room on case of Samuel Fuller. Court adjourned. In the office heard Bro[ther] Phelps read a deffinition of the Word Mormon — More-Good — corrected and sent to press. [*rest of page blank*] {page 210}

Sunday, May 21st 1843 10 1/2 [A.M.] Joseph arrived and after pressing his way through the crowd and getting on the stand said there were some people who thought it a terrible thing that any body should exercise a little power. [He] said he thought it a pity that any body should give occasion to have power exercised.

[Joseph] requested the people to get out of their alleys and if they did not keep them clear he might some time run up and down and might hit some of them and called on Bro[ther] Morey to constable to keep the alleys clear. {page 211} After singing Joseph read 1st chap[ter] 2d Epistle of Peter. W[illia]m Law prayed. Singing again.

When I shall have the opportunity of speaking in a house I know not. I find my lungs failing. It has always been my fortune almost to speak in the open air to large assemblies.

I have not an idea there has been a great many very good men since Adam. There was one good man, Jesus. /Many think a prophet must be a great deal better than any body else/ Suppose I would condescend. Yes, I will /call it/ condescend to be a great deal better than any of you, I would be raised up to the highest heaven, and who should I have to accompany me. {page 212} I love that man better who swears a stream as long as my arm and [is attentive to] administering to the poor and dividing his substance, than the long smoothed faced hypocrites.

I don't want you to think I am very righteous, for I am not very righteous. God judgeth men according to the light he gives them. We have a more sure word of prophecy, where unto you [would] do well to take heed, as unto a light that shineth in a dark place.

We were eyewitnesses of his majesty and heard the voice of his excellent glory, and what could be more {page 213} sure? Transfigured on the mount &c. and what could be more sure? Divines have been quarreling for ages about the meaning of this.

[I am like a] Rough stone rol[l]ing down [a] hill. [*several lines left blank*]

Three grand secrets lying in this chapter [2 Peter 1] which no man can dig out which unlocks the whole chapter. What is written are only hints of things which existed in the prophet's mind which are not written concerning eternal glory.

I am going to take up this subject by virtue of the knowledge of God in me which I have received from heaven. {page 214}

The opinions of men, so far as I am concerned, are to me as the crackling of the thorns under the pot, or the whistling of the wind.

Columbus and the eggs. Ladder and rainbow. Like precious faith with us. Add to your faith, virtue, &c. Another point after having all these qualifications he lays this inju[nc]tion, but rather make your calling and election sure. After adding all this virtue, knowledge, and make your calling sure. What is the secret? The starting point? According as his divine power which [he] hath given unto all things that pertain to life and Godliness. {page 215}

How did he obtain all things? Through the knowledge of him who hath called him. There could not any[thing] be given pertaining to life and Godliness without knowledge.

Wo, wo, wo to Christendom, the divine spirits, &c. If this be true, *Salvation* is for a man to be saved from all his enemies. Until a man can triumph over death he is not saved. Knowledge will do this.

Organization of spirits in the Eternal World. Spirits in the Eternal world are like spirits in this world. When those spirits have come into this [world] {page 216} risin and received glorified bodies, they will have an ascendency over spirits who have no bodies, or kept not their first estate like the devil. Devil's punishment, should not have a habitation like the other men. Devil's retaliation [was to] come into this world, bind up men's bodies

379

and occupy [them] himself. Authorities come along and eject him from a stolen habitation.

Design of the Great God in sending us into this world and organizing us to prepare us for the Eternal World. I shall keep [my spirit] in my own bosom. We have no claim in our eternal comfort in relation to Eternal things {page 217} unless our actions and contracts and all things tend to this end.

After all this make your calling and election sure. If this injuncti[o]n would lay largely on those to whom it was spoken. [Then] How much more there [is in this] to them of the 19[th] century.

1[st] Key—Knowledge in the power of Salvation.

2[nd] Key—Make his calling and Election sure.

3[rd] It is one thing to be on the mount and hear the excellent voice &c., &c. and another /to hear the/ voice declare to you, "You have a part and lot in the kingdom." {page 218}

[*several lines left blank*] Judge Adams arrived in Town. {page 219}

May 22nd, Monday Called at the office 9 A.M. Delivered 3 letters one from [Philadelphia] Concerning Benjamin Winchester [which I discussed] with Clayton. This morning received a large hickory walking stick, silver head with the Motto "BEWARE" from [*blank*]. [*rest page left blank*] {page 220}

Tuesday, May 23d 1843 At home in conversation with Judge Adams and others. Rode out to see the sick at 8 A.M. The Twelve [Apostles] met at Pres[iden]t J[oseph] Smith's office [at] 2 P.M. and ordained 4 Missionaries to the Sandwich Islands and set apart 2 to England. See minutes of Twelve [Apostles]. [*rest of page left blank*] {page 221}

Wednesday, May 24th 1843 Elder Addison Pratt, who was yesterday set apart for a mission to the Sandwich Islands presented the tooth of a whale, coral, Bones of an Albatros wing and skin of a foot, Jaw Bone of a porpoise, [and] tooth of a south sea seal as a beginning for a Museum in Nauvoo.

11 A.M. Court, Ferry vs Sam[ue]l Fuller. Decision Nonsuit. No notice having been given defendant. {page 222}

Thursday, May 25[th] 1843 [*entry left blank*] {page 223}

Friday, May 26th 1843 5 P.M. L. and Hiram and Judge Adams and Bishop Whitney, B[righam] Young, H[eber] C. Kimball, W[illard] Richards, and W[illia]m Law in council in upper room receiving instructions on the priesthood, the new and everlasting covenant [of celestial marriage], &c. &c. Adjourned to Sunday 5 P.M. [*rest of page left blank*] {page 224}

Saturday, May 27th 1843 2 P.M. the Twelve [Apostles] were in Council on B[enjamin] Winchester [case]. [Present:] Joseph, Hyrum, Judge Adams, Bishop Whitney, Sister Emma, Adams, and Jarman and G[eorge] J. Adams and others. Winchester was silenced. See minutes of the Twelve [Apostles]. /Adjourned to Monday 6 P.M./

A tremendous rain storm all day commencing with thunder in the morning. Joseph instructed the Twelve [Apostles] to call up[on] the whole Philadelphia Church while in the council. [*rest of page blank*] {page 225}

Sunday, May 28th Clouds and rain. Cold. 5 P.M. Adjourned council met in the upper room. Attended to ordinances and counselled and prayed that James Adams might be delivered from his enemies, that O[rrin] P. Rockwell [be released from prison in Missouri], and [that] the Twelve [Apostles] be prospered in collecting means to build the Nauvoo House. /Joseph and J. Adams <were married> [were sealed for eternity to their wives]/ ~~Adjourned to 9 o'clock Monday Morning~~ [*rest of page blank*] {page 226}

Monday, May 29th 1843 9 A.M. Met pursuant to adjournment. Hyrum, Brigham, Willard, and Sis[ter] Thompson <were married> and Heber and Newel K. [Whitney] [were] present. Also Joseph and James Adams. Singing and prayer by Elder Brigham Young. Conversation and instruction &c. teaching concerning the things of God. Had a pleasant interview.

Woodworth complaint: People vs James Thompson for assau[l]t [in] /Mayor's/ Court [at] 2 P.M. Fines Thompson $300. Gave instructions to have the account of Lawrence estate made out. Sister from Quincy visiting them. Pleasant but cool after the rain as it has been every rain this season. James Adams gave a deed of some 11 or 12 {page 227} quarter Sections of land on the prairie to trustee in trust.

6 P.M. the Twelve [Apostles] met and sent a mission to

Wisconsin and counselled the Philadelphia Branch to come to Nauvoo. See minutes /of the/ 12. [*rest of the page blank*] {page 228}

Tuesday, 30 May 1843 At the office about nine till noon looking at Nauvoo Stock and doing bisness [business] with the Twelve [Apostles] /and taking their bonds/. Directed a receipt to be written for their bonds by Phelps. [*rest of page blank*] {page 229}

Wednesday, May 31st 1843 Called at the office and court room before breakfast and conferred with Clerk W[illard Richards] on business. ~~Municipal Court~~ /City Council/ at 10. Leave of absence to sell some land to Backenstos. /Instructed Phelps to draft a city charter for the ferry/ Called at the store at 6 P.M. after riding on prairie with Clayton and others. City Council 6 [o'clock] Eve on Ferry Charter. Amaranth landed at Nauvoo with the Saints per Yorkshire under charge of T[homas] B[ullock] and R[ichard] R[ushton] [*rest of page blank*] {page 230}

Thursday, June 1st 1843 In City Council. Passed ordinance on Ferry to [grant exclusive ferrying rights to] Joseph Smith, perpetual succession. Gave a lecture on James Sloan's account [regarding] current [charges] for room candles &c. extra. Signed a conveyance of Eric Rhodes bonds to Joseph Smith to William Clayton 11 Oct[ober]. [*rest of page blank*] {page 231}

Friday, June 2d 1843 Closed the contract for 1/2 the steam boat "Maid of Iowa" in office with [Captain] D[an] Jones. A.M. Phelps drafted Bill of sale. Rode out in the P.M. Ordered W[illia]m Greenhalgh's wife to be sent for from England. [*rest of page blank*] {page 232}

Saturday, June 3d 1843 On "Maid of Iowa" with a pleasure party and the whole family for Quincy. [*rest of page blank*] {page 233}

Sunday, June 4th Returned from Quincy about 9 A.M. having tarried at Keokuk over night on account of wind &c. 10 A.M. in conversation with Priest D[e]Wolf of the Episcopal order. [*rest of page blank*] {page 234}

Monday, June 5th 1843 12 noon laid down to rest. [*rest of page blank*] {page 235}

Tuesday, June 6th 1843 [*entry left blank*] {page 236}

Wednesday, June 7th Arrived from Tennessee, John Workman and co[mpany] including 30 emigrants, all his own family except one widow. [*rest of page blank*] {page 237}

Thursday, June 8th 1843 Elias Higbee born Oct[ober] 23rd 1795, Died June 8th 1843, aged 48 years or 47 /yr/ 7 /mo/ 17 /days/ [of] Cholera morbus, inflammation, and mortification. [He was] one of the Temple committee.

Called at office just at night. Emma sick. P.M. Rode out on horseback. Called at garden where W[illard] Richards was at work. Asked who gave him leave to occupy that lot? Ans[wer], Your honer [honor]. [Joseph said,] "You are perfectly welcome to it so far as I am concerned." {page 238}

Friday, June 9th 1843 Rode out to look at lots in the city. P.M. mostly with Emma who was sick. Br[other] Lewis wanted to purchase. [*rest of page blank*] {page 239}

Saturday, June 10th 1843 At home. Bro[ther] Livingston and Goodrich from Petersboro, N[ew] H[ampshire] [arrived] in [the] city. [*rest of page blank*] {page 240}

Sunday, June 11th 1843 10 A.M. at the Temple stand. Hymn by the Quire. Read 23 Matthew. P[arley] P. Pratt Prayed. Singing.

Matt[hew] 23:37 [This] Subject [was just] presented [to] me since I came in this house. I [am] a rough stone. The sound of the hammer and chisel was never heard on me nor never will be. I desire the learning and wisdom of heaven alone. Have not the least idea but if Christ should come and preach such rough things as he preached to the Jews, but this Generation would reject him for being so rough. I never can find much to say in expounding a text. {page 241}

Never is half so much fuss to unlock a door if you have a key or [as] when you have not or have to cut it out with a jack knife.

O Jerusalem &c. Whence are [you] in the curse of Almighty God that was to be poured out upon the heads of the Jews? That they would not be gathered because they would not let Christ gather them. It was the design in the Councils of heaven before the world was that the principle and law of that Priesthood was predic[a]ted upon the gathering of the people in every age of the world.

Jesus did every thing possible to gather the people and they would not be gathered {page 242} and he poured out curses upon them. Ordinances were instituted in heaven before the foundation of the world in the priesthood for the salvation of men, not

383

[to] be altered, not to be changed. All must be saved upon the same principle.

That is only your opinion Sir, say Sectarians, [and I say] when a man will go to hell it is more than my meat and drink to help them to do as they want to. Where there is no change of priesthood there is no change of ordinances says ~~Jacob~~ /Paul/. If God has not changed the ordinances and priesthood, howl ye {page 243} sectarians. If he has, where has he revealed it? Have ye turned revelators? Then why deny it?

Men have thought many things insoluable in the last days, [for instance,] that he should raise the dead. Things have been hid from before the foundation of the [world] to be revealed to babes in the last days. There are a great many wise men and women to[o] in our midst. To[o] wise to be taught. They must die in their ignorance and in the resurrection they [will] find their mistake.

Many seal up the door of heaven by saying so, for God may reveal and I {page 244} will believe. Heirs of God &c. upon the same laws, ordinances, &c. of Jesus Christ. He who will not love it all will come short of that glory if not of the whole.

Ordinance of the baptism. God decreed before the foundation of the world that this baptism should be performed in a house prepared for the purpose.

Spirits of prison. The Holy Ghost reveals it. Spirits in the world of Spirits which Jesus went to preach to. God ordained that he who would save his dead should do it by getting together {page 245} as with the Jews. It always has been when a man was sent of God with the Priesthood and he began to preach the fulness of the gospel that [he] was thrust out by his friends. They are ready to butcher him if he teach[es] things which they had imagined to be wrong. Jesus was crucified upon this principle.

I will turn linguist. Many things in the Bible which do not, as they now stand, accord with the revelation of the Holy Ghost to me. Ponder "This day thou sha[l]t be with me in paradise." Paradise, [a] Modern word, don't answer to the original word used by Jesus. {page 246} Find the origin of Paradise. Find a needle in a hay mow. Here is a chance for a battle ye learned men. Said Jesus, for there is not time to investigat[e] this matter. For this day you will be with me in the world of Spi[ri]ts. Then I will teach you all about it. Peter says he went and preached to the world of Spirits so that they would receive it [and] could have it answered by proxey by those who live on the earth &c.

"Gathered you for baptism for the dead washing, anointing, &c." said Jesus to [the] Jews. At one time God obtained a house where Peter was[hed] and ano[inte]d &c. on the day of {page 247} pentecost.

Criticise a little further. Hell, [a] modern term, burning lake of fire and Brimstone. I would make you think I was climbing a ladder when I was climbing a rainbow. Who ever revealed it? God never did. Hades, I will hunt after Hades as Pat did for woodchuck. Sheol, who are you? God reveals, means a world of spirits. I don't think so says one. Go to my house I will take my lexicon &c. A world of departed spirits, [where] disembodied spirits all go, good, bad, and indiferent. Misery in a world of spirits is to know they came short of the glory others enjoy. They are their own accusers. {page 248}

One universal heaven and hell. Sup[p]ose honorable and virtuous and whoremonger all hudled together. Judged according to deeds done in the body. Shame, shame. Thus we can [have] mint and annice and cummin and long prayers, but touch not the law as Peter tells us.

Paul says [he was] caught up to 3d heaven and [if there are not three heavens] what [reason does the Bible have to] tell that Lie for Paul. Sun, Moon, and Stars. Many mansions. All one say Sectarians. They build hay, wood, and stubble, build on the old revelations without the spirit of revelation or Priesthood. If I had time I would dig into {page 249} Hell, Hades, Sheol, and tell what exists.

Heaven of Heavens could not contain him. He took the liberty to go into other heavens. I thought [the] Father, Son, and H[oly] Ghost [were] all stuck into one person. I pray for them, Father that we may be one. All stuffed into one God, a big God.

Peter [and] Stephen saw the Son of Man. [They] Saw the Son of Man standing on the right hand of God. 3 personages in heaven who hold the keys. One to preside over all.

If any man attempt[s] to refute what I am about to say after I have made {page 250} it plain, let him be accursed. As the Father hath power in himself so hath the sun [Son] power in himself to lay down his life. The Son doeth what he hath seen the Father do &c. Take his body and stuff it into the Father.

385

Gods have an ascendency over the angels. Angels remain angels. Some are resurrected to become Gods by such revelations as God gives in the most holy place, in his temple. Let them who are owing tithing pay it up and bring stone. What did Judge Higby [say? . . .] If those who {page 251} are owing would bring stone we could get the walls to the roof this fall or every as to let it down.

Closed about 12 [o'clock]. Bro[ther] Cutler said they could go but little further till they had the arch stone of the windows and they wanted immediately help on almost everything. [He] spoke about 15 [minutes].

Joseph gave notice the [that] Mr. DeWolf would preach this P.M. at his /own/ request. Singing. [*rest of page blank*] {page 252}

2 1/2 P.M. /After singing/, Joseph introduced Elder DeWolf [an] Elder of the Episcopal Church, requesting the most profound attention of the congregation. The day was pleasant and the walls of the building were nearly full. Elder DeWolf read the 6th [chapter] of Hebrews and kneeled and prayed, dressed in the black gown, the common clerical robe of the English Church. Choir sung.

[Elder DeWolf:] Heb[rews] 6:1, 2 The apostle speaks of the priesthood before the introduction of [the principles of the doctrine of Christ, saying that] their views [should] not [be] l[a]ying again the foundation of Repe[n]t[ance] &c from Dead work[s], works of Moses' law. Faith next. Next Baptism. You understand this doctrine. Plural number {page 253} [the doctrine of baptisms.] Baptism of water representation of that baptism which was to come. Holy Ghost raised from graves of ignorance. Water is significant figure. Fire of God's love, laying on of hand indication, sign, mark of the reception of the Holy Ghost. I perceive the doctrine of laying on of hand is perfectly understood here. Resurrection, Judgement day, resurrection previous /to/ and consummation of the earth.

I may never meet you all again this side of the eternal world, but I will appoint a meeting i.e., when the Lord Jesus shall descend with his angels to call the dead from their graves {page 254} and sit in Judgment.

Joseph gave [an] appointment for Elder Adams to lecture

on the Book of Mormon at 5 1/2 P.M. [*rest of page blank*] {page 255}

Monday, June 12th 1843 At the office in the A.M. P.M. called at the office for a warrant for Catherine Mulliner vs John Edger. Did not obtain it. <[Joseph Smith] married to Rhoda Richards and Willard Richards married to Susan[nah Lee] Liptrot>

That is about 40 Saints arrived from Peterboro, New Hampshire, among whom was Father Coles who had been absent on a mission. [*rest of page blank*] {page 256}

Tuesday, June 13th 1843 Joseph, Emma, and the children started north to see her sister. [*rest of page blank*] {page 257}

Wednesday, June 14th [*entry left blank*] {page 258}

Thursday, June 15th [*entry left blank*] {page 259}

Friday, June 16th 10 P.M. [Judge] J[ames] Adams wrote from Springfield that Governor Ford told him that he was obliged to issue a writ for Joseph and that it would start tomorrow. This Adams sent by express. [*rest of page blank*] {page 260}

Saturday, June 17[th] Heard that Lyman Wight had arrived. The people against [several individuals] on complaint of Joseph for riot tried before Esqu[ire] Robinson. No cause of action. [*rest of page blank*] {page 261}

Sunday, June 18[th] Jud[g]e Adams' message arrived early in the evening and a few minutes past ten. Clayton and Markham started to inform Joseph. Water had been rising in the river 3 or 4 days and is now 3 or 4 inches above high water mark. [*rest of page blank*] {page 262}

Monday, June 19th The laborers held a meeting in the grove to investigate the price and principle of labor. [*rest of page blank*] {page 263}

Tuesday, June 20th [*entry left blank*]. {Page 264}

Wednesday, June 21st 1843 [*entry left blank*] {page 265}

Thursday, June 22nd Another meeting concerning wages &c. [*rest of page blank*] {page 266}

Friday, June 23rd Judge Adams arrived from Springfield. This morning 8 o'clock a bee to remove the timbers from the Temple to the grove [to construct a bowery]. Joseph was taken by [Constable Harmon] Wilson [of Carthage, Illinois,] and [Sheriff Joseph] Reynolds [of Jackson County, Missouri], 12 miles to Dixon's Ferry then relieved by the citizens on Habeus Corpus and they [Joseph Smith, Wilson, and Reynolds] secured on 4 writs. P.M. It was reported in the city that Joseph was arrested. [*rest of page blank*] {page 267}

Saturday, June 24th Celebration of St. Johns [Day] in Nauvoo Laying the corner stone of the Masonic Temple on Main St[reet]. [*rest of page blank*] {page 268}

Sunday, June 25th 1843 Water fell in the Mississippi more than a foot since last Sabbath noon. The past week has been warm and pleasant. No rain. 6 or 8 Indians passed this morning. 2 P.M. Clayton arrived and Wilson Law started at 8 A.M. with 50 or 60 horsemen to find Joseph. Capt[ain] Jones with Maid of Iowa started with about 50 to go up Illinois. [*rest of page blank*] {page 269}

Monday, June 26th It is reported there are State writs in the city for Lyman Wight, P[arley] P. Pratt, and Allexander McRae. City watch this night. This morning 2 men came out of Davisis and went to upper landing. Met a boat with one man guarded by Lyman's son so reported. County assessor returned about nine. [*rest of page blank*] {page 270}

Tuesday, June 27th Reported to be many strangers in the city. Watch doubled in the city this night. Emma and family returned near night. Burned of[f] 1 wheel to their carriage coming home. [*rest of page blank*] {page 271}

Wednesday, June 28th Some anxiety about so many strangers and suspicious characters in this city. New ordinance proposed by some Aldermen. [*rest of page blank*] {page 272}

Thursday, June 29th 1843 Dr. Foster arrived in the city towards night and stated that Joseph would be in the next day and wanted the band to meet him at Hyrum's farm. [*rest of page blank*] {page 273}

Friday, June 30th 11 and 25 minutes [A.M.], Joseph in co[mpany] with Mr. Montgomery a friend from Lee Co[unty] in a buggy followed by stage and carriages containing [Sherriff] Reynolds [and] Wilson, 3 Lawyers, [Cyrus] Walker, [Shepherd G.] Patrick, and [Edward] Southwick, [with] Lucian [P. Sanger] the stage proprietor and others with a row of horses on each side about 40 in all.

A part of the train who went out had not found Joseph. The band and an immence carnival of people met the cavalcade at Hyrum's farm and escorted the Gene[ra]l to his [-] arriving at his house about 1 o'clock.

Reynolds and Wilson set at the head of the table. Municipal Court granted writ of Habeas Corpus and gave liberty till 8 [o'clock] next morning. [At] 5 P.M. [Joseph] gave an address at the Tempel [Temple] stand grove and turn[ed] the key according to the Priesthood that the Saints might defend themselves against the Missourians, mob laws, [and] Jos[eph] H. Reynolds the Missourian Kidnapper with Jerk of [a] sheriff. While Joseph was lecturing [Reynolds] went with Wilson to Carthage in co[mpany] with Esqu[ire] Davis. {page 274}

[*page left blank*] {page 275}

June 30th 1/4 [to] 6 [P.M.] Joseph commenced a lecture on the stand to many thousands by How do you do? I meet you with a heart full of gratitude to Almighty God. I am well, healthy, [and] strong as a giant. While I was on the road I pulled up the strongest man. Then they got 2 men and they could not pull me up. I have pulled mentally till I have pulled Missouri here.

There has been a great excitement in the country. I have been cool and dispassionate through all. Thank God I am now a prisoner in the hands of the Municipal {page 276} Court and not of a Missourian.

It was not as much my object to tell of my afflictions &c. or [as] to speak of the Habeas Corpus so that the minds of all may be corrected and know and publish that we have all power. There is a secret. The city has all power that the court's have given by the same authority — the Legislature.

I want you to hear O Israel this day, if this power is not sufficient we will claim higher power [from] the constitution of the State and the United [States]. I have dragged him [the sheriff] here by our {page 277} hand and will do it again but I swear I will never deal so mildly again.

Be cool, Be deliberate, be wise, and when you pull do it with sweepstakes. My lot has always been cast among the warmest kind of people.

The time has come when the veil is torn off from this state and let us mingle with the state of Ill[inois]. I should have been torn /from/ [my captors] with the extreme of life and blood if I had asked. I brought them [here as] prisoners and committed them as prisoners not of chai[n]s but of kindness to her [Nauvoo] from whom I was torn. {page 278}

There is no doubt I shall be discharged by the court. The writs are good for nothing, without form and void. Before I will be dragged again away among my enemies for trial I will spill the last drop of blood in my veins [and] see all my enemies in hell. Shall we bear it any longer? One universal "NO" ran through all th[e] vast assembly like a loud peal of thunder.

I wish the Lawyer who says we have no powers in Nauvoo may be choked {page 279} to death with his own words. Don't employ any Lawyers for their knowledge, for I know more [than] they all.

Go ye into all the world [and] preach the gospel. He that believeth in our chartered rights may come here and be saved and he [that] does not shall remain in ignorance.

One spiritual minded circuit Judge and several fit men.

Esqu[ire Cyrus] Walker [undeclared candidate for U.S. Congress] I have converted to the truth of Habeas Corpus. I got here by Law[ful] writ that [is] just as it should be.

In the midst of all your {page 280} indignation use not the hand of violence for I have pledged my honor. Will you all support my honor? "YES " universal by the audience. I have proof of your attachment.

When oppression rises again I have learned we need [not] suffer as we have. We can call others to our aid. Shall the prophecy of our enemies "We will establish our religion by the sword" be true? No.

If the Missourians oppress us more I this day turn the key by the authority of the Holy Priesthood {page 281} turn the key, unlock the door and motion you not rise up and defend yourselfs [on the first offense].

Always act upon the defence but if your enemies oppress you the 2d and 3d time, let it come and roar like thunder and you shall stand forth clean. Before the tribunal of any citizens of Illinois deny our right[s], let them go to hell and be damned. I give up my chartered right[s] at the sword and bayonets.

[The] Legislature [is] like the boy [who] say[s], "Dad[d]y, Daddy, I have sold my jackknife, got cheated, and want to get it back again." {page 282}

390   What can mobocrats do in the midst of Kirkpatrickites.

No better than a hunter being in a bear's claw. What could we do with them. Dung our garden with them. We don't want any excitement but after we have done all, rise up, break off the hellish yoke like Washington.

[The] day before I was taken I rode through Dixon and I said to my wife, I said, "Good people here." I was their prisoner [the] next day. Harmon T. Wilson said, "By God, we have got the Prophet now." I am prisoner to a higher court than a circuit court.

Defend yourselfs, says a law in {page 283} our Charter. Powers, same charter says Municipal Court, has powers to enact all laws &c. Dangerous power because it will protect the innocent and put down mobocrats. Constitution of U[nited] S[tates] say[s], "Habeas Corpus shall not be denied." Deny me the right of H[abeas] Corpus and I will fight with guns, sword, cannon behind and thunder [afore] till I am used up, like Killkenny Cats. We have more power because we have power to go behind the writ and try the merits of the case. {page 284}

I ask in the name of J[esus] Christ and all that is sacred that I may have your lives and all to carry out the freedom which is chartered to us. Will you all help me? All hands went up. Mr. Walker shall be presented for the Mormon's sake.

When at Dixon [I was] refused an interview with a lawyer. /Turned Markham out [of] doors [and] threatened my life/. [An] old gray headed man reared his ponny, came with Mr. Walker and I had Lawyers &c. enough. /Writ for Harmon Wilson/ [for] damages, assault, and Battery.

/[Had?]/ Habeas Corpus [and] got up to go {page 285} to Ottawa 22 miles[, stopped in] Pawpaw Grove. Thrust out all but Harmon Wilson [and delivered a sermon]. Esqu[ire] Walker sent Mr. Campbell [the local sheriff] to my rescue and [he] came and slept by me.

Morning certain men wanted to see Mr. Smith. They would not let me [until] an old man come to talk. Missourian interupted, [and the old man said,] "Stand off you puke [and let] Mr. Smith [have his say]. We have a [vigilance] committee in Pawpaw Grove. A court from whence there is no appeal."

My liberties began from that hour [when] they lost their pistols. [We've?] come direct to Nauvoo. When they began to suspect we were coming [here] they remonstrated. B[r]o[ther] Grover Came. {page 286}

[*page left blank*] {page 287}

[*page left blank*] {page 288}

Hosanna, Do., Do., to Almighty God who hath delivered us thus far out of the 7th trouble. 6:25 [P.M.]

(Esqu[ire] Walker was introduced [to the congregation, which, Joseph said,] as a body of people, [were] the greatest dupes that ever were or he is not as big a rouge [rogue] as he is supposed to be. 1/4 to 7)

Joseph[:] I told Mr. [Calvin] Warren [an attorney] I would not discuss the subject of religion with you. I understand the gospel and you [he] do [does] not. You [He] understand[s] Law [and] I do not. [*rest of page blank*] {page 289}

If the Legislature have granted Nauvoo the right of Habeas Corpus &c. it is no more than they ought to have done or more than our fathers fought for.

I swear in the name of the Almighty God with uplifted hand the Legislature shall never take away our rights. I'll spill my heart's blood first. [*several lines left blank*]

Evening at home before the Lawyers, "I prophecy in the name of the Lord God that Governor Ford by granting the write [writ] against me has damned himself {page 290} politically and ~~eternally~~. His carcass will stink on the face of the earth, food for the cairion crow and Turkey buzzard." [*rest of page blank*] {page 291}

July 1st 8 A.M. Trial presented. After a patient investigation and the pleas of Walker, Southwick, Patrick, Backman and Joseph, he [Joseph] was discharged and the court adjourned till Monday to make out the [w]riting or close the Records. (See records of court)

Strong wind, thunder, and rain in the P.M. Wind [from] N[orth] W[est]. [*rest of page blank*] {page 292}

Sunday, 2d July Esquire Southwick and Patrick spoke on the stand stating that Joseph had subjected himself to the law in all particulars and treated his per[se]cutors and kidnappers with respect.

Judge Adams come in from Carthage and stated that Wilson and Reynolds were exciting the people to mobocracy and about to send to Gove[nor] Ford for a possy to retake Joseph. [A]

Petition was immediately made out and signed by a great number of citizens. Also a remonstrance against Carthage proceedings signed by 150 and forwarded to Carthage and carried forward by Backenstos. [*rest of page blank*] {page 293}

Monday, 3d July By recommendation of Joseph, a special conference [was called] and selected many elders to go into the different countries and preach the gospel and disabuse the public mind with regard to the arrest or capture.

Hyrum commenced filling out his testimony. Mr. Walker wrote for [him]. [*rest of page blank*] {page 294}

July 4th Independance Elder O[rson] Hyde Lectured at the stand at 10 1/2 A.M., after which Joseph gave a short address concerning his arrest to correct Reports circulated by Reynolds [and] Wilson. A collection was then taken to help build O[rson] Hyde's house. At 12 1/2 [P.M.] meeting adjourned till 2 1/2 P.M.

It had been published that Elder G[eorge] J. Adams would preach in the P.M. but as he had gone to Springfield P[arley] P. Pratt preached on redemption.

During sermon a steam boat arrived from St. Louis with some 3[00] or 400 passengers. A pleasure party who were escorted by the band and some companies of Soldiers and seated near the center of the crowd. A boat had perviously arrived from Quincy and another from Burlington. The passengers on the three boats numbered from 8[00] to 1,000.

After sermon, President J[oseph] Smith gave a brief relation of his capture, detention, treatment, and trial (which will be given in full hereafter). All of which gave great satisfaction apparently to all parties and the visitors as well as Saints appeared highly gratified.

The day was pleasant. [The] sky [was] clear and nothing tendered to disturb the peace except one man in the crowd [who] said he would give $500 for Jo Smith's scalp. It was ordered he should be arrested, but was not to be found.

After Joseph's speach, O[rson] Hyde proposed, on his own responsibility, a collection to assist Gen[eral] Smith {page 293} in bearing the expenses of his persecutions which was taken accordingly and the meeting closed by singing [and] prayer about 7 o'clock.

Hyrum continued his testimony all [during the] meeting. [*rest of page blank*] {page 295}

July 5th 1843, Wednesday Hyrum continued his affidavit till near sunset when Joseph came in /and Mr. Walker read it/. Levie [Levi Richards] wrote Geo[rge] Pitkins' testimony.

Closed special conference at 11 A.M. commencing at 8 [A.M.]. Minutes printed in the [Nauvoo] Neighbor. Judge Adams and Esqu[ire] Southwick returned from Warsaw. [They] found but little excitment. Esq[ui]r[e] [Southwick] wrote a piece for Warsaw paper. [*rest of page blank*] {page 296}

July 6th, Thursday Hyrum finished his affidavit. B[righam] Young wrote his pie[ce]. [At] Walker['s request] Geo[rge] Pitkins rewrote [his account]. [*rest of page blank*] {page 297}

July 7th 1843, Friday /(Joseph at home since his return)/ A man came from the Governor for affidavits concerning the expulsion of the Mormons from M[iss]o[uri]. Geo[rge] Walker, Samuel Gully, [and] Joseph M. Cole copied the testimony given before the court all night in the office. Sloan also copied at home.

Between 4 and 5 [P.M.], B[righam] Young, Geo[rge] A. Smith, and W[ilford] Woodruff passed the office on [their way to] the steamer Rapids for the east.

Joseph and several others made affidavit[s] for the Gov-[ernor] which are filed in the Recorder's office. {page 298}

Saturday, 8th July 1843 Municipal Court set to examine the evidence of Joseph on Habeas Corpus. In the P.M. [heard] Shadrack Roundy /with/ Hyrum Smith, P[arley] P. Pratt, B[righam] Young, Geo[rge] W. Pitkins, and Lyman Wight's affidavits to the Governor &c.

Bishop Miller arrived from the Pinery with 157,000 feet lumber and $70,000 total shingle and loose boards. [*rest of page blank*] {page 299}

Sunday, July 9th 1843 /A.M. Backenstoes and Esqu[ire] Patrick returned from Springfield/ Joseph remarked that all was well between him and the heavens. That he had no enmity against any one and as the prayer of Jesus or his pattern so prayed Joseph, "Father forgive me my tresspasses as I forgive those who trespass against me." For I freely forgive all men. If we would secure and cultivate the love of others we must love others, even our enemies as well as friends.

"Why is it this babler gains so many followers and retains them?" because I possess the principle of love. All I can offer the world [is] a {page 300} good heart and a good hand. Mormons can testify whether I am willing to lay down my life for a Mormon. If it has been demostrated that I have been willing to die for a Mormon, I am bold to declare /before heaven/ that I am just as ready to die for a Presbyterian, a Baptist, or any other denomination. It is a love of liberty which inspires my soul. Civil and religious liberty were diffused into my soul by my grandfathers while they dandled me on their knees and shall I want friends? No!

"Where in do you differ from other[s] in your religion views?" In reality and essence we do not differ so far in our religious views but that we could {page 301} all drink into [from] one principle of love. One [of] the grand fundamental principles of Mormonism is to receive truth. Let it come from where it may.

We believe in the great Eloheim who sits enthroned in yonder heavens. So do the Presbyterians. If as a skillful mechanic in taking a welding heat I use a borax and allum &c. as succeed in welding you all together shall I not have attained a good object.

If I esteem mankind to be in error shall I bear them down? No! I will lift them up and [persuade a man] in his own way [and] if I cannot persuade him my way is better, I will ask no man to believe as I do. {page 302}

"Do you believe in Jesus Christ &c?" So do I. Christians should cultivate the friendship with others and [they] will [eventually] do it.

"Do you believe in the baptism of Infants?" says the Presbyterians. No. "Why"? Because it is no where written in the book, [and] communion is not baptism. Baptism is for remission of sins. Children have no sins. He /Jesus/ blessed them [and said,] "Do what you have seen me do." All [are] made alive in Christ.

[On] Faith and repentance we are agreed. Baptism, yes, by immersion. The Hebrew is the root, to bury immerse? Do you believe this? No, [then] I [say do you] believe in being converted. I believe in this tenaciously.

Holy Ghost by laying on of hands {page 303} Evidence — Peter on days of Pentacost might as well be baptised a bag of sand as a man if not done in view of the getting of the Holy Ghost. Baptism by water is but 1/2 a baptism and is good for nothing with[out] the other, the Holy Ghost. I am free to day. Messenger has returned with offers of peace from the Governor.

Except a man be born again of the water /and of the spirit/ can in no wise enter into the kingdom.

Though we or an angel from heaven preach any other gospel.

This evening Shadrach Roundy started for Springfield to see Gov[ernor] Ford and carry affidavits. {page 304}

Monday, July 10th [*entry left blank*] {page 305}

Tuesday, July 11th [*entry left blank*] {Page 306}

Wednesday, July 12th Received a Revelation in the office in presence of Hyrum and W[illia]m Clayton. [*several lines left blank*] This P.M. Adams and Hollister returned from Springfield. G. L. Wylie called for an interview. {page 307}

Thursday, July 13th Shadrach Roundy returned from Springfield. Reported the Gov[ernor] gone to Rock River and left affidavits to the care of Gen[eral] Adams (/all performed in/ less than 4 days). In conversation with Emma most of the day.

Roundy said it was reported that Gen[eral] Wilson of M[iss]o[uri] had started from the interior of Ill[inois] for Washington City. {page 308}

Friday, July 14th Introduced Mr. McNeal to the President. {page 309}

[*The following list of marriages is written on one of the last leaves of this journal:*]

\⁴Apr[il] [18]42 Marinda Johnson [Hyde] to Joseph Smith

1843

April 27th W[illia]m Clayton and Margaret Moon by J[oseph] S[mith] at H[eber] C. K[imball]'s

May 1st Lucy /W̶o̶o̶d̶w̶o̶r̶t̶h̶/ Walker and Joseph /See Clayton's Journal/

July 20[th] M. P. [Mary Ann Price?] to O[rson] Hyde

[July] 22[nd] W[illiam] Clayton and Ruth Moon

Oct[ober] 20[th] B[enjamin] F. Johnson and w̶i̶f̶e̶ Melissa LaBarron by Hy[rum] Smith

Nov[ember] 11[th] W[ilford] Woodruff and Ph[o]ebe W. Carter

[November] 21[st] Edward Lawrence and Marg[are]t Butterfield by W[illiam] Clayton

⁴ In the handwriting of Thomas Bullock.

1843-44

L ike the two preceding Nauvoo journals, the following document is in
the handwriting of Willard Richards, except where noted, and shares the
same strengths and weaknesses of its companion volumes. The original is
housed in the archives of the Historical Department, Church of Jesus Christ
of Latter-day Saints, Salt Lake City, Utah.

Saturday, July 15th 1843 At home. 6 P.M. with his [Joseph
Smith's] family and about 100 others took a pleasure excursion on
the Maid of Iowa from Nauvoo House Landing to the North part
of the city and back at dusk. (*Theatre in the evening by Mr. Chapman*). A shower this morning wet the ground 1 inch. {page 1}

Sunday, July 16th 1843 Preached all day or A.M. and
P.M. at the stand in the grove, near and west of the Temple concerning a man's foes being they of his own house, such as having
secret enemies in the city. Intermingling with the Saints &c. and
[said he would not prophesy anymore,] proposing Hyrum as a
prophet that he might be (a priest) so the hearers tell the story.
{page 2}

[*page left blank*] {page 3}

Monday, July 17th Mostly at home. Called at the office

once and in the evening was at the theatre in the store chamber, by Chapman and others. 4 days last past in <privacy[?]>says <William Clayton>. [*rest of page blank*] {page 4}

July 18th, Tuesday Making hay on the prairie. [*rest of page blank*] {page 5}

Wednesday, July 19th A gentle shower of rain in the P.M. [*rest of page blank*] {page 6}

Thursday, July 20th This evening borrowed $200 of Yearsly and furnished Bishop Miller $290 for the pinery expedition.

Mr. Divine [the] Fire King called on President. [*rest of page blank*] {page 7}

Friday, July 21st This morning Bishop Miller, Lyman Wight, and a large company including families started on the "Maid of Iowa" for the pinery in Wisconsin. [*rest of page blank*] {page 8}

Saturday, July 22[d] Saw Joseph 4 P.M. in a buggy at the store starting to ride out. [*rest of page blank*] {page 9}

[*page left blank*] {page 10}

Sunday, July 23rd P.M. Law and Prophets were until John and 18 Luke 16 v. Joseph preached introduction. It has gone abroad that I was no longer a prophet. I said it Ironically. I supposed you would all understand. I[t] was not that I would renounce the idea of being a prophet but that I would renounce the idea of proclaiming myself such, and saying that I bear the testimony of Jesus.

No greater love than that a man lay down his life for his friends. I discover 100s and 1000s ready to do it for me. {page 11}

In the midst of business, and find the spirit willing but the flesh is weak subject to like passions with other men. Although I am under the necessity of bearing the infirmities of other men, &c. On the other hand the same characters when they discover a weakness in brother Joseph, blast his character &c. All that law &c. [which has been revealed] through him to the church, he [Joseph] cannot be bourne with a moment.

Men mouth my troubles when I have trouble [but when] they [have problems they] forget it all. {page 12} I believe in a principle of reciprosiprocity. If we live in a devilish world &c.

398   I see no faults in the church. Let me be resurrected with

the Saints, whether to heaven or hell or any other good place—good society. What do we care if the society is good? Don't care what a character is if he's my firend. A friend, a true friend, and I will be a friend to him. Friendship is the grand fundamental principle of Mormonism, to revolution[ize and] civilize the world, [to] pour forth love. Friendship [is] like [the metals bonded in] Bro[ther] Turly['s] Blacksmith {page 13} shop. I do not dwell upon your faults. You shall not upon mine. After you have covered up all the faults among you the prettyest thing is [to] have no faults at all. Meek, quiet, &c. [If] Presbyterians [have] any truth, embrace that. Baptist, Methodist, &c. Get all the good in the world. Come out a pure Mormon.

Last Monday Morning certain men came to me. "Bro[ther] Joseph Hyrum is no prophet. He can't lead the church" You must lead the church. If you resign[, etc.] I felt curious and said here we learn in [the church about] a priesthood after the order of Melchisedeck—Prophet, {page 14} Priest and King, and I will advance from Prophet to Priest and then to King not to the kingdoms of this Earth but of the most High God.

If I should would there be a great many dissappointed in M[iss]o[uri]? Law and prophets &c. Suffereth violence and the violent taketh it by force. Heaven and Earth shall pass away &c. says Christ. He was the rock &c. Gave the law &c. Ex[odus] 30:31 v[erse] and thou shalt annoint A[a]ron &c. Last chap[ter] Ex[odus], 15th [verse] and thou shalt anoint them &c. A tittle of law which must be fulfilled, forever hereditary, fixed on the law of A[a]ron down to Zachariah the father of John. Zachariah had no child. /Had not/ God gave him a son? {page 15} Sent his angel to declare a son name[d] John with the keys. John [was a] King and lawgiver.

The kingdom of Heaven suffereth violence &c. The kingdom of heaven continueth in authority until John. The authority taketh it by absolute power. John having the power, take the kingdom by authority.

How do you know all this knowledge? By the gift of the H[oly] G[host. Jesus] arrested the kingdom from the Jews[, saying] of these stony Gentiles these dogs [he was] to raise up children unto Abraham. {page 16}

John [said] I must be baptized by you. [Jesus said you must baptize me.] Why, to answer my decrees. John refuses. Jesus had no legal administrator before John. No Salvation between the two lids of the Bible without a legal administrator.

Tis contrary to a Governor's oath to send a man to M[iss]o[uri] where he is prescribed in his religious opinions.

Jesus was then the legal administrator and ordained his apostles.

I will resume the subject at some future time. {page 17}

Monday, July 24th Exhibition of Divine, the fire king in the Mayor's court over the store. [*rest of page blank*] {page 18}

Tuesday, July 25th Saw Joseph in the middle room laying on the /low/ bed, gave him two dollars for room rent and $1.45 for benefit of Temple from Divine's exhibition. [*rest of page blank*] {page 19}

Wednesday, July 26th Shower of rain at twelve o'clock noon. [*rest of page blank*] {page 20}

Thursday, 27th Was at the store to pray for Sis[ter] Walker and anoint her finger, a phal[anx] broken. [*rest of page blank*] {page 21}

Friday, 28th [July] 1843 Mr. Sloan delivered the records at the Mayor's office, not [the] 29th as [recorded]. [*rest of page blank*] {page 22}

Saturday, July 29th Was at the office with Mr. [William] Clayton along. Went to Lodge I suppose. [Joseph] gave directions to send copy of certificates of trustee and Granger's power of Attorney to Rubin McBride [in] Kirtland.

(Noon James Sloan City Recorder /and Church Recorder/ brought the desk containing the city and church books and papers to the Mayor's office as he [Sloan] was about to leave for Ireland. 28 delivered) Sent Clayton to Hiram Kimball's to borrow $50. [*rest of page blank*] {page 23}

Sunday, July 30th Joseph sick. Lungs oppressed &c., over heated preaching one week before. J[ohn] Taylor preached A.M. After preaching President Marks called a special Conference to appoint Recorders for the baptism of the dead, Elder Sloan having started for Ireland. Willard Richards was appointed gen[eral] Church Recorder and Joseph M. Cole of the 4th ward and Geo[rge] Walker and Johnathan H. Hale and J. A. W. Andrews recorders for the baptisms of the dead.

P.M. the clerks met to organize and {page 24} prepare for recording baptisms. Joseph called Hyrum Smith, W[illia]m

Law, and W[illard] Richards to lay on hands and pray for him. [*rest of page blank*] {page 25}

Monday, July 31st Wilson Law and E[benezer] Robinson started for Chicago with W[illia]m Marks. Went on the Prairie. Newell Nurse called to get Joel Bullard confined. He is threatening, drinking, and probably delirious at first. [*rest of page blank*] {page 26}

Tuesday, Aug[ust] 1st 1843 Joseph sick. Esqu[ire] Walker gave a stump speech at the stand. [Joseph] Hoge [Walker's opponent in the congressional election] and Hyrum [Smith] called at the office. Hoge acknowledged the power of the Mormon Habeus Corpus.

News arrived from the Gov[ernor] that the writ was returned and killed. (Phelps translating)

The news above referred to was a private communication from Mr. Broman to Joseph by Mr. Backenstos and not [from] the Gov[ernor]. {Page 27}

Wednesday, Aug[ust] 2nd Some better. (Phelps translating) [*rest of page blank*] {Page 28}

Thursday, Aug[ust] 3d 1843 Not so well says Lorin. [*rest of page blank*] {page 29}

Friday, August 4th Health improving. [*rest of page blank*] {Page 30}

Saturday, August 5th [*several lines left blank*] 4 P.M. G[eorge] J. Adams, Hyrum, and W[illia]m Law spoke on the Election of Hoge and Walker. [*rest of page blank*] {page 31}

Sunday, August 6th /Emma started for St. Louis/ Zebedee Coltrin prayed. P[arley] P. Pratt preached on testimony. After sermon Joseph (for he came to the stand soon after Parly commenced) said he would preach his sermon next Sunday. He was not able to day. Would speak of another subject. [Regarding] The elections he was above the kingdoms of the world for he spake no laws [to the church to influence the election].

"I have not come to tell you /to/ vote this way, that way, or the other in relation to National matters. I want it to [go] abroad to the whole world that every man should {page 32} stand on his own merits. The Lord has not given me Revelation concerning politics. I have not asked the Lord for it. I am a third party [and] stand independant and alone. I desire to see all parties protected in their rights. In relation to Mr. Walker, he is a Whig candidate, a high minded man.

"Mr. Walker has not hung on to my coat tail to gain his election as some have said. I am going to give a testimony but not for electioneering purposes. {page 33} Before Mr. Walker come to Nauvoo rumor come up that he might become a candidate for Congress. Says I, he is an old friend [and] I will vote for him. When Mr. Walker come to my house, I voluntarily told him I was going to vote for him. When I dictated to him the laws of Nauvoo, he received them on my testimony. The rascals took Walker[']s and Montgomery['s] security [bond] /when I was arrested/. Walker made Reynolds come to me and beg my pardon for abuse /he gave me/ and /through his men/ took his pistols from the rascals and withdrew all claim to your vote and influence if it will be detrimental to your interest as a people. {page 34}

"Bro[ther] Hiram tells me this morning that he has had a testimony that it will be better for this people to vote for Hoge. I never knew Hiram say he ever had a revelation and it failed. [I] Never told Bro[ther] Law to tell my private feelings. (Let God speak and all men hold their peace) I utterly forbid these political demagog[u]es from using my name hereafter forever.

"It is my settled feeling that if Gov[ernor] Ford erred in granting a writ against me it is of the head and not of the heart, and I authorize all men to say I am a personal friend of Gov[ernor] Ford. {page 35}

"A cap to Parley's Sermon. Every word that proceedeth from the mouth of Jehovah has such an influence over the human mind, the logical mind that it is convincing without /other/ testimony. Faith cometh by hearing.

"If 10,000 men testify to a truth, [men whom] you know, would it add to your faith? No, or will 1,000 testimonies destroy your knowledge of a fact? No. I do not want anyone to tell I am a prophet or attempt to prove my word. I prophecy in the name of God Almighty. They shall bear off the palm." [rest of page blank] {page 36}

Hyrum Smith explained at some length concerning the election. [rest of page blank] {page 37}

Monday, Aug[ust] 7th Election of U[nited] S[tates] representatives and county officers. [several lines left blank]

The Democratic Ticket prevailed in Nauvoo by an over-whelming Majority. [*rest of page blank*] {page 38}

Tuesday, August 8th The court was posting the Election Books in the office, viz, Wells, Hale, Billings, and Phelps, [and] Walker clerks.

At the office 9 A.M. Staid 1/2 hour. [*rest of page blank*] {page 39}

Wednesday, Aug[ust] 9th [*entry left blank*] {page 40}

Thursday, Aug[ust] 10th 1843 [*entry left blank*] {page 41}

Friday, Aug[ust] 11th 1843 Brother James Adams very sick. 12 noon pulseless since morning. Eve[ning] gave instruction to grant licence to A. LaForest for his show on feats of strength tomorrow eve.

Gen[eral] James Adams died about 10 P.M. report says. [*rest of page blank*] {page 42}

Saturday, Aug[ust] 12th Emma returned from St. Louis. Joseph not well. Saw him at home 5 P.M. A. LaForest gave some experiments or exhibited some feats of strength as a public show man in the court room lifting cannon, anvils, men, &c.

Robert D. Foster [was] elected School commissioner and Geo[rge] W. Thatcher [elected] clerk of Co[unty] Commissioners court. Went to Carthage to give bonds and take oath of office. When before the court Harmon T. Wilson, John Wilson, Franklin J. Morrill, one Prentice and 12 or 15 others came in court, armed with hickory clubbs, knives, dirks, and pistols, and told the court they must not approve there bond or swear them into office. If they did blood would be spilt and pledged their word, honors, and reputations to keep them out of office and put down the Mormons. The bonds were accepted and the mob notified a meeting of the old citizens of Hancock County on Saturday next to consider about the Mormons retaining their offices. {Page 43}

Sunday, Aug[ust] 13th 1843 Joseph Pre[ached] in relation [to] the death of Judge [Elias] Higby. 2d Peter 3d C[hapter] 10-11 v[erses]. Text said he was not like other men. His mind was continually occupied with the business of the day, and he had to depend entirely upon the Living God for everything he said on such occasions.

The great thing for us to know is to comprehend what God did institute before the foundation of the world. Who knows it?

It is the constitutional disposition of mankind to set up stakes and set bounds {page 44} to the works and ways of the Almighty.

We are called thus [to] mourn this morning the death of a good man, a great man and a mighty man. It is a solemn idea that man has no hope of seeing a friend after he has lost him, but I will give you a more painful thought. The thought is simple and I never design to communicate no ideas but what are simple, for to this end I am sent. Suppose we have an idea of a resurrection &c. &c. and yet know nothing at all of the gospel and could not comprehend one principle {page 45} of the orders of Heaven, but found yourselves disappointed. Yes, at last find yourselfs disappointed in every hope or anticipation when decisions goes forth from the lips of the almighty at last. Would not this be a greater disappointment. A more painful thought than annihilation.

Had I inspiration, Revelation, and lungs to communicate what my soul has contemplated in times /past/ there is not a soul in this congregation but would go to their homes and shut their mouths in everlasting silence on religion till they had learned something. {page 46}

Why be so certain that you comprehend the things of God when all things with you are so uncertain. You are welcome to all the knowledge and [*several lines left blank*].

I do not grudge the world of all the religion the[y] have got. They are welcome to all the knowledge they possess.

The sound saluted my ears. We are come unto Mt. Zion &c. What could profit us to come unto the spirits of just men but to learn and come to the knowledge of spirits of the Just.

Where has Judge Higby gone? Who is there that would not give all his goods to feed the poor and pour out {page 47} his gold and silver to the four winds to come where Judge Higby has gone.

That which hath been hid from before the foundation of the world is revealed to babes and sucklings in the last days.

The world is reserved unto burning in the last days. He shall send Elijah the prophet and he shall reveal the covenants of the fathers in relation to the children /~~originally written~~/ ~~and the children~~ and the covenants of the children in relation to the fathers.

Four destroying angels holding power over the 4 quarters

of the earth until the {page 48} servants of God are sealed in their foreheads. What is that seal? Shall I tell you? No.

Doctrine [of] Election Sealing /of the servants of God/ on the top of their heads tis not the cross as the Catholics would have it. Doctrine of Election to Abraham was in relation to the Lord. A man wishes to be embraced in the covenant of Abraham. A man [like] Judge Higby in world of spirits, is sealed unto the throne, and doctrine of Election [is] sealing the father and children together. [*rest of page left blank*] {page 49}

To the mourner, do as the husband and the father would instruct you? [Then] You shall be reunited.

I have been acquainted with Judge Higby a long time. I never knew a more tender hearted man.

The President was much exhausted. G[eorge] J. Adams spoke about a contribution to get lumber for Bro[ther] Richard's house followed by P[arley] P. Pratt.

Elder G[eorge] J. Adams, after meeting was dismissed, called [and] read some charges which had been preferred by Chester A. Cowles against him and [said that he was] cited to appear before High Council for trial and called on all to bring forward their testimony, and prove their charge. Asked if they they did not, he should take the accusers for slander[ers]. {page 50}

[*several lines left blank*] 2 P.M. Joseph as Mayor instructed the Marshall to keep the Ladies['] camp ground clear of young men.

The city is enlarging very fast. We have so many learned men in this city and the height of knowledge is not [sufficient] to know enough to keep out of the way. I have been ferretting out grog shops, groceries, and beer barrels. {page 51}

Mr. Bagby[, county tax collector out] of Carthage, who has exercised more despotic power over the inhabitants of this city than any despot of the Eastern country I met. He gave me some abusive language [and] took up a stone to throw at me. I siezed him by the throat to choke him off. [*several lines left blank*]

At the Election /on the hill they/ got a Constable name of King. I don't know what need there was of a constable. Old Father Perry said why you can't vote in this precinct. King took me by the collar {page 52} and told me to go away.

All our wrongs have arisen under the power and authority of democracy and I have sworn that this arm shall fall from my shoulder and this tongue cleave to the roof of my mouth before I will vote for them unless they make me satisfaction and I feel it sensibly.

I was abused and regulated at the ground and there was not a man in the crowd to say, "This is Bro[ther] Joseph, this is the Mayor." Then spoke of the grog shops and the disturbance of the crowd in the street by Mosseur's grocery. Warned the grog shop[keepers] to be scarce after this time and the {page 53} peace officers to take notice of the grog shops and give him reasonable notice. Closed 20 mi[nutes] [past] 3 [o'clock].

Returned and said he had forgotten one thing. We have had certain traders in this city who have been writing falsehoods to Missouri. There is a certain man in this city who has made a covenant to betray and give me up and that too before the Gove[rnor] Carlin commenced his persecution. This testimony I have from gentlemen from a broad and I do not wish to give their names.

Sidney Rigdon, I most solemnly proclaim the withdrawal of my fellowship from this man /on the condition that the Judging be true/ and let the {page 54} Saints proclaim it abroad that he may no longer be acknowledged as my counselor and that all who feel to sanction my proceedings and views will manifest it by uplifted hands. It was a unanimous vote that Sidney Rigdon be disfellow[shipp]ed and his license demanded. [*several lines left blank*]

James Blakely commenced preaching at 3 P.M. and preached away most of the congregation. Afterwards a contribution of $4.60 was taken for Richard's house. Lydia Walker died at Joseph['s] about 9 o'clock. {page 55}

Monday, 14th August Rode out 9 A.M. At home 1 P.M. spoke to him [Joseph Smith] about recording Father Smith's blessing on the brethren. To the burying ground with Lydia Walker &c. LaForest lifted cannon. [-] [*rest of page blank*] {page 56}

Tuesday, 15[th] [*several lines left blank*] Evening at the exhibition of strength or feats of LaForest cannon and anvils &c. [*rest of page blank*] {page 57}

Wednesday, 16[th] 10 A.M. Attended funeral of Gen[eral] James Adams. I gave Esqu[i]r[e] Adams S[idney] Rigdon's affidavit to carry to Gov[ernor] Ford. LaForest played his feats. {page 58}

Thursday, Aug[ust] 17[th] In office 10 1/2 A.M. Trial [of] a case against Margaret Butterfield vs Alexander Mill. Also commenced a suit [of] Nauvoo vs Joel Bullard. Adjourned to 4 P.M. After dinner tried a case Nauvoo vs John Frizzacharly. 4 P.M. finished trying Butterfield[']s case.

9 P.M. Issued out a capius[?] before Alderman Harris vs A. LaForest and he was brought to court room and left $5 to secure for use of room till morning. P[arley] P. Pratt and O[rson] Hyde started for Boston by Chicago. {page 59}

Friday, Aug[ust] 18th 8 A.M. Conversing with Mr. Swartout. 10 [A.M.] with John D. Parker. I called with LaForest at his house. [rest of page blank] {page 60}

Saturday, Aug[ust] 19th 1843 Willard called on the President. Gave him $4.00 left as security by LaForest. LaForest left in the night leaving the cannon &c. in the store. /About/ 200 citizens assembled in Carthage to consult about the Mormons. [rest of page blank] {page 61}

Sunday, Aug[ust] 20th 1843 Saw the President [Joseph Smith] about 10 A.M. at home. [rest of page blank] {page 62}

Aug[ust] 21st, Monday Having received a letter from Esqu[ire] Patrick covering one from J. Hall Esqu[ire], Independance, M[iss]o[uri,] gave instruction to have them copied with some additional remarks and sent to Governor Ford. Copied accordingly.

Many folks at house. Rode out.

P.M. Held court Nauvoo vs Frederick J. Mosser on Temperance ordinance. Fined $3 and costs. [rest of page blank] {page 63}

Tuesday, 22[nd] [August] 1843 Sent a letter to Carthage by Sheriff Backenstos for Governor. Enclosed J. Hall's and Esq[ui]r[e] Patrick's [letters].

Fined Stephen Wilkenson $3 on confession for selling spirits. [rest of page blank] {page 64}

Wednesday, 23[rd] [August] 1843 Gave order for G[eorge] J. Adams to pass ferry free to Iowa. Also order for G[eorge] J. Adams to get some things for the Temple at Augusta.

Fined Mary Huxlaw $3.00 on confession for selling spirits.

Held court 4 P.M. City vs Joel Bullard, Larceny. No cause of action. Mrs. Mallory vs Pilkinton $45, cost. [*rest of page blank*] {page 65}

August 24th Gave a letter into office from Esquire Patrick for court papers on Habeus Corpus near noon. [*rest of page blank*] {page 66}

Friday, August 25th 1843 Hyrum in the office. Spoke of a new revelation.[1]

Rain in gentle showers through the day, the first water of much amount that has fallen since 1st June in Nauvoo. The Earth has been exceedingly dry, and the early potato [crop] nearly destroyed. Corn has been checked in its growth and even vines much injured by drouth [drought].

Saw the President at tea 5 P.M. {page 67}

Saturday, Aug[ust] 26th /1843/ About 3 o'clock P.M. Joseph came in the office. Clayton was in. In a few minutes went out and met Hyrum and returned.

Capt[ain] Black Hawk was in the street, yesterday returned from Council Bluff. Widow Granger was in to see about her deed for her lot. [*rest of page blank*] {page 68}

Sunday, Aug[ust] 27th 1843 10 A.M. President Marks prayed. Joseph said 2 weeks to day something said about Elder Rigdon. Vote taken [at that time] to take away his license on account of a report brought by Elder Hyde from Quincy. The letter [from former governor Carlin to Sidney Rigdon, produced by Rigdon in his defense,] is one of the most evasive things and carries with it a design to hide the truth[, according to Joseph Smith]. [The letter was read, dated] Quincy, Ill[inois] Aug[ust] 18, 1843 [It was] In answer to S[idney] Rigdon of the 15 inst[ant from] Thom[as] Carlin.

[Joseph then asked:] Has any man been concerned in a conspiracy to deliver Joseph Smith to M[iss]o[uri]? If so who? [Carlin's letter acknowledged only that Rigdon was not the "person in high standing in the church" who had "an interview" with him about how to have Joseph Smith "arrested and delivered into

---

[1] This is probably a reference to the revelation on eternal marriage and the "plurality of wives," recorded on 12 July 1843, and currently identified as section 132 in LDS editions of the Doctrine and Covenants. This section is not in RLDS editions.

the hands of the Missourians." Carlin did not tell who this individual was.] {page 69}

Read 7th Hebrews [regarding Melchizedek, king of Salem, who ordained Abraham a priest]. Salem is designed for a Hebrew term. It should be Shilom, which signifies Righteousness and peace. As it is, it is nothing. Neither Hebrew, Greek, Latin, French, or any other. To all those who are disposed to say [how] to set up stakes for the Almighty [they] will come short of the glory of God. To become a joint heir of the heirship of the son he must put away all his traditions.

I bear record this morning that all the combined powers of Earth and hell shall not over come this boy.

If I have sinned I have sinned outwardly, but secretly I have {page 70} contemplated the things of God. Told an annecdote of the Episcopalian priest who said he had the priesthood of Aaron but not of Melichisedek and bore this testimony that I never have found the man who claimed the priesthood of Melchisidek.

The law was given under Aaron for the purpose of pouring out Judgments and destructions.

The sectarian world are going to hell by 100s, 1,000s, 100,000!

3 grand orders of priesthood referred to here.

1st King of Shiloam [Salem had] power and authority over that of Abraham holding the key and {page 71} the power of endless life. Angels desire to look into it but they have set up to[o] many stakes. God cursed the children of Israel because they would not receive the last law from Moses.

By the offering of Isaac, if a man would attain [it], he must sacrifice all to attain to the keys of the kingdom of an endless life.

What was the power of Melchisedick[? It] was not P[riesthood] of Aaron &c. [but to be] a king and a priest to the most high God. A perfect law of Theocracy /holding keys of power and blessings/ [and] stood as God to give laws to the people, administering endless lives to the sons and daughters of Adam {page 72} kingly powers of anointing. Abram says Melchisedek [has priesthood. Before he sends me] away I [will] have a priesthood.

Salvation could not come to the world without the mediation of Jesus Christ. How shall God come to the rescue of this generation. He shall send Elijah[. The] law revealed to Moses in

409

Horeb. Never was revealed to the C[hildren] of Israel and he shall reveal the covenants to seal the hearts of the fathers to the children and the children to the fathers, /anointing and sealing/ called elected and made sure {page 73} without father &c. A Priesthood which holds the priesthood by right from the Eternal Gods and not by descent from father and mother.

2d Priesthood, patriarchal authority [to] finish that temple and God will fill it with power.

3d Priesthood[,] Levitical priest[hood.] Priests made without an oath but the Priesthood of Melchisedek is by oath and covenant. Holy Ghost.

Jesus Christ, men have to suffer that they might come up on Mt. Zion {page 74} exalted above the heavens. I know a man that has been caught up to the 3d heaven &c.

15 mi[nutes] past 1 o'clock.

Sidney Rigdon [said], "[I] never see [saw] Gov[ernor] Carlin but 3 times [and] never exchanged a word with any man living on this subject. I ask [your] pardon for having done any thing which should give a reason to make you think so."

[*written sideways on page*] /See letter on next page/ {page 75}

Evening Joseph, W[illia]m Law, W[illia]m Marks, Hyrum, N[ewel] K. Whitney, and Willard Richards were in Joseph's new house prayed that W[illia]m Law's father might live and receive the gospel and our families believe and rejoice and be saved.

Copy of the letter referred to on the previous page.

Quincy, Ill[inois] Aug[ust] 18th 1843

Dear Sir,

Yours of the 15th inst[ant] was received but not in time to answer it by mail. You say that "a Mr. Orson Hyde on board of the Steam Boat Anawawan a short time since was told by an officer of the boat that a Mr. Prentice in the vincinity of Quincy said that some person in high standing in the Church of Latter Day Saints in this place (Nauvoo) had an interview with you (me) said he would use all the influence /that/ his circumstances would admit of to have Joseph Smith arrested, and delivered into the hands of the Missourians &c."

This interview is said to have taken place at the
time the first warrant [was] issued against Smith, and
that since the last warrant was issued, that the same
person had written to you (me) or had an interview
with you giving the same assurances. It has been publicly said in this town that I (Sidney R[igdon]) was the
person who had this interview or interviews with you."

Now, Sir, it gives me pleasure to be perfectly able
to disabuse you. I have not seen you to my recollection,
nor had any correspondence with you until the present,
since 1839 and in all the intercourse I have had with
you, I have always looked upon you as one of the most
devoted followers of Joseph Smith and one of the pillars
of the Church of the Latter-day Saints. I never sought
through the aid of any person to entrap Joseph Smith.
A faithful discharge of my official duties was all that I
attempted or desired.

> Very respectfully
> your ob[edien]t servant,
> Thomas Carlin

Sidney Rigdon, Esq[ui]r[e] {page 76}
Monday, Aug[ust] 28[th] Delegation of Indians at Joseph's.
They wished him to become their great father. Geo[rge] Walker
wrote a deed in the office. [rest of page blank] {page 77}
Tuesday, August 29th Held court in the A.M. on
Hotchkiss. No cause of action. P.M. court City vs Erastus H.
Derby /bound to/ keep the peace 6 months, before trial gave up
his Elder['s] license to Recorder.
Court 4 P.M. Nauvoo vs Ira Miles. Fined $5 for swear-
in[g], [$] 25 [for] disorderly or breach of ordinance. [several lines
left blank] Walker wrote Copying Habeus Corpus court papers.
{page 78}
August 30th, Wednesday Office 10 A.M. Wanted Es-
qu[ire] Phelps to write a letter to Clerk to come in the city. [several
lines left blank] Walker continued on the court papers.
Thursday, Aug[ust] 31st Joseph called about 10 A.M.
and asked what the rent of house by the store was worth. About
these days was moving into the new house [Nauvoo Mansion] on

411

the Diagonal corner to commence keeping tavern. [*rest of page blank*] {page 79}

Friday, September 1st 1843 Coles vs G[eorge] J. Adams before High Council at the grove. Joseph and Emma there as witnesses on part of the council. G[eorge] J. Adams was discharged without reproof or censure by the High Council. [*rest of page blank*] {page 80}

Saturday, September 2d 1843 Joseph not well. Adjourned court till [*rest of page blank*] {page 81}

Sunday, September 3d [*several lines left blank*] 6 [o'clock] Eve[ning] Joseph, Hyrum, W. Marsh, N[ewel] K. Whitney, W[illia]m Law and Miller in council at Joseph prayed for Hiram['s] sick child and Whitney's &c. Much instruction from the President on future things. {page 82}

Monday, September 4th 1843 10 A.M. attended adjourned court Nauvoo vs A. Dodge, T. Dodge and Luther Purtelow. Fined 1st 2 $5.00 cash.[Fined the] Last 1 a cent. Called for a seal on a paper to go to England for Dr. Bennett shewing the death of a friend. 1 P.M. called to give licence to [Huroc?] and Maybe for a circus performance.

P.M. 2 1/2 till 5 [o'clock] attended circus with his family. [*rest of page blank*] {page 83}

Tuesday, Sept[ember] 5th Court 10 A.M. Foster vs Easton, Hamilton and adjourned till two. At 2 [p.m.] adjourned to next week. Joseph came in the office 9 A.M. with Hamilton of Carthage and wanted a bill of fare for tavern written. Also a deed Hamilton had of the Sheriff for Lot 2 Block 103 Nauvoo for taxes. Taxes has been paid. [*rest of page blank*] {page 84}

Wednesday, September 6th 6 or 7 A.M. come in before the Recorder was out of bed. Court at the old house. Nauvoo vs Joseph Owen. [*rest of page blank*] {page 85}

Thursday, September 7th Called [at] /office/ [at] 12 [o'clock]. Laid hands on Sister Partington and 2 children. Called P.M. enquired the news. Took home the letters written to Harrisburgs for the Church History. [*rest of page blank*] {page 86}

Friday, Sept[ember] 8th 1843 Emma sick. Joseph at home. Stephen Markham started for Lee County with court papers of Habeus Corpus as witness. Training of first cohort [of Nauvoo Legion]. [*rest of page blank*] {page 87}

Saturday, 9th Sept[ember] Emma a little more comfortable. Training. Clayton gone to A[u]gusta. Richards went to temple to pay 14 head of cattle. Cold, cloudy. City council did not form a quorum but adjourned. [*rest of page blank*] {page 88}

Sunday, Sept[ember] 10th 1843 Cold and considerable rain. Kindled a fire in the office for the first time this fall. This is the first rain of any consequence since the first of June. There has been occasional, say 3 or 4 slight showers, but not enough to wet the potato hills and the vegetables in the gardens have generally stopped growing on account of the drouth [drought]. Even [the] corn is seriously injured and much is injured by a worm in the ear. Early potatoes scarce[ly] worth digging. {page 89}

Monday, September 11th 1843 Early in the morning a petition was presented [to] Lieut[enant] Gen[eral Joseph Smith] to devise means to get the public arms of the state for the Legion. Election for Probate Justice. Weather cold. People cold. Greenleaff received most of the votes in Nauvoo, say 700 votes. Before noon L[i]eut[enant] General granted the petition and appointed W[illiam] W. Phelps, Henry Miller, and Hosea Stout a committee to wait on Governor Ford.

6 P.M. Joseph, Hyrum, W[illia]m Law, N[ewel] K. Whitney and Willard had a season of prayer in Joseph's east room New House for Laws little daughter who was sick and Emma who was some better. Woodworth very humble 3 or 4 days &c. {page 90}

Tuesday, Sept[embe]r 12[th] 1843 [*several lines left blank*] Wind east and south through the day. Rain commenced about 7 o'clock. [*rest of page blank*] {page 91}

Wednesday, Sept[ember] 13[th] 1843 Rode out on horseback 8 A.M. 2 o'clock and 10 minutes, Joseph introduced Mr. John Finch of Liverpool, England to give an address on his views of the social systems agreeable to Mr. Owen's System. 1. evils society is suffering. 2. causes which produce them. 3. best means of removing them. Spoke on the first two points. Joseph spoke and Finch replied &c. All pleasantly. [*rest of page blank*] {page 92}

September 14th 1843, Thursday 2 P.M. at the Temple stand. John Finch spoke on the 3d principle mentioned yesterday. 10 past 3 [P.M.], Joseph spoke 5 minutes. Told an anecdote of Sidney Rigdon and A[lexander] Cambell [about how they had first] got up a community at Kirtland. Big fish eat up the little. Did not believe the doctrine &c. Finch replied a few minutes.

Said he, "I am the cause of one crying in the wilderness and I am the Spiritual Prophet. Mr. Smith the Temporal Prophet."

Mr. Taylor commenced 3 1/2 [P.M.]. Spoke about an hour and 1/2. Finch spoke. Joseph closed about 6 [P.M.]. {page 93}

Friday, September 15th 1843 Mr. Finch left Nauvoo. Mailed letter to Clyde Williams and Co[mpany], Publishers, Harrisburgh, giving a history of the faith of the Church for their Book of Denominations Also power of attorney to Oliver Granger to Reuben McBride, Kirtland cirtified by the city Recorder. Joseph raised a sign [at the] *Nauvoo Mansion.* Resolutions of the Carthage Mob meeting arrived in town. Officer drill.

15 to 3 P.M. Rhoda Ann daughter of Willard and Jenneta Richards born. {page 94}

Saturday, September 16th 1843 General parade [of the] Nauvoo Legion near Gen[eral] Smith's farm. Went in co[mpany] with his staff to parade met by escort and arrived before the legion about 12 [o'clock]. [Joseph] Was received and saluted in military style. About 1 P.M. Legion was dismissed for 2 hours and I rode home to dinner. Returned about 20 minutes after 3 [P.M.]. Attend[ed] the review and inspection of the Legion with my staff. Gen[eral] Derby acting inspector. After which I took my part and gave orders. After which made a speech to the legion. Highly satisfied with officers and Soldiers {page 95} *and I felt extremely well myself.*

About sundown the Legion was dismissed and [I] rode home with some of my staff. Highly delighted with the day's performance and well paid for my services. The return will appear hereafter. [*rest of page blank*] {page 96}

Sunday, 17th September Was at meeting A.M. [and] gave some directions. While Almon Babbitt preached, I took my part as Mayor outside of the assembly to keep order and set pattern for the under officers. After preaching gave some instruction about order in the congregation. Men among women and women among men. Horses in the assembly Men and boys on the stand &c.

P.M. Mr. Blodget the Unitarian Minister preached. Was gratified with his {page 97} sermon in general, but differed in opinion on some points, on which I freely expressed myself to his great satisfaction on persecution, making the work spread by rooting up a flower garden or kicking back the sun. [*rest of page blank*] {page 98}

Monday, Sept[ember] 18th 1843 12 come in the city council at his old house a few minutes. Tried two causes in behalf of Nauvoo vs [—] Nauvoo vs Brinks. Fined defendant $3.00. [*rest of page blank*] {page 99}

September 19th, Tuesday Stand on steps at 2 [P.M.]. Gave Dr. Richards a cod fish. A.M. at home gave Letter to Bro[ther] Phelps from Governor to answer and answered it dated 20th with a paper containing the resolutions of Carthage meeting of Mobocracy.

Wrote to J[acob] B. Backenstos and lady to attend wedding of W[illia]m Backenstos 3 Sept[ember] [3 October 1843]. [*rest of page blank*] {page 100}

Wednesday, Sept[ember] 20th 1843 Rode out to his [Joseph's] farm. [*several lines left blank*] Very warm, wind south. [*rest of page blank*] {page 101}

Thursday, Sept[ember] 21st 1843 Made affidavit with Willard Richards and W[illia]m Clayton to auditor of State vs Walter Bagbee. About 11 A.M. called with his [Joseph's] Bro[ther] Samuel to see about getting a copy of Samuel's Blessing and wished the D[octo]r much joy in his new daughter. About noon went on board "Maid of Iowa" with Clayton. 1 P.M. thermometer stood at 100 in the shade at Esqu[ire] Phelps. [*rest of page blank*] {page 102}

Friday, September 22d 1843 About noon saw Joseph pass in a waggon with Hiram. [*rest of page blank*] {page 103}

Saturday, September 23rd Brother S[tephen] Markham returned from Dixon. The trial of Wilson and Reynolds will not come on till May [since] there were so many cases on the docket.

Saw the President riding down Main St. about 5 o'clock.

Bishop Miller returned from the pinery. Water so low in the upper river could not get a raft out. [*rest of page blank*] {page 104}

Sunday, Sept[ember] 24th 1843 Joseph preached about 1 hour from 2d chapter of Acts. Designed to shew the folly of common stock. In Nauvoo every one steward over their own. Amasa Lyman and Geo[rge] J. Adams continued the meeting. After preaching Joseph called upon the brethren to draw stone for the temple and gave notice for a special conference on the 6th Oct[ober]. Meeting adjourned on account of prospect of rain at about 1 P.M. Judge McBride and a lawyer from Missouri present at meeting. H[igh] Priests Quorum met in the store [and] ordained Bro[ther] [*blank*] {page 105}

Monday, Sept[ember] 25[th] Low[e]ring, wet day. Did not see the President. Heard he had conversation with a Missourian and Lorenzo Wasson called for constitution of the United States. [*rest of page blank*] {page 106}

Tuesday, September 26[th] 1835 [1843] Tried a case of Dana vs Leeches about 11 A.M. at old house. No cause of action. Called at store about 6 P.M. [and] directed a suit to commence Meddagh vs Hovey. [*rest of page blank*] {page 107}

Wednesday, September 27th 10 A.M. At home. Good feelings, gave Bro[ther] Phelps the privilege of occupying the small house near the store. [*rest of page blank*] {page 108}

Thursday, Sept[ember] 28[th] 1843 10 A.M. in the street going toward printing office. 11 1/2 A.M. Council over the store. Hyrum, Newell, Geo[rge] M[iller]., Wa<she>d. and An<oi>nt<e>d and J[ohn or Joseph] S[mith], J[ohn] T[aylor], A[masa] L[yman], L[yman] W[ight], J[ohn] M. B[ernhisel] an[oin]t[ed].

At 7 [o'clock in the] eve[ning] met at the Mansion's upper room front with W[illiam] L[aw] [and] W[illiam M[ark]. Beurach Ale [Joseph Smith] was by common consent and unanimous voice chosen President of the quorum [of the anointed] and anointed [second anointing] and ord[ained] to the highest and holiest order of the priesthood [as a king and priest] (and companion [as a queen and priestess]) [Present:] Joseph Smith, Hyrum Smith, Geo[rge] Miller, N[ewel] K. Whitney, Willard Richards, [Uncle] John Smith, John Taylor, Amasa Lyman, Lucien Woodworth, J[ohn] M. Bernhisel, W[illia]m Law, W[illia]m Marks. President [Joseph Smith] led in prayer that his days might be prolonged, have dominion over his enemies, all the households be blessed and all the church and world. {page 109}

Sept[ember] 29th 1843, Friday [*entry left blank*] {page 110}

Saturday, Sept[ember] 30th 1843 [*several lines left blank*] Rained this forenoon, wind east. [*several lines left blank*] P.M. wind west, very strong and cold. {page 111}

October 1st 1843, Sunday Wet and cold. Went to meeting A.M. Adjourned the meeting. P.M. More pleasant. People assembled, President [William] Marks, [Charles C.] Rich and Bishop Fouts preached. Eve[ning] Council met same as Thursday previous except [that Jane] Law, [Rosannah] Marks, [Elizabeth] Durphy, [and] Hiram's wife [Mary Fielding were initiated], Joseph &c. reanointed. Law &c. anointed counselors. Prayer and singing. Adjourned to Wednesday eve[ning]. [*rest of page blank*] {page 112}

Monday, Oct[ober] 2d 1843 At home. [*rest of page blank*] {page 113}

~~Wednesday~~ /Tuesday/, Oct[ober] 3rd 1843 At home. The brethren assembled with their wives to the amount of about 100 couples and dined at the Nauvoo Mansion as an "opening" to the house. A very pleasant day and all things passed off well. /See the [Nauvoo] Neighbor, Oct[ober] 4th 1843/ In the evening Mr. William Backenstos was married to Miss Clara M. Wasson at the Mansion. I solemized the marriage in presence of a select party. [*rest of page blank*] {page 114}

Wednesday, October 4th 1843 A.M. Joseph was sworn before Alderman Phelps at the Mansion to an affidavit concerning a suit in court. Clayton and Joseph vs Rhodes. /Gave Phelps orders to take such steps as were necessary to procure arms &c. for the Legion/ P.M. Esqu[ire] [Justin] Butterfield arrived and Joseph spent the P.M. in riding about the city with him and in the evening chatting.

Council of the quorum [of the anointed] adjourned to Sunday eve[ning], Hiram's child being sick. Towards night Joseph called to direct a license for an auction to be given E. Hovey and N. Heeper for the space of 10 days for $5.00. Granted accordingly and they were sworn to make due returns to the treasurer. {page 115}

Thursday, October 5th Morning rode out with Esqu[ire] Butterfield to farm &c. P.M. rode on prairie to shew some brethren some land. Eve[ning] at home. Walked up and down St[reet] with Scribe and gave instructions to try those who were preaching, teaching, or ~~practicing~~ the doctrine of plurality of wives on this Law. Joseph forbids it and the practice thereof. No man shall have but one wife. [*rest of page blank*] {page 116}

Friday, October 6th To special conference 11 1/2 [A.M.] So cold and windy few people [came] out. Gave notice President

417

Rigdon's case would be considered &c. Adjourned to morrow [at] 10 or 1st pleasant day. Walked towards home giving instructions to his scribe to cause all the paper relating to his 1/2 breed land in Iowa to be put in the hands of Esqu[ire] Butterfield. [*rest of page blank*] {page 117}

Saturday, October 6 /7/th 1843 Attended conference. See minutes on case of S[idney] Rigdon. [*rest of page blank*] {page 118}

Sunday, Oct[ober] 8th 1843 Slight frost last night. Conference A.M. Went in the P.M. Rain commenced and adjourned to Monday 10 A.M. Prayer Meeting at Joseph's. Quorum [of the anointed] present also in addition Sis[ters Harriet] Adams, [Elizabeth Ann] Whitney, Uncle John's wife [Clarissa], [and] Mother [Lucy Mack] Smith. Hiram and his wife were blessed, ord[ained], and anointed [to the fullness of the priesthood]. Prayer and singing. [*rest of page blank*] {page 119}

Monday, Oct[ober] 9th Conference [assembled.] [Alpheus] Culter, [Reynolds] Cahoon, and Hiram [Smith] spoke on the temple. P.M. Joseph preached funeral Sermon of Gen-[eral] James Adams. All men know that all men must die. What is the object of our coming into existence then dying and falling away to be here no more? This is a subject we ought to study more than any other, which we ought to study day and night. If we have any claim on our Heavenly Father for any thing it is for knowledge on this important subject. Could we read and comprehend all that has been written from the days of Adam on the relations of man to God and angels and the spirits of just men in a future state, we should know very little about it.

Could you gaze in[to] heaven 5 minutes you would know more than you ~~possibly~~ /would/ ~~can know~~ by read[ing] all that ever was written on the subject. We are one [and all] only capable of comprehending that certain things exist which we may acquire by certain fixed principles. If men would acquired salvation they have got to be subject to certain rules and principles which were fixed by an unalterable decree before the world was, before they leave this world. [Those of the ancient church claimed that they had "come unto mount Sion, and unto the city of the living God, the heavenly Jerusalem, and to an innumberable company of angels, to the general assembly and church of the firstborn, which are written in heaven, and to God the Judge of all and to the spirits of just men made perfect."] What did they learn by coming to the spirits of just men made perfect? Is it written, No! [What they learned cannot be written.] The spirits of just men are made ministering servants to those who are sealed unto life eternal. It is through them that the sealing power comes down.

The spirit of Patriarch Adam now is /one of/ the spirits of the just men made [perfect] and if revealed now, must be revealed in fire. And the glory could not be endured. Jesus shewed himself to his disciples {page 120} and they thought it was his spirit. They were afraid to approach his spirit. Angels have advanced higher in knowledge and power than spirits.

Judge Adams had some enemies, but such a man ought not to have had an enemy. I saw him first at Springfield, when on my way from M[iss]o[uri] to Washington. He sought me out when a stranger, took me to his house, encouraged and cheered me and give me money. When men are prepared, they are better off to go home. Bro[ther] Adams has gone to open up a more effectual door for the dead.

Flesh and blood cannot go there but flesh and bones quickened by the Spirit of God can. If we would be sober and watch in fasting and prayer, God would turn away sickness from our midst, Hasten the work of the Temple, and all the work of the Last Days. Let the Elders and Saints do away [with] light mindedness and be sober.

[The] Ship Timolian, Capt[ain] Plasket, sailed from New Bedford bound for Tahiti. Bro[thers] Rogers, Pratt, Hanks, an[d] Gravend sailed [for] their missions to [the] Sandwich Islands. {page 121}

Tuesday, Oct[ober] 10th 1843 Saw Joseph at dinner table. [He] said he would attend municipal court next morning [at] 10 o'clock. [*several lines left blank*] President Hyrum Smith was appointed by the voice of the spirit one of the Temple Committee in place of Judge Higby [Higbee] deceased. {page 122}

Wednesday, Oct[ober] 11th 1843 About home A.M. P.M. with Hiram, W[illia]m Law and ladies to John Benbow's. [*rest of page blank*] {page 123}

Thursday, [October] 12th 1843 Towards evening gave W[illiam] W. Phelps a letter from H[orace] R. Hotchkiss to be answered. ~~see~~ ans[wer] [*several lines left blank*] Eve[ning] prayer Meeting at Joseph's. Prayed for W[illia]m Marks [who is] sick. A[masa]

Lyman [and] John Taylor [were] absent. Cutler and Cahoon present [and initiated into quorum of the anointed]. {page 124}

Friday, Oct[ober] 13th 1843 First severe frost last night. Ice twice [the] thickness of window glass. At home, answered letter to H[orace] R. Hotchkiss. Gave Woodworth some instructions about food at the pinery. 10 A.M. presided at Municipal court. Horace Drown on Habeus Corpus. 1/4 past 12 adjourned for dinner till 2. In court again till 3[. Spent rest of afternoon] trying a span of grey horses in carriage. A Phrenologist came in and examined Joseph's head an hour. [*several lines left blank*] Very pleasant. {page 125}

Saturday, 14 Oct[ober] In the A.M. at home. Had a long conversation with a phrenologist and mesmerizer. [*several lines left blank*] From 11 to 1 in City Council. Appointed inspector of flour. [*rest of page blank*] {page 126}

Sunday, Oct[ober] 15th 1843 11 A.M. Cool, calm, [and] cloudy. Stand [erected at the] east end of the Temple. Singing. Prayer by P[arley] P. Pratt. Joseph preached: "It is one of the first principles of my life and one that I have cultivated from my childhood, having been taught it of my father, to allow every one the liberty of conscience.

"I am the greatest advocate of the C[onstitution] of [the] U[nited] S[tates] there is on the earth. In my feeling /the/ only fault I find with it is, it is not broad enough to cover the whole ground.

"I cannot believe in any of the creeds of the different denominations because they all have some things in them I cannot subscribe to, though all of them have some thruth [truth]. I want to come up into the {page 127} presence of God and learn all things, but the creeds set up stakes and say hitherto shalt thou come and no further, which I cannot subscribe to.

"I believe the Bible, as it ought to be, as it came from the pen of the original writers. As it read[s] it repented the Lord that he had made man. And also, God is /not/ a man that he should repent, which I do not believe. But it repented Noah that God made man. This I believe and then the other quotation stands fair.

"If any man will prove to me by one passage of Holy Writ one item I believe to be false I will renounce it [and] disclaim it far as I have promulgated it. The first principles of the gospel as I believe [are:] first Faith, [second] Repentance, [and third] Baptism for the remission of sins with the {page 128} promise of the Holy Ghost.

"Heb[rews] 6th [contains a] Contradiction 'Leaving the principle of the doctrine of Christ.' If a man leave[s] the principle of the doctrine of C[hrist] how can he be saved in the principle? A contridiction. I don't believe it. I will render it 'Therefore *not* leaving the P[rinciple] of the doctrine of Christ &c.'

"Resurrection of the dead and eternal judgment. [It is] one thing to see the Kingdom and another to be in it. [We] Must have a change of heart to see the kingdom of God and subscribe [to] the articles of adoption to enter therein.

"No man can /not/ receive the Holy Ghost without receiving revelations. The H[oly] G[host] is a revelator. {page 129}

"I prophecy in the name of the Lord God [that] anguish and wrath and trembulity [trembling] and tribulation and the withdrawing of the spirit of God await this generation until they are visited with utter destruction. This generation is as corrupt as the generation of the Jews that crucified Christ and if he were here to day and should preach the same doctrine he did then, why they would crucify him. I defy all the world and I prophecy they will never overthrow me till I get ready.

"On the economy of this city, I think there is to[o] many merchants among you. More wool and raw materials and [less manufactured goods. Let] the money be brought here to pay the poor {page 130} for manufacturing. Set our women to work and stop this spinning [of] street yarn and talking about spiritual wives. Send out /your money/ in the country, get grain, cattle, flax, &c.

"I proclaim in the name of the Lord God that I will have nothing but virtue and integripity [integrity] and uprightness. We cannot build up a city on merchandize. I would not run after the merchants, I would sow a little flax if I had but a garden and lot.

"The Temporal economy of this people should be to establish manufactoring and not to take usury for his money. I do not want to bind the poor here {page 131} and [see them] starve. Go out in the count[r]y and get food and /in/ cities and gird up your loins and be sober. When you get food return if you have a mind to. /Some say,/ "It is better to give [to] the poor than [give funds to] build the Temple." The building of the Temple has kept the poor who were driven from Missouri from starving. As has been the best means for the object which could be devised.

"All ye rich men of the Latter Day Saints from abroad I would invite [them] to bring up some of their money /and give to the Temple/. We want Iron, steel, powders, &c. A good plan to get up a forge, bring in {page 132} raw materials and manu[f]act[ur]ing establishments of all kinds and surround the rapids.

"I never stole the value of a pin's head or a picayune in my life. When you are hungry don't steal, come to me and I will feed you.

"The secrets of masonry is to keep a secret. It is good economy to entertain a stranger, to entertain sectarians. Come up ye sectarian priests of the everlasting gospel, as they call it and they shall have my pulpit all day.

"Wo to ye rich men. Give to the poor and then come and ask me for bread. Away with all your meanness and be liberal. We need purging, purifying, and cleansing. You have little faith in your Elders. {page 133} Get some little simple remedy in the first stages. If you send for a D[octo]r at all send in the first stages.

"All ye D[octo]rs who are fools, not well read, [and] do not understand the human constitution stop your practice.

"Lawyers who have no business only as you hatch [it] up, would to God you would go to work or run away."

1/2 past 2. Closed. [*rest of page blank*] {page 134}

Monday, Oct[ober] 16th 1843 About home attending to family concerns. Adjourned court till 17[th October at] 8 A.M. [*rest of page blank*] {page 135}

Oct[ober] 17th, Tuesday Municipal court 8 A.M. or 9 1/2 Drown discharged, no one appearing against him. [*rest of page blank*] {page 136}

Wednesday, Oct[ober] 18[th] [*several lines left blank*] Pleasant and comfortable. {page 137}

Thursday, Oct[ober] 19[th] 1843 [*several lines left blank*] O[liver] H. Olney married.[2] Warm and pleasant. The water has risen about 2 feet in the Missi[ssi]ppi and is rising. {page 138}

---

[2] This sentence is enclosed in a box in the original.

Friday, October 20[th] 1843 Heard that Joseph went to Ramus yesterday [and] has not returned. [*several lines left blank*]

Oliver H. Olney's Mormonism Exposed [*Absurdities of Mormonism Portrayed*] were found in the streets of Preston in great numbers. [*several lines left blank*]

John P. Green returned from a mission to the east N[ew] York with about 100 emigrants. Some of them from P[ennsylvani]a which he fell in with on the way.

Warm [and] smoky, and strong wind. Very dark evening. {page 139}

Saturday, 21st [*several lines left blank*] Ordained Joseph Coon in the office as he said by Hyrum's direction. Pleasant and cool. {page 140}

Sunday, Oct[ober] 22nd 1843 S[idney] Rigdon preached 1/2 hour on poor rich folks. At home all day. Prayer meeting at Mansion [at] 2 P.M. W[illia]m Marks and <wife anointed> [to fullness of the priesthood and quorum of the anointed] 24 present.

[Brigham] Young, [Heber C.] Kimball, Geo[rge] A. [Smith] and Daniel Spencer arrived about 11 A.M. on steam-[boat] Anawan and many saints. [*several lines left blank*] Pleasant [and] Cool. {page 141}

Monday, Oct[ober] 23rd \³ The following named deceased persons were sealed to me on 26th of October [1843]. [*See list on manuscript page 145.*] [*several lines left blank*]

\⁴ Hyrum began to act in his office as Temple committee. [*several lines left blank*]

It is reported that O[liver] H. Olney was married last Thursday eve[ning] to Miss Wheeler by Joseph Hacock. Cloudy, east wind. {page 142}

Tuesday, Oct[ober] 24th 1843 [*several lines left blank*] 1 P.M. W[illiam] W. Phelps and Col[onel] Dunham started for Springfield to see the Gov[ernor] and procure arms for the Legion. [*several lines left blank*]

A.M. warm and pleasant. P.M. wind west by north. 4 o'clock a little rain and some flakes of snow for the first [time] this fall. {page 143}

Wednesday, Oct[ober] 25th This morning cold. Ice 1/3

---

³ In the handwriting of Robert L. Campbell.
⁴ In the handwriting of Willard Richards.

of an inch thick in small bodies of water. Pleasant A.M. [*several lines left blank*] Eve[ning] cloudy [and] cold. {page 144}

Thursday, Oct[ober] 26th 1843 \⁵ The following named deceased persons were sealed to me (John M. Bernhisel) on Oct[ober] 26th 1843, by President Joseph Smith: Maria Bernhisel, sister; Brother Samuel's wife, Catherine Kremer; Mary Shatto, (Aunt); Madalena Lupferd, (distant relative); Catherine Bernhisel, Aunt; Hannah Bower, Aunt; Elizabeth Sheively, Aunt; Hannah Bower, cousin; Maria Lawrence, (intimate friend); Sarah Crosby, intimate friend, /died May 11[th] 1839/; Mary Ann Bloom, cousin.

\⁶ John M. Bernhisel

\⁷ Recorded by Rob[er]t L. Campbell, July 29th 1868.

\⁸ Warm and pleasant. Frost last night. {page 145}

Friday, Oct[ober] 27[th] 10 A.M. saw the President in his public room in conversation with Bishop Miller and Elder Hawes who have just returned from the south. Adjourned a court one week and renewed an execution. [*several lines left blank*]

Emigration has been great to Nauvoo for some few weeks.

Prayer Meeting in the evening at Joseph[ʼs]. Bis[hop] Whitney and <wife anointed> [to fullness of the priesthood]. Hiram /said his voice should be heard in the streets/. Joseph spoke and Cahoon. Warm and pleasant. {page 146}

Saturday, 28 Oct[ober] 1843 [*several lines left blank*] Cold east wind. Some rain. Eve west wind. Dark eve. {page 147}

Sunday, 29 Oct[ober] 1843 [John] Taylor and [Brigham] Young preached [at the] south side [of the] Temple from 11 A.M. to 2 P.M. Very pleasant.

Dr. Richards called for a collection to get $8.00 for a new Book for the history and obtained $3.00. Dr. R[obert] D. Foster voluntaryly came forward and gave $4.50. [He] Has given .50 in the subscription making $5.00 which is to be recorded on the book purchased. /not[e] its date/

2 P.M. or near 4 [P.M.], before all were ready prayer meeting at the mansion. 25 present [including] Sis[ters] Cutler,

---

⁵ In the handwriting of Robert L. Campbell.
⁶ In the handwriting of John M. Bernhisel.
⁷ In the handwriting of Robert L. Campbell.
⁸ In the handwriting of Willard Richards.

Cahoon, Woodworth. Adjourned Wednesday over Brick store. Joseph taught.

9 A.M. [Elders] Richards, Miller, and Haws ordained W[illia]m C. Steffey an Elder who was going to Texas on business. [*rest of page blank*] {page 148}

Monday, October 30th 1843 Saw Joseph at 9 A.M. at home. [He] Ordered court adjourned for one week and an execution renewed. [*several lines left blank*] 12 came to the office to attend a court. Parties agreed to leave it to Bro[ther] Flagg and he remitted. [*several lines left blank*] Eve[ning] ordered a warrant to arrest Morrie for breech of ord[i]nance. [*several lines left blank*] Pleasant and cold. Masons stopped work [on the Temple] mostly. {page 149}

Tuesday, October 31[st] 9 /A.M. Called at office. Retired immediately./ Moorie brought up [and] fined $5.00 by the Mayor. [*several lines left blank*] Some snow on the ground this morning. Cold east wind and rain through the day. {page 150}

November 1[st] 1843, Wed[nesday] [*several lines left blank*] Eve[ning]. Prayer Meeting of Mansion. 29 present. (Sister[s] Fielding, Richards, Taylor, Young, Kimball <anointed> &c. [*several lines left blank*] Letter and affidavit of E[dward] Southwick Esq[ui]r[e] handing [handed] in [to] the office for the Neighbor. [*rest of page blank*] {page 151}

Thursday, Nov[ember] 2[d] [*several lines left blank*] Joseph, Hyrum, [Brigham] Young, [Heber C.] Kimball, [John] Taylor, and [William] Clayton had council at 10. Agreed to write a letter to the 5 Candidates for the [U.S.] Presidency to enquire what their feeling[s] were or what their course would be towards the Saints if they were elected. [*rest of page blank*] {page 152}

Friday, Nov[ember] 3[d] 1843 [*entry left blank*] {page 153}

Saturday, Nov[ember] 4th [*several lines left blank*] 7 Eve Elder Taylor and Scribe called at the Mansion and read a letter to Clay, Calhoon, Johnson, Van Buren, [and] Cass, [the] candidates for the [U.S.] Presidency. [Letter] Approved. [*rest of page blank*] {page 154}

Sunday, Nov[ember] 5th 1843 Rode out with my Mother and others for her health. [Joseph] Was taken suddenly sick at the dinner table. Went to the door and vomited /all [his] dinner/. [His] jaws [were] dislocated and raised fresh blood. Every symptom of poison. [*several lines left blank*]

Prayer Meeting eve at the Hall over the store. <Joseph did not dress [in robes of the priesthood, as customary], nor Emma> [*several lines left blank*] Gave my clerk, Dr. Richards, to tell Mr. Cole he must find some other room for his school [than the hall over the store]. [*rest of page blank*] {page 155}

Monday, Nov[ember] 6th Busy with domestic concerns. [*several lines left blank*] P.M. listened to Phelps give a relation of his visit to the Governor and was pleased from 1 to 3 o'clock. [*several lines left blank*] Dr. R[ichards] gave Mr. Cole notice to find another room and in the eve prepared the tables to move them from the hall. [*several lines left blank*] Cool for same day. {page 156}

Tuesday, Nov[ember] 7th 1843 This morning Richards and others moved the tables from the hall. Mr. Cole moved them back while at 9 A.M. Richards /and Phelps/ called at the Mansion and stated that the school disturbed the history and prevented its progress. Joseph said tell Mr. Cole he must look out for himself. Your reasons are good. We must have the room. [*several lines left blank*] Very warm and pleasant. {page 157}

Wednesday, Nov[ember] 8th From 9 to 11 1/2 /A.M./ Interview with Phelps and Richards, clerks. Read and heard, read the history, then attended to setling some accounts with individuals who called. [*several lines left blank*]

P.M. Examined a sample of fringe designed for the Pulpits of the Temple. Conversed with Phelps, Lewis, Butler, and others from 2 to 3 o'clock. (Prayer Meeting in eve over store. Joseph not present.) {page 158}

Thursday, Nov[ember] 9[th] 1843 10 A.M. Called at the office with a letter from Ja[me]s A[rlington] Bennet and gave instruction to have it answered. [*rest of page blank*] {page 159}

Friday, Nov[ember] 10[th] [*entry left blank*] {page 160}

Saturday, Nov[ember] 11th 1843 [*several lines left blank*] Clear and cold. Freezing. {page 161}

Sunday, Nov[ember] 12th [*several lines left blank*] Prayer Meeting in the evening at S[outh] E[ast] Room [of] Jos[eph's] old house. R[eynolds] Cahoon and <wife anointed and Mother [Lucy Mack] Smith>. [*several lines left blank*] Clear [and] cold. {page 162}

Monday, Nov[ember] 13[th] 1843 Called at the office A.M. with Hyrum and heard Judge Phelps read letter to Ja[me]s A. Bennet and made some corrections.

In the morning Bro[ther] Phelps called at the Mansion and read a letter which I had dictated to Gen[eral] James Arlington Bennet which pleased me much.

P.M. Called again with Doct[or] Bernhisel and Clayton and read again. After wards called again and enquired for the Egyptian grammar. [*rest of page blank*] {page 163}

Tuesday, Nov[ember] 14th Absent most of the day. [*several lines left blank*] Evening called at the office to [-] Mr. Southwick of Dixon and hear my letter to Gen[eral] Bennet. [*rest of page blank*] {page 164}

Wednesday, Nov[ember] 15th 1843 At home. 10 A.M. Held court in the office. Erskine vs Pullen. Nonsuit. [*several lines left blank*] P.M. at the office. Suggested the idea of preparing a grammar of the Egyptian Language.

Prayer Meeting at the old house. A. Cutler and <wife anointed>. Spoke of Proclamation to the kings. Letter to Bennet and Petition to Congress &c. [*several lines left blank*] Warm and foggy. {page 165}

Thursday, Nov[ember] 16th At home. 9 1/2 Called at the office to hold court in case of Averill vs Bostwick hour [-] arrived. Walked up street with Hyrum a few minutes, returned and held court. [*several lines left blank*] Chilly East wind and fog. {page 166}

Friday, Nov[ember] 17[th] At home. Deeded W[illiam] W. Phellps' wife a lot. About 10 called at the office, with Es-q[ui]r[e] Southwick. Went into my scribe's room, Dr. Richards, to refresh ourselves an hour and conversed freely. [*several lines left blank*] Thunder, lightning, and rain last night. Morning warm and foggy. Day clear and warm. {page 167}

Saturday, Nov[ember] 18th Rode out on the Prairie with Southwick on horseback. [*rest of page blank*] {page 168}

Sunday, Nov[ember] 19th 1843 At home. [*several lines left blank*] 11 A.M. to 2 P.M. Prayer and fasting at the old house. Prayer meeting in the eve breaking bread &c. [*rest of page blank*] {page 169}

Monday, 20th Nov[ember] [*several lines left blank*] Monday evening 2 gentlemen from Vermont put up at the Mansion and in the evening several of the Twelve [Apostles] and others and my family sung hymns. Elder John Taylor prayed and gave an address. [*rest of page blank*] {page 170}

Tuesday, Nov[ember] 21st 1843 10 A.M. council of some of the Twelve [Apostles] and W[illiam] W. Phelps at the old house. Gave W[iliam] W. Phelps instructions to write an appeal to the citizens of Vermont and Richards, Phelps, Taylor, and Hyde instructions to write a proclamation to the Kings /&c./ of the Earth. [several lines left blank] Council in the eve in the old house [with] Richards, Turley, and others. [several lines left blank] The Ohio River will be froze up in a few days (prophecy). {page 171}

Wednesday, 22nd [several lines left blank] Prayer Meeting in the eve at [the] old house. B[righam] Young [was] <anointed and wife> &c. [rest of page blank] {page 172}

Thursday, 23th Nov[ember] 1843 [several lines left blank] 10 A.M. council in old house. Richards, Turley, &c. and walked down the river to look at the stream, rocks, &c. About 11 1/2 A.M. Suggested idea of petitioning Congress for grant to make a canal over the falls or a dam to turn the water to the city. Erect Mills &c. [rest of page blank] {page 173}

Friday, Nov[ember] 24th [entry left blank] {page 174}

Saturday, Nov[ember] 25th 1843 [several lines left blank] Mr. Frierson, United States Surveyor from Quincy arrived in Nauvoo. Evening the High Council set on the case of Harrison Sager for seduction. No action, but the President was present and the 12 [Apostles]. After this council, the President and 12 [Apostles] held a consultation and agreed to meet Mr. Frierson at the Nauvoo Mansion next morning. [rest of page blank] {page 175}

Sunday, November 26[th] Joseph, the Twelve [Apostles], Hyrum, [and] Phelps sat in council with Mr. Frierson at the Mansion concerning pet[it]ioning Congress for redress of [our] grievances.

At 11 A.M. O[rson] Pratt preached in the assembly room and in the eve Parley P. P[ratt] lectured at the Mansion. [several lines left blank] Rainy [and] Muddy. {page 176}

Monday, Nov[ember] 27[th] 1843 [entry left blank] {page 177}

[page left blank] {page 178}

Monday, Nov[ember] 27[th] 1843 At home quite unwell. [several lines left blank] Wet. {page 179}

Tuesday, Nov[ember] 28[th] At home. Mr. Frierson wrote a memorial to Congress. [several lines left blank] Cooler. {page 180}

Wednesday, Nov[ember] 29[th] 1843 At home. Mr. Frierson le[f]t for home taking a copy of the Memorial to get signers in Quincy.

/(The opinion of J[osiah] Lamborn[, attorney general of the state of Illinois,] and J. N. McDougall [writing to the state auditor at the request of the] attorney gener[a]l [regarding compensation for the Nauvoo Legion, was read while Joseph Smith's appeal for aid to the Green Mountain Boys] of V[ermon]t [was being prepared for publication. Lamborn's and McDougall's opinions] arrived in [Illinois state auditor] Ewing's Letter [of] No[vember] 30[th])/

4 P.M. A Meeting of citizens at the assembly room to appoint committee to get subscribers to the memorial [to Congress] &c. Joseph present. [*several lines left blank*] Clear and cold. {page 181}

Thursday, Nov[ember] 30th 1843 At home. 10 A.M. Rode out with Mr. Jackson. At home most of the day. [*several lines left blank*] In the evening sent to the office for the appeal to the Green Mountain boys, but a part of it had gone to press and it could not be had. [*several lines left blank*] Clear and cold. Froze some in the house. {page 182}

December 1st 1843 At home. 12 A.[M.] Sec[retary] called to get a petition for an appropriation from Congress to improve the rapids, but the Pres[ident] standing in the bar room said it was not [yet] written. Howard Corey started for Bear Creek to get subscribers. [*several lines left blank*] Clear and cold. Some ice floating in the river. {page 183}

Saturday, Dec[ember] 2nd 1843 Prayer Meeting at the assembly room (room over the store). P[arley] P. Pratt, O[rson] Hyde, W[ilford] Woodruff, Geo[rge] A. Smith, [and] O[rson] Spencer /were anointed preparatory [to receiving the fullness of the priesthood]/ and A[lpheus]. Cutler and [*blank* [Reynolds]] Cahoon were all present at the meeting which continued from 1 to 5 P.M. About 35 present. Adjourned to 10 next morning. [*rest of page blank*] {page 184}

Sunday, Dec[ember] 3d 1843 I arrived at the assembly room about 12 noon. Found all present, except Hyrum and his wife. He had slipped and turned his knee joint in backwards and sprained his large muscle, and I had been ministering to him, and Emma had been unwell during the night. Meeting orga-

429

nized. W[illiam] W. Phelps read Appeal to "Green Mountain Boys" which was dedicated by prayer after all had spoken upon it and prayed for Nathan Pratt, who was very sick. Hyrum and others [prayed for] {page 185}

Monday, Dec[ember] 4th [*several lines left blank*] 6 eve Attend[ed] the adjourned meeting of citizens in Assembly room. Phelps read appeal to "Green Mountain Boys". P[arley] P. Pratt his appeal to N[ew] York and W[illard] Richards the memorial to Congress. When I spoke 2 1/2 hours on Missouri persecution, the Government in gen[eral], men and measures &c. to a *crowded* and select congregation. Many could not get admission. Two Missourians [were] present. {page 186}

Tuesday, Dec[ember] 5th Mrs. Avery arrived from Bear Creek Precinct and made report her husband and son had been kidnapped by the Missourians. [*several lines left blank*]

At 6 eve met the 12 [Apostles], W[illiam] Phelps, [William] Clayton, and [Theodore] Turley in council in the office on important business. Advised the 12 [Apostles] to raise money to send Elder Hyde east to get paper to print Doctrine and Covenants [and to] Get new type and metal for stereotyping. {page 187}

Wednesday, Dec[ember] 6th 1836 [1843] At home. P.M. Dellmore Chapman made affidavit that Philonder Avery was decoyed from Bear Creek on 19 Nov[ember] /by one Richardson and/ by the Missourians. Run over the Missouri River and lodged in Monticello *gail* [jail] and his father Daniel Avery was taken by some of the same and some 30 citizens on the 2d Dec[ember] for the same purpose and served the same way. Affidavit to be sent the Gov[ernor]. [*several lines left blank*]

Esq[ui]r[e] Goodwin and others /not of the church/ petitioned the Gov[ernor] not to help Missouri persecute the Saints. {page 188}

Thursday, Dec[ember] 7[th] 1843 At home. 11 A.M. the citizens of Nauvoo assembled on the east side of this Temple. Organized, A[lpheus]. Cutler Chair/m[an]/, W[illard] Richards Sec[retary] and adopted resolution through their committee [comprised of] W[illiam] W. Phelps, Reynolds Cahoon and Hosea Stout, signed by Chair and Sec[retary] to be sent the Gov[ernor] to [be] sent by Woodworth. At 12 [P.M.] with petition from Goodwin and others and Dillman Chapman affidavit, all on file.

The German Brethren met at assembly room at 6 P.M. and chose Bishop Garn P. Elder to have preaching in their own language.

Joseph at home. 8 eve Having visited Bro[ther] Turley and found him destitute of food. Clear and cold. 10[:]00 {page 189}

Friday, December 8th 1843 At home. 11 A.M. in office giving instruction concerning dam across the Mississippi and other ordinance[s] and calling city council at four to be prepared for any invasion from Missouri.

Willard Richards and Philip B. Lewis made affidavit concerning Kidnapping by M[iss]o[urians]. Marshall was notified to see that ordinance were obeyed. Marshall made requisition on the Mayor for a portion of the Nauvoo Legion. Orders of L[i]eut[enant] Gen[eral] to Major General.

4 P.M. in city council. Passed an "extra Ordinance" and for Dam across Miss[issippi River]" and proposed to petition Congress to take the city under their protection. Receive the Legion as U[nited] S[tates] Troops assist in fortifications &c. Com[munication] approved. {page 190}

Saturday, Dec[ember] 9th 1843 At home. [*several lines left blank*] Prayer Meeting over the store. W[illia]m W. Phelps, L[evi] Richards, Lot [Smith], and Joseph Fielding [anointed]. [*rest of page blank*] {page 191}

Sunday, Dec[ember] 10th 1843 At home. [*several lines left blank*] Eve prayer Meeting over the store. Joseph not present. [*several lines left blank*] Warm and rainy. {page 192}

Monday, Dec[ember] 11th 1843 At home. [*several lines left blank*] Wrote the Gov[ernor] with Sission A. Chase's affidavit on kidnapping. [*rest of page blank*] {page 193}

Tuesday, Dec[ember] 12th 1843 At home. At 9 [A.M.] in the office. Directed a letter to be written [to] Uncle John Smith /granting the petition of the Macedon Branch — that Uncle John be ordained Patriarch/. At 10 [A.M.] in City Council in the office. Passed an ordinance for the health and convinience of Travellers &c. "For selecting 40 Policemen," and for amending an ordinance concerning the public revenue. [*rest of page blank*] {page 194}

Wednesday, Dec[ember] 13th 1843 At home. [*several lines left blank*] About this time Philander Avery having made his es-

431

cape from M[iss]o[uri] Jail arrived at Nauvoo. [*rest of page blank*] {page 195}

Thursday, Dec[ember] 14th At home. [*rest of page blank*] {page 196}

Friday, Dec[ember] 15th 1843 I [Joseph Smith] awoke this morning in good health, but was soon suddenly seized with a great dryness of the mouth and throat and sickness of the stomach, and vomited freely. My wife waited on me assisted by my scribe and Dr. L[evi] Richards, who administered to me herbs and mild drinks. I was never prostrated so low in so short a time before, but by evening was considerably revived. [*several lines left blank*] Very warm. {page 197}

Saturday, Dec[ember] 16th /This morning/ Considerably better. Arose at 10 and sat all day in the city Council which was held in my house for my accommodation. Passed an ordinance Regulating Merchants and grocers licences. Also "an ordinance concerning the landing of steam boats in Nauvoo" &c. Investigated the [p]etition to Congress for assistance to repeal mobs &c. The Mayor and council officially signed the Memorial to Congress for a redress of grievances. After council, had conversation with some of the Twelve [Apostles], [Theodore] Turl[e]y, &c. [at] 8 o'clock.

Prophecy before the City Council while discussing the Petition to Congress. Joseph [said,] "I prophecy by virtue of the Holy Priesthood vested in me in the name of Jesus Christ that if Congress will not hear our petition and grant us protection they shall be broken up as a government and God shall damn them. There shall nothing be left of them, not even a grease spot." Warm fogy and muddy. {page 198}

Sunday, Dec[ember] 17th 1843 At home. [*several lines left blank*] 4 P.M. prayer meeting at the Store [in the] Assembly room. Samuel Harrison Smith [was] admitted. Returned home at 7. [*several lines left blank*]

King Follet, Constable of Hancock County, with 10 men went this P.M. to arrest John Elliot [one of the] Kidnapper[s] of Daniel Avery with warrant of Esqu[ire Aaron] Johnson. [*several lines left blank*]

River clear of ice below the city and as far as up as stone tavern &c. {page 199}

Monday Dec[ember] 18th At home. After Dinner, Constable Follet returned with Elliot. Trial in the Assembly room for examination /before Aaron Johnson/. [Elliot was] found guilty of Kidnapping and bound over for trial to the Circuit Court in the sum of $3,000.

During the investigation testimony appeared to show Elliot had threatened my life and for this I brought him to trial /before R[obert] D. Foster, J[ustice] [of the] P[eace]/, immediately af[ter] the sentance of Esq[ui]r[e] Johnson. In testimony it appeared the prisoner had said in relation to myself "We will pop him over" as though he knew a plan had been laid to take my life by some body or co[mpany] of individuals.

Lawyers Marr and Stiles spoke in behalf of the State, followed by W[illiam] W. Phelps in a masterly speech in which he pourtrayed the enormyty of the offence in its true colors. {page 200} I followed in a lengthy speech in which I was engaged when at about 10 o'clock 2 young men arrived as express from Warsaw stating that the Mob were collecting at Warsaw. Also around Col[o-nel] Levi Williams [who was sought by the court as the principal in the kidnapping] and messengers had gone to M[iss]o[uri] to reinforce the mob.

/Before closing my speech I withdrew the action and told the court I would forgive Elliot and the 2 men who followed him from 4 1/2 miles below Warsaw [with the intent of recapturing him] and take them home [and] give them supper and lodging and breakfast and see that they were protected and the court discharged Elliot./

Esqu[ire] Johnson [who had issued a writ for the arrest of Levi Williams] made a demand on me as Mayor for a ~~detachment~~ /possey/ of to send to Hosea Sto[u]t's assistance whom he had sent with a workout this afternoon to apprehend Col[onel] Williams as being concerned in kidnapping Avery which demand I complied with. Gen[eral] Law, by my instruction, detached Col[o-nel] Markham with 1,000 men. Also an affidavit of Dr. Richards that the peace of the city was in danger. I, as {page 201} commander of the Nauvoo Legion, installed Gen[eral] Law to have the troops in readiness to repel invasion and returned home to rest about 1 o'clock in the morning of the 19th. [rest of page blank] {page 202}

Tuesday morning, Dec[ember] 19th 1843 At home. About 9 o'clock a part of the co[mpany] who went with Hosea Stout

433

returned and stated that they went within two miles of Col[onel] Williams, when they were informed that a body of men had collected around him armed with rifles, &c. &c. They judged it prudent to return for weapons and help. Also that Bro[ther] Loveland told them that he saw 30 armed men follow the Constable King [Follet] some miles on his way as he had charge of Elliot. Esq[ui]r[e] Johnson immediately wrote to Loveland to have him come to Nauvoo and Make affidavit of the War-like movements of the mob that he might send to the Gov[enor] & [*blank*]. {page 203}

 1 o'clock P.M. The Legion met near the Temple and &c. See Nauvoo Neighbor of the 20[th]. [*several lines left blank*]

 Took Amos S. Chase Affidavit. [*several lines left blank*] Clear and cold. {page 204}

 Dec[ember] 20[th], ~~Tuesday~~ /Wednesday/ At home. Counselling and attending to business in general in tolerable health and good spirits. Esq[ui]r[e] Johnson took the affidavit of Andrew M. Hamilton and James B. Hamilton concerning Daniel Avery's capture. Clerk of Municipal Court took Philonan Avery's affidavit to send to M[iss]o[uri]. [*several lines left blank*] Clear and cool. {page 205}

 Thursday, 21[st] Called on Bro[ther] Phelps before Sunrise and told him an alarm gun had been fired, but I believed nothing serious. Took the key and went into the office. A few citizens assembled but Bro[9] ~~Cairns had returned home and~~ all was peace. At 12 went into City Council and remained till 2 P.M. Passed [an] ordinance to prevent unlawful arrests and Sezure in Nauvoo. Read Memorial to Congress for Territorial powers &c. /Appointed O[rson] Pratt delegate to convey it/ Appointed J[ohn] P. Green Marshal &c. In the evening conversed with strangers in the bar room &c.

 J. Holman and E[lbridge] Tuftes left papers for history. Very warm and pleasant. {page 206}

 Friday, Dec[ember] 22nd 1843 At home. At nine o'clock while reading from a Magazine to my children, Bro[ther] Phelps come in and gave me the common Morning salutation, and I said, "God be with you" and he said "Amen." A little after 12 went into the store room occupied by Bulter and Lewis and com-

---

[9] This word was not crossed with the following, but context suggests that it should have been.

menced a labor with Dr. Charles to convince him that mobocracy is not justifiable and I did not deal in politics.

Near evening went to the printing office after my papers. Br[other] David Holman living about 2 miles from Ramus went out visiting with his family in the eve, when about 10 o'clock discovered his home on fire. Neighbors [had] inquired how long he would be gone. A man rode to Carthage. A co[mpany] went up, secured his provisions to themselves and fired the house. Very warm and pleasant. {page 207}

Saturday, Dec[ember] 23rd At home. Counselling the brethren who called on me and [visited while I was] attending to my domestic duties. [I was] making preparations for a Christmas dinner party. [*several lines left blank*]

Prayer Meeting in the Assembly room [above the store with] Isaac Morly and wife. O[rson] Pratt, Sister Lot, Fanny Murray, Sister Woodruff, Geo[rge] A. Smith's wife, Sister O[rson] Spencer, [and] Sister Phelp[s] [were anointed]. [*rest of page blank*] {page 208}

Sun[day], Dec[ember] 24th 1843 At home. Received a visit from Mr. Richards[, the] one who assisted to kidnap Avery. He manifested some repentance and promised to use his influence to prevent Avery's conviction by the Missourians. [*rest of page blank*] {page 209}

Monday, Dec[ember] 25th 1843 At home. About noon gave counsel to the brethren who called on me from the Morley Settlement. Told them to keep law on their side and they would come out well enough.

About 2 o'c[loc]k about 50 couple[s] sat down at my table to dine. While I was eating my scribe called on me to solemnize the Marraige of Doct[or] Levi Richards and Sarah Griffiths, but as I could not leave I referred the subject to Pres[i]d[en]t B[righam] Young who married them.

A large party supped at my house and spent the evening /in a most cheerful and friendly manner/ in Music, Dancing, &c. During the festivities {page 210} a man apparently drunk, with his hair long and falling over his shoulders come in and acted like a Missourian. I commanded the Capt[ain] of the police to put him out of doors. In the scuffle, I looked him full in the face and to my great surprize and Joy untold I discovered it was Orrin

435

Porter Rockwell, just arrived from a years imprisonment in M[iss]o[uri]. [*rest of page blank*] {page 211}

[*several lines left blank*] Daniel Avery was liberated on Habeus Corpus in M[iss]o[uri]. Warm and rain this eve. {page 212}

Tuesday, Dec[ember] 26th 1843 At home. [*several lines left blank*] I rejoiced exceedingly this day that Rockwell ~~and Avery~~ had returned and M[iss]o[uri] was again rid of the Brethren [*several lines left blank*] About dusk Bro[ther] Daniel Avery arrived in Nauvoo. Cloudy, wind N[orth] W[est]. Froze. {page 213}

Wednesday, Dec[ember] 27th At home. A little frost and ice in the river it having been clear some time past. [*several lines left blank*]

P.M. Bro[ther] Phelps called. I gave him a letter from Lewis Cass and one from John C. Calhoun. Ans[wer] to Letters I wrote them, and instructed him to answer them and shew them the folly of keeping p[e]ople out of their right[s] and that there was power in government to redress wrongs.

Mr. Keith gave a lecture and concert of music in the assembly room this eve. {page 214}

Thursday, Dec[ember] 28[th] 1843 At home. [*several lines left blank*] [Mr.] Keith lectured again in the Hall. {page 215}

Friday, Dec[ember] 29th At home. In the forenoon Bro[ther] Phelps called and gave us a lesson on eloquence and read my appeal to the Green Mountain boys, and also a New Year's Hymn without rhyme.

3 P.M. I related to Dr. Bernhisel and Joseph H. Jackson my commencement in receiving Rev[elation]. Mr. Jackson [who the following year wrote an expose entitled *A Narrative of the Adventures and Experiences of Joseph H. Jackson in Nauvoo, Disclosing the Depths of Mormon Villany*] said he was almost persuaded to be one with me. I replied I would to God he were not only almost but altogether.

At 4 P.M. in City Council 40 Policemen [were] sworn [in], whom I addressed at considerable length. See minutes of Council. Two petitions for licensing spirituous liquors. [*several lines left blank*] Cool, freezing. {page 216}

Saturday, Dec[ember] 30th 1843 9 A.M. Mayor's court in office. Two Boys, Roswell and Evander White, brought up for stealing 6 hens and Rooster. Sentence—pay for the hens and 10 days each hard labor on the road.

P.M. with the Quorum [of the anointed] in Assembly room. W[illia]m Law and wife were not present. [*several lines left blank*] Warm and rain. {page 217}

Sunday, Dec[ember] 31st At home. [*several lines left blank*] P.M. Called at Dr. Richards. Called again with Bro[ther] P[arley] P. Pratt to see his wife. To meeting early candle light till ten o'clock. Prayer Meeting. Sacrament [passed] after [which] I retired. [*several lines left blank*]

At 12 this night about 50 musicians and singers sung Phelp's New Year hymn under my window. Warm and rainy. No ice to be seen. {page 218}

January 1st 1844, Monday At sunrise Thomas Miller, James Leach, James Bridger, [and] John Frodsham were brought up before me by police for disorderly conduct. T[homas] Miller fined five dollars and cost. Others discharged. Wrote the Governor /T[homas] Ford/ See file. [*several lines left blank*]

A large party took a N[ew] Year supper at my house and continued music and dancing till morning. I was in my private room with my family and John Taylor &c. {page 219}

Tuesday, January 2d 1844 The party continued till morning. [*several lines left blank*] 2 P.M. Hiram Dayton was brought before Mayor Court for disorderly conduct in resisting and abusing the police in their duty. Fined $25.00 and cost. His son Lysander Dayton for same offence [was sentenced to] 10 days hard labor and subsequently for contempt of court 10 days more on the public streets. [*several lines left blank*] Cold, 1 inch [of] snow, first this winter of consequence. {page 220}

Wednesday, Jan[uary] 3d 1844 At home. [*several lines left blank*] 12 noon City Council. W[illia]m Law sworn, and Eli Norton concerning certain reports in circulation about a "doe" [dough] head [traitor] which proved to be all about nothing at all. [*several lines left blank*] Cloudy and cold. {page 221}

Thursday, January 4th 1844 At home. Another Tempest in a tea pot about nothing at all. W[illia]m Marks thought somebody had concluded he was the Brutus or doe head. Leonard Soby made affidavit that Warren Smith had said something about Law and Marks. Se[e] affidavit.

Took dinner in the North room. I was remarking to Bro[ther] Phelps what a kind, provident wife I had. That when I wanted a little bread and milk she would load the table with so many good things it would destroy my appetite. At this moment Emma came in and Bro[ther] Phelps in continuation of the conversation said, "You must do as [Napoleon] Bonaparte did [and] have a little table, just large enough for yourself and your order thereon." Mrs Smith replied, "Mr. Smith is a bigger man than Bonaparte. He can never eat without his friends." I remarked, "That is the wisest thing I ever heard you say." {page 222}

Friday, January 5th 1844 At home. 12 noon City Council. All about nothing at all. /W[illia]m Marks afraid Joseph had given some Saint[s the impression he was the traitor and that this] untruth [was communicated] to the police [who warmed themselves all night by a fire they had built just outside Marks's house.]/

4 1/2 [P.M.] adjourned. 5 went to my office. Bro[ther] Phelps made out commission for Joseph H. Jackson and Mariner J. Eaton as my aids as L[i]eut[enant] General. Returned home. [Spoke with] A number of gentlemen who had put up [boarded] with me and others. I sent for Bro[ther] Phelps who come in and read my letter to J[ohn] C. Calhoun. Dreamed about 2 serpents swallowing each tail foremost. [*several lines left blank*]

Commenced Snowing a little before sunset and continued all night. {page 223}

Saturday, January 6th At home. About ten o'clock rode out in a sleigh with Emma. Snow about 4 inches deep. [*several lines left blank*] Horace L. Eldridge county constable went to Carthage with a precept from R[obert] D. Foster, J[ustice] [of the] P[eace,] to apprehend Milton Cook in a case of Bastardy on complaint of Olive Smith, not a member of the Church. Eldridge made the arrest and the prisoner was taken from him by force of arms and he [Eldridge] returned to this city. [*several lines left blank*] Good sleighing. {page 224}

Sunday, January 7th 1844 At home in the morning. Rode out to my farm and preached at Bro[ther] Lot's. Also O[rson] Spencer and Reynolds Cahoon preached. [*several lines left blank*]

6 P.M. attended the prayer meeting in the assembly room. Law absent. Marks not present. [*several lines left blank*] Very cold. {page 225}

Monday, Jan[uary] 8th At home in the morning. 11 A.M. went to My office to investigate a difficulty between John D. Parker and his wife. Staid about 2 hours left the case to Bro[ther] Phelps, who labored to produce a reconciliation with good effect.

Each agreeing to promote each others happiness, which if they kept their covenant, Bro[ther] Phelps told them God would bless them and if they did not God would curse them.

Had an interview with W[illia]m Law in the street [in] front of Bro[ther] Phelps. Uncle John Smith come from Macedonia to day. Amos Fielding arrived from Liverpool and put up at Sniders.

Eldri[d]ge returned to Carthage with a possey of 11 men to apprehend Milton Cook. Could not get him and put up at Hamilton's for the night. Some snow this eve. {page 226}

Tuesday, Jan[uary] 9[th] At home. About 10 Bro[ther] Phelps called just as I was about to ride out. [*several lines left blank*] Eldri[d]ge and possey found Milton Cook in a grocery and arrest[ed] him and he was again taken from him. See "Nauvoo Neighbor" January 10[th] 1844 [for] Mr. Markam's account. {page 227}

Wednesday, Jan[uar]y 10[th] At home ordained Uncle John Smith a Patriarch. Enjoyed myself well in an interview with Brethren and concluded to take a ride part way with Uncle John who is about to return to Macedonia.

Lawyer Backman and another Lawyer viz Sherman, and Mr. Hamilton called on me from Carthage and stated that our late ordinance concerning search and Seizure of persons and property by forcing [outside law enforcement personnel to work through Nauvoo courts but refusing to recognize due] process [as executed by other courts] was the cause of dissatisfaction and what led them people to resist the Law. I explained it fully to them and called the City Council together at my house at 7 eve who passed an amendment [requiring cooperation with officers of the county and state in their official duties], see records, to satisfy the mobocrats and prevent mistakes among all.

Wrote a letter to Esq[ui]r[e] Backman to let him know I had called the council and fulfilled my promise. See file.

William Jones staid all night at Wilson's tavern in Carthage. Very cold. {page 228}

Thursday, January 11[th] 1844 At home. At 10 A.M. rode out and returned [at] 1 1/2 P.M. This morning W[illia]m Jones was arrested by Col[onel] Levi Williams and his company and kept him in custody without rations till noon. [*several lines left blank*]

The Twelve [Apostles] issued notices to the Saints at Nauvoo to cut and draw 75 or 100 cords of wood for the Prophet on the 15th and 16th January. [*rest of page blank*] {page 229}

Friday, January 12th 1844 [*several lines left blank*] Thaw, Snow nearly gone. {page 230}

Saturday, January 13th 1844 At home in the Morning. 10 o'clock went into City County [Council] and continued till sunset with one hour's intermission for dinner. Saw Petitions for Licence to retail spirits called up &c. [*rest of page blank*] {page 231}

Sunday, Jan[uar]y 14th 1844 At home. [*several lines left blank*] Prayer meeting at the assembly room. Did not go. \\[10]/H[eber] C. K[imball] and G[eorge] A. S[mith] in history office G[reat] S[alt] L[ake] City, Jan[uar]y 4[th] 1857 ~~that~~ //say// B[righam] Y[oung] and wife Mary Ann anointed/ \\[11]Warm, rainy towards night and evening. {page 232}

Monday, January 15th 1844 At home. Wrote Sister Martha L. Campbell, Almira, N[ew] Y[ork]. At 9 [A.M.] teams began to draw wood according to the appointment of the Twelve [Apostles]. At 10 Dr. Richards called and told me it was reported that Francis Higby was going to put me under $10,000 bond for speaking against him. At the same time Constable Eldridge summoned me to attend a court as witness before Esqu[i]r[e] Johnson and I went over accordingly to give my testimony. [*several lines left blank*]

I[n] the course of the day gave instructions to the Clerk of Municipal Court to Issue a Warrant for the arrest of Francis M. Higby on affidavit of Orson Pratt. [*several lines left blank*]

100 or 200 chopped in the woods. [*several lines left blank*] East wind in A.M. some rain. Wind N.W. in the P.M. very brisk. {page 233}

Tuesday, Jan[uary] 16th 1844 10 A.M. F[rancis] M. Higby was brought up on complaint of O[rson] Pratt before Municipal Court for absenting himself from City Council without leave—when [he should have been] in attendance as a witness—and for slanderous and abusive language towards one of the members of the Council. Court adjourned and City Council commenced their session and continued till two o'clock.

During which time a reconciliation took place with Francis

---

[10] Possibly in the handwriting of Thomas Bullock.
[11] In the handwriting of Willard Richards.

M. Higby who had written a slanderous letter concerning me and said many hard things which he acknowledged and I forgave him. I went before the Council and stated that all difficulties between me and Francis M. Higby are eternally buried and I am to be his friend forever. To which F. M. Higby replied I will be his friend forever and his right hand man.

Wrote James H. Lyman (in reply) Lenox, Ashtebulow, Ohio. At home, interviewed with Bro[ther] Phelps. [*several lines left blank*] Cold and windy. {page 234}

Wednesday, Jan[uary] 17[th] 1844 At home. [*rest of page blank*] {page 235}

Thur[s]day, Jan[uary] 18[th] At home. Wrote a letter to Joseph Coe, Kirtland. Also to Reuben McBride, Kirtland. Also to Clark Seal, Fountain Green and Justin Butterfield Esqu[ire], Chicago.

Toward night rode out. In the evening called at my office. [*several lines left blank*] A Cotillion Party at the Nauvoo Mansion in the Evening.

This afternoon Some one called on Bro[ther] Nelsen Judd and wanted to sell him some wood below Hibbards. He went to see the wood the man saying he would meet him at the place. When below Hibbards two men come up on horseback and told him they had a warrant for him for taking away Avery's things from Bear Creek. One shot at him twice and the other snapped at him twice each [with] his pistols. "Now tis my turn." said Judd, putting his hand in his pocket but having no pistols and the men fled. Moderate, thawed some. Eve cool and clear. {page 236}

Friday, January 19th 1844 At home. [*several lines left blank*] Rode out in the course of the day. [*several lines left blank*] In the evening gave a Lecture on the Constitution and candidates for the Presidency &c. Backenstos, clerk of the Co[unty] Court, [was] present. Bro[ther] Phelps and a great Co[mpany] in Bar Room. [*several lines left blank*] Mild weather, Cloudy P.M. and eve. {page 237}

Saturday, Jan[uary] 20th At home. Called at my office about ten [A.M.] to hold court. Adjourned till 4 P.M. 4 P.M. held court at office, City of Nauvoo vs Stephen Wilkison, /for breach of ordinance/ discharged by paying cost. [*several lines left blank*] Eve 6 Prayer Meeting. H[eber] C. Kimball and wife present [and anointed to the fullness of the priesthood]. I was at home. {page 238}

Sunday, January 21st 1844 Preached in front of Dr. Foster's Mammoth Hotel to several thousand people — although weather was somewhat unpleasant — on sealing the hearts of the fathers to the children and the hearts of the children to the fathers. [*several lines left blank*]

Prayer meeting over store. Parley P. Pratt present [and received second anointing]. Joseph not there. [*several lines left blank*] Mild weather. {page 239}

Monday, January 22d At home. Rain, wind Easterly. Rented the /Nauvoo/ Mansion house to Ebenezer Robinson for $1,000 per annum. [plus] Board for myself and family and horses, reserving myself 3 rooms in the house. [*several lines left blank*] Prayer Meeting at Pres[iden]t Young's, 10 present. [*several lines left blank*] Mud very deep. {page 240}

Tuesday, January 23[rd] 1843 [1844] At home. [*several lines left blank*] E[benezer] Robinson took possession of the /"Nauvoo/ Mansion" to continue it as a public house. [*several lines left blank*]

This day W[illiam] W. Phelps, N[ewell] K. Whitney, and W[illard] Richards priced the printing office and Lot at $1500, printing apparatus $950.00, Bindery [$] 112, foundry [$] 270. Total $2,832. Joseph being about selling to J. Taylor. [*several lines left blank*]

Cotillion party [met] in the evening at Nauvoo Mansion. [*several lines left blank*] Night clear and cold. Thawed some during the day. {page 241}

Wednesday, January 24th 1844 At home. [*several lines left blank*] Called at my office about 1 o'clock thought the apprisal of the printing office was too low. [*several lines left blank*] Very cold.

Thursday, Jan[uary] 25th 1844 At home. [*several lines left blank*] Prayer meeting at at Bro[ther] Brigham's. O[rson] Hyde [was] present. 8 of the 12 [Apostles were present]. [*several lines left blank*] Extremely cold. {page 242}

Friday, Jan[uary] 26th At home. [*several lines left blank*] 2 [P.M.] Afternoon reading the [Nauvoo] Neighbor. [*several lines left blank*] Went to the office and instructed Bro[ther] Phelps to write a piece on the situation of the nation — referring to the President's Messages &c. [*several lines left blank*]

Prayer meeting at Bro[ther] Young's. 8 of the [Twelve

Apostles were present]. O[rson] Pratt [was] present [and anointed to the fullness of the priesthood]. O[rson] Hyde [has] gone to Carthage to preach. [*several lines left blank*] Clear and cool. {page 243}

Saturday, Jan[uary] 27th 1844 [*several lines left blank*] Prayer Meeting at the Store chamber. W[illard] Richards present [and anointed to the fullness of the priesthood]. [*several lines left blank*] Extremely cold and clear. {page 244}

Sunday, January 28th 1844 At home. [*several lines left blank*] Had some company in the eve from Warsaw &c. Lectured to them on politics, religion, &c. [*several lines left blank*] Prayer Meeting at the store. Present W[ilford] Woodruff [who was anointed to the fullness of the priesthood]. [*several lines left blank*] Cold continues. {page 245}

Monday, January 29th 1844 At 10 A.M. The Twelve [Apostles] met at the Mayor's office [with] Joseph and Hyrum [and] J[ohn] P. Green. Moved by Willard Richards and voted unanimously that we have independent electors and that Joseph Smith be a candidate for the next presidency [of the United States] and that we use all honorable means to secure his election.

Joseph said to accomplish this you must send every man in the city who could speak throughout the land to electioneer, [to give] stump speech[es] — [about the] Mormon religion-election Laws &c. &c. Yearsly must go. Parley to N[ew] York. Snow to V[ermon]t. Rigdon to Pa.

"After the April conference we will have gen[eral] conferences all over the nation and I will attend them. Tell the people we have had Whig and Democrats [as] Presidents long enough. We want a President of the United States. If I ever get in the Presidential chair I will protect the people in their rights and liberties. I will not electione[e]r for myself, Hyrum, Brigham, Parley, and Taylor must go. The Whigs are striving for a king under the garb of Democracy. There is oretory enough in the Church to carry me into the Presidential chair the first slide." Cold, very. {page 246}

Mr. Bedell wanting an election at Warsaw, Benjamin Winchester was appointed to go. Capt[ain] White of Quincy was at the Mansion last night and this morning drank a toast: "May all your enemies be skined, their skins made into drum heads for your friends to beat upon. Also may Nauvoo become the empire seat of government." Capt[ain] White.

Clayton must go out or he will apostatize. Must. Also gave some instructions concerning an address to the paper for Bro[ther] Phelps to write — views on the powers and policy of the Government of United States &c.

A Millerite Lecturer come in to the office with Joseph and Clayton about 5 P.M. [and] had some conversation about Hades and Shaol &c. and Lectured in the evening in the Hall. [*rest of page blank*] {page 247}

Tuesday, January 30th 1844 11 A.M. went into the office with Col[onel] Jackson. [*several lines left blank*] 1 P.M. Court at my office, City versus Thomas Coates, fined $25 and costs for beating John Ellison. [*several lines left blank*]

A Millerite preached again in the assembly room [to a] full house and Elder Rigdon replied to him. Prayer Meeting at B[righam] Young's. John Taylor and wife present [and received second anointing]. [*rest of page blank*] {page 248}

Wednesday, January 31[st] At home. [*several lines left blank*] 11 o'clock A.M. called at the office. Told Ben[jami]n Winchester to go to Warsaw and preach the first principles of the Gospel &c. Get some Lexicons and returned home. [*several lines left blank*]

Prayer meeting at B[righam] Young's. Geo[rge] A. Smith and wife present [and anointed to the fullness of the priesthood]. /Geo[rge] A. Smith and wife Bathsheba W. Bigler received their Second Anointing which was administered by Brigham Young, Pres[iden]t of the Twelve [Apostles]/ {page 249}

Thursday, Feb[ruary] 1[st] 1844 At home. [*several lines left blank*] Cold. {page 250}

Friday, Feb[ruary] 2[nd] At home. [*several lines left blank*] 7 [P.M.] eve Dr. Richards called and read Phinehas Richard's appeal to the inhabitants of Mass for redress of M[iss]o[uri] difficulties. [*several lines left blank*]

Prayer meeting at Br[other] Young's. W[illiam] W. Phelps and wife [were anointed]. [*several lines left blank*] Cold. {page 251}

Saturday, Feb[ruary] 3rd 1844 At home. [*several lines left blank*] Prayer meeting over the Store in the P.M. Joseph not present. W[illia]m Clayton and Joseph Young and wife present [and anointed]. [*rest of page blank*] {page 252}

Sunday, Feb[ruary] 4th 1844 [*several lines left blank*] I attended in the [*blank*] [*blank*]. Evening at the prayer meeting [at the] Brick Store. Cornelius P. Lot and wife present [and anointed]. [*rest of page blank*] {page 253}

Monday, Feb[ruary] 5th 1844 Called at my office in the evening and heard read my views of the Gen[eral] Government. I was the first one who publicly proposed a National Bank on the principles I had advanced. [*rest of page blank*] {page 254}

Tuesday, Feb[ruary] 6th [*several lines left blank*] Evening with Hyrum and Sidney and the 12 [Apostles] and the wives at John Taylor's at 5 P.M. at supper. Very pleasant time. I prophesied at the table that 5 years would not roll round before the company would all be able to live without cooking. [*rest of page blank*] {page 255}

Wednesday, Feb[ruary] 7th [*several lines left blank*] Evening met the Twelve [Apostles] and Hyrum at my office /at their request/ to devise means to promote the interest of the gen[eral] Government. [*rest of page blank*] {page 256}

Thursday, Feb[ruary] 8th 1844 [*several lines left blank*] Court trial on 2 negroes trying to marry white women. Fined 1, $25.00 and 1, $5.00. Evening had a political Meeting in the assembly room and Br[other] Phelps publicly read my views of the Gen[eral] Government for the first time. Elders Hyde and Taylor made a speech and myself also. [*rest of page blank*] {page 257}

Friday, Feb[ruary] 9th 1844 At home. [*several lines left blank*] 1 o['cloc]k P.M. held Mayor's Court in dining room, Nauvoo vs W[illia]m Withers for assault. Suit withdrawn. [*rest of page blank*] {page 258}

Saturday, Feb[ruary] 10th At home. Held court, Nauvoo vs W[illia]m Withers for assault. Suit aborted, parties settled. Isaac Morley came and gave my clerks Phelps and Richards – 1 box [of] flour worth $4.50 – 2.50 himself, Gardner Snow $1.00, Henry Deam 1.00, 2 or 3 gallons of soap, a small [-], 4 brooms, a pound or two of butter from the brethren at Lima at the request of the 12 [Apostles], so that they might continue to write.

I instructed the Marshall to inform Mr. Cole the teacher that I must have the assembly room over the store for my own use for the future. [*several lines left blank*]

Prayer meeting [at] assembly Room [we] prayed for Sister Richards and others. {page 259}

Sunday, Feb[ruary] 11th 1844 At home. [*several lines left blank*] Pr[ayer] Meeting adjourned till Saturday next. [*rest of page blank*] {page 260}

Monday, Feb[ruary] 12th Sat in City Council. I suggested the repeal of the ordinances "Extra care of Joseph Smith," "unlawful search and seizure of person and property in Nauvoo," and "Regulating the currency" and they were repealed. Council signed the Memorial /to Congress/ of 21 December and instructed O[rson] Pratt to start immediately and told him how to proceed. Burned $81 [in] Scrip of the city according to ordinance. [*rest of page blank*] {page 261}

Tuesday, Feb[ruary] 13th 1844 At home. [*rest of page blank*] {page 262}

Wednesday, Feb[ruary] 14th 1844 At home. [*rest of page blank*] {page 263}

Thursday, Feb[ruary] 15th 1844 At home. [*rest of page blank*] {page 264}

Friday, Feb[ruary] 16th At home. [*several lines left blank*] This eve spent 2 hours in my office in conversation with Bro[ther] Phelps. [I] directed him to write a communication on Gov[ernor] Ford's Letter in the Warsaw Signal. [*rest of page blank*] {page 265}

Saturday, Feb[ruary] 17th 1844 At home. [*rest of page blank*] {page 266}

Sunday, Feb[ruary] 18th 1844 I preached at the Temple to a large collection. [*several lines left blank*]

4 P.M. Went to my office with Hyrum and 2 men from St. Louis. Heard Dr. Richards read my correspondence with Calhoun and Phelps [read] My views of the gen[eral] Government. I attended Prayer Meeting at seven over the store. Sister Hyde was there.

Fine warm weather for a week with cold nights. The ice left the south shore of the city this morning of many [-] extant. {page 267}

Monday, Feb[ruary] 19th 1844 9 A.M. went to my office with Dr. Bernhisel who proposed some alterations in my views of the government. Phelps read the same and the Doctor seemed better pleased with it than before. [*rest of page blank*] {page 268}

Tuesday, Feb[ruary] 20[th] 1844 At home. At 10 A.M. went to my office where the Twelve [Apostles] and some others met in council with Bro[ther]s Mitchel Curtis and Stephen Curtis who left the pinery, 1st of January, Black River. [They were] sent by Lyman Wight and Bishop Miller to know whither Lyman should preach to the indians. The Menominees and Chippeway having requested it. The Chippeways had given Bro[ther] Wight some wampum as token of peace and the brethren had given them 1/2 box flour and an ox to keep them from starving and Wight had gone through to Green Bay with them to mark a road.

I told them to tell Bro[ther] Wight I have no council to ~~shed blood~~ /give/ him. He is there on his own ground and he must act on his own responsibility and do what he thinks best and he shall never be brought into any difficulty about it by us.

I instructed the 12 [Apostles] to send out a delegation and investigate the locations of California and Oregon and find a good location where we can remove after the Temple is completed and build a city in a day and have a government of our own in a healthy climate.

Dr. Richards received a letter from Ja[me]s A. Bennet which /pleased me much. At office./ Warm. Ice began to come down from above in the river.

[*written sideways on the page*] /Visited at James Irvins this P.M. and evening/ {page 269}

Wednesday, Feb[ruary] 21[st] 1844 At home. [*several lines left blank*] Rev. De Wolf, Churchman, lectured in the assembly room in the eve. I attended and after sermon at his request spoke to the people to show them that to get salvation we must not only do some things but every thing which God had commanded to get salvation.

At the same hour, the Twelve [Apostles] met in my office and selected 8 men to fulfil the exploring expedition. I mentioned to them on the 20th and they adjourned to meet at the assembly room [on the] evening [of the] 23rd.

This day published a Pacific Inunendo [in the *Nauvoo Neighbor*] in concurrence with Governor's letter. Also letter to Mr. Taylor to let Warsaw Signal alone. [*several lines left blank*]

Ice left the west bank of the city opposite lower brick house. Very warm and pleasant. {page 270}

Thursday, Feb[ruary] 22nd 1844 At home. [*several lines left blank*] Ice continues to run in the river. Very pleasant. Cool night. {page 271}

447

Friday, Feb[ruary] 23rd 1844 W[illiam] W. Phelps re-[ceive]d letter from J[ohn] Whitmer on Church history &c. which Dr. Richards replied to. Letter on file—copy. [*several lines left blank*]

Met with the 12 [Apostles] &c. in assembly Room concerning the Oregon Expidition. I told them I wanted an exposition of all that count[r]y. Send 25 men. Let them preach the Gospel whereever they go. Let that man go that can raise $500, a horse or mule, a double barrel gun, one rifle, and one shot, saddle, bridle, [a] p[ai]r [of] 8 bore Pistols, Bowie knife, &c. Appoint a leader. Let him beat up for volunteers. I want every man that goes to be a king and Priest, when he gets on the mountains he may want to talk with his God. When with the savage nations have power to govern &c. If we don't get volunteers wait till after the election. Samuel Bent volunteered. Joseph A. Kilting volunteered. David Fulmer volunteered. [*several lines left blank*] Very pleasant. {page 272}

Saturday, Feb[ruary] 24[th] 1844 At home. Had an interview with Bro[ther] Phelps at 9 o'clock. [*several lines left blank*] Seth Palmer volunteered to go to Oregon. Amos Fielding volunteered. Cha[rle]s Shumway volunteered. John S. Fullmer volunteered. [*several lines left blank*]

1,500 copies of my views [*General Smith's Views of the Powers and Policy of the Government of the United States*] out of press. [*several lines left blank*]

Very pleasant the past two weeks. The pleasantest February I ever saw. {page 273}

Sunday, Feb[ruary] 25th 1844 I preached at or near the Temple. Hiram also preached. [*several lines left blank*] Eve[ning] Prayer Meeting over the store. Prayed that Gen[eral] Smith's views of the /power and policy of the U.S./ United States might be spread far and wide and be the means of opening the hearts of the people. Some rain this eve. Cloudy and foggy. {page 274}

Monday, Feb[ruary] 26th 1844 At home. P.M. Held Court at the Mansion. City of Nauvoo vs O[rsimus] F. Bostwick on complaint of Hyrum Smith for slanderous language concerning Hyrum and certain females of Nauvoo. Fined Bostwick $50.00 and costs.

F[rancis] M. Higbee, his attorney, gave notice he should appeal to the Municipal court and then to the circuit court. I told him what I thought of him trying to carry such a suit to Carthage. It was to stir up the mob, and bring them upon us &c. [*several lines left blank*]

Prayer Meeting over store. P.M. John Smith there. Eve[ning] Father Morley there. Had his second anointing in evening. John Smith and wife had their second anointing. Foggy. {page 275}

Tuesday, Feb[ruary] 27th 1844 At home. [*several lines left blank*] P.M. Went over to the printing press &c. Mailed Gen[eral] Smith's Views to the President and Cabinet, Supreme [Court] Judges, Senators, Representatives, principal papers in the U.S. all the Governors, and many postmasters and individuals. In all about 200. [*several lines left blank*] Cool and clear. River clear of ice. {page 276}

Wednesday, Feb[ruary] 28th 1844 At home. [*several lines left blank*] Phelps writing on O[rsimus] F. Bostwick for [the *Nauvoo Nieghbor* on behalf of the] women. 4 P.M. Steamer Gen[eral] Brooks passed up the river for the [first appearance of a] boat this season. No ice in sight. [*several lines left blank*]

Eve[ning], I sent Bro[ther] Coolidge to Bro[ther] Phelps to call the Brethren and pray for Bro[ther] Coolidge['s] sick child. He thought [it] could not live till morning. Bro[ther] Taylor, Phelps, and Richards prayed for him. Rainy day. {page 277}

Feb[ruary] 29[th] 1844 Thursday At home. [*several lines left blank*] Called at my office. Called out Bro[ther] Phelps and gave him the "Zanesville Gazette" on Jan[uar]y 31[st] containing the speech of Cassius M. Clay delivered in Scot County, K[entuck]y, Dec[ember] 30[th] 1843 on annexing Texas to the U[nited] S[tates] and instructed him to reply to the same, and gave him the matter and manner &c. and rode on with [Orrin] Porter Rockwell. [*several lines left blank*] Ohio Steamer went up the river. [*several lines left blank*] Rainy night. {page 278}

Journal

1 8 4 4

T his is the fourth and last of the jour-
nals Willard Richards kept for Joseph
Smith. *The original is housed in the archives of the Historical Department,
Church of Jesus Christ of Latter-day Saints, Salt Lake City, Utah.*

President Joseph Smith['s] Journal Kept by
W[illard] Richards
Vol[ume] 4 {cover page}
Commencing March 1st 1844

Friday, [1 March 1844] Spent the day in councilling. [*rest
of page left blank*] {page 1}

Saturday, March 2nd 1844 At home. [*several lines left
blank*] 10 A.M. Court at my office. [*several lines left blank*] /Pri-
vately in presence of Richards and Phelps/ reproved Bro[ther]
Stoddard for giving appearance of evil in attempting to be bail
for O[rsimus] F. Bostwick. Bro[ther] Stoddard explained and satisfied me. Interview with Richards and Phelps. [*several lines left
blank*] Cold night. {page 2}

Sunday, March 3d 1844 A little snow this morning. [*several lines left blank*] Prayer meeting a little while. {page 3}

Previous to the following meeting, Pres[iden]t Smith nominated /Ja[me]s/ Arlington Bennet [for] Vice Pres[iden]t.

Monday, March 4th 1844 At a meeting of the 1st Presidency, Twelve [Apostles], Temple Committee, &c. this eve at early candlelight. Geo[rge] Corey said he was sent by Lyman Wight to get sheep &c. to carry to the pine country to receipt it or agree to pay lumber.

Pres[iden]t Joseph said he did not know but it was best to let the Nauvoo House be till the Temple is completed. We need the Temple more than anything Else.

"Elder Hawes said there was some dissatisfaction about being sent from the pinery without accounts &c. and could not have credit on tithing. One month at the pinery is only called 15 days here." I [Joseph Smith] told them they should have their number of days in full. {page 4}

We will let the Nauvoo House stand till the Temple is done and we will put all our forces on the Temple. Turn all our lumber towards the Temple. Stock the lumber we want for the Temple, cover it this fall and sell the remainder to get Powder &c. When the Temple is completed, no man shall pass the threshhold till he has paid $5.00 and every stranger shall pay $5.00. I will not have the house dirted.

Let Woodworth go to the Pinery [and] take the things wanted and bring back the lumber and his wages [will] go on. Let a special conference be called on 6th April [and let] all the Elders [be] called here who can come. {page 5} Let the people of this city come together on Thursday 9 A.M. After 2 or 3 Lectures we will call in the people to fill up the [contribution] box.

Instructed a letter to be written to [James] Arlington Bennet, [informing that Joseph had] nominate[d] him for Vice Pres[iden]t. Election in Nauvoo, start the Herald and give a $1,000 [contribution] to the Temple. [*several lines left blank*] Temple committee offered to make [blasting] powder. [*several lines left blank*] Dr. Richards wrote [James] Arlington Bennet on his election to Vice Presidency. [*rest of page blank*] {page 6}

Tuesday, March 5th 1844 I saw Hiram Kimball at Bryants' Store an[d] gave him a lecture on his resisting the ordinances of the city by telling the Capt[ains] of the boats they need not pay wharfage &c.

Rode out with Emma. 2 P.M. in City Council. I called

to see whether the laws of the city [regarding wharfage fees] should be maintained which the Council decided should be and Water Street be opened from my store to the northern limits of the city. Heard Dr. Richards read his letter to [James] Arlington Bennet informing him of his nomination to the Vice Presidency, Dated 4th March. {page 7}

Wednesday, March 6th 1844 Went to my office [and] from there with Phelps to Bryants to see him about his uniting with [Hiram] Kimball and others to stay the ordinances of the city [regarding wharf tax]. [rest of page blank] {page 8}

Thursday, March 7th 1844 9 A.M. [rest of page blank] {page 9} I /Joseph/ presented to the meeting the proceedings of O. F. Bostwick and the Lawyers &c. [in which Bostwick was fined for saying that Hyrum Smith and the leading women of Nauvoo were promiscuous, and asked] for the people to speak out, say[ing] whether such men should be tolerated and supported in our midst. "From this time I design to bring such characters before the committee of the whole and if these things cannot be put a stop to, I will give them in to the hands of the mob. The hands of the officers of the /city/ falter, and are palsied by the conduct of such men.

"There is another I will speak about. He is a Mormon. A certain man who lived here before we come here. The two first letters of his {page 10} name are Hiram Kimball. When the city had passed an ordinance to tax steam boats, he goes and tells the captains of the steam boats that he owned the landing and they need not to pay tax and I am determined to use up such men if they will not stop their efforts. If this is not true, let him come forward and throw of[f] the imputation. When they appeal to Carthage I will appeal to this people, the highest court. I despise the Lawyers who lag on their Law suits. Kimball and Morrison say they own the wharfs, but the city own[s] the wharf, 64 feet from high water mark from printing office to the northern limits of the city. {page 11}

"Another thing I want to speak about the Lawyers of this city. I have good feelings and I will reprove them and the prophets always did say wo unto you ye lawyers. The Maratim[e] laws of the U[nited] S[tates] have ced[ed] up the tolls, wharfage, &c. to the respective corporation[s] who have jurisdiction &c.

"Shallow drafts intoxicate the brain &c. Look at the rea-

son. No vessel could land any where if subject to individual[s']
laws. [The] Corporation owns the streets of the city and have a
right to tax the Boats to make wharfs. The same as to tax citizens
to make roads. [I] Want every man in this city to stay at home
and let the Boat Captains, {page 12} peace officers, and every
body alone. [*several lines left blank*]

"Ho[w] are we to keep peace in this city, and defend our
selves against mobs, [unless I] disgrace every man by preaching
him on the house top, who will not be still, and mind their own
business. Let them alone to use themselves up.

"A couple of [dishonest] merchants in this city. I was told
by an old gentleman this morning /who told me/ that the spirit of
Mobocracy was almost subsiding. [But] These [local] mobocrats
have as the people abroad say, told the people that they need not
bring butter, eggs &c. /to Nauvoo/ [I] will not tell their names. If
they will not let the people bring in their produce, the people will
not buy their [the merchants'] goods. {page 13}

"Another man, [I] will not call his name, has been writing to New York Tribune some of the most disgraceful things possible to name. He has stated in that article that there are a great
many appropriations to the Temple applied some where else &c.
To stigmatize the Trustees and turn prejudice against us abroad.
If any man who has appointed any thing [to be applied to the
construction of the temple — an] old harness horses waggon &c.
/let him come forward [and I will show that there is not]/ the first
farthing and we cannot show where it has been appropriated, [or]
I will give him my head for a foot ball.

"He also states that the Temple cannot be built [because]
it costs so {page 14} much. Who don't know that we can put the
roof on this building this season? By turning all the means of the
N[auvoo] House and doubling our diligence we can do it.

"The best way for such men is to be still. If I did not love
men I would not reprove them, but [would] work in the dark as
they do. Read the Tribune and you see for yourself.

"[I will not say who wrote the article, but I will say that]
He is not a lawyer, he is nearer related to a Doctor, a small
man — 'Mr. McNiel — enquired if he was the man.' No did not
know you. You are a stranger." Joseph rested.

Pres[iden]t Hyrum spoke saying he wanted to make some
observations of a romantic turn. The character of such men {page

453

15} ought to be noted by every man[. If he] had a[n] old country [gift for metaphor, he would say he would] ferret them out like rats &c. You could describe them as you would a Hedgehog, in every hedge [you find them. An ambitious man is always] turning /himself/ [around, changing colors like a tree toad and stinking] like the skunk, like pollywogs running about with tail[s], drop[ping them] off [to become] toads &c. [A] soul [worth] $5.00 [is cheaper than a] gizzard.

Cha[rle]s Foster asked if Joseph meant him. Joseph said I will ask you a question[. Foster:] that is no way [to answer]. [Smith:] Yes, that is this way the Quakers do. Why did you denominate yourself. Jesus said whose image and superscription is it. [Foster:] Did you mean me. [Smith:] Why did you denominate yourself. [Foster:] /Then I understand/ you meant me. [Smith:] You said it. [Foster:] You shall hear from me. [Smith: As] Mayor I fine you $10.00 for that threat and disturbing the meeting. Doctor Foster[, his brother,] spoke to palliate and exhort him to await &c. {page 16} Doctor said he has not threatened you. Joseph says he has. Doctor[:] no one has heard him threaten you, and hundreds cried I have. Doctor continued to speak and Mayor ~~said stop~~ /order/ or I will fine you [as well].

W[illiam] W. Phelps read Gen[eral] Smith's views of the powers and policies of the Gen[eral] Government, after which it was voted unanimously with one exception, to uphold Gen[eral] Smith for the Presidency.

"A voice of Innocence from Nauvoo" [in response to Bostwick's allegations] was then read by W[illiam] W. Phelps and all the people [in the] assembly said Amen. Twice.

Doctor Foster read a letter from Thomas Ford Governor. {page 17} 30 minutes past 12. Adjourned till 2 P.M.

2 P.M. assembled according to adjournment. Singing and Prayer by O[rson] Pratt. Singing.

President B[righam] Young addressed the congregation to give his views on the Lawyers who first arose among the children of Israel to explain [God's law] to the common people. I am a Lawyer in Israel. My business is to make peace among the people, and men who takes any other course is out of the line of his duty. A Lawyer's duty is [to] tell what the Law is and then let the people go and act upon it and let them receive pay like any laboring man.

It is desirable for justices of the peace, when men call for writs to inquire into the case {page 18} and tell them how to settle, and thus put down law suits. To cure lawing, let us pay attention to our own business, when we hear a story never tell it again and it will be a perfect cure.

If your bro[ther] mistreats you let him alone. If your enemy cheats you let it go. Cease to deal with men who abuse. If all men had taken the course that some have we should not have such men in our midst. I have no objections to any mans coming here, but then I will have nothing to do with men who will stone me at midnight and at noon day &c.

Our difficulties and persecutions have always arisen from men right in our midst. It is the lust of individuals to rob us of every thing and build themselves up in our division.

I feel that I want that every man should stay and lift holy hands without wrath or dubiety {page 19} to the men who own land here, do not think you can sell your lands here and then go off and spend it in abusing the Mormons. Israel is the head and not the tale.

I expect the saints are so anxious to work and so ready to do right that God has whispered to the prophet, build the temple, and let the N[auvoo] House alone at present. I would not sue a man if he owed me 500 [dollars] or a thousand $ [dollars] and he come to me and told me he would not pay. [I would simply not do business with him again until he paid me.]

Bro[ther] Taylor said that it was said by some that the Municipal offices of the city were acting in an arbitrary manner, and which was false &c. and went on to explain the principles of democracy.

Stopped awhile for a contribution to get {page 20} fuse and powder. A boat was coming down and the messenger was waiting to go to St. Louis. Collected 50 or 60 dollars.

Bro[ther] Taylor continued his speech. When society was first organized they found themselves without Legislature Congress House of Lord or anything of the kind, every man was Lord over his own house.

Difficulties began to contend and combine together in governments bye and bye. Soon 2 or three requested they might return to their original customs and the government said they might. This is the situation of this city, in the main, [and why we] worked for a charter &c.

Of Gen[eral] Smith some are afraid. Think it doubtful about his election and like the ostrich stick their heads under a bush and leave their bodies out, and we can all see them and after this it will [be] a bye word that [that] man is an Ostrich who hides his head in this corner. {page 21} Spoke also on the going on with the Temple.

Pres[iden]t Young spoke. Men who have not paid their property tithing [should know] we shall call on them and take dinner and we had rather be saved that trouble and have them come up and pay.

Elder Cahoon said if any one had any doubt about the state of the temple, let them call and see the Books and where they have paid their tithing show it entered on the book paid in full for /the/ year &c.

Joseph said in relation to those who give property on the Temple, be careful into /whose/ hands it come into that it may be entered into the Church books. That those whose names are found in the Church books shall have the first claim in that house. "I intend to keep the door at dedication myself and not a man {page 22} shall pass who had not paid his bonus.

"I do not care 1/2 so much about the Pres[idential] election as I do the office I have got. We have as good a right to make political party to gain power to defend ourselves as for demagogues to make use of our religion to get power to destroy ourselves. We will whip the mob by getting up a President. When I look into the Eastern papers and see how popular I am I am afraid I shall be President.

"On the annexation of Texas, some object. The anti-Mormons are good fellows. I say it in anticipation they will repent. {page 23} Object to Texas on account of slavery. Tis the very reason why she should be received.

"Houston says, 'Gentleman, if you refuse to receive us we must go to the British' and the first thing they will do will be to set the negroes and indians [against us] and they will use us up. British officers running all over Texas to pick a quarrel with us[. It would be] more honorable for us [as a nation] to receive them and set the negroes free and use the negro and indians against our foes.

"Don't let Texas go lest our Mother and the daughters of the land will laugh us {page 24} in the teeth. If these things are not so God never spoke by any prophet since the world began. I have been [. . . [discreet about what I know]] [*several lines left blank*] [. . . [In the struggle between the north and the]] south, [if the south] held the balance of power &c. by annexing Texas[, this could still be remedied]. I can do away [with] this evil [and] liberate [the slaves in] 2 or 3 states and if that was not sufficient, call in Canada [to be annexed].

Send the negroes to Texas [and] from Texas to Mexico where all colors are alike. Notice was given for the Relief Society to meet Saturday 2 P.M. to adopt *"the voice of Innocence from Nauvoo"*

/Joseph stated the Mormon Zion has endured all animus. [- - - - - - - - - -]/

Singing and prayer by B[righam] Young. {page 25}

March 8th 1844 Bishop Miller arrived from the Pinery this morning. At 10 A.M. my scribe, W[illard] Richards, called to see me and told me James Arlington Bennet was a native of Ireland and could not be Vice President and wanted to know who should be the candidate. I told him he [should] council with others on that point. Said he, "I will call a council this evening." [*several lines left blank*]

7 eve [the] First Presidency, Twelve [Apostles], Bishop Miller, L[evi] Richards, W[illiam] Phelps, [and] Woodworth assembled in the Mayor's {page 26} office and W[illiam] W. Phelps read a pacific communication I had instructed him to write to U[nited] S[tates] Called *"A Friendly hint to Missouri."*

I[t] was said by Geo[rge] A. Smith that Bro[ther] Farnham had just returned from St. Louis and said the people in St. Louis were saying things have come to a strange pass. If Jo Smith is elected Pres[iden]t he will raise the devil with M[iss]o[uri] and [if] he is not elected he will raise the devil.

I[t] was agreed that Col[onel] Solomon Copeland, Parris, Henry co[unty], Tenn should be written to on the Vice Pres[iden]cy and that W[ilford] Woodruff should write. [*rest of page blank*] {page 27}

Saturday, March 9[th] 1844 In City Council. [*several lines left blank*] The Female Relief Society Met twice in the assembly room and sanctioned the voice of Innocence from Nauvoo and

457

adjourned 1 week to accomodate Members who could not get in. [*rest of page blank*] {page 28}
    [*page left blank*] {page 29}
    Sunday, March 10th 1844 /A.M./ I attended meeting at the Stand by the Temple and preached on the subject of the spirit of /Elias/ Elijah, and Mesiah clearly defining the offices of the 3 personages. The Savior will not come this year /nor 40 years to come/. The bow has been seen in the cloud and in that year that the bow is seen seed time and harvest will be, but when the bow ceases to be seen look out for a famine. [*rest of page blank*] {page 30}
    4 1/2 P.M. I met the 12 [Apostles] Bishop [George] Miller Temple Committee at Nauvoo Mansion. Letter was read from Lyman Wight and others Dated Feb[ruary] 15th 1844 to B[righam] Young, W[illard] Richards, &c. about removing to the table lands of ~~Texas~~ /Saxet [Texas]/ &c. &c. Also a letter to Joseph Smith &c. from Lyman Wight and others a committee of the branch at the pinery, Black River Falls, Feb[ruary] 15th 1844, on the [. . . [same issue]]
    Joseph asked, can this council keep what I say, not make it public, all held up their hands. [*several lines left blank* [Joseph then proceeded to organize the Council of Fifty to oversee the settlement of Texas and eventually to rule over the political Kingdom of God on earth.]]
    Copy the Constitution of the U[nited] S[tates], [*several lines left blank* [placed in the]] hands of a select committee [as a guide in drafting a constitution for the council]. {page 31}
    No laws can be enacted but what every man can be protected [from?]. [*several lines left blank*] Grant their petition, go ahead concerning the Indians and Southern states &c. [*several lines left blank*]
    Send 25 men by /the yrenip [Pinery]/ through to Santa Fee /Atnas Eef[Santa Fe] / &c, and if ~~Houston~~ /Notsuoh[Houston]/ will embrace the gospel [. . .] [*several lines left blank* [We]] can amend that constitution and make it the voice of Jehovah and shame the U[nited] S[tates.] {page 32} Parley Pratt in favor. Hyrum concured. Said Joseph, "Let us adjourn till after supper to the school room."
    7 Eve assembled at the assembly room over the store, Joseph, Hyrum, Brigham, 12 [Apostles], Temple committee,

Phelps, A. Fielding, J. Phelps, Wasson. ~~Joseph required perfect secrecy of them.~~

Evening in council over the store. [*rest of page blank*] {page 33}

Monday, 11 March 1844 At home. 9 A.M. in council [with Council of Fifty] in Lodge room. Henry Miller's. P.M. in council same place. [*rest of page blank*] {page 34}

Tuesday, 12 March 1844 At Home. 11 A.M. told Bro[ther] Cole I wanted the room over the store for more important purposes, not to break up the school and wished him to dismiss immediately which he did and called the council of the previous day which assembled in the P.M. and evening. Cole procured Henry Miller's brick house for his school. [*rest of page blank*] {page 35}

March 13th 1844, Wednesday In council 9 to 12 A.M. [*several lines left blank*] Joseph and Hiram Smith gave Amos Fielding a letter of Attorney to transact business in England.

In council on the "*The Kingdom of God*" [*rest of page blank*] {page 36}

Thursday, March 14th In council over the store from nine [A.M.] to one A.M. [P.M.]

2 to four P.M. went to see Bro[ther] [John] Wilkie. He had sent to me to come and see him. He wanted to know what he should do. I told him of the order of 1/10 [tithing] &c. Wanted I should come again.

4 to 7 P.M. in council. Adjourned till Tuesday 19th 9 A.M. Lucien Woodworth sent out on a mission [to Texas to negotiate a treaty in behalf of the Council of Fifty]. [*rest of page blank*] {page 37}

Friday, March 15th [*entry left blank*] {page 38}

Saturday, March 16th 1844 At home. [*several lines left blank*] Female Relief Society continued their meeting twice this day in assembly room to sanction the voice of "Innocence from Nauvoo" [*several lines left blank*]

1 P.M. Held a council with Bishop Miller, W[illard] Richards and Porter Rockwell. [*several lines left blank*] Very pleasant and warm for over 3 weeks. {page 39}

Sunday, March 17th At home. Last night was extreme strong wind from the west. Blew down the new house of the 70's [building project] just raised to the roof on Bain St. Very windy this day. [*several lines left blank*] Prayer Meeting adjourned 1 week. [*several lines left blank*] Some snow this evening. {page 40}

Monday, March 18th 1844 At home reciting German with [Alexander] Neibaur. Last night froze in the house. Considerable snow.

2 P.M. Secretary Richards called and gave me letter from [*blank*] and &c. which I read. [*several lines left blank*]

5 1/2 P.M. W[illiam] W. Phelps went past the office on the [way to board the] Leboner for St. Louis. [*rest of page blank*] {page 41}

Tuesday, March 19th 1844 9 A.M. in council [with Council of Fifty] in assembly room. [*rest of page blank*] {page 42}

[*page left blank*] {page 43}

Wednesday, [March] 20th 1844 A.M. and P.M. in assembly room studying the languages. [*several lines left blank*] Elder Woodruff read me a letter to Col[onel] Copeland (in my office) concerning his being Vice Pres[iden]t. [*several lines left blank*] "Voice of Innocence" [was published] in this days Neighbor. [*rest of page blank*] {page 44}

Thursday, [March] 21[st] 1844 In council [with Council of Fifty] over the store. [*rest of page blank*] {page 45}

Friday, March 22[nd] 1844 At home. [*several lines left blank*] 10 A.M. Held court in my office. [*several lines left blank*] Read German in the reading room. [*several lines left blank*] Cold and windy for some days. {page 46}

Saturday, March 23[rd] At home. Rode out and spent the day in councilling. [*several lines left blank*] Warmer. {page 47}

Sunday, March 24[th] 1844 10 A.M. I preached at the Temple stand followed by O[rson] Spencer, and Pres[iden]t Rigdon.

On the stand I related what was told me yesterday by Mr. Eaton that W[illia]m Law, Wilson Law, R[obert] D. Foster, Chaunc[e]y L. Higbee and Joseph Jackson had held a caucus designing to destroy all the Smith family in a few weeks [by revealing details of Nauvoo polygamy]. [*several lines left blank*]

After meeting I rode out with Emma and [upon return] held conversation with a large company at my door. [*rest of page blank*] {page 48}

Monday, March 25th At home in the morning. Rode out A.M. After dinner rode up to the upper landing to see the

"St. Louis Oak" steamer. Emigrants from England are expected soon. Called at my office on my return and read Memorial to Congress [requesting authorization to raise an army of 100,000 to explore and protect settlers in Oregon and Texas,] which my clerk had been writing as committee of council [of Fifty] of Thursday last. Was pleased with the instrument. [*rest of page blank*] {page 49}

Tuesday, March 26th 1844 From 9 to 12 in council [with Council of Fifty]. [*several lines left blank*] From 2 to 5 P.M. in council. [*several lines left blank*] Warm, some wet. {page 50}

Wednesday, March 27th 1844 This morning started to go to Ramus in co[mpany] with Bro[ther] Amasa Lyman but found it so muddy [we] turned back. [We] rode up as far as the Temple. [*several lines left blank*]

Issued warrant for Ianthus Rolf for stealing 2 stone cutter's tools on complaint [of] Vernon H. Bruce. [*several lines left blank*] This evening Dr. Reynolds of Iowa City lectured on Astronomy in my study. [*rest of page blank*] {page 51}

Thursday, March 28th 1844 [*several lines left blank*] Transferred Rolf's trial to Aaron Johnson Justice [of the] Peace. This afternoon had my study plastered where the same had been knocked of[f] &c. [*rest of page blank*] {page 52}

Friday, March 29th 1844 At home. [*several lines left blank*] This P.M. Mr. and Miss Cole had a public exhibition of their school in my reading room, which closed their 2d quarter. [*rest of page blank*] {page 53}

Saturday, March 30th 1844 This morning I heard there was some disturbance on the hill. Rode up and found it reported a robbery had been committed at the Key Stone Store. Mr Rollosson [had been robbed] of some $14[00] or [$] 1,500 and some goods and they were suspicious of a certain black man. I issued a general search warrant and returned to my office where I found the black man Chism [was in distress] with his back lacerated from his shoulders to his hips with 20 or more lashes. My clerk, Dr. Richards, kept him secreted and called Aaron Johnson a justice who issued his warrant for [*blank*] a Missourian who had boardered at my house a few days and on testimony fined him five dollars and cost for whipping Chism. One Easton a witness said he could not testify without implicating himself and he was

461

apprehended and held in custody. Marr Esq[ui]r[e] refused to testify because he was counsel. [rest of page blank] {page 54}

Sunday, March 31st 1844 At home this morning. At 9 [A.M.] went to my reading room and signed a Memorial to Congress for the privilege of raising 100,000 volunteers to protect the Texas, Oregon, &c. dated 26th. Also a Memorial to the Presi[dent] for the same purpose if the other fail and an introductory letter to Orson Hyde who was going to car[r]y the Memorials to Washington.

About noon the funeral of Gen[eral] Wilson Law's wife was attended.

About this time Bro[ther] Mills, one of the police, informed me that [blank [Chauncey]] Higby /&c/ drew a pistol on him the night before &c. I instructed him to make complaint to Esqu[ire] Wells and have him apprehended. [several lines left blank] A very cold time for a week past. {page 55}

Monday, April 1st 1844 Easton was brought up as being accessory to whipping Chism. I referred the case to Alderman Wells. On investigations, it appeared to the satisfaction of the court that he had been on trial for the same offence before Robert D. Foster and acquitted. It was evident to all present that it was a mock trial and so conducted designedly to frustrate the ends of justice, but it was thought best to acquit Easton and appeal from /to/ county court.

Francis L. Higby was fined $10.00 by Alderman Wells for abusive language to the Marshal. Francis L. Higby and Chaunc[e]y L. Higby were brought up for assualting the police before Wells and acquitted. [several lines left blank] Cool and windy. {page 56}

Tuesday, April 2d 1844 At home. Somewhat unwell and kept my house this day. John P. Green, Marshal and Andrew and John Lytle police force arrested by warrant of R[obert] D. Foster on complaint of F. M. Higby for false imprisonment. As case was going to trial the prisoners were taken by Habeus Corpus before Municipal court and tomorrow P.M. 1 o'clock set for trial. [several lines left blank] Strong wind. Warm this eve[ning]. {page 57}

April 3rd 1844, Wednesday [several lines left blank] 1 P.M. I presided in the municipal court. J[ohn] P. Green, Andrew Lytle and John Lytle on Habeus Corpus, taken away from R[obert] D.

Foster's court, where they had been arrained on complaint of Chaunc[e]y L. Higbee for false imprisonment. Prayer of Petitions [were] granted and court decided that Chaunc[e]y L. Higby was a very disorderly person. [*rest of page blank*] {page 58}

Thursday, April 4[th] 1844 In council [with Council of Fifty] in reading Room from 9 to 12 A.M. and from 1 to 4 P.M. O[rson] Hyde was at council and left for Washington immediately after council [to present Joseph Smith's memorial to Congress]. [*rest of page blank*] {page 59}

Friday, April 5th 1844 [*entry left blank*] {page 60}

Saturday, April 6[th] 1844 I made a few introductory remarks to an immense number of the saints assembled on the 14th anniversary of Church in the grove 1/4 miles east of the Temple on Young St. [at] 10 A.M. Weather warm. Brisk air from the South.

Prayer by W[illiam] W. Phelps. Singing. Pres[iden]t Sidney Rigdon arose and said it is 5 years to day since I met the saints on such an occasion on account of ill health and named for his text "The Church of Jesus Christ in the Last Days." Gave a brief history of the origin and progress of the Church. We *know* this is the Church of God.

/4 Lamanites [Indians] and interpreter came in and took a seat on the stand/ {page 61} [Rigdon] Referred to the wondrous wise men who had been in the Church [who] knew more than God himself. To those among us [who think they are wiser than the church, salvation requires subordination to the Kingdom of God. There are men who have] studied how to be [exempt] and know how far they could go and not get punished by the law.

12 [o'clock noon] Pres[iden]t Rigdon gave way and after singing Elder J[ohn] Taylor spoke. 1/4 to 1 [P.M.] Elder Taylor gave way for singing The Red Man ["O, Stop and Tell Me, Red Man"].

P.M. 1/4 to 3 Commenced by singing. Prayer by J[ohn] P. Green. Singing. President Rigdon resumed his subject of the morning, "The Church of Christ" [and how it will continue to] rise [because of its] authenticity. Light to those concerned. Those who have turned away and say they did not believe it like the adversary. Reasons of our secret {page 62} associations at the commencement nothing but what *will* become public property at the proper time. Sat with the President[, and others] before him [on the stand, in shackles in the Richmond Jail]. Before God under lock and keys for weeks. 30 men come upon them [shouting] God dam[n] you to hell /&c. &c/ [wrenched emotion] from every heart. While we were thus shut up the heaven's opens opened to us.

A gentleman from Mexico come and spent some days with us. He slipt out some dark night[. We] saw some armed men come in, armed themselves and chased them [him] 1/2 a mile, [and] after[wards] the mob tarred and feathered him &c. Mob us into the secret place and then say why don't you work in public. Men in your [. . .] {page 63} The kingdom of God is at the defiance of all earthly laws and yet breaks none.

A little before 5 o'clock the assembly were dismissed without ceremony /till 10 next morning/ on the appearance of a shower. The people had scarce time to retire before a heavy shower of rain, wind, thunder, and lightning followed. [*several lines left blank*] Leaves began to show themselves on the trees. {page 64}

Sunday, April 7th 1844 A very pleasant morning. The people began to assemble and by 10 o'clock there was the largest congregation ever seen in Nauvoo and the choir sang an hymn "Ye Slumbering Nation that have Slept a Long Night" when the meeting was called to order by the Marshal, and the choir sung "The Spirit of God &c".

President Rigdon presented the request of 3 or 4 sick and offered a prayer in their behalf /and all the congregation said Amen/ followed by G[eorge]. J. Adams in prayer and singing by the choir.

President Joseph Smith requested that the congregation would keep good order and in the name of the constitution, continental congress, and God Almighty I command the police to keep good order. {page 65}

President Rigdon arose and continued his subject "The Church of Christ." The kingdom of heaven is a government that enters into every principle of government. God has set up his kingdom to restore the power of salvation to the world. Salvation is a complete victory over every thing. The Gospel is to prepare the way for the kingdom of God. The salvation /of any man/ turns upon the si/m/ple act of the mind.

464 /After notice of attention of baptism during intermission

at the front of Main St. and singing/ [expression of] Faith, 12 o'clock, adjourned till 2 o'clock. [*rest of page blank*] {page 66}

3 1/4 P.M. Joseph commenced speaking on the subject of the Dead relative to the death of Elder King Follet who was crushed in a well by the falling of a tub of rock on him.

If men do not comprehend the character of God they do not comprehend themselves. What kind of a being is God? Eternal life [is] to know God. If man does not know God, [he] has not Eternal life. If I am so fortunate as to comprehend and explain the [*blank* [concept]] let every one sit in silence and never lift your voice against the servants of God again.

Every man has a right to be a false prophet as well as a true prophet. In the beginning before the world was Is a man like one of yourselves. Should you see him to day, you would see a man in fashion and in form. Adam was formed in his likeness.

Refute the Idea that God was God from all Eternity. Jesus said as the Father had power in himself even so hath the Son power to do what the Father did. Lay down his body, take it up again. You have got to learn how to make yourselves God, Kings, Priests, &c. by going from a small to a great capacity till they are able to dwell in everlasting burning and everlasting power.

How consoling when called to part with a dear friend to know their very being will rise to dwell in everlasting burning, heirs of God {page 67} and ascend [to] a throne as those who have gone before. I saw the Father work out his kingdom with fear and trembling. God is glorified in /salvation/ Exhaltation of his ancestors &c. Not all to be comprehended in this world. The head, as the head one, the head one of the Gods, brought forth the Gods. D[octo]rs and Lawyers that have persecuted [us should know that the Holy Ghost knows something about the topic]. The head one called the Gods together in grand council to bring forth the world. Example of error as [[follows] . . .]

~~Yacobam~~ /Jacob/ the son of Zebedee [is transliterated in the King James Bible] to form James the son of Zebedee, 4 Mat[thew] 21. Greek, Hebrew, German, and Latin [all say Jacob]. In the beginning the head of the Gods called a council of the Gods and concocted a scheme to create the world. Soon as we begin to understand the character of the Gods he begins to unfold the heavens to us. Doctors say, [God] created the Earth out of nothing. [The Hebrew word] Borau [is said to mean that God] creates it [when it] means to [be] organized. God has materials to organize the world. Element[s], [that] nothing can destroy. No beginning, no end.

The soul, [according to] doctors of Divinity, [is part of what] God created in the beginning[. I think this] lessens the character of man. Don't {page 68} believe it. Who told you God was self existent? Correct enough, in Hebrew [God created man and] put into him his spirit which was created before. Mind of man coequal with God himself. Friends separated for a small moment from their spirits coequal with God and hold converse when they are one with another [as we do on earth].

If man had a beginning he must have an end. Might proclaim [annihilation]. God revealed [that he did not have] power to create the spirit of man at all.

Inteligence exist[s] upon a self existent principle, no creation about it. All minds and spirit[s] God ever sent into the world are susceptible of enlargement. All things God has seen fit proper[ly] to reveal while dwelling in mortality are revealed. Precisely the same as though we were destitute of bodies[, these things are revealed to our spirits].

What will save our spirits will save our bodies. Our [actions in our earthly] tabernacles [will determine the future] for our spirits. All spirits who have not obeyed the Gospel must be damned[, all those] who have not obeyed the decrees of [the] Son of Man.

We are looked upon by God as though we were in Eternity. The greatest responsibility resting upon us is to look after our dead. They without us cannot be made perfect without us. Meet Paul 1/2 way. Hence the saying of Elijah. {page 69} God made provisions before the world was for every creature [to be saved;] in all sin[s] shall [man] be forgiven in this world or world to come, except one.

Salvation for all men who have not committed a certain sin[. God] can save any man who has not committed the unpardonable sin. Cannot commit the unpardonable sin after the dissolution of the body. Knowledge save[s] a man. [If one consents to obey the gospel, one is saved, otherwise one must be punished for sin.]

No way for a man to come to understanding but [to] give his consent to the commandment[s]. Damned by mortification. A lake as of fire of brimstone as exquisite [as] the dissappointment of the mind of man.

Why? Must commit the unpardonable sin in this world, [because a man] will suffer in the Eternal world until he will be exalted. [Jesus is the savior of all men who will obey him.]

Work of the Devil [is coercion]. The plans of the Devil laid to save the world [by force]. Devil said he could save them all. Lot fell on Jesus. All sin &c. forgiven except the sin against the Holy Ghost. [A man has] Got to deny the plan of salvation &c. with his eyes open. Like many of the apostates of Christ of the Church of Jesus Christ of [the] last Days.

Let all be careful, lest you be deceived. Best man brings forth best works. {page 70}

To the Mourners your friend has gone to wait the perfection of the reunion. The resurrection of your friend in felicity while [those of some] worlds must wait myriads of years before they can receive the like blessings. Leave the subject bless those who have lost friends, [they are] only gone for a few moments.

Shall mothers have their children? Yes. They shall have it without price. Redemption is paid[. The children who die will never grow but will be resurrected] possessing all the intelligence of a God. The child [will be] as it was before it died out of your arms. Thrones upon thrones. Dominion upon dominion just as you.

Baptism of water, fire, and Holy Ghost are inseparably connected. [I have] Found in the German Bible to prove what I have taught for 14 years about baptism. I baptize you with water, but when Jesus comes having the keys, he shall baptize you with the baptism of fire and Holy Ghost.

Leaving the principles of [the] doctrine of baptism &c. one God, one baptism, and one baptism i.e. all three.

Called upon all men Priests and all [men] to repent and obey the gospel. If they do not they will be damned. Those who commit the unpardonable sin are doomed to Gnolom without end. God dwells in everlasting burnings. Love all men but hate your [sinful] deeds.

You don't know me. You never will. I don't blame you for not believing my history had I not experienced it [I] could not believe it myself.

5 1/2 [P.M.] closed. Sang. {page 71}

[Evening of] 7 April [*page left blank*] {page 72}

Monday, April 8[th] 1844 10 A.M. Pres[iden]t Jos[eph] Smith called the congregation to order. Bro[ther] B[righam] Young, /W[illiam] W. Phelps/ read 15 chap[ter] 1st Corinthians from an old translation. Prayer for some 1/2 Doz[en] sick and opening [of the] meeting by B[righam] Young.

Pres[iden]t J[oseph] Smith said he must give up the subject of yesterday. Made a proclamation. "I have another great and grand Revelation. Great discussion [about] where Zion is. The whole America is Zion that is the Zion where the mountain of the Lord's House shall be, about the central part of N[orth] and South America soon as the Temple is finished. Lord hath ordained where these last and most important ordinances must be in a house, provided for the purpose when we can get a house built first there is the place[, then one can be] {page 73} Bap[tized,] washed, annointed, sealed &c. for the dead the same as for themselves.

"From henceforth the elders shall build churches where ever the people recieve the gospel[. If there are] sufficient [numbers] then build stakes to this place. I verily believe that God will establish this place for the salvation of the dead. Those who want to save their dead can come hither. Those who do not wish to come hither to live can bring their families and attend the ordinances and return." [*several lines left blank*]

20 mi[nutes to] 11 Elder G[eorge] J. Adams read /17th/ Obadiah "but upon Mount Zion shall be deliverance" Micah 3 chap[ter] latter part fore part [of chapter] 4" chap[ter] Gen[esis] 48 and 49 about to gather up his feet. Deut 33 chap[ter] {page 74} Isa[iah] 46:12, 13 Paul says as it is written deliverance shall come out of Zion.

Isa[iah] 17 [at the] close. Rushing of the nation [-] to the com[man]d &c. 48 Ps[alms,] 102d P.S.[alms] not give sleep to mine eyes &c. in the fields of the woods 1 Pet[er] 3 and 4 chap[ter]s 24 Isa[iah,] 2d Par[t] Cor[inthians] 15. I declare unto you I bless God for a prophet to tell us what the old Bible means where it don't tell what it means. Hosea [wrote,] "Ephraim what shall I do," quot[e]s him—Jer[emiah] 31 chap[ter] 1 /o'clock/ 16 mi[nutes] closed by A blessing from President Jos[eph] Smith through G[eorge] J. Adams and the conference referred to the Twelve [Apostles] and the Elders notified to meet in 2 hours. Baptism to be attended at 2 1/2 o'clock. {page 75}

Conference of the Twelve [Apostles] April 8, 1844

15 4 P.M. A large collection of Elders assembled at the stand. Addressed by Patriarch Hyrum Smith on Spiritual wife system. The first one we heard reporting such stories we will report him in the Time[s] and Seasons to come and give up his licence. He was decided against it in every form and spoke at length. President Rigdon Concurred in his remarks following Hyrum. 12 mi[nutes to] 6 adjourned to 8 A.M. tomorrow. [rest of page blank] {page 76}

April 9th 1844, Tuesday 8 A.M. The Elders assembled at the stand and Amasa Lyman addressed the Elders. After which President Young spoke at conciderable length on Elders preaching 1st principles alone when they go out.

Said the Prophet's declaration that all America was Zion was a perfect sweep stakes.

Referred to the building of the Temple and the branches around to send teams and provisions and work continually drawing stone and [seeing] to the election of Joseph.

11 mi[nutes to] 10 [A.M.] Hyrum referred to Joseph's proclamation concerning building up churches all over the land, also to the rights of franchise and the correct principles of electing good men for offices, especially [a] President[, we] want a Pres[iden]t of the U[nited] S[tates].

Pres[iden]t Young requested all who were in favor of electing Joseph to the Presidency to raise both hands which they [did] say 1,100 Elders and commenced clapping their hand[s] and gave many loud cheers. The opposite was called for and only one hand raised.

Elder Kimball spoke of a figure of the threshing flour mill, smut machine, grain heads &c. &c. never preached mysteries &c.

President Young corrected Bro[ther] Kimball and told about the mystery of Amasa Lyman [and Joseph's] breeches. Must al[l] take thought for thy brother. {page 77}

20 mi[nutes to] 11 [A.M.] A call was made for those who would volunteer to go preaching to pass out on[to] the green. A great company walked out then returned to their seats on the right of the stand and the names of those who could go 6 months were first taken /then 3 months/ viz. &c. 244 which were read

469

and corrected. After which W[illiam] W. Phelps made a few remarks in relation to principles.

20 mi[nutes] before 1 [P.M.] adjourned for 1 hour.

P.M. Met according to adjournment. Names of volunteers called and places assigned for their mission.

Pres[iden]t Young gave the brethren some good instruction to behave themselves and not come back crying can't you do something for me because they have been guilty of iniquity {page 78} and related several instances where God has heard the prayer of the brethren to defend us from our enemies [such] as Carlin, Reynolds, John C. Bennet[t].

Elder G[eorge] J. Adams said Lieut[enant] Smith had to raise $1750.00 this month and called on all who could give 5.00 each 1.00 each &c. and more than 50.00 were paid down 100.00 offered to be lent and the Elders agreed to sustain the President with uplifted hand. [*rest of page blank*] {page 79}

Wednesday, April 10th 1844 [*several lines left blank*] The Twelve [Apostles] were in council arranging for conference. [*rest of page blank*] {page 80}

Thursday, 11 April 1844 In council [with Council of Fifty] in the Masonic Hall A.M. and P.M. [*rest of page blank*] {page 81}

12th, Friday [*entry left blank*] {page 82}

Saturday, 13 April 1844 [*several lines left blank*] 1 P.M. Assembled in municipal Court in assembly Room. Joseph asked Dr. R[obert] D. Foster if he bore his [Joseph's] expence to Washington or any part thereof. Foster said he did not. Joseph said Dr. Goforth said that he was taken in a secret council and you [Foster] told him you had paid my expence &c. Dr. Foster said he never had a secret interview with Dr. Goforth and stated what he knew[?] {page 83} Joseph[:] have I ever misused you any way? Foster said I do not feel at liberty to answer this question under existing circumstances. Did I ever misuse you? [Foster: I] Do not feel at liberty to answer under existing circumstances.

Did I ever wrong you in deal personally [or] misused you in any shape? Foster[:] I do not feel at liberty to answer. I have treated you Christianly and friendly too, so far as I have had ability. Jo[seph:] tell me where I have done wrong and I will ask your forgiveness. I want to prove to this company by your own testimony that {page 84} I have treated you honorably. Foster[:] I shall testify no further at present.

Joseph[:] Justice Aaron Johnson did I ever make oath before you against Simpson[? Johnson:] not before the prosecution. Joseph told the whole story.

A. Colton come up on Habeus Corpus and was discharged on the insufficiency of the papers. After which Joseph preferred the following charge against Bro[ther] R[obert] D. Foster "for unchristian like conduct in general for abusing my character privately, for throwing out slanderous insinuation against {page 85} me, for conspiring against my peace and Safety, for conspiring against my life, for conspiring against the peace of my family" and "for lying." Joseph Smith [several lines left blank]

About 5 P.M. the "Maid of Iowa" Steamer arrived at the N[auvoo] House Wharf filled with passengers from England led by El[der] W[illia]m Kay. They started from Liverpool, 210 souls and nearly all arrived in good health and spirits. One smaller company arrived about one week before from Liverpool. {page 86}

Sunday, April 14th 1844 Rainy day. No meeting at the stand. [several lines left blank] Committee of the council [of Fifty] met in the P.M. at my office. [rest of page blank] {page 87}

Monday, April 15[th] 1844 At home. [several lines left blank] Rode out in the P.M. [rest of page blank] {page 88}

Tuesday, April 16[th] 1844 At home. [several lines left blank] 5 P.M. Had a long talk with Chaunc[e]y L. Higbee and Esq[ui]r[e] Marr in front of my house. Read to them Dr. Williams and Mr. Eatons affidavits before E[s]q[ui]r[e] Wells. [rest of page blank] {page 89}

Wednesday, [April] 17[th] 1844 P.M. Rode out. [several lines left blank] This days Nauvoo Neighbor printed Williams and Eatons affidavit about Jackson, Foster, Laws &c. and my reply to the Washington Globe. [rest of page blank] {page 90}

Thursday, [April] 18th 1844 9 A.M. Council [of Fifty] till 12 noon. At dinner made mention of the report that Foster, Higbee, &c. were paying some one's board at my table to catch something against me, so that if true they might have some thing to carry back.

2 P.M. to 5 1/2 in council [again]. 6 [P.M.] B[righam] Young, W[illard] Richards, J[ohn] Taylor, G[eorge] A. Smith, H[eber] C. Kimball, W[ilford] Woodruff of the 12 [and] A[lpheus]. Cutler, S[amuel] Bent, G[eorge] W. Harris, A. Johnson, W[il-

liam]. Marks, C[harles] C. Rich, A[masa] Lyman of the High Council, [and] W[illiam] W. Phelps, N[ewel] K. Whitney, Jno [John] Smith, J[ohn] M. Bernhisel, Jos[eph] Fielding, G[eorge] J. Adams, E[rastus]. Snow, R[eynolds] Cahoon, J. W. Coolidge, Jno [John] Scott, J[ohn]. D. Lee, L[evi]. W. Hancock, S. Williams, Jos[eph] Young, J[ohn] P. Green, J[ohn]. D. Parker, A[lexander]. McRae, Geo[rge] Watt, W[illiam] Clayton held council and unanimously cut off ananimously R[obert] D. Foster, Wilson Law, W[illia]m Law, Jane Law, and Howard Smith of Scott Co[unty], Ill[inois,] from the Church for unchristian like conduct. [rest of page blank] {page 91}

[page left blank] {page 92}

Saturday, April 20th 1844 Emma went to St. Louis. [rest of page blank] {page 93}

Sunday, April 21st At home. [several lines left blank] B[righam] Young at conference [in] Lima. Kimball [in] conference at Ramus. [several lines left blank] Rain this day. {page 94}

Monday, April 22nd 1844 Heavy rain this morning. River very high. All mills stopped in city.

This morning a man who had put up at my house told me he wanted to see me alone. I went into my room with him and he told me he was a prophet of God that he come from Vermont and he prophesied that this government was about to be overthrown and the Kingdom which Daniel spoke of was about to be established some where in the west and he thought in Illinois. [several lines left blank]

Bro[ther] W[illia]m Smith arrived from N[ew] J[ersey] with some 40 or 50 saints. I spent some time with him. [rest of page blank] {page 95}

Tuesday, [April] 23d 1844 At home. 9 [A.M.] to 12 in general meeting in hall to elect delegate to Baltimore convention 1st Monday [in] May. Hollister elected and Hyde and O[rson] Pratt from Washington.

P.M. 3 to 5 in Meeting. Again many speeches about Presidents &c. Appointed 2d Monday in May for state convention at Nauvoo. [several lines left blank] Eve[ning] sun set called at Carlos['s] widow with W[illia]m. Eve[ning] at Dr. Richards with Hiram. [rest of page blank] {page 96}

Wednesday, [April] 24th 1844 April At home and about the city. In the eve Bro[ther] Thayer and Dr. Richards and Dr.

Williams were in my room and a man who boarded at the Masonic Hall. I gave at their instigation a history of the Laws['s — William and Wilson] proceedings in past in trying to make difficulty in my family &c. [*rest of page blank*] {page 97}

Thursday, April 25th 1844 Emma returned from St. Louis. A brother of the St. Louis Gazetts come up at the same time and wanted to know by what principle I got so much power. How many inhabitants and armed men we had &c. I told him on the principle of truth and virtue which would last when I was dead &c.

Council [of Fifty met] from 10 [A.M.] to 12 and from 2 [P.M.] to 5. Adjourned sine die. Appointed a State convention at Nauvoo Friday after the 2d Monday in May the council to disperse abroad in the Nation.

Instructed my clerk Dr. Richards to make out a writ of Habeus Corpus for a Mr Smith of Iowa who was expecting to be arrested by the U[nited] S[tates] Marshal for getting money which was his due or he says at Washington.

A play of Rational amusement was to commence this eve but a tremendous thunder storm and rain commenced about 6 P.M. Mississippi River very high. Higher than known by the oldest inhabitants about. {page 98}

Friday, April 26[th] 1844 At home. 10 A.M. Marshal went up on hill to arrest Augustus Spencer for an assault on his Bro[ther] Orson Spencer for an assault in his own home. R[obert] D. Foster, Charles Foster, and Chaunc[e]y L. Higbee come down.

Charles Foster drew a pistol towards me on the steps of my office. I ordered him to be arrested and the pistol taken from him. A struggle ensued in which Charles Foster, R[obert] D. Foster and Chaunc[e]y L. Higbee resisted and I ordered them to be arrested. They resisted and I Mayor ordered the High policemen to be called and his possey and went on to try A[ugustus]. Spencer. Fined him $100 bound for to keep the peace 6 months.

$100 Bonds appealed to Municipal court at once [by] R[obert] D. Foster, Chaunc[e]y L. Higbee and Charles Foster[, arrested] for resisting the authorities of the city. O[rrin] P[orter] Rockwell sworn Marshal [John Greene] sworn. Said Dr. Foster swore by God he would not assist the Marshal and swore by God they would see the Mayor &c. in hell before they would go. {page 99}

473

Charles Foster drew a pistol. Dr. Foster interfered. Cha[r]les Foster and Chaunc[e]y L. Higbee said they would be God damned if they would not shoot the Mayor. Breathed out many hard threatening and menacing sayings. Would concider favored of God for the privilege of shooting or ridding the world of such a Tyrant referring to the Mayor. J. Coolidge confirmed. Tufts swore [and] confirmed the foregoing statements.

Fined R[obert] D. Foster, Charles Foster and C[hauncey] L. Higbee fined $100 each. Appealed to Municipal Court.

Issued a warrant for a R[obert] D. Foster on complaint of Willard Richards for breach of ordinance in that Foster, said to said Richards, "You," shakeing his fists in his face, "are another Damned black hearted villian. You tried to seduce *my* wife on the boat when she was going to New York and I can prove it. And the oath is out against you." Jos[eph] Smith, W[illard] Richards, John P. Green, Thayer, Elbridge Tufts. (~~Harding gave a writing to Kimball concerning Foster statement about Joseph &c. charging him with crime~~) {page 100}

Saturday, April 27th 1844 A large company of Gentlemen from St. Louis and other places on the river called at the Mansion and when they returned to the boat it was gone. They returned to the Mansion.

9 A.M. R[obert] D. Foster come up for trial. After much conversation with the Mayor in which he charged Joseph with many crimes [like] Daniteism in Nauvoo, and a great variety of vile and false Epithets and charges. Court adjourned to Monday 9 A.M. Foster agreed to meet Joseph on 2d Monday of May at the stand and have a settlement. Foster then said he would publish it [in the] Warsaw paper. Joseph told him if he did not agree to be quiet [and] not attempt to raise a mob and [threaten violence] he would not meet him. If he would be quiet he would publish it in Neighbor. Foster would not agree to be quiet and Joseph said he was free from his (Foster) blood had made the last overtures of peace, [and] delivered him into the hand of God and shook his garments against him.

Joseph continued in office some time in conversation and then went into the Big Room and read the Warsaw Signal about Mormonism.

Elder L. R. Foster arrived from N[ew] York. Elder Hiram Clark arrived from Liverpool with 150 passengers. Meeting at the stand at one o'clock to give instructions to the Elders going out Electioneering addressed by Pres[iden]t Rigdon and W[illia]m Smith. {page 101}

Sunday, April 28[th] 1844 At home. Hyrum preached at the stand. A.M. There was a meeting at Gen[eral] W[illia]m and Wilson Law's near the saw mill of those who had been cut off from the Church and their dupes. Several affidavits were taken and read against Joseph and others. W[illia]m Law, Wilson Law, Austin D. Cowles, John Scott Sen[ior]., Francis M. Higbee, R[obert] D. Foster, and Robert Pierce were appointed a committee to visit the different families of the city and see who would join the new Church (IE [i.e.,]) it was decided that Joseph was [a] fallen prophet &c. and W[illia]m Law was appointed in his place. Austin Cowles and Wilson Law Councillors. R[obert] D. Foster and F[rancis] M. Higbee to the 12 Apostles &c. as report says. El[der] James Blakely preached up Joseph in the A.M. and [in the] P.M. joined the anties [anti-Mormons]. Cha[rle]s Ivins Bishop. [several lines left blank]

Several were baptized in the river east of Main St[reet]. {page 102}

Sunday, 28[th] [several lines left blank] Suddenly sick eve could not attend Prayer Meeting eve. Prayed for our enemies. Lawsuits &c. &c. [rest of page blank] {page 103}

Monday, April 29th 1844 At home. Received a visit from L. R. Foster of N[ew] York who gave me a gold pencil case sent me by /Br[other]/ Theodore Curtis now in N[ew] York and the first I wrote with it was "God bless the Man"

At 11 [A.M.] R[obert] D. Foster come up for trial. Joseph transferred the case to Alderman Wm Marks. Foster objected to jurisdiction of court and informality. Court decided he had not foundation. Esqu[ire] Noble from Rock River assisted city attorney. Esq[uire] Patrick was present.

Lieut[enant] Williams filed affidavit (v.s.) Major Gen[eral] Wilson Law and he [Law] was suspended from office to await trial for ungentlemanly conduct &c. W[illia]m Law and Wilson Law were suspended for trial [before the Nauvoo Legion] about the same time. [several lines left blank]

Steamer Mermaid touched at Nauvoo House Landing 5 P.M. going down. {page 104}

Tuesday, April 30th 1844 At home. Counselling the brethren about many things. Much company &c. [*several lines left blank*]

Complaint was commenced (v.s.) W[illia]m and Wilson Law in the [court martial proceedings in the] Masonic Lodge &c. [*several lines left blank*]

The Osprey Steamer touched at N[auvoo] H[ouse] Landing eve. {page 105}

May 1[st] 1844, Wednesday /Heavy rain and wind last night/ At home. Much counsill[in]g with the brethren &c. this day. [*several lines left blank*] Rode out in P.M. [*several lines left blank*] Lyman Wight and George Miller arrived from Pine Country. {page 106}

Thursday, May 2d 1844 At home. Many called for Counsel. 10 A.M. Maid of Iowa started for Rock River after wheat for the Temple. Mr. Clayton and Col[onel] Markham went to attend court. Joseph vs. Wilson and Reynolds. [*several lines left blank*]

P.M. Went on to Prairie to see about selling land. While gone Lucian Woodworth returned from [T]exas. [*rest of page blank*] {page 107}

Friday, May 3d 1844 1 [P.M.] At home counselling the brethren &c. 2 P.M. In council. Lucien Woodworth gave a report of his [diplomatic] Mission [to the Council of Fifty]. Lyman Wight present. Adjourned. From 6 [P.M.] to 8 council. Adjourned till 10 next Monday.

Wrote a letter to Uncle John Smith to come to council. [*rest of page blank*] {page 108}

May 4th 1844, Saturday [*several lines left blank*] P.M. Rode out on the prairie to see some land and sell to [*blank*] [*several lines left blank*] 4 circular windows finished on the upper story of the Temple. [*several lines left blank*] Very plesant day. {page 109}

Sunday, May 5th 1844 At home. Instructed Dr. Richards, my clerk, to go to Quincy and pay Walsh 100 dollars due on my farm. Rain. Messenger did not go.

Elder Grant preached at the Mansion 2 P.M. A large co[mpany] in Bar Room. P.M. and eve. Joseph spoke a long time on petitions read F. Grierson's letter, Clay's letter, &c. [*several lines left blank*]

J[ohn] P. Green attended Conference at Quincy Saturday and to day. [*several lines left blank*] Rain continues. {page 110}

Monday, May 6th 1844 At home. 10 [A.M.] to 12 in

council [with the Council of Fifty]. 2 to 4 1/2 P.M. in council. Voted Almon W. Babbit go on a [diplomatic] mission to France. L[ucien] Woodworth on a [diplomatic] mission to Texas and Sidney Rigdon be candidate for the Vice Presidency of the U[nited] States.

Had a warrant served on me from Circuit Court on complaint of F[rancis] M. Higbee. Dam[ag]e[s] $5,000. Petition for writ of Habeus Corpus. Writ issued by clerk of Municipal Court.

6 eve in conversation with Jeremiah Smith and others in my office on Emma's correspondence with Gov[ernor] Carlin. [*several lines left blank*] Very pleasant. {page 111}

Tuesday, May 7[th] 1844 At home. Plesant Morning. Rode out on Prairie with 3 or 4 Gentlemen to sell them some land at 9 [A.M.]. 10 [A.M.] Municipal Court met. Adjourned till tomorrow 10 A.M. At one [o'clock] a severe storm of rain commenced with wind and I stopped at my farm over night. Storm abated about sun set.

An opposition printing press arrived at Dr. Foster's from Columbus, Ohio as reports says. Also that Esq[ui]r[e Daniel H.] Wells has issued a writ of ejectment on all those who bought land of Dr. Foster on Bench E[ast] of the Temple. Foster having given warrantee deeds but not having paid for the land. {page 112}

May 8th 1844, Wednesday Returned home. 10 A.M. went before Municipal Court on Habeus Corpus on complaint of Francis M. Higbee. See records [of the] court. Discharged on merits [of] case having proved Higbee's character &c. Court from 10 to 12 1/2 and from 2 to 5 P.M. Was released on merit case. See minut[e]s [of the] court.

Attended theatre [in the] eve[ning]. [*rest of page blank*] {page 113}

Thursday, May 9th At home. [*several lines left blank*] 9 A.M. A court Martial was held in my office on Mayor Gen[eral] Wilson Law. [*several lines left blank*]

In the eve I attended the Theatre. Pythias and Damon and the idiot witness were acted. {page 114}

Friday, May 10th 1844 At home. Rode out after Breakfast. [*several lines left blank*] In the course of the day went on the prairie with some brethren to sell them some land. [*several lines left blank*]

9 A.M. a court martial was held at the Mayor office on

R[obert] D. Foster for ungentlemanly conduct &c. [*rest of page blank*] {page 115}

Saturday, May 11th 1844 At home. 10 A.M. attended City council till 11 1/2. No Quorum present. /(During this time had conversation with [Mr.] Lines on Theatre)/ Council adjourned.

1 P.M. To my office a while and at [*blank*] to 6 a prayer Meeting. Elder Rigdon and J[ohn] P. Green admitted [to quorum of the anointed]. J[ohn] P. Green complained of James Blakesly and F[rancis] M. Higbee for abusing Joseph and the Twelve [Apostles] at Quincy in court House. [*rest of page blank*] {page 116}

Sunday, May 12th 1844 At home. 10 A.M. Preached at the stand touching many things. Hyrum spoke also Lyman Wight. [*several lines left blank*]

/Joseph/ 3 P.M. Prayer Meeting at council room. W[illia]m Smith and Almon /W./ Babbit were present [and initiated into quorum of the annointed]. A full room prayed for deliverance from our enemies and exaltation to such officers as will enable the Servants of God to execute Righteousness in the Earth. [*rest of page blank*] {page 117}

Monday, May 13th 1844 /Rain this morning/ At home. At 9 A.M. called a meeting of the [Council of Fifty of the] Kingdom [of God]. 10 A.M. went to my office conversed with several of the brethren.

Sold Ellis M. Sanders 100 acres of land. Rec[eive]d 300 dollars cash and his note for $1,000 and $20 for Temple. Paid Sisson Chase $298.00 and took up note of Kimball, Taylor, and Young given for money they had borrowed for me and $10.00 to H[eber] C. Kimball.

2 P.M. Meeting of Lyceum [Council of Fifty]. Letter of O[rson] Hyde April 25[th] and one [of the] 26th read [from the] city [of] Washington. Clerk [was] instructed to answer and Lyman Wight and H[eber] C. Kimball to go and carry it. See minutes of the meeting. Adjourned at 5 [P.M.] and letter of W[illard] Richards Sec[retary of the Council] to O[rson] Hyde and O[rson] Pratt, May 13th 1844.

6 P.M. Steamer of "Maid of Iowa" returned from Rock River with 400 bu[shels] corn [and] 200 wheat for Temple and some for St. Louis.

8 eve Joseph went on the Maid of Iowa with Dr. Richards
and returned in a few minutes. Pleasant weather. {page 118}

Tuesday, May 14th 1844 At home. Rode out early in the
morning say /about/ 7 o'clock. "Maid of Iowa" started for St.
Louis Capt[ain] Repshor, Bullock Clerk, about 9 nine A.M. [*several lines left blank*]

About noon it was reported that the Foster party were at
Marr's store sealing letters to the Governors of all the states.

This P.M. my Old Lawyer [John Reid] gave a lecture on
the stand stating the difficulties I had formerly encountered. I
spoke after he had closed and continued my history to the present
time.

4 P.M. Prayer Meeting, few present. Prayed for Bro[ther]
Woodworth's daughter who was sick. Lyman Wight was present
[and anointed]. [*rest of page blank*] {page 119}

Wednesday, May 15th 1844 At home. Much rain this
A.M. A son of John Quincy Adams, Mr. Quincy and Dr. Goforth
visited at the Mansion. [*several lines left blank*]

5 P.M. Went to my office and heard Bro[ther] Phelps
read my rejoinder to Clay's letter for the first time.

7 [P.M.] Rode to the upper landing with Mr. Adams,
Quincy and H[eber] [C.] Kimball. [*rest of page blank*] {page 120}

Thursday, May 16th Went to the office at 8 A.M. to
hear my reply to H[enry] Clay and letter of W[illard] Richards
clerk of council to O[rson] Hyde and O[rson] Pratt at 10 [A.M.].
Ordered Municipal court to convene. Spent the A.M. in reading
&c.

1 P.M. in Municipal Court. Jeremiah Smith Sen come
up on Habeus Corpus. He had been arrested by Jones and Mc-
[Cenie?] for procuring money at Washington under false pretences.
T. B. Johnson and Chaunc[e]y L. Higbee his Lawyers asked for
continuance from [lack of] Witnesses. Continued till next week
Thursday.

Rain continues. About home. Read proof of report of my
trial on Habeus Corpus on the 8th in the Neighbor. [*rest of page blank*] {page 121}

Friday, May 17[th] 1844 In convention of the state in my
office called to promote my Election Gen[eral] Brown Chairman,
Merryweather secretary. Minits [minutes] to be published in next
paper. Rode out towards night About 6 [P.M.].

Evening a caucus in my office. Dr. Goforth Chairman. Emma was sick and I could not attend. The people burned a barrel of Tar [in front of the Mansion], gave many toasts. Carried me on their shoulders twice round the fire and escorted me to my Mansion by a band of music.

Franklin D. Richards and Joseph A. Stratton were ordained High Priests and set apart on a mission to England by B[righam] Young, H[eber] C. Kimball, and W[illard] Richards of the Twelve [Apostles]. [*rest of page blank*] {page 122}

May 18[th] 1844, Saturday 9 A.M. With H[eber] C. Kimball to B[righam] Young's and af[ter]wards rode out to the regimental Taining and in the afternoon also on Jo Duncan about land &c. [*several lines left blank*]

5 P.M. 2 cannons were fired in front of my old home and regiment dismissed. [*rest of page blank*] {page 123}

Sunday, May 19[th] 1844 Cloudy morning. At home. Lyman Wight preached at the stand. Rain commenced about twelve. [*several lines left blank*] Bonney returned from the east. [*several lines left blank*]

Prayer Meeting at P.M. Was dispensed with. So muddy and rainy. About 12 men [and] 2 women attending. [*several lines left blank*]

Eve I talked a long time in the bar Room. Judge Phelps read my rejoinder to Clay. Esq[ui]r[e] Reid my old Lawyer present. [*several lines left blank*]

Fog[g]y and wet. "Maid of Iowa" has not arrived 10 o'clock. {page 124}

Monday, May 20[th] 1844 Emma continues sick. Am with her most of the time. 10 A.M. there was a public meeting on the Stand to obtain means for Lyman Wight to go to Washington. [*several lines left blank*]

Circuit Court. Bro[ther] Phelps and many brethren went. Phelps returned same day /or a summons was suffered to be issued for/ Joseph was summoned to appear on complaint of F[rancis] M. Higbee on same case. I was set free on habeus corpus on the 8 in[s]t[ant]. The Lawyers agreed to move an abatement. Judge Adams presiding. A good influence in favor of the Saints prevailed [and a change of venue to McDonough County was ordered]. [*rest of page blank*] {page 125}

Tuesday, May 21[st] 1844 At home. Very pleasant morning. Rode out with O[rrin] P[orter] Rockwell on horseback.

7 A.M. B[righam] Young, H[eber] C. Kimball, Lyman Wight, and about 100 Elders went on the Osprey for St. Louis. Maid of Iowa arrived.

At home towards night with Emma who is some better. Shovelled dirt on the ditch while Wasson stood on the corner of the fence to watch. A man came to find me having a summons and attachment to take me to Carthage. Could not find me. "Maid of Iowa" went up about 3 P.M. Rode out in the evening with W[illia]m Clayton to see Yearsly['s] little child who is sick. {page 126}

Wednesday, [May] 22nd 1844 At home. The officer after me from Carthage watching. At 10 [A.M.] about 40 Indians come up in front of the Mansion. 4 or 5 mounted among whom was Blackhooks['s] brother, Kiskishkee &c. I was obliged to send them word I could not see them at present and they encamped in the Council Chamber. P.M. to night with the police on duty some individuals lurking around. Loveland and others. [*several lines left blank*] Very pleasant day. [*rest of page blank*] {page 127}

Thursday, [May] 23d 1844 With my family reading Hebrew with [Alexander] Neibaur and counselling with various friends. Emma some better. /10 A.M. Municipal Court. N[ewel] K. Whitney adjourned 1 week./

1 P.M. Held council with the Indians Sac and Fox &c. in my back kitchen. They told me (Joseph) "You are a big chief. We are sons of /2 as/ big men /and Priests/ as ever inhabited this land. You preach a great deal so say great Spirit, you be as great and good as our fathers that will do. Our worship is different, but we are good as any other men. Before our nation were acquainted with white men, they were as great men as ever lived on the river, now live on Desmoines. 20 y[ea]rs ago [there was] 6,000 of us, now [we are a] small nation. 3 towns 2 [-] not over yesterday. They talk with big spirit. We have had possession of this land. Neohope is one of our principle men. We wish friendship with all men. Our chiefs done wrong in selling our country.

"Black Hawk's bro[ther] Maquisto Fox Nation worshipped on this piece of ground. When our Fathers first came here this was inhabited by Spanish. When driven off French came and then the English and Americans talk a great deal with the G[r]eat

481

spirit. We different colour, no difference. We all good men. Another said we have seen a great deal of pleasure on this piece of
land. Our fathers worshipped on this piece of land. English were
very friendly. Had good. We drove off a nation who was on their
river. This is the best country our fathers had seen. Fathers of the
2 old men were preachers. Wanted Joseph to be as {page 128}
good as they were. 2 Nations are brothers. Wanted Joseph to talk
right to be our big chief white men wear hats. Indians naked [-].
English, French, Indian all brethren. Don't expect to live long.
Don't care for any thing only for something to eat &c. Friendly
visit. 2 days. Sac chief sold their land again and would go to
M[iss]o[uri] in 2 years. We are very poor. Whites cheat us. But
no difference not long to live. We wanted to let you know we were
a Christian people."

I replied "We know you have been wronged, but we bought
this land and paid our money for it. Advise you not to sell any
more land. Cultivate peace with all men with the different tribes.
Great spirit wants you to be united and live in peace. Found a
book (presenting the Book of Mormon) which told me about your
fathers and Great spirit told me. You must send to all the tribes
you can and tell them to live in peace and when any of our people
come to see you treat them as we treat you."

3 P.M. Indians commenced a war dance in front of my
old house. Our people commencing with music and firing cannon. After the dance which lasted about 2 hours firing of cannon
closed the exercise. With our music marched back to office. Before they commenced dancing the Saints collected $9.45 cents for
to get them food. {page 129} Soon after the dance commenced,
[someone] come to my clerk Dr. Richards and told him an officer
was on the way with an attachment for him. He had come from
Carthage 12.30 mi[les] to bring the news. Dr. R[ichards] come to
my house and staid all night. Aaron Johnson come from Carthage and said Foster had been swearing that I swore to the affidavit on which Simpson was arrested &c. I instructed Johnson and
Rockwell to go to Carthage in the morning and have him indicted
for perjury as I never did swear to the complaint. His officer was
after John D. Parker also and /Report says B[righam] Young and
W[illia]m C. Kimball/. Past nine eve I walked a little way with
Dr. Richards for exercise. [*several lines left blank*]

482 Several police out during the night. Hyrum was in this

evening and cautioned me about speaking so freely about my enemies and in such a manner they could make it actionable. I told him 6 months would not roll over his head before they would swear 12 as palpable lies about him as they had about me. [*rest of page blank*] {page 130}

Friday, May 24th 1844 With my family. Aaron Johnson, and O[rrin] P[orter] Rockwell went to Carthage to get R[obert] D. Foster indicted but they returned as the grand jury had risen [to consider charges of adultery and perjury]. Joseph Jackson was there and swore vs. me.

Tarried with my family till 6 [P.M.]. Eve went into Dr. Bernhisels room. Had council with Bro[thers] Phelps and Richards. Ordered City council called tomorrow and protective ordinance passed on habeus Corpus. [*several lines left blank*]

Returned to my family. In about 1 hour central committee [of Council of Fifty] wrote to Hugh Clark Alderman, corner of 4th and Martin Streets, Phil[adelphia], P[ennslyvani]a on election. [*several lines left blank*]

Rain this eve. It has been very pleasant for some days. {page 131}

Saturday, May 25th 1844 At home. Keeping out of the way of expected arrests from Carthage. Towards night the grand jury [members] Hunter [and] Marks returned from Carthage also Marshal Green and A[lmon] M. Babbit. [They] informed me [there] were 2 indictments found against me. One for false swearing by R[obert] D. Foster and Joseph Jackson and one for polygamy or something else by the Laws, the particulars of which I shall learn more hereafter. Much hard swearing before Grand Jury. Francis M. Higby swore so hard that I [understand he] had to [be] removed[, he says that I steal] states property &c. His testimony was rejected.

2 P.[M.] Joseph Jackson come in town /as I heard/. I instructed the officers to have him arrested for threatening life &c. Had a long talk with Hunter Marks, Babbit, Hyrum, Bonney, Dr. Richards, Roundy &c. and concluded not to keep out of their way any longer.

2 P.M. Council [of Fifty met] in my north Room. Letter from Hyde. Ordered an answer. Also made arrangements to have me [succeed Rigdon as postmaster to] have [control of] post of-

483

fice. Adjourned /to Friday next/ week 2 o'clock. W[illard] Richards
writes to Hyde for Council [of Fifty]. {page 132}

Sunday, May 26th 1844 10 A.M. Preached at the stand
about /Joseph/ Jackson and the mobocrats. Rode out in the P.M.
Esq[ui]r[e] Richardson called on me with Babbit my Lawyers. A
man came to me and said Eagle with others were intending to
take Jeremiah Smith away in the night. I stationed the police to
protect him. [*rest of page blank*] {page 133}

Monday, May 27th 1844 About 8 o'clock I started on
horse back with a few friends and passing by the Temple pursued
my course to/wards/ Carthage thinking it best to meet my ene-
mies before the Court and have my Indictments investigated. After I had passed my farm on the prairie /most of/ the following
brothers joined me and the remainder soon after my arrival at
Carthage: Aaron Johnson, Dr. Bernhisel, Joseph Coolidge, John
Hetfield, O[rrin] P[orter] Rockwell, Lorenzo Rockwell, W[illia]m
Walker, Harrison Sagers, Hyrum Smith, J[ohn] P. Green, John
Green, Judge Richards, [Edward] Bonny, [Joseph B.] Nobles,
Shadrach Roundy, Theodore Turley, Jedediah Grant, John Lytle,
[Lucien] Woodworth, C[ornelius]. P. Lot, J[onathan]. Dunham
and 2 or 3 more.

Arrived at "A. Hamilton's Carthage Hotel" about noon.
Charles A. Foster come up with us 3 or 4 miles from the city and
accompanied us to Carthage. Had considerable conversation {page
134} and he appeared more mild than he had done [been] and as
though he was almost persuaded he had been influenced by false
reports to some extent.

Joseph Jackson, F[rancis] M. Higbee, and C[hauncey]
L. Higbee were in A. Hamilton['s] Hotel when we arrived. Soon
after our arrival Cha[rle]s A. Foster took me in a private room
/as a friend/ and told me there was a conspiracy against my life.
R[obert] D. Foster told some of the brethren there was evil determined against me (and that with tears in his eyes) and that there
were those who were determined I should not go out of the village
alive &c. Jackson was seen loading his pistol and swore he would
have satisfaction of me and Hiram. I had [a] short interview with
Judge Thomas who treated me with the utmost courtesy. He is a
great man and a gentleman. After dinner (at the 2d or 3d table)
we retired to our room and [as] Jackson who had been to the
court house come towards the Hotel, some one told him Hyrum

had arrived. When he turned immediately towards the Court House again. My Lawyers Messers Richardson, Babbit, and Skinner used all reasonable exertion to bring /forward/ my trial for Perjury but the prosecution party was not ready for trial. (One Withers a material witness was absent as they said) My attorney called frequently to report the state of the court {page 135} and I was ready to join but the case was defer[r]ed till next term and I was left to give bail to the Sherif[f] at his option and he told me I might go home and he would call and take bail some time.

We immediately called for our horses and while they were harnessing C[hauncey] L. Higbee come to me and wanted I should stay as a witness in a certain case where he was employed and urged me considerably but I told him I did not recollect the occurance particularly enough to testify on the case and got him to excuse me. 4 1/2 [P.M.] We started and when we had got to Bro[ther] Grant's the rain commenced and I went into the house while most of the brethren went into the barn. While the shower abated as we left the tavern and passed the court House there were many people about in groups and Jackson stood on the green with one or 2 men some distance off. After the storm had subsided, we went forward and I and Hyrum and some others arrived at home about 9 o'clock and my carriage and J. B. Nobles a little while after. My carriage was {page 136} upset on the Temple Hill but no one hurt. I rode on horseback all the way ([on] Joe Dunkin). Found Emma sick on my return.

While at Hamilton's C[hauncey] L. Higbee offered some insulting language concerning me to O[rrin] P[orter] Rockwell who resented it nobly as a friend ought to do. When Hamilton seeing it [he] turned Rockwell out of doors.

R[obert] D. Foster, Cha[rle]s A. Foster, Rolloson and Higbee were on the hill when I passed[, in the morning, and] as it was afterwards reported by Flack [they] gathered their pistols and horses and were in Carthage before me except Charles Foster.

Samuel Smith of Montebello heard at five in the morning that I had been taken prisoner to Carthage by mob [and] immediately gathered a co[mpany] of 25 men and arrived at Carthage about the time I did for the purpose of assisting me. [*rest of page blank*] {page 137}

485

Tuesday, May 28th 1844 At home. [*several lines left blank*] Rain in the P.M. {page 138}

Wednesday, May 29[th] 1844 At home. Dr. Luther W. Hi[ck]ock of Burlington, come in and arrested Jeremiah Smith on a warrant from Nathaniel Pope, Judge U. S. Circuit Court. During our conversation in the afternoon we learned to our Mutual joy that we were of one origin in our grandfathers, father Anthony Smith of Glasgow, Scotland. [*several lines left blank*] Rain A.M. {page 139}

Thursday, May 30th 1844 10 A.M. Municipal Court Jeremiah Smith Sen[ior] on Habeus Corpus discharged and Do. Another petition same case on arrest of Luther W. Hicko[c]k Burlington. Adjourned court 1 [P.M.] to 3. 3 to 4 1/2 in court. Jeremiah Smith discharged.

Evening [U.S. marshall] F. B. Johnson as was reported was going to Burlington. Jeremiah Smith swore out execution [paid] $77.75. Johnson come forward and acknowledged fee bill.

Hicko[c]k called for copy of proceedings. Johnson threatened to bring the draggons [dragoons] &c. to get [Jeremiah] Smith. [*several lines left blank*] Pleasant. {page 140}

Friday, May 31[st] 1844 9 A.M. Ordered a capias to arrest T[homas] B. Johnson for threatening the peace of the city with Draggon [dragoon] &c. H. Hugins made affidavit but Johnson had gone.

10 A.M. Called at my office and wrote. 1 P.M. was called to see Sister Richards who was very sick. Laid on hands. Directed some Raspberry tea and she was better. [*several lines left blank* [met with Council of Fifty]] 2 or 3 Indians stay in hall over night. [*several lines left blank*] Pleasant. {page 141}

Saturday, June 1st 1844 At home. Some gentle showers. [*several lines left blank*] 1 P.M. Rode out with Dr. Richards and O[rrin] P[orter] Rockwell called on Davis at the boat. /Paid Manhard $90.00/ Met G[eorge] J. Adams and paid him $50.00 to J[ohn] P. Green paid him and another bro[ther] $200.00 to [*blank*]. Excha[nge]d $100 Gold and a check. Drank a glass of beer at Moissers. Called at W[illia]m Clayton's while Dr. R[ichards] and Rockwell called at Dr. New House. Home 4 1/2 [P.M.]. [*several lines left blank*]

8 Eve Peter Maughn, John Sanders, and Jacob Peart called with Dr. Richards to consult about a coal bed on Rock River. I

suggested it would be profitable to employ the "Maid of Iowa" in the business of carrying the coal &c. Approved of this plan. [*rest of page blank*] {page 142}

Sunday, June 2[nd] 1844 At home. [*several lines left blank*] Pleasant day. {page 143}

Monday, June 3[rd] 1844 At home. Received letter this morning signed Francis that 600 men were coming to sack the city from Burlington and get Dr. Hicko[c]k. Rode out on the Hill about 9 o'clock on the Hill.

Municipal court set. Was not present. Augustin Spencer, C[hauncey] L. Higbee, C[harles] A. Foster, R[obert] D. Foster, and C[hauncey] L. Higbee had cases but failed to appear. Refer[r]ed back to low court. [*several lines left blank*]

5 [P.M.] read German with [Alexander] N[e]iba[u]r. [*rest of page blank*] {page 144}

Tuesday, June 4th 1844 At home. A. Morrison and Pulaski Cahoon proposed to give $100.00 per month for the use of the "Maid of Iowa" and made out their own bonds of their own security but I would not receive them. [*several lines left blank*]

P.M. Went out on my farm. Broke the whipple tree too my buggy. Wrote Mr Tewksbury, Boston. [*several lines left blank*]

6 to 7 eve in council with Taylor, Babbit, Hyrum, Richards, Woodworth, and Phelps &c. about prosecution [of Laws and Fosters] in behalf of Maria [Lawrence for slander]. Concluded to go to Quincy with Taylor and give up my Bonds of guardianship [of Maria Lawrence] &c. (Cutler and Cahoon are so anxious to get prope[r]ty they will all flat out as soon as the temple is completed and the faith of the Saints ceases from /Higbee and [*blank*]/. Walked out with Woodworth. {page 145}

Wednesday, June 5[th] 1844 Went on the prairie to show some land for sale. Returned towards night betwe[e]n 8 and 9 eve. Stood out to watch the lightning in the North. It was most beautiful and sublime, a little thunder. About 10 [P.M.] a shower of rain passed over with continued rumbling thunder. I told my clerk Dr. Richards it would be fair weather tomorrow. Received the Book of Denominations and answered by letter. Wrote I. D. Rupp (on file).

Very warm. Middle of the day thermometer stood at 94 1/2 degrees. No rain before this for some days. [*rest of page blank*] {page 146}

Thursday, June 6th 1844 At home. About 9 [A.M.] ordered my carriage which stood at the door till near noon, while I read my letter to H[enry] Clay to many strangers in the bar room among whom was one who advocated for H[enry] Clay. I argued long to show the subject in its true light and showed him that no man could honestly vote for a man /like Clay/ who had violated his oath and not acted on constitutional principles.

About 12 [P.M.] 1/2 D[imick] B. Huntington come and said R[obert] D. Foster felt bad and he thought there was a chance for him to return if he could be reinstated in his office in the Legion &c. that he had all the anties affidavits &c. at his control. I told him if he would return, withdraw all his suits &c. and do right he should be restored. Met Bro[ther] Richards coming from his garden with new potatoes. Told him to go to the High Council and have Bro[ther] Brown restored to the church and give him his licence. Rode out with several in my carriage an hour or so. [*several lines left blank*]

7 P.M. Heavy shower, thunder, lightning [and] rain and again about 9. {page 147}

Friday, June 7th 1844 At home. R[obert] D. Foster called professidly to make some concessions and return to the Church. [He] wanted a private interview which I declined. Told him I would choose individuals and he might choose others and we would meet and I would settle any thing on righteous principles. [*several lines left blank*]

Report was circulated in the evening that Foster said I would receive him on any terms and give him a hat full of dollars into the bargain.

1st number of Nauvoo Expositor published to day, ed-[ited] by Sylvester Emmons.

Went to the printing office about 2 o'clock and instructed Mr. Taylor to answer certain bill receipts of Geo[rge] W. Harris. [*several lines left blank*] Pleasant evening. {page 148}

Saturday, June 8th 1844 10 to one in city council. Burlington ferry Boat come down with a pleasure party and landed at N[auvoo] H[ouse] landing about 2 o'clock.

3 to 6 1/2 P.M. in /City/ Council. Made a long speech in favor of having an ordinance to suppress Libels &c. in Nauvoo and a committee was appointed to draft.

Counsellor [Sylvester] Emmons, Editor of the "Expositor,"

was cited to appear at the next regular term of the Council on impeachment. [*several lines left blank*] Elder Grant preached at the Mansion this eve. [*several lines left blank*] Thunder and Rain this eve and night. {page 149}

Sunday, June 9th 1844 At home. Health not very good. Lungs wearied. Hyrum preached at the stand. [*several lines left blank*]

2 P.M. Several passengers of the "Osprey" from St. Louis and Quincy put up at the Mansion. I helped carry in their trunks and chatted with them in the bar room. [*several lines left blank*]

Meeting at Mansion [at] 6 o'clock. [*rest of page blank*] {page 150}

Monday, June 10th 1844 In City Council from 10 to 1:20 P.M. and from 2:20 to 5:30 P.M. investigating the Merits of the Nauvoo Expositor, Laws, Higbee, Fosters &c. Council passed an ordinance concerning Libels and for other purposes, also issued an order to me to destroy the Nauvoo Expositor establishment as a nuisance. I immediately ordered the marshal to destroy it without delay. At the same issued an order to Jonathan Dunham, acting Major Gen[eral] Nauvoo Legion to asssist the Marshall with the Legion if called upon so to do. And about 8 o'clock the Marshall reported that he had removed the press, type, and printed papers and fixtures into the street and fired them.

This was done because of the libellous character of the paper. In slandering the Municipality of the city. The possey consisting of some hundred returned with the Marshal in front of the Mansion and I gave them a short address told them they had done right. That they had executed my orders required of me by the city council that I would never submit to have another libellous publication in [print] established in this city. That I cared not how many papers there were in the city if they would print the truth but would submit to no libe[l]s or slander from them. The speech was loudly greeted by 3 cheers 3 times. The posse dispersed all in good order.

Francis M. Higbee and others made some threats which will appear in due course of investigation. East wind very cold and cloudy. {page 151}

Tuesday, June 11th 1844 Spent the fore noon in council with the brethen at my house. 10 [A.M.] to 12 or thereabouts in my office with Hyrum, G[eorge] J. Adams, Dr. Richards, and others. Instructed Bro[ther] Phelps to write a proclamation to the citezens of Nauvoo to keep quiet &c. Had an interview with Elder Adams out doors returned home to dinner.

2 P.M. went into court. Many people present. Talked an hour or two on passing events the Mob party &c. and told the people I was ready to fight if the mob would compel me to. That I would not be in bondage. Asked the assembly if they would stand by Me and they cried yes from all quarters. Returned home. Dr. Richards come to me at my home as I was talking with Hyrum, Eaton, Bonny &c. And read a letter from Dr. Hicko[c]k Springfield June 6, that T. B. Johnson was about yet [and that] the [members of the Nauvoo] Municipal Court [had been] indicted [by the circuit court] from trying /Jeremiah/ Smith on Habeas Corpus. Instructed Dr. Richards to answer it, rode 1/2 hour with O[rrin] P[orter] Rockwell.

G[eorge] J. Adams preached at my house in the eve. Cloudy cool. {page 152} This fore noon Capt of Osprey called at printing office I called to see him rod[e] with him to his boat upper landing. When I come up Charles Foster called the passengers to come and see the meanest man. Rolloson attempted to draw a pistol but Eaton silenced him and kept them all down.

Harry Readfield said last evening F[rancis] M. Higbee said while speaking of the printing press of N[auvoo] E[xpositor] if they lay their hand upon it or break it. They may date their downfall from that very hour. And in 10 days there will not be a Mormon left in Nauvoo, what they do they may expect the same in return. Also Adrin Evert heard it.

Lanthus and Tallman Rolf said the city would be strung to the ground in 10 days and they would help do it (by Jason R. Luce, Moses Leonard and Joshua Miller).

Runners have gone in different directions to get up a mob &c. Mobites selling their houses. {page 153}

Wednesday, June 12th 1844 This morning was arrested by David Bettinos Constable of Carthage on complaint. F[rancis] M. Higbee before Morrison, J[ustice] [of the] P[eace]. I offered to go before any justice in Nauvoo but he swore he would carry me to Carthage. Took a writ of Habeus Corpus. Was tried before Municipal Court and discharged. See Docket. Some 15 others were in that same writ.

10 A.M. at my office. 1 [P.M.] to 2 Aaron Johnson

Habeus Corpus. At 4 to 6 went into court. Discharged at 8. [*several lines left blank*] Rain this night. {page 154}

Thursday, June 13th 1844 9 A.M. Presided in Municipal Court /at 70s Hall/ Hyrum Smith, J[ohn] P. Green, W[illiam] W. Phelps, Stephen Perry, J[onathan] H. Holmes, J[onathan]. Dunham, [Samuel] T. Bennett, W[illiam]. W. Edwards were arrested on complaint of F[rancis] M. Higbee before [Thomas] Morrison J[ustice] [of the] P[eace] of Carthage By David Bettisworth Con[stable] [of] Hancock County. They o[b]tained a Habeus Corpus were tried for a riot for burning the Nauvoo Expositor and set free by Municipal court. See Docket.

P.M. Attend[ed] meeting in 70s Hall. G[eorge] J. Adams preached after which I made some observations. [*several lines left blank*]

2 Brothers arrived from Carthage this eve and said about 300 mobbers were collected in Carthage to come upon Nauvoo. [Also that] Hamilton was paying [$] 1.00 [a] bu[shel] for corn and Jacob B. Backenstos [and the] clerk of the court had [prepared a transcript of the] trial [and the testimony] against us. Rain. {page 155}

Friday, June 14th 1844 Wrote to Gov[ernor] Ford explaining about the removal of the Nauvoo Expositor. Dr. Bernhisel also wrote the Gov[ernor] and Dr. J[oseph] R. Wakefield wrote [also]. All of which are on file. Read doings of /said/ City Council /till after dinner/ to Dr. Wakefield and gave him Vol[ume] of Times and Seasons.

About 4 P.M. rode out with Dr. Bernhisel. Pleasant and warm toward night. Some clouds.

Norton was tried for firing Foster's Printing office but [was] acquitted before Aaron Johnson, J[ustice] [of the] P[eace]. [*rest of page blank*] {page 156}

Saturday, June 15th 1844 At home. Two brethren come from Lima, said Col[onel] Levi Williams had demanded the Mormons' arms. Father Morley wanted to know what to do. I gave them answer where the brethren give up their arms, to give up their lives as dear as possible.

Report said there were 40 men training at Carthage. Mr Johnson come from Warsaw, said several boxes of arms had arrived at Warsaw from Quincy that there was some excitment but expected they were going to wait [for] the Meeting at Carthage middle of next week.

Maid of Iowa come down the river about 2 or 3 o'clock. While I was examining Benj[amin] Wests painting of Death on the Pale Horse which has been exhibiting in my reading room for 3 days. Lost their flat loaded with corn /sunk/ and a small robbery had been committed on board. Search was made at the landing by the police.

/This morning/ Samuel James started for Springfield to carry letters and papers to Gov[ernor] Ford concerning the destruction of the Expositor &c. About 7 rode out on horseback with O[rrin] P[orter] Rockwell. {page 157}

Sunday, June 16th 1844 Preached at the stand 10 o'clock A.M. Some rain. Some 40 individuals gentlemen from Madison, come down on the steamer to Enquire into our difficulties. Met them at Masonic Hall at 2 P.M. and gave them an explanation. The Clerk of City council Dr. Richards read the minutes of council deciding the Nauvoo Expositor a Nuisance. They were satisfied.

At the close of the Meeting repaired to the stand and met the brethren, some thousands. Instructed them to keep their cool prepare their arms for defence of the city, as it was reported a Mob was collecting at Carthage &c. Be quiet, make no disturbance. Instructed the meeting to organize and send delegates to all the surrounding towns and villages and explain the cause of the disturbance and show them all was peace at Nauvoo and no cause for Mobs.

Messengers arrived showing that the Clerk of the county court was expected to be driven out of Carthage next day and the only way to prevent sheding of blood was to get the Governor in person to come down with his staff. Wrote to Governor Ford stating the facts (on file). Brother from Bear Creek come and made affidavit before Recorder that 1,500 Missourians were to cross to Warsaw next morning on way to Carthage and (on file) Judge Thomas come and advised me go before some justice of the peace and have an examination, {page 158} and if acquitted or bound over, would allay all excitement or cut off all legal pretext for a mob and he would be bound to /order them to/ keep the peace.

Wrote a letter to Hugh McFall Adjutant Gen[eral] of Legion to carry letter to the Governor. He declined going. [*several lines left blank*]

Received letter from Issac Morl[e]y this date and answered it. [*rest of page blank*] {page 159}

Monday, June 17[th] 1844 Hyrum wrote letters to the Twelve [Apostles] but they were not sent. Wrote to Uncle John Smith.

This morning Joseph Smith, Samuel Bennett, John Taylor, W[illia]m W. Phelps, Hyrum Smith, John P. Green, Dimick B. Huntington, Jonathan Dunham, Stephen Markham, J[onathan] H. Holmes, Jesse P. Horman, John Lytle, Joseph W. Coolidge, Harvey D. Redfield, O[rrin] P[orter] Rockwell, and Levi Richards were arrested by Con[stable] Joel S. Miles on writ of D[aniel] H. Wells, J[ustice] [of the] P[eace] issued on complaint of Mr. G. Ware for riot on 10th inst[ant] in destroying Nauvoo Expositor. Were tried at Justice Wells 2 P.M. and discharged.

Edward Hunter Lewis and Major Bills started with letters &c. to Gov[ernor] Ford and officers of [*dash*] [*dash*] as stated on Sunday. Minutes [*dash*] rec[eive]d affidavit of Stephen Markham Mob was like to come upon us (on file) Issued order to [the Legion from the] Mayor to keep the peace to Jonathan Dunham acting commandant to assist the {page 160} Marshall also to be quiet and prevent all excitement, also to Col[onel] Rockwood to call my guard and Staff to head quarters (all on file). Ordered the Legion to parade 10 A.M. next day. Rec[eive]d letter from T. Hugins Esqu[ire] that Jeremiah Smith had got home clear and all excitement /survived by/ T. B. Johnson was allayed at Springfield. It was reported the Mob was still gathering at Carthage and that W[illia]m and Wilson Law had laid a plan to burn the printing office of Nauvoo Neighbor this night and strong police were on duty.

Capt[ain] of the Osprey called on me. Closed orders about 12 ready to retire. About eleven a negro came into my office with an open letter without date or name. Said Dr. Foster gave it to him at Madison to give Norton in that Foster said Dunham and Richards swore in presence of Temple they would kill him Foster in two days and a man at Madison would swear he heard them say so at Joseph's house. Pleasant night. {page 161}

June 18th 1844, Tuesday 9 A.M. [the Nauvoo] Legion assembled and organized. Just before was informed some boxes of arms were landed at the upper stone house and /were/ secured by the Marshal. Soon after it was discovered said arms (40 stands) were sent by [*blank*] and the Marshall bought them for the city.

About 2 P.M. the Legion was drawn up on the corner of the street by the Mansion. L[i]eut[enant] Gen[eral] Joseph Smith in uniform stood on the top of the gro[w]ing frame and addressed the Legion. /About 2 o'clock/ [Joseph] proclaimed the City under Marshal Law /and caused written orders to [be] issue[d] in his name/. Judge Phelps read the Warsaw "Signal extra" of the 17th inst[ant] when all the citizens were called upon [to] assist the mob. Gen[eral] J[oseph] Smith called upon all men from the Rocky Mountains to the ocean to come to his assistance.

About 3 [P.M.] [the] Legion marched up Main St[reet] under command of acting Major Gen[eral] Dunham. L[i]eut[enant] Gen[eral] [Smith] and staff [were] riding in front. The number was large and inspiring considering the number who were gone preaching. {page 162}

Truman Gillet Jun[ior] made affidavit /before the Recorder/ about W[illia]m Law (on file).

8 [P.M.] eve wrote to H. T. Hugins Esqu[ire] (and Dr. Hicko[c]k) in same [letter]. Sent per Dr. Wakefield to Burlington.

9 [P.M.] messengers arrived from Carthage. Mob had received inteligence from Gov[ernor] who would take no notice of them and they damned the Gov[ernor] as being as bad as Joe Smith. Did not care for him [and would] be as willing [to act even if] he would not help. Some 50 men in Carthage meeting at Fountain Green which attracted their attention. Reported by police Roundy.

At 10 o'clock after L[i]eut[enant] Gen[eral] had retired [it was reported] that Norton had threatened to shoot Joseph. Examination was immediately had but no proof found. [*rest of page blank*] {page 163}

Wednesday, June 19[th] 1844 [Legion] Troops come in from Green Plain about 11 A.M. L[i]eut[enant] Gen[eral] met them in front of his Mansion and an Escort came down from the parade below the temple and escorted them to the ground.

1 o'c[loc]k P.M. [Legion] troops arrived from Iow[a] and were escorted in. [*several lines left blank*] 9 Eve L[i]eut[enant] Gen[eral] at Head Quarters. All quiet. [*rest of page blank*] {page 164}

[*page left blank*] {page 165}

Thursday, June 20[th] 1844 At day break send the Guard out of the city /to pitch upon ground to/ to meet the enemy. 10 A.M. Southwick from Louisiana arrived [and] said a cannon from Quincy arrived at Warsaw. No excitement at St. Louis. [It was] reported to him a great excitement at Far West &c. 11 [P.M.] reviewed the troops facing the Mansion and went onto parade on the bank of the River.

Recorder took affidavit of Carlos W. Lyons wrote Ballentine and Slater at Doyles Mills for wheat. Wrote John Taylor [Tyler] Pres[iden]t [of the] U[nited] S[tates].

Willard Richards wrote [James] Arlington Bennet [and] Affidavit of John P. Green and John M. Bernhisel. Wrote the Twelve [Apostles] to come home.

[Theodore] Turley had orders to commence Making cannon. {page 166}

Friday, June 21[st] 1844 About 10 A.M. rode out with this guard. 2 1/2 [P.M.] returned to Head quarters with Col[onel] Freeman and Mr. [Bartlett with an] express from the Governor, he having arrived from Carthage. Letter on file. City Council called. Read affidavits of all before taken and 10 more. See record of city council. W[illard] Richards, J[ohn] Taylor, and D[r]. J[ohn] M. Bernhisel appointed by council to return with the express to the Gov[ernor] to Carthage. Taylor and Bernhisel went. Richards staid to prepare further documents. Took J[ohn] P. Green affidavits and Joseph Smith affidavit. Letter from councillor S[ylvester] Emmons resigned his office accepted.

W[illiam] W. Phelps took 2 affidavits of Joseph Jackson and 1 of James Clift. {page 167}

An officer of the U[nited] S[tates] Army arrested a deserter and staid at Joseph's all night. After news reached of the Gov[ernor] arrive[d] at Carthage sent an Express to Keokuk to stop the Express to the gov[ernor]. Col[onel] Brewer arrived at the Mansion about 9 eve with his Lady. [rest of page blank] {page 168}

Saturday June 22d, 1844 Wrote letter to Governor. Almon Babbit arrived from Carthage this morning at request of the Gov[ernor,] who thought it not wisdom to have Richards, Phelps &c. city council to go to Carthage and best to let people pass in and out of the city. Lucien Woodworth was delegated to go to the

Gov[ernor] in place of Dr. Richards. Dr. Robinson made affidavit. Joseph wrote to the Gov[ernor].

12 noon Woodworth started with Wood Esq[ui]r[e] of Burlington. [*several lines left blank*]

James Olive made affidavit [in the] Maj[or] Gen[eral's] office also Geo[rge] G. Johnstone and [*several lines left blank*] 7 P.M. issued Gen[eral] orders to Co[lo]n[el] Dunham [acting] Major Gen[eral] in command for intreachment [entrenchment]. [*rest of page blank*] {page 170}

[*several lines left blank*] 6 P.M. Prophesied that /in/ the sickly season that sickness would enter into their houses and vex them until they would fain repent in dust and ashes and they will be smitten with the scab &c.

7 [P.M.] received a written invitation from James Hamilton and 5 or 6 others to preach to morrow. {page 171}[1]

---

[1] At this point, the portion of the journal devoted to recording Joseph Smith's activities ends. Five days later, on 27 June 1844, Joseph and Hyrum Smith were shot and killed by members of a mob who had forced their way into Carthage Jail, Carthage, Hancock County, Illinois, where the Mormon leaders were being held. Joseph Smith was thirty-eight years old. The remaining pages of this journal are either blank or were used by Willard Richards and possibly others, from 1 September to 19 December 1844, to record their own activities.

INDEX

501

511

513

United States Government, 53, 210,
340, 368, 427, 443, 445
United States President, 443, 469, 495
Universalian, 58
Urim and Thummim, 52, 306, 339

Van Buren, Martin, 425
Van Hymon, Sister, 350
Vermont, 4, 428, 429, 443, 472
Vickers, Mr., 376
Vilanova, New York, 22, 71
Visions, 118-124, 130, 152, 155-8, 168,
see also Joseph Smith, Jr.,
revelations/translations/visions.

Wakefield, Dr. Joseph R., 491
Walker, Cyrus, 388, 390, 391, 392
Walker, George, 394, 400, 401, 402,
411
Walker, Lorin, 258, 272, 290, 375
Walker, Lucy, 396, 400
Walker, Lydia, 406
Walker, William, 484
Walsh, John C., 476
Ware, W. G., 493
Warren, Calvin, 306, 392
Warren (Worrin), Peter, 11
Wars (also Wars, Rumors of), 243, 332,
340, 350
Warsaw, New York, 22
Warsaw, Illinois, 394, 443, 491, 492,
494
Warsaw Signal, 446, 447, 474, 494
Washings, see Ordinances, Endowment.
Washington, D.C., 252, 419, 462, 463,
471, 472, 478, 479
Washington Globe, 471
Wasp, see also *Nauvoo Neighbor*, 286,
333, 346, 347, 375
Wasson, Clara M., 417
Wasson, Lorenzo, 416, 459, 481
Waterman, John O., 135
Watt, George, 472
Waterford, Canada, 13
Watts, Isaac, 145
Weaver, Russell, 99
Webb, John, 104

Webb, Milan, 350
Webster, Daniel, 313
Webster's English Lexicon, 66
Week, William, 359
Wells, Daniel H., 309, 313, 373, 403,
462, 471, 477, 493
West, Benjamin, 492
West Lodi, New York, 31
Western Agricultural Company, 205
Westfield, New York, 11, 21
Wheat, Almeron, 268
Wheeler, Miss, 423
Whigs, 402, 443
White, Evander, 436
White, Roswell, 436
Whitlock, Harvey, 60, 62-64
Whitmer, David, 34, 38, 39, 64, 74,
76, 101, 120, 131, 143, 152, 153,
156, 165, 166, 167, 172, 174, 187,
217, 223
Whitmer, John, 39, 49, 143, 153, 156,
166, 167, 171, 172, 187, 223, 448
Whitmer, Peter, 76, 269
Whitney, Elizabeth Ann, 244, 418, 424
Whitney, Bishop Newel K., 19, 25, 28,
37, 42, 65, 70, 85, 98, 100, 107, 163,
195, 196, 237, 247, 324, 327, 334,
381, 410, 412, 413, 416, 424, 442,
472, 481
Whitney, Samuel, 45
Wicliffe, Charles A., 368
Wight, Lyman, 46, 184, 186, 201, 204,
211, 212, 213, 372, 387, 388, 394,
398, 416, 447, 451, 458, 476, 478,
479, 480, 481
Wilcox, Brother, 236
Wilcox, Catharine, 104
Wild, Dr., 314, 322-23
Wilkie, John, 459
Wilkison, Stephen, 441
Williams, Clyde, 414
Williams, Dr., 471, 473
Williams, Dr. Frederick G., 10, 15, 19,
20, 25, 28, 29, 31, 36, 39, 40, 41,
42, 46, 65, 66, 70, 71, 72, 76, 91,
107, 110, 111, 114, 131, 138, 143,
152, 153, 156, 163, 194, 199

517